MAUI

KYLE ELLISON

MAUI

Maliko Bay

Haiku
36
Ulumalu

Waipi'o Bay

390
Haliimaile

Makawao

Keanae
Wailua

Pukalani
390
Olinda
394

Nahiku

37

East Maui

360

377

Kula

HANA AIRPORT
Wai'anapanapa State Park

Waiakoa
378

Hana

Haleakala

Pu'u 'Ula'ula
10,023 ft

National

Hamoa Beach

31

Park

Waimoku Falls

Polipoli Spring
State Recreation
Area

'Ohe'o Gulch

Kaupo

Kipahulu

31

'Alenuihaha Channel

Inset map

Kaua'i

Ni'ihau
Lihu'e
O'ahu

Ka'ula
Honalulu
Moloka'i
Kahului

Lana'i
Maui
Lahaina

Kaho'olawe

Waimea
Hilo

Hawai'i

0   100 mi

0   100 km

0   5 mi

0   5 km

© AVALON TRAVEL

Contents

There is a prominent Hawaiian saying about Maui: *Maui no ka oi,* "Maui is the best."

The endless stretches of golden sand are an obvious draw, but sand alone doesn't entice millions of visitors to a 727-square-mile dot in the middle of the Pacific. Perhaps it's more than just the thought of relaxing in a lounge chair with a mai tai in hand. Maybe it's also the way the trade winds blow across a beach of black sand at Wai'anapanapa State Park. Or it's the hope of a close encounter with a giant green sea turtle while snorkeling off the coast of Napili Bay. Maybe it's the way the setting sun reflects in the waters off Makena, both fiery and calm in the same fleeting moment.

Of course, Maui's magic is also found in the endless adventures to be embraced on the island. Hike through a thick bamboo forest and find yourself at the base of a 400-foot waterfall cascading down a rocky cliff. Ride your first wave and feel the thrill of the surf as you glide across a silky blue break. Wake at 3am to drive up a dark mountainside in the freezing cold to see the first rays of light illuminate Haleakala Crater. No matter what drew you to the island, the secret to Maui's allure lies in the many moments that stick with you long after you've left it behind.

Clockwise from top left: a local *keiki* at the beach; Hawaiian green sea turtle, or *honu;* Moloka'i waterfalls; winter surf at Pe'ahi, or "Jaws"; Mokulei'a Bay; paragliding above beautiful Upcountry.

Clockwise from top left: spinner dolphins off Lana'i; Maluaka Beach in Makena; 'Iao Valley; ziplining above Central Maui; St. Philomena Church, Kalawao.

Planning Your Trip

Where to Go

Lahaina and West Maui

West Maui pulses with a unique coastal vibe. The historic town of **Lahaina** was once the capital of the Hawaiian kingdom, and it retains a port town atmosphere. Warm weather and mostly dry conditions make this region a spectacular place for outdoor adventure. Snorkel with sea turtles at **Napili Bay,** lounge on the beach in **Kapalua,** ride the zipline above **Ka'anapali,** or hike to **Nakalele Blowhole.**

Central Maui

Central Maui is the island's population center and the seat of county government. Most visitors blow through town on the way to their beachfront resort, but Central Maui has its own set of sights off the regular trail. The twisting road into **'Iao Valley** is the region's most popular attraction. **Kepaniwai**

Heritage Gardens exhibits Maui's multicultural heritage, and down on the shore at **Kanaha Beach Park,** windsurfers and kitesurfers take to the waves along the stretch of Maui's north shore.

Kihei and South Maui

From the celebrity-laden resorts of **Wailea** to the condo-dwelling snowbirds of **Kihei,** South Maui is all about worshipping the sun and enjoying the procession of beaches. **Makena** remains South Maui's most adventurous venue, with snorkeling, scuba diving, hiking trails, kayaking, and some of the island's most photo-worthy beaches. Just offshore, **Molokini Crater** offers 100-foot visibility and the chance to snorkel with up to 250 species of fish.

Wailea Beach

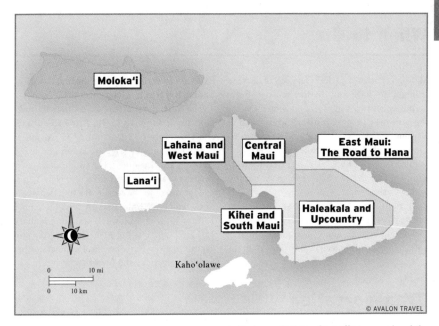

© AVALON TRAVEL

Haleakala and Upcountry

Rural, laid-back, and refreshingly cool, Upcountry is Maui's most underrated zone. Agriculture and produce dominate **Kula,** and everything from vegetables to vineyards, coffee, and goat cheese can be found in this rural and relaxing enclave. **Polipoli** is the island's little-known adventure zone, where mountain biking, paragliding, and hiking take place in a forest shrouded in mist. Watch the dramatic sunrise from the frosty peak of towering **Haleakala,** the sacred volcano from which the demigod Maui famously snared the sun.

East Maui: the Road to Hana

The New Age town of **Pa'ia** is as trendy as it is jovial. Surfers ride waves along undeveloped beaches, patrons shop in locally owned boutiques, and the town is home to some the island's best restaurants. Along the famous, twisting **Road to Hana,** tumbling waterfalls and rugged hiking trails await. The **Pools of 'Ohe'o** spill down cliffs to the sea. The hike through a bamboo forest

to the base of **Waimoku Falls** is considered the island's best trek.

Lana'i

Home to 3,500 residents and one large resort, this island is a playground of outdoor adventure. Learn about the island's history at the **Lana'i Culture and Heritage Center,** and make the journey down to **Kaunolu** to see an ancient village settlement frozen in time.

Moloka'i

Taking time to explore this island offers a chance to experience the roots of native Hawaiian culture. Take a guided tour into historic **Halawa Valley,** one of the oldest settlements in Hawaii, or ride on the back of a friendly mule as you visit the former leper colony of **Kalaupapa.** Watch the sunset from **Papohaku Beach,** one of the state's longest and most deserted stretches of sand, or climb your way high into the mists of the **Moloka'i Forest Reserve.**

When to Go

Maui isn't postcard-perfect every day of the year. It might not have four distinct seasons, but it definitely has two—summer and winter. During the **summer (May-October)**, areas such as Kapalua, Kahului, North Kihei, and Kaʻanapali are prone to trade winds that blow most afternoons. While Hana and Kapalua can see rain during summer, Lahaina and Kihei can go six months without a single drop.

During the **winter (November-April),** there can be plenty of rain. A winter day on Maui can mean light breezes, sunny skies, and a high of 78°F, but it can also mean cloudy skies and rain.

Experienced surfers will have the best chance of finding **big surf** in winter.

The **best, most affordable times** to travel to Maui are **January 15-30, April 15-June 5,** and **September 15-December 15.** Airfare is cheaper, occupancy rates are lower, and many activities are discounted. The two busiest weeks of the year are over Christmas and New Year's, and the two slowest weeks are the first two weeks of December. **Whale season** runs December 15-May 15, with peak whale-watching January 15-March 30. Visiting Maui during May and September gives you the benefit of summer weather with **lower prices** and **fewer crowds.**

Transportation

All flights from the continental United States arrive at **Kahului Airport** (OGG). Numerous rental-car options are available, and to save money when renting a car, consider renting from an off-site operator rather than a corporate chain. The rates are often much more affordable, and you get the benefit of a local-looking car. During the peak winter season and around Christmas holidays, reserve a rental car well in advance to ensure you get the best price.

The island is most easily explored by **car,** but if you only plan to stay in the resort areas, consider using **taxis** instead. With resort parking fees and fuel for the car, it can sometimes be cheaper to take taxis than rent a car. If there's a specific place you want to visit that requires a car, you can rent one for 24 hours and drop it off when you're done.

If your schedule is flexible and you aren't in a rush, the most affordable way to travel around the island is the **Maui Bus.** You can buy a day pass for only $4, and routes service much of the island.

If you're staying in West Maui, the small **Kapalua Airport** (JHM) has daily flights to Oʻahu, which can be convenient if you're hopping between islands and have a connection in Honolulu. The **Hana Airport** (HNM) has an afternoon flight that's just 20 minutes back to Kahului.

Halawa Valley

jumping from Pu'u Keka'a, also known as "Black Rock"

Best of Maui in 10 Days

Day 1

Given Hawaii's time zone, you may wake up before dawn. Take advantage by catching **sunrise at Haleakala.** Allow two hours of travel from Ka'anapali or Wailea and plan to arrive 30 minutes before sunrise. Spend an hour hiking into the crater. On your way down, have breakfast at **Kula Lodge** or **La Provence.** Spend the rest of the day relaxing poolside.

Day 2

Tackle another early morning activity such as a **snorkeling tour. Molokini** tours depart from Ma'alaea Harbor, while boats leave Ka'anapali Beach for **Olowalu** or **Honolua Bay.** Finish by 2pm and spend the afternoon relaxing on the beach.

Day 3

Enjoy **Lahaina,** ancient capital of the Hawaiian kingdom. Schedule a **surf lesson** or explore the town's **historic sites.** Grab lunch at **Aloha Mixed Plate** or **Cool Cat Café.** Then head north to world-famous **Ka'anapali Beach,** where you can snorkel, cliff-jump, play in the surf, or rent a cabana. Explore the shops in **Whalers Village,** dine at **Hula Grill,** and catch a showing of *'Ulalena* back in Lahaina that evening.

Day 4

Catch the 6:45am ferry to the island of **Lana'i.** Book a Jeep ahead of time and spend the morning exploring. Pick a remote beach such as **Polihua, Lopa,** or **Kaiolohia (Shipwreck Beach).** Then head back to **Lana'i City** for a plate lunch at **Blue Ginger.**

If you'd rather be **hiking,** call Rabaca's for a taxi up into town and the trailhead for the **Koloiki Ridge Trail.** Explore Lana'i City before catching a taxi down to **Hulopo'e Beach.** Snorkel along the reef or relax in the shade with a book. Hike around the corner to the **Pu'u Pehe Overlook,** keeping an eye out for the **spinner dolphins.** Rinse off at the beach shower, grab a drink at the **Four Seasons Resort,** and get back to the harbor to catch the 6:45pm ferry back to Maui.

Day 5

Sleep in before grabbing a late breakfast. Those staying in West Maui should dine at **The Gazebo,** followed by a stroll along the **Kapalua Coastal Trail.** Drive to **Kahakuloa,** stopping on the way at the **Nakalele Blowhole** or the **beach at Mokulei'a Bay.** If the conditions are calm and you can't get enough snorkeling, head to **Honolua Bay.** End the day with happy hour at the **Sea House** restaurant.

If you're staying in South Maui, brunch at **Kihei Caffe** before making the drive to **Makena.** Spend the day at **Maluaka Beach,** exploring to the end of the road, and walking the length of **Big Beach** just before sunset.

Day 6

Drive to **Pa'ia** and begin the day with a stroll down **Baldwin Beach,** followed by breakfast at **Café des Amis.** Enjoy the **Road to Hana** at a leisurely pace, taking time to hike to **Twin Falls** and explore the **Ke'anae Peninsula.** Check into your accommodations in Hana and enjoy sunset from **Hamoa Beach.**

Day 7

Catch the sunrise from **Wai'anapanapa State Park.** Visit the popular **Pools of 'Ohe'o** before day-trippers arrive around 11am. Spend a couple of hours exploring the pools and hiking the **Pipiwai Trail.** If the weather is nice, wrap around the back side of the island on the narrow and **rugged "back road."** Hike to **Alelele Falls,** grab a cold drink at the **Kaupo Store,** and experience a coast that feels like the end of the earth.

Day 8

Downtime: **Sleep in** as late as you'd like, lounge by the **pool,** get a **massage.** Breathe deeply.

Day 9

Spend the day in rural **Upcountry.** Enjoy breakfast on the lanai at **Grandma's Coffee House,** followed by a stroll down **Thompson Road.** Drive to **Ulupalakua** for a midday wine-tasting, and then double back the way you came to the town of **Makawao** for some **shopping** and lunch at **Polli's Mexican Restaurant.** Spend the afternoon in chic **Pa'ia,** although don't linger too long: You need to make it to the **Old Lahaina Luau** by 5pm to celebrate your last night on the island.

Day 10

Gradually make your way toward Kahului Airport. Stop in at the **Maui Ocean Center** for one last glimpse of marinelife. Continuing on to **Wailuku,** make the short drive into **'Iao Valley** to see the famous needle. At **Kanaha Beach Park,** watch the windsurfers. Think about how you'll miss Maui—and plan your next visit.

Hamoa Beach in Hana

Best Beaches

D. T. Fleming Beach Park

Fleming's offers some of the island's best bodysurfing, beachcombing, and coastal hiking. Public restrooms, showers, lifeguards, and parking make this a family-friendly beach. Surfers flock here in winter to tackle the large swells (page 40).

Ka'anapali Beach

Whether you're looking for snorkeling, stand-up paddling, cliff-jumping, or scuba diving, you'll find it at Ka'anapali Beach. This resort district is the see-and-be-seen shore for the island's West Side (page 42).

Napili Bay and Kapalua Bay

These two northwestern beaches offer protected snorkeling during summer. Swim with sea turtles at Napili and watch the sun go down from the deck of the Sea House restaurant with a drink in your hand (page 40).

Mokulei'a Bay

During summer, there are few better ways to start the day than by snorkeling at Mokulei'a. Tucked away at the base of the cliffs and hidden from the road, this is also a scenic and sandy spot for watching the large winter surf (page 41).

Keawakapu Beach

Enjoy a sunset stroll down Kihei's nicest beach, or spend your days snorkeling, stand-up paddling, or basking in the sun. Keawakapu has facilities on both ends of the beach, but despite the beach's popularity, there is always room to find your own section of shore (page 134).

Maluaka Beach

Maluaka is the most happening beach in Makena, where everything from kayaking to snorkeling and stand-up paddling are available. Public restrooms and showers make this a convenient spot for families, and you can walk down the road to historic Keawala'i Church (page 136).

Makena State Park

Wide, long, and completely **undeveloped,** aptly named **Big Beach** is a local favorite that comes alive at **sunset.** This legendary shore has a lengthy hippie history: **countercultural** visitors and nudists should visit neighboring **Little Beach** for Sunday night **drum circles** (page 137).

Baldwin Beach

This North Shore classic is a local favorite for **bodysurfing, bodyboarding,** and **scenic morning jogs. Undeveloped sand dunes** meld into **turquoise waters.** Families with **small children** will love the **cove at Baby Beach** with its protected **saltwater lagoon** (page 225).

Hamoa Beach

If your vision of paradise involves a book, a palm tree, and the sound of waves at your feet, you'll find it at Hamoa Beach, the **nicest beach in Hana.** Travelers from James A. Michener to Mark Twain have written of the beauty of its **sandy shore** (page 227).

Hulopo'e Beach Park

This **marine reserve** on the island of Lana'i has a **sandy cove,** a **vibrant reef,** and a **palm-fringed shore.** Summer months bring good **surfing** and **bodysurfing** and easy access to **coastal hiking trails.** Public restrooms, showers, and picnic tables make this a **family-friendly** outing (page 274).

Papohaku Beach

On most days your footprints will be the only set in the sand at Papohaku, one of the longest beaches in Hawaii. This westward-facing shore offers Moloka'i's **best sunsets.** It's perfect for anyone wanting to **escape** for a little while (page 300).

slate pencil urchin

ta'ape

Best Snorkeling and Diving

Honolua Bay
A world-renowned surf spot during winter, Honolua Bay has the island's best snorkeling during the calm, warm summer. Hawaiian **green sea turtles** are a common sight, as are **parrotfish, octopi,** and the rare **spinner dolphin** (page 45).

Puʻu Kekaʻa
The island's most famous snorkeling spot, also known as **Black Rock,** is one of its best. This rocky promontory on the Kaʻanapali strip is a magnet for **sea turtles** and **reef fish.** Morning hours offer the calmest conditions. Keep an eye out for the dozens of **cliff-jumpers** who throw themselves off the rock (page 48).

Napili Bay and Kapalua Bay
Within walking distance of each other on the island's northwestern coast, these two bays offer a sandy entry and **shallow, protected conditions.** Napili has more **turtles,** while Kapalua has more fish. Summer is the best time of year for calm and flat conditions (page 47).

Olowalu
Often known as **Mile Marker 14,** this historic shore along the side of the highway is great for **beginning snorkelers.** The best conditions are during the winter and earlier in the day. The outer reef is covered in **turtles** and is a playground of healthy coral (page 54).

Makena Landing
The volcanic Makena coast goes by many names; **Turtle Town** is perhaps the most relevant to snorkelers. It's pockmarked with **caves** that form the perfect shelter for sea turtles. Winter months are best along this southern shore. Everyone from scuba divers to kayak tours and snorkeling boats frequents the rugged coast (page 146).

Molokini Crater
A crescent-shaped volcanic caldera off the southern coast of Maui, Molokini Crater offers **crystal-clear waters** with 100-foot visibility most days of the year. Over a dozen snorkeling tours make the early morning pilgrimage to the crater, home to over **250 species of fish.** Companies such as **Trilogy Excursions** offer daily morning tours. For an extreme adventure, scuba divers should tackle the famous **Back Wall,** which drops straight down for nearly 300 feet (page 148).

Ulua and Mokapu Beach
These neighboring Wailea beaches are South Maui's most easily accessible, making them ideal for **beginning snorkelers.** The rocky point between the two beaches teems with **tropical reef fish** (page 145).

Hulopoʻe Beach Park
This Lanaʻi marine reserve has one of the **healthiest reefs** in Maui County and fronts a beach ranked as the nation's best. Come face-to-face with multihued **parrotfish** as they snack on colorful coral, or search the shallows for the *humuhumunukunukuapuaʻa,* Hawaii's state fish (page 278).

First and Second Cathedrals
These **offshore caverns** offer the best scuba diving on Lanaʻi. Beams of sunlight filter through the water, mimicking stained-glass windows—First Cathedral has even been the site of underwater weddings. You'll encounter everything from **frogfish** to **lobsters** and **spinner dolphins** (page 279).

Moku Hoʻoniki
Advanced scuba divers get their thrills on this Molokaʻi deep-water dive. It's home to a large population of **scalloped hammerhead sharks** (page 303).

Outdoor Adventures

PARAGLIDING IN POLIPOLI

Paragliding is Maui's most underrated adventure option. The Polipoli flying location has ideal conditions on a **cool mountain slope** with **views** gazing out over South Maui. The instructors at **Proflyght** will get you soaring (page 197).

KITESURFING AT KITE BEACH

Kitesurfing was born here on Maui. While experienced kiters can take straight to the water, schools such as **Hawaiian Sailboard Techniques** provide lessons for visitors who are looking to pick up a new sport (page 106).

STAND-UP PADDLING

Stand-up paddling (SUP) has its origins in Maui-- and it's popular all over the island. While seasoned pros will endure multiple-hour **downwinders**, even renting a board for an hour is a great introduction to the sport.

KAYAKING OR OUTRIGGER CANOEING

Many kayak tours combine snorkeling with an upper-body workout. Those looking for a **cultural connection** should snorkel from an **outrigger canoe,** ancient craft that date back to early Polynesia. **Hawaiian Paddle Sports** can get you on the water for a private paddling tour (page 63).

ZIPLINING ABOVE THE TREES

From **kid-friendly** short courses to stomach-churning screamers, ziplining has rapidly become one of the island's most popular activities. While all companies provide a thrilling experience, **Skyline Eco-Adventures** in Ka'anapali offers some of the best views (page 73).

sunrise SUP

WHALE-WATCHING IN KA'ANAPALI

Few things get your heart racing faster than a 50-ton animal leaping out of the water a few feet away. **Trilogy Excursions** offers **whale-watching charters** from both Lahaina and Ma'alaea. If luck is on your side, you just might end up on a boat that gets "mugged" (page 66).

MOUNTAIN BIKING MAKAWAO OR MOLOKA'I

The slopes of these islands are covered in **biking trails.** Makawao and Polipoli are the best spots on Maui, while Moloka'i's forest reserve is an **off-road playground.**

local Lahaina surfer

Best Surfing

Honolua Bay

Honolua Bay is a place of local legend, with one of the **best right-hand waves** in the world during winter. If you're an **expert surfer**—and show respect to locals by waiting your turn in the lineup—you could end up snagging the **wave of a lifetime** (page 58).

D. T. Fleming Beach Park

This Kapalua beach is popular with **bodyboarders** and is best during the winter. It's less crowded than neighboring Honolua, and much more user-friendly, but is for **intermediate to advanced** surfers (page 58).

Pohaku Beach Park

A **longboarder's** dream wave, **S-Turns** is the island's most user-friendly winter break and the most accepting of visiting **beginning surfers.** The long paddle out means a **long ride.** This rolling, forgiving wave is the perfect spot for honing your skills (page 57).

Ho'okipa Beach Park

The **most popular break** on the island's North Shore is also the center of the Pa'ia **surf scene.** Small days are acceptable for **beginners** who are still learning, but during the large swells of winter, this becomes an amphitheater of towering 20-foot surf for **experts** (page 229).

Pa'ia Bay

Walking distance from the center of town, Pa'ia Bay is one of the island's only real beach breaks. It's best for intermediate to advanced **shortboarding** and **bodyboarding** (page 228).

The Cove

The Cove is the **epicenter** of the bustling Kihei **surf scene.** The shallow, protected cove is home to the south side's numerous surf schools, with gentle waves that are perfect for **beginners** (page 153).

Lahaina Breakwall

Crowded, shallow, and nearly always sunny, the Lahaina Breakwall is where many visitors stand up and ride their first wave. **Surf schools** dominate the inside reef, while advanced surfers hang on the outside. While most days are calm with **gentle surf,** the large south **swells of summer** are for **advanced surfers** (page 59).

Launiupoko Beach Park

Keiki (children) learn to ride their first waves here at the most happening beach park on the road to Lahaina. **Longboarders** can choose from multiple peaks, while the **gentle waves** and calm conditions make it a perfect spot for **beginners** (page 60).

Hamoa Beach

More than just a beautiful beach, Hamoa has some of the best surf in East Maui. **Intermediate** and **advanced surfers** will find **wind swell** here any time of the year, even during summer when nowhere else on the island has waves (page 230).

Hulopo'e Beach Park

While it might not break often, Hulopo'e Beach has a **left-hand wave** on par with the best in the state—ideal for **intermediate** and **advanced surfers.** Summer is best for this south-facing shore on Lana'i. While spots on Maui can be crowded with 50 people, Hulopo'e will rarely ever have 10 (page 279).

Best Hikes

Sliding Sands Switchback Loop

This 12.2-mile sojourn crosses the floor of **Haleakala Crater** and weaves past **cinder cones** bursting with color. Keep an eye out for *nene* geese and glistening **silversword plants.** For a real thrill, hike by the light of the full moon (page 190).

Polipoli Spring State Recreation Area

Tucked in one of the least-visited corners of Maui, Polipoli looks more like the Pacific Northwest than a Pacific island. A **network of trails** weaves through **towering redwoods.** The silence in the forest is broken only by passing pheasants (page 191).

Na'ili'ili Haele

Known as the **bamboo forest,** this rugged, slippery trail on the **Road to Hana** hides a series of **waterfalls** set deep in the East Maui **rainforest.** The treacherous trail isn't for everyone, however: Hikers need to be in good physical condition (page 231).

Makamaka'ole Valley

Hidden along the twisting road between Kahului and Kahakuloa, Makamaka'ole offers some of the most accessible **waterfalls** in Central Maui. This **short, steep,** and **slippery** hike should only be attempted by physically fit hikers who are steady on their feet (page 109).

Hoapili Trail

Tucked away in the "deep south," the Hoapili Trail traces the winding **footpath of royalty** across **black fields of lava.** This winding, **rugged coastal track** is an enchanting time portal to ancient Hawaii. Mornings are best to beat the hot sun (page 159).

Pipiwai Trail

If expansive **banyan trees, dark bamboo forests,** and numerous **waterfalls** aren't enough of a thrill, this four-mile trail in Kipahulu reaches a dramatic terminus at the base of 400-foot **Waimoku Falls.** Often regarded as the island's best hike, this should be on every itinerary for a day spent in Hana (page 234).

Pipiwai Trail

Halawa Valley

Halawa Valley

More than just a hike to a **waterfall**, a trek in Halawa Valley on Moloka'i is a powerful journey to the **heart of Hawaiian culture**. Halawa Valley is one of the **oldest settlements** in the Hawaiian Islands. This valley is so **sacred** it can only be explored with a guide (page 308).

Munro Trail

Shaded by the boughs of Cook pines, this weaving dirt track on Lana'i climbs to the **summit** of 3,370-foot **Lana'ihale**. Views from this trail stretch toward Maui; on the clearest days, the summit is the only place in Hawaii where you can get a view of six islands at once (page 280).

Lahaina Pali Trail

Before the coastal road linking Kahului with Lahaina was created, this steep, hot, and dry trail was the preferred way to reach West Maui. The trail offers **panoramic views** and is perfect for **whale-watching, sunsets,** and working up a sweat (page 72).

Waihe'e Coastal Dunes and Wetlands Preserve

Hugging the shore of sleepy Waihe'e, this coastal track weaves its way past **ancient Hawaiian villages** along one the island's few remaining sections of **undeveloped coast** (page 108).

SUNRISES AND SUNSETS

Watch the sunset from the deck of a catamaran with a drink in one hand and your love in the other (page 64). Skip the early morning wake-up call for a sunrise trip and instead visit Haleakala for sunset (page 179). Spend the night in Hana to watch the sunrise from this eastern-facing shore, better known as Hana's Black-Sand Beach (page 218). Pu'u Pehe, often referred to as Sweetheart Rock, is visited by honeymooners who watch the sunset over the water from the panoramic overlook (page 281).

NATURAL WONDERS

The Phallic Rock is dedicated to Nanahoa, ancient Hawaiian god of fertility. Women traditionally visited this site in hopes of conceiving a child (page 296). Kiss beneath a waterfall on the Road to Hana (pages 213 and 214).

ROMANTIC UNWINDING

Old Lahaina's luau is the island's best; part of the show is devoted to couples who can dance together beneath the stars (page 79). Relax

Maui romance

after dancing the night away with a couples massage in an oceanfront cabana in Ka'anapali, Wailea, or Kapalua.

Best Historical and Cultural Sites

Bailey House Museum

Step inside this whitewashed missionary home to get a glimpse into 19th-century Maui. This museum also houses ancient Hawaiian artifacts, a surfboard ridden by Duke Kahanamoku, and one of the best bookstores for Hawaii-themed literature (page 98).

Alexander and Baldwin Sugar Museum

Within sniffing distance of the state's last sugar mill, this small museum takes an informative look at the island's multicultural plantation heritage (page 97).

Hui O Wa'a Kaulua Canoe Hale

The Hui O Wa'a Kaulua is an organization dedicated to the preservation of double-hulled Polynesian voyaging canoes. The group's canoe house is in Lahaina's Kamehameha Iki Park, where volunteers are happy to discuss

Kepaniwai Heritage Gardens

everything from Polynesian voyaging canoes to native Hawaiian culture (page 43).

Kepaniwai Heritage Gardens

Just a few minutes before ʻIao Valley, this small park parallels **ʻIao Stream** and features traditional housing of the island's **immigrant communities** (page 98).

Kalaupapa Peninsula

There was a time when a visit to Kalaupapa meant you'd just been handed a **death sentence.** Today, go to this **remote peninsula** on Molokaʻi to learn about the struggles of Hawaii's leprosy patients and **Father Damien,** the man who gave everything to try to save them (page 296).

Lanaʻi Culture and Heritage Center

This small, informative cultural center in the heart of **Lanaʻi City** traces the **island's history** from its original inhabitants through its era as the world's **largest pineapple plantation** (page 268).

Keʻanae Peninsula

This lush peninsula offers a refreshing glimpse into **"old Hawaii."** This taro-covered promontory is one of the island's last vestiges of indigenous Hawaiian culture (page 215).

Piʻilanihale Heiau

This towering, **50-foot-tall** *heiau* is the largest remaining religious structure in all of Polynesia. The surrounding area, **Kahanu Garden,** is largely unchanged from the **times of ancient Hawaii.** The stone platforms encompass an area the size of two football fields (page 217).

Respect

Although millions visit Maui annually and return home without incident, every year there is a handful who get hurt and end up in hospitals. Landowners get sued and access becomes restricted. Relations between locals and visitors have become increasingly strained. Litigation replaces handshakes, liability waivers become prolific, and warning signs stand where common sense once prevailed.

Healthy respect for the island and its nature, people, and culture is essential to a meaningful vacation. Just as each local is an ambassador for Hawaii, every visitor is a representative of the tourism industry. When visitors show respect for these islands, locals take notice. Some general guidelines:

RESPECT THE LAND

In traditional Hawaiian culture, the land is sacred above all. The earth and the sea provide us with sustenance, and to disrespect the land is the ultimate offense. The concept of landownership is foreign to traditional Hawaiian culture, which sees us as temporary stewards of the land. Pick up your *opala* (trash), stay off sensitive coral reefs, throw cigarette butts in proper receptacles, and help keep the valleys and shores as pristine as possible.

RESPECT LANDOWNERS' WISHES

Some unscrupulous travel publications encourage trespassing. As a result, far too many visitors walk across private land even when signs tell them not to. Poor behavior and lawsuits have led to restricted access for some formerly public sites. If you see a sign that says *Kapu* (keep out), No Trespassing, or Private Property, respect the landowners' wishes.

RESPECT NATURE

Many visitors' injuries are a direct result of failing to respect the power of nature. Waves are stronger than in other parts of the world, and flash floods, high winds, rough seas, and slippery rocks all claim lives annually. Respect warning signs. "If in doubt, don't go out."

RESPECT THE CULTURE

Hawaii has a culture that is unique in the world, and experiencing it is one of the best parts of visiting the islands. Tourism is the state's largest industry, but ultimately we are guests. Embrace the Hawaiian way of living and slow down for a little while.

Lahaina and West Maui

Highlights

★ **Nakalele Blowhole:** At this thunderous blowhole, pressure transforms incoming waves into a 100-foot geyser (page 30).

★ **Lahaina Courthouse:** With an art gallery in the basement, old photos on the ground level, and a museum on the third story, this is the best way to learn the unique history of Lahaina (page 36).

★ **Honolua Bay:** In summer, snorkel with sea turtles in this legendary protected bay. In winter, watch as the island's best surfers drop into waves over 20 feet high (page 45).

★ **Surfing Lahaina:** This ancient capital is one of the island's best places for learning the Hawaiian sport of kings (page 59).

★ **Sunset Cruises off Ka'anapali Beach:** Feel the trade winds in your hair as you literally sail into the sunset off West Maui's most iconic beach (page 64).

★ **Whale-Watching:** During December through April, the waters off Maui are home to the highest concentration of humpback whales on the planet. Head out for an up-close encounter with these 50-ton creatures (page 66).

★ **Kapalua Coastal Trail:** Spend an hour scouring the coast along this luxuriant yet rugged 1.75-mile trail. Along the way you will pass some of the Hawai'i's most beautiful beaches (page 69).

★ **Front Street:** Get your shopping,

© AVALON TRAVEL

people-watching, and dining fixes by walking the length of the island's most famous thoroughfare (page 76).

★ **'Ulalena and Maui Theatre:** The history of Hawaii is told through rhythms, dance, and creative special effects inside the impressive Maui Theatre (page 81).

The slopes and shores of West Maui are what many visitors picture when they close their eyes and envision paradise.

White sandy beaches, rocky coves, lush valleys, and oceanfront restaurants where the clinking glasses of mai tais and the smooth sounds of a slack-key guitar complement the setting sun—Maui is a magical place.

West Maui beaches are some of the best on the island. In winter, Honolua Bay shapes the kind of legendary right-hand point breaks that attract surfers from across the globe. In summer, this same bay offers some of the island's finest snorkeling, where bright parrotfish, shy octopi, and curious sea turtles occupy an expansive reef.

Hot, busy, and incomparably historic, Lahaina was once the whaling capital of the Pacific as well as the capital of the Hawaiian kingdom. Today, it's Maui's quintessential tourist town. The name "Lahaina" translates as "cruel, merciless sun," and, appropriately, almost every day is sunny in Lahaina. As a result, it buzzes with an energetic fervor that draws pedestrians to the streets, fishers to the harbor, and surfers to the breaks offshore.

Whether you're scouring the historic relics of Lahaina, swimming with reef fish at Napili Bay, stand-up paddleboarding along the Ka'anapali shore, or simply enjoying the sunset from an oceanfront luau, this is the Maui you were dreaming of.

ORIENTATION

West Maui, geographically, is an enormous swath of land. It technically begins once you pass through the tunnel and reach **Papalaua Beach,** and stretches all the way to **Kahakuloa** on the island's northern coast. With the exception of tiny **Olowalu village,** there's no development from the time you pass **Ma'alaea** until you reach **Lahaina.** Here you'll find Hawaii's ancient capital as well as restaurants, the harbor, and shops, whereas **Ka'anapali,** just up the road, is lined with world-class resorts. **Honokowai, Kahana,** and **Napili** meld together in a strip of oceanfront condos, and eventually give way to **Kapalua** resort about 20 minutes north of Lahaina. Past the resort, the coast gets wild and development comes to a halt,

Previous: Pu'u Keka'a, Ka'anapali; Honolua Bay. **Above:** inhabitant of the colorful West Maui reefs.

West Maui

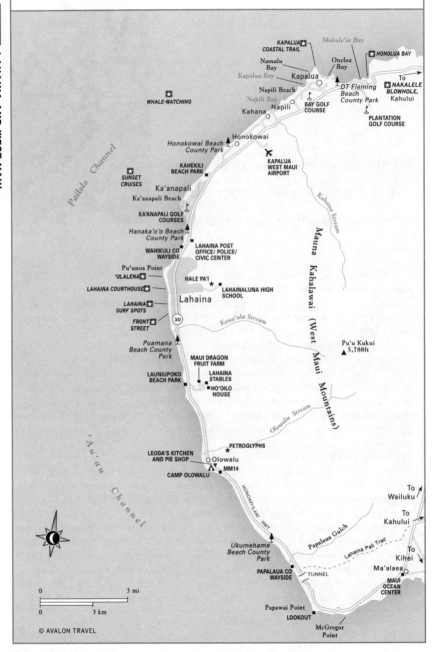

KAPALUA COASTAL TRAIL
Mokule'ia Bay
HONOLUA BAY
Namalu Bay
Oneloa Bay
Kapalua Bay
Kapalua
DT Fleming Beach County Park
To NAKALELE BLOWHOLE, Kahului
Napili Beach
Napili Bay
BAY GOLF COURSE
WHALE-WATCHING
Kahana
Napili
PLANTATION GOLF COURSE
Pailolo Channel
Honokowai Beach County Park
Honokowai
KAPALUA WEST MAUI AIRPORT
KAHEKILI BEACH PARK
SUNSET CRUISES
Ka'anapali
Kahana Stream
Ka'anapali Beach
KA'ANAPALI GOLF COURSES
Hanaka'o'o Beach County Park
WAHIKULI CO WAYSIDE
LAHAINA POST OFFICE/ POLICE/ CIVIC CENTER
Mauna Kahalawai (West Maui Mountains)
Pu'unoa Point
'ULALENA
HALE PA'I
LAHAINALUNA HIGH SCHOOL
LAHAINA COURTHOUSE
Lahaina
LAHAINA SURF SPOTS
Kaua'ula Stream
Pu'u Kukui 5,788ft
FRONT STREET
30
Puamana Beach County Park
MAUI DRAGON FRUIT FARM
LAUNIUPOKO BEACH PARK
LAHAINA STABLES
HO'OILO HOUSE
Olowalu Stream
'Au'au Channel
PETROGLYPHS
LEODA'S KITCHEN AND PIE SHOP
Olowalu
MM14
CAMP OLOWALU
HONOAPI'ILANI HWY
To Wailuku
To Kahului
Papalaua Gulch
Lahaina Pali Trail
To Kihei
Ukumehame Beach County Park
TUNNEL
Ma'alaea
PAPALAUA CO WAYSIDE
MAUI OCEAN CENTER
0   3 mi
0   3 km
Papawai Point
LOOKOUT
McGregor Point
© AVALON TRAVEL

Your Best Day in West Maui

Get up early and head to **The Gazebo** to be in line for the 7:30am opening. After breakfast drive up the road to **Kapalua Bay** and walk off the stack of macadamia pancakes with a stroll on the **Kapalua Coastal Trail.** Having worked up a sweat and soaked up the views, grab snacks and drinks at **Honolua Store** before embarking on the adventurous drive north.

If you feel like snorkeling and have your own gear, stop for an hour at **Mokulei'a Bay** and search for octopi and turtles, or simply take a stroll through the vines on a walk through **Honolua Valley.** Stop to photograph the world-famous bay when you reach the top of the hill, and then continue driving all the way toward **Nakalele Blowhole.** Watch your step as you clamber down to the thundering saltwater geyser, and if you're feeling up for it, continue driving to **Kahakuloa.**

By now it'll be getting late in the day, and you need to make it to **The Sea House** in Napili by 4:30pm for happy hour. Appetizers are 50 percent off, then enjoy a filling, early dinner overlooking Napili Bay.

Rainy Day? Grab breakfast at **Sunrise Café** and listen to the rain come down before escaping it by heading underwater on a tour with **Atlantis Submarines.** Get a burger at **Cool Cat Café,** and then brush up on your Hawaiian history inside the **Lahaina Courthouse.** Since there won't be much of a sunset, end the evening with dinner at **Thai Chef** and the show **'Ulalena.**

and sandy beaches give way to rocky coves and rugged cliffs.

PLANNING YOUR TIME

More people stay in West Maui than any other part of the island, and in many ways it feels separated from other parts of Maui. If you find yourself based here, it's easy to make simple, half-day jaunts to the beach, or go on tropical micro-adventures before lounging back at the resort. For other travelers who aren't based in West Maui, two full days is a good amount of time to experience the area's best sights, with one day spent in Lahaina and Ka'anapali and another exploring "up north." From Kahului Airport, it's about 40 minutes to Lahaina and an hour to Kapalua, though as the island grows, the traffic is getting particularly bad—and driving to Lahaina between 3pm and 5pm can often be bumper to bumper. Factor this in if you're trying to get to your 5pm oceanfront luau.

Sights

KAPALUA, NAPILI, AND HONOKOWAI

Exploring the island's northwestern coast is one of the island's best day trips—like a miniature Road to Hana without the waterfalls, but with far better beaches and views. If you continue all the way around the back of West Maui past the town of Kahakuloa (the road isn't limited to 4WD vehicles like your rental-car map might say, but it is far narrower, curvier, and scarier than the Road to Hana), you can combine the drive with the waterfalls of Makamaka'ole Valley in Central Maui for a full-day experience. This journey is not for the timid. Most turn back toward Kapalua once they reach Kahakuloa.

Makalua-puna Point

For spectacular views of the northwestern coast and white-sand Oneloa Bay, take a stroll on **Makalua-puna Point**—otherwise known as "Dragon's Teeth." The jagged rocks here have been dramatically sculpted by waves crashing on the coast, and there's a large labyrinth in the middle of the point for silently reflecting on the beauty. The trailhead is located by the small parking lot at the end of Office Road. Visit without leaving a trace; this point is sacred to native Hawaiians and access can be controversial, so tread lightly when you follow the trail out onto the windswept point.

Honolua Bay

Famous for its exceptional surfing and diving, **Honolua Bay** is also one of West Maui's most beautiful sights. There is a palpable magic in this bay, from the vine-laden valley that leads to the shore and the reef that's teeming with life, to the simply legendary right-hand wave that perfectly bends around the point. When visiting Honolua Bay—particularly when the surf is breaking—either stop at the overlook on the north side of the bay after climbing the short but steep hill, or drive down the bumpy dirt road that leads to the top of the bluff. To continue the Honolua adventure on foot, walk to the where the dirt road ends, where a very thin trail connects with a network of coastal trails that lead to views of the coast.

★ Nakalele Blowhole

Eight miles past the entrance to Kapalua, by mile marker 38, is the famous **Nakalele Blowhole.** Outside of Honolua Bay this is the most popular stop along this stretch of coast. It's about a 15-minute drive past the entrance to Kapalua if you go straight through without stopping. On the right days, the Nakalele Blowhole can jettison water upward of 100 feet into the air. The best conditions for witnessing Nakalele are when the trade winds are blowing and there's northerly swell. In the full throes of its performance, Nakalele Blowhole is a natural saltwater geyser erupting on a windswept outcropping, and it's one of the most powerful forces of the sea you can witness on the island. Visitors in the past have been killed by standing too close to the blowhole, so pay attention to warning signs in the area.

Finding the blowhole can be a challenge for those who don't know where to look. At mile marker 38 there is dirt pullout on the ocean side of the highway, although the trail from here that leads down toward the water will only take you as far as the decrepit old lighthouse and a marginal view of the blowhole. A better access point is 0.5 mile farther down the road where a second dirt pullout serves as the

Nakalele Blowhole

trailhead for the path leading to the blowhole. Between the two parking areas are dozens of dirt-bike tracks that don't lead anywhere, so the best thing to do is park by mile marker 38.5 and make your way down from there. The trail to the blowhole is just over 0.5 mile long, and the last half of the trail becomes a scramble down a moderate scree slope, which is best left to those who are steady on their feet. When you reach the bottom of the rocky trail, turn around and look behind you, facing away from blowhole. If you look closely, you'll find the **heart-shaped hole in the rocks** that's a Maui Instagram darling.

The Olivine Pools

A little over four miles past the Nakalele Blowhole, by mile marker 16, the **Olivine Pools**—traditionally called Mokolea—are one of the more unique and beautiful sights on the northwestern side of the island. The coastal panoramas from here are breathtaking, and even if you don't walk down to the pools, the views alone are reason enough to stop. For most visitors, though, the goal is to swim and bathe in the shallow tide pools perfectly perched on a lava rock outcropping. On rare calm days when the wind is light and the ocean is mellow and smooth, this can be one of the most serene perches you'll find anywhere on the island. However, the ocean is treacherous here, which makes swimming in the pools risky. A good rule of thumb is to sit and watch them for a while and wait to see if any waves are crashing into them. If the ocean is calm and isn't reaching the pools, then this is the safest time for swimming or wading. Visitors *have* died trying to reach the pools, so it is especially important to be aware of your surroundings at all times. If waves are washing into the pools, keep out. Park in the dirt area on the ocean side of the road, and follow the trail leading down toward the coast to access the pools. The trail will fork at a yellow sign that warns about the dangers of continuing. Follow the trail to the edge of the bluff and then proceed down the trail leading to the pools.

KA'ANAPALI
Pu'u Keka'a

Known to most visitors as Black Rock, **Pu'u Keka'a** is the correct name for this volcanic outcropping at the northern end of Ka'anapali Beach. Today the rock is a popular spot for snorkeling, scuba diving, and cliff-jumping, although the most popular time of day is about 20 minutes prior to sunset when a torch-wielding, shirtless member of the Sheraton staff scrambles onto the rock and lights a row of carefully placed tiki torches. Once all of the torches are lit, his flaming staff is ceremoniously chucked into the water moments before he performs a swan dive off the rock. More than just a creative marketing plan, the ceremony is a reenactment of the sacred belief that this is one of the spots on the island where a person's soul leaps from this world to the next immediately following death. For a prime perch to watch the show, grab a drink at the Cliff Dive Bar inside the Sheraton Maui.

Whalers Village Museum

There's actually more to Whalers Village than high-end luxury shopping and beachfront bars. On the third story, high above the fancy stores and bustling courtyard, the **Whalers Village Museum** (2435 Ka'anapali Pkwy., 808/661-5992, www.whalersmuseum.com, 10am-6pm daily, $3 adults, $2 seniors, $1 children) is the best resource for whale education on the island's West Side. Visitors can wander through the museum to learn everything from why whales were hunted in the first place to what life was like aboard a 19th-century whaling ship. There is a large display of scrimshaw art (drawings carved on whale's teeth), and there are also movies playing throughout the day that explore the dismal yet fascinating world of 19th-century whaling. During winter, a visit to the museum is the perfect way to reinforce the knowledge gained on a whale-watching excursion.

Tour of the Stars

For a truly unique Ka'anapali experience, stand on the roof of the Hyatt and stargaze

Ka'anapali

Continue Beach Walk

To Napili and Kapalua

HONUA KAI

'AINA GOURMET MARKET

DUKE'S

PAILOLO BAR AND GRILL

30

WESTIN KA'ANAPALI OCEAN RESORT VILLAS

KAI

ALA DR

PU'UKOLI'I STATION

KAHEKILI BEACH PARK

PU'UKOLI'I RD

Old Airport Beach

MAUI KA'ANAPALI VILLAS

ROYAL LAHAINA TENNIS RANCH

Keka'a Beach

ROYAL LAHAINA RESORT

Beach Walk

DR

MAUI ELDORADO

KEKA'A

SKYLINE ECO ADVENTURE

PU'U KEKA'A (BLACK ROCK)

SHERATON MAUI

FAIRWAY SHOPS

CJ'S DELI

SUNSET CRUISES OFF KA'ANAPALI BEACH

TIKI TERRACE

KA'ANAPALI BEACH HOTEL

TRILOGY OCEAN SPORTS

HULA GRILL

THE WHALER

Ka'anapali Beach

WHALER'S VILLAGE

LEILANI'S

WHALE MUSEUM

HONOAPI'ILANI HWY

SUGAR CANE TRAIN

Ka'anapali Golf Course

WESTIN MAUI

KA'ANAPALI

KA'ANAPALI ALII

ROYS

KA'ANAPALI GOLF COURSES CLUBHOUSE

PARKWAY

PARADISE GRILL

MAUI MARRIOTT

NOHEA KAI DR

Beach Walk

HYATT TENNIS CENTER

30

HYATT REGENCY

JAPENGO

0   0.25 mi

UMALU

To Lahaina

0   0.25 km

HANAKA'O'O BEACH PARK

© AVALON TRAVEL

through high-powered telescopes. Held at 8pm and 9pm every night, the **Tour of the Stars** (200 Nohea Kai Dr., 808/667-4727) allows small groups of 14 people to access the roof of the resort and peer through a 14-inch reflector telescope with the resort's director of astronomy. Tours are $25 for adults and $15 for children, and if you want to make it a romantic evening, join the nightly 10pm tour with chocolate-covered strawberries and champagne ($40 pp).

LAHAINA

From 1820 to 1845, this seaside town—which was originally called Lele—was the capital of the Hawaiian kingdom. At about the same time that the *ali'i* (nobility) and royalty were establishing their capital, fleets of New England whaling ships began anchoring in the Lahaina Roads. From 1820 to 1860, thousands of crusty whalers paddled ashore in wooden rowboats to reprovision their ships, soak their livers, and soothe their rusty loins. Answering the call to save these poor souls, Christian missionaries from New England began to arrive in the early 1820s, bolstered by the support of Queen Ka'ahumanu, who had embraced the values of Christianity. Lahaina became a battleground between drunken whalers and pious missionaries to win over the native Hawaiian populace, a Wild West of the Pacific. Today, scores of historic sites pertaining to this era are scattered around town.

Thanks to the tireless work of the Lahaina Restoration Foundation, many of the town's historic sites are well marked and accessible. Pick up a walking tour map from the Lahaina Visitors Center in the courthouse next to Lahaina Harbor or a *Mo'olelo O Lahaina* historical and cultural walking tour map from the offices of the Lahaina Restoration Foundation on the grounds of the Baldwin Missionary home.

The Banyan Tree

This magnificent tree is the most recognizable landmark in West Maui. You can't miss it at the corner of Hotel and Front Streets,

Parking in Lahaina

If you're looking for a good way to fight with your spouse, try finding parking in Lahaina while running late for an activity. A web of narrow streets and overpriced lots, Lahaina for most visitors is an expensive source of angst and confusion when it comes to parking.

But it doesn't have to be that way. Here are a few tips to help cut through the confusion.

- Most street parking in Lahaina is good for three hours, and there are no parking meters. If you know that you're only going to be a few hours, there is no need to pay for a parking lot. Free street parking can be found on Dickenson and Waine'e Streets, and there is a large, three-hour parking lot on the corner of Prison and Front Streets. The three-hour lot is heavily patrolled, however, so if you overstay, you'll likely end up with a $60 ticket.

- While there is also free street parking on Front Street, attempting to parallel park on Front Street is difficult and can block traffic. Save yourself the hassle and don't even try.

- If you're eating dinner in Lahaina, there is free parking at Lahaina Harbor between the courthouse and the harbor 7pm-7am daily, although you can't park in the back lot by the fishing boats because it's by permit only. On weekends and public holidays, there is free parking all day in the spaces in front of Kamehameha III School by the junction of Prison and Front Streets.

- There is also free all-day parking in the lot behind the Front Street tennis courts. The spaces when you first pull in are reserved for the cultural center, but there is a dirt parking lot in the back as well as a paved parking lot by the back tennis courts. There is a sizable homeless population there; don't leave valuables in your car.

- Parking in a paid parking lot doesn't make your car any more secure. Only a few of them are monitored, but car break-ins happen at hiking trailheads and beaches more than in central Lahaina in broad daylight. The only reason you would ever need to pay for parking in Lahaina is for the convenience of being closer to where you're trying to go. There is enough free parking for everyone. Essentially, paying for parking is a convenience, but not a necessity.

- Luakini Street, paralleling Front Street, is a one-way, with traffic running north to south on the south end of Dickenson, and south to north on the north end of Dickenson. Confused? Better to just avoid the street entirely.

- Allow yourself enough time. Parking may take 5 or 10 minutes, so factor this in when scheduling your day.

because it spreads its shading boughs over almost an acre. This tree is the **largest banyan in the state,** planted in April 1873 by Sheriff Bill Smith in commemoration of the Congregationalist Missions' golden anniversary. Every year in April a birthday party is held for the tree that draws hundreds of people to its shady confines. During most days you can find old-timers sitting here chatting, and artists gather on weekends to display their artwork under the tree's broad branches.

Fort at Lahaina

On the southwestern edge of the park are the restored coral remnants of the historic **Fort at Lahaina.** By 1825 the missionaries had convinced Hawaiian royalty that drunken sailors running amok in town was morally lamentable, so strict laws forbade native women from visiting the ships and whalers from coming ashore after nightfall. These rules, as you can imagine, proved a severe hindrance to lascivious pursuits, and riots frequently broke out between angry whalers and the missionaries. In 1827, whalers anchored offshore went so far as to lob cannonballs into the lawn of missionary William Richards's house, and it was decided by Hoapili—the governor of Maui—that a fort needed to be built to protect the town from the pent-up whalers. Hence, in 1832, a

Downtown Lahaina

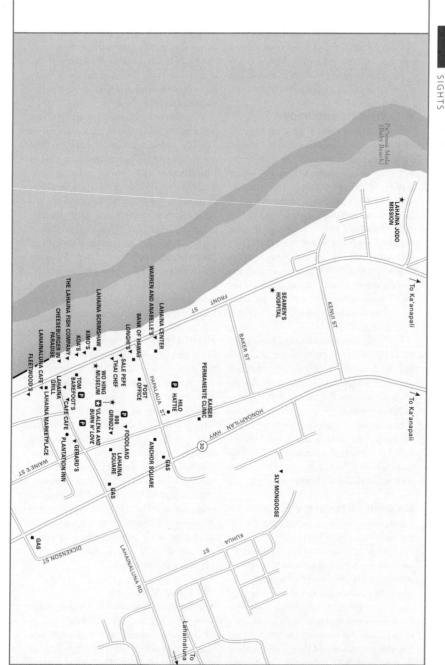

LAHAINA JODO MISSION ★

Pu'unoa Mala (Baby Beach)

To Ka'anapali

To Ka'anapali

SEAMEN'S HOSPITAL ★

FRONT ST

KENUI ST

BAKER ST

KAISER PERMANENTE CLINIC ■

HILO HATTIE ■

P

PAPALAUA ST

POST OFFICE ■

WO HING MUSEUM ★

808 GRINDZ ▼

'ULALENA AND BURN N' LOVE ★

P

FOODLAND ■

LAHAINA SQUARE ■

ANCHOR SQUARE ■

GAS

HONOAPI'ILANI HWY

30

SLY MONGOOSE ▼

KUHUA ST

LAHAINA CENTER ■

WARREN AND ANABELLE'S ▼

BANK OF HAWAII ■

LONGHI'S ▼

SALE PEPE ▼

THAI CHEF ▼

LAHAINA SCRIMSHAW ■

KIMO'S ▼

KOA'S ▼

THE LAHAINA FISH COMPANY ▼

CHEESEBURGER IN PARADISE ▼

LAHAINALUNA CAFE ■

FLEETWOOD'S ▼

TOM BAREFOOT'S ■

P

LAHAINA GRILL ▼

CAFE CAFE ▼

GERARD'S ▼

PLANTATION INN ●

P

LAHAINA MARKETPLACE ■

WAINE'E ST

GAS

GAS

DICKENSON ST

GAS

LAHAINALUNA RD

To Lahainaluna

To Lahainaluna

fort was constructed out of coral blocks with walls 20 feet high and laden with cannons, the restored remnants of which are still visible today. One of the cannons from the fort is across the street at Lahaina Harbor, facing out toward the water to serve as a reminder of the "tensions" that once gripped this town.

★ Lahaina Courthouse

The old **Lahaina Courthouse** contains the most informative museum in central Lahaina. During its tenure as the town's political center, it also served as governor's office, post office, customs office, and police station, complete with a jail in the underground basement. The jail is now home to the Lahaina Arts Society's **Old Jail Gallery,** and the society has its main **Banyan Tree Gallery** on the first floor. Since renovation in 1998, the **Lahaina Visitors Center** (808/667-9193, 9am-5pm daily) has also occupied a room on the main floor. Find tourist information and brochures about the town; numerous coupon books can help save a few dollars.

In the old courtroom on the second floor, the **Lahaina Heritage Museum** (9am-5pm daily, $3 donation) displays historical objects and old photographs, and there is even the original Hawaiian flag that was lowered from the courthouse on the day it was replaced in 1898 by the American stars and stripes. On the lower level there is also a small theater with informative documentaries about life in the islands. This is a must-stop for anyone with an interest in the history of Lahaina.

Baldwin Missionary House

On the inland side of Front Street, on the corner with Dickenson Street, you will notice the sprawling green lawn and whitewashed front of the historic **Baldwin Missionary House** (10am-4pm daily, $7 adults, $5 seniors). Established in 1834, this restored and peaceful property has stood since the days of the earliest missionaries and was the home of physician and reverend Dwight Baldwin, his wife, Charlotte, and their eight children. Baldwin was the first modern doctor and

dentist in Hawaii, having studied at Harvard, and in the back of the museum are his tools. Until 1868 this building also served as a dispensary, meeting room, and boardinghouse, and Baldwin was instrumental not only in educating scores of Hawaiians but also in helping to fight the smallpox epidemic that struck the island in 1853.

Various rooms contain period furniture and artifacts indicative of missionary life in Lahaina, and coin collectors will appreciate the array of historic coins that were used as legal tender in early Hawaii, including silver bullion minted in Bolivia as early as the 1500s. Entrance to the museum also covers the Wo Hing Museum up the street, and if you purchase a $10 Passport to the Past, admission to the A&B Sugar Museum in Kahului and the Bailey House Museum in Wailuku are also included. While visiting in the daytime is educational enough, for a true glimpse of missionary life, take part in a candlelit tour 6pm-8:30pm every Friday evening.

Plantation Museum

For a look at a period of Lahaina's history that didn't have to do with whalers, missionaries, or Hawaiian royalty, idle on over to the Wharf Cinema Center and climb the stairs to the third story for a glimpse inside the informative **Plantation Museum** (no phone, 9am-6pm daily, free). Although it isn't much larger than a closet, there are dozens of old photos showing life during plantation times as well as a video detailing harvesting sugarcane. The Pioneer Mill was the social and economic engine of the West Side for the better part of 100 years, and the plantation days are just as much a part of Lahaina's heritage as harpoons, grog, and Bibles. A visit only takes a couple of minutes and is worthwhile.

Wo Hing Museum

The **Wo Hing Museum** (858 Front St., 10am-4pm daily, $7) is a small Chinese museum sandwiched between the modern commercial ventures of Front Street. Built in 1912 as a social and religious hall for Chinese workers,

Moku'ula: The Ancient Capital of Hawaii

Until 1845, the town of Lahaina served as the royal capital of Hawaii. Generations of rulers from King Kamehameha on ruled the kingdom from this historic sun-drenched shore, and some of the most notable events in Hawaiian history were witnessed by this town.

If Lahaina was so important, you ask, where is the royal palace? Where is the seat of the monarchy? Where, exactly, was the capital? Unfortunately, when the capital was moved to Honolulu in 1845, the site of the former capital—Moku'ula—was abandoned and left to decay. Where once the home of ali'i and royalty existed, there is now an overgrown baseball field frequented by the island's homeless. If ever there were a fall from grace, it is the site of Moku'ula.

All hope is not lost for the former capital, however, as nonprofit group **Friends of Moku'ula** (808/661-3659, www.mokuula.com) is committed to restoring the nearly forgotten site, across from the area on Front Street where the 505 shopping center now stands. During the time when royalty called it home, there was a 25-acre *loko*, or fishpond, named Mokuhinia that was fed by the streams flowing from Mauna Kahalawai. In the middle of this pond was a small island— Moku'ula—and only the highest chiefs and Hawaiian royalty were allowed to set foot on it. Within walking distance of the ocean and framed by the mountainous backdrop, it must have been a sight to behold.

When the capital was moved, the stream was diverted to irrigate the sugar crop, and the Mokuhinia fishpond became a festering swamp of mosquitoes and bugs. Taking matters into their own hands, mill workers filled the pond with dirt in 1914. The ballfield and parking structures that stand in its place were subsequently constructed on top.

Just because Moku'ula isn't visible, however, doesn't mean that it's gone. Archaeologists estimate that the site still exists about three feet below the surface, and digs have yielded artifacts that show evidence of the ancient fishpond. The Friends of Moku'ula are working to raise awareness and raise funding for a major restoration of the former royal site. The group envisions the site as a historic landmark as well as an educational resource about Hawaiian culture.

For a more in-depth look at both the history and future of Moku'ula, take one of the **Maui Nei** (505 Front St., 808/661-9494, www.mauinei.com) two-hour cultural walking tours ($50 adults, $24 ages 6-12), which not only cover many of the historic sites of Lahaina but also spend ample time discussing Moku'ula. For a truly in-depth cultural experience, book one of the 3.5-hour Discover Old Hawaii tours ($150 pp), where you'll participate in creating cultural arts at Lahaina's most sacred places. If you have an interest in Hawaiian history, there are few tours that will provide the level of insight offered on these tours.

it's been placed on the National Register of Historic Places, showcasing Chinese immigration history on Maui, as well as Chinese cultural traditions. Downstairs are displays, and upstairs is the temple altar. In the cookhouse next door, you can see film clips of Hawaii taken by Thomas Edison in 1898 and 1906. On Chinese New Year, the Wo Hing Museum is the center of the activities that play out on Front Street. The entrance fee also covers entrance to the Baldwin House.

Hale Pa'ahao

Where Luakini crosses Prison Street, turn left and walk a few yards to **Hale Pa'ahao** (no phone, 10am-4pm daily, free), better known as Lahaina's old prison, one of the more historically informative sites. The peaceful courtyard inside the prison walls is a place of serenity and calm, where benches rest beneath the shade of a mango tree, but this compound once housed dozens of sailors and Hawaiians who broke the laws set out by the royals and their missionary advisors. To get an idea of an offense that would land you in the Lahaina slammer, read the list from the 1850s posted on the wall of one of the whitewashed wooden cells.

Lahaina Jodo Mission

On the northern end of Lahaina by Baby Beach and Mala Wharf, **Lahaina Jodo Mission** (12 Ala Moana St., 808/661-4304, sunrise-sunset daily) is found by turning off Front Street where a sign over a building reads "Jesus Coming Soon." Turn left toward the beach and you'll immediately spot the three-tiered wooden pagoda at the end of the road. The temple bell welcomes you at the entrance gate, and a giant bronze Buddha sits exposed to the elements on a raised stone platform nearby. The largest Buddha outside Asia, this seated Amita Buddha image was dedicated in 1968 in commemoration of the centennial of the arrival of Japanese workers in Hawaii. You may stroll around, and while the buildings are closed to the public, you can climb the steps of the main building to peek into the temple. It's the perfect spot for solitary meditation if you've had enough of frenetic Lahaina. Buddha's birthday is celebrated here every April.

Hale Pa'i Printing Museum

All the way at the top of Lahainaluna Road on the grounds of Lahainaluna High School, which is the oldest high school west of the Rocky Mountains, having been founded in 1831, **Hale Pa'i Printing Museum** (808/667-7040, Mon.-Wed. 10am-4pm, free) provides a phenomenally informative view into the literary past of the Hawaiian Islands. If you're involved in the education field or interested in history, this is a must-stop for a look at the history of Hawaii's printed past.

In addition to the old printing press, there are a host of native Hawaiian artifacts. This small, out-of-the-way museum in the school's parking lot provides excellent insight into the development of modern Hawaii.

SOUTH OF LAHAINA
Olowalu Petroglyphs

For every 1,000 people who snorkel at Olowalu, probably only one makes it back to the *ki'i pohaku*, the petroglyphs behind the Olowalu General Store. Hidden 0.5 mile back in the recesses of Olowalu valley, the 70 rock carvings on the face of Pu'u Kilea date to nearly 300 years ago, when there was no written form of the Hawaiian language. The Olowalu valley is heavily steeped in Hawaiian history, and even though a century of sugar cultivation and the encroachment of modern development has eroded traditional village sites, a number of families living back in the valley aim to perpetuate the lifestyle of their ancestors.

To find the petroglyphs, drive on the road behind the Olowalu fruit stand at mile marker 15 and proceed on the paved segment, which runs back toward the valley. After 0.5 mile are signs for the Olowalu Cultural Reserve, and when the road turns to dirt, the petroglyphs are about 200 yards farther, on the rock face. Unfortunately, some of the petroglyphs have been vandalized, so visitors are asked to keep a respectful distance from them.

Maui Dragon Fruit Farm

The **Maui Dragon Fruit Farm** (833 Punakea Loop, 808/264-6127, www.mauidragonfruit. com), in the Launiupoko subdivision, makes for a curious combination of agriculture and adventure. With the consistency of an apple but the look of an exotic poppy-seed muffin, dragon fruit is tropical and native to Central and South America, although it's most often seen in Southeast Asia. In addition to dragon fruit, various other crops are grown on this certified organic farm.

Guided farm tours ($15 adults) take place at 10am and 1pm daily. Additional adventure activities include a 450-foot-long zipline (10am, 11:30am, 2pm, and 4:30pm daily, $80 adults, $50 children) and an enormous plastic "Aquaball" (10am, 11:30am, 2pm, and 3:30pm daily, $90 adults, $70 children) filled with water and then rolled 450 feet downhill with you inside. Combine the farm tour, zipline, and the Aquaball for $140 adults or $100 children.

Missionaries: "Came to Do Good and Stayed to Do Well"

All around West Maui, from the Baldwin House in central Lahaina to the fallow fields of former sugar plantations, island visitors are surrounded by signs of the missionary influence.

The first Protestant missionaries arrived from New England in 1820 aboard a wooden brig named *Thaddeus* after a tortuous journey around Cape Horn. Led by Hiram Bingham (whose grandson would go on to "discover" Machu Picchu), the original missionaries immediately set to work crafting a moral compass for the wayward Hawaiians, who had abandoned their centuries-old religious system only a year earlier. A written form of the Hawaiian language was created, Bibles were printed, and within a few years a number of the Hawaiian nobility were converted to Christianity.

It didn't take long for the missionaries to start having children. In the same year of their arrival, the first nonindigenous child was born in the Hawaiian Islands. The introduction of progeny would not only alter the social structure of the mission, but change the political and economic course of the kingdom of Hawaii.

In 1848, the American Board of Commissioners for Foreign Missions, which had founded and funded the endeavor, agreed to allow missionaries to engage in economic pursuits—including owning property. A momentous event known as the Great Mahele was planned by the Hawaiian monarchy, and according to the terms of the Mahele—or division—a system of land ownership was established in Hawaii to subdivide lands between the crown, the chiefs, and private citizens. Though native residents had two years to lay claim to their *kuleana,* or homestead lands, many citizens literally "didn't get the memo." By 1850 much of these lands became available for foreign purchase. Suddenly, what was once a religious mission began to take on the form of a colony.

Though their parents remained dutifully devoted to the faith, the Hawaii-born children of missionaries instead focused on economic opportunity. Samuel Alexander and Henry Baldwin—children of missionaries who arrived in 1831 and 1832—pooled their money in 1869 to buy 12 acres of Makawao sugar land for $110. Today, the Alexander & Baldwin company has over 88,000 acres of land and assets of over $1.4 billion, is traded on the New York Stock Exchange, and has been listed as one of the 1,000 largest companies in the United States.

Another missionary child—Sanford Dole—became a central figure in the 1893 overthrow of the Hawaiian government and ultimately the president of the short-lived Republic of Hawaii. His cousin, James Dole, turned the island of Lana'i into the world's largest pineapple plantation.

Today, the legacy of Hawaii's missionaries lives on in the real estate, business, agriculture, and ranching industries of Hawaii. Names such as Baldwin, Dole, Cooke, Castle, and Rice are plastered on everything from arts centers to high schools to public parks.

Think about this while you stand in the Baldwin Missionary House. The people who founded and inhabited these sites would ultimately end up changing the course of Hawaii's history—for better or for worse.

Beaches

KAPALUA, NAPILI, AND HONOKOWAI

Known to locals simply as "up north," the beaches along this stretch include tropical turquoise coves sandwiched between condos and luxurious homes. Napili and Kapalua beaches are the most popular, but past the entrance to Kapalua, the shore gets wilder and the crowds start to thin. The wind can howl in the afternoons and massive surf crashes into the coast October-April. Over the winter the shorebreak often grows to 10 feet or larger.

Honokowai Beach Park

The farthest point south, Honokowai Beach Park is a narrow stretch of sand at the northern edge of Ka'anapali. While the beach here is far from the nicest on the island, there is a large, grassy park with a playground for small children and a couple of shops across the street.

Napili Bay and Kapalua Bay

There is a lot of debate about which beach is better: Napili Bay or Kapalua Bay. There are a couple of factors that distinguish one from the other. Although a mere 0.25 mile from each other, the shore-break at Napili Bay can be larger in the winter, whereas Kapalua is more protected. The snorkeling between the two reefs is a toss-up, although Kapalua often has more fish while Napili has more sea turtles. Napili Bay is a little larger, although it can also become more crowded. If you are traveling with children, Kapalua Bay is the better bet since the water is calmer and there is easy access to beach showers and restrooms.

Your best chance for finding parking at Napili Bay is either along the side of Lower Honoapi'ilani Road between Napili Kai and the Kapalua Tennis Club, or on the south end of the beach, where there is some beach parking at the bottom of Hui Drive. The beach parking lot at Kapalua Bay fills up early. If you can't find a parking place, drop all of your beach gear by the stairs leading down to the sand and then circle back to find a parking spot along the road.

Oneloa Bay (Ironwoods)

Hidden from view from the road through Kapalua, Oneloa Bay is virtually always empty. This epic expanse of shore sits right along the Kapalua Coastal Trail, although since the swimming is poor and it's out of sight, it's also out of mind. Mornings on Oneloa can be calm and still, and this is a popular spot for sunset wedding photo shoots. Oneloa is a great beach for those who just want to commune with nature and need a bit of an escape. To reach Oneloa, either park at the lot for Kapalua Bay and walk 15 minutes along the Kapalua Coastal Trail, or follow Lower Honoapi'ilani Road into Kapalua; a small beach access path and parking lot are located across from The Ridge. While there is a small beach shower for rinsing off, the nearest public restrooms are at Kapalua Bay.

D. T. Fleming Beach Park

D. T. Fleming Beach Park was the most

Oneloa Bay or "Ironwoods"

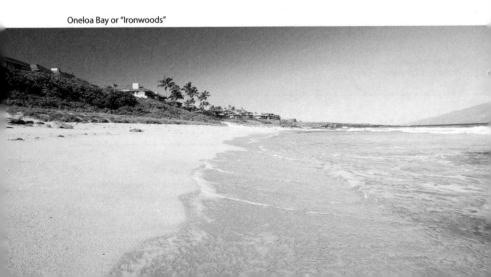

The Best Beach in America

If a friend quizzes you on which beach in Maui was named the number-one beach in the United States, and you have to choose among Kapalua Bay, Ka'anapali Beach, D. T. Fleming Beach, Wailea Beach, and Hulopo'e Bay on Lana'i, the correct answer would be . . . all of them.

Since the rankings began in 1991, each of the five beaches listed above has held the title as the number-one beach in America, and Hamoa Beach in Hana is consistently ranked in the top five. So how, exactly, is the number-one beach determined?

The person behind the rankings is Stephen P. Leatherman, otherwise known as Dr. Beach. He has compiled a sophisticated ranking system of 50 different criteria to measure hundreds of beaches, including natural factors such as softness of the sand and width at low tide as well as human factors such as the availability of lifeguards and ease of public access. Water samples from each beach are collected to determine turbidity, suspended human material (sewage), and the amount of algae.

So why is there a different winner every year? Once a beach has won the title it is subsequently retired from future consideration. With that thought in mind, wouldn't it make sense that the best of the best would be the beach that was voted number one when the rankings first started?

If this were the case, the top beach in the United States when the rankings began in 1991 was Kapalua Bay, so the granddaddy of the best beaches in America is here on Maui.

recent of Maui's beaches to be named number-one beach in the United States, garnering the title in 2006. Fleming's is a hybrid stretch of sand where the southern half is dominated by Ritz-Carlton resort guests and the northern half is popular with locals. This is one of the best beaches on the island for bodysurfing and bodyboarding, although the surf here can get rough and dangerous in the winter. Luckily, this is one of the only beaches on the West Side with lifeguards. There are restrooms and showers at the northern end. To access D. T. Fleming Beach Park, take Honoapi'ilani Highway (Hwy. 30) past the main entrance to Kapalua 0.9 mile and turn left at the bottom of the hill. The road dead-ends in the lot.

Mokulei'a Bay (Slaughterhouse)

Mokulei'a Bay was once a secret, since you can't see it from the road, but has recently become so exceptionally popular it can be tough to find a place to park. Tucked at the base of dramatic cliffs, Mokulei'a offers some of the best snorkeling on the West Side. It's known to locals as Slaughterhouse Beach, but the name is less sinister than it sounds: a slaughterhouse was once located here but is now long gone. The bay is part of the Honolua Bay Marine Life Conservation District, so no fishing or spearfishing—or any other kind of slaughter—is allowed. This is also a popular beach for bodysurfing, although the surf can be treacherous during large winter swells. This beach is nearly always deserted in the early morning hours, but lately is packed by 11am. To reach Mokulei'a, travel 2.5 miles past the entrance to Kapalua and park on the left side of the road, where you will notice a paved stairway leading down to the beach, as well as a sign that details the rules of the marine reserve.

Punalau Beach (Windmills)

Sandy, serene, and almost always empty, Punalau is little visited by tourists—but not for lack of beauty. The local name, Windmills, is derived from an old windmill that once stood here but has long since been destroyed. This is now a popular place for advanced surfers and ambitious beachcombers who scour the shore for flotsam and shells. The road down to the shore can often be rough, so unless you have a high-clearance vehicle, it's best to leave your car parked by the highway and make the five-minute trek on foot. Bring all of your valuables with you, and also pack a blanket or towel for lying in the sun and soaking up the silence. Since the reef is shallow and can be razor sharp, don't snorkel or swim here. This is also one of Maui's best spots to watch large winter surf, and the left break at the far southern end has been referred to as Maui's version of the Pipeline.

KA'ANAPALI

The beaches in Ka'anapali are long, wide, and lined by resorts. Much like Kapalua, however, the wind can often be a factor here in the afternoon, so it's best to get your water activities in early before the trade winds start blowing.

Ka'anapali Beach

Few stretches of Maui shore are more iconic than famous **Ka'anapali Beach.** This long, uninterrupted expanse of sand is lined from end to end with world-class resorts, was named the number-one beach in the United States in 2003, and is the pulsing epicenter of the West Side's see-and-be-seen crowd. It should come as no surprise that the area is a constant hotbed of activity. Pick any island beach activity—surfing, snorkeling, scuba, snuba, paddleboarding, volleyball, parasailing (summer), or whale-watching (winter)—and you'll find it on Ka'anapali Beach. A paved pathway runs the length of the beach and is popular with joggers in the morning.

The best snorkeling is found at Pu'u Keka'a (Black Rock) in front of the Sheraton at the far northern end of the beach. Most of the water sports, such as surf lessons, take place at KP Point in front of the Ka'anapali Ali'i, and the beach volleyball court is in front of the Sheraton on the north end of the beach. For bodyboarding, the best area is between Whalers Village and Pu'u Keka'a. Since the beach faces directly west, it can pick up waves any time of year. Be careful on days with big shore-break, however, and use common sense.

Another favorite activity at Ka'anapali Beach is cliff-jumping off Pu'u Keka'a. While this 20-foot jump is popular with visitors and locals, the rock is one of the most sacred places on the island for native Hawaiians, who believe it's an entry point for a person's soul passing from this world into the next. To jump off Pu'u Keka'a is to mimic the soul at the moment of death, a legend still told during the evening torch-lighting ceremony that takes place before each sunset.

Since Ka'anapali Beach is exposed to the afternoon trade winds, the weather can often be wetter and windier than down the road in Lahaina. The morning hours are best for paddleboarding or snorkeling, and if the wind is blowing too hard by the Sheraton, you can find a pocket of calm at the southern end of the beach by the Hyatt. Also, if you plan on going for a morning swim, realize that there are two areas where large catamarans come ashore to pick up passengers, so be alert when you're in the water in front of Ka'anapali Beach Hotel or Whalers Village.

Unless you're staying at one of the resorts along the Ka'anapali strip, parking is going to be a challenge. Free public parking can be tough to come by, since most public spots are taken by 9am. There is one small public garage between the Sheraton and the Ka'anapali Beach Hotel, a lot between Whalers Village and the Westin, a handful of beach parking stalls in the front lot of the Ka'anapali Beach Hotel, and a small public lot on Nohea Kai Drive just before the Hyatt. While there's always a chance that you'll luck out and snag a spot, more often than not you'll end up having to pay to park in the garage of Whalers Village. Remember, however, that if you end up shopping at a store or eating at a restaurant in Whalers Village, you can get the parking ticket validated.

Kahekili Beach Park (Airport Beach)

There was a time not too long ago when **Kahekili Beach Park,** named after the great king of Maui, was an undeveloped scrubland of *kiawe* (mesquite) trees that paled in comparison to Ka'anapali Beach. Over time, there has been so much development at Airport Beach (also known as

sunset at Makila Beach

LAHAINA

The beaches of Lahaina are the most underrated on the island. The swimming is poor due to the offshore reef, but they are sunnier, less crowded, and more protected from the wind than most other beaches on Maui. If it's raining in Kapalua or Napili, or windy on Ka'anapali Beach, 90 percent of the time it's going to be sunny and calm on the beaches of Lahaina.

Makila Beach

Also known as **Breakwall, 505,** or **Shark Pit,** this is the most happening stretch of sand in Lahaina. Most visitors access the beach from Kamehameha Iki Park, and there is beach parking in a small lot or in the back of the Front Street tennis courts. This is the area where most of the surf schools set out from. There is also a beach volleyball court, which can get busy during the afternoon. Visitors are encouraged to marvel at the Polynesian voyaging canoes on display as part of the **Hui O Wa'a Kaulua Canoe Club.** Visitors rarely wander to the south end of the beach where palm trees hang over a secluded cove. Locals call this area Shark Pit for the harmless reef sharks that hang around the offshore ledge. The swimming is poor due to the offshore reef, although it provides calm water for wading with small children. There is one shower but no restroom.

Pu'unoa (Baby Beach)

On the northern end of Front Street, the beach that runs along Pu'unoa Point (and known to locals as **Baby Beach**) is an oasis of tranquility where you have to ask yourself if you're still in Lahaina. Shielded from visitors by its residential location—and protected from surf by the offshore reef—the sand running along this lazy promontory is the perfect spot for sitting in a beach chair and listening to the waves. Numerous trees provide shade, and the calm waters are ideal for beachgoers with young children or those who want to tan on a raft.

Finding the beach can be a challenge, and parking can be an issue. For the access point

Ka'anapali North Beach) that it's almost as busy as neighboring Ka'anapali. Yet Kahekili still has a family-friendly atmosphere where locals lounge on the grassy area in front of the beach pavilion or snorkel the offshore reef. The beach here is just as long as Ka'anapali Beach, although the steep grade of the shore makes it difficult for jogging. Most visitors use the boardwalk along the shore, and if you're up for a stroll, you can follow it as it weaves through the Royal Lahaina and Sheraton parking areas to meet up with the Ka'anapali beach path. There are public restrooms, and there is a large public parking lot at the Kai Ala entrance from the highway. If the lot is full, there's more parking on the north end of the beach, accessible from Lower Honoapi'ilani Road. The swimming here is much better than at Ka'anapali since there isn't as much catamaran traffic. If Ka'anapali Beach is too busy for you, you'll enjoy how Kahekili offers a world-class beach atmosphere at a slower pace.

with the largest amount of parking, turn off Front Street onto Ala Moana Street by the sign for Mala Ramp. Instead of heading down to the boat launch, proceed straight on Ala Moana until the road ends by the Jodo mission. From here you will see the beach in front of you. The best section of beach is a five-minute walk to the left along the sand. Transients sometimes hang out around this parking lot; don't leave any valuables in your car. If you're walking from central Lahaina, the quickest access to the nicest part of beach is to turn off Front Street onto Kai Pali Place, where you will notice a shore access path. If you are coming from central Lahaina, this turn will be about three minutes after you pass the Hard Rock Café.

Wahikuli and Hanakao'o Beach Parks (Canoe Beach)

On the northern tip of Lahaina, these two beach parks are the strip of land between Front Street and Ka'anapali. **Wahikuli** is closer to Lahaina, and **Hanakao'o** is at the southern edge of the Hyatt. Of the two beaches, Wahikuli offers better swimming, although a secret about Hanakao'o is that on the days when the main stretch of Ka'anapali Beach is windy, Hanakao'o sits tucked in a cove where the wind can barely reach. Hanakao'o is also known as Canoe Beach, since this is where many of the outrigger canoe regattas are held on Saturday mornings. A beach path allows you to walk or ride bicycles from the south end of Ka'anapali through Hanakao'o, Wahikuli, and down to Front Street in Lahaina.

SOUTH OF LAHAINA

On the stretch of shore between Lahaina and Ma'alaea are a grand total of zero resorts. Paddleboards and fishing poles rule this section of coast, and even though the swimming is poor, there is one spot that offers good snorkeling. Most visitors pass these beaches without giving them another thought, but if you do decide to pull over to watch the whales, visit the beach, or photograph the sunset, don't stop in the middle of the road. If you're headed in the Lahaina direction, it's easiest to pull off on the right side of the road and wait for traffic to clear before crossing.

Olowalu

Known to visitors as Mile Marker 14, the real name of this beach is **Olowalu,** after the village that stretches back into the valley. The snorkeling here is the best south of Lahaina, although plenty of beachgoers—particularly

hidden lagoon at Olowalu

those with young children—come simply to wade in the calm waters. While the water may be calm, it's also shallow, and the swimming area is nonexistent during low tide. Parking is along the side of the highway, although it's easy to get stuck in the sand.

Launiupoko Beach Park

Located at the only stoplight between Ma'alaea and Lahaina, **Launiupoko** is the most family-friendly beach park on the West Side of Maui. It has a protected wading area for small *keiki* (children), a decent sandy beach on the south end of the park, a wide, grassy picnic area, and numerous surf breaks that cater to beginner surfers and stand-up paddle surfers. This park is so popular with the weekend barbecue crowd that local families arrive before dawn to stake their claim for a birthday party with a bouncy house. There is a large parking lot as well as restrooms and showers, and since most of the

parking spots are taken by 8am, there is an overflow lot on the *mauka* (mountain side) of the highway. The water is too shallow for swimming and the snorkeling is poor, but this is a good place to put your finger on the local pulse and strike up a good conversation.

Puamana Beach Park

While there is a private gated community that goes by the same name, the public can visit the small **Puamana Beach Park** one mile north of Launiupoko. As at other beaches in the area, the swimming is poor, although the tables provide a nice setting for a picnic. For a stroll down the beach, the sandy shore fronting the condos is public property, so at low tide you can walk from the beach park to the other end of the private, gated section, although the grassy area is private. There aren't any restrooms at the beach park, but there's a refreshing shower in the parking lot with a serious nozzle.

Snorkeling

Snorkeling is the most popular activity in West Maui. Hundreds of people ply the waters of the island's western shore, flipping their fins as they chase after schools of yellow and black *manini* (convict tang). But there is always room to find your own section of reef, and the waters of West Maui teem with everything from graceful green sea turtles to the playfully named *humuhumunukunukuapua'a*—the Hawaiian state fish, whose name translates as "big lips with a nose like a pig."

Mornings are the best time of day for snorkeling. Different times of year also mean different snorkeling conditions. During the winter, places such as Honolua Bay and Napili can be dangerous due to the huge surf, so summer is the best time for exploring these reefs. Similarly, snorkeling spots on the south shore such as Olowalu can be prone to large surf during summer, although with much less frequency than the northern

beaches in winter. If the surf is too big or the conditions too poor, there is probably another place that is calm and beautiful just a 20-minute drive away.

KAPALUA, NAPILI, AND HONOKOWAI
★ Honolua Bay

When it comes to snorkeling along Maui's shore, **Honolua Bay** is the gold standard. This wide, scenic cleft in the coast is not only a biodiverse marine reserve, it's also protected from the afternoon trade winds. Honolua Bay is one of the most sacred and revered spots on the West Side of the island, and there has been a herculean movement over the last decade to "Save Honolua" and spare the area from development. The valley, bay, and shore exude a supernatural beauty. Somewhere between the lush green foliage of the valley and the shimmering turquoise waters is a palpable magic unlike anywhere else.

As the highway morphs into a rural county road, the first glimpse of Honolua is from the paved overlook 1.8 miles past the entrance to Kapalua. This is a nice place to pull over for a picture, but there are better lookouts a mile later. Toward the bottom of the hill, parking for the shore is in a lush and shaded valley where you might encounter some merchants selling their crafts. To reach the water, find a parking spot wherever you can (all the trails along a 0.5-mile stretch eventually lead to the shore), grab all of your snorkeling gear, and make a short five-minute trek through a dense green understory that chirps with activity and drips with vines.

The "beach" is more a collection of boulders. If you are facing the water, the right side has a much larger snorkeling area and a greater concentration of marinelife. The center of the bay has a sandy bottom and is mostly devoid of marinelife, so it's best to trace the shore and snorkel around to the right. If there aren't any charter boats tied up on the right side of the bay between 9am and noon, it means that the conditions aren't good enough to bring paying snorkelers here. Also, if you see breaking waves out toward the point and there are more than 20 surfers in the water, it means that the visibility is going to be less than stellar and conditions will be dangerous. If it isn't raining on the shore but the stream on the left side of the bay is gushing with brown water, it means that it's raining farther up the mountain and the runoff is emptying into the bay, which also makes for subpar conditions.

If, however, the sun is shining brilliantly, here's your guide to the best snorkeling area: When you enter the water from the rocky shore, swim straight out for about 20 yards and then turn right toward the shore. You'll want to hug the shore in 5 to 10 feet of water and follow it in a ring around the right side of the bay. If you're on a mission to find Hawaiian green sea turtles, the best spot to check out is the **turtle cleaning station** on the right center of the bay. It's about 200 yards out from the boat ramp, in line with the bend in the cliff on the right side of the bay, in about 15 to 20 feet of water. If you snorkel Honolua Bay during winter, dive a few feet underwater to listen for the distant song of humpback whales. Keep a keen eye out for boat traffic, as a number of catamarans make their approach through the middle of the bay.

Mokulei'a Bay

Parking for **Mokulei'a Bay** is along the highway 1.5 miles past the entrance to Kapalua, and the best snorkeling is in the cove on the right side of the bay. Even though Mokulei'a is still a part of the Honolua Marine Life Conservation District, the reef is completely different than at Honolua Bay, so you're likely to see different species. There's still the likelihood of seeing a sea turtle, a chance for some spotted eagle rays swimming over the sand by the end of the point, and perhaps an octopus clinging to the wall at the far end of the cove. Mokulei'a is more exposed to the afternoon trade winds, so morning hours during flat, calm days are the best time for snorkeling.

Namalu Bay

While Honolua and Mokulei'a Bays are far from secret, for a hidden, out-of-the-way snorkeling experience in a rocky, almost Mediterranean cove, the craggy shore of **Namalu Bay** is one of West Maui's best spots. There isn't much in the way of live coral, but you can spot green sea turtles, reef fish, and the occasional eagle or manta ray. The center of the bay is about 40 feet deep, and the areas ringing the shore are a more manageable 5 to 15 feet. As a bonus, the rocks also make for some enjoyable cliff-jumping.

Accessing the bay can be challenging, and while strong swimmers can access Namalu Bay by swimming around from Kapalua Bay, this is a long swim over deep water that's only possible when it's calm. The more practical way to reach Namalu Bay is via the dirt pathway that follows the coast. The closest public parking is at the Kapalua Bay Villas in a hidden, little-known location. To find the eight public parking spots, turn into the parking area for the Montage Hotel and make an immediate right toward the Kapalua Bay Villas. Then make a left, following the sign for beach access parking, and notice the small public parking area seemingly orphaned among the private residential lots. From here it's a short walk down to the shore and the access for the Kapalua Coastal Trail.

Now that you've found the trailhead, to find the actual snorkeling area, make your way past two brown "Trail" markers and then notice the trail goes in three different directions. The trail to the right is the Kapalua Coastal Trail; the gravel trail leading straight heads to Hawea Point, the westernmost point on the island and a great place for spotting sea turtles from shore; and the grassy trail that bends off to the left leads toward Namalu Bay. Follow the trail as it wraps to the left, past the signs that say "Proceed at your own risk." In 30 seconds you'll find yourself standing atop the cliffs overlooking hidden Namalu Bay, wondering how a place this beautiful can be so isolated and unknown.

Kapalua Bay

Kapalua Bay is a sandy cove that is a favorite for snorkeling with small children. Its relatively small size means it is easy to scour the entire bay, and you can expect to see colorful parrotfish, lots of goatfish, and even the occasional green sea turtle. Although depths rarely exceed 20 feet, the best snorkeling is found along the right side of the bay where the rocks extend out to the distant point. If you're a strong snorkeler and the conditions are calm, you can even snorkel around the northern point into neighboring Namalu Bay.

Napili Bay

A short walk from Kapalua Bay is neighboring **Napili Bay.** You can easily snorkel at both bays without even reparking your car. Napili Bay doesn't have quite as many fish as Kapalua Bay, but there is a higher likelihood of finding a green sea turtle. While many snorkelers hug the wall on the right side of the bay, there is another reef in the center of the bay that's almost exposed during low tide. About 20 yards farther out is a second, less visited reef, and although it's deeper, at about 15 to 20 feet, it has the highest concentration of fish. This outer reef is far from shore, so if you're uncomfortable in the water, stay on the inside reefs and enjoy the shallower areas.

Rental Shops

In Napili, **Water Works Sports** (5315 Lower Honoapiʻilani Rd., 808/298-2446, www.water-workssportsmaui.com, 8am-5pm daily) inside Napili Shores has snorkel rentals for $7.50 per day or $25 per week. They can give you tips on current conditions, and also have snorkeling gear for sale.

In Kahana, **Maui Dive Shop** (4405 Honoapiʻilani Hwy., 808/669-3800, www.mauidiveshop.com, 8am-9pm daily) is within the Kahana Gateway Center and offers a full range of rentals as well as information on dive and snorkeling charters to Molokini and Olowalu.

In Honokowai, locally run **All About Fish** (3600 Lower Honoapiʻilani Hwy., 808/669-1710, www.mauifish.net, 9am-5pm Mon.-Sat., noon-4pm Sun.) in the 5A Rent-A-Space mall offers affordable rentals on a full range of dive equipment. This is a good option if you're staying in a condo in Honokowai and looking for local advice on snorkeling conditions. Snorkeling gear runs $8 per day or $25 per week, and the atmosphere is relaxed.

KAʻANAPALI
Kahekili Beach Park

In the northern part of Kaʻanapali, **Kahekili Beach Park** offers decent snorkeling off the park and at the far southern end of the beach. The reef extends from the shore out to about 25 feet of water. Expect to see a healthy amount of herbivorous reef fish. The moderate depth and easy entry make this a user-friendly snorkeling spot during the early morning hours. At the far southern end of the beach is a rock jetty that also offers good

Mokuleiʻa Bay

snorkeling. The rocky promontory here is the "back" of Puʻu Kekaʻa (Black Rock).

Puʻu Kekaʻa (Black Rock)

The best snorkeling in Kaʻanapali is at **Puʻu Kekaʻa,** better known as **Black Rock.** At the far northern end of Kaʻanapali Beach in front of the Sheraton, this area offers the most consistently beautiful snorkeling conditions and a relatively easy entry. The morning hours are best, and the best chance for seeing sea turtles is during high tide, when the water comes up on the side of the rock and all the *limu* (seaweed) falls into the water. Since this is a favorite delicacy of the green sea turtles, occasionally three or four of them congregate in the shallow cove in only 5 to 10 feet of water. Since the cliff is also a favorite place for cliff-jumping, steer clear of the immediate landing zone, and if you see the wind whipping up whitecaps out by the point, stay in the cove, protected from the wind and with gentler currents.

Snorkeling 101

Every year, thousands of island visitors strap on a mask for a peek at the underwater world. For those who have never snorkeled, however, the act of breathing through a tube in the middle of the ocean can be harrowing. Follow these basic snorkeling tips for a better first-time experience.

1. Choose the right equipment. Any successful snorkeling mission begins with the proper equipment. Make sure the mask fits by holding it to your face and sucking in with your nose. If the mask stays without you touching it with your hands, it means you have a good seal. For snorkels, no matter what the store clerk says, you don't have to get one with all the bells and whistles. A simple J-shaped snorkel is all that's needed, although some people like the feature where if water gets in the top of the snorkel it won't continue down toward your mouth. For fins, unlike shoes, you want to make sure you have a tight fit around your heel instead of around your toes. If your heel lifts up while the fins are on, it means the fins are too big. If they feel slightly tight when you test them out on land, remember that the water will lubricate the area once you get in the ocean.

2. Learn how to put on the gear. Before getting in the water, put a defog solution in your mask to keep it from clouding up. Even better than snorkel shop gels is a homemade solution of baby shampoo and water. For new masks, use toothpaste. Also, to keep your eyes from stinging, don't put sunscreen on your forehead immediately prior to snorkeling, since it will end up running into your eyes. When placing your mask on your head, brush all of your hair back so none gets into the mask. If hair gets caught in the mask, it will break the seal and allow water to leak in. Next, ensure the mask strap is high on the crown of your head. If the mask strap is touching your ears, it means the mask is too low (young children love to put the mask strap below their ears, which is why their masks always seem to leak). Remember that your nose is inside a mask, so you need to get used to the sensation of only breathing through your mouth.

Fins are meant for swimming, not walking, so once you fall down with fins on, it's almost impossible to stand back up. The number-one rule in Hawaii is never turn your back on the ocean—that's precisely what happens when you put on your fins on the beach and back your way into the water. Instead, try holding your fins under your arm (after having put your mask on while onshore), walking out to chest-deep water, and putting your fins on once there.

3. Less is more. If you are breathing, and you see fish, you're doing it correctly. Take long, slow, relaxed breaths in and out of your mouth, and when you swim, use scissor-style kicks with your hands behind your back. Excessive movement will scare away the fish. If you float on the surface (particularly easy with a flotation belt), you'll see more of them.

4. Don't panic. When water ends up in your snorkel, don't panic! To clear the snorkel of water, your options are to either say "two" loudly to shoot the water out the top of your snorkel, or pop your head out of the water, remove the snorkel from your mouth, and turn the mouthpiece upside down to drain it. Similarly, if water gets in your mask, instead of removing the whole mask, pull the bottom of the mask away from your face and let the water drain out.

Keep an eye on where you're swimming, don't overexert yourself, and most important, have fun.

Ka'anapali Point

On the other end of Ka'anapali Beach is the reef at **Ka'anapali Point,** in front of the Marriott. It's not nearly as popular as the reef at Pu'u Keka'a but covers a larger area and isn't nearly as crowded. If Pu'u Keka'a is a flotilla of fins, take a 10-minute stroll to the southern end of the beach and try your luck at this less visited spot.

Rental Shops

Every major resort along the strip of Ka'anapali has a rental shack by the sand. Prices vary slightly among the operators, but expect to pay higher resort prices compared to what you'll find off the strip. The best deal in Ka'anapali on rental gear is at **The Snorkel Store** (2580 Keka'a Dr., 808/333-3705, www.thesnorkelstore.com, 8am-5pm daily), in the

Fairway Shops by the highway. A full snorkel setup is around $10 per day or $27 per week, provided you book ahead online or fill out a coupon in the store. While here, ask about their guided **Snorkel Safari** ($75), where a local guide takes your party snorkeling at a spot along the shore, providing individualized attention you won't find on larger boats. It's a great option for beginner snorkelers and a nice way to find new spots.

Snorkeling Charters

A number of catamarans depart directly from Ka'anapali Beach on half-day sailing excursions along the West Maui coast. For trips to either Lana'i or Molokini Crater, you still need to go to the Lahaina or Ma'alaea harbors. For boats departing from Ka'anapali Beach, the preferred snorkeling destination is Honolua Bay. Since the surf at Honolua Bay during winter can get huge, the alternate destination is Olowalu on the south shore. Most days of the year these sleek sailing yachts are able to pull right up on the sand and load passengers directly from the beach, although on days with large surf, the shore-break can be too rough, and the trip might be moved to Lahaina Harbor. If a member of your party has restricted mobility, trips out of Lahaina Harbor are a safer option.

Of the charters departing from Ka'anapali Beach, **Trilogy** (808/874-5649, www.sailtrilogy.com) loads in front of the Ka'anapali Beach Hotel and offers 8am snorkeling trips, making them the first boat to reach Honolua Bay. The tours from Ka'anapali are usually aboard the *Trilogy IV*, a few feet smaller than other boats along the beach. The maximum capacity is about 35 people. All the food is made fresh on board. Both the Trilogy crew and the level of customer service are widely regarded as the best in the industry. Due to its slightly smaller size and its light weight, the *Trilogy IV* is the fastest of the Ka'anapali sailboats. Half-day charters are $119 for adults, include all food and equipment, and usually return to the beach around 1:30pm.

On the stretch of sand in front of Whalers Village, **Teralani** (808/661-7245, www.teralani.net) has two boats that regularly make excursions along the West Maui coast. The Teralani boats are larger than Trilogy's and cap their trips at 49 people. The main snorkeling tour departs at 9:30am and returns to the beach around 2:30pm. A shorter trip departs at 11am and returns to the beach at 3pm. All food and equipment are included in the rates. There's also an open bar once you've finished snorkeling, whereas Trilogy charges $5 per drink. With the open bar, however, the rates are also higher, at $139 for adults on the longer sail and $112 on the four-hour cruise.

Other catamarans departing from Ka'anapali Beach include **Gemini** (808/669-0508, www.geminicharters.com), which loads on the stretch of beach in front of Leilani's restaurant and is just as large as Teralani's boats. It offers a similar trip, departing at 11am and returning to the beach between 3pm and 3:30pm. Equipment, food, and an open bar are included in the tour for $115 for adults.

Hula Girl (808/665-0344, www.sailingmaui.com), which also loads on the stretch of beach in front of Leilani's restaurant, is an ornately painted boat that takes a different approach: The $98 for the five-hour tour (9:30am-2:30pm) doesn't include food, but the boat has a kitchen on board where chefs make food to order. There is also free Wi-Fi for anyone who wants to immediately upload camera footage of an encounter with a sea turtle. Scuba diving is offered for an additional cost for both certified ($69) and introductory ($80) divers.

LAHAINA
Wahikuli Beach Park

Most of Lahaina is ringed by a barrier reef, and there are surprisingly few options for decent snorkeling. One exception is **Wahikuli Beach Park,** between Ka'anapali and Lahaina, where you can find sea turtles, corals, and large schools of goat fish at a reef just a short swim offshore. For the best results, snorkel around the north end, about 10 yards off the rocks in about 5 to 10 feet of water.

Don't Stand on the Reef!

At West Side snorkeling spots, signs warn against standing on the reef. While everyone knows to avoid stepping on sea urchins and sharp rocks, the signs are about harm to the reef rather than your feet.

Unlike beaches with rocky or sandy bottoms, reefs in Maui are made up of fragile corals, living animals with hard exoskeletons—just as alive as the fish swimming above them or the eels inhabiting their crevices. Corals easily die, and one of the biggest threats is the number of visitors who stand on the reefs. Many snorkelers who stop to fix their snorkel masks or readjust their hair ties don't realize they're killing the ground they're standing on.

Snorkeling areas such as Honolua Bay, Kahekili Beach Park, and Olowalu have seen the most damage in recent years. Estimates from recent studies suggest that West Maui has lost as much as 25 percent of live coral in the last decade alone. There are other factors involved, such as sedimentation, overfishing, algal blooms, pesticide-laden runoff, and even the petroleum-based sunscreen that washes off swimmers' shoulders and ends up settling on the sensitive polyps. Visitors can do their part in protecting this fragile ecosystem by eliminating contact with the reef altogether. Adjust your snorkel mask in waist-deep water, and don't stand on the reef to take photos.

Even if you only snorkel once on the island, the health and protection of the coral reefs is something we can all work on to protect our coast's future.

Mala Wharf

In Lahaina, the best snorkeling spot is **Mala Wharf,** and since it is a functioning small-boat harbor, you have to keep an eye out for boat traffic. The reward, however, is a snorkeling site where legions of sea turtles and numerous reef sharks live under the pilings littering the ocean floor. This site is most often accessed by boat, but the easiest way to reach it from shore is to park in the public parking area and cross to where the pier meets the sand. From here, it's a kick out to where the pier drops into the water. While conditions are nice year-round, the only time you don't want to snorkel here is when the river draining into the bay is a torrent of runoff.

To find the parking for Mala Wharf, turn off Front Street onto Ala Moana Street, following the signs for Mala Ramp, just on the south side of the bridge from the Lahaina Cannery Mall. Once you turn, make an immediate right down toward the boat ramp, where there are restrooms, showers, and a moderate amount of parking.

Rental Shops

Lahaina Divers (143 Dickenson St., 808/667-7496, www.lahainadivers.com, 8am-8pm daily) is a full-service dive shop but has everything you need for snorkeling. Come if you're looking to own gear for an extended period of time. Since the staff are all divers themselves, they can give you up-to-date information on the current conditions around the West Side.

If you're just looking for cheap rental gear to get through your vacation, both **Boss Frog's** (150 Lahainaluna Rd., 808/661-3333, www.bossfrog.com, 8am-5pm daily) and **Snorkel Bob's** (1217 Front St., 808/661-4421, www.snorkelbob.com, 8am-5pm daily) provide economical rentals as low as $2 per day. Remember, however, that you get what you pay for, and you will be pitched activities and upsold on fancier equipment. If you aren't picky about a mask fitting perfectly or are on a budget, the offerings are fine and will get you through a couple of sessions at the beach.

For a similar operation in the center of Lahaina, check out **The Snorkel Store** (840 Waineʻe St., 808/669-1077, www.thesnorkelstore.com, 8am-5pm daily), a small but friendly shop squirreled away in the Lahaina Square Center a block inland from Front Street. There are often 2-for-1 specials on snorkeling gear if you book online, and prices can be as low as $10 to $25 per week.

Snorkeling Charters

Before sunrise, Lahaina Harbor teems with activity as fishers fuel their boats and charter captains prepare for the day. Lines form and re-form, food coolers are slung across the docks, and fresh fish is set on ice. Most snorkeling charters depart from behind the banyan tree on Front Street; a few set out from Mala Ramp on the northern edge of town. Snorkeling charters in Lahaina run the gamut from small inflatable rafts to massive two-tiered catamarans. It's important to find a tour company with the type of experience you want.

SAILBOATS

The company with the largest number of snorkeling charters from Lahaina Harbor is **Trilogy** (808/874-5649, www.sailtrilogy.com), which offers all-day cruises to Lana'i ($205 adults, $149 teens, $100 children) as well as a four-hour snorkel along the West Maui coast ($110 adults, $83 teens, $55 children). While a couple of other boat companies also travel to Lana'i to snorkel for the day, Trilogy is the only one with a commercial permit to have crew and facilities based on the island. The company has been running the trip to Lana'i for 45 years, and the all-day experience is far better than any other snorkel charter option.

Departing from Lahaina Harbor at 10am (during busier times of the year there can also be a 6:30am departure), the 60-foot sailing catamarans travel to Manele Harbor on Lana'i, where passengers disembark to snorkel at Hulopo'e Bay. Since Hulopo'e faces south, during summer there are a few days with large surf, so the snorkeling can be subpar. Winter is nearly guaranteed to have pristine conditions. On the beach, Trilogy has exclusive access to the left side of Hulopo'e Bay and it is the only company with lifeguards, beach mats, beach chairs, refreshments, beach volleyball, and all the snorkeling gear right on the beach. Also included in the rates is an optional guided van tour of Lana'i City.

The other sailing catamaran departing from Lahaina Harbor to Lana'i is *Sail Maui* (808/244-2087, www.sailmaui.com), a 47-foot boat that takes just 24 passengers and is the island's fastest catamaran. The seven-hour, $190-trip departs at 8:30am and docks at Manele Harbor on Lana'i. You're unsupervised while you snorkel, since the crew doesn't have permission to operate on shore, and you're given a picnic lunch to the enjoy while at the beach. The trip returns to Lahaina around 3:30pm, and the crew might even hook an *ono* or a mahimahi while trolling the fishing lures under sail.

While it mostly focuses on sunset sails and sailing charters, *Scotch Mist II* (808/661-0386, www.scotchmistsailingcharters.com) is a 50-foot Santa Cruz monohull that also operates four-hour sailing and snorkeling charters along the western shore of the island for $109.

POWERBOATS

Of the larger diesel boats that operate out of Lahaina Harbor, **Pacific Whale Foundation** (612 Front St., 808/942-5311, www.pacificwhale.org) offers the most options. Its large boats can fit 149 people, and while that's a crowd, there's simply no beating the price: $83 for adults on the 9am five-hour tour to Lana'i, and each paying adult is allotted one child free of charge. Unlike other boats that dock at Manele Harbor, these cruises snorkel off the boat, with the two preferred destinations being either Kaunolu (Shark Fin Cove) or the Manele reef outside of the small boat harbor. The level of customer service on a boat this size isn't the same as on the sailing vessels, but for families who are on a budget and want to go snorkeling for the day, it's more affordable. Pacific Whale Foundation guests check in at the storefront across the street from the famous banyan tree, and loading is by the main dock at the harbor, where you wait for a crewmember to escort you to the boat.

Many of these boats go whale-watching in the winter, but during summer, **Hawaii Ocean Project** (808/6617-6165, www.hawaiiaoceanproject.com) has a fleet of aging but functional diesel boats that offer snorkeling charters ($89 adults, $57 children) to Lana'i and along the coast of West Maui. The cost is affordable, and trips are offered at 7:30am Monday, Wednesday, and Friday.

For private excursions, **Captain Woody's** (808/667-2290, www.captainwoody.net) operates charters of only six people and leaves from Mala Ramp. Fishing, snorkeling, and seasonal whale-watching can all be included in these small group tours, which usually last six hours.

RAFTS

For those who don't like crowds, there are a number of rafts with small group sizes that place you closer to the water than any other type of vessel. Due to their bouncy nature, however, rafts aren't recommended for pregnant women or anyone with back problems. If you're prone to seasickness, the waters often become rough during the afternoon. Some companies swap their snorkeling charters for whale-watching during winter, however, so check ahead.

Of all the rafts, **Ultimate Snorkel Adventure** (808/667-5678, www.ultimate-whalewatch.com) is the best option, though it only offers snorkeling trips May-November. It operates out of slip 17 of Lahaina Harbor. Group sizes are kept to 16, and this rigid

inflatable is the fastest boat in Lahaina Harbor, at speeds over 35 mph. Snorkeling locations are chosen off the island of Lana'i based on the best conditions, and unlike some of the other options that go ashore on Lana'i, this excursion snorkels off the raft. Due to its small size, it can navigate close to the shore of Lana'i to find blowholes or follow pods of spinner dolphins hanging out by the rocks. Five-hour snorkeling trips are $139 for adults, and this is a great option for a semi-private tour with a relaxed but professional captain and crew.

Departing from Mala Ramp at 6:30am, **Maui Ocean Riders** (808/661-3586, www.mauioceanriders.com, $139 adults, $119 children) is the only boat to circumnavigate Lana'i. Covering an astounding 70 miles over the course of the trip, this excursion features multiple snorkeling spots and the opportunity to witness little-seen areas of Lana'i, such as the waters off Shipwreck Beach, Polihua Beach, and the snorkeling area known as Three Stone. On calm days this excursion is the best of all the rafting options. On days when the trade winds are blowing early in the morning, the ride can get rough.

For a raft that docks at Manele Harbor and spends time on Lana'i, **Maui Adventure**

snorkeling in Honolua Bay

Cruises (808/661-5550, www.mauiadventure-cruises.com) operates two trips from Lahaina Harbor, one of which allows passengers to spend three hours of beach time at Lana'i's Hulopo'e Bay. This excursion ($139 adults, $109 children) operates Monday, Wednesday, and Friday, docks in Manele Harbor, and allows guests to walk Hulopo'e Bay unsupervised. Breakfast, snacks, and a deli lunch are included. Excursions depart at 7am and 9:30am from slip 11 in Lahaina Harbor. On Tuesday, Thursday, and Saturday, an abridged 4.5-hour trip ($99 adults, $79 children) is offered, where you'll travel to Lana'i and snorkel off the boat rather than docking at the harbor.

SOUTH OF LAHAINA

The best snorkeling south of Lahaina is at Olowalu, otherwise known as Mile Marker 14. The reef here is a wide expanse of coral heads. The outer reef is popular with tour and dive boats, and the inside sections can teem with large parrotfish and Hawaiian green sea turtles. Directly out from the mile marker is a sand channel that leads through the shallow reef and allows access to deeper water. If you venture out from a random spot along the coast, there is a good chance you will get trapped in a maze of shallow coral heads where the water is often murky and the snorkeling is poor. If possible, get here in the morning before the winds pick up.

Scuba Diving

Scuba diving from the West Side of the island involves one of two options: Departing from a West Side harbor for an excursion to Lana'i or diving along the West Maui shore. While certified divers should seek out a dive charter, there are also a number of shore operators that offer introductory dives. If you're a certified diver and planning on diving independently, ask at the rental shop about current conditions, and always use a dive flag. Dive spots along the northern section of the island are inaccessible during winter due to large surf. Summer is the best time for diving up north.

KAPALUA, NAPILI, AND HONOKOWAI
Dive Sites

The best shore dive in West Maui is **Honolua Bay,** although slogging all of your gear down to the water can be an exhausting undertaking. If you're diving from shore, launch from the center of the beach and hug the right side of the bay where the reef drops off into the sand channel. Maximum depth can reach about 40 feet, and you can expect to see green sea turtles and a wide variety of reef fish, and you may even have a rare encounter with

spinner dolphins. Of the boats offering dive trips to Honolua Bay, *Hula Girl* (808/665-0344, www.sailingmaui.com) offers scuba diving as an add-on to the regular snorkel charter, although most dive charters head elsewhere along the West Side.

For a beginner-friendly introductory dive, **Kapalua Bay** can offer everything from a shallow dive of 25 feet to a more advanced dive of 40 feet rounding the corner toward neighboring Namalu Bay. There are showers and facilities as well as easy sandy-beach entry.

Dive Operators

Down in Honokowai, **Tiny Bubbles Scuba** (3350 Lower Honoapi'ilani Rd., 808/870-0878, www.tinybubblesscuba.com, 8am-5pm daily) operates shore dives along the West Maui coast. Under the lead of the vivacious and knowledgeable instructor Timmerz, all of the instructors for Tiny Bubbles have been diving the Maui shore for over a decade and are acquainted with the nuances of Maui diving. Introductory courses are $109, and certified divers can participate in a private guided beach dive for $89. Night dives and scooter dives are also offered. Depths on these shore dives rarely exceed 40 feet. All gear is included, and while the business is run out of the Ka'anapali Beach Club, the exact dive site is determined by the conditions.

Also operating out of Honokowai, **Scorpion Scuba** (3600 Lower Honoapi'ilani Rd., 808/669-1710, www.mauifish.net) is another trusted operator with years of experience on the shores of West Maui. The dives are an exceptional value: Introductory dives are $98, and certified beach dives are $78, with all gear included. Inquire about their certification classes, night dives, and scooter dives. The scuba operation is run out of the All About Fish store in Honokowai, where you can pick up any gear you need or ask about dive sites and conditions.

KA'ANAPALI
Dive Sites

The northernmost dive site in Ka'anapali and the one preferred by independent instructors is **Kahekili Beach Park.** The depth is shallow, rarely exceeding 35 feet, and the coral begins immediately. The reef parallels the shore, with the greatest diversity of life found at 15 to 25 feet. The beach is long, and the healthiest amount of coral is found right off the beach park. It is uncrowded compared to neighboring Ka'anapali Beach, and there is easier parking for lugging gear from the car. Showers and restrooms are conveniently located in the middle of the beach park.

The best dive in Ka'anapali, however, is **Pu'u Keka'a,** also known as **Black Rock.** Despite the relative ease of the dive and the fairly shallow depths, the rocky promontory draws all sorts of marinelife. Although not always guaranteed, divers frequently sight sea turtles, reef fish, eels, octopuses, and rare squid or cowries. The best way to dive Pu'u Keka'a is to do a drift dive from the southern end of Kahekili Beach Park and swim around to the front of the rock, or enter the water in front of the Sheraton, swim partway around the rock, and then double back the way you came. This is a great dive for those who have

just been certified. For a real treat, consider a night dive.

To dive away from the crowds, head to the large reef at **Ka'anapali Point,** stretching from the Marriott down toward the Hyatt. The depth ranges 10-30 feet. You'll likely see a large number of turtles, corals, and technicolor parrotfish.

Dive Operators

The Ka'anapali resort diving scene is dominated by **Five Star Scuba** (www.5starscuba. com), which has operations at many of the Ka'anapali resorts. Options include pool sessions, one-tank dives, certification, and night dives. A single one-tank dive for certified divers is about $89, with the exact dive location determined by where you're staying and the conditions.

In front of Ka'anapali Beach Hotel, **the kiosk** (808/661-7789) also offers one-tank dives, pool classes, and certification courses. Introductory dives are $110, and certified dives are only $79. For a Maui dive you'll never forget, book a night dive at Pu'u Keka'a ($89).

LAHAINA
Dive Sites

Within walking distance of southern Ka'anapali, **Hanakao'o Beach Park** is the northernmost beach in Lahaina and the site of many introductory dive classes. This is a good dive if you're practicing your skills over sand. The shallow area is also good for spotting turtles and colorful reef fish, and you can find turtles if you follow the rocks south toward Wahikuli Beach Park.

The best dive in Lahaina is **Mala Wharf,** although it's most often accessed as a boat dive. When Hurricane Iniki came storming through in 1992, the 30-foot waves it created were strong enough to destroy the outer half of Mala Ramp. Today the collapsed pilings are still lying in 25 feet of water, and the result has been decades of live coral development on what is now one of the island's best artificial reefs. The caverns of the pilings are home to numerous turtles and whitetip reef sharks, some of which can reach up to six feet. Even though the depth never exceeds 35 feet, this is a favorite of island dive charters due to its proximity to the harbors and wealth of marinelife.

The *Carthaginian* is an old whaling ship that was scuttled in 100 feet of water by Atlantis Submarines about 0.5 mile offshore from Puamana. A couple of West Side dive charters include this deep-water dive, with a maximum depth of 100 feet, in their weekly schedule. The *Carthaginian* hasn't yet developed the same amount of live coral as neighboring Mala Ramp, and it's the deepest dive in the area. Winter dives are punctuated by whale song—and you might even spot one underwater.

Dive Operators

Lahaina Divers (143 Dickenson St., 808/667-7496, www.lahainadivers.com) has the largest number of dive options available in Lahaina. Two custom-built 46-foot dive boats, departing from Lahaina Harbor, are the largest on Maui. Two-tank dives range from $149 for dives off Lana'i to $199 for a dive off Moku Ho'oniki (Moloka'i), famous for hammerhead sharks. There are also trips to the Back Wall of Molokini Crater as well as four-tank dive trips. The full-service dive shop in Lahaina has equipment sales and rentals. Since the availability of dives varies by day, inquire ahead of time.

On the north end of Lahaina at Mala Ramp, **Extended Horizons** (94 Kupuohi St., 808/667-0611, www.extendedhorizons.com) is another reputable operation that offers tours to Lana'i and the west shore of Maui. Extended Horizons takes only six passengers, and it's the only charter boat on the island to run completely on biodiesel. Morning tours

check in at 6:30am at the Mala boat ramp for two-tank dives to Lana'i ($159). Other dive options include trips along the Maui shore as well as night dives, beach dives, and certification classes.

A smaller operation offering scuba tours of Lana'i, **Dive Maui** (1223 Front St., 808/661-7333, www.hawaiianrafting.com) departs from Mala Ramp aboard a rigid aluminum inflatable vessel. Group sizes are small, and a deli lunch is included with the two-tank dive. The shop is conveniently located within walking distance of Mala Ramp.

SOUTH OF LAHAINA
Dive Sites

Known to some operators as Turtle Reef or Turtle Point, **Olowalu** is an offshore, turtle-laden area popular with charter boats on the offshore reefs. Maximum depths are about 30 feet, and on nice days the visibility is close to 100 feet. This area is also popular with independent dive operators as a confined-water area for practicing dive skills. If you are shore-diving independently, the easiest way to get to deeper water is to enter around the Mile Marker 14 sign and swim in a straight line until you reach depths of 20-25 feet. When navigating your way through the coral heads, it's imperative to make sure that your gear doesn't drag across the reef, and bring a dive flag with you so that boats know you're below.

Ukumehame is a special spot accessible only by boat charter. Huge manta rays congregate here to be cleaned by reef fish who nibble algae off their wings, and the depths are a moderate 30-60 feet. It can't be done as a shore dive because the manta ray area is about a 25-minute surface swim from shore, and it takes trained dive instructors to determine if the water clarity is good enough for diving.

Waves in Hawaiian Scale

Hawaiians are weird when it comes to their waves. Not because a high surf advisory is a legitimate excuse for missing work, school, or even jury duty, but rather because Hawaiians measure the size of waves differently.

Unlike places that measure the face of the waves, Hawaiian surfers measure the back of the wave. The resulting number is about half what it would be if measured elsewhere. A six-foot wave in California is a three-foot wave in Hawaii.

The history of this is foggy at best. One theory suggests that Hawaiian surfers underestimated wave size in the 1950s as a humble response to the bravado of California surfers who boasted about the size of the waves they caught. Another theory is that since Hawaiian lifeguards would be forced to work instead of surf when the waves reached a certain height, they invented a separate scale so that it would require larger waves before they had to go to work.

Whatever the reason, the practical implication is that when you're looking at a surf forecast, you need to know if it's being measured on the Hawaiian scale or by face height. On websites such as Omaui.com, the forecast is given in face height, while on Hawaiiweathertoday.com, the forecast is in the Hawaiian scale.

If you ask a local surfer what the conditions are like, you'll get a reply of either "3 feet Hawaiian" or "3 feet," when the head-high waves are obviously larger. Australians have also adopted the Hawaiian scale system of measurement. While confusion reigns, all that matters is assessing your own ability when paddling out to the lineup.

Surfing

Surfing is more than a hobby in West Maui— it's a way of life. In Lahaina, legions of longboarders begin each morning by watching the sunrise from the water, and flotillas of surf schools operate throughout the day. Up north, Honolua is the proving ground of the island's burgeoning surfers, and whenever "The Bay" starts breaking, a palpable buzz runs through the community. Not all breaks are suitable for beginners, and only a handful of breaks are included in this guide. Practice common etiquette, and enjoy the serenity that comes with surfing one of the most beautiful spots in the world.

KAPALUA, NAPILI, AND HONOKOWAI

Winter is the best time for surfing "up north," and the waves get larger the farther north you go. With the exception of S-Turns, however, most of the breaks on the Upper West Side are for experienced surfers. Beginners will have better luck at the breaks south of Lahaina.

Surf Spots

Pohaku Beach Park in Kahana is the epicenter of the West Side's longboard community. The break, commonly known as **S-Turns,** is perfect for beginners. Travel on Honoapiʻilani Highway until you reach the intersection with Hoʻohui Street, with the McDonald's on the corner. Turn toward the ocean, and make a left once you reach the bottom of the hill. Drive for 0.25 mile and find the parking lot for S-Turns on the right. From the parking lot, you can see two distinct breaks. To the right is Mushrooms, which can be a fun wave, but it's shallow on the inside section. To the left is S-Turns, where you'll notice a couple of A-frame peaks a long paddle offshore. Surfing at S-Turns is as much a paddle workout as a surfing workout, and you can be forgiven if you need to stop to catch your breath on the way out. Beginners stay on the inside section, while more experienced surfers favor the outer peaks. Also, there have been some shark issues at S-Turns in the past, so be wary if the water is murky and no one else is out. S-Turns starts breaking on a moderate northwest swell, and on the largest of days can reach a few feet overhead.

The surf break at **D. T. Fleming Beach Park** is at the far northern end of the beach. The wave here is a combination of a beach break and a point break, and it can get crowded with bodyboarders during weekends. This is one of the few places on the West Side that picks up wind swell, so if it's windy and there aren't waves anywhere else, check Fleming's.

If you're an avid surfer, **Honolua Bay** needs no introduction. The wave here is truly one of the best in the world, holding almost religious significance for the locals. Honolua is for experienced surfers, but even nonsurfers should come here during a large swell to watch the island's best pull into the gaping, barreling perfection. Honolua can become crowded, and if you paddle out and nobody recognizes you, your chances of getting a wave decrease significantly. Granted, on days when the surf is only about head high and the crowd isn't too thick, there can still be enough waves for everyone—provided you know what you're doing.

Windmills is a surf break suited to experienced surfers and an epic spot for watching the island's best. The massive left tube barrels with such ferocity it has been called Maui's Pipeline. Many professional surf films have been shot here, and the best vantage point is on the side of the road about one mile after the dirt turnoff for the bluffs at Honolua Bay.

Rental Shops

Experienced surfers will get the best selection with **808 Boards** (808/283-1384, www.808boards.com, 7:30am-5pm daily, $25-35 per day), who will pick up and drop off the board at no additional charge.

Rent a board at the **Boss Frog's** locations in Napili (5095 Napilihau St., 808/669-4949, www.bossfrog.com, 8am-6pm daily) and Kahana (4310 Lower Honoapi'ilani Rd., 808/669-6700, www.bossfrog.com, 8am-5pm

daily). Rates are around $20 per day for soft-top longboards or $25 per day for fiberglass boards.

For the cheapest boards you'll find on this side of the island, little-known **A&B Ocean Rentals** (3481 Lower Honoapi'ilani Rd., 808/669-0027, 9am-4pm daily) is hidden in Da Rose mall in Honokowai on the ocean side of the highway. Surfboards can be as cheap as $15 per day or $70 for the whole week.

KA'ANAPALI
Surf Spots

The only surf break in Ka'anapali is **Ka'anapali Point,** in front of the Marriott on Ka'anapali Beach. This is where the Ka'anapali surf lessons take place, although the wave here is tricky because it bends at a weird angle. Also, the inside section can be shallow and rocky, so surf school students are given booties. Ka'anapali Point can pick up both southwesterly and northeasterly swells, which means there can be surf any time of year.

Rental Shops and Schools

While the waves in Lahaina are more amenable to learning, there are still a number of operators along Ka'anapali Beach for those who would prefer to walk directly from the resort to a lesson. Since Ka'anapali gets windier than Lahaina, it's important to book the first lesson of the day for the best conditions.

Two-hour lessons ($79) can be booked at the beach shack in front of the Ka'anapali Beach Hotel. **Island Style Adventures** (808/244-6858, www.isasurfschool.com) in front of the Westin also offers two-hour lessons ($75). For rentals by Ka'anapali Point, expect to pay $20-40. Booties are included in the price of all lessons and rentals.

LAHAINA

Lahaina and areas south have small waves breaking during most of the year, while summer has the most consistent surf. Most days will only have waves in the waist-high range, but the best swells of summer can reach overhead.

Two-hour lessons are $65 pp, and the owner, Tim, often enjoys time on the water as the private surf coach for Jimmy Buffett.

One block away on Prison Street are **Royal Hawaiian** (117 Prison St., 808/276-7873, www.royalhawaiiansurfacademy.com, 7am-7pm Mon.-Fri., 7am-3:30pm Sat.-Sun.) and **Maui Wave Riders** (133 Prison St., 808/875-4761, www.mauiwaveriders.com, 7am-9pm daily). Both have been operating since the mid-1990s, and all of the instructors are competent and patient professionals guaranteed to get you up and riding. Group rates run $65 pp, and for rentals, expect to pay $20 for three hours or $30 for the whole day.

To get away from the Breakwall crowds, **Maui Surfer Girls** (808/214-0606, www.mauisurfergirls.com) is the island's premier female-only surf camp operator, although they also offer coed group lessons for $85 pp. It costs a few dollars more than in town, and lessons take place a few miles south of town along a mellow stretch of beach. At certain times of year, all-inclusive one- and two-week classes are offered to empower teenage girls through learning surfing. Lessons are offered at 8am, 10:30am, and 1pm daily.

Also south of town is **Hawaiian Paddle Sports** (808/442-6436, www.hawaiianpaddlesports.com), which offers completely private two-hour lessons ($189, $129 for 2-4 people, $109 for groups of 5 or more) and includes free photos of your time on the water. For something completely different that you'll never forget, try out **canoe surfing in an outrigger canoe** ($119-149 pp).

SOUTH OF LAHAINA

For beginning surfers and longboarders, the mile-long stretch of coast between **Puamana** Beach Park and **Launiupoko Beach Park** has numerous breaks with mellow waves for beginners. In between the two parks are peaks known as **Guardrails, Woody's,** and **Corner Pockets.** The beach parks and Guardrails have parking on the ocean side of the road, and parking for Woody's is in a dirt lot on the inland side of the highway. There can be small waves here most times of year, although summer sees the most consistent surf. If you're slightly more advanced, park in the lot for Puamana Beach Park and walk the length of shore all the way to the right along the Puamana condominium complex. At the far northern end of the beach is another break known as **Beaches or Hot Sands** that offers a fun right point welcoming to visitors.

If you're experienced and prefer to ride a shortboard, the wave at **Olowalu** offers two A-frame peaks that are popular with locals and can get crowded. In a different location than the snorkeling spot of the same name, the Olowalu surf break is by mile marker 15.5.

At mile marker 12, **Ukumehame Beach Park** is another break that caters to beginners and longboarders but requires a much longer paddle than places such as Guardrails or Puamana. However, the longer effort means a longer ride. This is a favorite of island longboarders. While the beach itself is fairly long, the best waves are found directly in front of the small parking lot.

Tucked right at the base of the cliffs by mile marker 11, **Grandma's** is the name of the break on the far southern end of Papalaua Beach Park. This is a playful wave that caters to beginners and longboarders.

Stand-Up Paddling

KAPALUA, NAPILI, AND HONOKOWAI

One of the best stretches of coast for paddling is the section between Kapalua Bay and Hawea Point. The sandy entry at Kapalua Bay makes it easy to launch a board into the water. Napili Bay is another popular spot for morning paddles. Never bring a stand-up paddleboard into Honolua Bay. It's heavily frowned upon by locals and you'll likely be sent back to the beach by the surfers in the water.

Rental Shops

In Napili, rent stand-up paddleboards ($20 per hour, $40 per day) from **Water Works Sports** (5315 Lower Honoapi'ilani Rd., 808/298-2446, www.waterworkssportsmaui.com, 8am-5pm daily) inside the Napili Shores building. Be sure to get out early before the wind picks up.

If you'd prefer to have your boards delivered, **1-800-Snorkel** (800/766-7535, www.1-800-snorkel.com) offers stand-up paddleboard delivery to your hotel ($45-50 per day, depending on the type of board). Let them know before the morning you'd like to go, and they'll deliver it to the hotel lobby.

KA'ANAPALI

Sandy Ka'anapali is the perfect spot for stand-up paddling, but only during the morning hours before the wind picks up. On winter days, the water can be as smooth as glass, with dozens of whales breaching around you. Being out on the water during whale season can be an exciting adventure, but the same laws apply to stand-up paddlers as to boats: Stay 100 yards from humpback whales—unless, of course, they swim over to you.

Rental Shops

Almost every hotel along the main strip has activity huts offering paddleboard rentals. At **the kiosk** (808/661-7789, 8am-5pm daily) in front of the Ka'anapali Beach Hotel, boards are $25 for the first hour and $15 per additional hour. Or get them delivered to your hotel ($45 per day) from either **808 Boards** (808/283-1384, www.808boards.com) or **1-800-Snorkel** (800/766-7535, www.1-800-snorkel.com).

Start the day by stand-up paddling off Ka'anapali.

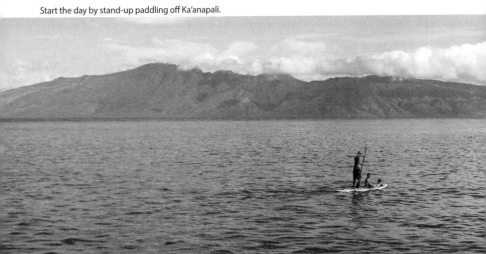

Tips for Stand-Up Paddling

Stand-up paddling is very popular in Hawaii. While taking a lesson is always the best way to ensure success, here are a few tips if you'd rather rent a board and set out on your own.

- Paddle in the morning before the wind comes up.

- When first getting in the water, start on your knees to get the feeling for the board.

- When you stand up, keep your feet shoulder-width apart. You want to be standing in the middle of the board about where the handle is.

- A stand-up paddleboard is like a bicycle; you need momentum for balance, so if you stop paddling, it's like trying to balance on a bicycle without pedaling. When you first stand up from your knees, take a couple of paddles quickly to build up enough momentum so that you won't fall.

- Use the correct side of the paddle. Paddles are like an extension of your hand; you want to use the side of the paddle that would be your palm as opposed to the back of your hand.

- Instead of placing both hands on the shaft of the paddle, put one on the top and the other on the shaft. To keep a straight line you must alternate paddling on both sides of your body by taking a few strokes on your left and then a few strokes on your right, much like you would in a canoe.

- When paddling, make long, full strokes. Many first-time paddlers have a tendency to poke at the water with short little strokes. Since this doesn't create much momentum, the board becomes wobbly and you're liable to fall. By taking long strokes you create enough momentum for a stable platform and a much more enjoyable paddle.

- Use a leash. A leash is your lifeline if you fall off the board. If you are not sure which ankle to put the leash around, act as if you're going to do a cartwheel, and whichever foot you put backward is the one you should attach the leash to.

- If you are paddling where there are waves, make sure that your board is pointing either into the waves or away from them. When waves hit the side of your board, there is a good chance you'll end up falling.

- When you fall off your board (don't worry, it happens to the best of paddlers), the best thing to do is just let it happen. Most paddleboarding injuries occur when people try to save themselves from falling and end up going down awkwardly. Accept your fate and fall gracefully into the water.

- Only competent surfers should ever try to surf on their paddleboards. Large, heavy boards can become dangerous in a surf lineup if they go crashing through a crowd, and a spate of injuries related to stand-up paddlers and their large boards have created a rift in the island surfing community. Common surf etiquette is to share the waves with surfers and stay out of the way. In the event you do fall down, make sure that your board doesn't hit someone.

LAHAINA

Lahaina is ringed by a barrier reef, which can make it shallow and dangerous for paddling. The trained instructors, however, know all of the *pukas* (holes) in the reef, and by allowing them to lead the way, you'll be awarded with sweeping views of the island's West Side. When you are over the Shark Pit, there's a decent chance you'll encounter an endangered Hawaiian monk seal or a harmless whitetip reef shark. While the 505 area can be a little difficult to navigate, it has the added benefit of being protected from the wind and will usually have calm, flat conditions when Ka'anapali is rough and blustery.

If you've rented your own board, the best place in the immediate area for stand-up paddling is the stretch of shore between Puamana and Launiupoko Beach Parks, where the water isn't nearly as shallow and it's still protected from the afternoon trade winds.

Rental Shops and Schools

Stand-up paddling lessons are offered in the Lahaina Breakwall area by **Royal Hawaiian** (117 Prison St., 808/276-7873, www.royalhawaiiansurfacademy.com, 7am-7pm Mon.-Fri., 7am-3:30pm Sat.-Sun.), **Goofy Foot** (505 Front St., 808/244-9283, www.goofyfootsurfschool.com, 7am-9pm daily, lessons Mon.-Sat.), and **Maui Wave Riders** (133 Prison St., 808/875-4761, www.mauiwaveriders.com, 7am-9pm daily). Rather than mingling with all the surf school students, the stand-up paddling tours go the other direction from the Lahaina Breakwall down to the section of beach known as Shark Pit. For rentals, expect to pay in the $35 range for three hours to $45 for all day.

For more personalized service in an area that isn't as crowded, **Maria Souza Stand-Up Paddle School** (808/579-9231, www.standuppaddlesurfschool.com) and **Hawaiian Paddle Sports** (808/442-6436, www.hawaiianpaddlesports.com) both offer lessons on beaches south of Lahaina, run by instructors who have a deep-rooted respect for the island, the environment, and Hawaiian cultural history. While they're more expensive, these tours will leave you with a deeper appreciation for the ocean. Lessons with Maria Souza's are $159 pp, and with Hawaiian Paddle Sports $189 for a private lesson, $129 pp for 2-4 people, or $109 pp for groups of five or more.

Kayaking and Canoeing

West Maui has numerous options for both kayaking and outrigger canoeing. While kayaking isn't as hard on the shoulder muscles and allows you to hug the coast, outrigger canoeing is a culturally rich experience unique to Polynesia. The morning hours are the best time to paddle, with most operators offering an early morning tour followed by another later in the morning.

KAPALUA, NAPILI, AND HONOKOWAI

The most popular kayak trip on the Upper West Side of the island is the paddle from D. T. Fleming Beach Park to Honolua Bay. Along this stretch of coast, you pass rugged rock formations inaccessible from the road, and you'll hug this dramatic coast past Mokulei'a Bay and into Honolua. Because of the high surf during winter, these tours are only offered in summer, and all trips depart D. T. Fleming Beach Park in the early morning hours before the afternoon trade winds pick up. Snorkeling in Honolua Bay is included in the excursions, and you are likely to encounter Hawaiian green sea turtles or potentially even Hawaiian spinner dolphins.

The best company offering tours up here is **Hawaiian Paddle Sports** (808/442-6436, www.hawaiianpaddlesports.com), with completely private excursions for kayaking ($149 pp) and outrigger canoeing ($159 pp). The educational component and respect for culture are superior to other operations.

KA'ANAPALI

Off Kahekili Beach Park in front of the Westin Villas, **Maui Paddle Sports** (808/283-9344, www.mauipaddlesports.com) offers two-hour outrigger canoe rides in a six-person outrigger ($85 pp). Trips run at 8am and 9:30am daily. This is a convenient option if you're staying in the area off Kahekili Beach.

SOUTH OF LAHAINA

The main areas for kayaking south of Lahaina are either Olowalu (mile marker 14) or Coral Gardens, off Papalaua Beach Park (mile marker 11), where you can paddle along the rugged sea cliffs that plunge down into the sea. This is a popular area for kayaking in winter since the large surf on the northern shores makes kayaking there impossible, and these are fantastic reefs for spotting Hawaiian green sea turtles. **Hawaiian Paddle Sports** (808/442-6436, www.hawaiianpaddles-ports.com, private tours $119-199 pp) offers three-hour tours in this area. For a more budget-friendly operation, **Kayak Olowalu** (808/661-0606, www.kayakolowalu.com) offers 2.5-hour tours ($65 pp adults).

Other Water Activities

★ SUNSET CRUISES

Few Maui activities are more iconic than a sunset sail off the West Maui coast. The feeling of the trade winds in your hair as you glide along is a sensation of freedom you can't experience on land. Watch as the setting sun paints the sky every shade of orange and pink. On most days you can make out a rainbow hovering over the lush valleys of Mauna Kahalawai.

Ka'anapali

A **sunset sail off Ka'anapali Beach** can be the most magical moment of your vacation, but there are a few things to understand to make the most of the magic. Make sure to ask when you need to check in, as departure times for sunset sails are different in summer and winter. Secondly, while it's always nice to dress up a little, remember that you're going on a boat and should be outfitted accordingly. The Ka'anapali boats are all sailing catamarans, which are boarded from the sand, and since some days can have moderate shore-break, there's a good chance you'll end up wet from the shins down. Your shoes are collected prior to boarding (to prevent sand tracking onto the boat), so don't put too much effort into matching them with your outfit.

There's even a chance that the departure will be moved to Lahaina Harbor due to large

view of Maui from a sunset sail

surf on the beach. Since this isn't possible to predict until the day before the sail, it's a good idea to double-check on the morning of your sail to confirm where the boat will be loading. The northerly trade winds can often be chilly, so it's a good idea to bring a light jacket. Finally, remember that you'll be sailing. Even though the vessels are wide, stable catamarans, it may be difficult to move around, and spray may come over the sides. If your idea of a sunset sail is a stable platform that putts along at three knots, the dinner cruises from Lahaina are a better bet.

Trilogy (808/874-5649, www.sailtrilogy. com) offers sunset sails ($69) on Tuesday, Thursday, and Saturday as well as an Aloha Friday sunset sail ($79) that features live music and Pacific Rim pupus. Trilogy's sail isn't marketed as a booze cruise, but three premium alcoholic beverages are included in the rates, including mixed drink cocktails like the Moloka'i Mule. Unless the surf is high and they need to load from Lahaina Harbor, the check-in for all Trilogy tours is in front of the Ka'anapali Beach Hotel.

In front of Whalers Village, **Teralani** (808/661-7245, www.teralani.net) offers two different sails departing nightly during the busier times of year. The original sunset sail ($71 adults) includes a pupu menu as well as an open bar of beer and mixed drinks. For those who would rather dine on board, the full dinner sail ($94 adults) is 30 minutes longer and includes a filling menu.

Gemini (808/669-0508, www.geminicharters.com) similarly offers sunset sails ($75 adults) that feature a pupu menu as well as Maui Brewing Company beer and mai tais.

The most yacht-like experience departing from the beach is on the *Hula Girl* (808/665-0344, www.sailingmaui.com), which not only offers the newest boat but also luxurious upgrades like throw pillows, free Wi-Fi, panoramic viewing from the fly-bridge, and high-tech sailing. Regular sunset sails ($68) are offered Monday, Wednesday, and Friday, but you have to buy your food and drinks. For a full-service dinner cruise, *Hula Girl*

also offers cruises on Tuesday, Thursday, and Saturday ($80 adults) featuring upscale Pacific Rim dining options made fresh in the onboard kitchen. In many ways, it's more like a floating restaurant with an $80 cover charge. Menu items range $5-23, and a full-service bar slings top-shelf cocktails.

Lahaina
DINNER CRUISES

A sailboat is a better venue than a powerboat for a sunset cruise, but for those who would rather be on a large, stable diesel vessel instead of a catamaran, the best dinner cruise from Lahaina is offered by **Pacific Whale Foundation** (612 Front St., 808/942-5311, www.pacificwhale.org). The power catamaran used for this charter is the nicest of the large diesel boats, and the menu includes locally sourced produce and sustainably harvested seafood. Regular seats are $88, but if you don't want to share a table with another party, upgrade to the premium seating ($108 adults). Three alcoholic beverages are included in the cruise, as is live music.

SAILBOATS

If you know what it means to "shake a reef," you'll be much happier watching the sunset aboard a small sailboat than on a large motorized platform. The fastest sailing catamaran offering sunset sails ($65 adults) from Lahaina is *Sail Maui* (808/244-2087, www. sailmaui.com), which provides sailing, pupus, beer, wine, and mai tais. Trips run Monday-Saturday, and maximum capacity of the cruise is just 24 people.

The newest catamaran in Lahaina Harbor is *Ocean Spirit,* part of the **Pacific Whale Foundation** (612 Front St., 808/942-5311, www.pacificwhale.org) fleet that sailed to Hawaii from St. Croix in only 42 days. The two-hour sunset sails ($69) include locally sourced pupus and three alcoholic beverages.

If you're a monohull sailor, *Scotch Mist II* (808/661-0386, www.scotchmistsailingcharters.com) offers evening sunset sails ($69)

Whale-Watching FAQ

The waters off Maui have the highest concentration of humpback whales anywhere on the planet. Commonly asked whale-watching questions:

Q: What kind of whales are around Maui?

A: Although there are rarely seen species such as pilot whales and false killer whales that inhabit the waters off Maui year-round, 99 percent of the time you will see North Pacific humpback whales.

Q: Where are these whales from?

A: They were born here in the warm protected waters of Hawaii. The humpbacks then migrate 3,000 miles to their summer feeding grounds in Alaska, where they gorge themselves on small fish and krill, and return again in the winter to mate and give birth.

Q: Why don't the whales mate in Alaska?

A: Since baby humpbacks are born with minimal amounts of fat, the water is too cold in Alaska.

Q: Do the whales eat at all in Hawaii?

A: No. While there's no evidence to suggest that whales wouldn't eat if given the opportunity, the waters off Maui don't contain the same amount of zooplankton and marine organisms that humpback whales feed on. Adults go for months at a time without eating, losing up to one-third of their body weight.

Q: How much do humpback whales weigh?

A: At birth, humpback whales are 10-12 feet long and weigh about a ton. Full-grown adults weight about one ton per foot, which means that a 45-foot humpback weighs about 90,000 pounds.

Q: Are males or females bigger?

A: Females are a little bit larger than males, which is known as reverse sexual dimorphism, a technical way of saying "I need to give birth to a 2,000-pound animal, so I need to be bigger than you."

Q: How quickly do whales swim?

A: Although they can sprint up to about 20 mph, on average humpback whales travel at a steady rate of 3-5 mph.

Q: How long does it take them to get to Alaska?

A: Whales spend 6-8 weeks migrating between Alaska and the Hawaiian Islands.

Q: Are whales more active in the morning?

A: No. Since whales only take short "cat naps," there isn't a set time of day when they are asleep. Mornings are often best for whale-watching because the water is calmer and the whales are easier to spot.

Q: What is "getting mugged?"

A: "Getting mugged" refers to the fact that all boats are required to maintain a 100-yard distance from humpback whales. Should the whales decide to approach the boat, it is out of your hands. You need to wait until the whale loses interest. This can take 45 minutes or more.

aboard a Santa Cruz 50-foot racing boat, which departs from slip 2.

★ WHALE-WATCHING

Any vessel that floats is going to be offering whale-watching between December 15 and April 15. Even though whale season officially lasts until May 15, the whales aren't encountered with enough regularity after mid-April to guarantee sightings. The peak of the season for whale-watching is January through March, and simply being out on the water turns any trip into whale-watching.

Most snorkeling and sailing operators offer whale-watching during winter, with most boats carrying whale naturalists well-versed in the study of these gentle giants. Since most prices are about the same, the choice ultimately comes down to what sort of vessel best suits your comfort level. Small rafts from Lahaina Harbor place you the closest to the water. Sailboats also offer whale-watching trips from both Lahaina Harbor and Ka'anapali Beach. The large 149-passenger diesel boats in Lahaina provide the most affordable rates, but you'll be sharing the vessel with over 100 other people and won't get 360-degree views.

SUBMARINE

If riding a submarine is on your bucket list, **Atlantis Submarines** (Slip 18, 808/667-2224, www.atlantisadventures.com/maui, 9am-2pm daily) operates regular charters ($105 adults, $35 children) from Lahaina Harbor to the *Carthaginian,* a sunken whaling ship in 100 feet of water. Check-in is at the Atlantis shop inside the Pioneer Inn. Trips last two hours.

For those who are a little nervous about descending completely underwater and want to see fish without snorkeling, *Reef Dancer* (Slip 6, 808/667-2133, www.mauiglassbottomboat.com) is a yellow "semi-sub" that remains partially submerged for its journey along the coast. While there is an above-deck portion of the sub that never goes underwater, passengers are seated in an underwater cabin that offers 360-degree views of the underwater world. All of the boat staff double as scuba divers who can point out anything that might be living along the reef such as eels, octopuses, turtles, or urchins. This is a great way for young children, elderly visitors, and nonswimmers to enjoy Maui's reef system without having to get their hair wet. Sixty-minute tours ($35 adults, $20 children) run three times each morning, with a longer 90-minute tour ($45 adults, $25 children) departing Lahaina Harbor at 2:15pm daily.

FISHING

In no place is Lahaina's port town heritage more evident than at dingy yet lovable Lahaina Harbor. The smell of fish carcasses still wafts on the breeze, and shirtless, tanned, sweat-covered sailors casually sip beer as they lay the fresh catch on ice. Some days you can buy fresh mahimahi or ono straight from the folks who caught it, or, if you'd rather take your shot at reeling one in yourself, there are a slew of sportfishing boats ready to get you on the water.

The charters that have the best chance of catching fish are those that leave early and stay out for a full day. These are more expensive, but during a full-day charter you're able to troll around the buoys on the far side of Lana'i or Kaho'olawe. On half-day charters,

diving deep on Atlantis Submarines

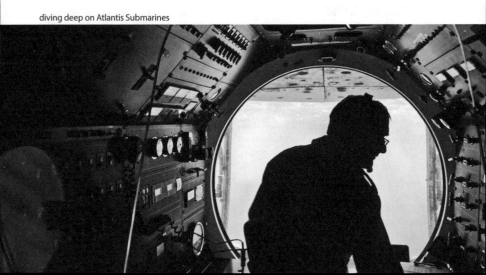

you're confined to shallower water where the fish aren't biting as much, particularly during the winter. On virtually all charters you need to provide your own food and drinks. Don't bring bananas on board, since it is considered bad luck. Most boats will let you keep what you catch so you can cook it the same night.

Of all the boats in the harbor, *Start Me Up* (808/667-2774, www.sportfishingmaui.com) has the best reputation. Prices range from $129 pp for two hours to $279 pp for an eight-hour charter. Catch a 500-pound marlin, and your trip is free!

A boat with a sterling reputation is *Die Hard* (808/344-5051, www.diehardsportfishing.com), run by the legendary Captain Fuzzy. Rates for these charters vary, but expect to pay $200 pp for six-hour charters and $220 pp for full-day, eight-hour charters.

Down at the south end of the harbor, away from many of the other boats, **Luckey Strike** (808/661-4606, www.luckeystrike.com) has two different boats and operates on the premise that using live bait for smaller fish is better. Captain Tad Luckey has been fishing these waters for over 30 years, and as with most captains in the harbor, he has an enviable and well-earned amount of local knowledge to put into every trip.

PARASAILING

Parasailing isn't possible December 15-May 15. Since the waters off West Maui are part of the Hawaiian Islands Humpback Whale National Marine Sanctuary, all "thrill craft," such as high-speed parasailing boats, are outlawed during the time of year when the whales are nursing their calves. During the summer or fall, however, parasailing is a peaceful adventure option for gazing at West Maui from hundreds of feet above the turquoise waters. It's one of the best views you'll find on the island.

Ka'anapali

UFO Parasail (800/359-4836, www.ufoparasail.net) is one of the two operators departing from Ka'anapali Beach, in front of Leilani's

These are the best seats in the house!

restaurant. Only eight people are on the boat at a time, which means that your overall time on the water is only a little over an hour. Of that hour, your personal flight time lasts 10-12 minutes, depending on the length of your line (you'll end up being 400-500 feet off the water). The staff and captains who run these tours do hundreds of trips over the course of the season, and from a safety and efficiency standpoint, the crew has it down to a science. Taking off and landing on the boat is a dry entry and exit, and you will be blown away by the serenity you experience up in the air. Prices range $85-95 depending on your height; you must weigh at least 130 pounds to fly alone, and trips usually start around 9am.

In front of the Hyatt, **West Maui Parasail** (808/661-4060, www.westmauiparasail.com) offers similar tours at $75 for 800 feet or $85 for 1,200 feet. If you aren't staying in the Ka'anapali resort area, a perk of going with West Maui Parasail is that free, convenient parking can be found in the Hanakao'o Beach Park area just a three-minute walk from the Hyatt.

Lahaina

The only parasailing operation in Lahaina is **West Maui Parasail** (808/661-4060, www.westmauiparasail.com) out of slip 15. The prices are the same as at the Ka'anapali operation, but a benefit of parasailing from Lahaina is that the water is consistently calmer and glassier than in neighboring Ka'anapali.

JET SKIING

Just like parasailing, Jet Skiing is only possible May 16-December 14. During summer, the island's only Jet Ski operation is **Maui Watersports** (808/667-2001, www.mauiwatersports.com), in Ka'anapali, just south of the Hyatt. Even though the area is relatively protected from the wind, morning hours are still the best for the calmest conditions. Rates are $79 for a 30-minute ride and $119 for a full hour, although you can save money by booking online.

WAKEBOARDING

Captain Ryan at **Wake Maui** (808/269-5645, www.wakemaui.com) offers wakeboarding trips in the flat water between Lahaina and Ka'anapali. Wake Maui provides the only service of its kind, where a six-passenger ski boat is equipped with all the wake toys for a fun day on the water. Since Maui's winds can often be extreme, however, wakeboarding charters usually depart early to capitalize on glassy conditions. Other toys include waterskiing and wakesurfing equipment, or you can simply charter the boat ($214 for 1 hour, $428 for 2 hours, $791 for 4 hours) if you want to go whale-watching in winter.

SPEARFISHING

To take snorkeling to the next level and maybe take home dinner, **Maui Spearfishing Academy** (808/446-0352, www.mauispearfishing.com, $169) teaches visitors how to spearfish and eradicate invasive species, and can teach you the technique behind holding your breath to spear-dive and target the right fish.

Hiking and Biking

HIKING

There aren't nearly as many hiking trails on the West Side of the island as you might expect. Much of the access in West Maui is blocked by private land or lack of proper trails. Also, since much of West Maui sits in the lee of Mauna Kahalawai, there aren't any accessible waterfalls, as there are in East Maui. Nevertheless, the hiking options in West Maui offer their own sort of beauty, from stunning coastal treks to grueling ridgeline hikes.

Kapalua, Napili, and Honokowai
★ **KAPALUA COASTAL TRAIL**
Even though it's only 1.75 miles long, the **Kapalua Coastal Trail** might just be the best coastal walk in Hawaii. The trail is bookended on each side by beaches that have each been named the number-one beach in the United States: Kapalua Bay and D. T. Fleming Beach Park. While most walkers, joggers, and hikers begin the trail at Kapalua Bay, you can also access the trail from other junctions at the Kapalua Bay Villas, Oneloa Bay, the Ritz-Carlton, and D. T. Fleming Beach Park.

What makes the Kapalua Coastal Trail legendary are the various environments it passes through. If you begin at Kapalua Bay, the trail starts as a paved walkway paralleling the beach and weaves its way through ultra-luxurious residences. At the top of a short hill, the paved walkway reaches a junction by the Kapalua Bay Villas, where the path suddenly switches to dirt. Signs point to the continuation of the trail, and a spur trail leads straight

Pu'u Kukui: One of the Wettest Spots on Earth

Three hundred eighty: That's how many inches of rain fall annually on the 5,787-foot summit of Mauna Kahalawai. That's over 31 feet. For those more familiar with snow, going off the general estimate that one inch of rain is equal to a foot of snow, that's about 380 feet of snow—higher than the tallest point in the state of Florida.

The summit of Mauna Kahalawai—known as Pu'u Kukui—is really wet. There aren't many days when you can see Pu'u Kukui, so if you get a clear morning, take a picture. Even on days when it's sunny along the coast (Lahaina only gets about 13 inches of rain per year), you can see rain clouds hanging in the valleys of the lushly forested interior. There aren't any roads back here, and there are barely even hiking trails; it's just too wet.

Mount Wai'ale'ale on Kaua'i is regarded as the wettest place in Hawaii, with an average annual rainfall of 390 inches. Even though a remote area in East Maui known as the Big Bog is alleged to be even wetter, with 404 inches mean over the last 30 years, Pu'u Kukui still holds a number of rainfall records that no other spot can beat. In March 1942, rain gauges at Pu'u Kukui recorded 101 inches of rain in a single month. In 1982, over 704 inches of rain were unleashed on the summit. According to statistics provided by the Weather Channel, both are U.S. records.

out toward Hawea Point, a protected reserve that is home to the island's largest colony of 'ua'u kani (wedge-tailed shearwaters). If you follow the grass trail to the left of the three-way junction, it connects with the trail to Namalu Bay—the rocky, Mediterranean cove hidden in the craggy recesses.

Continuing along the main Kapalua Coastal Trail leads over a short rocky section before emerging at a smooth boardwalk along Oneloa Bay. The boardwalk here was constructed as a means of protecting the sensitive dunes of Kapalua, and in the morning Oneloa is one of the most gloriously empty beaches you'll find on Maui. At the end of the boardwalk, the trail leads up a flight of stairs and eventually connects with Lower Honoapi'ilani Road. From here, take a left and follow the sidewalk as it connects with the trail running in front of the Ritz-Carlton before finishing at the water's edge at D. T. Fleming Beach Park. For a side trip, hike out parallel to the golf course to **Makalua-puna Point**—otherwise known as Dragon's Teeth (page 29).

VILLAGE WALKING TRAILS

The **village walking trails** are the next most popular hikes in the Kapalua resort

area. Weaving their way up the mountainside through the cool and forested uplands are the 1.25-mile Cardio Loop or the 3.6-mile Lake Loop, an uphill, butt-burning workout popular with local joggers. More than just a great morning workout, there are also sections of the trail that offer sweeping views looking out toward Moloka'i and the area around Honolua Bay. To find the access point for the trails, park in the lot for the Kapalua Village Center (between Sansei Restaurant and the Kapalua Golf Academy) and follow a paved cart path winding its way down toward an underpass, where you will find the trailhead for both loops.

MAHANA RIDGE TRAIL

The **Mahana Ridge Trail** is the longest continuous trail in the Kapalua resort area and the best option for serious hikers. Though you can access the Mahana Ridge Trail from the village trails, a less confusing and more scenic trailhead is in the parking lot of D. T. Fleming Beach Park along the access road from the highway. The trailhead is a little hard to find, so look for the thin trail leading up the inland side of the road about 20 yards back from the parking lot. This trail climbs up the ridge for nearly six miles, all the way to the Maunalei Arboretum, and is a proper hiking trail with narrow sections, moderate uphills, and sweeping views of the coast. It is an out-and-back trip, and maps are available online at www.kapalua.com.

MAUNALEI ARBORETUM TRAIL

To climb even farther up the mountainside, follow the **Maunalei Arboretum Trail** as it winds its way through a forest planted by the great D. T. Fleming. The manager of Honolua Ranch during the 1920s, Fleming forested the mountainside with numerous plant species from across the globe in an effort to preserve the watershed. Today, over 85 years after the arboretum was established, hikers can still climb the ridges of this historic upland and be immersed in a forest of wild banyan trees as well as coffee, guava, and bo trees. Trails in the arboretum range from short 0.5-mile loops to a moderate 2.5-mile round-trip that winds down Honolua Ridge. To reach the trails, you have to hike six miles up the scenic Mahana Ridge Trail, or book a guided hiking tour ($99) through **Ambassadors of the Environment** (808/669-6200) at the Ritz Carlton.

OHAI TRAIL

The 1.2-mile **Ohai Trail** awards hikers with panoramic vistas of the island's North Shore. This area is often windy, and the way in which the wind drowns out all other sounds makes it a peaceful respite on the northern coast. The Ohai trailhead is 10 miles past the entrance to Kapalua, by mile marker 41, between the Nakalele Blowhole and Olivine Pools. Along the moderate, winding trail are a few placards with information on the island's native coastal plants. This is also a great perch to watch for tropical seabirds soaring on the afternoon breeze. There isn't any readily available water on this stretch of coast, so be sure to pack a water bottle with you. There is sometimes a vendor selling drinks in front of Nakalele Blowhole, or a food truck (Mon.-Sat.) parked by Kahakuloa.

Ka'anapali

KA'ANAPALI BOARDWALK

The southern terminus of the three-mile-long **Ka'anapali Boardwalk** is in front of the Hyatt resort, and the easiest public beach parking is at Hanakao'o Beach Park along the highway between Ka'anapali and Lahaina. From here the boardwalk runs north all the way to the Sheraton, about 1.5 miles, although

Kapalua Coastal Trail

if you follow the paved walkway through the lower level of the Sheraton and through the parking lot, you will notice the trail re-forms and starts skirting the golf course. The walkway then runs through the Royal Lahaina resort and the parking lot of adjoining hotels. Following the Beach Walk signs, you eventually join another boardwalk that runs all the way down to the Honua Kai resort.

South of Lahaina
LAHAINA PALI TRAIL

Hot, dry, and with incomparable views, the **Lahaina Pali Trail** is a walk back in time to days when reaching Lahaina wasn't quite so easy. This five-mile, three-hour (one-way) hike is the most strenuous trek in West Maui, as the zigzagging trail climbs 1,600 vertical feet before reaching a crest by the Kaheawa Wind Farm. While torturous on both your legs and your thirst, the reward for the uphill slog is panoramic views over the central valley and dozens of humpback whales off the coast during winter.

Tracing its way over a part of the island that receives less than 10 inches of rainfall annually, this trail was originally constructed about 400 years ago during the reign of Pi'ilani, who envisioned a footpath wrapping around the island. When a dirt road was constructed along the coast in 1911, the trail fell into disrepair. Nevertheless, hikers still encounter evidence of ancient activity, such as stone shelters and rock walls. It's surreal to imagine that only 100 years ago this was the preferred route to reach Lahaina. To get the most out of this hike, pick up the hiking guide that the Na Ala Hele trail system has published, titled *Tales from the Trail*. It provides an interactive historical tour aligned with markers along the trail. Copies are available at the Department of Land and Natural Resources building in Wailuku (54 High St.), or, if you have a smartphone, download it as a PDF (www.mauiguidebook.com/hikes/lahaina-pali-trail).

The downside of this trail is that since it's a one-way hike, it can take some logistical planning. The Ukumehame trailhead on the Lahaina side is at mile marker 10.5, about 0.5 mile past the tunnel in a small dirt parking lot on the inland side of the highway. If you depart from the Ukumehame trailhead, the path ascends moderately and offers pristine views of the coral reefs below. After the trail levels out at 1,600 feet, when you reach the crest by the wind farm, it descends steeply and sharply to the opposite trailhead between Ma'alaea

mountain views from the Maunalei Arboretum Trail

Surfing Etiquette

Surfing is a highlight of a visit to Lahaina, and it's important to have a basic grasp of etiquette out in the water.

1. Always wear a leash. Errant boards in the lineup can be dangerous. Nothing ruins a session like having to swim after your board.

2. Stay out of the way of any surfer on a wave. While this can sometimes be difficult when paddling out from shore, the best thing to do is either stop paddling so the surfer can navigate around you, or aim for a line behind the board so it ends up passing in front of you.

3. Offer a simple "hello" and a smile to your fellow surfers. It may or may not be returned, but it's a way of signaling "friend" instead of "foe."

4. At more advanced breaks, don't paddle directly to the peak of the wave. Instead, wait for a while on the shoulder to let the local surfers have a turn. In more advanced lineups such as Honolua Bay and the outer reef at Breakwall, waves are earned instead of given, so it's best to keep a low profile. Share the waves. If you just got the last one, don't turn around and take the next one.

5. It's never alright to "drop in" on another surfer. Although it might seem like a free-for-all out there, surfing etiquette dictates that the surfer closest to the breaking part of the wave has the right-of-way. To initiate a ride in front of this surfer is the worst of surfing offenses and a surefire way to get the "stink eye." As a general rule, if you're paddling for a wave, there is already someone riding that wave, and if you can see that person's face, choose a different wave.

6. Don't throw your board. Sometimes in larger surf your board can get ripped away from you, but it's heavily frowned upon to "duck dive" a wave by throwing your board to the side and swimming under the wave. Instead, either duck dive your shortboard under the wave, or, if on a longboard, try to "turn turtle" by flipping upside down with your board and letting the wave crash over you while holding it with your hands. In the event you are riding a wave and fall, to keep the board from shooting out and hitting someone in the face, reach down and try to grab the part where your leash connects to minimize the distance it can go flying.

7. Don't stare at people. This is especially true at more advanced breaks such as Honolua Bay. Even if you like someone's tattoo or are trying to read the brand of someone's board shorts, it comes off as threatening.

8. Assess your own abilities. Surfing is meant to be fun and enjoyable. Paddling out into conditions that are beyond your ability level is a good way to get in trouble. Sit and watch the waves for a few minutes before paddling out, assess the vibe once you're out there, and as long as you follow proper surf etiquette, you'll end up having an epic time on the water.

★ Surfing Spots

The most popular surf break in Lahaina is **Lahaina Breakwall,** located between the 505 shopping center and Lahaina Harbor. This is where most of the Lahaina surf schools operate. All of the surf schools hang out in the shallow inside section, and more experienced surfers sit farther outside. The outside section at small levels can be either a left or a right, although when it gets big on a large summer swell, it can turn into a huge left that can grow to 10 feet or more. During low tide it can get shallow enough here that you need to paddle with your fingertips and your skeg can scrape the bottom, so high tide is the optimal time for those who are concerned about falling. It shouldn't come as a surprise that this spot can get crowded, a fact of life that has earned it the moniker "Snakewall." If you're a beginner, you're better off going a few miles south to Puamana Beach Park or Guardrails.

Rental Shops and Schools

Inside the 505 shopping center, **Goofy Foot** (505 Front St., 808/244-9283, www.goofy-footsurfschool.com, 7am-9pm daily, lessons Mon.-Sat.) has helped over 100,000 students ride their first wave since opening in 1994.

and the junction of Honoapi'ilani Highway (Hwy. 30) and North Kihei Road. Your four options for the return route are to leave a car at the opposite trailhead, hike back the way you came, hitchhike back to the original trailhead, or turn back the way you came once you reach the wind farm (which is the shortest and most practical option).

If you plan on only hiking half the trail, setting out from the Ma'alaea trailhead offers better views of the valley and Kealia Pond, whereas departing from the Ukumehame trailhead offers better views of the coast and whale-watching opportunities. For the intrepid and those equipped with headlamps, the Ukumehame side is the best sunset perch on the West Side. Since there is absolutely no shade on this hike and it can get brutally hot, it's imperative to avoid the middle of the day and to pack more water than you would normally need. You'll be passing over rocky, rugged terrain, so wear closed-toe shoes.

BIKING

Whether you're going for a 60-mile ride around the West Maui Mountains or a leisurely ride down Front Street on a beach cruiser, biking on the West Side of the island means cycling on roadways. For serious cyclists looking to rent a road bike, **West Maui Cycles** (1087 Limahana Place, 808/661-9005, www.westmauicycles.com, 9am-5pm Mon.-Sat., 10am-4pm Sun.), in the industrial park of Lahaina, is the best bike shop on the West Side. Mountain bikes and high-performance road bikes range $50 per day to $285 per week; basic beach cruisers are $15 per day.

Closer to the center of Lahaina, **Boss Frog's Cycles** (156 Lahainaluna Rd., 808/661-1345, www.mauiroadbikerentals.com, 8am-5pm daily) also offers beach cruisers ($15 per day, $60 per week) and high-performance road bikes ($45 per day). While this location is closer to town and more convenient, die-hard cyclists will appreciate the passion for the sport found at West Maui Cycles.

Adventure Sports

Even though water sports dominate the recreation options on the island's West Side, there are still a number of places where you can get a thrill on the land or over the water.

ATV RIDES

The best ATV ride on the West Side of the island is with **Kahoma Ranch** (808/667-1978, www.kahomaranch.com), to get dirty and rip across dirt roads on your own ATV ($222) or a shared ATV ($149). At the end, when you're all hot and sweaty, you can take a plunge down one of three different waterslides. Tour participants are awarded with views looking out at the island of Lana'i and back into Kahoma Valley. The tour area is closed to the public, so this is the only way you will see these views.

The waterslides look like little more than tarps stretched over a hole in the ground, but the speeds you can achieve are much faster than you'd expect. Children are $82, and those as young as age five can accompany a driver of legal age. Tours take place at 7:30am, 10am, 1pm, and 4pm daily, although the 7:30am tour doesn't include the waterslides.

ZIPLINING

The largest ziplining tour in West Maui is **Skyline Eco-Adventures** (2580 Keka'a Dr., 808/878-8400, www.zipline.com, 7am-6pm daily, $150), a company that was the first zipline operator on Maui. Each of the eight zip lines has a historical, environmental, or cultural connection explained by the guides, and the main draw is the view toward Lana'i and Moloka'i across the royal-blue channels.

These tours are so popular they run eight times a day, with the earliest starting from the Fairway Shops office at 7am daily. The benefit of an early tour is that temperatures are still cool and winds are calm, although there can sometimes be some lingering morning showers, and the dirt roads can be muddy from this moisture. Try to get on the 8am or 9am tour, although there is never a bad time to be up here ziplining. Children must be 10 years of age for the Ka'anapali course, closed-toe shoes are required, and the maximum weight is 260 pounds. To combine ziplining with splashing in the reservoirs, try the four-line **Zip N' Dip** tour, where you zip right into the water.

Up north, **Kapalua Ziplines** (500 Office Rd., 808/756-9147, www.kapaluaziplines.com) has a seven-line course that differs from Skyline in Ka'anapali in that all the lines are tandem. You can zip next to your loved one and watch them grimace with glee as you soar up to 2,100 feet across the Kapalua mountainside. You'll walk over one of Hawaii's longest suspension bridges and ride an ATV to the summit. Tours ($207) are offered five times per day. Since the tours can sometimes be canceled due to wind, try to go early in the morning.

Golf

KAPALUA, NAPILI, AND HONOKOWAI

For serious golfers, the name Kapalua should be synonymous with the **Kapalua Plantation Course** (2000 Plantation Club Dr., 808/669-8044, www.golfatkapalua.com). This 7,411-yard, par-73 course is the island's most famous and is the site of the Hyundai Tournament of Champions. With the course's fame come big greens fees: $299, but discounted to $239 if you are staying in the Kapalua resort. Greens fees decrease as the day wears on, as low as $139 in the late afternoon for nine holes, but expect the wind to be howling. Club rentals ($70) include two sleeves of balls, and shoe rental is $15. To find the clubhouse, travel along Honoapi'ilani Highway (Hwy. 30) for one mile past the main entrance to Kapalua resort and make a right onto Plantation Club Drive. Continue up the hillside; the clubhouse is on the right.

The **Kapalua Bay Course** (300 Kapalua Dr., 877/527-2582, www.golfatkapalua.com) along the Kapalua shore is more forgiving at par 72 and 6,600 yards. While all of the holes offer resort-quality play, the highlight is hole 5, where the green is sandwiched between Oneloa Bay and D. T. Fleming Beach Park and you are surrounded by 270 degrees of brilliant blue ocean. The Bay Course is windy in the afternoon, so early mornings are best for calm conditions. Greens fees are $219, discounted to $199 for those staying in Kapalua resort. The fees decrease through the day, to as low as $109 for nine holes. To find the clubhouse, turn on Kapalua Drive from Lower Honoapi'ilani Road, across the street from Oneloa Bay (Ironwoods Beach). Travel up the road by the tennis center to the clubhouse on the right.

KA'ANAPALI

The courses in Ka'anapali are cheaper than in Kapalua and closer to most resorts. Perhaps most important, they're less prone to wind and rain, and it takes the trade winds about two hours longer to reach Ka'anapali than Kapalua. What this means is that an 8am tee time at Kapalua gets blustery around the sixth hole, whereas at Ka'anapali, you could be well into the back nine before the wind becomes a factor. The sacrifice in Ka'anapali is that the views aren't quite as nice—although they are still spectacular by normal standards—and the greens are slightly less manicured.

Of the two courses in Ka'anapali, the nicer is the **Royal Ka'anapali** (2290 Ka'anapali Pkwy., 808/661-3691, www.kaanapaligolf-courses.com), with the best views. In addition to paralleling the Pacific Ocean, this 6,700-yard, par-71 course is also the island's original course, opened in 1962. Greens fees are $255 for nonguests; those staying in Ka'anapali can play for $169. For those willing to tee off after 1pm, greens fees drop to $129.

Most of the holes on the course at **Ka'anapali Kai** (2290 Ka'anapali Pkwy., 808/661-3691, www.kaanapaligolfcourses. com) are on the inland side of the highway. The fairways aren't as nicely maintained as at the Royal, but the elevation provides classic ocean views. Greens fees are $205 for nonguests and $129 for those staying in Ka'anapali. Greens fees drop to $99 after 1pm, club rental is $55, and shoes are available for $10.

Both Ka'anapali courses check in at the same clubhouse. If you're looking for something just a little bit different, **Foot Golf** is offered on the Ka'anapali Kai course after 4pm; for $15 you play a modified course using a soccer ball and only your feet.

Spas

While the spa and massage services in this section are broken down by their geographic location, if you would rather enjoy an in-room, mobile massage, **Na Ali'i Massage** (808/250-7170, www.mymauimassage.com) will meet you anywhere on the West Side and offers rates much lower than the resorts or local massage parlors. A 60-minute massage is $85, and they offer a full range of other services, such as body scrubs, reflexology, and hand and foot treatments.

KAPALUA, NAPILI, AND HONOKOWAI

The best spa on the northwest side is the fantastically luxurious **Spa Montage** (100 Bay Dr., 808/665-8282, www.montagehotels.com, 9am-7pm daily), a wellness retreat unlike any other, incorporating state-of-the-art workout equipment with peaceful surroundings looking out toward Kapalua Bay. When your treatment is through, you can use the facilities or sit by the edgeless pool. A 60-minute massage runs $210. For one of the island's best spa deals, purchase a day pass for $55, which gives you access to the facilities, including the fitness center, hydrotherapy circuits, and impossibly calming surroundings. A week-long pass is $250, or $350 for two people.

For a spa experience outside a resort, **Zensations Spa** (3600 Lower Honoapi'ilani Rd., 808/669-0100, www.zensationsspa.com, 10am-5pm Mon.-Sat., 9am-7pm Sun.) in the 5A Rent-A-Space mall in Honokowai, offers 60-minute massages for $99 as well as a full range of aromatherapy and facial and body treatment options. The spa is within walking distance of many Honokowai condos.

KA'ANAPALI

While nearly every resort in the Ka'anapali complex has a spa or beauty center, there are a couple that stand out. At the Westin Maui next to Whalers Village, **Heavenly Spa** (2365 Ka'anapali Pkwy., 808/661-2588, www.westin-maui.com, 8am-7pm daily) has been lauded as one of the top spas in the United States and has 50-minute massages beginning at $155. For slightly more affordable rates, the **Spa at Black Rock** (2605 Ka'anapali Pkwy., 808/667-9577, www.blackrockspa.com, 8:30am-7pm daily) offers 50-minute massages beginning at $140.

Shopping

KAPALUA, NAPILI, AND HONOKOWAI

Shopping in the northwestern corner of the island is utilitarian, paling in comparison to the shops of Ka'anapali and Lahaina. Nevertheless, there are still a few stores worthy of a mention if you're staying in the area and need some emergency retail therapy.

In Kapalua, the **Honolua Store** (502 Office Rd., 808/665-9105, 6am-6:30pm daily) has a small apparel and souvenir section to accompany the food market, and if you save your receipt from any purchase, you will receive a free gift the next time you shop here.

Down the road in Kahana, **Women Who Run With Wolves** (4310 Honoapi'ilani Rd., 808/665-0786, www.womenwhorunwithwolves.com, 10am-6pm daily), downstairs in the Kahana Manor, has the best women's apparel and accessory shopping that you'll find on the northwest side.

KA'ANAPALI
Whalers Village

Without a doubt, the undisputed epicenter of the Ka'anapali shopping scene is **Whalers Village** (2435 Ka'anapali Pkwy., 808/661-4567, www.whalersvillage.com, 9:30am-10pm daily), smack in the middle of Ka'anapali Beach between the Whaler Hotel and the Westin Resort. With three levels of restaurants, clothing boutiques, jewelry galleries, and kiosks, Whalers Village is the see-and-be-seen spot for all of your island souvenir shopping. While many of the stores are name-brand outlets you're already familiar with, there are still a handful of locally run stores. Get your parking validated, since the garage rates are expensive.

If you park in the Whalers Village garage, you can't help but walk directly past **Totally Hawaiian** (808/667-4070, www.totallyhawaiian.com), a gift gallery featuring the wares of over 100 local artists. Works such as

hand-painted Hawaiian gourds are on display, as is an impressive collection of Ni'ihau shell jewelry. There's also a fascinating array of ancient Hawaiian weapons handcrafted from shark's teeth and wood.

Sand People (808/662-8785, www.sandpeople.com) is a "coastal lifestyle emporium" featuring home decor and furnishings inspired by the ocean. This is a good place to find that whitewashed driftwood picture frame you've been searching for.

Other popular apparel favorites include **Blue Ginger** (808/667-5793, www.blueginger.com), a store specializing in women's and children's resort wear, and **Maggie Coulombe** (808/344-6672, www.maggiecoulombe.com), a world-renowned dress fashionista who has clothed top celebrities. A wide variety of pearl shops, jewelry stores, and surf outlets round out the popular mall.

LAHAINA

Frenetic and fast-paced, Lahaina is the shopping capital of Maui. The section of Front Street between the Old Lahaina Center and the 505 shopping center is where you'll find the majority of shops.

★ Front Street

Front Street is a sight in itself that centers around commerce and a voracious love of shopping. It has been listed as one of the "Great Streets in America" by the American Planning Association. Walking the length of this vivacious thoroughfare is one of the West Side's most popular activities. Along the flat oceanfront stretch, you'll find art galleries, surf shops, and more compressed in a nonstop string of merchandise. Most shops are open 9am-10pm daily.

The **Wyland Gallery** (711 Front St., 808/667-2285, www.wyland.com) offers the artist's trademark array of marinelife scenes in a perfect oceanfront location. On the

What's with All the Cheap Activity Signs?

Walking around Front Street in Lahaina, it only takes about three minutes to notice that every other shop is offering discount activities at rates that are too good to be true. A helicopter ride for $49? Bike down the volcano for $29? A luau for $9? There's got to be a catch.

Yes, there is a catch, but it doesn't mean the rates aren't real. In order to cash in on the advertised rates, you are essentially signing yourself up to endure a time-share presentation, separate from the activity, that lasts a couple of hours. While no one plans on going to a meeting while on vacation, it could end up saving you a bundle on many of your island activities.

A word of caution, however, before you start committing to everything on the whiteboard. The activity providers (particularly the Molokini snorkeling tours) are with companies that aren't the best in their field, so comb over the particulars of the agreement (90 percent of afternoon Molokini snorkeling tours don't end up going to Molokini). Before committing to a discounted luau, find out which luau it is to see if it's one you want to attend.

Even though you might not plan on buying a time-share, many of these closers could sell ice to an Eskimo. You could end up walking out with the most expensive luau you'll ever attend, but now you "own a piece of Maui."

opposite side of the street, acclaimed photographer **Peter Lik** (712 Front St., 808/661-6623, www.peterlik.com) has a popular showroom of his oversize art, with the ability to transport you directly into the photograph. Other galleries of note are **Sargent's Fine Art** (802 Front St., 808/667-4030, www.sargentsfineart.com), on the corner of Lahainaluna Road; the **Village Gallery** (120 Dickenson St., 808/661-5199, www.villagegalleriesmaui.com); and **Martin Lawrence** (808/661-1788, www.martinlawrence.com). Those with a passion for art should also remember that every Friday night is art night in Lahaina, when many galleries put on their finest show, featuring artist appearances or live jazz, 7pm-10pm.

Bella Lulu (626 Front St., 808/667-5657) and **Serendipity** (752 Front St., 808/667-7070, www.serendipitymaui.com) offer unique female apparel. **Hale Zen** (180 Dickenson St., 808/661-4802, www.halezen.com)—a two-minute walk up Dickenson Street—is a local favorite for everything from homewares to candles, lotions, and crafts from local artists. Just across the street, by Lahaina Divers, **Goin Left** (143 Dickenson St., 808/868-3805, www.goinleft.com, 10am-8pm Mon.-Sat., 11am-6pm Sun.) is a relatively new shop with apparel and accessories

that are catered around the modern board sports lifestyle.

For jewelry, stop into **Glass Mango Designs** (858 Front St., 808/662-8500, www.glassmango.com) for a colorful selection of "wearable art." For a shop that's stuffed with work from local artists, **Maui Memories** (658 Wharf St., 808/298-0261, www.mauiislandmemories.com, 9am-8pm daily) is across from the Banyan Tree and has island-themed clothing, accessories, and gifts from dozens of Maui artists.

Classic retail outpost **Lahaina Scrimshaw** (845 Front St., 808/667-9232, www.lahainascrimshawmaui.com) showcases the seafarers' craft of carving scenes on ivory.

505 Front Street

Down at the southern end of Front Street, most shops are open 9am-9pm daily, including several art shops, clothing shops, and a **Whalers General Store** for sundries.

Banyan Tree Market

While the Friday art nights are always festive, those who prefer lesser-known artists are encouraged to visit the fair beneath the banyan tree, held 9am-5pm on various weekends throughout the year. For a full schedule on when the art fair is on, visit www.lahainaarts.com.

Lahaina Cannery Mall

Enough visitors still frequent **Lahaina Cannery Mall** (1221 Honoapiʻilani Hwy., 808/661-5304, www.lahainacannery.com, 9:30am-9pm Mon.-Sat., 9:30am-7pm Sun.) to keep a few stores open. Stores of note include **Honolua Surf Co.** (808/661-5777, www.honoluasurf.com), which has the same apparel as you would find in Whalers Village or on Front Street for slightly reduced rates, and **Maui Toy Works** (808/661-4766), for children's gifts.

SOUTH OF LAHAINA
Olowalu General Store

The only shopping to be found south of Lahaina is at **Olowalu General Store** (820 Olowalu Village Rd., 808/667-2883, 5am-7pm daily), where you can pick up affordable, island-themed clothing that no one else will have. This store is a classically local operation where you can support the local economy.

Entertainment

West Maui is the island's entertainment hot spot, with the island's best luaus and most happening bars. You can't walk more than 10 yards in Lahaina without tripping over an evening drink special. More than just booze, West Maui is also home to family entertainment options ranging from free hula performances and whale lectures to evening magic performances.

Despite the happening surroundings, however, if you're the clubbing type who likes to party into the wee hours of the morning, you're out of luck since most bars close by 11pm, and only a handful stay open later than 1am. Also, even though almost all of the nightlife options involve bars and pubs that have lively atmospheres, the options for dancing are woefully inadequate. For the most up-to-date info on the latest evening scene, pick up a free copy of *Maui Time* newspaper or check out "The Grid" section on the website at www.mauitime.com.

KAPALUA, NAPILI, AND HONOKOWAI
Evening Shows

Can't get enough of *ki hoʻalu* (slack-key guitar)? The **Masters of Slack Key** (5900 Lower Honoapiʻilani Rd., www.slackkeyshow.com, 7:30pm Wed.) performance at the Aloha Pavilion of the Napili Kai Beach Resort is the best show you'll find on the island. Tickets can either be purchased online or at 6:45pm, when the doors first open. Prices for the show are normally $38, although you can also book a package dinner combo for $95, which includes a sunset dinner at the Sea House restaurant immediately before the show.

Bars, Live Music, and Nightlife

The late-night karaoke sessions at **Sansei** (600 Office Rd., 808/669-6286, www.sanseihawaii.com, 5:30pm-10pm Mon.-Thurs., 5:30pm-1am Fri.-Sat.) restaurant in the Kapalua resort are the most happening evenings on the northwestern side. This popular sushi and sake bar stays open until 1am during karaoke night, and the main draw is the award-winning late-night menu (10pm-1am) that offers dozens of sushi plates at heavily discounted rates.

A short walk away at the Ritz-Carlton hotel you can find live music in the **Alaloa Lounge** Thursday-Monday evenings. It has the most consistent live music in the Kapalua resort.

In the Kahana Gateway Center, **Maui Brewing Company** (4405 Honoapiʻilani Hwy., 808/669-3474, www.mauibrewingco.com, until midnight daily) is a happening brewpub that's packed with hop-soaked locals. Sit at the bar so you can keep your beer cold on the slab of ice that's inside the bar.

Over a dozen beers are available on draft, many of which are only found at the brewery.

Dollie's (4310 Lower Honoapi'ilani Rd., 808/669-0266, www.dolliespizzakahana. com, until midnight daily) is the West Side's de facto sports bar, where cheap beer and good pizza are served throughout the night. This is where island locals come to watch Sunday and Monday football games. Fifteen different televisions also show NBA, hockey, college sports, and whichever game you're hoping to catch.

KA'ANAPALI
Whalers Village

The center stage area at Whalers Village constantly teems with free events. Stalwarts of the entertainment schedule include lei-making classes, hula classes, arts and crafts sessions, and live music on most weekend nights. Since the schedule of events is constantly shifting, visit www.whalersvillage. com for an up-to-date calendar of the current month's activities. The center underwent an enormous renovation in 2016, but by 2017 the regular performances should be rocking on their regular schedule.

For drinks, every resort in Ka'anapali has fantastic and expensive drinks, but **Pailolo Sports Bar** (808/667-3200) at the Westin Ka'anapali Villas is the island's only place that serves beer by the pitcher.

Magic Dinner Theater

The only show in Ka'anapali that isn't a luau is the **Kupanaha Magic Dinner Theater** (2525 Ka'anapali Pkwy., 808/262-8450, www. kupanaha.com, 4:45pm-7:30pm Tues.-Sat., $79 adults, $65 teens, $49 children), which is a great choice if you want to experience a hula performance as well as a magic show but only have a single night to do so. Located inside the Ka'anapali Beach Hotel, this three-hour show features everything from tableside magic during dinner to an illusionist sawing a person in half.

To add some cultural flare, the Kupanaha hula dancers chant and dance their way through ancient Hawaiian lore, and you're treated to an authentic cultural performance without leaving your seat. The food is as good as at a nice Ka'anapali restaurant, and this show is a great value for family entertainment, considering all that is included.

Luaus

There is no shortage of luaus along the Ka'anapali strip. The best on the island, the Old Lahaina Luau, is in nearby Lahaina, but there are four luaus in Ka'anapali. If the only reason you want to go to a luau is for the fire dancing, choose one in Ka'anapali. All will feature buffet food mass-produced for 100 people as well as local craft artisans, and all will offer premium seating for an added price. In my opinion it isn't worth the extra cost, since it usually means you get only slightly better seats and are first in line for the food. Most shows begin at either 5pm or 5:30pm. Ka'anapali can experience higher winds and a greater likelihood of rain than nearby Lahaina, so the chances of the luau needing to be moved inside or cancelled are higher. Most nights are gorgeous, but if you want to guarantee calm conditions, you'll have better luck in Lahaina.

Of the numerous luaus in Ka'anapali, the best show is the **Wailele Polynesian Luau** (2365 Ka'anapali Pkwy., 808/667-2525, www. westinmaui.com, $115 adults, $65 children) at the Westin Maui resort. The fire dancers are the best, and the food is above average compared to the other options. Shows take place Tuesday and Thursday evenings as well as Sunday during busier times of the year, although the schedule varies. If you're driving to Ka'anapali, the one downside of this show is that parking can be challenging. Try to find free beach parking in the lot between Whalers Village and the entrance to the Westin. If you can't find a free spot, the most economical option is to park in the Whalers Village garage and then buy an ice cream or a quick beer after the show to get your parking validated for three hours.

Ka'anapali Sunset Luau at Black Rock (2605 Ka'anapali Pkwy., 808/877-4852, www.sheratonmauiluau.com, $108 adults, $60 children) is Monday and Wednesday evenings at the Sheraton resort. The crowds aren't quite as large as other shows, and the grassy luau grounds are more spacious. While the food is fine and the dancers are entertaining, the best part is the atmosphere, looking out at Pu'u Keka'a and experiencing the torch-lighting ceremony. While children are welcome, it mainly caters to couples and adults.

At the far end of the beach at the southern tip of Ka'anapali, the **Drums of the Pacific** (200 Nohea Kai, 808/667-4727, www.drumsofthepacificmaui.com, Mon.-Sat., $99 adults, $69 children) takes visitors on a journey through numerous Polynesian cultures. This is Ka'anapali's largest luau, and the fire dancing and the performance are on par with other shows. If you book directly on the luau website, you can sometimes get a deal of one child admission free with each paying adult.

On the northern side of Pu'u Keka'a, facing out toward the ocean, the **Myths of Maui Luau** (2780 Keka'a Dr., 808/661-9119, www.mythsofmaui.com, Sun.-Fri., adults $90, children over 5 $35, children under 5 free) at Royal Lahaina is a favorite option for those traveling with children. This is the island's longest-running luau (but don't confuse it with Old Lahaina Luau, which is better), and while there's no shaking the tourist kitsch, there's a palpable charm that goes along with the old-school venue. Everything over on this side of "the rock" is more laid-back than along the main Ka'anapali strip. Although the show doesn't face the beach, it's nevertheless set along a wide stretch of sand, and guests are encouraged to watch the sun go down while sipping a drink from the luau grounds. The show features a fire dance finale, and the entertainers bring children on stage for an impromptu hula lesson. The food is average, and while it isn't very Hawaiian, children enjoy the macaroni and cheese. Mai tais and Blue Hawaiians are included in the price of the ticket, but premium drinks cost extra at the bar.

Bars, Live Music, and Nightlife

Most of the bar scene in Ka'anapali plays out at the pool bars within the resorts. My favorite is the **Grotto Bar at the Hyatt** (200 Nohea Kai Dr., 808/661-1234), tucked beneath two different waterfalls. While the happy hour and dinner scene can be fun, if you're looking for anything later than 10pm, you're going to have to get a cab down to Lahaina. **Hula Grill** (808/667-6636) in Whalers Village has live music every afternoon and evening, and neighboring **Leilani's** (808/661-4495) occasionally has live music during happy hour.

Friday through Sunday, the West Side's best nightclub is the **Black Rock Lounge** (2605 Ka'anapali Pkwy., 808/662-8053), inside the Sheraton Maui, where DJs and fog machines combine to create a sexy venue for singles. The club stays open until 2am, and on Friday and Saturday the $10 cover is waived before 11pm.

During the week, the only place in Ka'anapali with anything that resembles proper nightlife is **Paradise Grill** (2291 Ka'anapali Pkwy., 808/662-3700, www.paradisegrillkb.com, until 2am), featuring live entertainment 10pm-1:30am daily. Paradise Grill and the associated Mello's Bar are on the corner of Ka'anapali Parkway and Honoapi'ilani Highway, the first building you see at the main entrance to the Ka'anapali resort. Most of the late-night entertainment takes place downstairs in Mello's, while the upstairs section of the restaurant usually has live music during dinner hours (6pm-9pm daily). Expect to find acoustic music upstairs during dinner, and rock, reggae, and karaoke later downstairs.

LAHAINA
Hula Shows

For a heavy heaping of Hawaiian cuteness, the free *keiki* hula shows at the **Lahaina Cannery Mall** (1221 Honoapi'ilani Hwy., by Safeway) take place at 1pm Saturday-Sunday on the center stage.

Magic Dinner Theater

At **Warren and Annabelle's** (900 Front St.,

808/667-6244, www.warrenandannabelles. com, 5pm and 7:30pm Mon.-Sat., $64-104), any skepticism you might have had about attending a magic show in Maui will immediately be erased. Much more than a simple sleight-of-hand show, this enchanting evening revolves around the legend of Annabelle, a ghost whose swanky parlor you have the pleasure of dining in for the evening. After making your way through a secret entrance, you are welcomed into a plush lounge where the sound of piano keys accompanies the clink of oversize wine glasses.

The high level of service starts when you enter, and the refined waitstaff zip about with the air of a caffeinated butler. Settling into an overstuffed chair, guests can relax with some beverages from the bar and dine on gourmet pupus. Once dinner is through, it's on to the intimate 78-seat theater, and be warned, if you sit in the front row, you'll end up becoming a part of the show. Two parts magic and three parts comedy, this show will leave you laughing. Rates are $64 for the show only, but do yourself a favor and spend the extra $40 for the cocktails and appetizers package. Due to Maui County liquor laws, this show is only for ages 21 or older. The 7:30pm show is added during busier times of the year. Reservations are strongly recommended.

★ 'Ulalena and Maui Theatre

'Ulalena (878 Front St., 808/856-7900, www. mauitheatre.com, 6:30pm Mon.-Fri., $60-80) is a captivating and sophisticated show that details the history of the Hawaiian Islands through chant, dance, and visual effects in the 680-seat Maui Theatre. Performed without words, it utilizes over 100 different instruments played live. The most expensive tickets allow you to spend 20 minutes with the cast. If you're a fan of musicals or have an interest in Hawaiian history, this isn't an evening to be missed. A new show called Kahiko O Lahaina opened at the Maui Theatre, featuring the fascinating history of Lahaina.

Also at the Maui Theatre, Elvis fans will think they've died and gone to Graceland when they see a performance of Burn'n Love (878 Front St., 808/856-7900, www.mauitheater.com, 7:30pm Mon.-Tues. and Thurs.-Fri., $60-85) by the talented Darren Lee, a longtime Elvis impersonator so convincing you'd swear you were looking at The King.

Art Night

Friday night is Art Night in Lahaina. In keeping with Lahaina's status as the cultural center of Maui, three dozen galleries open their doors 7pm-10pm, throw out the welcome mat, set out food and drink, provide entertainment, and usually host a well-known artist or two for this weekly party. Take your time to stroll Front Street from one gallery to the next. Stop and chat with shopkeepers, munch the goodies, sip the wine, look at the pieces on display, corner the featured artist for a comment on his or her work, and soak in the music of the strolling musicians. People dress up, but don't be afraid to come dressed casually.

Luaus

Lahaina is the best place on the island to attend a luau. It's dry and calm and has beautiful sunsets, and the island's best luau is here.

Old Lahaina Luau (1251 Front St., 800/248-5828, www.oldlahainaluau.com, daily, $110 adults, $75 children) is hands down the best on Maui. The food is the best, the luau grounds are immaculate, and everything from the show to the service runs like a well-oiled machine. Despite the fact that the luau seats 440 people, it still manages to retain an intimate atmosphere. You are greeted with a lei made of fragrant fresh flowers. Premium bar selections are included in the rates. There is a large imu (underground oven) for the pig, although it gets insanely crowded, so hang by the imu early if you want to get a good view of the unearthing. The private oceanfront setting provides the perfect perch for watching the sun go down. There is ample free parking, or if you plan on having more than a couple of drinks, it's a short cab ride from Ka'anapali. One downside is that there isn't any fire dancing, since fire dancing isn't Hawaiian (it's

Samoan), and the show specifically focuses on the history of Hawaii. While kids are welcome, it caters more to couples and adults.

For seating, choose either traditional *lauhala* mats (closest to the stage) or at tables with chairs, which still provide a good view. The only places where it's hard to see the show are the seats in the far corners. Seating preference is given to those who book first. Remarkably, shows are offered seven days a week.

At the southern end of Front Street, the **Feast at Lele** (505 Front St., 808/667-5353, www.feastatlele.com, $125 adults, $93 children) is a luau on the oceanfront in the 505 shopping center. Lele is the ancient Hawaiian name for the town of Lahaina, and this show begins with dance native to Hawaiian culture. The event then migrates through various Polynesian cultures, including those of Aotearoa (New Zealand), Tahiti, and Samoa. The combination of cultures makes for a fast-paced, fiery, and heart-pumping performance capped off by everyone's favorite, Samoan fire and knife dancing. Unlike the other luaus on the island, the food features dishes from around Polynesia that reflects the show.

Bars and Live Music

Rooted in the grog-shop days of its boisterous port-town past, Lahaina is Maui's nightlife capital—unless you want to go dancing. Most places close by 11pm, but that doesn't mean you can't find live music.

For free, family-friendly live music in a historic outdoor setting, the Lahaina Restoration Foundation hosts a **Hawaiian Music Series** (http://lahainarestoration.org, 6pm-7:30pm last Thurs. of every month) on the lawn of the Baldwin House (Dickenson St. and Front St.) in the center of town. Musical artists vary from month to month, but most sessions involve live music and *kanikapila* storytelling. Seating is limited at this popular event, and attendees are encouraged to bring a blanket or beach chair to enjoy the show.

The family-friendly **Friday Town Party** (www.mauifridays.com, 6pm-9pm 2nd Fri. of every month) is held between the Baldwin

House and Wharf Cinema Center. Part of the Maui Fridays series, the free event features everything from live music and *keiki* competitions to silent auctions and dance performances. Various bars and restaurants feature live music, and most restaurants offer specials valid that night only.

One of the best spots for live entertainment in Lahaina is **Fleetwood's** (744 Front St., 808/669-6425, www.fleetwoodsonfrontst.com), a two-story bar and restaurant that offers the only rooftop perch in Lahaina. This bar was opened by legendary rock musician Mick Fleetwood, and Mick himself has been known to jump in with the band for some impromptu percussion. Live music is offered most frequently on the rooftop bar, beginning around 7pm.

If you're looking to dance with a young crowd of locals, **Lulu's Lahaina Surf Club** (1221 Honoapi'ilani Hwy., 808/661-0808, www.luluslahaina.com, until 2am) is the town's only dance club, located in the Lahaina Cannery Mall. There is usually a $5 cover Saturday night. Other nights of the week sporadically feature live music. While the dance floor is large and there are a couple of pool tables in the back, the mall location detracts from the vintage Lahaina experience. Another problem here is fights.

Both **Cool Cat Café** (658 Front. St., 808/667-0908, www.coolcatcafe.com) and **Kimo's** (845 Front St., 808/661-4811, www.kimosmaui.com) provide live music during the dinner hour seven nights a week. There isn't an official dance floor, so the atmosphere is relegated to drinks and mingling.

For **karaoke,** the most happening place in Lahaina for late-night sake and singing is **Kobe** (136 Dickenson St., 808/667-5555, www.kobemaui.com, until 1am), a steak house, from 9:30pm Friday-Saturday.

If you're a night owl, Lahaina has a couple of watering holes that stay open until 2am. On Front Street, **Spanky's Riptide** (505 Front St., 808/667-2337, www.spankysriptide.com) in the 505 shopping center on the far southern end is a good place to grab a cheap goblet of

PBR, play pool, and engage in conversation with a colorful cast of characters.

For a truly local experience, the legendary dive bar **Sly Mongoose** (1036 Limahana Place, 808/661-8097) is in the Lahaina industrial park on the inland side of the highway, where visitors don't go. This is a no-nonsense dive where the beer is cold, the drinks are cheap, and the patrons are regular. This bar isn't within walking distance from Front Street, so you'll have to take a cab.

Food

The number of dining options on the West Side is overwhelming. In most places you pay a premium for the location, so prices may seem high at ocean-view tables. That said, it's still possible to get a meal for under $10 pp outside the main visitor areas. While there is an overabundance of places on the West Side to sit and casually dine, there are only a handful of decent places for an affordable lunch on the run.

KAPALUA, NAPILI, KAHANA, AND HONOKOWAI
American
Overlooking the Plantation golf course, the **Plantation House** (200 Kapalua Dr., 808/669-9600, www.theplantationhouse.com, 8am-9pm daily, $10-22) offers spectacular views with succulent food to match. Considering the luxurious venue, the affordable breakfast and lunch menu makes you feel like you're getting away with something, as selections from the Benedict menu are only $13. Breakfast is served until 3pm, and for dinner, you can pair fresh fish such as ahi and monchong with a glass from the extensive wine list.

Breakfast
One fact about Maui is that ★ **The Gazebo** (5315 Lower Honapi'ilani Rd., 808/669-5621, 7:30am-2pm daily, $9-14) restaurant has the island's best breakfast. This isn't a secret, however, and there is a line out the door by 6:45am. What makes this spot so popular is not only the oceanfront location, gazing out toward Moloka'i, but also the famous macadamia nut pancakes and enormously filling portions. Lunch is offered until closing at 2pm, and by then the line has shrunk. Finding parking can be challenging; try for a spot along Napili Place, or park by the Napili Bay beach access on Hui Drive and walk to the restaurant across the sand of Napili Bay. From the beach, looking toward the water, the Gazebo is on the point to the left.

Affordable, easy, and convenient, the **Honolua Store** (502 Office Rd., 808/665-9105, 6am-8pm daily) in Kapalua has some of the island's best deals. Breakfast runs 6am-10:30am daily, and if you're tight on cash, a filling to-go container of *loco moco* is only $6.

Brewpub
A visit to ★ **Maui Brewing Company** (4405 Honoapi'ilani Hwy., 808/669-3474, www.mauibrewingco.com, 11am-midnight daily, $12-15) should be at the top of every beer lover's island to-do list. This is the island's original brewpub, and while you can find a number of the beers in local supermarkets, at least a dozen more can only be found on tap when you visit. The interior is basic, but this isn't a place you come to for the decor. Even though the beer is the main draw, the Hawaiian beef burger, sliders, and coconut porter beef stew are all hearty accompaniments to a rich pint of stout. There are also filling and affordable pizzas and vegan or gluten-free options.

Coffee Shops
At the Kahana Gateway Center, **Hawaiian Village Coffee** (4405 Honoapi'ilani Hwy.,

808/665-1114, www.hawaiianvillagecoffee.net, 5:30am-6pm Mon.-Sat., 5:30am-5pm Sun.) is a classic coffee shop with a strong local following and good community vibe. This is the earliest place to open on the northwest side, and the sunrise hours feature a collection of late-shift police officers refueling after a long night and sleepy-eyed locals stopping in on their way to work. Although small, the shop has a welcoming atmosphere for reading the morning paper or checking your email on the free Wi-Fi.

Hawaiian Regional

★ **Merriman's** (1 Bay Club Place, 808/669-6400, www.merrimanshawaii.com, 3pm-9pm daily, dinner from 5:30pm daily, $25-49) is one of the most scenic dining spots on the island. Arrive early to enjoy a glass of wine while watching the sunset from the oceanfront fire pit, and then enjoy a menu of farm-to-table fare, where over 90 percent of the ingredients are sourced from local farmers, fishers, and ranchers. Acclaimed chef Peter Merriman is one of the founders of the Hawaiian Regional movement, and his genius is evident in everything from the Keahole lobster and avocado salad to the Sichuan peppered day-boat mahimahi. For pairings, there are probably nations with constitutions shorter than the wine list, which features over 40 different varietals. Reservations are strongly recommended.

In Kapalua, the ★ **Banyan Tree** (1 Ritz Carlton Dr., 808/665-7096, 5:30pm-9:30pm Tues.-Sat., $25-50) restaurant inside the Ritz Carlton has phenomenally come back to life. Pair a glass from the extensive wine list with a pupu of *opakapaka* ceviche, and then treat your palate to charred ahi steak, served with bok choy and bacon. Much of the food is sourced here on island, including herbs from the garden. End the evening with a lava cake with *lilikoi* and coconut ice cream.

Another restaurant making waves in Kapalua is spectacular **Cane and Canoe** (1 Bay Dr., 808/662-6600, 7am-11am and 5pm-9pm daily), located inside the Montage Kapalua Bay looking out toward Moloka'i,

with an acoustic guitar player perched beneath the trees. Order from a menu of Hawaiian regional cuisine with a slightly Italian twist: Pacific Rim cioppino of lobster, shrimp, and mahimahi, or soba gnocchi with exotic mushrooms, served with a porcini puree. For breakfast, order the $19 local rice bowl or $28 ahi Benedict.

For one of the island's best breakfasts and happy hours, **The Sea House** (5900 Lower Honoapi'ilani Rd., 808/669-1500, www.seahousemaui.com, 7am-9pm daily, $12-45) restaurant at Napili Kai is right on the sands of Napili Bay and is a longtime island classic. Happy hour runs 2pm-5pm with half-off pupus, and if you sit down and order at 4:30pm, you can often enjoy a sunset dinner for half price. For the island's best date night, book the dinner and show package for the Wednesday-night Masters of Slack Key.

Japanese

Ask any local where to get sushi, and they'll tell you ★ **Sansei** (600 Office Rd., 808/669-6286, www.sanseihawaii.com, 5:30pm-10pm Sat.-Wed., 5:30pm-1am Thurs.-Fri., $8-30), a legendary outpost on the main entrance road to Kapalua resort. If you want to maximize your Sansei experience, call ahead for reservations for 5:30pm on Thursday or Friday evening. When the restaurant opens, they usually run an early-bird special for the first 30 minutes, with selected dishes half off. If you miss the early bird wave and would rather wait a few hours, the same specials are often offered 10pm-1am Thursday-Friday.

If Sansei is too packed, or for a more intimate venue, **Miso Phat** (4310 Lower Honoapi'ilani Hwy., 808/669-9010, www.misophat.com, 11:30am-9pm daily) has exceptionally fresh sushi and phenomenal rolls in a humble Kahana location. Best of all, it's BYOB.

Local Style

From the outside, you might wonder what's so special about the hole-in-the-wall ★ **Honokowai Okazuya and Deli** (3600

Lower Honoapiʻilani Rd., 808/665-0512, 11am-2:30pm and 4:30pm-8:30pm Mon.-Sat., cash only, $9-15). Even though the front door is often closed and it's in a strip mall next to the 5A Rent-A-Space, inside you'll find huge portions, great local food, and budget-friendly prices. There are a few seats inside for dining, but most visitors order takeout to enjoy back at the condo. The food rivals any on the island, and the prices can be half as much as food served with an ocean view. Try the lemon caper mahimahi or the chicken *katsu*.

Mexican

In Honokowai, **Ohana Tacos** (3600 Lower Honoapiʻilani Rd., 808/283-7768, 11am-9pm Sun.-Thurs., 11am-8pm Fri.-Sat., cash only, $7-11) is a family-run restaurant with a badge of authenticity: It's frequented by local Latin Americans. This is one of the few places on the island where you can order *sopes* or choose *lengua* as a meat option. There are only a few outdoor tables.

Natural Foods

One of the few places to pick up a healthy meal on the go is **Honokowai Farmers Market** (3636 Lower Honoapiʻilani Rd., 808/669-7004, 7am-7pm daily, $6-9), located across from Honokowai Beach Park. There is a hot bar, a salad bar, a full health-conscious market, and a counter serving açaí and pitaya bowls.

KAʻANAPALI
American

In front of the Honua Kai resort, **Duke's** (130 Kai Malina Pkwy., 808/662-2900, www.dukesmaui.com, 7:30am-9:30pm daily, $10-25) is moderately priced. Affordable breakfasts include banana and macadamia nut pancakes, while lunches tend toward sandwiches, burgers, and fish tacos. Dinner entrées are more expensive. Duke's sources ingredients from over 20 different local farms, and the Bloody Marys are always a good idea. Afternoon trade winds can make the outdoor dining frustrating, so go for breakfast before 10am or for dinner after sundown.

Poolside at the Westin Maui, **Relish Burger Bistro** (2365 Kaʻanapali Pkwy., 808/667-2525, www.westinmaui.com, 6:30am-10pm daily) has Kobe beef burgers and ahi *poke* tostadas as well as succulent pulled pork sliders that are served on a purple taro roll. Lunch prices ($15-19) are relatively affordable, considering you're at a resort.

For the most affordable and convenient meal in Kaʻanapali, **CJ's Deli** (2580 Kekaʻa Dr., 808/667-0968, www.cjsmaui.com, 7am-8pm daily) in the Fairway Shops has burgers, meatloaf, deli sandwiches, and comfort food ($9-15). It's also BYOB, and there's a general store a few shops down if you want to grab a drink. Up early from jet lag? You can get breakfast for under $8, beginning at 7am.

If you worked up an appetite while snorkeling at Puʻu Kekaʻa, **Hank's Haute Dogs** (2605 Kaʻanapali Pkwy., 808/661-0031, www.hankshautedogs.com, 11am-3pm daily, $12-15), inside the Sheraton Maui, has a full menu of gourmet hot dogs that were featured on the *Man v. Food* television program.

Hawaiian Regional

Even though every resort in Kaʻanapali has some sort of Hawaiian Regional option, none can hold a candle to world-famous ★ **Roy's** (2290 Kaʻanapali Pkwy., 808/669-6999, www.royshawaii.com, 11am-9:30pm daily, $15-45). The location, inside the golf clubhouse, would be nicer if it had an ocean view, but for what the restaurant lacks in decor, it makes up for in flavor. Chef Roy Yamaguchi was one of the founders of the Hawaiian Regional movement, and his mastery is evident in the *misoyaki* butterfish and honey mustard-braised short ribs. Even though there are over 30 Roy's locations around the country, every restaurant has a menu and a style unique to the venue. Dinner entrées are pricey; ordering sandwiches, salads, and appetizers off the lunch menu is more affordable. The chocolate soufflé will change your life. Order it halfway through your meal since it takes 20 minutes to prepare.

★ **Hula Grill** (2435 Ka'anapali Pkwy., 808/667-6636, www.hulagrillkaanapali.com, 11am-11pm daily, $13) in Whalers Village is a place that exudes the carefree nature of being on vacation in Hawaii. Sink your toes down into the sand of the outdoor barefoot bar, which has a better vibe than the pricier indoor dining room. There's live music in the afternoons, and the Kapulu Joe pork sandwich and the kalua pork and pineapple flatbread are two affordable options along an otherwise expensive shore.

Across the Whalers Village walkway, **Leilani's on the Beach** (2435 Ka'anapali Pkwy., 808/661-4495, www.leilanis.com, 11am-11pm daily, $19) serves the best fish tacos on the island. The tacos are enormous, served Cajun style, and accompanied by a special sauce that brings it all together. They've become a bit expensive, but are heavily discounted on Tuesday afternoons. Whether you dine on the casual patio or upstairs in the dining room, save room for a world-famous Hula Pie with macadamia nut ice cream and chocolate cookie crust; it's big enough to share.

At the far southern end of the Ka'anapali strip, **Japengo** (200 Nohea Kai Dr., 808/661-1234, www.japengomaui.com, 5pm-10pm daily, $25) has enormous and affordable sushi rolls that compete for best on the island. There's live music every night and an ocean view from the bar, and at sushi school (3pm-4:30pm 2nd and 4th Sat. of the month, $35 pp), you can learn to make hand rolls from one of the restaurant's master chefs.

Natural Foods

The best gourmet natural foods market on the West Side, **'Aina Gourmet Market** (130 Kai Malina Pkwy., 808/662-2832, www.ainagourmet.com, 7am-9pm daily) is tucked away in the lobby of Honua Kai Beach Resort. 'Aina is in the same restaurant group as Pacific'O as well as O'o Farms, and this is a great place for grabbing a cup of 100 percent Maui coffee, organically raised produce, or a healthy *panini* made from locally sourced ingredients. There are a few tables, or you can enjoy your meal on the beach.

LAHAINA
American

We'll come right out and say that ★ **Lahaina Grill** (127 Lahainaluna Rd., 808/667-5117, www.lahainagrill.com, 6pm-10pm daily, $25-49) is the best restaurant in Lahaina. Opened on Valentine's Day 1990, this restaurant continues to be one of Lahaina's most romantic evenings. The ambience, service, and extensive wine list are what you would expect of a fine-dining experience. The only thing missing from the classy bistro setting is an ocean view. The food is a combination of new American cuisine infused with Pacific Rim favorites, where meat dishes include the coveted Kona coffee-roasted rack of lamb, and seafood selections include sesame-crusted ahi filets and crisp fried lobster crab cakes. Much of the produce is sourced locally from independent farmers. Reservations are recommended.

Hands down, the best burger in Lahaina is at ★ **Cool Cat Café** (658 Front St., 808/667-0908, www.coolcatcafe.com, 10:30am-10:30pm daily, $10-25). Overlooking the banyan tree, the inside portion of the restaurant is decorated in 1950s decor, while the outdoor patio is livelier. Cool Cats is consistently voted as the island's best burger, surpassing Cheeseburger in Paradise, which is located right down the street. All of the meat is massaged with a secret seasoning, and specialty burgers like the Don Ho (teriyaki and pineapple burger), Luna (covered in avocado), and Frisco (served on sourdough bread with grilled onions and jack cheese) are what make it such a legendary choice. There are also fish sandwiches, blackened fish tacos, salads (get the Buddy Holly with chicken strips on top), and a popular bar. It's extra to add fries to your meal (and cheaper to get a basket for the table than to add to each burger separately). This is where you'll find Lahaina Harbor boat crew spending their tips at the bar.

Along with Kimo's, the Front Street restaurant with the best tableside views is **Koa's Seaside Grill** (839 Front St., 808/667-7737, www.koasgrill.com, 9am-9pm daily), where the deck extends out over the water and views stretch out toward Lana'i. Breakfast—served until 1pm—is one of the best in Lahaina, and fish tacos are only $12 every day 2pm-5pm.

One of Lahaina's best-kept secrets is **Lahaina Coolers** (180 Dickenson St., 808/661-7082, www.lahainacoolers.com, 8am-midnight daily, $27), a laid-back local favorite that can rival anywhere in town. All three meals are a reason to visit, particularly breakfast. The dinner menu is just as good as at more upscale places in town. There are also pizzas, pastas, and an affordable bar menu where kalua pig tacos are only $11.

If you're strolling down Front Street and need a casual meal, **Lahainaluna Café** (790 Front St., 808/757-8286, www.lahainaluna-cafe.com, 10:30am-9pm daily) has affordable plates in an open-air outdoor courtyard. Two mahimahi fish tacos are $11, and so is the barbecue kalua pulled pork sandwich—served on a Sugar Beach Bake Shop sweet roll.

Coffee Shops

For a quick coffee on the run, **Sir Wilfred's** (707 Front St., 808/661-0202, www.sirwilfreds.com, 8:30am-9pm daily) is the island's original coffee shop, having opened its doors in 1976. In 1979 Sir Wilfred's introduced the island's first espresso machine, and the Front Street store is still one of the best spots in Lahaina to stop in and buy some locally grown beans or inquire about fine cigars. Those in need of an early wake-up, however, will unfortunately have to wait until the 8:30am opening time.

If you're looking for a place you can linger, grab breakfast, get free Internet access, and sip on a proper espresso, try **Café Café** (129 Lahainaluna Rd., 808/661-0006, www.cafecafelahaina.com, 7am-7pm daily) on Lahainaluna Road. There are a few outdoor tables for sipping your macchiato, and you can also pick up organic, locally sourced, open-face bagel sandwiches ($5-7).

French

If you take your fine dining seriously, then you're going to love **Gerard's** (174 Lahainaluna Rd., 808/661-8939, www.gerardsmaui.com, 6pm-8:30pm daily, $50) in the Plantation Inn. Chef Gerard Reversade has been serving French food with an island twist for over 30 years and was one of the pioneers of Hawaiian Regional cuisine. Classics such as foie gras and escargot punctuate the appetizer menu, and favorites include the roasted lamb in lemon/peppermint jelly accompanied by potato au gratin, as well as the fresh fish that changes with the day's selection. Gerard's has received the *Wine Spectator*'s Award of Excellence 19 times for its extensive collection of French and American labels. Ignore the cost and let your taste buds take over. Reservations are imperative.

Hawaiian Regional

In the 505 shopping area, ★ **Pacific'O** (505 Front St., 808/667-4341, www.pacificomaui.com, 11:30am-10pm daily, $29-46) is one of the best venues in Lahaina for enjoying an oceanfront meal. Many of the ingredients are grown at the organic O'o Farm in Kula. The seaside patio is the perfect lunch spot for pairing a sesame fish salad with a crisp glass of white wine, and the fish tacos are affordable at $16.50. Reservations are necessary for dinner, when you can feast on entrées such as seafood risotto or *hapa* tempura—sashimi-grade fish wrapped in nori. Aside from the food, the wine list is one of the most comprehensive on the West Side.

On the far northern end of Lahaina, ★ **Honu** (1295 Front St., 808/667-9390, www.honumaui.com, 11am-9:30pm Mon.-Sat., 11am-9pm Sun., $18-45) offers locally sourced food in an oceanfront setting. *Honu* is the Hawaiian name for sea turtle, and there's a strong likelihood that you'll spot a turtle coming up for a breath at some point during your meal. Chef Mark Ellman, one of the original founders of the Hawaiian Regional movement, has created a menu where butternut squash coconut soup complements main courses ranging from lentil quinoa burgers to pork osso bucco. The pizzas are similarly delicious. The extensive craft beer selection features over 50 different microbrews—a rarity among island restaurants. If there's a wait, try sister restaurant **Mala,** next door.

In the heart of Front Street, **Kimo's** (845 Front St., 808/661-4811, www.kimosmaui.com, 11am-10pm daily, $25-32) has a deck looking out over the waters of the Lahaina Roadstead and moderately priced lunch items ($15-18) such as coconut-crusted fish sandwiches or beach bunny turkey burgers. The dinner entrées in the dining room are pricier, including the signature Molokini Cut, a 14-ounce prime rib served with an au jus. The staff at Kimo's is as professional as they come, and the happy hour (3pm-5pm daily) has some of Lahaina's best deals.

Italian
The culinary brainchild of a chef who arrived via Brooklyn, and before that Milan, **Sale Pepe** (878 Front St., 808/667-7667, www.salepepemaui.com, 5pm-10pm Mon.-Sat., $15-30), by the Maui Theatre, is one of Lahaina's new hot spots. The authentic Italian dishes use only the freshest island ingredients, and what isn't sourced from local farmers is brought all the way from Italy.

Japanese
If there were an award for best cuisine in the most unlikely of locations, ★ **Star Noodle** (285 Kupuohi St., 808/667-5400, www.star-noodle.com, 10:30am-10pm daily, $12) would win. This popular noodle establishment on an obscure corner at the top of the Lahaina Gateway industrial area has been sculpted by Sheldon Simeon, a local chef who made it to the final three on the reality show *Top Chef.* The Asian-infused menu is spectacularly affordable, with bowls of *udon,* plates of pad thai, and dishes such as miso salmon or chicken in *ponzu* sauce. If the wait is too long (which it usually is), sit at the bar and order from the main menu.

Local Style
Believe it or not, there's a place in Lahaina where you can eat by the water and the bill won't give you a heart attack. At the northern end of Lahaina next to the Old Lahaina Luau, with which it's affiliated, ★ **Aloha Mixed Plate** (1285 Front St., 808/661-3322, www.alohamixedplate.com, 8am-10pm daily, $8-12) offers affordable plate lunches in a casual oceanfront setting. The private setting is among the most scenic in Lahaina, the food is some of the best local fare you'll find outside a luau, and it's cheap. For lunch and dinner you can sample luau items such as *lomilomi* salmon or poi. For the main course, get a kalua pig plate lunch (with two scoops of rice and macaroni salad) or spring for the Aloha Mixed Plate of *shoyu* chicken, teriyaki beef, and fresh fish served with rice and mac salad. Breakfast is just as affordable with omelets and *loco moco* dishes. There's a full bar, although alcohol isn't served at the oceanfront tables.

For breakfast where all the locals go, ★ **808 Grindz** (843 Waine'e St., 808/280-8914, www.808grindzcafe.com, 7am-2pm daily) is a hidden hole-in-the-wall by Nagasako supermarket, where an entire menu of omelets and *mocos* is only $8.08.

Market
Believe it or not, the **seafood counter** at the back of **Foodland Farms** (345 Keawe St., 808/662-7088, 6am-7pm daily, $8) serves one of the island's best *poke* bowls. Order a bowl of ahi *poke,* served on a bed of brown rice, and then head down to Wahikuli Beach Park for a picnic out on the sand.

Natural Foods
To the delight of those who care about what they put in their bodies, ★ **Choice** (1087 Limahana Place, 808/661-7711, www.choicemaui.com, 8am-9:30pm Mon.-Sat., $8) is devoted to the benefits of a healthy, active lifestyle. When you walk in the door (where a sign informs you this is a "bummer-free zone"), you can sense the antioxidants flowing. The smoothies use all-natural superfood ingredients (spirulina, açaí, coconut meat, and almond milk), so your body will thank

you. Make your smoothie "epic" by adding superfoods such as kale and blue-green algae. A large selection of freshly made kale salads are available after 11:30am each day.

Shave Ice

There are few things better than a cold shave ice on a hot Lahaina day, and the best shave ice in Lahaina is at **Local Boys West** (624 Front St., 808/344-9779, www.localboysshaveice. com, 10am-9pm daily), across the street from the banyan tree. In addition to the copious array of flavors, what makes Local Boys great is the way they offer free Roselani (made on Maui) ice cream, Kaua'i cream, and adzuki beans at the bottom of the shave ice, which as any island local knows is the only way to enjoy it.

Thai

The best Thai food on the West Side is at **Thai Chef** (878 Front St., 808/667-2814, www. thaichefrestaurantmaui.com, 11am-2pm and 5pm-9pm Mon.-Fri., 5pm-9pm Sat., $14), a small hole-in-the-wall restaurant squirreled away in the parking lot between Longhi's and the Maui Theatre. The family-run restaurant is BYOB if you'd like to accompany your chicken pad thai with a Singha beer; beer and wine are available at Foodland across the parking lot. Vegetarians can order plenty of spicy tofu and vegetable dishes. It's not fancy, but you won't be disappointed. Takeout is available; reservations are recommended.

SOUTH OF LAHAINA
American

The only restaurant between Lahaina and Ma'alaea is ★ **Leoda's Kitchen and Pie Shop** (820 Olowalu Village Rd., 808/662-3600, www.leodas.com, 7am-8pm daily, $8-12), in the Olowalu store building. Using many sustainable ingredients from local farms, this sandwich and pie shop has quickly become an island favorite. The deli sandwiches, pot-pies, and baked goods are so good, however, that you'll often find a line stretching out the front door. Try the veggie burger for a healthy lunch, or a savory chicken pot pie.

Getting There and Around

AIR

Above Kahana is the small **Kapalua-West Maui Airport** (JHM, 4050 Honoapi'ilani Hwy., 808/665-6108), which is a convenient option for those commuting to Honolulu. The interisland fares ($70-80 one-way) are often a little higher than at the larger Kahului Airport, but when you factor in the hour of driving you save, it's worth the few extra dollars. This small airport is used principally by Mokulele Airlines, but it's also used by small commercial tour companies. Surrounded by former pineapple fields, the single airstrip is short and used by small propeller aircraft only. The check-in counters, inspection station, boarding gate, and baggage claim are only a few steps from each other.

Mokulele Airlines (866/260-7070, www. mokuleleairlines.com) has seven flights a day between Kapalua and Honolulu. The earliest flight departs at 9:10am, and the last flight of the day is at 5:40pm. Outside those times, you'll have to go to Kahului. There's also a 5:15pm flight to Moloka'i, but there aren't any flights to Lana'i.

CAR
Car Rentals

The largest car rental providers on the West Side are in Honokowai, equidistant between Lahaina Harbor and Kapalua Airport. Here you'll find both **Avis** (11 Halawai Dr., 808/661-4588, 7am-5pm daily) and **Budget** (11 Halawai Dr., 808/661-8721, 7am-5pm daily). Provided you arrive at the harbor or

Northwest Coast Mileage Guide

To use this mileage guide for Maui's northwestern coast, zero your trip odometer when you pass the entrance to Kapalua resort.

- 1 mile: D. T. Fleming Beach Park

- 1.6 miles: Mokulei'a Bay (Slaughterhouse Beach)

- 2.3 miles: Parking area for Honolua Valley and Honolua Bay snorkeling

- 2.7 miles: Honolua Bay Overlook and dirt access road to surf spot

- 3.7 miles: Overlook for Windmills surf spot

- 4 miles: Punalau Beach access road (Windmills)

- 5 miles: Honokohau Bay Overlook

- 5.8 miles: Honokohau Bay

- 7.4 miles: mile marker 38 and trail to lighthouse

- 7.9 miles: mile marker 38.5 and trail to Nakalele Blowhole

- 10 miles: Ohai Trail

- 12 miles: Olivine Pools

- 12.8 miles: Road becomes one lane and scary!

- 13.3 miles: Braddah Chics food truck ($12 garlic shrimp!)

- 13.5 miles: Kahakuloa Village

Kapalua Airport during business hours, they have a shuttle that will pick you up.

In the Sheraton resort in Ka'anapali, **Enterprise** (2605 Ka'anapali Pkwy., 808/661-8804, 7am-5pm daily) has a service counter and will pick you up anywhere from Lahaina Harbor to Kapalua.

Taxi

In West Maui, taxi options include **West Maui Taxi** (808/661-1122), **AB Taxi** (808/667-7575), and **Paradise Taxi** (808/661-4455). A ride from Lahaina to Ka'anapali is about $15, and from Ka'anapali to Kapalua about $25. Going rates for a cab ride to Kahului Airport from Ka'anapali are about $100, so you might want to think twice about taking a cab to the hotel.

Shuttle

The free **Kapalua Shuttle** (808/665-9110)

runs throughout the resort for guests on an on-demand basis 7am-11pm daily. In Ka'anapali, the **resort shuttle** offers free transportation across the resort and runs on a set schedule 9am-9pm daily. For a shuttle to the airport, **Speedi Shuttle** (877/242-5777, www.speedishuttle.com) offers shared ride services that range from around $50 pp in Lahaina to $65 pp from Ka'anapali.

Motorcycle and Moped

If you want the wind whipping through your hair, there are a number of different motorcycle, Harley, and moped rentals scattered across the West Side. The place with the largest selection of bikes is **Aloha Motorsports** (30 Halawai Dr., 808/667-7000, www.alohamotorsports.com, 8am-5pm daily), in Honokowai, across the highway from the Honua Kai resort. The company offers free pickup and drop-off on the West Side. Rates for mopeds can be as low as $49 for 24 hours, and Harley rentals average around $159 for 24 hours. During slower times of the year there can be specials available.

In central Lahaina, the best option for hopping on a Harley is at **Cycle City Lahaina** (602 Front St., 667-2800, www.cyclecitymaui.com, 8:30am-6pm daily), steps from the banyan tree. This is a satellite operation of a larger store in Kahului. Rates are usually around $140 for 24 hours, although lower specials are often advertised.

If you don't need a full-on hog and just want a moped for the day, check out **Motoroshi** (129 Lahainaluna Rd., 808/661-0006, www.motoroshi.com, 7am-7pm Mon.-Sat.) moped rentals on Lahainaluna Road. Only a few steps off Front Street in the parking lot of the **Café Café** coffee shop, mopeds are available for $39 for 12 hours, $49 for 24 hours. There are also a number of Vespa scooters that range $75-95 per day, depending on the size of the bike.

BUS

The cheapest way to get around West Maui, albeit slowly, is the **Maui Bus** (808/871-4838, www.co.maui.hi.us/bus). There are four different routes in West Maui, and departures are once per hour. All trips cost $2 pp per boarding, and you can buy a day pass for $4. The bus stations in Lahaina are in the back of the Wharf Cinema Center across the street from the banyan tree, and on the intersection of Front Street and Papalaua Street across the road from the Hard Rock Café. To get from one side of Lahaina to the other, bus 23 makes various stops around town 8am-11pm daily.

From Napili or Kahana to Whalers Village in Ka'anapali, where you can connect with buses to Lahaina and beyond, bus 30 begins service at 5:30am daily at the Napili Kai Beach Resort and makes various stops along Lower Honoapi'ilani Road until 9pm. Bus 25 connects Whalers Village in Ka'anapali with the Wharf Cinema Center in Lahaina 6am-9pm daily, and bus 20 connects the Wharf Cinema Center with Queen Ka'ahumanu Mall in Kahului, making a stop in Ma'alaea to transfer to a bus down to Kihei.

Since a taxi from Napili to Kahului Airport costs about $120, if you need to get from Napili to the airport and don't have a car, the cheapest way is to buy a $4 day pass and take bus 30 to Whalers Village, change to bus 25 to the Wharf Cinema Center, hop on bus 20 the Queen Ka'ahumanu Mall, and then take bus 40 to the Kahului Airport. Total transit time for this sojourn is 2 hours and 10 minutes, but for $4, who's complaining? You aren't allowed to have more luggage than you can place on your lap or under your seat.

SEA

Not many visitors access West Maui from the water, but those traveling from the islands of Lana'i or Moloka'i will arrive at Lahaina Harbor by interisland ferry. **Expeditions** (808/661-3756, www.go-lanai.com) ferry runs five times daily between Manele and Lahaina Harbors, and the *Moloka'i Princess* (877/500-6284, www.molokaiferry.com) ferry runs four times per week between Kaunakakai and Lahaina. From Lana'i, the earliest arrival time in Lahaina is 9am, and the latest is 7:45pm. Traveling from Moloka'i, ferries arrive around 6:30pm. When arriving in Lahaina by ferry, you'll find there are a large number of taxis to get you to your resort. If you plan on renting a car, call ahead to the rental-car offices and they'll pick you up. If you are traveling from Lana'i, the rental-car offices are closed if you arrive on the last ferry of the day.

Central Maui

C entral Maui is industrial, urban, and most importantly, real. The site of Kahului International Airport, Central Maui is the first part of the island most visitors encounter.

It's more built up than you'd expect of "paradise," but beyond the traffic lights, box stores, and increasing lanes of asphalt, Central Maui is the beating heart of the island's cultural past. It's also rich in natural beauty, with muddy trails leading deep into the mountains and miles of sandy shore. It's home to the island's widest array of multicultural cuisine. The sport of kitesurfing was invented here on the shores of Kanaha Beach Park. While there might not be any palm-lined resorts or tropical beach bars with mai tais, there's something that travelers might find much more interesting: a true sense of island community.

ORIENTATION

Central Maui comprises two main towns: **Kahului** and **Wailuku.** The communities of **Waihe'e, Waikapu,** and **Waiehu** are almost completely residential, and when combined with larger Kahului and Wailuku, contribute to a Central Maui population of 57,000. This is Maui's most populated region. It doesn't become rural until you pass **Waihe'e** on **Kahekili Highway.** The airport and cruise port are both in **Kahului,** and the tightest cluster of shopping and restaurants is around **Market Street** in Wailuku.

PLANNING YOUR TIME

Most visitors experience Central Maui when they drive away from the airport or take a day trip to 'Iao Valley before rushing off someplace else. Rather than devoting an hour, however, first-time visitors should spend at least half a day experiencing Central Maui's sights, whereas returning visitors looking to see new sights could easily spend two days: one day hiking, exploring the beaches, or seeing the most popular sights, and another in museums and enjoying the abundance of food.

Previous: Maui Tropical Plantation; windsurfing off the North Shore. **Above:** Kepaniwai Heritage Gardens.

Look for ★ to find recommended sights, activities, dining, and lodging.

Highlights

★ **Maui Arts and Cultural Center:** Seeing a movie or live performance in this state-of-the-art facility is one of the best nights out on Maui (page 96).

★ **Alexander and Baldwin Sugar Museum:** Peer into the daily lives of plantation laborers and read about an era that is coming to a close on Maui after 145 years (page 97).

★ **Bailey House Museum:** See authentic Hawaiian artifacts, a surfboard ridden by Duke Kahanamoku, and the best compilation of Hawaiiana literature on the island (page 98).

★ **Kepaniwai Heritage Gardens:** This small riverside park is dedicated to Maui's immigrant communities. Sample the traditional architecture of the island's "mixed plate" community (page 98).

★ **'Iao Valley State Park:** Learn about King Kamehameha's decisive victory at the Battle of Kepaniwai and snap a photo of the iconic 'Iao Needle (page 99).

★ **Maui Tropical Plantation:** Once seemingly left for dead, this colorful agricultural land has experienced a rebirth, with ziplining, a coffee shop, a farm stand, shopping, and a phenomenal restaurant (page 100).

★ **Kanaha Beach Park:** Watch the world's best windsurfers and kitesurfers zip through the air at this unheralded beach park (page 102).

★ **Waihe'e Coastal Dunes and Wetlands Preserve:** Hike the trail of this

undeveloped preserve as it passes by the ruins of Kapoho fishing village and its associated *heiau* (page 108).

★ **Waihe'e Ridge Trail:** Hike above 2,500 feet elevation to commune with the ferns and the clouds on this exceptionally scenic but muddy trail above the Waihe'e shore (page 109).

Central Maui

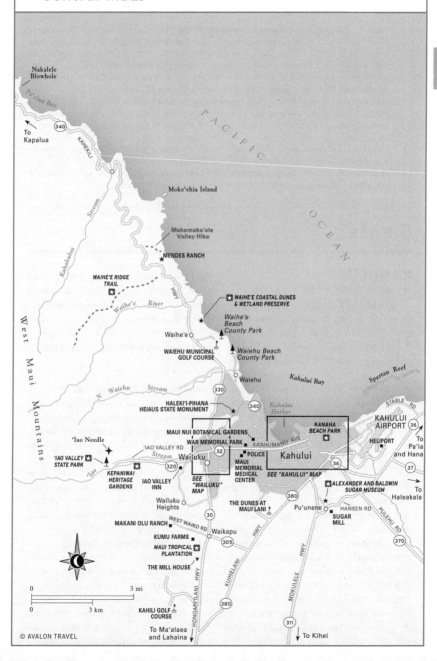

Nakalele
Blowhole

Pōʻelua Bay

To
Kapalua

340

KAHEKILI

PACIFIC

OCEAN

Moke'ehia Island

Makamaka'ole
Valley Hike

MENDES RANCH

WAIHE'E RIDGE
TRAIL

Waiheʻe River

HWY

WAIHE'E COASTAL DUNES
& WETLAND PRESERVE

Waiheʻe
Beach
County Park

Waiheʻe

Waiehu Beach
County Park

WAIEHU MUNICIPAL
GOLF COURSE

N Waiehu Stream

Waiehu

Kahekili

Kahului Bay

Spartan Reef

330

STABLE RD

HALEKI'I-PIHANA
HEIAUS STATE MONUMENT

340

Kahului
Harbor

KAHULUI
AIRPORT

36

KANAHA
BEACH PARK

To
Pa'ia
and Hana

MAUI NUI BOTANICAL GARDENS

HELIPORT

West Maui Mountains

'Iao Needle

'IAO VALLEY RD

'IAO VALLEY
STATE PARK

'Iao Stream

WAR MEMORIAL PARK

Wailuku

32

KA'AHUMANU AVE

POLICE

Kahului

36

SEE
"WAILUKU"
MAP

MAUI
MEMORIAL
MEDICAL
CENTER

SEE "KAHULUI" MAP

37

KEPANIWAI
HERITAGE
GARDENS

IAO VALLEY
INN

320

ALEXANDER AND BALDWIN
SUGAR MUSEUM

To
Haleakala

Wailuku
Heights

THE DUNES AT
MAUI LANI

380

Pu'unene

HANSEN RD

SUGAR
MILL

MAKANI OLU RANCH

WEST WAIKO RD

Waikapu

30

KUMU FARMS

305

MAUI TROPICAL
PLANTATION

370

THE MILL HOUSE

0   3 mi

0   3 km

KAHILI GOLF
COURSE

HONOAPI'ILANI HWY

KUIHELANI HWY

MOKULELE HWY

PULEHU RD

380

311

To Ma'alaea
and Lahaina

To Kihei

© AVALON TRAVEL

Your Best Day in Central Maui

Begin the day early with coffee and breakfast from **Wailuku Coffee Company,** or stop at **Maui Coffee Roasters** if approaching from Kahului. By 9am you'll be lacing up your boots to hike the **Waihe'e Ridge Trail,** or stroll the **Waihe'e Coastal Dunes and Wetlands Preserve** if you'd rather stay by the shore. After working up a sweat and snapping some photos, grab some lunch at **The Farmacy** in Wailuku and drive up to **'Iao Valley,** stopping at **Kepaniwai Heritage Gardens** and the **Bailey House Museum.**

Or, if you'd prefer an afternoon at the beach, grab some lunch in Kahului at **Poi by the Pound** or **Da Kitchen,** and head to Kanaha to watch the windsurfers and kitesurfers race across the waves. Finish the day with dinner at **The Mill House** at the Maui Tropical Plantation, enjoying the culinary genius that Chef Jeff Scheer puts on the plates.

Rainy Day? Follow the breakfast plan above, but instead of hiking or heading to the beach, visit the **Alexander and Baldwin Sugar Museum** and **Bailey House Museum** in Wailuku, spend the afternoon on **Market Street** with shopping and lunch at **Aria's,** and check the **Maui Arts and Cultural Center**'s schedule of events for that night.

Sights

KAHULUI
★ Maui Arts and Cultural Center

One of the reasons that Maui is *no ka oi* (the best) is that it truly does have a little of everything: tropical weather, world-class beaches, and live entertainment and cultural exhibitions on par with any urban center. Though the island has multiple venues for events, none offer the professionalism of the **Maui Arts and Cultural Center** (1 Cameron Way, 808/242-7469, www.mauiarts.org), massively renovated in 2012.

Although it doesn't look like much from the highway, when you first step inside the Castle Theater or wander through the Schaefer Gallery, you quickly realize that this is a place you would expect to find in a metropolis. The 1,200-seat Castle Theater has three levels of seating, and the acoustics are designed in such a way that an unamplified guitar can be heard from each seat. The 250-seat McCoy Studio is a black-box theater that hosts smaller plays and theatrical events, while the 5,000-seat A&B amphitheater has drawn some of the world's biggest musical talent, from Elton John to The Eagles. The

Maui Film Festival is partially held here on a screen inside the Castle Theater, and movies regularly show throughout the year. The constantly changing schedule of performances is listed on the website, and rarely is there a night there isn't something happening at the MACC.

Maui Nui Botanical Gardens

For anyone with an interest in Polynesian flora or sustainable farming techniques, the **Maui Nui Botanical Gardens** (150 Kanaloa Ave., 808/249-2798, www.mnbg.org, 8am-4pm Mon.-Sat., free) is an absolute must-stop. From the moment you walk in, native trees and their informational placards are displayed, and small signs warn you to watch out for falling *ulu,* or breadfruit, which populate the treetops above.

On the self-guided walking tour, signs discuss the differences between endemic, indigenous, and introduced plant species, and a central theme is the way traditional irrigation techniques maximize the ability to farm. Freshwater was precious to Polynesian farmers, and more than 70 species of dryland *kalo,* or taro, are successfully growing in a

Maui Sugar

On January 6, 2016, Maui was sent into a frenzy that few people saw coming. After 145 years of producing sugar on Maui, Hawaiian Commercial & Sugar Company dropped the bomb that after 2016, the era of sugar on Maui would officially end. Within minutes the island was consumed by the news: What will happen to all the land, and what does it mean for Maui?

HC&S had 36,000 acres of sugarcane on Maui—about 5 percent of the nation's production. In addition to the 175,000 tons of sugar produced each year, the Pu'unene Mill—the last in the state—annually produced 52,000 tons of molasses and provided 6 percent of the island's energy by burning bagasse, or spent cane. By their own estimates, however, HC&S was losing $30 million annually due to underproduction, and they lost a lucrative Maui Electric Company contract worth upward of $19 million per year. Coupled with rising costs of operation, it was decided sugarcane would no longer be planted.

There was also an environmental outcry, as the plantation, opponents claimed, polluted the air with smoke each time they conducted a burn. Vocal residents were fed up with what they believed were outdated practices, and while the facts are disputed, what can't be argued is that the sugarcane plantation helped sculpt the island as it is today. It's because of the laborers in the island's sugar mills—which at one point numbered 14—that Maui has an ethnically mixed community.

Many see the end of sugar in Hawaii as a blow to cultural heritage, whereas others see the dawn of a bright new era where small-scale, sustainable organic farms will help reduce the need to import 85 percent of our food. Taro farmers are hoping that waters are restored to East Maui's streams, which have been diverted for decades to quench the thirst of Central Maui cane fields. Others are wary that GMO seed companies will quietly take over the fields, turning Maui into an outdoor laboratory for experimental chemicals and crops. HC&S says they'll try new crops—potentially sorghum or hemp—or even use the fields for cattle grazing to bolster the island's beef industry. If there's one thing nearly everyone agrees on, it's that we don't want to see more development, and we'll miss the fields of waving green sugar.

dry coastal dunes system. Although not as expansive as the botanical gardens in Kula, the gardens espouse the Polynesian view that humans are but stewards of the land—placed here on this earth to help protect it for future generations.

★ Alexander and Baldwin Sugar Museum

There's no place on the island where you can gain a better understanding of Maui's plantation heritage than at the **Alexander and Baldwin Sugar Museum** (3957 Hansen Rd., 808/871-8058, www.sugarmuseum.com, 9:30am-4pm daily, $10), a small, worn-down building in Pu'unene. This town, which was once the beating heart of Maui's sugar industry, has been reduced to a faint pulse: a post office, a bookstore, the museum, and the stinky sugar mill are all that remain, and

even the mill is scheduled to close at the end of 2016.

The $10 entrance fee gets you a yellow booklet called "Passport to the Past," which also includes entry to the Bailey House Museum in Wailuku, as well as Lahaina's Baldwin Home Museum and Wo Hing Museum. Here in the Sugar Museum, exhibits discuss everything from sugar's Polynesian roots to historical profiles of the island's first sugar barons. Many of the businessmen who made their fortunes in sugar—Samuel Thomas Alexander and Henry Perrine Baldwin included—were the children of New England missionary families who "came to do good and stayed to do well." Alexander and Baldwin actually met as children while growing up in Lahaina, and the 12 acres of Makawao land they purchased in 1869 would grow into a business that at one point was ranked as one of the 900 largest in the country.

In addition to educating visitors about the growth of the sugar industry, what makes the museum a must-see attraction is the window it provides into the daily lives of workers from around the globe. The cultural exhibits within the museum include everything from the hand-sewn Japanese clothing used to protect workers from centipedes to Portuguese bread ovens used by immigrants from the Azores to make their famous staple. There's even an exhibit on Filipino cockfighting.

Now, with the announcement that sugar operation will cease on Maui at the end of 2016, the museum will commemorate an era that's officially history—145 years of sugar, literally gone up in smoke.

WAILUKU
★ Bailey House Museum

Regardless of whether or not you're a museum person, every visitor to Maui should see the **Bailey House Museum** (2375-A Main St., 808/244-3326, 10am-4pm Mon.-Sat., $7 adults, $2 ages 7-12) on the road to 'Iao Valley. It's listed on the National Register of Historic Places, and Duke Kahanamoku's redwood surfboard is outside on the lawn. Handcrafted

in 1910 for Hawaii's "Ambassador of Aloha," the surfboard rests near a 33-foot-long canoe that's made from a single koa log, built around 1900 and one of the last of its kind.

Inside the museum, the Hawaiian Room houses artifacts of precontact Hawaii such as wooden spears, stone tools, knives made from conch shells, and daggers made from shark's teeth. In the same room are stone *ki'i*, or statues, depicting the Hawaiian war god Ku; expertly crafted wooden calabashes; and an exhibit of artifacts found on the island of Kaho'olawe from both the pre- and post-bombing eras. If you need a good book or are interested in learning more about Hawaiian history and culture, the museum bookstore has the island's best selection of Hawaiian historical texts.

★ Kepaniwai Heritage Gardens

Like peanut butter to jelly—or spam to *musubi*—**Kepaniwai Heritage Gardens** (870 'Iao Valley Rd., 7am-7pm daily, free), goes hand in hand with a visit to 'Iao Valley. Tucked on the banks of 'Iao Stream, this simple but informative cultural park is far more interesting than it looks, as it details Maui's "mixed plate" culture. In addition to pavilions

Bailey House Museum

The Battle of Kepaniwai

Given the calming nature of Kepaniwai, it's tough to believe this narrow river canyon was the site of one of Hawaii's fiercest conflicts. Before King Kamehameha united all the islands under a single crown in 1810, opposing chiefs frequently waged battles in an effort to expand their influence. Having already conquered much of the island of Hawaii, Kamehameha sailed to Maui in 1790 with 1,200 warriors and landed at the protected waters of Kahului Bay. Though Kahekili—the reigning chief on Maui—was away on Oʻahu at the time, Kamehameha met fierce opposition from the Maui warriors who, under the leadership of Kahekili's son Kalanikupule, had positioned themselves just a few miles away at the entrance to ʻIao Valley.

Using wooden spears and clubs spiked with shark's teeth, Kamehameha's forces chased Kalanikupule's warriors deep into the valley in an evenly matched battle. After two days of fighting, neither side could claim victory. It's said that on the third day of battle, Kamehameha employed two cannons he had acquired from Western explorers. The spears and stones of the Maui warriors were no match for the explosive cannons, and by the end of the third day, Kamehameha's forces had gained a hard-won victory. Over the course of the battle, not only did ʻIao Stream run red with the blood of the vanquished, but the bodies of the deceased formed a natural dam that blocked much of its flow. This dark history lives on today in the name Kepaniwai, which translates as "damming of the waters."

that make great picnic spots (and double as great drinking spots for locals), the park features a small monument devoted to each of the island's plantation-era immigrant communities—Japanese, Chinese, Puerto Rican, and Portuguese, each monument with a small dwelling constructed in traditional style.

Along the stream are a few places where you can swim in the shallow (and cold!) waters, although use some caution when scrambling down the bank as there aren't any official trails. Unless you're a major history buff, 30 minutes here will suffice.

★ ʻIao Valley State Park

This is one of those Maui attractions you can wrongly turn into a dud—particularly if you focus on the destination, rather than enjoying the journey. Much like driving the Road to Hana and not stopping until you get there, traveling to **ʻIao Valley State Park** (end of ʻIao Valley Rd., 7am-5:30pm daily, parking $5) simply to see the park is the wrong way. Rather, the journey begins the moment you leave the streets of Wailuku and make the turn down ʻIao Valley Road through a thick canopy of trees. Here you'll find chickens crossing

the road, rural houses, fields, and farms at the base of vertical cliffs.

Crane your neck and look skyward toward peaks that tickle the passing clouds, and embrace the feeling you've suddenly traveled 100 years back in time. When you reach the park at the end of the road, rather than hastily parking, walking, and rushing to see the ʻIao Needle, take a moment to read the history of all that's happened in the park, from the gruesome and bloody Battle of Kepaniwai to how soldiers would use the valley ridgelines to spot warriors approaching from sea.

When you do begin to hike the "trail," a walkway with 133 steps, admire the landscape that lines the edge of the stream. Once you conquer the stairs, you're met with a view of Kukaʻemoku—better known as ʻIao Needle—rising 2,250 feet above the distant shore. While most visitors tend to photograph the needle, what's more spectacular is the rugged ridgelines and isolated interior of the mountain, which is so inaccessible and so untouched it's believed the bones of Hawaiian royalty are buried deep inside caves—so remote and shrouded in secrecy that they'll never be disturbed.

★ Maui Tropical Plantation

Talk about a place that's come back to life: There was a time when the **Maui Tropical Plantation** (1670 Honoapi'ilani Hwy., 808/242-8983, www.mauitropicalplantation. com, 9am-5pm daily, free) was a popular Maui highlight, but gradually the luster started to fade and the clientele grew old. That's changed now that new owners have set up new features such as zipline tours (page 112), a coffee shop, an ice cream stand, an art gallery, and a fresh organic farm stand. Best of all, the palate-bending Mill House restaurant is located on the property, and much of the food served is sourced right here on the farm (page 120).

The longtime draw is the **Tropical Express Tram Tour** ($20 adults, $10 children), otherwise known as "the train," a 40-minute ride that runs seven times 10am-4pm daily, making a loop through the surrounding fields as the driver discusses the crops. While children will be excited to ride on a train (it's the island's last), adults will enjoy the informative commentary. Once finished with the tram, linger for a while in the plantation store and the adjoining **Rebecca Lowell Art Gallery,** and visit the shed with historical photos and information about the plantation.

If it happens to be open, be sure to swing by **Kumu Farms** (808/244-4800, 10am-4pm Tues.-Sat.), to the right of the parking lot entrance. This fantastic certified-organic market is one of the island's best, where you can purchase food grown on property at a fraction of store prices. Produce is literally picked 25 feet from the farm stand, so there isn't anywhere else in Maui with produce this fresh. The farm features cilantro, peppers, chard, eggplant, carrots, and the famous sunrise papayas that are grown at the sister store on Moloka'i. You can also purchase homemade mac nut basil pesto, or cuts of grass-fed Waikapu beef for around $6 per pound. If you're staying on the West Side of the island and plan to cook in your condo, there's no better place to pick up your produce on your drive from Central Maui.

Say It Right: 'Iao Needle

Given that not many English words are entirely composed of vowels, it's understandable that the name of this valley can give some visitors fits.

The most common mispronunciation of this word is "eye-ow," as in "Ow, I hurt my eye." The first step toward wrapping your tongue around the proper pronunciation is understanding that vowels are different in Hawaiian than in English. In Hawaiian they are "ah, eh, ee, oh, oo," similar to Spanish. Once you have this vowel structure in mind, it's easy to see that 'Iao Needle is properly pronounced "ee-ow."

If all else fails, remember what you would say if you sat on a 1,200-foot-tall needle: "Ee-ow!"

Haleki'i and Pihana Heiau

Few island visitors stop at the **Haleki'i and Pihana Heiau,** which is a shame, considering their historical importance. This site is officially classified as a Hawaii state park, but the gate to the *heiau* is no longer open for vehicular access and its condition has fallen into disrepair. Nevertheless, it's still easy to park on the street in front of the *heiau* and make the five-minute walk up the hill.

In ancient Hawaii these two *heiau* served as the religious center of the entire Wailuku *ahupua'a,* or land division. Many of Maui's ruling *ali'i* came here to either honor their deceased or commune with religious deities. It's believed that Keopuolani, the woman who would become queen, was born here at Pihana *heiau,* a site that is also believed to have been a *luakini heiau,* used for human sacrifice. Hawaiian scholars believe that one of the last human sacrifices on the island was performed here at Pihana in 1790 by King Kamehameha after his victory at the Battle of Kepaniwai. Much of Pihana *heiau* was destroyed during the 19th century when the Hawaiian monarchy converted to Christianity, but numerous walls and terraces from Haleki'i still remain.

To reach the *heiau,* travel along Waiehu Beach Road until you cross the bridge over 'Iao Stream. On the other side, make the first left onto Kuhio Place and then the first left onto Hea Place. Since the access gate to the *heiau* will likely be locked, park on the street and walk up the access road. Don't be surprised if the neighbor's dog barks—just keep walking up the hill.

Kahakuloa

Technically Kahakuloa is part of Wailuku, but this old fishing village is an entity to itself. Lonely and remote, there are few places left in Hawaii that are quite like Kahakuloa. Many choose to get to Kahakuloa from the West Side of the island by following the road past Kapalua, Honolua Bay, and Nakalele Blowhole, but because this road is a loop, Kahakuloa can similarly be accessed from Wailuku. It will take you 30-45 minutes to reach Kahakuloa from Wailuku—and there aren't any gas stations—so be sure you have at least half a tank of gas before driving along the coast.

Following Kahekili Highway (Hwy. 340) past Mendes Ranch and Makamaka'ole Valley, the road becomes narrow and the foliage

dense. The first stop is **Turnbull Studios** (5030 Kahekili Hwy., 808/244-0101, www. turnbullstudios.org, 10am-5pm Mon.-Fri.), an eclectic sculpture garden with handmade crafts by local Hawaiian artists. The artist has been making sculptures at this mountainside garden for over 25 years. There are only a few parking spaces, and if it's been raining heavily, think twice before going down the short but steep driveway in a low-clearance rental car.

Farther down the road you'll reach the **Kaukini Gallery** (808/244-3371, www. kaukinigallery.com, 10am-5pm daily), inside a mountaintop home overlooking Kahakuloa Valley. The gallery features more than 120 local artists and their paintings, jewelry, and crafts, and the views from the parking lot looking up the valley make it the most scenic gallery on the island.

Finally, after a few hairpin turns on a narrow one-lane road, you reach the village of Kahakuloa, accurately called "old Hawaii" and "a place that time has forgotten." The town offers visitors a unique opportunity to glimpse Hawaiian traditions, still in practice, which managed to evade modernity. If you continue driving, you'll reach Kapalua in approximately 14 miles.

early morning at Haleki'i and Pihana Heiau

Beaches

The little-known beaches of Central Maui are defined by wind and water sports. You won't find any tiki bars or rows of beachfront cabanas, but you will find narrow stretches of sand where the world's best boarders hang out.

KAHULUI

★ Kanaha Beach Park

Kanaha Beach Park, located right next to the airport, is one of those places where you ask yourself, "How did I not know this was here?" For what it lacks in visitor friendliness (it's a frequent hangout for the homeless), the park makes up for with vibrant energy—particularly in the afternoon. You'll find windsurfers, kitesurfers, paddleboarders, and surfers out riding the waves, and on Sunday the park is bumping with barbecues and pickup games of beach volleyball.

In the early morning, before the wind picks up, this is the perfect place for a long stroll on the string of sandy beaches, where the dramatic ridgelines of Mauna Kahalawai rise from the turquoise waters. In the afternoon, the cobalt waters become flecked with whitecaps and dozens of colorful sails as windsurfers and kitesurfers race across the water—particularly in summer, when it's windier. The large, grassy beach park has showers and restrooms, and there's even a roped off area for swimming if you want to cool off or wade. It's also a convenient place to hang out if you've already checked out of your hotel and are killing time before an evening flight, since it's only minutes from the airport.

To reach Kanaha from Hana Highway, make a right at the stoplight for Hobron Avenue and then another right onto Amala Place. Drive for about 1.5 miles. The best entrances for Kanaha Beach Park are the two at the end of the road. For a shortcut, loop through the airport, past Arrivals and Departures, and make a right onto Ka'a Street, continuing past the rental-car counters until you reach the end of the road. Turn right; the beach park is on the left.

Kite Beach

Located next to Kanaha Beach Park, **Kite Beach** is the place on the island for Maui's kitesurfing crowd. The narrow strip of sand has multiple entrances—all with sand or dirt parking lots—and you can expect kitesurfers to start launching between 11am and noon.

Stable Road

If you're looking to really get away from it all and just relax on an empty patch of sand, the string of beaches off **Stable Road** are a bit of a local secret. You'll find fishers casting rods and dropped tailgates with coolers, but if you walk a couple of yards down the beach, you can usually find your own patch of sand that's perfect for a chair and book. Afternoons are often windy—and don't expect any snorkeling—but a couple of spots are deep enough for swimming, and days with light wind are gorgeous. To reach Stable Road, drive on Hana Highway (Hwy. 36) in the direction of Pa'ia, and 1.4 miles from the junction with Haleakala Highway (Hwy. 37), make a left onto a narrow paved road. From here, travel about 0.5 mile until you see sandy parking lots on the right side.

Kahului

© AVALON TRAVEL

ONEHE'E

KEA ST

To Waihe'e

340

Kahului Harbor

KA'AHUMANU AVE

32

UH MAUI COLLEGE

MAUI ARTS AND CULTURAL CENTER

FOOD TRUCKS

KAHULUI BEACH RD

LEI'S FAMILY CLASS ACT

QUEEN KA'AHUMANU CENTER

FOODLAND

KAMEHAMEHA

WAKEA AVE

HINA AVE

KANE ST

BEACH HOTEL

MAUI SEASIDE HOTEL

GAS STATION

LIBRARY

BISTRO CASANOVA

Ho'aloha Park

Kahului Bay

LANA'I AVE

LONO AVE

KANE ST

KAHULUI SHOPPING CENTER

ICHIBAN

KAULAWAHINE ST

BANK OF HAWAII

WHOLE FOODS

MAUI MALL

CENTRAL MAUI

BEACHES

HOBRON AVE

32A

CATHOLIC CHURCH

POST OFFICE

MAUI MEDICAL CENTER

To Lahaina

350

PU'UNENE AVE

PIZZA IN PARADISE

HO'OHANA ST

POI BY THE POUND

BRIGIT AND BERNARD'S GARDEN CAFE

RESTAURANT MATSU

SAFEWAY

WINDSURF SHOPS

HUI'ILI ST

LALO PL

BISTRO MANILA

AMALA

To Kihei

ANIMAL COFFEE

HOME DEPOT

MAUI HARLEY-DAVIDSON

PAPA PL

DAIRY RD

DOWN TO EARTH NATURAL FOODS

WINDSURF SHOP

MAUI COFFEE ROASTERS

DA KITCHEN

Kanaha Pond State Wildlife Sanctuary

Kahului Bay

380

WAL-MART

MAUI DOWNHILL

MAUI MARKETPLACE

GAS STATION

'ULULANI'S SHAVE ICE

GAS STATION

ISLAND BIKER

WINDSURF SHOP

KMART

COSTCO

OBSERVATION PAVILION

FOOD TRUCK PARK

Kite Beach

HANA HWY

HALEAKALA HWY

COURTYARD MARRIOTT

AMALA ST

To KANAHA BEACH PARK
Kanaha Beach County Park

Entrances

HO'OKELE ST

370

PULEHU RD

KEOLANI PL

KAA ST

To Kahului Airport

36

To Hana

0   0.25 mi
0   0.25 km

Wailuku

To West Maui
Backside

Happy Valley

'Iao Stream

330

'ULEI PL

MAKUA ST

KONAHEA ST

KAHAWAI ST

N MARKET ST

POST OFFICE

WILI PA LOOP RD

KALA ST

SAM SATO'S ▼

MAUI VISITOR'S BUREAU ■

To Steel Horse Saloon, Home Maid Bakery, and Tiffany's

TASTY CRUST ▼

MILL ST

KANIELA ST

MISSION ST

■ BANANA BUNGALOW

NORTH ST

CENTRAL AVE

SIMPLY SWEETS ▼

NANI ST

NORTHSHORE HOSTEL ●

ARIA'S

SAENG'S THAI CUISINE ▼

N HIGH ST

PUBLIC PARKING ■

CHURCH ST

'IAO THEATER ■

WAILUKU COFFEE BAR ■

IF THE SHOE FITS ▼

A SAIGON CAFE ▼

32

To Kahului

THE FARMACY HEALTH BAR ■

JINI'S CURRY ▼

MAUI THING ■

NATIVE INTELLIGENCE ■

VINEYARD ST

CHURCH OF THE GOOD SHEPHERD ■

MAUI MEDICAL GROUP ■

GAS STATION ▼

REQUESTS ■

GAS STATION ■

▼ 808 ON MAIN

E MAIN ST

GIANOTTO'S PIZZA ▼

WELLS ST

Wells Park

To 'Iao Needle

320

KA'AHUMANU CHURCH ★

MARKET ST

S

KANOA ST

WAI'ALE RD

✚ BAILEY HOUSE MUSEUM

PAKAHI ST

AUPUNI ST

PALUA ST

'IAO SCHOOL ■

KOELI ST

WAILUKU PUBLIC LIBRARY ■

UNION CHURCH ■

ICHIBAN OKAZUYA ▼

KAOHU ST

KALUA ST

■ WAILUKU PUBLIC SCHOOL

30

MALAKO ST

KAHO'OKELE ST

● OLD WAILUKU INN

To Lahaina

MAKAHALA ST

0   0.25 mi

0   0.25 km

© AVALON TRAVEL

The Road to Kahakuloa

If driving to Hana was the scariest thing you've ever done, you might want to take a rain check on the Road to Kahakuloa. There are sheer drop-offs with no guardrails, completely blind turns, and the occasional rockslide that will send boulders down onto the highway. The narrowest section of the road is between Mendes Ranch and Kahakuloa village, which leads many visitors to travel from Kapalua and then retreat the way they came. If you're up for a bit of adventure, however, and want to drive the whole way, then this is one of the most scenic, hair-raising drives you can take in Hawaii.

That said, there's a lot of confusion surrounding the drive. Some rental car maps show the road as for 4WD vehicles only. Others say that it's one lane. Still others say you shouldn't drive it at all. This road can be narrow, frustrating, and downright scary, but if you utilize a few simple techniques, what was once a white-knuckle drive through the wilderness becomes one of the island's best day trips.

Despite the dangers, incidents are rare. The road does not require a 4WD vehicle. It's paved, although some sections can be bumpy. The road is narrow, and at some places is only wide enough for one car.

So how do you drive on a one-lane road? Go slowly around corners and honk your horn on those you can't see around. Turn the radio off so you can hear if anyone is honking from the other direction. If you need to take a break, use one of the gravel pullouts on the side of the road and let the cars behind you pass. Watch the road that's directly in front of you, but also look across the valley for oncoming traffic that might still be 0.5 mile away. If you notice that there is an oncoming truck, use the next pullout, wait 20 seconds for the oncoming traffic to pass, and then continue on your way. If you do encounter another car at a narrow spot, you might have to slowly reverse to the nearest pullout and give the other car room to pass. The number-one rule is, don't sightsee and drive at the same time. If you're the driver, keep your eyes firmly glued to the road. If you want to take photos, pull over.

If you want, take this adventurous back road, which direction should you approach from? If you're departing from West Maui and moving clockwise around the mountain, you have the benefit of being on the inside lane and away from the steep cliff faces. This is the most popular way to visit, after an outing to Nakalele Blowhole. Then again, since you are pressed against the mountainside instead of against the ocean, you run the risk of falling rocks coming down after a heavy rain. If you approach from the Wailuku direction and move in a counterclockwise direction around the mountain, be sure the person in the passenger seat isn't afraid of heights.

Buckle up, hold on, and get ready for a ride to remember.

Surfing

The majority of surfing on this side of the island takes place from October to April. Some eastward-facing locations can pick up wind swell during the summer months, but it's choppy and sloppy. There are no surf schools that operate along this stretch of coast, and anyone opting to surf around here needs to be at least an intermediate surfer. On the biggest winter swells, teams of professional surfers have been known to tow-surf the outer reefs here, where waves can reach 70 feet. Thanks, but we'll be watching from shore.

SURF SPOTS
Kahului

For longboarding and stand-up paddle surfing, **Lowers** at Kanaha Beach Park (page 102) is a popular North Shore favorite. When standing on the sand, look for the lifeguard tower, which is where you'll paddle out. The wave at Kanaha breaks on an offshore reef and requires an arm-burning paddle, but a long paddle means a long ride, and the surf usually won't close out until the faces reach 10 feet. Mornings are best before the wind picks up, which is usually around 11am.

Wailuku

The most popular surf break in Wailuku is **Big Lefts** in Paukukalo. This is a long left-hand wave that can get very big on north and northeasterly swells, although it's for advanced surfers only and is heavily localized. To access the surf break, turn onto Waiehu Beach Road and then make a right on Ukali Street, following it to the end. The surf break is in front of the parking lot. Don't leave any valuables in your car, give locals the set waves, and stick to hopping the shoulder.

For a mellow longboarding wave, there's a break in front of **Waiehu Beach Park** that usually has fewer people than neighboring Paukukalo. The wave quality isn't as good, but this is still a good wave in the early morning during any north swell. To reach Waiehu Beach Park, travel along Waiehu Beach Road before taking a right turn on Lower Waiehu Beach Road, and follow it to the parking lot at the end.

WINDSURFING

Maui is one of world's top destinations for windsurfing, and at **Kanaha Beach Park,** the trade winds are so consistent during the summer months that they arrive like clockwork around 11am. In winter, the trade winds are a little less consistent, and waves can reach 15 feet or higher.

There's strictly no windsurfing before 11am, and Kanaha is split into two main launching areas conveniently named **Uppers** and **Lowers.** Many of the windsurfing schools operate by Uppers at a cove known as Kook's Beach. Lowers is located in the area by the lifeguard tower, the preferred launching point. If there are waves breaking on the reef, you'll notice a channel off the lifeguard stand where you can get past the break and out beyond the surf.

For more information on Maui windsurfing, go to www.mauiwindsurfing.net for photos, rental operators, and descriptions of the various launching sites. For a live cam of the conditions at Kanaha, check out www.mauiwindcam.com.

KITESURFING

The best place for kitesurfing on Maui is at the aptly named **Kite Beach** (page 102) a

dawn patrol at Paukukalo

Stand-Up Paddling: The Maliko Run

In the sport of downwind stand-up paddling, there's no stretch of water more legendary and hallowed than the nine-mile-long Maliko Run. It's the spot where downwind racing was born, and the place where the world's best train for the professional tour.

In a "downwinder," paddlers position the wind at their backs and glide on the open ocean, connecting "bumps," or ocean swells, that pass beneath the board. When done properly, it's possible to feel like you're surfing on a wave that virtually has no end, and your mind and body are exceptionally aligned with the ocean movements beneath you. In the Maliko Run, paddlers begin at Maliko Gulch to the east of Ho'okipa Beach Park, and paddle downwind to either Kahului Harbor or the beach at Kanaha Beach Park. On a typical day, paddlers will be up to a mile offshore and in winds of 30 mph, riding on ocean swells that can range from knee-high to a couple of feet overhead. Average paddlers complete the nine-mile run between Maliko and the Harbor in a little under two hours, whereas the world's top paddlers can finish the course in a little over an hour—a seven-minute mile.

Maliko Runs are a favorite weekend activity of the island's water sports enthusiasts, and over 200 racers gather each year for the professional races, with one of the largest being the OluKai race at the end of April. A Maliko Run isn't an activity for anyone who isn't an avid stand-up paddler, but for stand-up paddling enthusiasts, this is the Holy Grail.

If you're a competent paddler and have lots of experience in the ocean, **Moore Water Time** (www.moorewatertime.com) has a shuttle service ($15-17 pp) with daily runs to Maliko that leave from Kanaha and Kahului Harbor. For boards, an increasing number of Kahului shops are now renting race boards, and a couple of schools will even provide lessons where an experienced instructor can accompany you.

place of hallowed ground where the sport was born. This is the beach where all kitesurfing schools operate, and just as at neighboring Kanaha, the crowd is international. Even if you aren't a kitesurfer, this is a fantastic spot to sit and watch as dozens of colorful kites zip through the gusty trade winds. Since Kite Beach is so close to Kanaha, the unwritten rule is that kitesurfers are supposed to stay downwind (closer to Kahului Harbor) of the windsurfers to avoid high-speed entanglement. Even though this is one of the premier spots on the planet for kitesurfing, unless you're an experienced kitesurfer, lessons are imperative.

For more information about kitesurfing on Maui, check out www.kitesurfmaui.org. For a webcam of current wind and weather conditions, go to www.kitebeachcam.com.

RENTAL SHOPS

Of all the rental shops in Kahului, **HI-Tech Surf Sports** (425 Koloa St., 808/877-2111, www.surfmaui.com, 9am-6pm daily) has the largest selection of surfboards ($25 per day) and stand-up paddleboards ($35 per day), with discounts for longer rentals.

Other reputable rental spots include the **Naish Pro Center** (111 Hana Hwy., 808/871-1503, www.naishmaui.com, 9am-5pm daily), **Second Wind** (111 Hana Hwy., 808/877-7467, www.secondwindmaui.com, 9am-6pm daily), and **Kanaha Kai** (96 Amala Place, 808/877-7778, www.kanahakai.com, 9am-5pm daily), which is the closest shop to the beach. Expect stand-up paddleboards to cost about $35 per day, and downwind boards $35-55. Windsurfing rigs should be about $55, and kitesurf rigs about $85.

SCHOOLS AND LESSONS

When it comes to windsurfing and kitesurfing in Maui, one class isn't enough. Ideally you want to book at least a five-hour package to maximize your investment, although every school offers a single-session option if you just want to test the waters.

One of the best schools on the island is **Hawaiian Sailboard Techniques** (425 Koloa St., 808/871-5423, www.hstwindsurfing.com), located inside HI-Tech Surf Sports. Founder Alan Cadiz has been teaching windsurfing on Maui since 1985, making this the longest-running outfit on the island's North Shore. Cadiz was one of the first instructors to teach the sport to others, and an instructor will accompany you on a stand-up paddleboard. Three-hour kitesurfing lessons are $255, and private windsurfing starts at $99. Stand-up paddle lessons begin at $89 for a two-hour class, and if you're experienced, ask about doing the Maliko Run along with a professional guide.

One of the largest schools is **Action Sports Maui** (808/871-5857, www.actionsportsmaui.com), where kiting lessons range from $199 for a 2.5-hour intro class to $2,195 for a 10-day, 30-hour intensive training package. Windsurfing lessons range from $89 for 2.5 hours to a five-day course ($395 pp group, $725 private).

Kitesurfing School of Maui (808/873-0015, www.ksmaui.com) focuses specifically on kitesurfing, and offers a $199 three-hour beginner package, or $680 for eight hours (a better option for actually learning the sport).

Aqua Sports (808/242-8015, www.mauikiteboardinglessons.com) is right on Kite Beach and offers a $195 one-day beginner special. If you just want to get the feeling for what it feels like to kitesurf without taking an entire lesson package, check out **Kiting.com** (808/852-1938, www.kiting.com) for a 30-minute tandem-kitesurfing experience ($99) riding with a professional instructor who handles the board and the steering. If you decide you're hooked on the sport, lesson packages are available.

Hiking and Biking

HIKING
'Iao Valley

From the winding drive back into the mountains, you would think that popular 'Iao Valley would offer some good hiking. In reality, the only hike is the paved walking trail that leads to the 'Iao Needle lookout.

If you want to swim in 'Iao Stream, the best place for accessing the swimming holes is from Kepaniwai Heritage Gardens, where short trails lead down to the refreshing—and cold—water.

★ Waihe'e Coastal Dunes and Wetlands Preserve

Here's a hike that's wildly underrated: Set on land protected by the Hawaiian Islands Land Trust, the two-mile trail in the **Waihe'e Coastal Dunes and Wetlands Preserve** runs the length of one of Maui's last undeveloped shorelines. Within the 277-acre preserve are the remains of the Kapoho fishing village as well as two different ancient *heiau* (temples). Scholars estimate that the Waihe'e area was populated as early as AD 300-600, which is not surprising, as the freshwater streams, fertile valleys, and lush uplands provide all the natural resources to sustain life. In modern times this area was once slated for development as a golf community, although by raising funds through events such as the annual Buy Back the Beach dinner, the land trust was able to preserve this culturally rich shore and honor its history.

The trail parallels the shore and passes by a couple of abandoned houses before reaching the cultural relics at Kapoho. Expect the round-trip journey to take a little over an hour; add 30 minutes to explore the coast or ruins. To reach the trailhead, make a right on Halewaiu Place off Kahekili Highway (Hwy. 340) and follow the signs for Waiehu Golf Course. When the road makes a sharp turn to the right and starts heading toward the golf course, notice an unmarked dirt road going to the left. Park here, because around the corner is a stream crossing that's unsuitable for rental cars. Traveling on foot, the trailhead will be on the left, just uphill from the stream crossing. Avoid leaving valuables in your car.

★ Waihe'e Ridge Trail

The parking area for the **Waihe'e Ridge Trail** is at mile marker 7 of Kahekili Highway, across from Mendes Ranch. If the gate is open, which it usually is 7am-5pm daily, continue driving for another mile to the upper parking area. This 2.5-mile trail starts on a steep concrete incline, but fear not—if you can make it up this, you can make it the rest of the way. Eventually the trail levels out a bit

and the concrete changes to dirt, which can often lead to muddy conditions, particularly if it has recently rained. But oh, the views! This trail rises to 2,560 feet elevation, the highest hiking trail in West Maui, and offers sweeping views into Waihe'e and Makamaka'ole Valleys. In the distance, Makamaka'ole Falls tumbles dramatically through the forest; look the other direction, and the turquoise waters of the Waihe'e shore form a dramatic backdrop. The trail continues to Lanilili summit, where you can see the northern slope of the mountain on clear days. If you start hiking before 9am, you'll usually get clear conditions. This trail takes some energy, so count on three hours for the five-mile trip.

Makamaka'ole Valley

There aren't many waterfalls in Central Maui that you can access, but one exception is at **Makamaka'ole Valley,** off the side of Kahekili Highway. Approaching from Wailuku, the discreet trailhead is 0.8 mile past Mendes Ranch. At this point the road has climbed in elevation and narrowed in places to a single lane. You'll pass a sharp turn in the valley, and when the road starts pointing back toward the ocean, you'll notice a small

rainbow over Waihe'e Coastal Dunes and Wetlands Preserve

West Maui's Backside

Pailolo Channel

To Kapalua

HONOLUA BAY
(MARINE LIFE
CONSERVATION
DISTRICT)

PACIFIC OCEAN

Honolua

Honokohau Bay

Honokohau

NAKALELE
BEACON SITE

Nakalele Blowhole

Gulch

30

Po'elua Bay

Ohai Trail

Hononana Bay

Keahikano
2,017ft

Mokolea Point

Anakaluahine

Blowhole

Honolua
2,627ft

Honokohau Stream

Kahakuloa Bay

Kahakuloa

KAUKINI
GALLERY

Kahakuloa Stream

KAHEKILI HWY

TURNBULL
GALLERY

Makamaka'ole
Valley Trail

MALUHIA BOY
SCOUT CAMP

MENDES
RANCH

WAIHE'E
RIDGE TRAIL

Lanilili
2,627ft

WAIHE'E COASTAL DUNES
& WETLANDS PRESERVE

Waihe'e
Point

*Waihe'e
Beach
County Park*

Waihe'e

WAIEHU MUNICIPAL
GOLF COURSE

*Waiehu
Beach
County
Park*

Happy Valley

Waiehu

HALEKI'I-PIHANA HEIAU
STATE MONUMENT

Wailuku

0   2 mi

0   2 km

To
Lahaina

© AVALON TRAVEL

dirt pullout that can accommodate four or five vehicles.

The trailhead is a very narrow but well-defined dirt pathway that heads downhill into the brush. There's also a false trailhead that departs from the same parking area but only goes for a few yards. If the trail suddenly ends, turn around and look for the other one. Once you are on the correct trail, it will wind its way downhill for about 10 minutes before arriving at a small swimming hole, where you'll find a rushing waterfall and a rope swing. Along the way you're rewarded with a dramatic view of Makamaka'ole Valley as it weaves toward the ocean below.

After the first swimming hole, the trail continues deeper into the valley toward a waterfall more dramatic than the first. You have to climb over a large boulder and move branches aside to keep following the trail, which then parallels the stream over some slippery rocks. The mosquitoes can be vicious in this shaded section, so be sure you're covered. After five minutes, the trail ends at a large banyan tree whose serpentine roots snake down a near-vertical cliff face. In order to reach the pool below, climb down using the roots of the banyan as if descending a ladder. This maneuver requires athletic ability and skill, so it should only be attempted by those who are agile and accepting of the risks. The reward, however, is a small swimming hole where you can bathe beneath a waterfall in a hidden tropical setting.

HIKING TOURS

Guided hiking tours of the Waihe'e area are available through **Mendes Ranch** (3530 Kahekili Hwy., 808/871-5222, www.mendes-ranch.com). Prices range from $65 for the 1.5 hour Mendes Cliff hike to $115 for 3.5 hours on the Waihe'e Ridge Trail. Both hikes offer spectacular views, and the guides have lots of local knowledge and stories.

BIKING

The lone Central Maui mountain biking trail is in the **Kahakuloa Game Management**

Area, where a five-mile-long 4WD road rises 1,600 vertical feet. Wear bright-colored clothing because it's also a hunting area. The turn-off from Kahekili Highway is between mile markers 40 and 41.

The **road bike ride to Kahakuloa** is one of the best on the island, where cyclists are treated to quad-burning ascents, hairpin turns through the rainforest, and sweeping views of the entire North Shore. Sharing the road with cars can be tough, considering how narrow it gets, but most cars are traveling so slowly around the tight turns that altercations are rare.

If you would prefer to be on a designated bike path that stays on level ground, the **North Shore Greenway** runs from the last parking lot at Kanaha Beach Park all the way to the town of Pa'ia. To reach the Kahului terminus of the bike path, follow Amala Place all

the way to the end and park in the last parking lot of Kanaha Beach Park. Parts of the bike path go directly behind the airport runway. This ride is best in the morning hours before the wind picks up.

Rental Shops

At **Crater Cycles** (400 Hana Hwy., 808/893-2020, www.cratercycleshawaii.com, 9am-6pm daily), mountain bike and road bike rentals begin at $65 per day, with discounted prices for multiple days. The staff love cycling and can offer inside info on current trail conditions and tips for enjoying your ride.

Across the street from K-Mart, **Island Biker Maui** (415 Dairy Rd., 808/877-7744, www.islandbikermaui.com, 10am-5pm Mon.-Fri., 9am-3pm Sat.) offers rentals that begin at $60 per day or $210 per week. Mountain bikes and road bikes are available.

Horseback Riding and Bird-Watching

HORSEBACK RIDING

You know a ranch is the real deal when you can smell it before you see it. The family-run **Mendes Ranch** (3530 Kahekili Hwy., 808/871-5222, www.mendesranch.com, $110), on the road toward Kahakuloa, has managed 300 head of cattle since the 1940s, when it was just a homestead. Today, aside from the sweeping ocean views and trails that run along the coast, what makes Mendes such a popular option is that rather than nose-to-tail riding, you can run the horses on a 1.5-hour authentic *paniolo* (cowboy) experience of life on a working ranch. Rides depart at 9am and 12:30pm Monday-Saturday.

More centrally located is **Makani Olu Ranch** (363 W. Waiko Rd., 808/870-0663, www.makanioluranch.com), a working cattle ranch in Waikapu Valley with nearly 100 longhorn cattle. Rides accommodate four people at most, and since the entire ride is at a walking pace, this is a great option for novice riders who just want the view from the saddle.

The ride traverses Waikapu Valley and crosses Waikapu Stream, allowing you access to a part of the island you'd otherwise never see. From the lookout points, the views are back toward the central isthmus, as well as up the valley walls leading deep into the heart of the mountains. Two-hour rides are $105, and you can upgrade to a three-hour ride ($125) that includes lunch while riding through the valley. If you're nervous about getting on a horse, the Makani Olu Ranch Ride ($150) includes a 45-minute lesson before heading out on the trail. Because it's located in the middle of the island, the ranch is only 25 minutes from Wailea, and 35 minutes from Ka'anapali.

BIRD-WATCHING
Kahului

Despite being smack in the middle of town, the **Kanaha Pond State Wildlife Sanctuary** houses as many as 90 species of native and migratory birds. Only five minutes from the Kahului airport, this area was once a royal fishpond that was built in the 1700s. It provided the island's *ali'i*, or chiefs, with a consistent supply of mullet, although the dredging of Kahului Harbor in 1910 altered the natural flow of water.

Today this is where you'll spot the endangered Hawaiian stilt (*ae'o*), a slender, 16-inch bird with sticklike pink legs that, according to most recent population estimates, numbers around 2,000 statewide. The Hawaiian coot (*'alae ke'oke'o*), a gray-black duck-like bird that builds large floating nests, may also be seen here, and the sanctuary is open free of charge August 31-March 31. In summer, when the sanctuary is closed for nesting season, an observation pavilion is maintained on the pond's south edge, which is open year-round. To access the trails inside the sanctuary, entry is through the gates on Amala Place on the road to Kanaha Beach Park.

Wailuku

The best places for bird-watching in Wailuku are the **Waihe'e Coastal Dunes and Wetlands Preserve** (page 108), where you can spot seabirds in the low grass, and the **Waihe'e Ridge Trail** (page 109), where the song of indigenous Hawaiian forest birds might accompany your hike.

Adventure Sports

ZIPLINE TOURS

For travelers who only go big or go home, the eight-line **Flyin Hawaiian Zipline** (1670 Honoapi'ilani Hwy., 808/463-4786, www.flyinhawaiianzipline.com, $185) covers 2.5 miles of West Maui mountainside and finishes in a different town. The most enticing reason to book this tour is the ultra-long, cheek-clenching, three-screamer zipline that runs for more than 3,600 feet—the longest on the island. The lines aren't parallel, and the height off the ground isn't as high as the fifth line at Pi'iholo, but you also get a short ATV ride at the end as they shuttle you back where you started.

In addition to views toward Haleakala, this zipline ecotour incorporates elements of habitat restoration for Hawaii's native plants and works to remove nonnative species. The company champions sustainable, educational tourism, and the ecological element of the organization isn't just something done to appear green—it's the real deal. Expect the tour to take 4-5 hours. Small snacks are included. Riders must be 10 years old and weigh 75 to 250 pounds. Guests meet at the Maui Tropical Plantation for a 4WD ride back into Waikapu Valley, where you suit up for your midair journey across the mountain. This tour often sells out well in advance, so reservations are a must.

If you'd rather ease into it, or are traveling with children, the most beginner-friendly zipline in the central valley is **Maui Zipline** (1670 Honoapi'ilani Hwy., 808/633-2464, www.mauizipline.com, $110), on the grounds of the Maui Tropical Plantation. Children as young as five and as light as 45 pounds can take part in this five-line adventure; children under age 11 must be joined by an adult. Because the course caters to young children, it isn't as extreme as some others, but the guides introduce educational elements to the program, such as the weather patterns of the area and lessons on plant species, making this a great option for families. Cable lengths range 300 to 900 feet, and there are two cables running parallel to each other, so you can go two at a time.

HELICOPTER RIDES

You heard it here first: Helicopter tours are the island's best splurge. They're expensive, and some people find them scary, but they are the best way to experience Maui's beauty. The majority of the island is only accessible by helicopter, and until you've seen waterfalls powerfully plunging through hidden mist-shrouded valleys, or buzzed below the world's tallest sea cliffs and seen humpback whales from the air, you'll never know the breadth of beauty that Maui really has to offer.

All pilots have logged thousands of flying hours and put an emphasis on safety, and when narrating the tours, most also provide information on geology, biology, and history. Morning tours are best because they offer the clear conditions necessary for visiting spots such as 1,100-foot Honokohau Falls or peering into Haleakala Crater. All helicopter flights depart from the **Kahului Heliport** (0.5 mile from the junction of Hana Hwy. and Haleakala Hwy.), and the two most popular tour options are those combining the West Maui Mountains with Moloka'i, and East Maui (Hana) with Haleakala. Regardless of which operator you choose, inquire about getting the two front seats next to the pilot, since it's much easier to take photos. If you're really serious about photos, wear long sleeves and dark-colored clothing to avoid reflection in the window, and to get really pro, consider wearing gloves. Remember that you cannot have been scuba diving within 24 hours before the flight (although snuba is OK). All prices listed are for advance online reservations.

Air Maui (1 Kahului Airport Rd., Hangar 110, 808/877-7005 www.airmaui.com) has a perfect safety record and has options you won't find elsewhere, including the West Maui and Moloka'i tour with a sunset dinner landing ($428 pp), where you tour the mountains and marvel at thundering waterfalls, then land for a private sunset dinner in the mountains above Kapalua. More affordable options are the 30-minute Maui Lite trip ($188 pp), occasionally offered for $100 for last-minute single seats. There are also standard West Maui-Moloka'i and Hana-Haleakala tours, including one with a cliff-side landing on the back side of Haleakala. All helicopters are the A-Star variety, which seat up to six.

The largest operator on the island, with cheaper flights, is **Blue Hawaiian**

Helicopters (1 Kahului Airport Rd., Suite 105, 808/871-8844, www.bluehawaiian.com), operating both A-Star and more expensive Eco-Star helicopters, with individual bucket seats and larger viewing windows. Options include a 30-minute flight of West Maui (Eco-Star $185 pp, A-Star $153 pp) and a 1.5-hour complete island tour with a landing at Ulupalakua Ranch ($321-396 pp). For a multi-island adventure, cross the channel to the Big Island for a tour of North Kohala (sorry—no volcanoes or lava) before returning over Hana for a two-hour flight ($453-510 pp).

Also flying Eco-Star helicopters is **Sunshine Helicopters** (1 Kahului Airport Rd., Suite 107, 808/270-3999, www.sunshinehelicopters.com), which charges extra for seats in front. Tours include a 45-minute Hana-Haleakala flight ($225 pp) and a 70-minute complete island flight with deluxe seating ($480 pp). To save a little, flights are discounted $50 before 8am and after 2pm. If Mendes Ranch horseback riding or the Atlantis Submarine are also on your list of activities, you can book them as a combo package through Sunshine Helicopters and save a little on both.

After 20 years of operating flights on the Mainland, **Maverick Helicopters** (1 Kahului Airport Rd., Suite 108, 808/893-7999, www.maverickhelicopter.com) is the island's newest operator, with Eco-Star flights that include a 45-minute Hana-Haleakala tour ($329 pp) and a 70-minute complete island tour ($399 pp).

To get really extreme and have no glare in your photos, **Pacific Helicopters** (808/871-9771, www.pacifichelicoptertours.com) can fly without the doors to enjoy the dramatic scenery with no obstructions. Tours average $293-323 pp, depending on length of the tour, and since the helicopter only has room for three passengers, it's cheaper for a party of three to charter a flight ($800).

FLIGHTSEEING TOURS

If you're staying on Maui and want to see lava (which isn't guaranteed), the only way to see Kilauea volcano is with a flightseeing tour in an airplane. There aren't any helicopter companies from Maui that visit Kilauea volcano, although there are a couple of fixed-wing options from Kapalua and Kahului airports. **Royal Pacific Air** (808/838-7788, www.royalpacificair.com) begins its flights at Honolulu and makes stops at Kapalua Airport ($449 pp) and Kahului Airport ($425 pp) before continuing on to the Big Island. If you're staying in Ka'anapali, Napili, or Kapalua, the Kapalua airport is only a 10-minute drive, an amazingly convenient option. In addition to active Kilauea volcano, you'll experience hidden waterfalls on the Big Island as well as Hana and Haleakala Crater. It isn't cheap but compares to the most expensive helicopter tours.

The other option is **Maui Air** (808/877-5500, www.volcanoairtours.com), offering tours of the volcano. The plane can accommodate 10 passengers, and fares are about $385 from Kahului Airport and $425 from Kapalua Airport.

Golf

If you don't want to pay resort prices for golf but still appreciate a course that's well cared for, the three courses in Central Maui have some of the island's best deals. All have affordable restaurants with ice-cold beer. Prices listed are summer rates; expect higher costs in winter (approximately $20-25 higher per round).

KAHULUI

The **Dunes at Maui Lani** (1333 Maui Lani Pkwy., 808/873-0422, www.dunesatmauilani. com, 6:30am-6pm daily) is a Scottish-style links course that weaves through natural sand dunes. Course designer Robert Nelson utilized the natural topography of the dunes in creating this 6,841-yard course, so it includes a healthy number of bunkers. On the 18th hole, which is par 5, two pot bunkers short of the green famously challenge even those with the lowest of handicaps. The afternoon trade winds can make this course difficult, and the greens fees are priced accordingly: $89 for morning rounds, $79 after 1pm. Club rental

teeing off at Waiehu Golf Course

is $35, and the central location makes it easy to sneak in a round before the 10-minute drive to the airport.

WAILUKU

On the hillside in Waikapu, the 6,554-yard **Kahili Golf Course** (2500 Honoapi'ilani Hwy., 808/242-4653, www.kahiligolf.com, 6am-6pm daily) is one of the island's best golf values. Greens fees for visitors are $99, although if you tee off after 2pm, it drops to $59; club rentals are $35. The bicoastal views are better than at Maui Lani, although instead of links-style golf, the course is set on a gently sloping hillside. Kahili is a 35-minute drive from Ka'anapali, 25 minutes from Wailea.

If you just want to tee up the municipal course, **Waiehu Golf Course** (200 Halewaiu Rd., 808/243-7400, 6:45am-5pm Mon.-Fri.,

6am-5pm Sat.-Sun.) is a 6,330-yard, par-72 course that's wildly popular with locals. Visitor greens fees are $50, although you can sneak in nine holes for only $10 if you tee off after 3pm. Cart rentals are $20 for 18 holes, and hand carts are only $4. Club rentals are $20, and a couple of the holes have oceanfront tee boxes and sweeping, resort-quality views.

Rental Shops

Regardless of where you're golfing, you can save on rental clubs by stopping at **Roger Dunn Golf Shop** (293 Dairy Rd., 808/873-5700, 9am-7pm Mon.-Fri., 9am-6pm Sat., 10am-5pm Sun.), just a couple of minutes from the airport. Rental rates start at $20 per day or $60 per week—far more affordable than the $60-75 you would pay at resorts.

Shopping

KAHULUI

Kahului has the island's largest amount of shopping, though it's mainly the box-store variety. The two-story **Queen Ka'ahumanu Shopping Center** (275 W. Ka'ahumanu Ave., 808/877-4325, www.queenkaahumanucenter. com, 9:30am-9pm Mon.-Sat., 10am-5pm Sun.) is Kahului's largest mall, though many of the stores are large corporate chains. That said, there's still one shop, **The Story of Hawaii Museum** (808/283-3576, www.storyofhawaiimuseum.com, 10am-5pm daily) that sells Hawaiian prints and doubles as a Hawaiian history museum. In addition to maps and Hawaiian giclées, visitors will find exhibits on everything from Maui's involvement in World War II to the route of Hawaii's King Kalakaua—the first monarch to circumnavigate the globe.

Across town, the open-air **Maui Mall** (70 E. Ka'ahumanu Ave., 808/877-8952, www.mauimall.com, 10am-6pm Mon.-Thurs. and Sat., 10am-8pm Fri., 10am-4pm Sun.) has a

couple of surf shops and clothing boutiques, and is convenient for anyone visiting on a cruise ship that's docked at Kahului Harbor.

For a classic Maui shopping experience, head to the Saturday **Maui Swap Meet** (310 W. Ka'ahumanu Ave., 808/244-3100, www.mauiexposition.com, 7am-1pm Sat., $0.50 adults, free under age 13) at UH Maui College, where over 200 local vendors gather to sell their foodstuffs and crafts. You can find everything from homemade jams to hand-turned koa wood bowls—often at prices much reduced from what you'd find in the stores.

Kahului also has the greatest concentration of water sports shops on the island, many of which are near the corner of Hana Highway and Dairy Road. Stop here for surf clothing, accessories, board shorts, or equipment sales. Favorites include **HI-Tech Surf Sports** (425 Koloa St., 808/877-2111, www.surfmaui.com, 9am-6pm daily), **Neilpryde Maui** (400 Hana Hwy., 808/877-7443, www.neilprydemaui. com, 9am-6pm daily), and **Maui Tropix** (261

Dairy Rd., 808/871-8726, 9am-8pm Mon.-Sat., 9am-6pm Sun.), which sells the ubiquitous "Maui Built" wear.

WAILUKU

Sleepy Wailuku is turning into a hot shopping outpost. With a tight little cluster of shops, Market Street rivals Lahaina, Paia, and Makawao for shopping and strolling. The difference here, however, is that many of the stores have authentic local connections—either selling products from local vendors or traditional Hawaiian crafts.

At **Native Intelligence** (1980 Main St., 808/249-2421, www.native-intel.com, 10am-5pm Mon.-Fri., 10am-4pm Sat.), visitors will find what's arguably the island's most culturally authentic store, perpetuating traditional Hawaiian culture and values, and selling everything from textbooks printed in Hawaiian to traditional lei-making supplies. You'll also find hand-carved weaponry, jewelry, and immaculate colorful feather-work, and occasional classes help introduce visitors to traditional Hawaiian culture. For anyone with an interest in traditional culture, this store is a must-visit.

Near the corner of Market and Main Streets is **Maui Thing** (7 N. Market St., 808/249-0215, www.mauithing.com, 10am-5pm Mon.-Fri., 10am-4pm Sat.), a clothing store that focuses on Maui-themed clothing and has Hawaiian books for the *keiki* (kids). This is a great store for unique Maui clothing you won't find anywhere else on the island.

Just next door is **If the Shoe Fits** (21 N. Market St., 808/249-9710, www.teriedmonds. com, 10am-5pm Mon.-Fri., 10am-2pm Sat.), which has specialty footwear and repairs.

For men's aloha shirts and women's clothing, **Ha Wahine** (53 Market St., 808/344-1642, 11am-3pm Mon.-Sat.) is a clothing boutique featuring clothes made on Maui, with many featuring native designs and traditional Hawaiian patterns.

Across the street is a longtime Wailuku institution, **Request Music** (10 N. Market St., 808/244-9315, 10am-6pm Mon.-Sat.), the last holdout of true island record shops, kept alive by loyal music lovers who still want to feel the vinyl, admire the album covers, and talk with people who *really* love music. Most of the merchandise caters to the reggae and roots lifestyle, but the basement is filled with music that goes back decades.

Just a few doors down, **Sandell Artworks** (34 N. Market St., 808/249-2456, hours vary) brings creative color and flare to funky Market Street, where paintings and prints run the gamut of characters and oddities of Maui.

At the far end of Market Street are two local water sports stores, **TriPaddle Maui** (54 N. Market St., 808/243-7235, www.tripaddlemaui.com, 10am-5pm Mon.-Fri., 10am-3pm Sat.), which specializes in accessories for outrigger paddle sports, and **Maui Sporting Goods** (92 N. Market St., 808/244-0011, 9am-6pm Mon.-Fri., 9am-5pm Sat.), the de facto fishing headquarters for most of Maui's anglers.

The string of pawn shops along Market Street always have some good deals, and at **Kama'aina Loan** (98 N. Market St., 808/242-5555, www.kamaainaloan.com, 9am-5pm Mon.-Fri., 10am-4pm Sat.-Sun.), you'll find everything from surfboards to ukuleles to ritual drums used by Nepalese shamans.

Entertainment

KAHULUI
Daytime Entertainment

There are free hula shows at the **Maui Mall** (70 E. Kaʻahumanu Ave., 808/877-8952, www. mauimall.com) at 11am Sunday, and a calendar of other events can be found on the website. Across town, the **Queen Kaʻahumanu Shopping Center** (275 W. Kaʻahumanu Ave., 808/877-3369, www.queenkaahumanucenter.com) offers free hula shows at 10:30am Monday, followed at 12:30pm by Polynesian crafting. Similarly, a full calendar of events can be found on the website.

Evening Shows

The best option for evening entertainment in Kahului is the **Maui Arts and Cultural Center** (1 Cameron Way, 808/242-7469, www.mauiarts.org), where a constantly changing schedule of live concerts, movies, exhibits, comedy shows, and family events takes place most nights of the week. Multiple events often happen on the same evening. Check the website for a list of upcoming events.

Bars

The best bar in Kahului is the **Kahului Ale House** (355 E. Kaʻahumanu Ave., 808/877-9001, www.kahuluialehouse.com, 11am-midnight Mon.-Sat., 7am-midnight Sun.), which has live music every night and 24 beers on draft. There are 40 TVs for watching the game, as well as ice-cold beer, surprisingly good sushi, and happy hours 3pm-7pm and 9:30pm-11:30pm.

If you would rather visit a smaller bar in a darker, more intimate setting, **Koho's Grill and Bar** (275 W. Kaʻahumanu Ave., 808/877-5588, 7am-10pm Sun.-Thurs., 7am-11:30pm Fri.-Sat.) inside the Queen Kaʻahumanu Shopping Center is a longtime local favorite, with daily drink specials and a casual crowd of margarita-sipping locals.

WAILUKU

Market Street is closed to vehicular traffic 5:30pm-9pm the first Friday of every month, and the area becomes a festive pedestrian thoroughfare. There's live music in Banyan Tree Park, street performers, food concessions from local restaurants, activities for children, and a beer garden for the adults. This is the original and most popular of the **Maui Friday Town Parties** (www.mauifridays. com/wailuku).

Shows

A couple of times per year, theatrical shows take place inside historic **ʻIao Theater** (68 N. Market St.), a Spanish mission-style theater that was opened in 1928. Listed on the National Register of Historic Places, the ʻIao is Hawaii's oldest theater and has hosted performers such as Bob Hope and Frank Sinatra over its lengthy history. For updated showtimes, visit **MauiOnStage** (www.mauionstage.com).

Bars

If you're a fan of completely unpretentious dive bars, **Steel Horse Saloon** (1234 Lower Main St., 808/243-2200, 10am-2am daily) is where Wailuku locals go to let off some steam. With pool tables, karaoke, live music, and TVs, the Steel Horse Saloon has the comfortable feel of a casual corner bar, where everyone seems to know everyone's name, yet visitors are certainly welcome. The drinks are cheap (none of those tourist prices around here), and you'll get the chance to mingle with locals instead of lei-wearing visitors. It's open late, there are occasionally DJs, and it's the place to go to get weird.

Just down the street, **Tiffany's Bar and Grill** (1424 Lower Main St., 808/249-0052, www.tiffanysmaui.com, 10:30am-2am daily, food until 11:30pm Mon.-Sat., 10:30pm Sun.) is another longtime Lower Main Street institution that caters to a heavily local crowd. Karaoke is the name of the game here, and unlike the Steel Horse, this has a full-service restaurant that serves surprisingly good local food.

Food

KAHULUI

American

If hunger strikes on the way toward Lahaina, a convenient option is **Café O'Lei** (1333 Maui Lani Pkwy., 808/877-0073, 8:30am-4pm Mon., 8:30am-7:30pm Tues.-Sun.) in the Dunes at Maui Lani clubhouse. There's an outdoor patio that looks out over the golf course as well as a full bar. Sandwiches and burgers are an affordable $8-10, and entrée items such as tiger shrimp linguine are $12-14. Breakfast is served until 10:30am.

Coffee Shops

For local coffee beans, head to **Maui Coffee Roasters** (444 Hana Hwy., 808/877-2877, www.mauicoffeeroasters.com, 7am-6pm Mon.-Fri., 8am-5pm Sat., 8am-2:30pm Sun., $9), the best little coffee shop in town. In the same shopping complex as Marco's Grill and Deli, Maui Coffee Roasters has an assortment of brews made from Maui, Kona, Kaua'i, and Moloka'i beans. The full breakfast and lunch menu features bagels, breakfast wraps, sandwiches, and salads, and there are multiple tables and free Wi-Fi. It's five minutes from the airport.

If you're just trying you get a quick cup on the go, **Akamai Coffee** (100 Pakaula St., 808/575-9891, www.akamaicoffee.com, 6am-5pm Mon.-Fri., 6:30am-5pm Sat., 7am-1pm Sun.) is a drive-through coffee shop in the Home Depot parking lot that has some of the island's best coffee, despite the location. The beans are grown and roasted on Maui. To really save time, call in your order ahead of time, and it's ready in 15 minutes.

Culinary Academy

To play a role in the next generation of Maui's most talented chefs, reserve a table at ★ **Lei's Family Class Act** (310 W. Ka'ahumanu Ave., 808/984-3280, www.mauiculinary.sodexomyway.com/classact, 11am-12:30pm Wed. and Fri.), where students of the Maui Culinary Academy gain real-world experience. The students perform all roles and serve a four-course Latin, Asian, Italian, French, or Moroccan fine-dining menu that changes each week. See the website, updated each semester, for specific menus and dates. Since it's only open twice per week, advance reservations are strongly recommended. Depending on the entrée, the prix fixe menu ranges $29-41 pp, and there's no corkage fee if you bring your own wine.

Filipino

For Filipino dishes that are so authentic you would think you were in Manila, **Bistro Manila** (230 Hana Hwy., 808/871-6934, 10am-2pm and 5pm-8:30pm Mon.-Sat., $9-15) is where the top island chefs go to get some culinary inspiration. While there is no liquor license, you are free to pair your *pancit, sisig,* or pan-fried *bangus* with beer or wine that you bring in yourself.

German

Industrial Kahului is the last place you would expect to find a Bavarian après-ski lodge, but **Brigit and Bernard's Garden Café** (335 Ho'ohana St., 808/877-6000, 11am-2:30pm Mon., 11am-2:30pm and 5pm-9:30pm Tues.-Fri., 5pm-9:30pm Sat., www.brigitandbernards.net, $16-32) pumps out authentic stick-to-your-ribs German fare. The vaulted A-frame ceiling is hung with colorful steins, cross-country skis, and posters of alpine ski resorts. Order a massive plate of bratwurst or schnitzel served with a huge potato *rosti* and wash it down with a Bitburger brew.

Hawaiian

Usually the only time you get Hawaiian food is when you attend a luau, but here at humble ★ **Poi by the Pound** (385 Hoʻohana St., 808/283-9381, 10am-8pm Mon.-Thurs., 10am-9pm Fri.-Sat., $12-20), in industrial Kahului, the kalua pig, *lau lau, poke,* and poi are just as good—if not better—than food you'd find at a luau. To go full-on local, order the Hawaiian Plate ($19), packed with Hawaiian favorites, or get teriyaki chicken or *kalbi* ribs, made to order on the grill. Fresh poi is available for purchase, and pick up a block of sweet *kulolo,* made from taro and coconut milk.

Italian

The finest restaurant in Kahului, **Bistro Casanova** (33 Lono Ave., 808/873-3850, www.bistrocasanova.com, 11am-9:30pm Mon.-Sat., $14-38) livens up downtown with a fusion of Mediterranean and Italian cuisine. The tapas menu, served after 3pm, has crostinis, gnocchi, and grilled calamari, and a swanky bar attracts the after-work cocktail crowd.

For a quick slice of pizza, check out **Pizza in Paradise** (60 E. Wakea Ave., 808/871-8188, www.pizza-maui.com, 11am-9pm Mon.-Thurs., 11am-10pm Fri.-Sat., $13-26), a family-run joint that makes its own dough and sauce. Whole pies are available, but the "by the slice" option is nice for lunch on the go. The menu also has subs and pasta, but it's the pizza that keeps locals walking through the door. The location is obscure; parking is around back.

Japanese

The best Japanese in Kahului is at **Ichiban Restaurant** (65 W. Kaʻahumanu Ave., 808/871-6977, 7am-2pm and 5pm-9pm Mon.-Fri., 11:30am-2pm and 5pm-9pm Sat., $8-12) in the Kahului Shopping Center. Rainbow rolls and heaping bowls of *udon* punctuate

the menu, and cap it all off with a Kirin beer or a cup of sake.

For the Japanese restaurant equivalent of a dive bar, **Restaurant Matsu** (161 Alamaha St., 808/871-0822, 10am-3pm and 5pm-7:30pm Mon.-Fri., 10am-2pm Sat.) is a local favorite for affordable ramen and plate lunch. Try the flavorful *shoyu* ramen or a spam *katsu musubi,* and order at the counter before settling in for an authentic, surprisingly good meal.

Local Style

Let's get one thing straight: The enormous plate lunch dishes at ★ **Da Kitchen** (425 Koloa St., 808/871-7782, www.da-kitchen.com, 11am-9pm Mon.-Sat., $10-17) are the best on the entire island. Da Kitchen is the gravy-covered gold standard that all other plate lunch is measured by—it even helped serve the food at President Obama's first inauguration.

Da Kitchen is tucked in the same strip mall as HI-Tech Surf Sports and Denny's—just look for the huge sign that says "Restaurant"—and despite the somewhat obscure location, the place is always packed. Some of the items are big enough to split (lunch for under $20), and for a tasty albeit artery-clogging meal, go all-in with fried spam *musubi* followed by Polynesian Paralysis Moco: fish tempura, kalua pork, two eggs, onion, mushrooms, and gravy over fried rice.

Mexican

For quick and authentic Mexican food, visit **Las Piñatas** (395 Dairy Rd., 808/877-8707, www.pinatasmaui.com, 8am-8pm Mon.-Sat., 9am-8pm Sun., $7-10), next to Kinko's off Dairy Road. The Kitchen Sink burrito is so big that a growing teenager will have trouble cleaning the plate. Pair with a bottle of beer or *horchata.*

Just down the road from Las Piñatas is **Amigos** (333 Dairy Rd., 808/872-9525, www.amigosmaui.com, 10am-9pm Mon.-Fri., 9am-9pm Sat.-Sun., $8-12), where daily specials (two burritos for $14) make this a cheap place to eat while in town. The main difference between Amigos and Las Piñatas is that Amigos features a small bar where you can order a margarita, get Mexican beers on draft, or cap off your *carnitas* with a shot of Patrón.

Natural Foods

If you're vegetarian or vegan, you'll love the deli inside ★ **Down to Earth** (305 Dairy Rd., 808/877-2661, www.downtoearth.org, 7am-9pm Mon.-Sat., 7am-8pm Sun.) grocery store. At only $8, the "Fresh Mex" burrito is both filling and affordable, and you can save time by ordering online at www.dtedeli.org. Since it's on the road between the airport and Lahaina, this is one of the few places in Kahului for a quick and healthy meal on the go.

The other option is **Alive and Well** (340 Hana Hwy., 808/877-4950, www.aliveandwell-inmaui.com, 8am-7pm Mon.-Fri., 8am-6pm Sat., 10am-5pm Sun.) a health emporium that has deli sandwiches, organic juice, and smoothies. There's also *kombucha* on tap!

Shave Ice

If you find yourself driving to the airport and suddenly realize you never got shave ice, the most popular place in town is **Ululani's** (333 Dairy Rd., 808/877-3700, www.ululanis-shaveice.com, 10:30am-6pm daily), located in a kiosk by the Wow-Wee Maui Kava Bar and Grill.

WAILUKU

Old-school Wailuku is quietly becoming one of Maui's best places for food. Don't expect oceanfront tiki torches like you'd find at restaurants in Lahaina, since the atmosphere here is far more "authentic" in the run-down and real local sort of way. Prices are lower because rents are lower, and the wealth of affordable international cuisine is starting to garner attention.

American

Located inside the Maui Tropical Plantation, ★ **The Mill House** (1670 Honoapiʻilani Hwy., 808/270-0333, www.mauitropicalplantation.com, 11am-3pm and 5pm-9pm Mon.-Sat., 8pm-close Sun.) has gone completely next-level with the concept of farm-to-table. Nearly everything is sourced on the island, with much of it grown on the farm, and it's the island's only restaurant where the meat arrives as a whole animal and is processed on-site. Aside from the freshness, there's a creative and innovative culinary genius to all of the flavorful plates, ordered tapas-style and shared around the table. While the menu changes around what's in season, favorites include the pork *ragù* gnocchi or the beet pickled egg salad, and an extensive wine list, with 60-plus wines, accompanies the French-press coffee. Hard-core foodies can attend the **Maui Chef's Table** (6pm-9pm Fri.-Sat., $150 pp), where executive chef Jeff Scheer prepares dishes that were thought up just hours before and have yet to make it on the menu. This exclusive event only has 36 seats, and reservations are strongly recommended.

The "fanciest" food in Wailuku is **Aria's** (2062 W. Vineyard St., 808/242-2742, www.ariasmaui.com, 10am-3pm and 5pm-8:30pm Mon.-Fri., 8:30am-3pm and 5pm-8:30pm Sat., 8:30am-2pm Sun.), a white-linen restaurant with resort-quality food at affordable Wailuku prices. The $11-13 lunch sandwiches include braised lamb and cucumber tzatziki, and dinner has entrées like scallop linguine for only $19. It's a surprising find in a funky part of town.

Just half a block from Market Street is **808 on Main** (2051 Main St., 808/242-1111, www.808onmain.com, 10am-7pm Mon.-Fri.), where you can get filling *paninis,* sandwiches, and salads with creative culinary flare. Try the chicken mango chutney *panini* served on sourdough with pepper-jack cheese ($10), or a toasted wasabi hoagie roll with roast beef and wasabi aioli ($11). In addition to standard wine ($7 per glass) and beer, you'll also find a Beer & a Shot menu with drink combos ($8). Angry Orchard and Crown Royal, anyone? Historic black-and-white photos of Wailuku are the basic decor.

Central Maui Food Trucks

Central Maui is the island's epicenter for quirky gourmet food trucks, and the prices compare with most of the island's budget restaurants. Expect entrées to cost $8-13, and while locations can vary, here's where you can usually find them:

FOOD TRUCK PARK ACROSS FROM COSTCO

Only five minutes from the airport, this tight little cluster of food trucks has everything from fried *poke* and ahi *katsu* at local favorite **Like Poke?** to $10 plates of chicken pad thai at the **Thai Me Up** food truck. You'll also find local plate lunch at **Mama T's Molokai Grindz,** and three tacos for $5 at **Maui 8 Wonder Tacos.** The food truck park (10am-4pm Mon.-Tues., 10am-8pm Wed.-Fri.) is located across from the Costco gas station on Haleakala Highway.

KAHULUI HARBOR

In the dirt parking area across from the Maui Arts and Cultural Center you'll find **Geste Shrimp Truck** (Kahului Beach Rd., 808/298-7109, 10:45am-5pm Tues.-Sat., cash only), where $12 gets you 12 pieces of shrimp served with crab macaroni salad and two scoops of rice. Based on the aroma of shrimp emanating from the white truck, it's no surprise that it often runs out of food before 5pm. Next door, you'll find **Lau Hee Chicken Hekka** and their local-style plate lunch of sweet salty chicken, as well as a handful of other trucks that occasionally set up shop.

MAUI FRESH STREATERY

With its rotating menu of global cuisine, **Maui Fresh Streatery** (137 Ka'ahumanu Ave., 808/344-7929, 11am-1pm Mon., Wed., and Fri.) has reached legendary status in Maui's food truck community. Just how popular is this gourmet food truck with the obscure Kahului location? It's only open six hours per week and never has trouble selling out. For nearly 10 years, chef Kyle Kawakami was a teaching professor at Maui's Culinary Academy, and he's now the overlord of a global menu that changes by the week, including chicken *katsu* curry and Furikake Fries as well as the Tres Cerditos Cubano pork sandwich. The tip jar is donated to local nonprofits, and nothing on the menu costs over $10. Since the schedule can be irregular, check ahead on social media for location and hours; you can usually find it in the parking lot of the Shell gas station.

For a Wailuku classic that's easy on the wallet, **Tasty Crust** (1770 Mill St., 808/244-0845, 6am-3pm Mon., 6am-10pm Tues.-Thurs., 6am-11pm Fri.-Sat., cash only) is an old-school working-class diner in a working-class part of town that has been feeding Wailuku for over 50 years. Breakfast is the time to stop by for a stack of their famous hotcakes. Not only are the banana pancakes tasty and filling, but at $5.50 they're also affordable. Best of all, breakfast is served all day, and this is a true local dining experience with local people.

Bakeries

Wailuku is the island's epicenter for bakeries, and none is more popular than **Home Maid Bakery** (1005 L. Main St., 808/244-7015, www.homemaidbakery.com, 5am-10pm daily), which has been serving their famous *malasadas* and *manju* since 1960. Plain *malasadas* cost $0.86, cream-filled are $1.35, and both are available 5am-10am and again 4pm-10pm.

For pumpkin scones that might change your life, visit **Simply Sweets** (1910 E. Vineyard St., 808/269-2113, 6am-3pm Sun.-Fri.), which is little more than a take-out stand with a lone seat out front. You'll also find cream-filled *malasadas* ($2), cream puffs, and other baked goods. This corner stand is a local favorite for pastry patrons in the know.

Coffee Shops

Wailuku Coffee Company (26 N. Market St., 808/495-0259, 7am-5pm Mon.-Sat.,

8am-3pm Sun., $5-8) is where "the hip come to sip." For breakfast, served until 10:30am, try a bacon, tomato, and avocado bagel served with a layer of cream cheese ($9), and for lunch try a gluten-free Life Foods burger ($11), made on Maui. You'll also find pastries, Wi-Fi, smoothies, and "pitza" served on pita bread.

Fijian

The only place on the island for Indo-Fijian cuisine is **Jini's Curry** (2050 Main St., 808/243-3454, www.fijiindianfood. com, 10:30am-3:30pm Mon., Wed., and Fri., 10:30am-6:30pm Tues. and Thurs., 11:30am-3:30pm Sat.), in the Wailuku Promenade, a small food court on Main Street in the heart of historic Wailuku. The spices are subtler, or "island style," compared to traditional Indian, and roti is used instead of naan to accompany the flavorful curries. For an affordable snack, grab a $3 vegan samosa that's topped with mango chutney.

Italian

Family-owned ★ **Giannotto's Pizza** (2050 Main St., 808/244-8282, www.giannot-tospizza.com, 11am-9pm Mon.-Sat., 11am-8pm Sun., $7) serves up homemade Italian recipes "just like Mama used to make." Located next to the Wailuku Promenade, this place is as authentic as the "Joisey" accents emanating from the kitchen. Photos of mafiosi adorn the wall, pizza by the slice is $2-4, and there's free delivery on orders over $20.

Local Style

At ★ **Sam Sato's** (1750 Wili Pa Loop, 808/244-7124, 7am-2pm Mon.-Sat., bakery until 4pm, cash only, $6), you'll probably wonder if this is really the famous restaurant, hidden deep with the Wailuku mill yard in a building you can't even see from the road. This family-run institution has been providing Wailuku plate lunch and famous *manju* pastries since the 1930s. It's the dry noodles that make Sam Sato's legendary, served with a side of homemade broth and topped with char

siu pork and sprouts, making an affordable and addictive meal.

To order lunch like a Wailuku local, **Ichiban Okazuya** (2133 Kaohu St., 808/244-7276, 10am-8pm Mon.-Fri.) has arguably the best chicken *katsu* on Maui. You can also get tempura shrimp and veggies piled high with rice. This authentic hole-in-the-wall is takeout only. At peak times the line can be out the door, though the staff is surprisingly fast.

Natural Foods

For your daily fix of açaí and kale, head straight to ★ **The Farmacy Health Bar** (12 N. Market St., 808/866-4312, 7:30am-5:30pm Mon.-Fri., 9am-5pm Sat., 10am-4pm Sun., $6-9), where you can also score a dragon fruit smoothie or an açaí bowl with poi. Expect GMO-free organic ingredients and a strong community following.

Thai

A funky hole-in-the-wall that really has some good food in the heart of run-down Vineyard Street, ★ **Saeng's Thai Cuisine** (2119 W. Vineyard St., 808/244-1567, 11am-2:30pm and 5pm-9:30pm Mon.-Fri., $9-12) has pad thai and curries that are as tasty and authentic as they come. Pair your meal with a Singha beer or a glass of surprisingly good wine. The peaceful setting is a hidden find in the heart of industrial Wailuku.

Vietnamese

Sandwiched between a bridge and a low-income housing unit is one of Maui's most popular Vietnamese venues, ★ **A Saigon Café** (1792 Main St., 808/243-9560, 10am-9:30pm Mon.-Sat., 10am-8pm Sun., $9-15). From the moment you step inside this place, you feel like you're in Vietnam, and it's a cultural as well as culinary experience that's well off the tourist radar. Opt for $12 clay pot dishes with rice, chicken, and vegetables, or try the *pho, banh hoi*, or tasty Vietnamese soup. The portions are enormous, the place is always packed, and if locals recommend eating at "Jennifer's," this is the place they mean.

Getting There and Around

CAR
Rental Cars

At the Kahului Airport, **Hertz** (808/893-5200), **Avis** (808/871-7575), **Budget** (808/871-8811), **Enterprise** (808/871-6982), **Alamo** (888/826-6893), and **Thrifty** (808/847-4389) all offer the standard corporate options for island rental cars. Other options in Kahului (which are often cheaper) include **Maui Car Rentals** (181 Dairy Rd., 808/877-3300, www.mauicarrentals.net), **Aloha Rent A Car** (190 Papa Place, 808/877-2436, www.mauirentacar.com), **Kimo's Rent A Car** (440 Alamaha St., 808/280-6327, www.kimosrentacar.com), and the budget service **Discount Hawaii Car Rental** (800/292-1930, www.discounthawaiicarrental.com).

If you're thinking of getting a 4WD vehicle, don't—you won't need it. The only time you need 4WD in Maui is for Skyline Drive in Polipoli, or for peace of mind on the back road to Hana. Many visitors spend a lot of money on 4WD, often double the price of a regular car, and never end up using it. Rent a 4WD vehicle just for the day if you need it.

MOTORCYCLE

If the idea of zipping ocean-side on a massive Harley is your preferred method of getting from A to B, **Maui Harley Davidson** (150 Dairy Rd., 808/831-2614, www.hawaiiharleyrental.com, 9am-5pm daily) offers rentals from the Kahului shop only five minutes from Kahului Airport.

BUS

The Queen Ka'ahumanu Shopping Center is the central hub of the **Maui Bus,** and if you are connecting from one bus to another, there is a good chance that you'll end up making a stop at the mall. All segments on the bus cost $2 pp (or $4 pp for a day pass), and this is the terminus and starting point for routes heading up-country as well as to Kihei and Lahaina.

If you're just trying to get across town, buses on the Wailuku Loop (bus 1) make various stops around Wailuku and run hourly 6:30am-9:30pm daily. Similarly, buses on the Kahului Loop (bus 5) make various stops around Kahului and run hourly 6:30am-9pm daily. If you're trying to get to the Kahului Airport from Queen Ka'ahumanu, you have to get on the Upcountry Islander bus (bus 40), which runs every 90 minutes 6:10am-9:10pm daily. For more information, a full schedule, or to see routes to other parts of the island, visit www.mauicounty.gov and navigate to "For Residents" and then "Maui Bus."

Kihei and South Maui

If one word defines South Maui, it's "beaches." South Maui is graced with dozens of sandy stretches just waiting for your footprints.

The island's longest beach is Sugar Beach; one of its smallest is Pa'ako Cove. The sound of waves lapping against the palm-lined sand is a year-round reality in South Maui. There are enough beaches that a three-week vacation isn't enough time to possibly see them all. Because much of South Maui actually faces west, the end of each day is punctuated by a sunset that somehow outdoes the last.

It's also one of the state's hottest areas, particularly in Kihei, where the smell of coconut oil wafts on the late-morning trade winds. Mornings are for stand-up paddling and snorkeling, whereas afternoons are for finding a cold drink and settling in for the sunset. At the Maui Ocean Center in Ma'alaea, you can explore the beauty of the underwater world regardless of the conditions outside, and at Molokini Crater, set just offshore, you can snorkel, dive, splash, and swim in Maui's clearest waters.

This is also Maui's fastest growing zip code, where rows of condos and luxury resorts seem to populate every shore. Despite the hypercharged growth, however, there's still a wild side in South Maui once you venture south toward Makena, where nudist drum circles still take place on the hidden sands of Little Beach, and hiking trails follow a rocky shore that was once the pathway of kings.

ORIENTATION

South Maui runs in a long narrow column and is never far from the coast. To drive from Ma'alaea, the northernmost part, to the end of the road in Makena, takes approximately 30 minutes and passes through Kihei and Wailea. The high-end resorts are found in Wailea, whereas Kihei is laden with oceanfront condos and more affordable options for dining. Makena is where the coast gets wild and development disappears, yet it is close enough to the Wailea resorts to reach by pedaling a bike. Kihei, the commercial hub of South Maui, is sandwiched in a strip between South Kihei Road and Pi'ilani Highway, whereas Ma'alaea is the site of the harbor and the windy gateway to West Maui.

Previous: Keawakapu Beach at sunrise; a Hawaiian green sea turtle, or *honu*, off Wailea. **Above:** playing in the waves.

Highlights

★ **Maui Ocean Center:** Surround yourself with sharks, eagle rays, and dozens of fish, all without getting your hair wet (page 129).

★ **Hawaiian Islands Humpback Whale National Marine Sanctuary Visitors Center:** Learn about Maui's most exciting winter visitors in an oceanfront setting by Koʻieʻie Fishpond (page 130).

★ **Keawakapu Beach:** While the northern end of Keawakapu Beach teems with activity, the southern expanse is a peaceful getaway for a blanket and a book (page 134).

★ **Maluaka Beach:** The perfect place for a morning stand-up paddle is along Makena's historic coast (page 136).

★ **Makena State Park:** There are actually three beaches within the state park, known to most locals simply as "Big Beach." The sunsets are legendary (page 137).

★ **Molokini Crater:** The water inside this offshore caldera is some of the clearest in the world. The snorkeling ranks as some of the best in the state, and the scuba diving is some of the best in the world (page 139).

★ **Ulua Beach and Mokapu Beach:** These protected, sandy beaches offer friendly snorkeling conditions and an abundance of marinelife (page 145).

★ **Hoapili Trail:** This ancient footpath of kings meanders through the island's most recent lava flows. Wander deserted Hawaiian fishing villages whose stone foundations stand frozen in time (page 159).

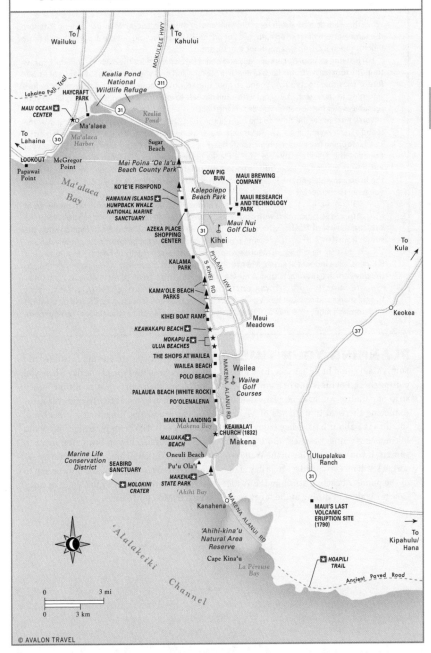

South Maui

To Wailuku

To Kahului

MOKULELE HWY

Lahaina Pali Trail

Kealia Pond National Wildlife Refuge

311

HAYCRAFT PARK

31

MAUI OCEAN CENTER

Kealia Pond

Ma'alaea

To Lahaina

30

Ma'alaea Harbor

Sugar Beach

LOOKOUT

McGregor Point

Mai Poina 'Oe Ia'u Beach County Park

COW PIG BUN

MAUI BREWING COMPANY

Papawai Point

Ma'alaea Bay

KO'IE'IE FISHPOND

Kalepolepo Beach Park

MAUI RESEARCH AND TECHNOLOGY PARK

HAWAIIAN ISLANDS HUMPBACK WHALE NATIONAL MARINE SANCTUARY

AZEKA PLACE SHOPPING CENTER

Maui Nui Golf Club

31

Kihei

To Kula

KALAMA PARK

S KIHEI RD

PIILANI HWY

KAMA'OLE BEACH PARKS

KIHEI BOAT RAMP

Maui Meadows

Keokea

KEAWAKAPU BEACH

37

MOKAPU & ULUA BEACHES

THE SHOPS AT WAILEA

MAKENA ALANUI RD

WAILEA BEACH

Wailea

POLO BEACH

Wailea Golf Courses

PALAUEA BEACH (WHITE ROCK)

PO'OLENALENA

MAKENA LANDING

Makena Bay

KEAWALA'I CHURCH (1832)

MALUAKA BEACH

Makena

Oneuli Beach

Ulupalakua Ranch

Marine Life Conservation District

SEABIRD SANCTUARY

Pu'u Ola'i

31

MAKENA STATE PARK

MOLOKINI CRATER

'Ahihi Bay

MAKENA ALANUI RD

Kanahena

MAUI'S LAST VOLCANIC ERUPTION SITE (1790)

'Alalakeiki Channel

'Ahihi-kina'u Natural Area Reserve

To Kipahulu/ Hana

Cape Kina'u

La Pérouse Bay

HOAPILI TRAIL

Ancient Paved Road

0   3 mi

0   3 km

Your Best Day in South Maui

While there are dozens of different combinations for the perfect South Maui day, all tend to follow the same pattern of wake up early, get out on the water, and round out the day with beach time, lunch, more beach time, happy hour, and sunset.

For just one example, wake up early and board *Kai Kanani* for the 6:30am Molokini Express tour. The tour leaves from Maluaka Beach in Makena and gets you out to **Molokini Crater** before all the other boats arrive. Spend an hour snorkeling and enjoy continental breakfast before returning to the beach at 8:30am with a full day left to explore. If you get a chance, fill up your reusable water bottle before you depart the boat.

You'll next make the drive to the "end of the road," hugging the coast and passing over the island's most recent lava flow. To stretch your legs, hike for 30 to 45 minutes on the **Hoapili Trail,** stopping to photograph the sandy beaches and watch for dolphins or whales. Back at your car, make the drive to **Makena State Park,** better known as **Big Beach,** and grab a quick lunch from whichever food truck is parked outside the First Entrance. Spend an hour strolling the beach or watching the local bodyboarders, and drive back to Maluaka Beach in Makena if you need to shower off.

At 4:30pm, park in the lot for Ulua Beach and walk to the Wailea Marriott, where dishes at **Migrant** are 50 percent off with drink specials until 6pm. Finish the day with a stroll along the **Wailea Coastal Walk,** where you can walk north past **Mokapu Beach** and watch the sunset from **Keawakapu**—leaving time to get back to your car before it's completely dark.

Rainy Day? Rain in South Maui is exceptionally rare, and virtually unheard of in summer, but if it rains, dine indoors at **Chez Meme** with French toast made with homemade brioche. On the drive north to Ma'alaea, stop at the **Hawaiian Islands Humpback Whale National Marine Sanctuary Visitors Center** before continuing on to the **Maui Ocean Center** to ogle sharks and rays. Get lunch downstairs at **Beach Bums Bar and Grill,** and on the drive back through Kihei, stop at **Maui Brewing Company** for a pint at their indoor tasting room.

PLANNING YOUR TIME

South Maui could be either your base for exploring the rest of the island or a sunny, sandy strip of paradise you have no plans to leave. Exploring the wild hinterlands of Makena should take about half a day, enjoying the hiking, snorkeling, beaches, and legendary sunsets. If you aren't staying in the Wailea resort, it's still nice to spend a whole day at one of the popular beaches, strolling the Wailea Coastal Walk and dining at the fancy resort restaurants. If you are staying in Wailea, do yourself a favor and spend one day where you don't leave the resort—just pool time, beach time, and maybe a massage to enjoy the luxurious surroundings. Kihei, on the other hand, deserves two days: two mornings to try out two different beaches and two afternoons to try out two different lunch spots. Ma'alaea requires only a few hours, as the only reason to go is to visit the Maui Ocean Center or catch a boat to Molokini Crater.

Sights

MA'ALAEA
★ Maui Ocean Center

There isn't a snorkeling spot on the island where you're going to see as wide a range of marinelife as at the **Maui Ocean Center** (192 Ma'alaea Rd., 808/270-7000, www.maui-oceancenter.com, 9am-5pm daily Sept.-June, 9am-6pm daily July-Aug., $28 adults, $20 children). This three-acre marine park has the nation's largest collection of live tropical coral, and small children will enjoy the tide-pool exhibits and the green sea turtle lagoon. Experience the 54-foot-long acrylic tunnel beneath a 750,000-gallon aquarium filled with dozens of rays and sharks, standing in a dry space and watching a tiger shark float right over you, or contemplating how spotted eagle rays look like birds as they buzz circles just a few feet from your head.

The center is deeply committed to educating visitors about the unique marine ecosystem. Did you know, for example, that nearly 25 percent of Hawaii's fish and coral species are found nowhere else on earth? The center is also a fantastic resource for learning about native Hawaiian culture, with exhibits on everything from Polynesian wayfaring to ancient Hawaiian fishponds. The center is set up to provide the animals with a realistic environment, and trained naturalists wander the grounds and give periodic talks about the various exhibits.

This is one of the island's best attractions for children as well as a rainy-day activity. Its popularity can mean crowds, however, so visit in the morning when the facility opens. There's a self-guided tour through the exhibits, and if you want to have some of them all to yourself, head directly to the last exhibit and work your way backward toward the front. Expect to spend about two hours, and if you purchase your tickets online beforehand, you can also add transportation ($5 pp). Book online for the family pass to save up to 15 percent.

Kihei

Kihei's main draws are the beaches and weather, and in the morning it can seem like half the town is running, snorkeling, or

underwater magic at the Maui Ocean Center

stand-up paddling. In ancient Hawaii, the Kihei area was called Kamaole, which translates as "barren." Even during World War II, the soft, gently sloping beaches were used by the military as practice zones for amphibious landing craft, since no one was around. Today there are a sea of snorkelers, boogie boarders, and beach umbrellas. Even with the recent growth, however, there are still a few places to get back to nature or catch a glimpse of the past.

Kealia Pond National Wildlife Refuge

The road between Maʻalaea and North Kihei passes through a large mudflat that parallels the shore. Most of this area is dry during summer, but on the inland side of the highway is 200-acre **Kealia Pond National Wildlife Refuge** (www.fws.gov/kealiapond). Visit to catch a glimpse of native bird species such as the *aeʻo* (Hawaiian stilt) and *ʻalae keʻokeʻo* (Hawaiian coot). Even if you aren't an avid birder, the boardwalk off North Kihei Road is an informative place to stretch your legs and learn about the threats facing the island's species.

Koʻieʻie Loko Iʻa Fishpond

Inside Kalepolepo Beach Park in North Kihei, the **Koʻieʻie Loko Iʻa Fishpond** is the most prominent example of ancient Hawaiian life between Maʻalaea and Wailea. Estimated to be around 500 years old, it covered six acres and produced about 2,000 pounds of fish annually. It was formed by rocks passed by hand from the uplands to the sea, and thanks to the hard work of the **ʻAoʻao O Na Loko Iʻa O Maui** (726 S. Kihei Rd., 808/359-1172, www.maui-fishpond.com)—volunteers who have been working since 1996 to restore the ancient fishpond—it can be viewed any time by visiting Kalepolepo Beach Park. For a unique experience, the organization offers guided cultural canoe trips at 8am Monday, Wednesday, and Friday for those who prearrange a visit.

★ Hawaiian Islands Humpback Whale National Marine Sanctuary Visitors Center

Right next door to Kalepolepo Beach Park is the **Hawaiian Islands Humpback Whale National Marine Sanctuary Visitors Center** (726 S. Kihei Rd., 808/879-2818, www.hawaiihumpbackwhale.noaa.gov, 10am-3pm Mon.-Sat., 10am-3pm Sat., free), a phenomenal educational resource for anyone with an

Kealia boardwalk

interest in humpback whales. You can find plates of baleen, krill in a jar, and free binoculars out on the deck to view the whales in winter. There are also displays on turtles, dolphins, and teams that untangle whales, and while it's a bit out of the way in North Kihei, it's an easy stop when traveling from Ma'alaea back to Kihei or Wailea. Aside from the exhibits, the center also boasts some unique architecture: the 1940s-era coastal clapboard structure, seemingly better suited to Nantucket than North Kihei. The Ko'ie'ie fishpond is in front of the compound, which makes this a fun and educational side trip when visiting Kalepolepo Beach.

Makena

Makena has the most evidence of ancient culture and history in South Maui. This rugged, lava-strewn shore was home to a thriving population of ancient Hawaiians, and was believed to be the most populated region in South Maui during pre-contact times. When diseases and foreign plant and animal species were introduced by European explorers, however, the combination of outside forces ravaged the indigenous population, and many of the villages in Makena were abandoned. In a fitting twist to the tale, Makena is also the landing site of the first European explorer to set foot on Maui's shore—French explorer Jean-François de Galaup, compte de Lapérouse, in 1786. Despite the amount of history in Makena, many of the archaeological and cultural remnants are either on private land, in cordoned-off sanctuaries, or scattered along the shore in areas such as the Hoapili Trail. One site is open to visitors, and it parallels the plight of Makena's indigenous people.

Keawala'i Church

In an area of the island that's developing rapidly, there's a timeless beauty to **Keawala'i Church** (5300 Makena Rd., 808/879-5557, www.keawalai.org). Set on a palm- and *ti*-lined cove and bathed in the gentle sound of the surf, Keawala'i was founded in 1832 and constructed in 1855. The original structure was made of *pili* grass, and this Protestant church served as one of the main centers of worship in southern Maui. The grass was eventually replaced with coral, and in 1856 the church raised $70 to purchase a bell from the United States, then a different country. It took that bell almost three years to travel to Hawaii, and in February 1862 it was lifted into the belfry, where it still hangs today.

historic Keawala'i Church in Makena

Ma'alaea Harbor

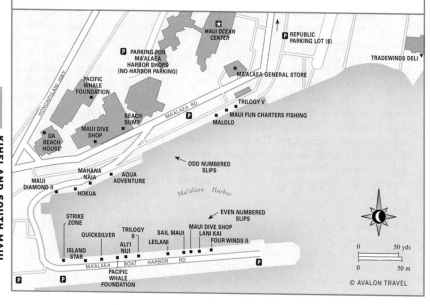

Unfortunately, in the mid-1800s, when Makena's streams began to run dry from excessive logging upslope, much of Makena's population moved elsewhere. Keawala'i slid into disrepair, and when it was pillaged by thieves in the years after World War II, the community opted to band together to bring the church back to life. Today, after 50 years of renovations, Keawala'i is as beautiful as at its height. United Church of Christ services are conducted in the Hawaiian language at 7:30am and 10am Sunday, although visits to the church grounds are possible any time of day.

Beaches

When it comes to beach weather, even though South Maui is dry, other elements such as the wind and clouds can greatly affect the comfort level. The closer you are to Ma'alaea, the earlier in the day it gets windy—particularly in the summer. Since the afternoon trade winds begin their march in Ma'alaea, they progressively move from north to south through Kihei, Wailea, and ultimately Makena. During trade-wind weather patterns, the "Makena cloud" forms over Haleakala and extends out toward the island of Kaho'olawe, although this doesn't normally happen until the early afternoon. Consequently, the morning hours are the best time to hit the beach. In the afternoon, the pocket of beaches in south Kihei and Wailea have the best chance of being sunny and calm. Winter months aren't as windy, and this is also when humpback whales can be seen leaping offshore. Is it any wonder so many snowbirds choose to spend the winter here?

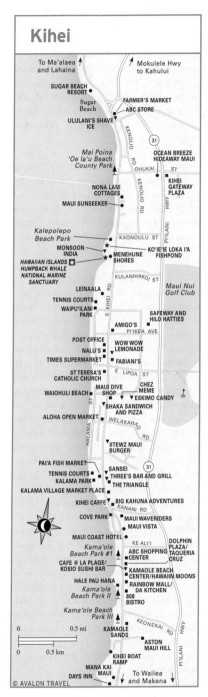

Kihei

To Ma'alaea and Lahaina
Mokulele Hwy to Kahului
SUGAR BEACH RESORT
Sugar Beach
FARMER'S MARKET
ABC STORE
ULULANI'S SHAVE ICE
KENOLIO RD
31
OCEAN BREEZE HIDEAWAY MAUI
Mai Poina 'Oe Ia'u Beach County Park
OHUKAI ST
KIHEI GATEWAY PLAZA
NONA LANI COTTAGES
KENOLIO RD
MAUI SUNSEEKER
PI'ILANI HWY
Kalepolepo Beach Park
KAONOULU ST
MONSOON INDIA
KO'IE'IE LOKA I'A FISHPOND
MENEHUNE SHORES
HAWAIIAN ISLANDS HUMPBACK WHALE NATIONAL MARINE SANCTUARY
KULANIHAKO'I ST
LEINAALA
Maui Nui Golf Club
S KIHEI RD
TENNIS COURTS
WAIPU'ILANI PARK
AMIGO'S
SAFEWAY AND HILO HATTIES
PI'IKEA AVE
POST OFFICE
WOW WOW LEMONADE
NALU'S
TIMES SUPERMARKET
FABIANI'S
ST TERESA'S CATHOLIC CHURCH
E LIPOA ST
CHEZ MEME
MAUI DIVE SHOP
WAIOHULI BEACH
ESKIMO CANDY
SHAKA SANDWICH AND PIZZA
ALOHA OPEN MARKET
HALAMA ST
WELAKAHAO RD
STEWZ MAUI BURGER
PAI'A FISH MARKET
SANSEI
31
TENNIS COURTS
THREE'S BAR AND GRILL
KALAMA PARK
THE TRIANGLE
KALAMA VILLAGE MARKET PLACE
KIHEI CAFFE
BIG KAHUNA ADVENTURES
KANANI RD
COVE PARK
MAUI WAVERIDERS
MAUI VISTA
MAUI COAST HOTEL
KE ALI'I
DOLPHIN PLAZA/ TAQUERIA CRUZ
Kama'ole Beach Park #1
ABC SHOPPING CENTER
CAFE @ LA PLAGE/ KOSIO SUSHI BAR
KAMAOLE BEACH CENTER/HAWAIIN MOONS
HALE PAU HANA
RAINBOW MALL/ DA KITCHEN
Kama'ole Beach Park II
808 BISTRO
Kama'ole Beach Park III
KEONEKAI RD
0   0.5 mi
KAMAOLE SANDS
0   0.5 km
ASTON MAUI HILL
KIHEI BOAT RAMP
PI'ILANI HWY
MANA KAI MAUI
DAYS INN
To Wailea and Makena
© AVALON TRAVEL

MA'ALAEA
Sugar Beach

If your picture-perfect vision of Hawaii is enjoying a long, lonely stroll down an isolated beach, **Sugar Beach** is going to be your favorite spot on the island. Bordered on one side by Kealia Pond National Wildlife Refuge and the waters of Ma'alaea Bay on the other, this undeveloped strip runs for five miles all the way to North Kihei.

There isn't any snorkeling here, although there can sometimes be waves for boogie boarding during summer. Rather, the main attraction here is taking a long, quiet stroll, and since most afternoons have very fierce trade winds, early morning is the best time to visit. To access Sugar Beach you can begin at the northern terminus at Haycraft Beach Park, the southern terminus in North Kihei, or at numerous entry points along North Kihei Road. If you park at Haycraft, be sure to lock your car—there are hidden homeless camps nearby.

KIHEI
Mai Poina 'Oe Ia'u Beach Park

On summer days with northerly winds, **Mai Poina 'Oe Ia'u Beach** is known as the "Kanaha of Kihei" for the windsurfing and kitesurfing crowd. In the morning hours, before the wind comes up, this beach is a nice place for taking a stroll and wandering around the dunes, and while there isn't any swimming and snorkeling is poor, there are picnic tables and pavilions for a meal by the water, and good stand-up paddling in the morning.

Kalepolepo Beach Park

Right next to the Hawaiian Islands Humpback Whale National Marine Sanctuary, **Kalepolepo Beach Park** is Kihei's most underrated beach. What makes this little-visited enclave so special is Ko'ie'ie Fishpond (page 130), which has been masterfully restored in recent years by local volunteers. Aside from its rich historical value, the fishpond is great for families with young children since it's a protected area for swimming.

Waipuilani Beach Park

Less beach and more park, this shoreline park in central Kihei is known to most locals as the dog park, since it's a popular place to run the family pet. It's a popular local gathering place—particularly for watching the sunset—and is one of North Kihei's most popular beaches, even though there's hardly any sand. To reach the parking area, turn on Waipuilani Road at the corner of South Kihei Road and the Maui Sunset condo.

The Cove

Otherwise known as "the surf lesson spot," this beach at the south end of Kalama Park is known for its top-notch people-watching. The beach itself is just a small strip of sand, but it provides a front-row view for watching people surf. There's a volleyball court and shops across the street, and while it isn't Kihei's nicest beach, it's an action-packed hub of surfers, paddlers, and beachgoers soaking up rays.

Kamaole I, II, and III

The **Kamaole Beach Parks** form the core of Kihei's beach scene. Grassy areas run parallel to the roadway, and all of the parks have showers, restrooms, picnic tables, and barbecue grills for a relaxing sunset meal. Kam I has a beach volleyball court on the north side of the park. The best way to experience these beaches is to take a stroll along the coast and link all three together. The lava rock headlands can be rough on your feet and *kiawe* (mesquite) trees drop thorns, so wear footwear if you plan on walking all three beaches. The tide pools between Kam II and Kam III are a particularly nice place to explore, and when you reach the southern end of Kam III, there's a walking trail that runs for 0.75 mile to the Kihei Boat Ramp.

Mornings are the best time for stand-up paddling and snorkeling, and by noon the wind can pick up and turn the surface to whitecaps. These are great beaches for bodysurfing almost any time of year, but sometimes waves can get dangerously large on the biggest summer swells. Kam I and Kam II have street parking, whereas larger Kam III has its own parking lot exclusively for beachgoers. Kam III is also the party spot where locals truck in horseshoes, ice chests, and bouncy houses for their three-year-old's birthday party. If you can't find parking, there's overflow parking between Kam III and the boat ramp.

Sometimes you will hear locals say they enjoy spending time at **Charley Young Beach;** this is just another name for the northern end of Kam I. It's protected from the wind when the southern section of the beach is choppy. Parking for Charley Young is along Kaiau Place, which is a small offshoot of South Kihei Road not far from the Cove Park.

★ Keawakapu Beach

Aside from Kam III, **Keawakapu** is Kihei's most popular beach. This long stretch of sand is more protected from the wind than the beaches farther north, and a small shop on the north end of the beach rents out stand-up paddleboards, kayaks, and snorkeling gear. In morning, before the wind picks up, this beach is a bustle of snorkelers entering the water and kids splashing in the surf, and by late afternoon, it changes into the perfect perch for the sunset. Snorkeling is best around the north and south headlands, and if you're feeling up for a really long stroll, you can connect with the Wailea Coastal Walk (page 158) at the southern end of the beach.

The north end of the beach has ample parking, and the lot is located off South Kihei Road on the north side of the Days Inn. To reach the south end of Keawakapu—which is much calmer—when South Kihei Road begins to head uphill, continue driving straight until the road dead ends in a small parking lot. There aren't many parking spaces here, although there is a small shower for hosing off. There's also a central entrance to Keawakapu that's known as Sidewalks, with public parking on the corner of Kilohana Drive and South Kihei Road.

Wailea

To Kihei and Ma'alea
To Kihei and Kahului

MANA KAI MAUI RESORT
MAUI MANGO COTTAGES
31
MAPU ST
FIVE PALMS
DAYS INN
SARENTO'S ON THE BEACH
KILOHANA DR
PI'ILANI
AKALA
MAPU ST
KEAWAKAPU BEACH
EKAHI VILLAGE
Maui Meadows
OKOLANI DR
S KIHEI RD
WAILEA ALANUI RD
Beach Walk
MIKIOI ST
MOKAPU BEACH
ULUA BEACH
MARKET BY CAPISCHE
WAILEA TENNIS CLUB
THE SHOPS AT WAILEA
WAILEA TOWN CENTER
WAILEA GATEWAY CENTER
WAILEA BEACH MARRIOTT
WAILEA IKE DR
MONKEYPOD KITCHEN
WAILEA BEACH VILLAS
MANOLI'S PIZZA COMPANY
Wailea Beach
GRAND WAILEA RESORT HOTEL AND SPA
WAILEA EKOLU VILLAGE
KALAI WAA DR
FOUR SEASONS RESORT MAUI AT WAILEA
FAIRMONT KEA LANI
CAPISCHE?
Polo Beach
KAUKAHI ST
HOTEL WAILEA
POLO BEACH CLUB
MULLIGAN'S ON THE BLUE
0   0.5 mi
0   0.5 km
Palauea Beach (White Rock)
Po'olenalena Beach
GOLD AND EMERALD COURSES CLUBHOUSE
GANNON'S
MAKENA SURF
To Makena
Chang's Beach
PACIFIC OCEAN
MAKENA ALANUI
WAILEA ALANUI RD
© AVALON TRAVEL

WAILEA
Ulua Beach and Mokapu Beach

Ulua and **Mokapu** are the northernmost of Wailea's beaches, separated by a small grassy headland. Mokapu is on the north side of the hill, Ulua is on the south, and the point that separates the two is one of Wailea's best snorkeling spots. Ulua is slightly larger than Mokapu and more protected from the surf. Mokapu Beach is also the northern terminus of the Wailea Coastal Walk, although the trail technically crosses the sand dune and continues to the southern end of Keawakapu. Restrooms and showers are available. A large public parking lot is at the bottom of Ulua Beach Road, just north of the Shops at Wailea.

Wailea Beach

Home to Maui's "see and be seen" crowd, **Wailea Beach** epitomizes Wailea. Fronted by the Grand Wailea and the Four Seasons Maui, this is a beach where CEOs and professional athletes mingle with regular travelers. The beach is constantly abuzz with activity, as there's snorkeling around Wailea Point, stand-up paddleboard rentals, outrigger canoe tours, and dozens of visitors playing in the surf who are happy to just be in Maui. Despite the private nature of the resorts, public access to the beach is quite easy, as there is a large public parking lot just before the entrance to the Four Seasons. In the parking lot are public restrooms and showers.

Polo Beach

Polo Beach is the southernmost of Wailea's resort beaches, and is the southern terminus of the Wailea Coastal Walk. The cloud-white Fairmont Kea Lani dominates the shore, its Arabian spires providing a unique backdrop to the shimmering blue waters. Of all of Wailea's beaches, Polo Beach is the most popular with locals due to the large public parking area being a convenient place for launching stand-up paddleboards and kayaks. There are public restrooms, showers, and one small barbecue grill. Polo Beach can also be good for boogie boarding in summer, and there is a small activity booth on the north side of the beach if you want to rent a paddleboard or kayak. To reach Polo Beach, travel south along Wailea Alanui Road before making a right on Kaukahi Street and following it to the end.

MAKENA AND BEYOND
Palauea Beach (White Rock)

If you're looking for a beach that isn't as crowded as Wailea or Polo Beach, stroll south to **Palauea Beach,** otherwise known as **White Rock.** For decades this area was about bonfires and guitars rather than gates and security cameras, but recently the megamansion sprawl has found its way to the shore. Parking for Palauea is along the side of Makena Road, and public access is at the southern end of the beach, next to the lonely portable toilet. Snorkeling is good around both ends of the beach, and while there aren't any facilities, restrooms, or showers, you can find all of those at Polo Beach just a five-minute walk away.

Po'olenalena Beach

Once frequented only by locals, **Po'olenalena Beach** can now get so busy it's tough to find a space in the potholed parking lot. There are volleyball games on Sunday afternoon, and the beach is a favorite for watching the sunset. On the north end, a small trail leads from the parking lot around a rocky point, bringing you to a cove that isn't visible from the road. There are usually about 10 percent of the people on the cove beach as on Po'olenalena. It's the perfect spot to escape with a beach chair, an umbrella, and a good book.

To find Po'olenalena, travel on Wailea Alanui Road until you see Wailea Golf Club Drive on the left. Continue straight for one more minute to see the parking area for the beach on your right. For the public parking lot on the south end of the beach, look for the lot just before Makena Surf on the right side of the road. Barely visible and with only 10 spots, it's next to the yellow fire hydrant numbered 614.

Chang's Beach

If you're looking for a pocket of sand with exceptional snorkeling and not too many people, **Chang's Beach** will be your favorite spot in Makena. Not many make it here because it's hidden from the road. Chang's Beach is about 1.5 miles past the Fairmont Kea Lani on Makena Alanui Road. Look for the small parking lot immediately past Makena Surf. If you find a spot in the parking lot *before* the Makena Surf building (the one by fire hydrant 614), walk south for 100 yards past the gated entrance, and another parking lot with six spaces is on the right, by fire hydrant 616. From here a paved walkway leads down to the shore and the fingernail of sand.

★ Maluaka Beach

Directly in front of the Makena Beach and Golf Resort, **Maluaka Beach** is everything you've ever wanted in a beach. Locals refer to it as Prince Beach, since the hotel used to be called the Maui Prince. There's good snorkeling around the north end, fun waves for boogie boarding during the summer, ample

Big Beach at Makena State Park

Makena

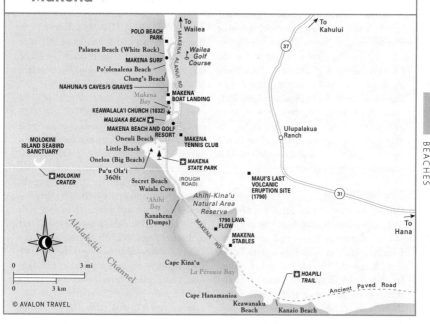

parking, restrooms and showers, and a grassy area for relaxing.

Maluaka Beach has two different entrances. On the north side, coming in on Makena Alanui, make a right on Honoiki Street, then a left onto Makena Road, to the public parking lot across from Keawala'i Church. For the south entrance, continue on Makena Alanui until you pass the entrance for the Makena Beach and Golf Resort, then continue past the turnoff for the golf and tennis club. As the road bends around to the right, you'll see a sign for Makena Keone'o'io on the right. Make a right, and follow it to the parking area.

★ Makena State Park

Among the string of golden shores, none can hold a sandy candle to **Oneloa,** or **Big Beach.** As the largest beach in Makena State Park, this mile-long stretch of sand has avoided the rush of development, much of which is attributed to the grassroots movement to "Save Makena."

In the early 1970s this area was a famous hippie commune where hundreds of draft-dodgers, nudists, and dropouts camped out back in the *kiawe* trees. Although Big Beach visitors have since put their pants on, the same can't be said for neighboring **Little Beach**—the island's official clothing-optional establishment located just over the north side of the bluff. There's an anachronistic aura that permeates Little Beach, where simply clambering from one side to the other can transport you back to an era when life was easy and it was hip to be free. For an authentic Maui counterculture experience, check out the Little Beach Sunday night drum circle (page 168).

Before you get in the water at Makena, understand that the shore-break here is more powerful than anywhere on the island. There should be a spinal clinic here for the number of back and neck injuries, and this isn't the place to splash in the waves with a boogie board from the ABC store. There are lifeguard towers in case of emergency, but think twice before entering the water on days when there's any surf.

To reach Big Beach and Makena State Park, travel on Makena Alanui road for one mile past the entrance to the Makena Beach and Golf Resort. There are three entrances; the First and Second Entrances have large parking areas, and Third Entrance is just dirt on the side of the road. The closest parking spots are at First Entrance, and be sure not to leave any valuables in your vehicle. Despite its popularity, there still are no showers at Big Beach, and the nearest place to wash off the sand is at Maluaka Beach, 0.5 mile north.

Oneuli Beach

You did it—you found a black-sand beach. The famous black-sand beach is in Hana, at Wai'anapanapa State Park, and **Oneuli Beach** in Makena State Park is dark brown and less famous. This hidden spot is a popular place for locals to kick back and fish, and there's good snorkeling at the south end of the bay only on the clearest and calmest days. The main draw, aside from the sand, is the lack of crowds, but note that the access road is potholed and bumpy. To reach Oneuli Beach, turn right off Makena Alanui Road 0.2 miles past the turnoff for Maluaka Beach, and 0.2 miles before the first entrance to Big Beach.

Pa'ako Beach (Secret Cove)

If you want to go back home and tell your friends you found the "secret beach" on Maui, take the time to visit this gem. The problem is that even though **Pa'ako Beach** is also called **Secret Cove,** the tiny inlet of sand is anything but secret. Weddings take place on a daily basis, and the chances of having it to yourself are slim. To access the beach, you have to walk through a hole in a lava rock wall just south of the Third Entrance for Big Beach. Watch carefully to find the tiny opening. As you climb up and over a little hill where Big Beach ends, you will notice a lava rock wall running along the right side of the road. Next to the speed table is a blue Beach Access sign and a shoulder-width opening in the lava rock wall. If you're not sure if you're at the right spot, a telephone pole on the other side of the street has the code E2 3 written on it. The easiest access is to park at the Third Entrance for Big Beach and walk the rest of the way. As you might expect, sunsets here are as epic as they get.

Secret Cove

What Molokini Snorkelers Need to Know

During about 80 percent of the year, the trade winds are so strong that Molokini Crater is filled with four-foot waves by noon, so boats **go there early in the morning.** A discount tour to Molokini that departs at 2pm, conditions permitting, is a scam, since conditions will rarely be permitting. You might get lucky, but chances are you'll end up snorkeling at a spot named Coral Gardens.

Most of the year, and every day in summer, **the ride back to Ma'alaea Harbor is very rough,** with 30-knot winds and sheets of spray coming over the bow. Some people love the ride, and although it's not dangerous, others are terrified. Grab a sheltered seat toward the back of the boat and brace yourself.

The water temperature in Maui fluctuates between 73°F in winter and 79°F in summer—colder than the Gulf of Mexico, but still warmer than most oceans. If you go on one of the large diesel boats, you will be asked if you want to rent a wetsuit. The crew receives a commission, so expect a sales pitch. **Don't rent a wetsuit** unless you think you will actually need one.

Molokini Crater offers dozens of species of fish, impossibly clear water, and healthy, vibrant corals, but **there are no green sea turtles.** All of the turtles are found along the southern shore, so if you want to see some turtles, book a charter that stops along the shore.

If there is large surf along the southern shore (more frequent in summer than winter), **the water color at Turtle Town will be closer to green than blue.** If the visibility along the shore isn't what you expected, it's due to increased surf.

Even if you book an early tour to beat the afternoon's trade winds, if the wind is blowing out of the north, Molokini isn't accessible. Often this wind switch can occur within minutes, so **there is a chance you'll end up snorkeling at a secondary spot,** which usually still ends up being a good trip.

Molokini Crater is a tightly controlled marine reserve. Feeding fish or stepping on coral can carry heavy penalties. **Don't feed the fish!**

Keawanaku Beach

If you're up for an epic hiking adventure to a beach hardly anyone knows about, put on your hiking boots and make the trek to **Keawanaku Beach.** The round-trip journey takes at least two hours on the Hoapili Trail (page 159).

Snorkeling

MA'ALAEA

Although you'll often see little red dive flags fluttering in the wind off the harbor at **Ma'alaea Bay,** these are local spearfishers who are diving for *tako* (octopus). Don't mistake this for a nice snorkeling spot. Although Ma'alaea Bay once had a teeming reef prior to the 1990s, nearly 100 percent of it has died due to invasive species of algae. It has been a case study for what will happen to all the island's reefs if environmental dangers go unmitigated.

★ Molokini Crater

When it comes to snorkeling, what Ma'alaea is known for is the harbor that serves as the starting point for boats to **Molokini Crater,** a half-submerged volcanic caldera that rises in 300 feet of water. Visibility here can be 100 feet or better nearly every day of the year. Nowhere else in Hawaii has water this consistently calm and clear. The back of Molokini Crater drops to almost 300 feet, but inside the bowl, where snorkel boats tie up, is only about 40 feet deep, and the best snorkeling is along the rim of the crater in 15 feet of water. At Molokini you have a great chance of finding colorful parrotfish, endemic reef species, octopuses, eels, and—if you're lucky—maybe a harmless whitetip reef shark. One species notably absent from Molokini, however, are Hawaiian green sea turtles—although most tour operators combine a trip to Molokini with a second snorkeling spot along the coast of Maui so that you can check turtles off your list.

Because it's so massively popular, however, Molokini is a place where it can sometimes seem like there are far more humans than fish. To avoid the crowds, book your trip for as early as possible before most other boats arrive. Schedule this activity early in your trip, since you'll probably be waking up early anyway with a little bit of jet lag. If you visited Molokini 20 years ago and are returning for a second trip, you might notice there are fewer fish. Fish feeding, a popular activity during the 1980s, completely disrupted the area's natural food chain, and a handful of species took over the reef. In an effort to return the crater to its former health, Molokini is now a tightly controlled marine preserve, and you'll be required to fill out a form that outlines the rules for visiting.

Boats to Molokini fall into three categories: small, medium, and large. The cheaper the ticket to Molokini, the more people there are going to be on the boat, which also means the more people there are going to be snorkeling with you. The larger boats, which are diesel catamarans, carry 150 people during busier months. There are three sailboat companies that carry 20 to 50 people. Three raft companies carry up to 24 and get you to Molokini quickly and easily. These trips can be economical, and the small group size ensures personalized service, but the tradeoff is that the food won't be as good as on larger boats, and the restroom situation can be tight. Rafts aren't recommended for anyone who is pregnant or has back or neck problems.

Nearly all boats leave for Molokini from Ma'alaea Harbor. Note that Lahaina Harbor

morning snorkel

is not a departure point for Molokini Crater. Three rafts and most scuba-diving boats leave from Kihei Boat Ramp. At Makena, the sailing catamaran *Kai Kanani* departs from Maluaka Beach; its early trip is one of the first to arrive at Molokini.

Rental Shops

The best place for renting snorkel gear in Ma'alaea is at **Maui Dive Shop** (300 Ma'alaea Harbor Rd., 808/244-5514, www.mauidiveshop.com, 6am-6pm daily) in the Ma'alaea Harbor Shops. There is a wide range of snorkeling equipment for rent or purchase, and you can pick up an optical mask if you normally wear prescription glasses.

Snorkeling Charters

Trilogy Excursions (Slip 62 and Slip 99, 808/874-5649, www.sailtrilogy.com) has been the gold standard for charter boats in Maui for 45 years. Their Molokini trip ($129 adults) is pricier than the budget options, but you get what you pay for: Trilogy boats have only 40

How to Avoid Being Eaten by a Shark

Sharks get a really bad rap, even though they're important to a healthy marine ecosystem and pose minimal danger to humans. That said, if you're still concerned about sharks in Maui when you're snorkeling, swimming, or diving (and, don't worry, you're not the only one), here are a couple of tips to minimize the minuscule chance of getting bitten:

- Stay out of the water after a heavy rain, when the water is murky and brown.

- Avoid swimming near stream mouths or river mouths that empty into the ocean.

- Avoid swimming at dawn and dusk, when sharks are slightly more active.

- Swim in a group—or at least with a buddy—if you plan to swim far offshore.

- If you encounter a shark while paddleboarding, drop to your knees, keep your eyes on the shark, and use your paddle as a weapon.

By following some basic ocean safety, you minimize the risk of an attack. If the sun is shining, the water is blue, and conditions are shallow and calm, you run a much greater risk of getting a sunburn than getting attacked by a shark.

to 50 passengers, snuba is available as an upgrade, and you get to enjoy a sailing catamaran to feel the breeze in your hair. The 7am trip on the *Trilogy V* departs from Slip 99, and the 8am trip is on the larger and newer *Trilogy II* from Slip 62. On Monday, Wednesday, and Friday, Trilogy also offers the adults-only Captain's Dinner Sail ($129), focusing on luxury dining and drinking.

Sail Maui (Slip 72, 808/244-2087, www.sailmaui.com) offers a great trip for anyone whose priority is sailing, making only one snorkeling stop, almost always Molokini. The emphasis on the trip back toward Ma'alaea is racing at top speed on their high-performance 47-foot catamaran; it can reach upward of 20 knots. The boat carries just 20 to 30 people. Trips ($120 adults) depart at 7:30am and last five hours. On Tuesday, Thursday, and Saturday, a three-hour afternoon trip to Coral Gardens (1:30pm-4:30pm, $70 adults), along the West Maui coast, is offered.

Along with *Trilogy II* and *Kai Kanani* in Makena, *Ali'i Nui* (Slip 56, 808/875-0333, www.aliinuimaui.com) is a sailing catamaran that is closer to a yacht than a regular charter boat. With sleek black-and-white trim, this 65-foot catamaran is also one of the island's widest, at 36 feet, providing a more stable platform. *Ali'i Nui* is affiliated with Maui Dive Shop, and while their snorkeling excursion ($175 adults) is more expensive than others, they also include complimentary transportation to and from your hotel if you're staying on the west or south side of Maui. *Ali'i Nui* offers snuba—but calls it "huka"—for $65 extra, whereas other companies have switched to snuba. *Ali'i Nui* visits Molokini five times per week, but on Wednesday and Friday they sail to Olowalu (or, as they call it, "Turtle Point"). The Monday sail ($165) only visits Molokini and is approximately five hours long.

The company with the largest presence in Ma'alaea Harbor is **Pacific Whale Foundation** (300 Ma'alaea Boat Harbor Rd., 808/249-8811, www.pacificwhale.org), a nonprofit organization that has its headquarters in the Ma'alaea Harbor Shops. Instead of checking in down at the harbor, check in at the shop. These cruises are more economical than some of the higher-priced excursions, although on busy days you could be sharing the boat with more than 100 people. Note that the boat cruises, Pacific Whale Foundation Eco-Adventures, are a for-profit business, and the nonprofit arm of the company is funded by merchandise sales and gear rentals.

The standard Pacific Whale itinerary for

trips to Molokini ($94 adults) departs at 7am and features two snorkeling spots. A smaller vessel, with no more than 34 passengers, is the 7:30am Molokini Wild Side excursion ($114 adults), which spends a greater amount of time focusing on the marine and bird species. May to November, when whale-watching trips aren't running, there are a greater number of options for snorkeling times and charters.

The *Pride of Maui* (101 Ma'alaea Boat Harbor Rd., 808/242-0955, www.prideofmaui.com) offers a five-hour excursion ($101 adults) aboard a large power catamaran that features a glass-bottom viewing area and a large top deck for sunning. Trips depart at 8am next to the U.S. Coast Guard station. This popular boat can frequently load over 100 passengers. During the summer and fall months, when it isn't whale season, there's also a 3.5-hour afternoon snorkel trip ($50 adults) to a location along the West Maui shore.

The catamaran *Four Winds II* (Slip 80, 808/879-8188, www.fourwindsmaui.com) offers excursions in the morning (7am daily, $105 adults) to Molokini and in the afternoon ($49) to Coral Gardens. The catamaran has a mast, but it's often so windy in Ma'alaea Bay that the boat isn't able to sail. Small children will love the glass-bottom part of the boat when stopped at Molokini, and unlike other boats that also make a stop along the shore, *Four Winds* makes Molokini its only stop, so you have plenty of time to relax and explore the crater at your own pace. The downside is that you won't get the chance to snorkel with turtles, although you do make a stop at a "turtle cleaning station" to view the turtles from above.

One of the cheapest trips to Molokini ($60 adults) is on *Malolo* (Slip 87, 808/661-3333, ext. 8, www.bossfrogs.com), a boat that's owned by Boss Frog's snorkel shop. You can sometimes finagle a cheaper fare if you rent snorkeling gear in the store. The focus is on quantity, but if you're just looking for a trip to the crater, it's an affordable option. A higher quality boat that also carries more passengers is the sister ship *Quicksilver* (Slip 44,

808/442-3267, www.quicksilvermaui.com), whose Molokini snorkeling trip ($110 adults) visits two spots. *Quicksilver* is known for its semiformal dinner cruise ($90 adults), which features live music and often tucks around the corner of West Maui to get a good angle on the sunset and shelter from the wind.

If you want to visit Molokini from Ma'alaea but don't want to spend a lot of time getting there, the *Aqua Adventure* (Slip 51, 808/573-2104, www.mauisnorkelsnuba.com) leaves at 7:15am and cruises at speeds much faster than the larger boats. The small number of passenger, capped at 40, is also a plus, and snuba gets people in the water. You can choose to snorkel, but if your main priority is getting to Molokini quickly to snuba dive, this trip ($108 adults) visits two snorkeling spots and offers an additional upgrade for snuba. Trips return by noon.

A similar operation that features snuba and small crowds is **Lani Kai** (Slip 76, 808/244-1979, www.mauisnorkeling.com), a trip ($109) that departs at 7am and visits two snorkeling locations. Lani Kai also has an afternoon charter ($51) that cruises the cliffs over to Coral Gardens and ties up next to *Four Winds* and *Malolo,* with the difference being there are far fewer people on the boat.

KIHEI

Mornings are the best time of day for snorkeling in Kihei, before the wind picks up. Winter mornings offer light winds, clear visibility, and calm water, and as an added bonus, if you dive down a few feet while snorkeling, you're guaranteed to hear whale song reverberating in the distance. Summer can have intermittent periods of high surf, which can affect visibility.

Snorkeling Spots

The northernmost beach in Kihei to snorkel is **Charley Young Beach,** also known as the north end of Kamaole I. There's a rocky point on the right side of the beach that offers good snorkeling, and at the southern end of the beach, the rocky points between

What Is Snuba?

On many of the boats that visit Molokini Crater, you can upgrade to a snuba dive, but what exactly does that mean?

Snuba (SNOO-Bah) is the safest, easiest, and fastest way to experience what it's like to breathe underwater. It is similar to scuba diving in that you breathe through a regulator, but instead of having to wear pounds of gear, take an in-depth class, and swim with a tank on your back, on a snuba dive the air tank sits on a raft above the surface, and the only equipment you wear are a weight belt and a lightweight shoulder harness. A 10-foot-long hose descends from the inflatable raft above you and connects to your regulator, so it's almost like snorkeling. Since snuba is more user-friendly than scuba diving, it's the perfect option if you like snorkeling but are hesitant about full-on scuba diving.

Some commonly asked questions:

Q: What is the minimum age for snuba?
A: Eight.

Q: How deep will I go?
A: Up to 20 feet; at Molokini Crater, 10 feet.

Q: How long can I stay underwater?
A: In most cases you share an air tank with another diver, and most dives last 20 to 25 minutes.

Q: Do I need to know how to swim?
A: Yes. Flotation devices would defeat the point of the activity.

Q: I've never snorkeled before. Can I still snuba?
A: It's helpful to have snorkeled, but not necessary. As a quick self-test, pinch your nose and breathe through your mouth for 30 seconds. If this feels awkward, you might want to pass on snuba diving.

Q: Can I fly or travel to Haleakala after a snuba dive?
A: Yes. Since you don't descend as deep as in scuba diving, your body doesn't accumulate enough nitrogen for flying to be a problem.

Q: Do I need to be in good health to snuba?
A: Although snuba is more amenable to physical limitations than scuba diving is, you still need to complete a standard medical form.

Q: If I'm congested, can I snuba dive?
A: Not unless you want to have unbearable sinus pain.

Q: My ears hurt when I dive underwater. Can I still snuba?
A: Yes. Your instructor will teach you how to equalize the air spaces in your ears so that you won't feel any pressure.

Q: How much does snuba diving cost?
A: While every operation is different, most boats offer snuba as a $59-69 upgrade.

Kamaole I and Kamaole II, and Kamaole II and Kamaole III, have colorful reef fish and turtles.

Keawakapu beach, 0.5 mile south of Kamaole III, has good snorkeling on both the north and south sides of the bay. The north end can get crowded due to the large public parking lot and bustling activity stand, and if you want to escape the crowd, either get here early, before everyone arrives, or just snorkel the outer edge of the reef in front of the Mana Kai hotel. To combine a morning snorkel with a stroll, park at the northern end of Keawakapu Beach and walk to the southern point. There are fewer crowds, it has a larger area for snorkeling, and the walk back to your car is one of the island's best beach walks.

Rental Shops

Choosing where to rent snorkels in Kihei can be overwhelming, and before you go flinging open the nearest door, it's important to understand the nature of the snorkel rental business on Maui: Most snorkel shops and activity stands in Kihei are fronts for activity sales and timeshare presentations, so expect a sales pitch for a helicopter ride or vacation rental, even if your only intention is to go snorkeling. As a general rule, if it seems too cheap, there's probably a catch.

Maui Dive Shop (1455 S. Kihei Rd., 808/879-3388, 7am-9pm daily) is a reputable option for anything related to snorkeling or diving, and **Boss Frog's** (main office 1770 S. Kihei Rd., 808/874-5225, www.bossfrog.com, 8am-5pm daily) has three locations in Kihei and some of the island's cheapest rentals. The company is heavily embedded in the activities sales market, so expect a sales pitch.

Snorkel Bob's has multiple stores in Kihei, including the Kamaole Beach Center (2411 S. Kihei Rd., 808/879-7449, www.snorkelbob.com, 8am-5pm daily), and another in the Azeka II shopping area in Central Kihei (1279 S. Kihei Rd., 808/875-6188, 8am-5pm daily). Snorkel Bob's is a statewide chain that also incorporates activity sales, and you're sure to see their quirky ads if you flip through any island visitors magazines. Snorkel Bob's is known for selling gear they design themselves, and a nice feature of the operation is that you can rent gear on one island and return it on another island free of charge. Packages range from $2 per day for a basic mask and snorkel rental to $44 per week for a package that includes prescription lenses and fins.

Snorkeling Boats

The great thing about the snorkeling charters from Kihei Boat Ramp is it only takes 15 minutes to reach Molokini Crater (compared to an hour from Ma'alaea Harbor). The rafts only carry about 24 people, so if you don't like crowds, these are the trips for you, unless you're pregnant or have back or neck problems.

Blue Water Rafting (808/879-7238, www.bluewaterrafting.com) meets at the boat ramp at 6:30am. If you've already been to Molokini and are looking for an adventure snorkel, Blue Water has a trip to the Kanaio Coast, where you can snorkel along a volcanic coast most

visitors will never see. This forgotten southwestern coast is pockmarked with thundering sea caves and jagged lava formations, and there are multiple places where you can see the remnants of ancient fishing villages. The captains are geologists, historians, and marine naturalists, skilled enough to hug the coast so closely you could almost reach out and touch it. The waters in this area can be rough, however, so this isn't the best trip if you're prone to motion sickness. Book the four-hour Kanaio Coastline tour ($110 adults, $89 children) or combine it with an 11am excursion to Molokini ($135 adults, $110 children). A two-hour tour to Molokini ($55 adults, $45 children) departs at 11:30am and is one of the most affordable options for visiting the crater. There is no breakfast, coffee, or restroom on board, and the minimum age for children is four.

The other primary snorkeling option from Kihei Boat Ramp is **Redline Rafting** (808/757-9211, www.redlinerafting.com), which differs from Blue Water Rafting in that they go to Molokini first, even taking time to snorkel the backside of the crater in 300 feet of water. From there they motor down toward Keone'o'io (La Perouse Bay) to snorkel and search for dolphins, and then explore the northern fringes of the rugged Kanaio Coast. Because this tour visits Molokini, it doesn't go as far south as Blue Water Rafting, although it is one of the earliest boats to the crater. Tours ($135 adults, $110 children) meet at 6:30am and include breakfast, coffee, and a boat with a restroom.

Seafire (808/879-2201, www.molokinisnorkeling.com) offers a trip ($65) at 7:30am on its orange and silver jet-drive raft that not only looks like a Coast Guard boat but is driven by a member of the Coast Guard Reserve. Trips last for three hours, and it's one of the best budget options for reaching Molokini Crater. On the way back toward the Kihei Boat Ramp, you'll stop at a spot along the coast to look for Hawaiian green sea turtles, or maybe even stop at the wreck of the *St. Anthony,* scuttled off the Kihei coast.

WAILEA
★ Ulua Beach and Mokapu Beach

The best locations for snorkeling in Wailea are **Ulua Beach** and **Mokapu Beach,** listed together because the rocky point that separates them is where you'll find the most marinelife. Ulua, the southernmost, is more protected and offers a gentle, sandy entry. This is the perfect spot for beginning snorkelers. Morning hours are calm and are the best time for finding turtles. Winter months have the best visibility, and if you're staying at one of the Wailea resorts, you can reach the beaches by strolling along the Wailea Coastal Walk. If you are driving, there are two small public parking lots that fill up early; arrive before 9am. To reach the parking area, turn on Ulua Beach Road off Wailea Alanui Drive just north of the Shops at Wailea, and follow the road down to the parking lots at the end.

Wailea Point

The second most popular spot for snorkeling in Wailea is **Wailea Point,** a rocky promontory rife with green sea turtles that separates the Four Seasons and Fairmont Kea Lani. The easiest point of entry is from the south side of

Wailea Beach in front of the Four Seasons, but be prepared for a five-minute swim over sand.

Rental Shops

You could pay $25 per day for a set of snorkeling gear from a stand on Wailea Beach, or you could make the short walk over to **Maui Dive Shop** (3750 Wailea Alanui Rd., 808/875-9904, www.mauidiveshop.com, 8am-9pm daily), inside the Shops of Wailea, where snorkeling gear is $9 per day or $25 per week.

MAKENA AND BEYOND

While Makena offers some of the south side's best snorkeling, the entry and exit points can be a little more challenging than at Kihei or Wailea beaches. Makena is more exposed to southerly swell than the beaches to the north are, so visibility is affected and waves can sometimes crash into the lava rocks with such fury that it's the last place you want to be. Assess the conditions and your own abilities before venturing into the water.

Snorkeling Spots

The best place for beginner snorkeling in Makena is **Maluaka Beach,** in front of the Makena Beach and Golf Resort. There's a rocky point that wraps around the north end

Mokapu Beach

The Aquarium Is Closed

Many outdated guidebooks claim the best snorkeling in South Maui are at two spots in the Ahihi Kinau Natural Area Reserve known as the Aquarium and the Fishbowl, hidden near the end of the paved road and accessible via a trail through the island's most recent lava flow.

These areas became too popular, and what was once a sensitive and protected part of the island was overrun by visitors who would leave trash, introduce pollutants to the water such as petroleum-based spray-on sunscreens, and destroy sensitive ponds. It seemed the only solution for keeping troublemakers out was to keep all visitors out, so the area was closed in 2008.

The area still hasn't recovered from overuse, and you can incur a hefty fine if you're found snorkeling in this area. Sneaky visitors sometimes try to enter by sea via a long swim from La Perouse Bay, but this is dangerous. There are many other spots for good snorkeling along the island's south side.

Respect the closure in the Natural Area Reserve.

of the beach, and the entry from the sand into the water is gentle.

While Maluaka might be the easiest place to snorkel in Makena, the best snorkeling is at **Makena Landing.** The entry can be a little challenging, but once you make it out past the shallow areas, you'll be glad you made the effort. There are multiple entry and exit points for Makena Landing, the most common being the public parking area off Makena Road. To reach the parking area, drive along Makena Alanui until you reach Honoiki Street and the turn for Keawala'i Church. When you reach the bottom of Honoiki, turn right and follow the road 0.25 mile until you see a parking area on the left.

Once in the water, hug the coast toward the point on the right, and when you have rounded the tip, you'll notice there is a long finger of lava underwater that extends out toward Molokini. This is what's known as the South Finger, and there's a sea cave here that houses green sea turtles. This area is referred to as **Turtle Town** by many snorkel boat operators, and unless you want to share the water with 200 other snorkelers, try to be out here before 10am. If you swim

north from the South Finger, you will pass over lime-green coral heads. Keep an eye out for moray eels or the strange-looking flying gurnard. Eventually you'll come to the North Finger, another underwater lava formation that houses many turtles. This finger is covered in bright-red slate-pencil urchins that the ancient Hawaiians used for red dye. Eagle rays and manta rays are sometimes seen off the deeper end of the finger.

An alternate entry point for Makena Landing is via the north side at a spot known as **Five Graves.** Parking is scarce, and the entry can be challenging, but it's a much shorter swim to reach the fingers. Instead of turning into the parking lot on Makena Road, continue driving up and over the hill. When the road drops back down to the shore, park in a dirt area on the right that can fit about five cars. On the other side of the street is a small trail. You'll know this is the right path if you see five graves in a small graveyard on the left. Follow this trail to the shore. The easiest place to get in and out of the water is a protected nook in the rocks on the right. Although the beach area to the left of the trail looks like it would be easier, it's shallow for a long way out, and you don't want to contend with the breaking waves. On calm days this is the quickest means of reaching the fingers. On days with surf, forget about it.

Moving south, inside **Makena State Park,** the best snorkeling is at the point that separates Big Beach from Little Beach. Park in the First Entrance to Big Beach, and turn right when you hit the sand. This leads to the far northern end of the beach, where you can enter the water to snorkel around the point. The surf can get big here in the summer, so this is only possible on a flat day. For more direct access to the reef, clamber up and over the hill to Little Beach and snorkel in the cove off the left side of the bay. If there are waves in the bay, however, it's best to go elsewhere, because this puts you in the path of oncoming boogie boarders—some of whom swim naked.

While there have been lots of complaints about the parts of Ahihi Kinau Natural Area Reserve that are closed, parts of the beautiful coast are still open, including **Waiala Cove,** a small, rocky, and mostly protected bay with crystal clear water for snorkeling. Since this area is so popular, and the road so narrow, it's common for there to be traffic jams, so rather than trying to park on the road, continue driving 0.2 miles to the parking lot for Kanahena Cove. Here you'll find a gravel trail that winds its way back toward Waiala Cove. The best entry is on the northern side, just a few feet off of the road. While Waiala has great snorkeling when the water is calm, if waves are breaking inside the bay, it's best to go someplace else. At **Kanahena Cove,** follow the trail from the large parking lot down to the rocky coast to snorkel the reef that's known to local surfers and divers as **Dumps.** This spot gets very busy, especially in winter, and in summer there is frequently large breaking surf that makes it too dangerous to snorkel.

For a map of the Makena area, staff with the Department of Land and Natural Resources have a small office in the parking lot. They've also erected signs with yellow fish that show the best places to snorkel (for the record, the fish is the *lauwiliwilinukunuku'oi'oi*—say that 10 times fast). To reach the Kanahena parking lot, travel 2.5 miles past Makena Beach and Golf Resort, or about 1 mile past Makena State Park. Because break-ins have been a problem, don't leave any valuables in the car.

Finally, just when you think the road will never end, the asphalt gives way to a gravel parking lot in a spot known as **Keone'o'io,** or **La Perouse Bay.** The lava field that you drive over on the way to La Perouse is the remnants of Haleakala's last eruption. The bay is named for the French explorer Jean-François de Galaup, compte de Lapérouse, who in 1786 was the first European to set foot on Maui at this very spot. As you enter the parking area, there's a stone structure memorializing this event.

The snorkeling in La Perouse Bay can be phenomenal, although there are also times when it can be a total bust. Early mornings are best, before the trade winds fill the bay with whitecaps, and summer can bring large surf, which turns the shore into a cauldron of white water. On calm days, however, the best snorkeling is found to the right of the parking lot, where you must scramble across a lava rock point to reach the protected inlet. The water here is an enchanting turquoise against the young black lava rock.

Snorkeling Boats

Kai Kanani (808/879-7218, www.kaikanani.com) is the snorkeling boat leaving from Makena. Only a few years old and still sparkling, it has all the added amenities you would expect from a luxury yacht, with top-notch captains. *Kai Kanani* departs directly from Maluaka Beach in front of the Makena Beach and Golf Resort, which, if you're staying in Makena, or even Wailea, makes it a far more convenient option for sailing to Molokini than driving to Ma'alaea Harbor.

If that weren't enough, they also offer free transportation to the beach from Wailea resorts. If Molokini was too crowded the last time you visited, *Kai Kanani*'s early-morning Molokini Express charter ($75 adults) departs the beach at 6:30am and guarantees you're the first boat at the crater, since it only takes about 15 minutes to motor across the channel. This trip is just over two hours long, and while the second trip of the day ($150 adults) visits the crater when it's more crowded, the fact that it's four hours long as opposed to two allows for twice the amount of snorkeling time in twice the number of spots. If you're concerned about getting seasick, the journey time from Maluaka Beach to Molokini is much shorter than the journey between Molokini and Ma'alaea. On Monday, Wednesday, and Friday, they also offer a champagne and cocktail sunset cruise ($91 adults).

Scuba Diving

South Maui has some of the island's best shore diving, and with so many locations and so many different operators, planning your dives can be overwhelming. The information in this section will help you find the operations and locations that suit you best.

MA'ALAEA
Dive Sites

While **Molokini Crater** can be a great place to snorkel, to truly experience the crater's magic, you have to put on a tank. For experienced divers Molokini ranks among the best dive locations around the world, and for novices it's a window into a new aquatic universe. Only certified divers are allowed to dive at Molokini. If you aren't certified but want to experience it from below, sign up for a 20-minute snuba dive to depths of up to 10 feet.

What makes the crater such an exceptional dive spot is the combination of its pelagic location, where it's possible to see anything, and the multiple dive spots within the crater that cater to a wide range of ability levels. Novices will enjoy either Middle Reef or Reef's End, as depths don't usually exceed 70 feet. **Middle Reef** is home to pelagic species such as jacks and reef sharks, and the sand channel

exploring the contours of South Maui's shore

houses curious-looking garden eels. There's also a huge drop-off at the Middle Reef section where it can be easy to exceed your depth.

Similarly, at **Reef's End,** the dive traces the wall of the underwater caldera to the point where it drops off into the abyss. Since this underwater promontory sits on the fringe of the crater, this area has the best chance of sighting bottlenose dolphins, manta rays, humpback whales, and even the occasional whale shark.

The best and most advanced dive in Molokini Crater is a drift dive of the legendary **Back Wall.** Beginning at Reef's End, divers follow the current along the back of Molokini, where a vertical wall drops 250 feet to the ocean floor. If you use nitrox or mixed gases, this is the deepest dive available anywhere in Maui County.

Even though diving at Molokini offers a chance of seeing sharks, if you want a guarantee of diving with them, the most unique dive on the island is at the **Maui Ocean Center** (192 Ma'alaea Rd., 808/270-7000, www.mauioceancenter.com), where you can

Don't Feed the Fish!

There was a time when bread crumbs, frozen peas, and fish food were as integral to a snorkeling outing as a mask and fins. Though other places in the world still allow fish feeding for the enjoyment of snorkelers, here in Hawaii, feeding fish has had a devastating effect on the marine ecosystem—particularly on coral reefs.

You shouldn't feed fish in the ocean for the same reason you don't feed bears in the woods: It isn't their normal diet. The next time you go snorkeling in Hawaii, in addition to looking at the colorful aquatic species, listen to what you hear underwater. The snap, crackle, and pop sounds are the reef fish feeding on algae. When herbivorous reef fish gorge themselves on the outside food you introduce into the water, they become full and stop eating the algae. Consequently, the reef's coral polyps become so overgrown that they struggle to breathe and ultimately die.

Aside from the adverse effect on the coral, larger fish species have been known to drive out the smaller fish species in areas where people feed fish. Many visitors to Molokini notice there are fewer fish than when they visited in the 1980s. This is the reason for the stringent restrictions currently in place.

If that isn't enough to deter you, remember that some fish have really sharp teeth. Many visitors have oval-shaped scars on their fingers from introducing food into the water. For your own safety and the health of the reef, don't feed the fish!

go diving *inside the shark tank.* As part of its Shark Dive Maui program, certified divers are able to spend 30 to 40 minutes surrounded by various species, including hammerhead and tiger sharks. The dive ($199) has a limit of four divers and is only offered on Monday, Wednesday, and Friday mornings. The cost includes the tank and the weight, although divers have to provide the rest of their gear. Although diving at an aquarium might seem like cheating, even some of Maui's most seasoned divers claim it's a great dive. More than just a novelty, this is your best opportunity to be completely surrounded by the ocean's most feared and misrepresented creatures.

One of the island's newest wreck dives is a **Helldiver** World War II airplane that was abandoned by a pilot on a training run off Sugar Beach. When the pilot ejected, his plane sank in 50 feet of water, and for the better part of 60 years it sat forgotten in the mudflats. When a local fisher tipped off a Kihei dive instructor that there was probably something down there, the exploratory dive mission yielded a historical discovery that is now property of the U.S. military. While there isn't an overwhelming amount of marinelife here, this is a unique dive you won't find in many

people's logbooks. There aren't any regularly scheduled trips to the Helldiver, but many South Maui operators periodically plan excursions to the site, so inquire about when the next outing might be.

Rental Operators

The only retail operator in Ma'alaea that rents out dive gear is **Maui Dive Shop** (300 Ma'alaea Harbor Rd., 808/244-5514, www. mauidiveshop.com, 6am-6pm daily) in the Ma'alaea Harbor Shops. Although most dive operations furnish their own gear, this is a good place to pick up equipment if you're diving at the Maui Ocean Center or need accessories.

Dive Boats

Although most Molokini dive boats depart from the Kihei Boat Ramp, two that depart from Ma'alaea Harbor are the 48-foot *Maka Koa,* operated by Maui Dive Shop (808/875-1775, www.mauidiveshop.com), as well as the 40-foot *Maui Diamond II* (Slip 23, 808/879-9119, www.mauidiamond.com). Maui Dive Shop offers two-tank trips to Molokini Crater six times per week, and the second dive is either along the shore of Maui or at the *St.*

Anthony wreck off Kihei. Rates for a two-tank dive are $150, and renting a buoyancy control device and a regulator is an additional $30. Snorkelers are allowed to accompany divers for $90. The trip is a good option for novice divers who want to explore in the 65- to 70-foot range. An added perk of booking with Maui Dive Shop is that they provide transportation from your hotel to Ma'alaea Harbor. Check-in is at 6:15am at the store in the Ma'alaea Harbor Shops.

For a few dollars less, *Maui Diamond II* offers two-tank trips to Molokini and the South Maui shore ($139), and rental of a buoyancy control device and a regulator is an additional $20. If you aren't a certified diver, you have the option of partaking in a Discover Scuba Diving introductory class, where you will snorkel at Molokini and then dive with an instructor at the second spot along the shore. The cost of the snorkel and introductory dive combo ($155) includes all your equipment.

a friendly critter of the reef

KIHEI
Dive Sites

The only real dive site in Kihei is the *St. Anthony Wreck* off the south end of Keawakapu Beach. Maui Dive Shop offers dives to this part of a massive artificial reef system twice weekly as part of a two-tank excursion combined with Molokini.

Rental and Shore-Dive Operators

If you need to rent gear, get gear serviced, pick up tanks for a shore dive, or book a guided shore dive with an instructor, there are a number of different retail operators throughout Kihei. My top pick is **Maui Dreams** (1993 S. Kihei Rd., 808/874-5332, www.mauidreamsdiveco.com, 7am-6pm daily) in the shop across from the southern end of Kalama Park. These guys love to dive and offer a full range of excursions, including scooter dives ($99), night dives ($79), and regular introductory dives ($89). Guided shore dives for certified divers are $69. Maui Dreams is also the only PADI Five-Star Instructor Development Center in

South Maui, so these guys literally instruct the instructors. If you want to complete your scuba certification, you can do so for as little as $299 if you've already completed the E-Learning section that's found on the PADI website.

Inside the Azeka Makai shopping center, **B&B Scuba** (1280 S. Kihei Rd., 808/875-2861, www.bbscuba.com, 8am-6pm Mon.-Fri., 8am-5pm Sat.-Sun.) offers guided shore dives ($65), night dives ($75), and scooter dives ($119) along the South Maui shore. Other operators focus on recreational diving, but B&B offers PADI certification classes and IANTD tech diving classes with trimix, nitrox, and rebreather training. They also provide gear rental and tank pumping.

Dive Boats

All dive boats in Kihei leave from Kihei Boat Ramp, just south of Kamaole III Beach. Parking is tight in the main lot, so head to the overflow lot on the right. The scene at the boat ramp in the morning can be hectic—especially in the dark. Most boats offer coffee aboard if you still need a wake-up, and most boats have private restrooms. Since a number of boats that leave from Kihei Boat Ramp don't have offices, bring a credit card or cash so you can pay on board. If you plan on diving during your time in Maui, bring your certification card.

Of all the choices in Kihei, the top pick among locals is **Mike Severn's** (808/879-6596, www.mikesevernsdiving.com), Kihei's original dive-boat operation. A number of the other operators in Kihei provide exceptional service, but it's impossible to beat Mike Severn's. An instructor will sit down with you, take out a book, and thoroughly explain the species you just saw. At Mike Severn's, the instructors wrote those books. Since Mike Severn's caters to seasoned divers, the instructors don't mandate "follow the leader," giving you the freedom to enjoy the dive at your own pace. Two-tank dives are $139, plus $15 for gear rental. Meet at 6am at the Kihei Boat Ramp aboard the 38-foot *Pilikai.*

Also among South Maui's best, **Ed Robinson's** (808/879-3584, www.mauiscuba.com) caters to advanced divers and underwater photographers. Meet at 6:30am at the Kihei Boat Ramp. Regular two-tank dives ($129) are offered Monday, Thursday, and Saturday. More advanced two-tank drift dives ($129) are offered Sunday and Friday, and a three-tank dive ($169) Tuesday. Experienced divers can join an Adventure X dive ($149) on Wednesday. Ed Robinson's has a shop in an industrial yard in central Kihei (165 Halekuai St.) that also serves as a dive museum.

Pro Diver (808/875-4004, www.prodivermaui.com) is one of the last dive boats to cap its trips at 6 divers (other boats usually take 12 with 2 instructors), which guarantees a personal experience. The 34-foot boat meets at 6am at Kihei Boat Ramp. Two-tank dives are $139, and it's $15 for gear rental if you didn't bring your own.

In addition to offering shore dives and rental options, **B&B Scuba** (1280 S. Kihei Rd., 808/875-2861, www.bbscuba.com) also has a dive boat that does two-tank dives ($119) from Kihei Boat Ramp aboard the 40-foot *Kilikina II.* They're out on the water by 5:45am daily, and since the goal is to beat the crowds, don't show up late. The payoff for the early wake-up is that you reach your first dive site before other boats, and if that first dive site is Molokini, there is a certain magic to the solitude most visitors never get to experience. You're usually back to the dock by 10am. The wallet-friendly cost is also a strong selling point.

WAILEA
Dive Sites
Unlike Ma'alaea or Kihei, which serve as departure points for diving elsewhere, Wailea offers shore dives with shallow depths for beginners. The entry points in Wailea are sandy and easy; the best place to enter the water is the north end of **Ulua Beach.** This is where most dive operators bring students during their certification courses, as the maximum depth is about 35 feet. Expect to see turtles, reef fish, lobsters, and perhaps a rare spotted eagle ray. There is ample parking at the bottom of Ulua Beach Road, and the concrete walkway down to the shore is convenient for hauling tanks and gear.

The next best option is **Wailea Point,** off the south side of Wailea Beach. The nearest parking lot is between the Grand Wailea and Four Seasons resorts. Expect to see more green sea turtles than you can count, since they love the lava rock caves.

Rental Operators
The only dive shop in Wailea is **Maui Dive Shop** (3750 Wailea Alanui Rd., 808/875-9904, www.mauidiveshop.com, 8am-9pm daily), within the Shops at Wailea. You can pick up dive-related accessories and inquire about current conditions. If you're in need of gear and tank rental, you're better off visiting one of the larger outlets in Kihei.

Top Pick for Water Sports

When it comes to water sports in South Maui, the choices can be overwhelming, with dozens of rental shops and operators to help you get out on the water. To filter through the options, my top pick for water activities on Maui is the team at **Hawaiian Paddle Sports** (808/442-6436, www.hawaiianpaddlesports.com). You'll be hard-pressed to find a company that does more to give back to the island.

Hawaiian Paddle Sports is one of only five companies on Maui that are certified by the Hawaii Ecotourism Association, an organization that sets stringent standards for sustainable and cultural practices. They don't use single-use plastics on their tours (think metal water bottles instead), and they don't touch or disturb marinelife, like pulling octopuses from their holes.

They're also involved in the local community, donating every year to community groups and nonprofits, and their staff is involved in island cleanups and service projects. In 2015 they became Maui's first certified B Corporation business—joining a network of over 1,500 businesses around the world dedicated to using business for environmental and social change.

In South Maui, Hawaiian Paddle Sports offers surf lessons, stand-up paddleboard tours, kayak tours, outrigger canoe tours, as well as an adventurous "Molokini Challenge" paddle to Molokini Crater and back. All tours are private, so you aren't combined with another group, and the price per person decreases with the number in your group. It tends to be more expensive than the "get 'em in, get 'em out" budget options, but as the saying goes, you get what you pay for.

- Stand-up paddleboard tours and lessons: $189 for 1 person, $129 pp for 2-4 people, $109 pp for 5 or more
- Surf lessons: $189 for 1, $129 for 2-4, $109 for 5 or more
- Kayak tours: $199 for 1, $149 for 2-4, $119 for 5 or more
- Outrigger canoe tours: $149 pp
- Molokini Challenge: $199 pp

MAKENA AND BEYOND
Dive Sites

In addition to being one of the best shore dives in Makena, **Nahuna,** also called **Makena Landing, 5 Caves,** and **5 Graves,** also has the greatest number of names. The general area is also referred to as **Turtle Town,** a name created by charter boat companies to sell snorkeling tours.

What makes this dive so fantastic is not only the turtles but also the possibility of seeing pelagic species like spotted eagle rays and 'awa (milkfish). Divers are surrounded by whale song in winter, and you can also find nudibranchs, harlequin shrimp, flying gurnards, and eels. On calm days the visibility can reach 100 feet, although on days where there is a south swell, usually in summer, visibility can be reduced to 20 feet at best.

From shore, the easiest place to enter the water is the park at Makena Landing. Once in the water, turn right and follow the coast until you reach a long finger of lava. This is what's known as the South Finger, and the depth is only about 15 feet. Follow the South Finger away from the shore, and halfway to the end you will notice a large cave that you can swim through from below. There are numerous turtles that hang out here, and almost always a whitetip reef shark under a ledge. Emerging on the other side of the cave, kick your way parallel to the shore for three minutes until you reach the North Finger, which is where you're sure to find Hawaiian green sea turtles.

Another nice shore dive is **Waiala Cove,** 1.5 miles past the First Entrance for Big Beach. The depth goes to about 40 feet. Since this cove is protected from the wind, it offers pristine diving conditions as long as the surf isn't up. Expect to find green sea turtles and the rare spinner dolphin on the outer edge of the reef. Entry can be tricky since you have to navigate your way over slippery rocks, but you don't need to worry about boats in this cove, although it is often packed with snorkelers. Parking is 0.2 miles down the road at the Dumps, the Kanahena parking lot.

Surfing

If you look at a map of South Maui, you'll notice that much of it actually faces west. This means that South Maui can get waves at any time of year. The southwest swells of summer bring the best waves, but large northwest winter swells can also wrap into select areas to provide the occasional out-of-season surf. If you're a complete beginner, the only spot in South Maui you should attempt to surf is The Cove in South Kihei, but if you're an intermediate or advanced surfer, there are other spots to check out.

MA'ALAEA

Ma'alaea is one of the few spots on Maui that faces almost due south, which means that summer is the only time there will be waves.

Surf Spots

The most consistent wave in Ma'alaea is a spot known as **Off the Wall.** This is an A-frame, shifty peak that breaks directly in front of the harbor wall, and you can usually only surf here in the morning hours before the wind starts howling. To access Off the Wall, park in the dirt parking area at the end of the break wall ($0.50 per hour), and paddle to the shifty peak—which definitely beats jumping off the wall. Expect short but fun rides, and while it isn't the best break on this side of the island, it's a nice place to get wet.

Half a mile up the highway in the direction of Lahaina is **McGregor Point,** a right-hand point break. Although McGregor's rarely gets bigger than head-high, the spot can offer a long wave and is best in the early morning. Parking for McGregor's is in a dirt lot on the road heading toward the lighthouse. Be careful when pulling off the highway as it

is a difficult turn. To get down to the shore, you have to clamber down a steep and narrow trail, which can be tough if you're surfing with a longboard. McGregor's only breaks on the biggest of south swells, but is an island classic when it does.

Rental Shops

The only rental shop for surfboards ($30 per day) and stand-up paddleboards ($40 per day) in Ma'alaea is **Da Beach House** (300 Ma'alaea Rd., 808/986-8279, www.dabeachhousemaui.com, 10am-5:30pm daily), inside the Ma'alaea Harbor Shops. There are also boogie boards and beach chairs, and this is a good place to pick up a board if you're planning on surfing some of the breaks on the road toward Lahaina.

KIHEI
Surf Spots

The surf epicenter of Kihei is **The Cove,** at the southern end of Kalama Park, where all of the surf schools give lessons. While the waves are gentle, the downside is that it can get crowded. On some days you'll swear you could walk on water across all of the longboards crammed into the small area, but in the early morning hours, before all the surf schools show up, this is still a fun, albeit small, wave. If your goal in Hawaii is to try surfing for the first time, this is where to come.

For more advanced surfers, the best wave in Kihei is an A-frame that breaks next to the **Kihei Boat Ramp.** This is a fickle wave that needs a big southwest or west swell to start working, and you need to be cautious of the boat traffic coming in and out of the harbor area. Access can be tricky, since you're asked to not walk in the sand dune area that runs along the shore. If you're on a longboard and are up for a paddle, you could always paddle from the far southern tip of Kamaole III Beach.

Shortboarding in Kihei can be found at **Sidewalks** on the south-central end of Keawakapu Beach. This is a beach break that offers a fast wave, and the vibe here isn't nearly as localized as at the boat ramp or farther south. Nevertheless, it's still an intermediate wave that isn't suitable for longboards or beginners. Parking for Sidewalks is at the public lot on the corner of Kilohana Drive and South Kihei Road.

Rental Shops and Schools

In the area surrounding The Cove there are five or six operators crammed into the same city block. Even with the wide selection, it's best to make a reservation. Nearly all lessons take place in the morning between 8am and noon, before the trade winds fill in, and all operators offer standard two-hour lessons. If you've moved past the phase of learning how to pop up and ride straight, most operations also offer "surf safaris," where they act as your personal surf guide for the day.

The shop with the largest presence is **Maui Wave Riders** (2021 S. Kihei Rd., 808/875-4761, www.mauiwaveriders.com, 7am-3pm daily) who have a brand-new surf shop and building directly across from The Cove. The company also has a Lahaina location and has helped thousands of visitors ride their first wave since opening in 1997. Lesson rates are $65 pp in a group of up to six people, $85 pp for a semiprivate lesson, and $145 for one-on-one instruction.

Closest to Kalama Village is **Big Kahuna Adventures** (1913 S. Kihei Rd., 808/875-6395, www.bigkahunaadventures.com, 7:30am-7pm Mon.-Sat., 7:30am-5pm Sun.), inside Kihei Kalama Village. Lessons are the standard $60 pp for two hours and take place at 8am and 10:15am daily. Meet at the surf truck parked across the street from the shop.

Surf Shack (1993 S. Kihei Rd., 808/875-0006, www.surfshackmaui.com, 7:30am-3pm daily) is across the street from The Cove. Park inside the Island Surf building. Lessons are $59 pp in a group of up to six people, or $125 for a private lesson, and $350 for a private lesson for four.

Although they function on a smaller scale, another operation providing lessons in Kihei as well as on the West Side is **Maui Beach Boys** (808/283-7114, www.mauibeachboys.com), a company that offers rates in the same range, $70 pp for a group lesson and $95 for a semiprivate lesson.

If you're a beginner and need a basic Soft Top longboard, head to one of the three **Boss Frog's** (www.bossfrog.com, 8am-5pm daily) around town. It's cheaper than renting from the surf schools ($20 per day, as opposed to $25), and the surf school rentals often cap the rental period at four hours, whereas Boss Frog's is open until 5pm. There are three locations in Kihei, including the stores in Dolphin Plaza (2395 S. Kihei Rd., 808/875-4477), across from Kukui Mall (1770 S. Kihei Rd., 808/874-5225), and in the Long's Shopping Center (1215 S. Kihei Rd., 808/891-0077).

If you need a pro board, the best service is from **808 Boards** (808/283-1384, www.808boards.com, 7am-5:30pm daily), who will drop off and pick up the board where you're staying for no extra charge. You can get a beginner board ($25 per day, $100 per week) or a premium fiberglass board ($35 per day, $140 per week).

Similarly, **Island Surfboard Rentals** (808/281-9835, www.islandsurfboardrentals.com) rents longboards ($30 per day, $180 per week) and provides free delivery and pickup. Shortboards ($22 per day, $130 per week) include a leash, some wax, and inside knowledge.

WAILEA
Surf Spots

On the north side of Mokapu Beach, **Stouffer's** is a local A-frame peak for intermediate shortboarders. It can pick up southwest swells in summer and large west swells in winter. Parking is at the south lot of Keawakapu Beach or in the public parking at the bottom of Ulua Beach Road.

On the southern end of Wailea is a punchy little left on the southern end of **Polo Beach** that's good for intermediate shortboarding.

MAKENA AND BEYOND
Surf Spots

There aren't any beginner surf breaks in Makena. If you're an intermediate or advanced surfer and have always wanted to surf naked, try **Little Beach**, a left that breaks on large southern swells. To reach the wave, you need to carry your board up and over the hill that separates Little Beach from Big Beach.

Stand-Up Paddling

KIHEI

Kihei is one of the best spots on the island for stand-up paddling, and all of the major surf schools also offer paddleboard services. Getting out on the water in the morning is imperative because once the trade winds pick up, it can become impossible to paddle upwind. For a truly meditative experience, rent a board the evening before and get up early for a sunrise paddle. You can always putt around by the Kamaole parks and stop at whichever beach is calling your name.

Rental Shops and Schools

Learning to stand-up paddle often takes just a single lesson. Professional instructors can give you all the pointers you need—where to stand on the board, how far apart to keep your feet, and the correct side of the paddle to use. After that you should be solid enough to paddleboard on your own.

For lessons and rentals, **Maui Stand-up Paddleboarding** (808/568-0151, www.mauistanduppaddleboarding.com) offers private lessons and guided tours ($189 for 1 person, $139 pp for 2-4 people, $119 pp groups more than 5). The professional guide also brings along a GoPro and provides free photos of you and your group. They also offer rentals ($55 per day) with a minimum rental of

There is no shortage of board rentals in Kihei.

three days, and uniquely offer inflatable Naish boards, which are convenient if you're staying upstairs or in a place without much space.

Of the schools by The Cove, **Maui Wave Riders** (1975 S. Kihei Rd., 808/875-4761, www.mauiwaveriders.com) offers 90-minute lessons ($65 pp group, $85 semiprivate).

You can also try out a multisport operator such as **South Pacific Kayaks and Outfitters** (808/875-4848, www.southpacifickayaks.com), which offers two-hour lessons ($75 pp group, $99 semiprivate, $139 private). They also offer surf lessons, kayaking tours, hiking tours, and kitesurfing lessons.

If you don't feel like being packed in with the rest of the students around The Cove, you can opt for a multisport operator such as **Blue Soul** (3414 Akala Dr., 808/269-1038, www.bluesoulmaui.com) that offers private lessons ($169 for 1 person, $129 for 2-3 people, $99 pp groups of 4 or more). Blue Soul also offers surf lessons, canoe tours, hiking tours, and adventure tours to spots all over the island. Or, bundle it all together in a "Maui Adventure Day" ($950).

Away from The Cove, you can also find a popular rental stand on the north end of Keawakapu Beach. **808 Boards** (808/283-1384, www.808boards.com, 7am-5:30pm daily) offers stand-up paddleboard rental ($45 per day, delivery included).

WAILEA

When compared to neighboring services, stand-up paddleboard rentals in Wailea are egregiously expensive. Then again, you're paying for the convenience of just walking out your door and renting a board on the sand, but prepare to pay upward of $50 per hour.

If you would prefer to take part in a guided tour, **Paddle On** (888/663-0808, www.paddleonmaui.com, $139-159) offers early-morning tours from Polo Beach in front of the Fairmont Kea Lani. There are numerous options, from Paddleboarding 101 to guided paddles down the coast, and for a morning experience you'll never forget, inquire about sunrise yoga tours that are as meditative as you can get.

Kayaking and Canoeing

When all factors are considered, Makena is the best area for kayaking and paddling. Not only is it far richer culturally, but it takes the wind about an hour longer to reach it than neighboring Kihei or Wailea.

KIHEI

The best outrigger canoe tour in Kihei is with **'Ao'ao O Na Loko 'Ia O Maui** (808/359-1172, www.mauifishpond.com) at Ko'ie'ie Fishpond. This cultural tour is run by a nonprofit that's working to restore the fishpond, and along with the workout you get serious culture. Learn how this fishpond was built over 500 years ago, and be a part of the cultural awakening that's helping to bring it back to life. Affordable tours ($40) are offered at 8am Monday, Wednesday, and Friday. Meet

in the parking lot of the Hawaiian Islands Humpback Whale National Marine Sanctuary Visitors Center.

WAILEA

While there are a number of options for paddling tours in Wailea, the one that focuses the most on Hawaiian culture is **Hawaiian Outrigger Experience** (808/633-2800, www.hoemaui.com), operating from Wailea Beach. A play on words, the acronym HOE translates as "paddle!" in the Hawaiian language. From the moment you begin this tour, you will realize this is as much a cultural experience as it is about the water. You'll spend time snorkeling with Hawaiian green sea turtles and gain authentic cultural insight from instructors who exude the genuine spirit of aloha. Options include a 30-minute tour ($69) and a 90-minute tour ($119) of paddling, snorkeling, and in winter, whale-watching.

If a full-on paddling tour is too much exertion, another activity with cultural roots is the family-operated **Maui Sailing Canoe** (808/281-9301, www.mauisailingcanoe.com, $99 adults, $79 children), which departs off Polo Beach. The distinctly red sail of the *Hina* is visible off Wailea most mornings. This is the only tour where you can harness the light breeze to slowly sail along the coast like the Polynesians who voyaged here centuries ago. Snorkeling time is also included in the tour, combined with paddling, sailing, and relaxing in the sun. With a maximum of only six people, this is a perfect adventure for families wanting to do something different.

MAKENA

The rocky shore of Makena Landing is the preferred spot of other kayak operators, most of whom also have operations elsewhere on the island. While my top pick is **Hawaiian Paddle Sports** (808/442-6436, www.hawaiianpaddlesports.com), **Aloha Kayaks Maui** (808/270-3318, www.alohakayaksmaui.com) is another operator that employs sustainable practices, and you can also choose from **Kelii's Kayaks** (808/874-7652, www.keliiskayaks.com) as well as **South Pacific Kayaks and Outfitters** (808/875-4848, www.southpacifickayaks.com) Most tours are $65-85 for 2.5 hours and $95-110 for 4 hours. There are usually two tours offered per day. If you plan on kayaking from Makena Landing, book the early tour to beat the wind and the crowds of snorkel boats that converge on the area later in the morning.

exploring the Makena coast by kayak

Fishing

MA'ALAEA

For four hours of recreational fishing ($159 pp), the most personalized service you'll find in Ma'alaea Harbor is **Maui Fun Charters** (Slip 97, 808/572-2345, www.mauifuncharters. com). An important difference between this boat and others is that they focus on bottom fishing instead of sportfishing, so instead of spending hours trolling in circles in hopes of catching the big one, you drift closer to shore and will catch a greater number of varied, albeit smaller, fish. If your goal is to take something home to fry up for dinner, this is your best bet.

If you want to try your luck at reeling in a trophy fish, **Strike Zone** (Slip 40, 808/879-4485, www.strikezonemaui.com) offers bottom fishing as well as sportfishing excursions. Morning charters ($168 adults) leave at 6:30am Tuesday, Thursday, and Sunday and last six hours. On Monday, Wednesday, and Friday, 2-4 hour private afternoon charters are available. This boat can accommodate up to 28 passengers and is a good option for larger groups.

KIHEI

If you want to get really adventurous, **Local Fishing Knowledge** (808/385-1337, www. localfishingknowledge.com) offers kayak fishing and fly fishing excursions for the experienced and passionate angler. If you just want to rent a rod for casting in the surf, the "beach bum" setup is perfect for anglers on the sand.

Hiking and Biking

HIKING
Kihei

Hiking in Kihei is barefoot sandy strolls down the beach. For the island's longest uninterrupted beach walk, five-mile-long **Sugar Beach** runs between Kihei and Ma'alaea. You can access the beach from Haycraft Park on the Ma'alaea side, from Kenolio Park on the Kihei side, or at any of the access points along North Kihei Road.

Another popular **coastal walk** in Kihei connects the trio of Kamaole Beaches, following the trails around their headlands. Starting at Charley Young Beach on the north end of Kamaole I (parking is in a public lot on Kaiau Place), you can walk to the south end of Kamaole III along the shore and around the rocky points. Although it's always nice to feel the sand between your toes, the rocks around the headlands can be sharp, so it might be best to bring footwear.

If you want to extend the coastal walk just a little bit farther, there is a short 0.5-mile **walking path** that parallels the coast from the southern end of Kamaole III Beach to the Kihei Boat Ramp. Along the way you will pass informative signs about the coastal dune system and the *u'au kani* seabirds that nest in the dunes. There are a few benches sprinkled along the walking path to rest or, in winter, watch for whales.

Wailea
WAILEA COASTAL WALK

If your idea of a hike means throwing on some Lululemon, talking on your iPhone, and stopping to pick up some Starbucks, then the paved, 3.5-mile (round-trip) **Wailea Coastal Walk** is going to be your favorite hike on the island. The pathway runs from Ulua Beach to Polo Beach and is undeniably gorgeous, passing a host of native coastal plants put in to revitalize the area's natural foliage. You'll also

hiking the Hoapili Trail

the road took on a structure that remains untouched to this day. The trailhead for Hoapili (also known as the "King's Highway") is in the parking lot of La Perouse Bay snorkeling area, 3.1 miles past the First Entrance to Big Beach. To find the trail, drive south on Makena Alanui Road until the it dead-ends.

From the La Perouse Bay parking lot, you'll see the trail paralleling the shore and weaving south along the coast. Before you set out, remember that there is no shade and the trail traverses jagged 'a'a lava that's so sharp you'll want proper hiking boots. Since much of this hike is outside cell phone range, it's important to be prepared with food and water. Reduce the chance of overheating by starting early in the morning.

After you've followed the shoreline for 0.7 mile, passing a couple of pockets of sand and sometimes feral black goats, you'll see an abandoned lava rock structure off the right side of the trail. This is the popular surfing spot known as Laps (short for La Perouse), and on large south swells you can see death-defying surfers riding waves over jagged sharp lava. After the surf spot, the trail climbs for 10 minutes before arriving at a junction and veering off to the left. There is a sign informing you that you're entering the King's Highway and to respect the historic sites. The sign will also indicate that Kanaio Beach is two miles ahead.

On the inland section of trail where the path deviates from the coast, there's a short spur trail that leads down to the lighthouse at Cape Hanamanioa, although there isn't much to see except the old weathered light. A better side trip is the short spur trail 20 minutes later that leads down to Keawanaku Beach, where you're almost guaranteed to have the beach to yourself. To find the beach, look for a short lone palm tree springing from the black lava field surrounded by a grove of kiawe trees, then keep an eye out for the trail down to the shore. Although rocky, the trail is noticeable, and if you find yourself asking "Am I still on the trail?" then you probably aren't. After Keawanaku, the trail continues for 20 minutes to the coast at Kanaio Beach, a salt- and

pass the Grand Wailea, Four Seasons, Kea Lani, Marriott, and Wailea Beach Villas. To reach the "trailhead" for the walkway, park in the public lot at Ulua Beach, at the bottom of Ulua Beach Road, or in the public lot on the southern end of the trail at Polo Beach, at the bottom of Kaukahi Street. At the far northern end, the walkway becomes sand and traverses the dunes past Mokapu Beach, where it links to Keawakapu in Kihei. In front of the Marriott, you can watch whales in winter through rented binoculars ($0.50).

Makena and Beyond
★ HOAPILI TRAIL

Hot, barren, and in the middle of nowhere, the **Hoapili Trail** isn't as much about hiking as about stepping back in time. Although the 5.5-mile trail (round-trip) takes about four hours, even an hour introduces you to a side of the island most visitors never see.

The trail was once an ancient Hawaiian walking path reserved for royalty. In 1824, sections of the trail were reconstructed, and pepper-colored shore of black lava rock and sun-bleached coral. You'll notice the remnants of multiple structures, once part of an ancient fishing village.

Although Kanaio Beach is the turnaround point for most hikers, the King's Highway continues to Highway 31 on the "back road to Hana." To reach the highway, however, requires an overnight stay along the trail; camping is permitted along the shore from points east of Kanaio Beach. To travel just a little farther, however, a sandy road continues from Kanaio Beach and winds along the coast. Another 20 minutes of walking from Kanaio brings you to a shore that's completely bathed in bleached white coral, and on the southern end of the "white beach" is an ancient Hawaiian *heiau* set out on the point that looks much the same now as it must have when it was built.

BIKING

For a casual bike ride in South Maui, it doesn't get better than renting a beach cruiser and pedaling to beach-hop, bar-hop, and coolly cruise the strip, not worrying about traffic or finding parking. For an epic half-day road biking adventure, ride from Kihei to Makena and the lava-strewn "end of the road," where you can cycle across the island's last lava flow and relax at beaches as you go.

Kihei

If you're a hard-core cyclist, head to **South Maui Cycles** (1993 S. Kihei Rd., 808/874-0068, www.southmauibicycles.com, 10am-6pm Mon.-Sat.), across the street from Kalama Park to rent road bikes ($22-60 per day, $99-250 per week). This is a full-service bicycle shop that also offers sales and repairs.

To beach-hop for a while, beach cruisers ($15 per day, $50 per week) are available from **Boss Frog's Bike Shop** (1770 S. Kihei Rd., 808/661-3333, www.bossfrog.com, 8am-5pm daily). There are also mountain bikes, hybrid bikes, and proper road bikes. You can also pick up a cruiser at another Boss location in the Dolphin Plaza, across from the southern end of Kamaole II Beach Park.

Golf

KIHEI

If you just want to play a relaxing round without shelling out resort prices, **Maui Nui Golf Club** (470 Lipoa Pkwy., 808/874-0777, www.mauinuigolfclub.com) is one of the island's best values. The views look out toward Molokini Crater, and while this course isn't as challenging as the Wailea Gold course, it still provides an enjoyable round. Club and equipment rentals are available from the pro shop, and there's a driving range for working on your stroke before your round. The afternoon trade winds can have a major effect on play, reflected in the greens fees for morning rounds (from $119) and afternoon tee times (as low as $42). To save a few dollars, check the website for online specials. On a winter day with light winds, you can sneak in an enjoyable twilight round after a morning at Molokini Crater. As an added bonus, your first beer at Kono's Green—the golf course's 19th hole—is the same price as the score for your round—just present your completed scorecard.

WAILEA

Without question, the **Wailea Gold** (100 Wailea Golf Club Dr., 808/875-7450, www.waileagolf.com) is the best golf course in South Maui, where the pros play when they come to town. The 7,000-yard-plus course and 93 bunkers challenge even those with low handicaps. Guests at the Wailea resort complex can play a morning round for $199, and nonguests pay $215. The May 1 to December 20 rates are only $179-189, and sunset twilight play at 3:30pm can be as low as $99. Club rental and practice facilities are located at the main Wailea clubhouse.

If the Gold course is intimidating, the **Wailea Emerald** (100 Wailea Golf Club Dr., 808/875-7450, www.waileagolf.com) is far more forgiving. The course isn't quite as long, but it is still a proper resort course with technical challenges and amenities, so you still need to bring your A-game. Greens fees are the same as the Gold course.

The **Wailea Old Blue** (100 Wailea Golf Club Dr., 808/875-7450, www.waileagolf.com) course, constructed in 1972, is Maui's second golf course after Ka'anapali. Not only is Old Blue an easier course, it's also substantially cheaper ($185 nonguests, $99 Super Twilight). In summer you can sneak in nine holes after 2pm for only $60. After you card your best round of your vacation, head down to Manoli's to celebrate at the bar.

Spas

KIHEI

To save money over the pricey resorts (but also sacrifice ambience), there are a handful of places off South Kihei Road to get a relaxing massage. A popular choice is **The Hidden Spa** (1993 S. Kihei Rd., 808/214-6862, www.obhiddenspa.com, 9am-7pm Tues.-Sat., 10am-6pm Sun.-Mon.), with 30-minute ($30) and 60-minute ($60) massages.

If you're staying in Ma'alaea or North Kihei and don't want to travel to South Kihei or Wailea, **Massage Maui** (145 N. Kihei Rd., 808/357-7317, www.massage-maui.com, 8am-9pm daily) is a low-key massage option where you can either meet the masseuse in the Sugar Beach location ($95) or arrange for an outcall massage where the therapist visits you in your condo ($115).

WAILEA

When it comes to choosing South Maui's best spa, it's tough to beat a 50,000-square-foot luxury arena that has been voted the best spa in Hawaii and among the top 10 in the United States. **Spa Grande** (3850 Wailea Alanui Dr., 808/875-1234 x 4949, www.grandwailea.com/spa, 8am-7pm daily), the palatial spa inside the Grand Wailea completely redefines the concept of pampering. It's Hawaii's largest spa, and all guests are advised to arrive an hour early to enjoy a casual complimentary

soak in the hydrotherapy baths before your treatment.

Can't decide among the Roman hot tub, Japanese *furo* baths, or honey-mango loofah exfoliation? Do them all as a package! A 50-minute massage treatment runs $185 on average, and an 80-minute *lomilomi* massage is $260. Along with an enormous selection of facials and treatment options, there's also a beauty salon and fitness center.

Down the beach at the Fairmont Kea Lani, the **Willow Stream Spa** (4100 Wailea Alanui Dr., 808/875-2229, www.fairmont.com/kea-lani-maui, 7:30am-7pm daily) has also been voted among the best in Hawaii, and they work to incorporate plants grown on property in many massages and services. During the 120-minute Natural Hawaiian Journey, pamper yourself with a clay body mask and an invigorating Hawaiian salt scrub before a therapist wraps you in a resort-grown *ti* and administers a scalp and face massage. Finish off by rinsing yourself in a rain-inspired shower, and then slink down to the pool.

As you might expect, **The Spa at Four Seasons** (808/874-8000, www.fourseasons.com, 8am-9pm daily) is just as lavish and over the top, and a nice perk here is the option of getting a massage in an oceanfront cabana. The prices are often higher than Spa Grande, but the offerings of wellness options, body treatments, and massage are no less impressive.

For guests of the Marriott, there's the **Mandara Spa** (3700 Wailea Alanui Dr., 808/891-8774, www.mandaraspa.com, 8am-8pm daily), or to spend 30 minutes with an apothecary consultant who personalizes your experience with herbs, head to the **Awili Spa** (Andaz Maui, 3550 Wailea Alanui Dr., 808/573-1234, www.maui.andaz.hyatt.com) for a unique approach to well-being.

Aroma Stone Wailea Healing Center (161 Wailea Ike Place, 808/264-9999, www.aromastonewailea.com, 10am-5pm Mon.-Fri., 10am-4pm Sat.) is another out-of-resort option that only requires a five-minute drive yet saves enough money almost to come back for a second round. Close to the Wailea Tennis Center, in between the Shops at Wailea and the Wailea Gateway Center, this healing zone offers 60-minute massage treatments ($105) that are infused with essential oils and hot stones.

Horseback Riding and Bird-Watching

HORSEBACK RIDING
Makena and Beyond

The only horseback riding in South Maui is *way* south, at the end of the road at **Makena Stables** (8299 S. Makena Rd., 808/879-0244, www.makenastables.com), a family-run outfit that has been leading horseback riding tours since 1983. The trails meander over Ulupalakua Ranch, only accessible on a private tour. Along the way there's a good chance of spotting axis deer or wild goats that clamber across the jagged *'a'a* lava.

This is one of the few horseback riding operations on the island with the possibility of riding your horse along the shore. Not only do the views stretch out toward Kaho'olawe in the distance, but you ride directly through the island's most recent lava flow, taking time to stop at Kalua O Lapa, the volcanic vent from which Madame Pele leaked her fiery liquid. Group sizes are capped at six, and riders must be under 205 pounds. To escape the brutal South Maui sun, take a sunset ride during the coast's most romantic hour.

BIRD-WATCHING
Kihei

If South Maui had a mascot, it would be the *kolea*, or Pacific golden plover, since it leaves its summer home in the Arctic for winter in Maui.

For exceptional bird watching, the **Kealia Pond National Wildlife Refuge** (www.fws.gov/kealiapond), between Ma'alaea and Kihei, is 700 acres of open wetlands with over 30 species of birds, including the *ae'o* (Hawaiian stilt), *'alae ke'oke'o* (Hawaiian coot), and *koloa maoli* (Hawaiian duck). The greatest number of species is found in winter. There are short walking trails that leave from the visitors center (mile marker 6 on Mokulele Hwy.) into the Kealia Pond area. There's also a short boardwalk from Ma'alaea to North Kihei that parallels the shoreline and offers a number of informative placards about the island's native wildlife. The boardwalk takes about 30 minutes to walk to the end and back. It's best to approach from the Ma'alaea side of the road because there's no left turn allowed into the parking lot off North Kihei Road.

Another place to try your luck is on the beach walk between the Kihei Boat Ramp and the south end of Kamaole III Beach. The coastal dune system here is home to *'ua'u kani* (wedge-tailed shearwaters), and the fledgling season is usually October-December. Although **Molokini Crater** is best known for snorkeling, few people know that the 161-foot-tall islet is also a seabird sanctuary, home to a healthy population of *'ua'u kani* as well as soaring frigates. If you're an avid birder and are planning a trip to Molokini, bring binoculars to check out what's happening above water, not just down on the reef.

Those with an interest in Maui County's seabirds should check out the **Maui Nui Seabird Recovery Project** (www.mauinuiseabirds.org).

Makena and Beyond

The best place for bird-watching in Makena is at **Oneuli Beach** by Makena State Park. Although the chances of seeing many species of birds are slim, this coastal wetland area is home to avian species such as the *'auku'u* (black-crowned night heron), *'alae ke'oke'o* (Hawaiian coot), and *ulili* (wandering tattler).

Shopping

MA'ALAEA
Ma'alaea Harbor Shops

The handful of shops at **Ma'alaea Harbor Shops** (300 Ma'alaea Rd., 808/242-8900) have periodic craft fairs. The most popular retail outlet is **Da Beach House** (808/986-8279, 10am-5:30pm daily), with a surprising assortment of beach and surf wear to accompany a wide range of accessories.

KIHEI
North End

At the far northern end of Kihei is the **Sugar Beach General Store** (145 N. Kihei Rd., 808/879-9899, 8am-8:30pm daily) within the Sugar Beach Resort. It can fill your basic sundry needs.

Up on Pi'ilani Highway, the **Kihei Gateway Plaza** is a sprawling semi-industrial compound with a smattering of clothing shops. Of the main stores in the plaza, the largest is **Maui Clothing Outlet** (362 Huku Li'i Place, 808/875-0308, 9am-8pm Mon.-Sat., 10am-6pm Sun.), with an enormous selection of resort wear and island-themed clothing at discount prices. One of the sister stores in the same area is **Pretty Wahine** (362 Huku Li'i Place, 808/879-1199, 10am-6pm daily), with women's boutique clothing options.

If you turn up Pi'ikea Avenue between the Azeka Mauka Center and the Long's Shopping Center, you'll quickly come to the **Pi'ilani Village Shopping Center** (291 Pi'ikea Ave., 808/874-5151), which has the most relevant shopping options in North Kihei. A big draw

is the **Hilo Hattie's** (808/875-4545, 9am-9pm daily) clothing store, with a wide range of men's and women's apparel. If you need a swimsuit, **Maui Waterwear** (808/891-8319, 9am-9pm Mon.-Sat., 9am-7pm Sun.) specializes in women's bikinis and beach accessories.

Central Kihei

Central Kihei is the land of the roadside shopping stall. One exception is the **Local Motion** (1819 S. Kihei Rd., 808/879-7873, www.localmotionhawaii.com, 9am-8pm Mon.-Sat., 9am-5pm Sun.) surf shop inside the Kukui Mall, one of longest-running surf shops in Kihei and an undisputed local favorite, carrying a large collection of surfing and board accessories. Across the parking lot, **The Bikini Market** (1819 S. Kihei Rd., 808/891-8700, www.thebikinimarket.com, 8am-6pm daily) caters to a female clientele and promotes high-end swimwear and pieces designed by local artists.

Across the road from Kukui Mall is the **Aloha Open Market** (1794 S. Kihei Rd., 9am-7pm daily), which has grown over the years from tents and roadside crafts to a legitimate retail outlet. The most popular shop is **Maui Mana** (808/875-7881), a head shop.

The largest concentration of shopping in Kihei is in the **Kihei Kalama Village** (1941 S. Kihei Rd., 808/874-0003, 10am-7pm daily), with over 40 businesses, the most notable being **Da Beach House** (808/891-1234, www.dabeachhousemaui.com) for surf-themed apparel, **Mahina** (808/879-3453,

Did Menehune Build the Ko'ie'ie Fishpond?

In Hawaiian lore, Menehune are the mythical little people of the Hawaiian Islands who are believed to be mysterious, mischievous, and quick in their work. While stories about Menehune abound, the most commonly told one involves the building of stone fishponds across the Hawaiian Islands. In a story similar to those found on Kaua'i and Moloka'i, Ko'ie'ie Fishpond in North Kihei is believed to have been built by Menehune in the course of a single night.

Don't pass this off as a playful legend, however; history supports the claim. It's believed by many scholars that the Hawaiian Islands were populated by seafaring voyagers from the Marquesas Islands around AD 400-600, and that these original small-in-stature inhabitants were supplanted in AD 1100 by much larger settlers from Tahiti. As it turns out, the Tahitian word for "commoner" is *manahune*, and it's believed that the ruling Tahitian class put the Marquesans to work on building the fishponds.

As Hawaiian society progressed and the centuries wore on, it's theorized that the *manahune* remained lower-class citizens. Much of the evidence for this theory is derived from a census on the island of Kaua'i in 1820, where, in a tantalizing fusion of history and lore, 65 citizens classified themselves as being *manahune*.

So, did magical little people build Ko'ie'ie Fishpond, or did a diminutive class of indentured workers stack all the stones in the sea? Since there was no written language at the time of its construction, believed to be AD 1400-1500, all we are left with are the legends, the stones … and the Menehune Shores condominium on the shore.

www.mahinamaui.com) for women's apparel, **Serendipity** (808/874-8471, www.serendipitymaui.com) for fine women's clothing, and **The Love Shack Maui** (808/875-0303, www.loveshackmaui.com) for intimate moments. There are also myriad kiosks and stands where you can get henna tattoos or play with a digeridoo. This shopping area is within walking distance of the Cove Park, where most of the surf rentals take place, so if part of your group is out surfing, you can wander down here for some souvenir browsing while they are on the water.

South End

In the **Kamaole Beach Center,** the main retail outlet is **Honolua Surf Company** (2411 S. Kihei Rd., 808/874-0999, 9am-9pm daily), specializing in high-quality surf clothing. You can occasionally get the same Honolua-brand clothing cheaper than at Whalers Village in Ka'anapali or at the nearby Shops at Wailea.

Rainbow Mall is home to **Maui Fine Art & Frame** (2439 S. Kihei Rd., 808/222-3055, www.mauiartframe.com, 11am-8pm daily), one of the few art galleries in Kihei. In

addition to numerous island-themed paintings and ceramics, the frames that encompass the artwork are an art form unto themselves.

WAILEA

While all of the high-end luxury resorts have a decent amount of shopping, particularly the Grand Wailea, the majority of retail on this side of the island is at the shopping centers and shops.

Shops at Wailea

Any longtime visitor to Maui will remember when the **Shops at Wailea** (3750 Wailea Alanui Dr., 808/891-6770, www.theshopsatwailea.com, 9:30am-9pm daily) were a plantation-style shopping complex with wide grassy areas and free hula shows from local *halau* (hula schools). These days, the complex has gone upscale. Inside you'll find art galleries such as **Ki'i Gallery** (808/874-1181) and **Dolphin Galleries** (808/891-8000) accompanying surf shops like **Billabong** (808/879-8330) and **Honolua Surf Company** (808/891-8229). You can often spot celebrities hanging out in luxury stalwarts such as **Tiffany and Co.** (808/891-9226), **Gucci** (808/879-1060), or **Louis Vuitton** (808/875-6980).

Aside from the high-end chain stores, you can also find a few island-themed shops offering unique and boutique souvenirs. At **Sand People** (808/891-8801, www.sandpeople. com), you can pick up coast-inspired gifts and home decor, and **Martin & MacArthur** (808/891-8844, www.martinandmacarthur. com) showcases Hawaiian-made crafts and an assortment of koa woods. If you're missing something from your cosmetics kit, **Cos Bar** (808/891-9448, www.cosbar.com) carries makeup lines, such as Bobbi Brown, that you won't find anywhere else on the island. If you're in need of a fancy gift, **Na Hoku** (808/891-8040) offers unique Hawaiian-inspired jewelry.

Wailea Gateway Plaza

Although it doesn't have anywhere near the glitz and glamour of the Shops at Wailea, the awkwardly placed little **Wailea Gateway Center** (10 Wailea Ike Dr.) still has a couple of boutique shops worth a visit. One of those is **Otaheite Hawaii** (808/419-6179, www.otaheitehawaii.com, 10am-9pm Mon.-Sat., 10am-6pm Sun.), which specializes in chic island-lifestyle beach clothing. Local

designer Tiare Lawrence customizes the fabrics around her love for the ocean and traditional Hawaiian background, which means lots of creative swimwear and sundresses to accompany the gifts and accessories.

If your sweet tooth is aching, **Sweet Paradise Chocolatier** (808/344-1040, www.sweetparadisechocolate.com, 10am-8pm daily) will lure you with the scent of rich chocolate. In addition to an ornate spread of fine chocolates, all the items are made on the island, and some of the cacao is even grown in Hawaii—the only U.S. state currently growing cacao.

Next door, **Panties in Paradise** (808/879-5057, 11am-9pm daily) has soft and sensual lingerie, lace, and negligees, and is easily the sexiest shop in Wailea—and just happens to be next to a chocolate store.

Wailea Town Center

Although this is mostly an office complex, one retail outlet worth a mention is **Wailea Wine** (161 Wailea Ike Place, 808/879-0555, www.waileawine.com, 10am-6pm Mon.-Fri., 10am-5pm Sat.), with an exceptional selection of wines from across the globe and one of the largest on the island, along with gourmet culinary options.

Entertainment

MA'ALAEA
Live Music

In the downstairs section of the Ma'alaea Harbor Shops, **Beach Bums** (300 Ma'alaea Rd., 808/243-2286, until 9pm daily) has live music 5pm-8pm daily, which coincides with the 3pm-6pm happy hour and $2.75 PBR pints. If you're staying in one of the condos at Ma'alaea, this is your best bet for a happening atmosphere and the chance to mingle with boat crews who are drinking through that morning's tips.

KIHEI
Events

The largest and most popular event in South Maui is the **Fourth Friday** celebration, held 6pm-9pm on the fourth Friday of the month at the Azeka Mauka shopping complex. There are multiple live music performances and beer gardens scattered throughout. It's a surprisingly well organized affair that's fun for the entire family.

For an artistic event that happens most nights, **Island Art Party** (1279 S. Kihei Rd., 808/419-6020, www.islandartparty.com,

No Dancing!

The best place to go dancing in Maui is at the Kihei Kalama Village (aka the Triangle), since it's home to nearly all the places on Maui where you're legally allowed to dance. That's right—believe it or not, dancing in Maui is technically illegal at most of the island's bars.

In order for an establishment to legally permit dancing, there needs to be a designated area that is either roped off or separated in some way from the designated drinking area. There are to be no drinks on the dance floor, and randomly choosing to shake your rump while waiting in line at the bar is strictly verboten and can get you thrown out.

So why the strict rules? When it comes to the law, the dancers themselves won't get in trouble, but rather the licensed establishment can potentially lose its liquor license. The strangest part is that there is no legal definition for what constitutes dancing. Consequently, anything that involves rhythmic or purposeful movement, from a shoulder shake to a toe tap, can be construed as illicit, dangerous, and legally unacceptable. Unless, of course, you put down your drink and make your way to the designated dance floor.

Local dance advocate groups have been recommending bills to the state legislature for years in an effort to change the law (or at least define dancing), but for reasons that continue to defy logic, dancing remains an often forbidden pursuit.

10am-9:30pm) is a unique venue where you can join an instructor-led painting class while sipping a glass of wine. It's one of the island's best rainy-day activities and is for ages 16 and up.

Live Music and Dancing
INSIDE THE TRIANGLE

The majority of Kihei's nightlife takes place at the Triangle, as in, the *Barmuda* Triangle, where you could end up getting lost for days. This collection of bars within the Kihei Kalama Village can almost seem like a tropical fraternity row, with each house on the street having a different theme party.

If you're starting your night early, check out **Haui's Life's A Beach** (1913 S. Kihei Rd., 808/891-8010, www.mauibars.com, until 2am daily), aka **The Lab.** This rockin' beach bar has an outdoor patio that looks toward South Kihei Road and is a great place for people-watching. There is live music most nights, or you can shoot some pool, watch some sports, and eavesdrop on local happenings.

The best venue within the Triangle for live music is **Three's Bar and Grill** (1945 S. Kihei Rd., 808/879-3133, www.threesbarandgrill.com, until 1:30am daily), a semiformal dining establishment that also has a VIP Surf Lounge with a built-in stage area

and lighting. Weekdays often have music around dinner time, and weekend shows begin around 10pm and usually stretch until closing.

The most popular club in the traditional sense of the word is the **South Shore Tiki Lounge** (1913 S. Kihei Rd., 808/874-6444, www.southshoretikilounge.com, until 2am daily), where resident DJs play for a small but crowded dance floor. This place gets popular on weekends with its thumping house beats and young singles.

Across the parking lot, swap your draft beer for some cutting-edge mixology at **Ambrosia** (1913 S. Kihei Rd., 808/891-1011, www.ambrosiamaui.com, until 2am daily), a small martini bar that specializes in "upscale drinking." DJs spin on many nights of the week, and the vibe is decidedly classier and more refined than at some of the neighboring venues.

For an authentic dive bar—not the fashionable kind—**Kahale's Beach Club** (36 Keala Place, 808/875-7711, until 2am daily) is a working-class bar with live music, cheap drinks, and a decidedly local atmosphere. The beer is some of the cheapest on the island, and you won't find grass skirts, convertibles, or timeshare salespeople within a respectable radius.

Finally, for a good old-fashioned touch of the *craic*, **Dog and Duck Irish Pub** (1913 S. Kihei Rd., 808/875-9669, until 2am daily) is a small gathering place where you can throw darts, eat bangers and mash, drink Guinness, rock out to live music, or take part in the popular quiz nights. To switch up the drinking venue, right next door is the recently opened **What Ales You** (808/214-6581, www.whatalesyoumaui.com, 11am-10pm daily), a small tap house with 16 beers on tap and about 20 wines on the wine list.

OUTSIDE THE TRIANGLE

At the other end of the parking lot of the Azeka Mauka is **Diamonds Ice Bar** (1279 S. Kihei Rd., 808/874-9299, www.diamondsicebar.com, until 2am daily), a small establishment tucked in the end unit that offers live music most nights. If you have a large group, there's a private VIP room. While it doesn't see the same amount of crowds as down at the Triangle, it can still be a happening place if the right band is playing.

Moose McGillicuddy's (2511 S. Kihei Rd., 808/891-8644, until 2am daily) harnesses the late-night crowd in South Kihei who are looking for cheap drink specials and an old-fashioned good time. This sports bar cranks up the music at 9pm and caters mostly to the single crowd that's looking to get a bit weird.

WAILEA
Shows

Surprisingly there aren't that many dinner shows on Maui, but one that will wow you is the **Willie K Dinner Show** held at Mulligan's on the Blue (100 Kaukahi St., 808/874-1131, www.mulligansontheblue.com, 6:30pm Wed., $65). Even if you've never heard of Uncle Willie K, once you see him play, you'll never forget him. An insanely talented local Hawaiian musician who grew up on Maui, Willie K's prowess stretches across a wide range of genres, from blues to Hawaiian to rock-and-roll and opera. The show usually happens on Wednesday, but since the schedule can vary, check the online calendar.

If you're on a budget and looking for a free public show, **Wailea Leʻa** (6:30pm-8pm 3rd Wed. of the month) at the **Shops at Wailea** (3750 Wailea Alanui Dr., 808/891-6770, www.theshopsatwailea.com) usually features free performances by famous Hawaiian artists.

Luau

The best luau on the island is Old Lahaina Luau in Lahaina, but if you're staying on the south end of the island and don't want to drive that far, there are two options in South Maui. My top pick is **The Grand Luau at Honuaʻula** (3850 Wailea Alanui Dr., 808/875-7710, www.honuaula-luau.com, 4pm Mon. and Thurs.-Sat., $105 adults, $57 children) because the show focuses more on Hawaiian history than the South Pacific in general. The luau takes place on the grounds of the Grand Wailea; Honuaʻula is a name given to this section of the island by the original Polynesians who migrated here centuries ago. Call in advance to check the schedule, which can vary.

Just a few steps down the coastal walkway is **Te Au Moana** (3700 Wailea Alanui, 877/827-2740, www.teaumoana.com, 4:30pm Mon. and Thurs.-Sat., $110 adults, $63 children), at the Wailea Beach Marriott. Showtimes overlap with neighboring Grand Wailea. This show focuses more on the dance and mythology of greater Polynesia than on Hawaii, but it's still a highly entertaining performance, particularly if it's your first luau. The stage backs up to the shore in front of the hotel. The backdrop of the setting sun creates a panorama you would expect from a luau in paradise.

Live Music

For live entertainment after the sun goes down, the most popular place in Wailea is **Mulligan's on the Blue** (100 Kaukahi St., 808/874-1131, www.mulligansontheblue.com, until 1am daily). This Irish pub is owned by a real Irishman, and aside from the Willie K dinner show, the next most popular evening is at 7pm Sunday, when the Celtic Tigers Irish folk band takes to the stage. There are also periodic performances by award-winning local artists, so pick up a copy of a local entertainment catalog to see what the happenings are.

At **Monkeypod** (10 Wailea Ike Dr., 808/891-2322, www.monkeypodkitchen.com, until 10:30pm daily) restaurant in the Wailea Gateway Center, not only do they have Wailea's best beer selection, but there's also live music every day beginning at 1pm.

You can also find live music inside hotel lobbies, with one of the best being the **Lobby Lounge** (3900 Wailea Alanui Dr., 808/874-8000, 5pm-11:30pm daily) bar inside the Four Seasons Wailea, with hula dancers performing around sunset and live music each night. Just down the beach walk, at the Grand Wailea, the **Botero Lounge** (800/888-6100) has live music and a lively bar 5pm-10pm daily.

Bars

For a traditional bar scene, head to **Manoli's Pizza Company** (100 Wailea Ike Dr., 808/874-7499, www.manolispizzacompany.com, until midnight daily), where, in addition to draft and bottled beers, there are 20 organic or sustainable wines. Late-night happy hour is 9pm-midnight daily, and it's within walking distance of many of the resorts.

By the clubhouse of the Wailea golf course—which requires a short drive from the resort strip—the Red Bar at **Gannon's** (100 Wailea Golf Club Dr., 808/875-8080, www.gannonsrestaurant.com, until 9pm daily) pairs the sexiest drinks in Wailea with a stunning ocean view. Choose from affordable draft beers, an extensive list of over 100 wines, and enticing cocktails made with everything from sweet tea vodka to açaí liqueur. There's also occasional live entertainment, usually paired with the 3pm-8pm happy hour.

Makena and Beyond

On Sunday nights, the most happening thing in Makena is the drum circle at sunset on Little Beach. More of a drug-infused people-watching spectacle, the event features drummers, fire dancers, hippies, nudists, and curious onlookers. It definitely isn't for everyone, but if you want a bit of counterculture or are up for enlightening conversation, climb the trail to Little Beach in the hour just before sunset. If you plan to stay late, park outside the gate of the First Entrance of Makena State Park.

Food

MA'ALAEA
American

If your idea of the perfect lunch is clutching a pint of PBR with barbecue-covered fingers, **Beach Bums Bar and Grill** (300 Ma'alaea Boat Harbor Rd., 808/243-2286, 8am-9pm daily, $8-25), downstairs in the Harbor Shops, is the perfect spot. It's a festive open-air sports den of pulled pork sandwiches, barbecue ribs, and sweet potato fries.

For lunch on the go, **Tradewinds Deli** (20 Hauoli St., 808/242-9161, 9am-6pm Mon.-Sat., 9am-4pm Sun.) has bowls of chili and rice ($6) and sandwiches ($8.50). This old-school store has been around for 35 years. You'll find it

tucked in the Ma'alaea Mermaid condo right next to Ma'alaea Harbor.

KIHEI
American

One of the best breakfast finds on the south side is ★ **Kihei Caffe** (1945 S. Kihei Rd., 808/879-2230, www.kiheicaffe.net, 5am-2pm daily, $7-10), which gloriously opens at 5am if you're waking up early from jet lag. The portions are enormous, and breakfast is served all day. Try a generous omelet or gargantuan breakfast burrito, and since the atmosphere can be hectic, get here early to beat the crowds.

One of the best things to happen to Kihei in recent years is ★ **Nalu's South Shore**

Grill (1280 S. Kihei Rd., 808/891-8650, www. nalusmaui.com, 8am-9pm daily). Many of the ingredients are local or organic, and the seared ahi club ($14) is Kihei's best sandwich. Located in the Azeka Mauka shopping center, order at the counter.

For refined and relaxing comfort food in a hidden South Kihei garden, ★ 808 Bistro (2511 S. Kihei Rd., 808/879-8008, 7am-noon and 5pm-9pm daily) offers welcome serenity from the bustle out on the street. Located across from Kamaole II Beach, the restaurant can be hard to find; walk past Fred's Mexican Café to find the bistro around back. Breakfast has omelets and banana bread French toast ($7-10), and dinner is American comfort food at prices cheaper than in Wailea. Bonus: It's BYOB.

For gourmet burgers and a lengthy Scotch list, Cow Pig Bun (535 Lipoa Pkwy., 808/875-8100, www.cowpigbun.com, 11am-midnight daily, $14-19) is a strangely named restaurant with curiously amazing food. Try the burger on a brioche bun with pepper jack, mushroom, pickled onions, and a touch of Sriracha aioli.

Finally, if you just want a quick and filling burger, Stewz Maui Burgers (1819 S. Kihei Rd., 808/879-0497, www.stewzmauiburgers. com, 11am-8:30pm daily) in Kukui Mall is a take-out window with local grass-fed beef from Maui Cattle Company ($9).

Brewery

Maui Brewing Company (605 Lipoa Pkwy., 808/213-3002, www.mauibrewingco.com, 11am-10pm daily) is slowly beginning to dominate Hawaii's beer scene. They're already the largest craft producer in the Aloha State, and with their shimmering new Kihei brewery, with 36 of their own beers on tap, this island favorite is rapidly turning into a major player. Tours of the brewery (noon-3:15pm daily, $15 pp) are offered six times per day and include a souvenir glass and a token for a pint. Need some food to soak up the suds? There's a rotating schedule of food trucks outside 11am-10pm daily.

Coffee Shops

The most modern coffee shop in Kihei is Java Café (1279 S. Kihei Rd., 808/214-6095, www. javacafemaui.com, 5am-9pm daily, $7-9), in the Azeka Mauka shopping center; 75 percent of the coffee served is grown in Hawaii. You can also buy bags of beans from coffee farms on Maui, Kaua'i, Moloka'i, and the Big Island. Flatbreads and *paninis* are available for lunch; there's also a large selection of breakfast bagels.

For a coffee shop with a quirky French twist, Café@La Plage (2395 S. Kihei Rd., 808/875-7668, www.cafealaplage.com, 6:30am-5pm daily) is located in Dolphin Plaza across from Kam I beach. In addition to the menu of coffee and espresso, breakfast bagels and sandwiches average $6-8.

Delivery

Too tired to go out for food? There's a new service on Maui called Hopper Maui (808/214-6171, www.hoppermaui.com) where you can order from one of 20 different restaurants and have it delivered to your door. You'll pay a 15 percent fee on top of your meal, which doesn't include a tip for the driver, but in terms of convenience, it's tough to beat.

French

Completely hidden in central Kihei is cozy Chez Meme (115 Kio Loop, 808/879-5425, www.baguettebistromaui.com, 7am-2pm daily, $10-25), a French bistro that makes its own jam and bakes its own bread and brioche. Try the French toast, since breakfast is served all day, and lunch has French favorites like ratatouille and beef bourguignon.

Hawaiian Regional

Since most of Kihei's restaurants are in strip malls, there isn't an overabundance of fine dining. The exception, however, is ★ Sarento's on the Beach (2980 S. Kihei Rd., 808/875-7555, www.sarentosonthebeach.com, 7am-11am and 5:30pm-10pm daily, $28-49), on the water at the north end of Keawakapu Beach. You won't find a more romantic or relaxing spot in Kihei. Start off with the seared ahi or beef carpaccio before moving on to the pan-roasted island snapper or rack of lamb Placourakis. Valet parking is free, and if you show up about an hour before sunset, you'll probably get a seat with a fiery view during dessert.

Another local favorite is **Three's Bar and Grill** (1945 S. Kihei Rd., 808/879-3133, www. threesbarandgrill.com, 11am-9:30pm Mon.-Tues., 8:30am-9:30pm Wed.-Sun., lunch $10-15, dinner $20-25), inside the Kihei Kalama Village. Opened by three chefs who each boast their own culinary specialty—Hawaiian, Southwestern, and Pacific Rim—the restaurant has lunch and appetizer items such as Hawaiian-style ribs and kalua pig quesadilla. Dinner menu entrées feature chicken roulade and a raw bar of sushi and *poke*.

Japanese

★ **Sansei** (1881 S. Kihei Rd., 808/879-0004, www.sanseihawaii.com, 5:30pm-10pm daily, $16) has been a South Maui favorite since 2002. Award-winning dishes such as the *panko*-crusted ahi rolls and signature shrimp dynamite keep locals flocking to this nondescript spot. For a night on the town, hit up the half-priced sushi menu after 10pm Thursday-Saturday, where the *unagi* and rainbow rolls will leave sushi-lovers feeling like kids in a candy store. Late nights can be noisy, with sake and karaoke.

Koiso Sushi Bar (2395 S. Kihei Rd., 808/875-8258, 6pm-10pm Mon.-Sat., $10-32) on the other hand, is a boutique sushi bar with only 15 seats that you'd expect to find in a city. The *nigiri* and sashimi are astoundingly fresh. Connoisseurs will by surprised by this hidden Kihei find.

Local Style

The only true local-style plate lunch in Kihei is at ★ **Da Kitchen** (2439 S. Kihei Rd., 808/875-7782, www.da-kitchen.com, 9am-9pm daily, $8-15), toward the back of the Rainbow Mall in South Kihei. Although the restaurant isn't as large as its Kahului counterpart,

the portions are enormous enough that you could split them and still walk away full. This hole-in-the-wall strip-mall special is one of the best deals in town. If you're looking for a place where locals eat, this is it.

Mexican

At the very authentic **Taqueria Cruz** (2395 S. Kihei Rd., 808/875-2910, www.taqueriacruz. com, 11:30am-8:30pm Mon.-Fri.) you can hear the *norteño* music from the kitchen before it even opens. Tucked in the back of Dolphin Plaza across from Kam I beach, this is reminiscent of a roadside taqueria you might find on the back roads of Baja. The BYOB capability means you can enjoy your fish tacos with a Pacífico from your own cooler. There are taco specials ($2), burritos ($9), and live music 6:30pm-8:30pm Tuesday night.

On the weekend, get a margarita from the bar at **Amigos** (1215 S. Kihei Rd., 808/879-9952, www.amigosmaui.com, 8am-9pm daily) located in the Long's Shopping Center in the heart of central Kihei.

Natural Foods

The best natural foods market for organic, raw, or gluten-free fare is **Hawaiian Moons** (2411 S. Kihei Rd., 808/875-4356, www.hawaiianmoons.com, 8am-9pm daily, $5-15), within the Kamaole Beach Center across from Kamaole I. The hot bar serves up filling lunches.

In the Azeka Mauka shopping center, ★ **Wow Wow Hawaiian Lemonade** (1279 S. Kihei Rd., 808/344-0319, www.wowwowhawaiianlemonade.com, 7:30am-4pm daily, $8-12) has açaí bowls with *haupia* or poi, topped with locally grown fruits. This local company is working to source all their fruits from Hawaiian farmers and is committed to bettering the local community in addition to serving great food.

Pizza

While it may sound counterintuitive, Kihei's best pizza is at the **South Shore Tiki Lounge** (1913 S. Kihei Rd., 808/874-6444, www.

southshoretikilounge.com, 11am-2am daily, $18-27) in the Kihei Kalama Village. Pies are handcrafted with local ingredients and wheat flour; sit outside on the garden-view deck for a relaxing place to dine.

Another favorite for south shore pizza is ★ **Fabiani's Bakery and Pizza** (95 E. Lipoa St., 808/874-0888, www.fabianis.com, 7am-9:30pm daily, $10-12) in central Kihei. Located in a strip mall, it's tough to find, but once you get there, you'll realize why it's a local hangout: Lunch and dinner are dominated by fresh, tasty pizzas and *paninis* crafted by a chef from Italy. There's also a decent wine selection, and the atmosphere inside is nicer than the exterior suggests. The fresh breakfast pastries are a local secret, and the 50-percent-off pizzas at the 3pm-5pm daily happy hour are one of the best deals in Kihei.

Shaka Sandwich and Pizza (1770 S. Kihei Rd., 808/874-0331, www.shakapizza. com, 10:30am-9pm Sun.-Thurs., 10:30am-10pm Fri.-Sat.) has been around for over 25 years and is the south side's original pizza joint. The homemade 18-inch Italian pies are big enough to fill two hungry teenagers, and the cheese steak supreme hoagie is a local favorite. Pizzas run $21-31, and by the slice is only $3.

Seafood

Hidden back in the central Kihei industrial yard is ★ **Eskimo Candy** (2665 Wai Wai Place, 808/879-5686, www.eskimocandy.com, 10:30am-7pm Mon.-Fri., $10-17), Kihei's best local secret for fresh seafood. Try the seafood chowder, fish-and-chips, and *poke*, featuring four different styles of seasoned ahi tuna. There are only a few tables outside for dining, and they also have wholesale rates on fish for grilling back at your condo. To find it, make the turn off South Kihei Road by Maui Dive Shop and the Avis car rental outlet, continuing toward the end of the road; the restaurant is on the right.

In Kihei Kalama Village, **Paia Fish Market** (1913 S. Kihei Rd., 808/874-8888, www.paiafishmarket.com, 11am-9:30pm

daily) now has a Kihei outlet for their mouth-watering $10-12 fish burgers, and it's a casual spot for grabbing some lunch after a morning of surfing at The Cove.

For fish tacos, **Coconut's Fish Café** (1279 S. Kihei Rd., 808/875-9979, www.coconutsfishcafe.com, 10am-9pm daily) serves tacos piled high with 17 different ingredients, and is a casual stop in the Azeka Mauka shopping center.

WAILEA

Prices in Wailea are much higher than in other parts of the island, and double the cost in Kihei. You're often paying for master chefs, exceptional service, and unparalleled ambience in world-class resorts.

American

The first restaurant you'll encounter in Wailea approaching from Pi'ilani Highway is ★ **Monkeypod Kitchen** (10 Wailea Ike Dr., 808/891-2322, www.monkeypodkitchen.com, 11:30am-10:30pm daily, $13-35), the brainchild of renowned Maui chef Peter Merriman. Ingredients are all sourced locally, supporting sustainable farming and ensuring fresh, healthy meals. Dinner options range from sesame-crusted mahimahi to *bulgogi* pork tacos in an Asian pear aioli, or an organic spinach and quinoa salad big enough to share. The craft beer list is the best in Wailea. To save a few bucks, visit during happy hour, 3pm-5:30pm and again 9pm-11pm daily, when appetizers are 50 percent off and pizzas are only $9.

Hawaiian Regional

At the Four Seasons, **Duo** (3900 Wailea Alanui, 808/874-8000, 6:30am-11am, 5:30pm-9pm daily, $30-50) ranks in the upper echelon of fine island cuisine. The dinner menu is dominated by steak and seafood options such as Brandt True filet mignon and *shiso panko*-crusted ahi. For something light, try the lobster bisque. The breakfast buffet is lauded as the best in Wailea.

At the beautiful Grand Wailea, **Humuhumunukunukuapua'a** (3850 Wailea Alanui Dr., 808/875-1234, www. grandwailea.com, 5:30pm-9pm daily, $30-49) is not only one of the hardest restaurants to pronounce, it's also one of the most popular. Named after the state fish, "Humu" sits in a thatched-roof Polynesian structure afloat on its own million-gallon saltwater lagoon. Large plates include the famous Hawaiian spiny lobster dish, where you can choose your lobster from the lagoon, as well as crispy mahimahi or fresh *opakapaka*. The sunset view looking over the lagoon is the classic image of paradise. The third Thursday of every month is the **Ka Malama Dinner** ($150), where the head chef, Mike Lofaro, teams with the resort's Hawaiian Cultural Ambassador to create a meal that's based around the traditional Hawaiian lunar calendar. The concept for the meal was so successful that it led to a television show, *Search Hawaii*, that's a fusion of culture and food.

Inside of the Marriott, **Migrant** (3700 Wailea Alanui Dr., 808/875-9394, www.migrantmaui.com, 4pm-10pm daily) is the brainchild of chef Sheldon Simeon of Star Noodle and *Top Chef* fame. The menu is inspired by dishes sourced from Maui's ethnic community, and chow fun noodles and *tocino* Filipino sweet pork are some popular local favorites. The food is so fresh that the menu lists the mileage to the farms where the food was sourced. To save a few bucks, visit the "Be Happy Hour," 4pm-6pm daily, when dishes are 50 percent off. There's also a sake bar and 36 beers—8 of which are on tap.

For more plantation-inspired cuisine, **Ka'ana Kitchen** (3550 Wailea Alanui Dr., 808/573-1234, 6:30am-11am and 5:30pm-9pm daily), inside the Andaz, is popular for both breakfast and dinner, where the chefs prepare food in an open-air kitchen you can see from your table. For breakfast, try the kalua pork Benedict with *ponzu* hollandaise ($22), and for dinner, abalone risotto ($31) or tender *wagyu* beef cheeks ($47).

Italian

Wailea's best pizza, ★ **Manoli's Pizza Company** (100 Wailea Ike Dr., 808/874-7499, www.manolispizzacompany.com, 11:30am-10pm daily, $16-22) is walking distance from many of the hotels, across from the Shops at Wailea. It serves 14-inch thin-crust pizzas, with organic and gluten-free options and toppings that include shrimp, pesto, kalamata olives, artichoke hearts, and feta cheese. There are salads, pasta, and a selection of 20 wines, and specials at happy hour, 3pm-6pm and again 9pm-midnight daily.

At the luxurious Four Seasons Resort, the tables at ★ **Ferraro's Bar e Ristorante** (3900 Wailea Alanui Dr., 808/874-8000, 11:30am-8pm daily, $30-50) are close enough to the ocean that you can dine to the sound of the waves. Clink glasses beneath the stars and savor the authentic *cucina rustica* while listening to a live violin. Lunch is more casual, with wood-fired pizzas, and why not some pinot gris?

Up on the hill at Hotel Wailea, **Capische?** (555 Kaukahi Rd., 808/879-2224, www.capische.com, 5pm-9:30pm daily) has a sweeping sunset view from the balcony looking over Wailea, and tremendously fancy Italian fine dining with a wine list that runs for miles. The service is spectacular, and much of the produce and herbs for the dishes are sourced on the property. Reservations are advised, and the menu changes seasonally.

Markets

For a quick meal in Wailea, there are thankfully some affordable options. At the **Island Gourmet Market** (3750 Wailea Alanui Dr., 808/847-5005, www.islandgourmethawaii.com, 6:30am-10:30pm daily) inside the Shops at Wailea, you can find breakfast ($6-8), chili and rice ($6) for a filling lunch, açaí bowls ($7) that provide a little health, and poke bowls ($7) for a fish power lunch. There's a coffee shop inside the store as well as a decent wine selection.

Up the hill, at **The Market by Capische?** (10 Wailea Ike Dr., 808/879-2433, 8am-7:30pm daily), the sandwich, smoothie, and coffee offerings are a little more gourmet, with prices that are reasonable for Wailea. Recharge with a Kumu Kale smoothie ($8), or sink your teeth into sourdough topped with cured meats, olives, and horseradish ($12). The Market is located inside the Wailea Gateway Plaza, directly under Monkeypod.

Seafood

In the Fairmont Kea Lani, **Nick's Fishmarket**

(4100 Wailea Alanui Dr., 808/879-7224, www. nicksfishmarketmaui.com, 5:30pm-9:45pm daily, $30-50) has whitewashed walls, a vine-covered trellis, and Mediterranean ambience. Selections include *opah,* mahimahi Kona *kampachi,* and Moroccan spiced salmon, along with creative sides like wasabi mashed potatoes and mango peppercorn chutney. Reservations are recommended.

Getting There and Around

South Maui is easily navigable by car, although there are parking challenges. Anyone staying at a Wailea resort will likely pay a parking fee upward of $25 per day. Inquire whether your resort has a parking fee and factor this into the cost of the rental. When it comes to parking in Kihei, spots along the street in the Kamaole II area can be tough to find in the middle of the day, so either arrive at the beach early or be prepared to do a little walking. Parking at Ma'alaea Harbor costs $0.50 per hour, although you can find a handful of public spots on the northern side of Hauoli Street. While a car is a necessity to go exploring, those who just want to relax on the beach and make sporadic ventures elsewhere can get by with a combination of walking, shuttles, public buses, and taxis.

CAR
Rental Cars

If you've already made your way to Kihei and decide you need a rental car, there are a number of local options. One of the most popular is family-owned **Kihei Rent a Car** (96 Kio Loop, 808/879-7257 or 800/251-5288, www. kiheirentacar.com), which can arrange a free pickup or drop-off at the Kahului Airport for rentals longer than five days. The rates are often better than the major corporate competitors.

In North Kihei, **Ohana Rent a Car** (411

Huku Li'i Place, 808/419-7401, www.ohana-rentalcar.com, 8am-5pm Mon.-Fri., 8am-noon Sat.) has affordable rates and a complimentary shuttle within the South Maui area.

If you would rather get those corporate rewards points, **Avis** (1455 S. Kihei Rd., 808/874-4077, 8am-5pm Mon.-Fri., 8am-4pm Sat.-Sun.) has an outlet in central Kihei next to Maui Dive Shop and Pizza Madness.

Taxi

To have someone do the driving for you and not worry about parking, directions, or sobriety, the best taxi service in Kihei is **MJ Taxi Service** (808/280-9309, www.mjtaxi.com).

SHUTTLE

For a ride to the airport, contact **Roberts Hawaii** (808/954-8630, www.robertshawaii. com). Fares run $18-26 pp one-way, depending on where you're staying.

MOTORCYCLES AND MOPEDS

In the Azeka Mauka shopping center in North Kihei, **Hawaiian Island Cruisers** (1280 S. Kihei Rd., 808/446-1111, www.hawaiiancruisers.com, 9am-5pm Mon.-Sat.) offers mopeds ($35 per day) and Harleys ($150 per day).

In the Kukui Mall in central Kihei, **Maui Boy Mopeds** (1819 S. Kihei Rd., 808/874-8811, www.mauiboymopeds.com, 8am-5pm daily) rents mopeds ($20 for 2 hours, $300 per week) and usually offers the most competitive rates.

In the Kamaole Shopping Center, **Aloha Motorsports** (2463 S. Kihei Rd., 808/667-7000, www.alohamotorsports.com, 8am-5pm daily) has a wide range of Harley, Honda, and Suzuki bikes ($99-159 per day) and sometimes offers free hotel pickup.

BUS

Maui Bus operates a number of lines throughout South Maui. All rides are $2 per boarding, or you can also buy a $4 day pass if you know you'll be hopping on and off a lot. The Kihei Villager (bus 15) runs between Ma'alaea Harbor Village and Pi'ilani Shopping Center 6:05am-8:30pm daily with various stops in between. The Kihei Islander (bus 10) runs between Wailea Ike Drive by the Shops at Wailea and Queen Ka'ahumanu Center in Kahului 5:30am-9:30pm daily. If you are trying to get to North Kihei or Ma'alaea, you can transfer at Pi'ilani Shopping Center to the Kihei Villager (bus 15).

Haleakala and Upcountry

Look for ★ to find recommended
sights, activities, dining, and lodging.

Highlights

© AVALON TRAVEL

★ **Haleakala National Park:** Watch the sunrise and then spend the day hiking across the crater floor. Or visit for sunset and stay for the stars, camping overnight (page 179).

★ **Hali'imaile Distillery:** Sample vodka made from pineapples as well as flavored whiskey and rum (page 183).

★ **Kula Country Farms:** Pick up fresh produce, drink in the views, and support the island's farmers (page 185).

★ **Surfing Goat Dairy:** It's the only tour on Maui with gourmet cheese and the chance to hand-milk a goat (page 186).

★ **Maui Wine:** Sip on Maui-made wine and finish it off with an elk burger (page 187).

★ **O'o Farm:** Enjoy a romantic freshly cooked lunch in the middle of an eight-acre farm with a glass of wine, a private chef, and a vine-covered trellis (page 188).

★ **Historic Makawao Town:** Boutiques, art galleries, and ranching history—all in a two-street town (page 198).

U pcountry is Maui's little secret that's just now starting to get out.

Here's a place where the smell of euca-lyptus replaces the rustle of palms and truck-driving farmers with scuffed boots replace the pool boys with towels.

Upcountry is where you throw on a flannel shirt and go for a morning drive, perhaps stopping to relax on the porch of a small family-run coffeehouse. It's a place to go hiking through forests of pine trees or sip on Maui-made wine and watch the day begin or end over Haleakala Crater. It's seeing a Sunday polo game and wandering through Makawao's galleries and buying vegetables straight from the source at a stand on the side of the road. It's eating doughnuts at a family bakery that's been serving them for over a century or settling in for a colorful sunset over bicoastal views each night. Most of all, it's slowing down and taking time to breathe the mountain air and trading the glamour of beachfront resorts for the charm of a small town.

ORIENTATION

Generally speaking, Upcountry comprises Makawao, Pukalani, Kula, Keokea, and Ulupalakua. At an elevation of 1,500 to 4,000 feet, it's also home to the 10,023-foot summit of **Haleakala Crater.** From sea level, the 38-mile drive to the summit is the shortest climb to 10,000 feet of any paved road in the world. From Makawao or Kula, reaching the summit of Haleakala Crater is about an hour's drive, and from Ka'anapali or Wailea takes a little over two hours. The drive from Makawao to Ulupalakua takes 35 minutes, versus 10 minutes to the beach in Pa'ia or 15 minutes to Kahului Airport. **Makawao** has the greatest selection of restaurants, shops, and a defined center, whereas **Kula** is a patchwork of houses, farms, and restaurants that are fairly spread out. Tiny **Keokea** is the gateway between Kula and the winery in **Ulupalakua,** where the road continues all the way around to Kaupo and the "back way" to Hana.

PLANNING YOUR TIME

While it's possible to experience Upcountry's highlights in a single day, try to spend two full

Previous: Kula Country Farms's pumpkin patch; Ulupalakua storefront. **Above:** wine tasting at Maui Wine.

Upcountry

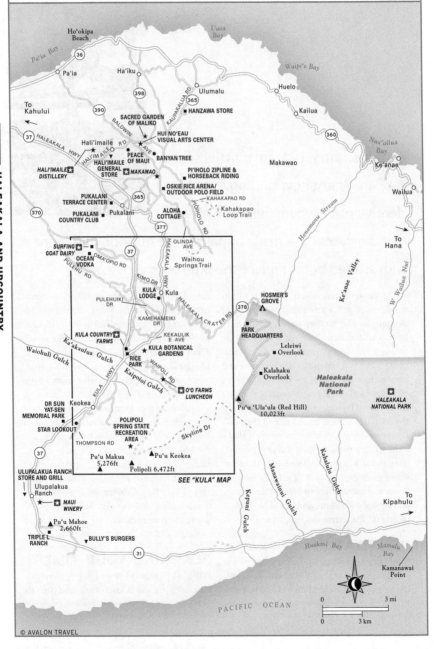

Ho'okipa Beach

Pa'ia Bay

Uaoa Bay

Pa'ia Bay

36

Pa'ia

Ha'iku

Waipi'o Bay

398

365

Ulumalu

Huelo

To Kahului

390

HANZAWA STORE

Kailua

37 HALEAKALA HWY

SACRED GARDEN OF MALIKO

360

BALDWIN

Hali'imaile

HUI NO'EAU VISUAL ARTS CENTER

Nua'ailua Bay

HALI'IMAILE RD

PEACE OF MAUI

Makawao

Ke'anae

HALI'IMAILE DISTILLERY

HALI'IMAILE GENERAL STORE

BANYAN TREE

MAKAWAO

Wailua

PUKALANI TERRACE CENTER

PI'IHOLO ZIPLINE & HORSEBACK RIDING

365

OSKIE RICE ARENA/ OUTDOOR POLO FIELD

370

PUKALANI COUNTRY CLUB

Pukalani

ALOHA COTTAGE

KAHAKAPAO RD

Kahakapao Loop Trail

To Hana

377

PIIHOLO RD

Homomanu Stream

OLINDA AVE

SURFING GOAT DAIRY

37

Waihou Springs Trail

Ke'anae Valley

OMA'OPIO RD

OCEAN VODKA

KIMO DR

HOSMER'S GROVE

PULEHU RD

PULEHUIKI DR

KULA LODGE

Kula

378

W Wailua Nui

HALEAKALA HWY

KAMEHAMEIKI DR

HALEAKALA CRATER RD

PARK HEADQUARTERS

KULA COUNTRY FARMS

KEKAULIK E AVE

Leleiwi Overlook

Ka'akaulua Gulch

KULA BOTANICAL GARDENS

Waiohuli Gulch

RICE PARK

WAIPOLI RD

Kalahaku Overlook

Kaipoioi Gulch

Haleakala National Park

KULA HWY

O'O FARMS LUNCHEON

DR SUN YAT-SEN MEMORIAL PARK

Keokea

HALEAKALA NATIONAL PARK

STAR LOOKOUT

POLIPOLI SPRING STATE RECREATION AREA

Pu'u 'Ula'ula (Red Hill) 10,023ft

THOMPSON RD

Skyline Dr

37

Pu'u Makua 5,276ft

Pu'u Keokea

SEE "KULA" MAP

Polipoli 6,472ft

Kepuni Gulch

Manawainui Gulch

Kahalulu Gulch

ULUPALAKUA RANCH STORE AND GRILL

To Kipahulu

Ulupalakua Ranch

MAUI WINERY

Pu'u Mahoe 2,660ft

Huakini Bay

Mamalu Bay

TRIPLE L RANCH

BULLY'S BURGERS

Kamanawai Point

31

PACIFIC OCEAN

0   3 mi

0   3 km

Your Best Day in Upcountry

Begin the day in Keokea with breakfast at **Grandma's Coffee House.** Walk it off with a 30-minute stroll on neighboring **Thompson Road** before continuing on to **Ulupalakua** and a visit to **Maui Wine.** Have lunch at the **Ulupalakua Ranch Store and Grill** (try the home-made chili) before stopping for produce at **Kula Country Farms** on the drive to **Makawao** for shopping. When it's time for dinner or happy hour, head to **Polli's Mexican Restaurant** for a mango margarita, or **Casanova** at 5pm for $5 carafes of wine.

If you start your day with a **Haleakala sunrise,** spend an hour at the summit area hiking on **Sliding Sands Trail.** On the way back down, grab breakfast at **Kula Lodge** and shop at the **Kula Marketplace.** Monday through Thursday, skimp on the hiking atop the crater to squeeze in an earlier breakfast so you can make it out to **O'o Farm** for the 10:30am lunch tour. When the tour finishes at 2pm, choose to either go shopping in Makawao or drive out to **Maui Wine**—depending on how much energy you have after the early morning wake-up.

Rainy Day? Start with breakfast at **Kula Lodge** and a piping cup of hot chocolate, and head downstairs to look at the artwork of Curtis Wilson Cost. Drive to Makawao for an hour of shopping and have lunch at **Polli's Mexican Restaurant,** where a lively crowd often gathers whenever the rain is coming down. Drive 10 minutes to **Hali'imaile Distillery** for an hour-long tasting and tour before treating yourself to a nice dinner at **Hali'imaile General Store.**

days seeing the area—one day at Haleakala Crater either watching the sunrise and exploring Upcountry on the way back down, or gradually visiting Upcountry sights before heading to Haleakala for sunset. On the second day, start with horseback riding or ziplining, and then see the sights you didn't get to see the day before. While many people drive Upcountry from the beach, there are numerous lodges and bed-and-breakfasts to base yourself on the hill. It's also possible to visit Upcountry when driving the "back road" from Hana, but by the time you get here after a full day in Hana, there's really only time for the winery.

Sights

★ Haleakala National Park

"Hale-a-ka-la," House of the Sun. Few places are more aptly named than this 10,023-foot volcano. Believed to have been dormant since 1790 (the summit area has been inactive for 600 years), when measured from the seafloor, Haleakala is 30,000 feet tall—surpassed only by the peaks on the Big Island as the tallest mountain on earth.

Given its size and spellbinding nature, it's little wonder the mountain is considered sacred to indigenous Hawaiians. This is where the powerful volcano goddess, Pele, crafted her colorful cinder cones, and a *wahi pana,* or

sacred place, only inhabited by the gods. It's where the demigod Maui lassoed the sun to slow its path across the sky so his people could have time to grow their crops and dry their cloth in the sun. It's also a fragile ecological treasure, with more endangered species than any other national park.

Today, the most popular activity for visitors to Maui is visiting Haleakala for sunrise—but there's far more to this national park than simply the light of dawn. Over 30 miles of hiking trails crisscross the crater, where backcountry cabins and campgrounds provide a classic wilderness experience. The sunsets and stargazing are as spectacular as viewing the crater at sunrise, and even the drive leading up to park—where the road gains 10,000 vertical feet in only 38 miles—is part of the magical, mystical experience of standing atop Haleakala.

When to Visit

The biggest question surrounding Haleakala is not if you should visit, but when. Sunrise is the most popular option, and although everyone should experience a Haleakala sunrise at least once, it's not the only time to visit. Sunrise is crowded, tough to find parking, requires waking up at 3am, and is often near or below freezing. Sunset is a display nearly as colorful but without all the crowds. You don't get the benefit of watching the sun emerge from the horizon, but there are often only 20 people instead of 400, and it isn't as cold. If you plan on hiking the crater floor, arrive at the summit in the middle of the day and time your exit for sunset.

The weather, unfortunately, can be unpredictable. Rain and even snow can fall at any time of year, but summer typically has better conditions. Statistically, on 85 percent of mornings, it's clear enough to see the sunrise. For sunset, a good rule of thumb is that if you can't see the mountain from below,

you probably shouldn't bother. On the other hand, if you can see the mountain, but not the top, the sunset will seem to float on a colorful sea of clouds. To take the guesswork out of the equation, call the National Weather Service **Hotline for Haleakala Summit** (808/944-5025, ext. 4) for an up-to-date weather forecast. You can also check out the University of Hawaii astronomy website (www.ifa.hawaii.edu/haleakalanew/weather.shtml) for up-to-the-minute weather data, including windchill, visibility, and rainfall, before heading to the summit.

Admission and Hosmer's Grove

Admission ($15 per car) to **Haleakala National Park** (www.nps.gov/hale) is good for three days and includes the Kipahulu section past Hana, home to the Pools of 'Ohe'o. If you're driving for sunrise, head straight to the summit; if you have time to explore, take the side trip to **Hosmer's Grove,** just past the park entrance (page 190).

Continuing straight past the Hosmer's Grove turnoff, you'll soon arrive at **Park Headquarters** (808/572-4400, 7am-3:45pm daily) at an elevation of 6,800 feet. Stop for information, camping permits, gifts, toilets,

Prepare for crowds and cold at sunrise.

BRRR...

On any given morning at the top of Haleakala there is always at least one unfortunate person shivering in a tank top. People forget that Haleakala is over 10,000 feet high, which means the temperature is 30 degrees colder than it is back down on the beach. And, even though Haleakala is the "House of the Sun," the morning windchill—particularly in winter—can often be below freezing. Ice on the road is common in winter, and every few years the summit gets snow that stays for a couple of days. Naturally, whenever it snows on Haleakala, hundreds of locals rush to the summit to help their children build snowmen, and then, of course, immediately rush home to put the photos online.

Most mornings at Haleakala Crater are between 30°F and 50°F, so consider packing pants, gloves, a hat, and a jacket. No winter clothing? Use the hotel's blankets, but be sure to return them in good condition in order to avoid fees. Temperatures rise into the 60s by noon, but sunrise and sunset visitors should prepare to bundle up.

For current weather info at Haleakala summit, visit www.ifa.hawaii.edu/haleakalanew/weather.shtml or call 808/944-5025, ext. 4.

and a pay phone. There are some 'ahinahina (silversword) plants outside, and sometimes nene (Hawaiian geese) frequent the area.

On the road toward the summit, **Leleiwi** (page 188) is an overlook that's a great alternative at sunrise. **Kalahaku,** on the other hand, is another overlook that's popular at sunrise but can only be accessed when traveling downhill.

Visitors Center and Summit Observation Building

Near the end of the road is the **Visitors Center,** at 9,740 feet. It's about 10 miles up the mountain from headquarters, about a 30-minute drive. This is where all of the bike tour companies bring you for sunrise, as it's the best view looking down into the crater. It's open sunrise-3pm daily and contains clear and concise displays on the geology of Haleakala. Maps and books are available, and a 30-minute ranger-guided walk takes place most days at 10am and 11am.

If you want to top out above 10,000 feet and officially summit Haleakala, **Pu'u 'Ula'ula** (Red Hill) is the highest point on Maui at 10,023 feet. Here you'll find a glass-sided observation area that's open 24 hours daily. The view of the Big Island and coast of Maui is better than at the Visitors Center below. The lava rock ridge just in front of the parking

area is the best place to watch the sunset. For perspective, it's 100 miles from the top of Haleakala to Mauna Loa in the distance.

Close to the summit is the **Maui Space Surveillance Complex** (www.ifa.hawaii.edu/haleakala), aka Science City. It's closed to the public and highly controversial, with protests over the construction of a telescope on culturally sacred land.

Camping and Cabins

To really appreciate Haleakala's beauty, you need to stay overnight. The most accessible campground is at **Hosmer's Grove,** where you don't even need a permit. There are a handful of tent sites, a few barbecue grills, a pit toilet, and running water. You can drive up to the campsites, which makes it an easy option. The campground is at 6,800 feet, so nights can get close to freezing. It also makes a great staging ground for driving to the summit for sunrise.

For a rugged overnight backpacking experience, there are **wilderness campsites** inside the crater at both Holua (elevation: 6,940 feet) and Paliku (6,380 feet). Camping in the crater requires a permit, which can be picked up for free from the park headquarters before it closes at 3:45pm. Both campsites have pit toilets and nonpotable water, and although the sites are first-come,

Makawao

To Ha'iku

ST JOSEPH'S
■ CATHOLIC CHURCH

KAUPAKALUA RD

390

To Pa'ia

BREWER RD

BALDWIN AVE

VOLCANO SPICE COMPANY

SIP ME ▼

JORDANNE GALLERY AND STUDIO ■

MAKAWAO ▼ STEAK HOUSE

HOMME BY NATURE ■

PINK BY NATURE ■

365

MARKET FRESH BISTRO/ VIEWPOINTS GALLERY/ HOT ISLAND GLASS ■

GOODIES ■

RODEO GENERAL STORE ■

MAKAWAO GARDEN CAFÉ ▼

DESIGNING WAHINE ■

MAUI MASTER JEWELERS ■

SHERRI REEVE GALLERY COLLECTIONS ■

NAKUI ST

MAKAWAO FINE ART GALLERY ■

THE MERCANTILE ■

DRAGON'S DEN ▼

KOMODA'S ■

LITTLE TIBET ■

POLLI'S MEXICAN RESTAURANT ■

JULIE GALEEVA FINE ART GALLERY

FLEUR DE LEI ■

CASANOVA ▼

JEWELS OF THE WHITE TARA ■

OLINDA RD

MAUI HANDS ■

PUANA ST

LIBRARY ■

LIQUOR SHACK AND GRINDS ■

Parking

KRANK CYCLES ■

STOPWATCH ▼ BAR AND GRILL

GAS STATION ■

AI ST

POST OFFICE ■

365

MALU ST

390

PIZZA FRESH ■

MAKAWAO AVE

KESHAU PL

SCALE NOT AVAILABLE

© AVALON TRAVEL

PAKANI PL

To Pukalani ↓

first-served, they can accommodate up to 25 people and are rarely full. Maximum stay is three nights in a 30-day period, and no more than two nights in a row at the same site. Holua is accessible by a 3.7-mile hike down Halemau'u Trail and is set in a field of subalpine scrub brush looking toward the Ko'olau Gap. Paliku, on the other hand, requires hiking 9.2 miles from the Sliding Sands Trail at the summit (or a 10.3-mile hike on Halemau'u Trail), and is wet, lush, surrounded by foliage, and a good place for spotting *nene*. This is also the preferred area for hikers opting to walk out the Kaupo Gap.

In addition to campgrounds, **backcountry cabins** ($75) are available at Holua, Kapalaoa (7,250 feet), as well as Paliku. Due to their popularity, however, securing reservations can be difficult. Reservations can be made up to 180 days in advance by creating a profile on www. recreation.gov and searching for Haleakala National Park (Cabin Permits). Cabins are often booked four months in advance, so if you want to include this on your trip to Maui, plan ahead and be flexible. Cabins include 12 padded berths, a wood-burning stove, and basic kitchen utilities. Pit toilets and nonpotable water are available, and all trash must be packed out.

MAKAWAO
★ Hali'imaile Distillery

When was the last time you tried vodka made from pineapples? **Hali'imaile Distillery** (883 Hali'imaile Rd., 808/633-3609, www.haliimailedistilling.com, tours every 30 minutes 10am-4pm Mon.-Fri., $10) is the only place in the world you'll find the sugary spirit. The team in this Quonset hut are completely redefining cocktails, from the world's only vodka aged in French oak to Kona coffee-flavored whiskey and chocolate macadamia nut vodka. Master distiller Mark Nigbur helped pioneer the process of distilling with glass, instead of copper or steel, and he's partnered with Sammy Hagar, his wild blond doppelgänger, to create Sammy's Beach Bar Rum. Tours last an hour and pass through the distillery, which is sandwiched between Hawaii's only sugar plantation and America's only pineapple plantation. Notable brands are Pau Maui Vodka and Paniolo Whiskey, and the tour is capped off by three-quarter-ounce pours for visitors over age 21.

Hui No'eau Visual Arts Center

About one mile downhill from Makawao is the **Hui No'eau Visual Arts Center** (2841 Baldwin Ave., 808/572-6560, www.huinoeau.com, 10am-4pm Mon.-Sat., $2 donation), located on a gorgeous 10-acre estate owned by the Baldwin family. The centerpiece is the neo-Spanish mansion built in 1917 and transformed in 1934 into a spectacular center for the arts. Touring the grounds is free, as is perusing the gallery, which hosts the work of local artists and has rotating exhibitions. You can pick up a self-guided tour ($6) of the property or take an hour-long guided tour ($12). History buffs should head directly to the room full of old black-and-white photographs that show what it was like to live on the estate 100 years ago.

Makawao History Museum

If you're curious how Portugal's Azores Islands are tied to Makawao's pastures, or wonder what it was like to live on a ranch in 19th-century Maui, a short visit to the **Makawao History Museum** (3643 Baldwin Ave., 808/572-2482, 10am-5pm daily,

Sample the spirits at Hali'imaile Distillery.

Kula

OCEAN VODKA

SURFING GOAT DAIRY

OMA'OPIO RD

PULEHU RD

37

KULA HWY

HALEAKALA HWY

377

ENCHANTING FLORAL GARDENS

KIMO DR

LOWER KULA RD

MAUI NUI FARM AND THAI FOOD

Kula

KULA LODGE RESTAURANT

GAS

KULA LODGE

KULA SANDALWOODS CAFE

KULA MARKETPLACE

PULEHUIKI DR

KAMEHAMEIKI DR

SUNRISE PROTEA FARM

PONY EXPRESS TOURS/ SKYLINE ECO-ADVENTURES

To Haleakala National Park

HALEAKALA CRATER RD

378

HOLY GHOST CATHOLIC CHURCH

POST OFFICE

MORIHARA STORE

KULA BISTRO

COPP RD

UPCOUNTRY B&B

KEKAULIKE AVE

PULUKE FARMS B&B

KULA COUNTRY FARMS

KULA BOTANICAL GARDENS

G AND Z GUESTHOUSE

O'O FARM

PROFLYGHT PARAGLIDING

ALII KULA LAVENDER

WAIPOLI RD

Waiakoa Loop Trail

Waiakoa Trail

KULA HWY

FONG STORE

CHING STORE

GAS

THOMPSON RANCH

Upper Waiakoa Trail

Skyline Trail

GRANDMA'S COFFEE HOUSE

Keokea

THOMPSON RD

Trail

Boundary Trail

Waiohuli Trail

KAHUA RD

Redwood Trail

POLIPOLI SPRING STATE RECREATION AREA

Pu'u Keokea

Tie Trail

Poli Poli Trail

Plum Trail

Haleakala Ridge Trail

Pu'u Makua 5,276ft

Polipoli 6,472ft

0   1mi

0   1 km

© AVALON TRAVEL

donation) is an easy way to find out. Located in historic Makawao town amid art galleries and boutiques, the small museum has won awards for historic preservation. Look at old black-and-white photos of early Makawao ranches and read profiles of community members who helped to shape the town. The museum is completely volunteer-run and supported in part by donations. Pick up a cookbook of family recipes from Makawao's original families.

KULA

On the slopes of Haleakala between 2,000 and 4,000 feet elevation, Kula is the hub of Maui's rural and agricultural life. Tractors drive on two-lane roads where stands sell local produce, and flannel-clad farmers lament how deer are getting into their cabbage. For visitors, the bicoastal views are reason enough to drive here, but so are the farm tours, the winery, the shops, and the laid-back small-town vibes.

★ Kula Country Farms

Kula Country Farms (Kula Hwy., past mile marker 13, 808/878-8381, www.kulacountryfarmsmaui.com, 10am-5pm Tues.-Fri., 8am-4pm Sat.-Sun.) perfectly captures Kula's agricultural spirit. Stop in for affordable produce where colors explode off the shelves. Buy a healthy snack to enjoy with the ocean view. In October the farm gets festive and features a corn maze and an eight-acre pumpkin patch, although the main reason to visit is to support local farmers.

Ali'i Kula Lavender Farm

If you've ever wanted lavender tea . . . or lavender sunscreen, lavender body butter, or lavender scones, **Ali'i Kula Lavender Farm** (1100 Waipoli Rd., 808/878-3004, www.aliikulalavender.com, 9am-4pm daily, $3) is worth a stop. Located at the top of Waipoli Road on the way up toward Polipoli, the views at 4,000 feet elevation stretch all the way to the ocean. The air is crisp for walking around the farm, and the shrill calls of ring-necked pheasants echo above the pastures. The farm itself is 13.5 acres, and guided walking tours ($12) are given at 9:30am, 10:30am, 11:30am, 1pm, and 2:30pm daily. A small café serves scones and tea. The view, the serenity, and a warm cup of tea make this a relaxing stop.

Botanical Gardens

By Waipoli Road, the **Kula Botanical Garden** (638 Kekaulike Ave., 808/878-1715,

fresh produce at Kula Country Farms

www.kulabotanicalgarden.com, 8am-4pm daily, $10 adults, $3 children) is a 19-acre private garden with 2,500 species of plants. There are over 90 varieties of protea alone, and the self-guided walking tour takes 45 minutes. If you're on your way down from Haleakala and didn't get to see a *nene* goose, the botanical garden has two, which means you can at least get photos. You'll also find a chameleon exhibit, a Christmas tree farm, three carved wooden tiki gods, and coffee that's grown on the farm.

★ Surfing Goat Dairy

While it's a bit out of the way, eccentric **Surfing Goat Dairy** (3651 Omaopio Rd., 808/878-2870, www.surfinggoatdairy.com, 9am-5pm Mon.-Sat., 9am-2pm Sun.) is a must-see. Where else are you going to get the chance to hand-milk a goat and then feast on gourmet cheese? Three miles down Omaopio Road off Kula Highway (Hwy. 37), a line of enormous palms provides what's probably the most regal entrance to a goat dairy anywhere. There are 30-plus flavors of gourmet goat cheese and over 25 types of goat cheese truffles. The best reason to visit is the 3:15pm tour. "Casual" tours ($12) run every 30 minutes 10am-3pm daily, but the 3:15pm tour ($17) allows you to hand-milk a goat.

Ocean Vodka Organic Farm and Distillery

It isn't a vacation until you're sipping vodka at 10am. Located next door to Surfing Goat Dairy, **Ocean Organic Vodka Farm** (4051 Omaopio Rd., 808/877-0009, www.oceanvodka.com, 9:30am-5pm daily, $10) offers tours of their fully sustainable farm that produced organic vodka. The facility's energy is provided by 240 solar panels, and 30 types of Polynesian sugarcane provide the juice for vodka and rum that's distilled and bottled here. All the cane is hand-harvested, bottles are labeled by hand, and leftovers are used as organic mulch, while chickens take care of the pests.

Meet the goats at Surfing Goat Dairy.

At the outdoor thatched-roof tasting room, amid fields of waving sugarcane, sip on samples of vodka and rum sourced from different types of sugar. Some have flavors of banana and coconut despite not containing them. Even stranger, the water that's used in distilling the spirits is sourced from 3,000 feet below sea level, where heavy mineral-laden water has spent 2,000 years drifting from Greenland to the coast of the Big Island (really). Tours begin at 9:30am daily and run every 30 minutes until 4pm.

KEOKEA AND ULUPALAKUA

Once you pass Rice Park and the turnoff for Highway 377, the road begins to take on a different feel. The elevation slowly drops, the jacaranda trees provide shade over the road, and the views of South Maui begin to open up before you. Life is slow up here, in this hangout of artists, farmers, and lifelong ranchers. You'll know you've reached the community of Keokea when you see **Keokea Park** on the left, a small field that also has a playground and public restrooms.

Across from Grandma's Coffee House is the turnoff for **Thompson Road,** a one-lane pasture-lined country road that offers one of the island's best views and a leisurely spot for a stroll. By mile marker 18, on the way to Ulupalakua, is the small **Sun Yat-sen Park,** named for the revolutionary who helped found modern China. Sun Mei—Sun Yat-sen's brother—immigrated to Hawaii in 1871 to work as a rice farmer on O'ahu. He moved to Maui and opened a shop, eventually starting a ranch in Keokea that sprawled over 3,900 acres. He was soon known as the "King of Kula," and with the wealth he'd amassed from his business ventures, Sun Mei paid to have his younger brother educated on O'ahu. Despite the fact that he spoke no English when he arrived from China, Sun Yat-sen eventually graduated with the highest scholarly distinction.

After finishing medical school back in China, and having witnessed modern governments on his many travels abroad, Sun Yat-sen envisioned modern China free of imperial rule. Back in Hawaii in 1894, he formed the Hsing Chung Hui, or Revive China Society, which aimed to further China's prosperity through the development of modern governance. When a revolution in Guangzhou failed spectacularly in 1895, Sun Yat-sen's family fled China to the ranch in Keokea. Forced into exile, Sun Yat-sen spent 16 years in Japan, London, and Hawaii, during which time he staged nine more revolutions—all of them massive failures. Through each failed attempt he regrouped here in Keokea, though the successive failures, funded by Sun Mei, eventually left the businessman bankrupt and forced him off the island.

Despite the failures, Sun Yat-sen had successfully sown the seeds of revolution, and having kept the movement financially alive from this ranch in Keokea, Sun Yat-sen watched as his fellow revolutionaries finally overthrew the Qing Dynasty in October 1911. Immediately returning to China from exile,

he was elected on December 29 as the provisional president of the new Republic of China.

★ Maui Wine

Yes, there is actually a winery on Maui, and yes, it's actually good. Once considered an island novelty that only served pineapple wine, **Maui Wine** (14815 Pi'ilani Hwy., 808/878-6058, www.mauiwine.com, 10am-5:30pm daily), like a fine wine, is getting better by the year. There are three varieties of pineapple wine, but there's also grenache, malbec, syrah, viognier, and chenin blanc. Aside from the wine and complimentary tastings, what makes the winery a must-see is its history and beauty.

The tasting room bar is 18 feet long and made from a single mango tree. The guest cottage where King Kalakaua stayed when he visited the ranch in 1874 is now the tasting room. There's a small historical room attached to the tasting area that details the history of the ranch (allegedly Kalakaua had too much cheer and wagered Molokini while gambling), and free tours trace the ranch's progression from potatoes to sugarcane to wine. Wondering about the cannon sitting in the yard? It was fired to greet King Kalakaua as part of his regal arrival. Today, that heritage is carried on with the "King's Visit"—a private tasting, booked in advance, that pairs the fine estate wines with meat and produce sourced from the ranch and prepared by a private chef.

TOURS
Makawao

If you think pineapples grow underground or on trees, you should probably spend a couple of hours on the **Maui Pineapple Tour** (875 Hali'imaile Rd., 808/665-5491, www.mauipineappletours.com, 9:30am and 11:45am daily, $65). Learn why Maui's pineapples are sweet and taste like golden candy. Everyone gets a free pineapple, and you can eat Maui gold in the fields until your gums tingle. Bring a camera for the sweeping views, and don't forget the sunscreen. The minimum age is five, and the pineapple tour conveniently aligns with distillery tours next door.

For customized private tours of the island, **Open Eye Private Tours** (808/572-3483, www.openeyetours.com, from $725 for 1 or 2 adults) is based in Makawao and led by Pono, a guide who's been offering tours of Maui since 1983. The tours have an emphasis on Hawaiian culture, and through contacts built up over the years, he's able to bring visitors to properties you otherwise wouldn't get to visit. For example, a Hana tour bus won't stop at a taro field to help pull taro with the owners, but Pono will. As a former teacher, he also specializes in arranging activities for children.

Kula
★ O'O FARM

For a romantic Maui luncheon in the middle of a farm, where you can sip wine beneath a vine-covered trellis and dine on fish or chicken prepared by a chef in an outdoor kitchen, check out the **O'o Farm Gourmet Luncheon Tour** (651 Waipoli Rd., 808/667-4341, www.oofarm.com, 10:30am-2pm Mon.-Thurs., $58), where visitors take a tour around the eight-acre farm and choose from 60 different crops while picking a salad in the fields.

The air up here is misty and cool, at least when the clouds roll in, and there's nothing like a cup of French-pressed coffee. The first hour is spent touring the farm and meeting the on-site chef, who arrives at the farm at sunrise to source ingredients from the fields. Much of the produce used travels a total of 400 feet. Instead of a farm-to-table restaurant, the table has been brought to the farm. The wine is BYOB, and there's also a **"Seed to Cup" Coffee Tour** with coffee grown on the farm (8:30am-10:30am Tues.-Wed., $50).

For a smaller, more intimate, one-man operation of coffee, protea, and produce, the **Shim Farm Tour** (625 Middle Rd., 808/876-0055, www.shimfarmtour.com, 9am-5pm daily, reservations required, $7) runs February-June. Learn the history of the Chinese people in Kula on the affordable one-hour family-run tour.

Hiking and Biking

HIKING
Haleakala National Park

Thanks to the colorful cinder cones and trails that crunch underfoot, anyone who hikes across Haleakala Crater will swear they could be on the moon. Covering a total of 19 square miles, the crater basin is a vast wilderness with 30 miles of trails. It's a place of adventure, mythology, and silence—and home to Maui's best hiking. If you love the outdoors, no trip to Maui is complete without a spending a day on the crater floor.

Hikers need to be prepared, however, as temperatures can range from 30°F to 80°F over the course of a single day. The hiking is at high elevation, 7,000 to 10,000 feet, and hiking back up generally takes twice as long as the hike down. **Hike Maui** (808/879-5270, www.hikemaui.com, $165) is the only company that offers commercially guided hiking tours. Should you go on your own, here's a rundown of the most popular hikes, listed from shortest to longest. All mileage is round-trip.

PA KA'OAO (0.4 MILE)

If you don't feel like watching the sunrise with 200 other people, huff your way up this five-minute trail that leaves from the Visitors Center parking lot. The view from the top looks down toward the crater, and it's better than from the parking lot. Bring a flashlight for the walking the trail before sunrise.

LELEIWI OVERLOOK (0.5 MILE)

Running late for sunrise? Consider hiking to **Leleiwi Overlook** (8,840 feet). Located by

Haleakala National Park

© AVALON TRAVEL

NOTE: BE AWARE OF FREE RANGE
CATTLE ALONG THE HALEAKALA
HIGHWAY, ESPECIALLY AT NIGHT

SKYLINE DR.

PARK
HEADQUARTERS

HALEAKALA (378)

▲ 6,849ft

Hosmer's Grove Loop Trail

△ HOSMER GROVE
CAMPGROUND

Supply Trail

Leleiwi
Overlook

Kalahaku Overlook
9,324ft

Halemau'u Trail

Pu'u 'Ula'ula
(Red Hill)
10,023ft

MAUI
SPACE
SURVEILLANCE
COMPLEX

VISITOR
CENTER

White
Hill

Kamoali'i

Ka Lu'u
O Ka 'O'o

HALEAKALA
WILDERNESS

Pu'u O Maui

Kawilinau
(Bottomless Pit)

Halali'i

△ HOLUA
(CABIN)
CAMPSITE)

Silversword
Loop

Ko'olau Gap

Pu'u
Kumu

▲ 8,907ft

Ka Moa
O Pele

Pu'u-O-
Pele Sliding

Pu'u
Naue

Manu Hina

Haupaakea Peak
9,157ft

KAPALAOA
(CABIN)

Pu'u-O-
Pele

Namana
O Ke Akua

Pu'u
Maile

Honokahua

O'ilipu'u

Kaluaiki

8,105ft ▲

Sands

Trail

Kalapawili Ridge

▲ 8,201ft

Kaupo Gap

Kaupo Trail

▲ 4,772ft

△ PALIKU
(CABIN/CAMPSITE)

▲ 6,300ft

Scientific Research

Area (Closed)

To Kaupo
and Hwy 31
(4 miles)

Koukou'ai

Ka'apahu

Kipahulu Valley

Palikea
Stream

Paliku

Palikea
2,224ft

Kipahulu Area

'One'o Gulch

Makahiku
Falls

Waimoku
Falls

△ KIPAHULU
CAMPGROUND

To
Kaupo

(31)

△ RANGER
STATION

To
Hana

0   1 mi
0   1 km

.e marker 17.5, Leleiwi has smaller crowds .nd is usually warmer. The view looks down on the crater floor and the sheer multihued cliffs, although since the lookout faces east, it isn't as good for sunset.

HOSMER'S GROVE NATURE TRAIL (0.5 MILE)

Unlike other trails in the park, the **Hosmer's Grove Nature Trail** is at the park's lower boundary just after you enter the park. The short trail loops through a dense grove of trees, planted in 1910 as part of an unsuccessful experiment to test the viability of the lumber industry. Surrounded by sweet-smelling pine and fir, grab a fleece and go for a stroll through the 20-plus species of trees, listening for forest birds that flit around in the treetops. To reach the trailhead, make a left on the road pointing toward the campground immediately after entering the park. The walk, over mostly level ground, should take 30 minutes. To extend the trip, hike the **Supply Trail** for 2.3 miles to where it meets with the crater rim.

HALEMAU'U TRAIL (SWITCHBACK TRAIL) (7.5 MILES)

Beginning from an altitude of only 7,990 feet, the first 1.1 miles of this trail meander through scrub brush before bringing you to the edge of a 1,000-foot cliff. The view down into the Ko'olau Gap is better here than from the summit, and although the trail is well-defined, the drop-offs can be a bit disconcerting. After 3.7 miles—and a 1,000 foot drop—the trail passes Holua Cabin, where you can turn around. Tack on another mile by continuing to Silversword Loop, a section of the crater known for its numerous 'ahinahina, or endangered silversword plants.

KEONEHE'EHE'E TRAIL (SLIDING SANDS TRAIL) (8 MILES)

Starting at the summit visitor center at 9,800 feet, Keonehe'ehe'e descends 2,500 vertical feet to the crater floor below. This trail is barren, windswept, without shade, and a stunning conduit to the cinder cones. You can turn around anytime you want to hike out. Continuing to Kapalaoa Cabin adds 3.5 miles round-trip.

SLIDING SANDS SWITCHBACK LOOP (12.2 MILES)

If you're in good shape and have a full day to devote to exploring the crater, this is hands-down the best day hike in the summit area. Park at the Halemau'u trailhead, then hitch a ride to the top, where you'll hike down to the crater floor on the Sliding Sands Trail. Follow the signs toward Holua Cabin and the Halemau'u Trail, where a leg-burning, switchbacking, 1,000-foot climb leads back to the car.

If you really want an island adventure that you'll never forget, consider hiking the trail at night in the light of a full moon. For this night hike, bring a backpack of extra clothing, carry extra water and a flashlight, and dress for windchill that can drop below freezing any time of year.

KAUPO GAP

Of all the hikes in Haleakala Crater, none are more legendary, or more extreme, than "shooting" the Kaupo Gap, a two-day trip, with a stay at Paliku campground, that drops 9,500 vertical feet over 17.5 miles. Permits are required for camping at Paliku, in the crater's remotest corner, 9.2 miles from the Sliding Sands trailhead.

On the second day of the hike, you'll descend from Paliku outside the national park boundary, and legally continue across private land until you reach Kaupo Store. Along the trail, keep an eye out for goats and deer that roam the windswept grasslands. When you finally finish the hike in Kaupo, it's best if you've prearranged a ride. If not, you may have to convince the rare passerby to shuttle your sweaty body all the way to the other side of the island. Despite the logistical challenges and the grueling backcountry terrain, this is a unique and memorable hike.

Polipoli: The Last Frontier

While no official statistics are kept, there's a good chance that **Polipoli Spring State Recreation Area** is Maui's least visited corner. Even a place as desolate as Kaupo sees more people. High above the protea farms, the lavender farm, the disc golf course, and even the paragliding school, Polipoli is almost an afterthought, so far removed from the rest of the island that most visitors don't even know it's there.

This isolation makes Polipoli an enchanting place. Set between 5,300 and 7,100 feet elevation, there are sweeping views down to the shore, and trails completely enveloped in trees and thick mists. Bathed in the scent of redwood and pine (yes, there are redwoods on Maui), it's a magical, spooky, and refreshing place.

This 10-acre recreational area of the Kula Forest Reserve was extensively logged during the 1930s by the Civilian Conservation Corps (CCC). A large clearing at 7,000 feet is nicknamed "The Ballpark," where corps members would gather on their lunch break to play high-altitude baseball. Today Polipoli is frequented by hikers and hunters looking for wild boars, goats, and pheasants. In 2014, Hurricane Iselle downed so many trees that it looked like a fallen box of toothpicks, but after a seven-month cleanup, the trails and campground are open again, albeit with fewer trees. This is also the island's premier mountain biking destination, where a forested woodland of downhill and single-track provides a ride akin to Oregon or Northern California.

Mornings offer the clearest views for hiking in Polipoli, and for anyone wanting to hit the trails early, there's a small campground ($12) and a rustic cabin ($90) that can accommodate up to 10 people (no electricity). Both are reachable along the steep, switchbacking Waipoli Road, 9.7 miles uphill from Kekaulike Highway (Hwy. 377). The last four miles are unpaved and require a 4WD vehicle. For cabin reservations, contact the **Division of State Parks** (54 S. High St., Suite 101, Wailuku, 808/984-8109, 8am-3:30pm Mon.-Fri.). Make campground reservations online at www.hawaiistateparks.org.

Polipoli Spring State Recreation Area

For a place to escape and commune with the serenity of nature, channel your inner Emerson or Thoreau, and meditate up in the mists, get a 4WD vehicle and head to **Polipoli Spring State Recreation Area**, an out-of-the-way forested spot with some of the island's best hiking. Trails pass through old-growth redwoods, eucalyptus, ash, and pines. Be sure to wear bright colors, since hunters are frequently in the area.

After ascending the switchbacking pasture-lined road that continues up from the lavender farm, the first hike is the **Waiakoa Loop Trail,** which begins by the hunters check-in station. The trailhead technically doesn't begin for 0.75 mile down the hunting access road, but if you don't have a 4WD vehicle, it's better to park at the hunters station and walk to the trailhead. Once you're here, a three-mile loop with a moderate elevation change of 400 feet passes through lowland brush and pines.

Farther up the road, just past the cattle guard where the road eventually turns to dirt, you'll find the trailhead for the **Boundary Trail,** a 4.4-mile one-way trail that descends to the lower fence line. This trail offers sweeping views of South Maui, and since it's 1,000 vertical feet lower than other trails, it won't leave you as winded. It can either be done as an out-and-back hike or combined with other trails as a loop. The shortest loop is up the **Lower Waiohuli Trail,** which intersects the Boundary Trail at the 2.6-mile mark. Turning left on the Lower Waiohuli Trail, it's 1.4 miles back uphill to the main road, then a 2.5-mile trek back along the dirt road to your car.

If seven miles seems too far, most of the shorter walks in Polipoli begin and end at the campground. While some are only a mile long, the best hike in the park for first-time visitors is the 5.3-mile loop trail formed by connecting the **Haleakala Ridge Trail, Polipoli Trail, Redwood Trail,** and **Plum Trail.** Driving all the way to the campground requires a 4WD vehicle.

It's possible to hike all the way from Polipoli to the summit of Haleakala. Follow the 6.8-mile dirt road, known as **Skyline Drive,** a "back entrance" to Haleakala National Park. If it has snowed recently atop Haleakala and the rangers have closed the road, this is an alternative way to hike into the park and be the only person there. Even on regular days, however, Skyline is a strenuous hike providing panoramic views down the mountain's southwest rift zone. Though Haleakala has been dormant for more than 220 years, volcanologists claim that when the mountain erupts again, magma will cover the barren landscape that's visible from this trail. To reach the trailhead for Skyline Drive, turn left at the fork that leads down to the campground from the main dirt road. From here, the road continues climbing and begins to double back toward the north, along the way passing the trailhead for the 1.8-mile **Mamane Trail.** Eventually you'll reach a locked gate at an area known as the Ballpark (7,000 feet). From here it's a 3,000-vertical-foot switchbacking trail to the summit. Pack plenty of water and warm clothing, and be aware of the challenges of hiking at altitude.

Makawao

In the heart of the Makawao Forest Reserve, the **Kahakapao Loop Trail** is popular with mountain bikers and families walking their dogs. This forested 5.7-mile loop weaves through eucalyptus and pines, and the air is cool at just over 3,000 feet elevation. To reach the trailhead from Makawao, follow Makawao Avenue toward Ha'iku for 0.3 mile before turning right on Pi'iholo Road. After 1.5 miles, just past the Pi'iholo zipline tours, take a left at the fork in the road and follow it for 0.5 mile. Here you'll make a right onto Kahakapao Road and drive 1.5 miles on a narrow uphill until you reach a metal gate (open 7am-7pm daily). From the gate, a steep asphalt

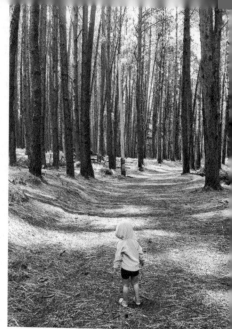

hiking on the Waihou Spring Trail

road continues for another 0.5 miles until it reaches a gravel parking lot. Expect to encounter some cyclists while hiking, since it's a multiuse network of trails.

If you don't feel like dealing with throngs of bikers, head to the **Waihou Spring Trail,** toward the top of Olinda Road. This two-mile trail is only open to hikers and doesn't have as steep an elevation gain as at Kahakapao. It's uniquely situated among an experimental planting of pine trees, and while the wooded trail is nice enough for walking, the treat is at the end, where a steep switchback leads to a hidden gulch. Here you'll find a 30-foot vertical rock face with tunnels bored through, and if you have a flashlight, you can climb in the tunnels and follow them for a short distance. To reach the trailhead for Waihou Springs, go to Makawao's only intersection and follow Olinda Road uphill for five very curvy miles.

Bike Down Haleakala

You've seen the brochures, you've heard

the hype; here's the deal with cycling down Haleakala volcano:

It's imperative to be confident and competent on a bicycle. It is marketed as beginner-friendly, but in reality, dozens of people are seriously injured each year. In almost all cases it's because they took their eyes off the road or were riding too fast.

That said, watching the day begin from Haleakala Crater and the crisp air in your face as you weave through cow-speckled pastures is magical. Visit the shops of Makawao town and finish the ride close to the beach. A wide range of operators have different options, and the key to an enjoyable trip is choosing carefully. Decide whether you want to include sunrise at Haleakala Crater. This means waking up early, with pickups at 2am. After watching the sunrise, it's back in the van for the drive down to 6,500 feet, where all the tours begin the cycling portion, outside the national park. If you opt for a tour that doesn't include sunrise, you'll be driven to this spot, usually arriving about 10am. The next option is whether to ride with a guide. The benefit is safety, but it means you have to follow the pace of the group. For independent-minded travelers, it's probably best to choose a company that lets you ride on your own.

The third option to consider is where the tour ends: in Upper Kula with a zipline combo, or all the way to the beach. It's possible to ride from the summit to the beach with your own car and bike. **Krank Cycles** (1120 Makawao Ave., 808/572-2299, www.krank-maui.com, 9am-6pm daily) and **Haleakala Bike Company** (810 Ha'iku Rd., Suite 120, 808/575-9575, www.bikemaui.com) offer independent rentals, although **Maui Sunriders** (71 Baldwin Ave., 866/500-2453, www.mauisunriders.com) is the most convenient, as their shop is near the beach.

With those options in mind, here are some of our top picks:

Maui Easy Riders (808/344-9489, www.mauieasyriders.com, $119) is a small operation run by two brothers, both named Billy (really). Group size is small, only eight people, and tours begin at 9am in the parking lot of Pa'ia Bay. The ride begins at 6,600 feet, just above where other companies begin, and the 25-mile ride to the beach is longer than any other company. This guided tour makes a stop in Makawao for 30 minutes of exploring on foot, and at the end you can literally jump off your bike and into the waves.

The other top pick for guided tours is the ride with **Bike It Maui** (808/878-3364, www.

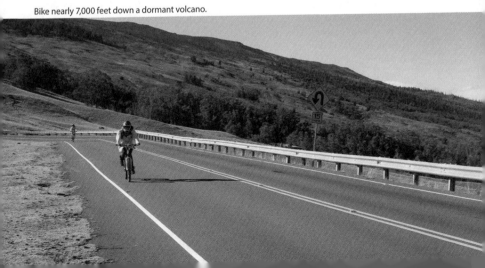

Bike nearly 7,000 feet down a dormant volcano.

Tips for Biking the Volcano

- If you go with a tour, you can't ride from the summit. If you want to bike from the summit, you have to provide your own bicycle and transportation.

- Seeing the sunrise isn't guaranteed: 15 percent of the time the crater is clouded in. Variations in the weather aren't seasonal, so all you can do is hope for the best.

- If you want to spend more than 15 minutes at Haleakala after sunrise, save sunrise for a separate trip and book a midmorning bike ride. The trip will be cheaper, and you'll be able to hike and explore the crater without having to rush back to the van.

- Be prepared to wake up *really* early for a sunrise tour. Companies collect guests from the farthest hotels first, so if you're staying in Makena or Kapalua, expect to meet your driver as early as 1:45am.Try to book this excursion early in your trip, when you're still jet-lagged and waking up early.

- If you're on a budget, opt for a midmorning tour. It isn't as cold, you don't have to wake up as early, it isn't as crowded, and the trips are substantially cheaper. Companies charge more for the sunrise tours because they're popular.

- Remember that you're sharing the road with cars. There are no bike lanes, so be sure to keep your eyes on the road at all times.

- Pack closed-toe shoes, long pants, a rain jacket, and warm clothing. Early morning temperatures often dip below freezing at the summit. Although many tour companies provide rain gear, the more protection you have against the elements, the better.

- Don't expect to get any sleep in the van ride up. The road switchbacks incessantly, and drivers entertain the riders with island history and jokes.

- If you're skittish, go with a guided group. If you're an independent person, choose an independent company so you can ride without a guide.

- Don't schedule your bike ride for the day after scuba diving; decompression sickness can kill.

bikeitmaui.com), whose sunrise tour ($140) also includes breakfast afterward. Their van is the most comfortable for the ride up the mountain, and their bikes are exceptionally well maintained. The ride ends in Lower Kula.

Other providers who ride to the beach include **Mountain Riders** (800/706-7700, www.mountainriders.com) and **Cruiser Phil's** (808/893-2332, www.cruiserphil.com).

For an independent ride, **Maui Sunriders** (71 Baldwin Ave., 808/579-8970, www.mauisunriders.com) has sunrise tours ($125) that start from and end at their shop in Pa'ia, as well as an affordable "Express" tour ($76). Visitors can explore Pa'ia once the ride is over.

Other independent tours include **Haleakala Bike Company** (810 Ha'iku Rd., Suite 120, 808/575-9575, www.bikemaui.

com), offering a sunrise tour ($135) and a "Haleakala Express" ride ($75) that end at Ha'iku Marketplace.

MOUNTAIN BIKING

The mountain biking on Maui is really good. The two main areas Upcountry are the **Makawao Forest Reserve,** about 15 minutes above Makawao, and **Polipoli,** above Kula. Thanks to the team at Krank Cycles, the Makawao Forest Reserve has recently undergone over $500,000 in trail work, which means Makawao has some of the best trails in Hawaii. With 16 miles of trail in total, there are terrain parks, single-track, two-mile climbs, and even a 30-foot banked wooden wall you'd expect to find in a place like Whistler. The "Pineapple Express" is

Paniolo Country

Anyone headed Upcountry is sure to hear the term *paniolo* at least a couple of times—particularly when wandering around Makawao. While most locals will tell you that *paniolo* is simply Hawaiian for "cowboy," the term also encapsulates a unique portion of Hawaii's ranching heritage.

In 1793, on the Big Island of Hawaii, British explorer George Vancouver gifted King Kamehameha I some cattle. Kamehameha placed a *kapu*—a taboo—on the killing of cattle so the population could expand. By 1830, when the *kapu* was lifted, tens of thousands of wild cattle ran amok over the Hawaiian Islands, destroying crops and endangering human lives. Kamehameha III sent an adviser to California to seek help with the cattle explosion. He brought back three Mexican *vaqueros,* who taught Hawaiians how to rope cattle. Spanish, spoken by the *vaqueros,* is the root of the Hawaiian word *paniolo,* today's word for Hawaii's cowboys.

The *paniolo,* predating the cowboys of the U.S. West, set up ranches on Haleakala's slopes. Ikua Purdy, a *paniolo* from the Big Island, won the World Championship of steer roping at the Cheyenne Frontier Days in 1908, and was the first Hawaiian elected to the National Rodeo Cowboy Hall of Fame.

This ranching heritage continues Upcountry, where *paniolo* work Haleakala Ranch (30,000 acres), Ulupalakua Ranch (20,000 acres), Ka'ono'ulu Ranch (10,000 acres), Thompson Ranch (1,400 acres), and Pi'iholo Ranch (800 acres). One of the largest annual Upcountry events is the Fourth of July Makawao Rodeo. Upcountry cherishes its *paniolo* past, and ranching and agriculture still continue as staples of Upcountry life.

two miles of downhill, and the west loop on the Kahakapao Trail is the most popular trail for climbing.

Polipoli, on the other hand, offers rugged downhill mountain biking, with a network of trails that switchback through redwoods, lava flows, and wide-open plains. You'll need a 4WD vehicle to reach some trailheads, and forget about visiting after a rain, since you'll get stuck in the mud. For a classic climb and single-track descent, park where the **Mamane Trail** meets the road toward the campground. Start by riding in the direction of the campground and turn uphill at the fork, where you'll climb along the spine of the mountain before the two-mile Mamane Trail drop.

For the island's longest off-road descent, the chance to bike from 10,000 feet, have someone drive you to Haleakala for the start of **Skyline Drive.** The unpaved road begins by Science City and switchbacks its way across desolate cinder that looks like the surface of the moon. Watch for wild goats and hunters, and definitely wear bright clothing. After six

miles, turn down the Mamane Trail for two fast miles of single-track. For a full 7,000-foot vertical descent, continue riding all the way down to Highway 37, then turn left for the two-mile ride on pavement to Grandma's Coffee House. Arrange to have your ride pick you up here.

For Upcountry bike rentals, **Krank Cycles** (1120 Makawao Ave., 808/572-2299, www.krankmaui.com, 9am-6pm daily) is located in Makawao and offers half-day (9am-1pm or 1:30pm-5:30pm, $35) and full-day ($75) rentals. Half day rentals are enough time for the Makawao trails, but not for Polipoli. These guys are Maui's most dedicated mountain bike shop; check out their website for current trail conditions.

To ride on 80 acres of farmland with seven miles of trails, **Bike Park Maui** (3725 Baldwin Ave., 808/740-8405, www.bikeparkmaui.com, 10am-5pm Sat.-Sun., $10) is five minutes from Makawao, with a terrain park, plank bridges, and jumps. Mountain bike rentals ($50 adults, $35 children) are available.

Horseback Riding and Bird-Watching

HORSEBACK RIDING

Upcountry is horse country, and in the rolling Upcountry pasturelands, horseback riding is a slice of authentic Upcountry life. All of Upcountry's horseback options are on working ranches, which mean you're dealing with real *paniolo* who still ranch, wrangle, and ride.

For a small-scale intimate experience in the most beautiful pastures on Maui, **Thompson Ranch** (Middle Rd., 808/878-1910, www.thompsonranchmaui.com, $125, cash only) offers guided trail rides on their Keokea ranch. This is a family-run working cattle ranch that's far from touristy, and the ranch owners love their horses. The view here is unforgettable, with green pastures rolling down to the blue Pacific. The climb is steep, and the maximum weight for riders is 200 pounds.

In Makawao, **Pi'iholo Ranch** (808/270-8750, www.piiholo.com, 8:30am-1pm Mon.-Sat.) offers horseback tours on their 800 acre spread. Options include a two-hour ride across cattle-filled pastures ($229) and a three-hour ride with lunch at a private cabin ($349). Roping sessions are often held in the arena on Thursday afternoons. To reach Pi'iholo Ranch, go 1.5 miles up Pi'iholo Road before branching left onto Waiahiwi Road. Follow this for 0.5 mile; the sign for the ranch is on the left.

For a ranch adventure unlike any other, book the half-day Kanaio Beach ride (4.5 hours, $285) with the crew at **Triple L Ranch** (15900 Pi'ilani Hwy., 808/280-7070, www.triplelranchmaui.com, 8am-6pm daily). Located four miles past the Maui winery on the back road toward Hana, the ranch is set in windswept Kanaio, the youngest part of Maui. The cattle are all free range and roam the mountain without fences. There's no denying the magic of riding a horse to an isolated beach, even though it's rocky and lacking sand. Kanaio is laden with archaeological sites and abandoned lava-rock fishing villages. Maximum weight is 220 pounds, and minimum age is 12. Group size is limited to two or three.

nene

BIRD-WATCHING
Haleakala National Park

If you're an avid bird-watcher, just get in the car, drive uphill, and don't stop until you reach the entrance of **Haleakala National Park.** Given Hawaii's extreme isolation, 71 different species of birds were once endemic to the islands. Of those species, 23 have gone extinct, and dozens more are critically endangered due to mongooses, feral cats, and the gradual loss of habitat. Endangered species such as *'akohekohe* find themselves clinging to a fragile existence on Haleakala's slopes.

One of the best bird-watching places is at **Hosmer's Grove** on the moderate 0.5-mile loop trail. Even if you don't see native honeycreepers (birds whose bills have adapted to extract nectar from native plant species), the treetops chirp with birdsong different from anywhere else on the planet.

While casual hikers might spot an *'i'wi* or *'apapane* (scarlet Hawaiian honeycreeper), the best way to spot rare species is to take the three-hour ranger-led **guided walks** (808/572-4400, 8:45am Thurs.) into the neighboring privately owned **Waikamoi Preserve.** Reservations are essential. On a less frequent basis, hikes into the preserve are arranged by the **Maui Forest Bird Recovery**

Project (808/573-0280, www.mauiforest-birds.org).

Moving higher up toward the summit, bird-watchers should look for two endangered species: the *'u'au* (Hawaiian petrel), which burrows in areas near the summit Visitors Center, and the *nene* (Hawaiian goose), which can be spotted along park roadways and the valley floor. The *nene* is Hawaii's state bird, and one of the best places to spot them is in grasslands surrounding Paliku Cabin.

Adventure Sports

PARAGLIDING

When was the last time you ran off a hill and experienced total silence? Or saw Maui from a bird's eye view without the whir of a chopper? **Proflyght Hawaii Paragliding** (1598 Waipoli Rd., 808/874-5433, www.para-glidemaui.com, 7am-7pm daily) is Hawaii's only paragliding school, and thanks to Maui's

optimal conditions, flights are possible about 330 days per year. The launch and landing sites are perfect for learning, and nearly every flight takes place in the morning before the clouds fill in. Tandem flights drop 1,000 feet ($95) or 3,000 feet ($185) over the Polipoli treetops. This unforgettable island experience is highly recommended.

paragliding in Polipoli

ZIPLINE TOURS

Believe it or not, Upcountry is where ziplining was born in the United States. In 2002 **Skyline Eco-Adventures** (12 Kiopaʻa Place, 808/878-8400, www.zipline.com, 7am-7pm daily) opened in Kula's misty uplands, the first in the country. Today, Skyline offers a five-line course best for beginners, since the length of the lines and vertical drops aren't dramatic. There's also the option to combine a zipline with a sunrise Haleakala bike tour, although the bike ride only descends 2,500 feet, so the combo is best for people who just want a sample of both activities. The course is located on the road toward Haleakala at approximately 4,000 feet elevation, and the lines run through misty, cloud-shrouded groves of eucalyptus and koa. Once you unhook from the final line, which is the longest and easily most thrilling, stroll through the neighboring lavender farm with a warm drink from the café.

In the forests above Makawao, 20 minutes away, **Piʻiholo Zipline Tours** (799 Piʻiholo Rd., 808/572-1717, www.piiholozipline.com, 7am-9pm daily) takes the adrenaline up a notch. This is the site of the island's longest side-by-side parallel zipline, which means you can watch Mom scream in terror for 2,300 feet. At one point your feet are 600 feet above the ground, and occasionally in winter there are small waterfalls that splash through the rocky ravines. Piʻiholo can often be rainy, particularly in winter. Visitors can choose either four or five lines, but since the fifth line is the 2,300-foot screamer, it's best to get the full experience. There's also a seven- or eight-line excursion that weaves through the treetops, a great option for families with kids who aren't quite ready for the screamer.

YOGA, FITNESS, AND SPAS

Located in Makawao next to Casanova restaurant, **Mangala Yoga** (1170 Makawao Ave., 808/359-2252, www.mangalayoga.com) offers drop-in classes ($18) or a five-class package ($85). A full class schedule is available on the website.

On Piʻiholo Road, **Hale Hoʻomana** (1150 Piʻiholo Rd., 808/573-8256, www.halehoomana.com) is a day spa in the soothing uplands, where services aim to combine cultural Hawaiian values with the healing properties of massage.

For one of the island's most affordable massage deals, call the **Maui School of Therapeutic Massage** (1043 Makawao Ave., 808/572-2277, www.massagemaui.com) to inquire about student clinics, which have prices a fraction of those at the resorts. Clinics are usually held weekday evenings or Thursday afternoon.

Shopping

★ HISTORIC MAKAWAO TOWN

If you want to make someone from Makawao cringe, refer to Historic Makawao Town as a smaller version of Lahaina. The galleries and boutiques here are on par, if not better, than the shops and galleries on Front Street, and you don't have the cruise ships unloading at the shore. Instead, Makawao exudes its own unique vibe, where you might find yourself standing on the creaky wooden deck of a fashionable women's clothing boutique, allowing a misty rain shower to pass while sipping a coffee or tea, or chatting with a friendly Portuguese ranch hand, chuckling at the colorful rooster that's managed to bring traffic to a halt.

It's a town of laughter, smiles, and curious moments, where a truck might pass with a goat in the back with a tailgate made out of rope, and where locals can't stroll two blocks without waving at three people they know. It's a hive of artistic, creative individuals, with strong *paniolo* ranching heritage and hitching posts lining the wood shingled storefronts that don't see much use anymore. Find a roadside parking spot and stroll around town.

Art Galleries

For Polynesian jewelry, visit **Maui Master Jewelers** (3655 Baldwin Ave., 808/573-5400, www.mauimasterjewelers.com, 10am-5pm Mon.-Fri., 10am-4pm Sat.) where works by over 30 local artists are on display. They are the island's leading source for New Zealand bone and jade carvings and also offer Tahitian pearl jewelry.

Sherri Reeve Gallery (3669 Baldwin Ave., 808/572-8931, www.sreeve.com, 9am-5pm Mon.-Fri., 10am-4pm Sat.-Sun.) showcases this ebullient Makawao artist whose distinctive floral designs have graced shirts, cards, paintings, and prints since it opened in 1997. This is a worthwhile stop among the large number of galleries in town.

At **Jordanne Gallery and Studio** (3625 Baldwin Ave., 808/563-0088, www.jordannefineart.com, 10:30am-5pm daily), meet a plein-air painter who decided at the airport during a family trip to Lana'i that she wasn't getting back on the plane. With little money and no plan, her painting talents paved an unforeseen path.

In the Courtyard shopping area, **Viewpoints Gallery** (3620 Baldwin Ave., 808/572-5979, www.viewpointsgallerymaui.com, 10am-6pm daily) is a large, clean space that features a rotating array of artists, predominantly painters.

Back behind the gallery next to Market Fresh Bistro is **Hot Island Glass** (3620 Baldwin Ave., 808/572-4527, www.hotislandglass.com, 9am-5pm daily), the island's best-known glass studio, where you can watch artists blow glass (10:30am-4pm Mon.-Sat.). Call ahead to check the demonstration schedule.

For original oil paintings from over a dozen artists, check out the intimate **Makawao Fine Art Gallery** (3660 Baldwin Ave., 808/573-5972, www.makawaofineartgallery.com, 11am-5pm Mon.-Sat., noon-5pm Sun.),

open since 1986. The gallery is a collector's haven for limited-edition pieces.

On a corner in the center of town, **Julie Galeeva Fine Art** (3682 Baldwin Ave., 808/573-4772, www.juliegaleeva.com, 10am-5pm Mon.-Sat.) showcases the highly textured paintings of this talented Russian-born artist and Maui resident.

Clothing and Gifts

You know those people who casually exude the trendy essence of cool? There's a good chance they're shopping for clothes at Makawao's fashionable boutiques. Working your way down Baldwin Avenue from the center of town, **Collections** (3677 Baldwin Ave., 808/572-0781, www.collectionsmauiinc.com, 9am-6pm Mon.-Sat., 11am-5pm Sun.) has been providing men's and women's clothing and boutique home furnishings since 1975.

The Mercantile (3673 Baldwin Ave., 808/572-1401, 10am-6pm daily) specializes in boutique women's clothing, and **Pink by Nature** (3643 Baldwin Ave., 808/572-9576, 10am-6pm Mon.-Sat., 11am-5pm Sun.) has a chic selection of the newest and trendiest styles. Its brother store, **Homme by Nature** (3643 Baldwin Ave., 808/572-3456, 10am-6pm Mon.-Sat., 11am-5pm Sun.) is a rustic yet modern wood-paneled enclave of vintage menswear and home decor.

The collection of clanging wind chimes announces your arrival at **Goodies** (3633 Baldwin Ave., 808/572-0288, 10am-6pm daily), an eccentric but genuinely artsy clothing boutique for women. **Designing Wahine Emporium** (3640 Baldwin Ave., 808/573-0990, 10am-6pm Mon.-Sat., 11am-5pm Sun.) offers something for everyone, including a selection of men's aloha shirts.

To pick up a rub for a sunset barbecue, the **Volcano Spice Company** (3623 Baldwin Ave., 808/575-7729, www.volcanospicecompany.com, hours vary, usually 10am-5pm Mon.-Sat., 11am-3pm Sun.) is a small shop full of spices made on the property. Try the coffee barbecue rub and the original volcano spice blend.

Protea

Protea

Protea are large flowers that bloom in dark brown, brilliant orange, bright yellow, and pale pink. Natural or hybridized, some have pincushion-like heads, others have tops that resemble a bunch of wispy feathers, while others look like bottlebrushes. Originally from South Africa, these beautiful flowers have been grown on Maui since the mid-1960s and are now big business as the state's showiest of flowers. Dozens of hybrids have been created for their long stems, colors, and the size and shape of the petals. Kula and environs, at 3,000 feet elevation, has perfect growing conditions, with sunny days, crisp nights, and even temperatures that don't usually go above 80°F. Upcountry boasts numerous protea growers, some with shops, and many of whom ship.

On a corner in town is **Little Tibet** (3682 Baldwin Ave., 808/573-2275, 10am-5pm Mon.-Sat.), where an array of colorful gemstones and crystals warrant a look. Across the street is the **Dragon's Den** (3681 Baldwin Ave., 808/572-2424, www.thedragonsden-herbshop.com, 9:30am-6pm Mon.-Sat., 11am-4pm Sun.), an herb shop that's been here since 1982, with organic superfoods and medicine, and now serving herbal tea.

If you find yourself enjoying Makawao's vibe to the point you want to take it home with you, **Jewels of the White Tara** (3682 Makawao Ave., 808/573-5774, 10am-6pm Mon.-Sat., 11am-5pm Sun.) has exotic New Age furnishings. This import store features home decor and international clothing items, with pieces from India, Indonesia, Laos, and Vietnam, among others.

Fleur de Lei (1169 Makawao Ave., 808/269-8855, 10:30am-6:30pm daily) is an eco-boutique with clothing items made from organic cotton, as well as "sail bags" made from recycled windsurfing and kitesurfing sails. The store promotes fair trade and sustainable practices, and if you aren't familiar with vegan leather, stop in and ask.

For Maui-made arts and crafts such as paintings, woodwork, and jewelry, **Maui Hands** (1169 Makawao Ave., 808/572-2008, www.mauihands.com, 10am-6pm Mon.-Sat., 11am-5pm Sun.) is on Makawao Avenue right next to the Makawao library.

KULA
Art Galleries
There's only one artist on the island who really nails Upcountry. Driving past the Kula

Lodge to Haleakala, make a stop at the **Curtis Wilson Cost Gallery** (15200 Haleakala Hwy., 808/874-6544, www.costgallery.com, 8:30am-5pm daily), tucked neatly beneath the restaurant. The vibe is like a fine wine cellar filled with exceptional art. Having painted the island's rural corners for over 40 years, Cost now has the longest-running one-man gallery in Hawaii. Art can be ordered with custom koa frames or individually commissioned, and the work of his daughter, Julia Cost, is also displayed.

Worcester Glassworks (4626 Lower Kula Rd., 808/878-4000, www.worcesterglassworks.com, hours vary, usually 10am-5pm Mon.-Sat., by appointment Sun.), by Kula Bistro restaurant, is a well-lit gallery inside a rustic studio mostly occupied by industrial machinery used in the glass blowing process. The resident glassblowers, Bill and Sally Worcester, operate this family-run studio and welcome guests "most days."

Gifts and Flowers
Right next to Kula Lodge is the **Proteas of Hawaii Gift Shop** (15200 Healakala Hwy., 808/878-2533, www.proteasofhawaii.com, 8am-4pm daily), where you can pick up a bouquet of freshly cut protea ($75-140) grown only half a mile away.

Down the driveway from Kula Lodge is the exceptional **Kula Marketplace** (808/878-2135, www.kulamarketplace.com, 8am-7pm daily), an oasis of gifts from over 200 local artists, including jams, honey, coffee, music, and clothing. It's a great place to wander while digesting breakfast from neighboring Kula Lodge.

KEOKEA AND ULUPALAKUA
Art Gallery and Fine Furniture
Next to Grandma's Coffee House, tiny little

Keokea Gallery (9230 Kula Hwy., 808/878-3555, 9am-5pm daily) has linocut collages, handmade frames, and a collection of painted surfboards. The affable artist in residence, Sheldon, is always up for a chat, and the works here are surprisingly good considering the rural location.

To return from vacation with a desk so beautiful it will make your coworkers cry, walk to **The Kingswood Shop and Gallery** (8900 Kula Hwy., 808/878-3626, www.kingswoodshop.com, 10am-4pm Wed.-Sat.), not far from Keokea Park. The legendary woodworker Peter Naramore has exquisite pieces of koa wood furniture and exceptional heirloom antiques, and can also commission custom pieces unique to your tastes.

Clothing and Gifts
All the way out here in "deep Upcountry," the only real place for clothing and gifts is the **Ulupalakua Ranch Store** (14800 Pi'ilani Hwy., 808/878-2561, www.ulupalakuaranch.com/store, 9:30am-5:30pm daily), open for 150 years. The store features products from a dozen local vendors, and since it is on a working ranch, you'll find Wranglers and belts rather than aloha shirts and sunscreen. Consider buying a hat or shirt to help the ranch stay afloat, which helps keep the open spaces and *paniolo* heritage alive.

Visitors to Keokea should look inside **Ching Store** (9212 Kula Hwy., 808/878-1556, 7am-5:30pm daily) and **Fong Store** (9226 Kula Hwy., 808/878-1525, 7:30am-5:30pm Mon.-Sat., 7:30am-3pm Sun.). These family-run businesses are fascinating time portals, where oversize cigarette boxes still serve as decor. Mrs. Fong will be quick to point out that this store is in the "new" location, since 1932; the original store opened in Keokea in 1908.

Food

MAKAWAO
American

The two best things about **Market Fresh Bistro** (3620 Baldwin Ave., 808/572-4877, www.marketfreshbistro.com, 9am-3pm Tues.-Sat., 9am-2pm Sun., dinner 6pm-8:30pm Thurs., $12) are the courtyard setting and the salmon and tomato Benedict. Emphasis is on local ingredients, and breakfast is the most popular meal, served until 11am.

A true hole-in-the-wall favorite, the **Makawao Garden Café** (3669 Baldwin Ave., 808/573-9065, www.makawaogarden-cafe.com, 11am-3pm Mon.-Sat., $6-9) is hidden in an alcove next to the Sherri Reeve art gallery. The café only offers outdoor seating, which means that when it rains, the restaurant closes. Laid-back and open only for lunch, options include a baby brie and bacon sandwich or quinoa salad with goat cheese. Cool down with a refreshing smoothie—flavored with mango or *lilikoi*.

If you're in the mood for a turkey or club sandwich paired with freshly squeezed juices, the deli counter inside **Rodeo General Store**

(3661 Baldwin Ave., 808/572-1868, 6:30am-10pm Mon.-Sat., 6:30am-9pm Sun., $8-10) is great for lunch on the run. The homemade chili ($4) is filling and affordable, or boost your energy with a "Green Machine"—an all-natural collection of celery, apple, parsley, cucumber, and kale thrown in the juicer.

For a juicy steak in a ranching town, **Makawao Steak House** (3612 Baldwin Ave., 808/572-8711, www.cafeoleirestaurants.com, 5pm-9pm Tues.-Sun., $25-30) has a dimly lit, dark-wood interior that makes you want to order red wine and a bowl of Maui onion soup. The steaks are expertly prepared, and this longtime local date-night venue is the most upscale restaurant downtown.

Bakery

To act like an Upcountry local, start your morning with a doughnut from ★ **Komoda Store and Bakery** (3674 Baldwin Ave., 808/572-7261, 7am-4pm Mon.-Tues. and Thurs.-Fri., 7am-2pm Sat.). Komoda's *defines* Upcountry, and the unmistakable aroma of its cream puffs wafts on the predawn air.

famous Komoda stick donut

Welcome to Keokea, Maui's Chinatown

Ask any local for directions to Chinatown and they'll probably point you toward Honolulu. While Hawaii's capital has one of America's oldest Chinatowns, few people are aware that Maui's Chinatown is in Keokea. Don't expect swinging red lanterns or dim sum carts on the street; this Chinatown was initially founded on potatoes.

Arriving in the 1820s on ships engaged in the sandalwood trade, many of Maui's Chinese immigrants ended up working in sugar mills. Laboring hard on the fledgling plantations, Chinese farmers saved up to buy land in Keokea, which paid off when potatoes were needed to feed prospectors in the California gold rush. At one point, Kula farmers were shipping such a steady stream of potatoes to the ports of California that the area was referred to as "Nu Kaleponi"—Hawaiian for "New California."

Meanwhile, back in China, 2,000 years of imperial rule ended when the Qing Dynasty fell in 1911. The roots of the revolution can be traced to the rural slopes of sleepy Keokea and sometime resident Sun Yat-sen.

Today, local Chinese history is evident in the town's two mom-and-pop stores, Fong Store and Ching Store. The staff at either will be more than happy to talk about the area's heritage. The Chinese community has also constructed buildings in Keokea such as the Kwock Hing Society and St. Joseph's Church.

There's a line out the door before 7am, and popular items like baked butter rolls sell out within hours. Spring for the classic Komoda "stick doughnut." Fittingly, this 100-year-old store operates without computers, so expect to pay cash.

Coffee Shops

Need to perk up after a Haleakala sunrise? **Casanova Deli** (1188 Makawao Ave., 808/572-0220, www.casanovamaui.com, 7:30am-5:30pm daily) is a Makawao classic that's been slinging cups of caffeinated cheer since 1986. Breakfast sandwiches, *paninis,* and omelets are paired with eccentric locals, and the people-watching from a front porch stool is some of the island's best.

At the edge of town, down Baldwin Avenue, **Sip Me** (3617 Baldwin Ave., 808/573-2340, www.sipmemaui.com, 6am-5pm daily) is Makawao's newest spot for espresso, Wi-Fi, and treats. It's Upcountry's earliest coffee shop to open, and 90 percent of the baked goods are gluten-free. Coffee is made from organic beans roasted on Maui, and you'll find healthy organic smoothies ($7) made from local ingredients. Best of all, there's a lovable "Pay It Forward" wall where you can buy a

stranger a coffee—and maybe even receive one yourself if you meet the random criteria.

For a quick coffee on the go, there's a small coffee shop inside **Rodeo General Store** (3661 Baldwin Ave., 808/572-1868, 6:30am-10pm Mon.-Sat., 6:30am-9pm Sun.) that serves organically roasted local coffee along with organic milk.

Food Tour

For a food, history, and walking tour through the heart of Makawao town, **Local Tastes of Maui** (808/446-1190, www.localtastesofmaui.com, 9:30am-11:30am daily, $45) offers tours of Makawao (Thurs.) as well as Pa'ia, Lahaina, and Kihei. Portions of proceeds are donated to local animal welfare organizations.

Hawaiian Regional

The ★ **Hali'imaile General Store** (900 Hali'imaile Rd., 808/572-2666, www.bevgannonrestaurants.com, lunch 11am-2:30pm Mon.-Fri., dinner 5:30pm-9pm daily, $22-42), which serves gourmet food in an old-school roadhouse that was once a general store, is easily the island's most unlikely location for food of this caliber. Master chef Beverly Gannon—frequently voted Maui's top chef and a founder of the Hawaiian regional cuisine movement—crafts appetizers such as sashimi Napoleon and famous crab pizza. Entrées include *paniolo* barbecue ribs and coconut seafood curry. Portions are plentiful.

Italian

On the corner at Makawao's only intersection, **Casanova** (1188 Makawao Ave., 808/572-0220, www.casanovamaui.com, lunch 11:30am-2pm Mon.-Tues. and Thurs.-Sat., dinner 5:30pm-9:30pm daily, $18-34) offers wood-fired pizzas and Italian classics like *linguine pescatore*. Easily Makawao's sexiest venue, it feels like a date-night place in a city. There's a great wine list, a $20 corkage fee if you bring your own bottle, and $5 wine carafes 5pm-6pm. On selected nights, Casanova becomes Maui's best nightclub, with Wednesday "Ladies Night" the place where singles come to party. Friday and Saturday feature Reggae or Latin from around 10pm. Cover is about $10.

Mexican

Mix some mango margaritas, a seafood burrito, and a great community atmosphere, and it's obvious why ★ **Polli's Mexican Restaurant** (1202 Makawao Ave., 808/572-7808, www.pollismexicanrestaurant.com, 11am-10pm daily, $11-22) has been a Makawao classic since 1981. Portions are enormous for the seafood enchilada, chicken burrito supreme, sizzling beef fajita, and "Makawowie" nachos appetizer. Polli's also offers Maui Cattle Company cheeseburgers, barbecue pork sandwiches, a heaping array of vegetarian options, and baby back ribs that fall off the bone. The festive interior is decorated with photographs from Mexico, surf photography from Hawaii, and authentic souvenirs from all over Latin America.

KULA
American

The **Kula Lodge** (15200 Haleakala Hwy., 808/878-1535, www.kulalodge.com, 7am-8:30pm daily, breakfast 7am-10:45am daily, $12-34) has been welcoming hungry patrons into its rustic interior for so long it's become synonymous with Kula dining. Inside a 1940s private home, this panoramic mountainside perch hasn't changed much since. At 3,200 feet elevation, it's a little bit cooler, and the dark-wood interior is a perfect fit with the low temperatures and clouds. Paintings by Curtis Wilson Cost adorn the wooden entrance (his gallery is beneath the restaurant). The Lodge is a filling breakfast stop on the way down from Haleakala.

For an affordable, laid-back, and welcoming vibe, **Kula Sandalwoods Café** (15427 Haleakala Hwy., 808/878-3523, www.kulasandalwoods.com, 7am-3pm Mon.-Sat., 7am-noon Sun., $9-11) serves breakfast until 11am. While the outdoor lanai is nice, the cozy interior has a small fireplace with country music on the radio. For breakfast, try the Keokea omelet; at lunch, go for the kalua pig sandwich.

French

A tucked-away outdoor patio in the middle of a Kula pasture, **La Provence** (3158 Lower Kula Rd., 808/878-1313, www.laprovencekula.com, 7am-2pm Wed.-Sun., $11, cash only) is a boutique French restaurant and local Kula favorite. On Lower Kula Road just past the True Value hardware store, La Provence offers flaky croissants, café au lait, and affordable filling crepes. Order a vegetable and goat cheese crepe or a tomato and avocado Benedict, accompanied by a side of Kula greens and a cluster of roasted potatoes. Weekends can be busy, so don't come if you're in a rush. There's an ATM at the hardware store if you find yourself without cash.

Italian

For Italian food paired with local favorites, ★ **Kula Bistro** (4556 Lower Kula Rd., 808/871-2960, www.kulabistro.com, 7:30am-8pm daily, breakfast 7:30am-10:30am Tues.-Sun., $12-30) surpasses all others. Tasting the pesto chicken flatbread or jumbo lobster ravioli, it's obvious that owner Luciano Zanon has been perfecting this cuisine since his childhood in Venice. Maui-grown coffee is served at breakfast, and lunch has kalua pig *paninis* and filling hamburger steak. Most ingredients are sourced locally, the desserts are baked fresh daily, and there's no corkage fee. To pick up some booze for the BYOB, Morihara Store across the street has a decent selection.

Markets

If Kula had a center, it would be at **Morihara Store** (4581 Lower Kula Rd., 808/878-2578, 6:30am-8pm Mon.-Sat., 7:30am-8pm Sun.)—the family-run store that services most of Kula's general needs. There are basic condiments, to-go items for lunch, and beer and wine. The store is a refreshing old-school throwback to simpler times.

KEOKEA AND ULUPALAKUA
American

If hunger strikes on the back road from Hana or while at the winery, head to the **Ulupalakua Ranch Store and Grill** (14800 Pi'ilani Hwy., 808/878-2561, www.ulupalakuaranch.com, 10am-5pm daily)—a carnivorous carnival of ranch-grown meats eaten on the wooden front porch. The grill

features venison, lamb, elk, and beef, all raised on the 20,000 acres surrounding the store. Everything is made from scratch. Try the filling and affordable Uncle Mike's Steak Chili & Rice Bowl ($9), or an Ulupalakua Elk Burger ($12). There's also a Fresh Maui Taro Burger ($9) if you don't eat meat.

The other burger spot on the back road to Hana is **Bully's Burgers** (15900 Pi'ilani Hwy., 808/268-0123, www.triplelranchmaui.com, hours vary, usually 11am-6pm Wed.-Sun.) in Kanaio. This exceptionally simple roadside shack has grass-fed burgers ($10), raised on Triple L Ranch. Bully's is four miles past Maui Wine heading in the direction of Hana, and while there aren't any restrooms and the hours are irregular, the burgers don't disappoint.

Coffee Shop

While it doesn't look like much from the outside, there's a simple romance to ★ **Grandma's Coffee House** (9232 Kula Hwy., 808/878-2140, www.grandmascoffee.com, 7am-5pm daily, breakfast 7am-11am Mon.-Fri., 7am-noon Sat.-Sun.) that makes it Maui's best coffee shop. "Grandma" started brewing her own coffee back in 1918, and locally grown beans are roasted in the kitchen

Grab brunch and coffee at Grandma's Coffee House.

using her 100-year-old roaster. The beans are still harvested and processed by four generations of her family. For breakfast, order a Keokea crepe ($14) and enjoy it out on the porch, where slack-key musicians periodically offer live music on weekend mornings. Or grab a cup of coffee to go and enjoy a stroll on Thompson Road across the street. The only downside is that the restrooms are located at Keokea Park, a five-minute walk.

Getting There and Around

CAR

With the exception of central Makawao, where it's possible to walk between shops, Upcountry can only be visited by car. There aren't any rental agencies for cars or mopeds, and parking is free. The main road that leads to Upcountry is Highway 37, with Highway 377 forming a loop through Kula. Haleakala National Park is up Highway 378. There aren't any gas stations in Upper Kula or on Highway 378. From Kula, expect it to take about an hour to drive to the summit of Haleakala, and from Ulupalakua over to Makawao, the drive is about 30 minutes.

BUS

Some parts of Upcountry are served by the **Maui Bus** (808/871-4838, www.co.maui.hi.us/bus), with the Upcountry Islander (bus 40) connecting Upcountry with downtown, and the Kula Villager (bus 39) connecting all the way to Kula. For the Upcountry Islander, bus stops are in front of the Pukalani Community Center, the Makawao Library, and in the center of Hali'imaile. Rates are $2 pp, and the bus makes stops at the Kahului Airport as well as at Queen Ka'ahumanu Mall, where you can link up with other lines. The earliest bus leaves from Pukalani Community Center at 6:30am daily, and later buses run every 90 minutes until 9:30pm.

East Maui: the Road to Hana

Look for ★ to find recommended sights, activities, dining, and lodging.

Highlights

★ **Ke'anae Peninsula:** This fertile peninsula provides a glimpse into one of the last holdouts of an ancient way of life (page 215).

★ **Kahanu Garden and Pi'ilanihale Heiau:** Take a journey back to ancient Hawaii and gaze upon the largest *heiau* in the state (page 217).

★ **Wai'anapanapa State Park:** Swim inside hidden caves, bask on the shores of a black-sand beach, and walk in the footsteps of kings (page 218).

★ **Pools of 'Ohe'o:** At Maui's iconic **Seven Sacred Pools,** you can swim beneath waterfalls that tumble down to the ocean and hike through a bamboo forest (page 222).

★ **Baldwin Beach:** Start your journey to

Hana on the right foot with an early morning stroll down this undeveloped white-sand shore (page 225).

★ **Hamoa Beach:** Surf or snorkel at a beach that Mark Twain and James A. Michener both recognized as one of the most beautiful they'd ever seen (page 227).

★ **Twin Falls:** Swim beneath waterfalls in an accessible, family-friendly setting (page 231).

★ **Na'ili'ili Haele:** Trek through a bamboo forest punctuated by waterfalls, guava trees, and natural swimming holes (page 231).

★ **Hang Gliding in Hana:** See the volcanic coast from the air and soar past hidden waterfalls while learning the basics of hang gliding on flights from the Hana airport (page 236).

East Maui is more than a destination. It's a different mind-set. Lush, tropical, and riddled with waterfalls,

East Maui is the location of the famous Road to Hana and where Maui locals come to escape for a few days. From the windswept taro patches of the Ke'anae Peninsula to the empty pastures of Kaupo, time in East Maui ticks by at a slower place. By no means, however, does that make East Maui lazy. It's the island's adventure center, where an average day could consist of trekking to remote waterfalls, cliff-jumping in a bamboo forest, spelunking hidden caves on a black-sand beach, or body-surfing off sandy shores.

Many who drive the legendary Road to Hana ask "This is it?" and "Where is the rest of town?" Hana is not a destination—it's famous for what it isn't more than for what it is, a sleepy little fishing hamlet. Neighbors still talk to each other and wave as they pass on the street, fishing nets hang in front yards, and the fish end up on the table. You don't come to Hana to reach something; you come out here to leave everything else behind.

East Maui is also home to Pa'ia (Pa-EE-ah), a trendy, funky, and sexy town nominated by *Coastal Living* magazine as one of the "happiest seaside towns in America." Laid-back and worry-free, Pa'ia skanks to the beat of its own bongo. It also has the island's best shopping and food—even better than Lahaina—and the beaches are undeveloped and unheralded sanctuaries of calm.

ORIENTATION

East Maui comprises Pa'ia, Ha'iku, and the famous Road to Hana. **Pa'ia** is a hippie town that has become coastal beach chic, and **Ha'iku** is mostly residential, with the exception of some restaurants and B&Bs. The **Road to Hana** stretches 45 miles from Pa'ia to the center of **Hana,** but continues another 37 miles around the island's back. Pa'ia is only 10 minutes from Kahului Airport, although reaching Hana takes at least a couple of hours—or 20 minutes by plane. The Hana region is spread out over 22 miles from **Nahiku** to **Kipahulu,** over an hour's drive. If you're staying overnight in Hana, be sure to check exactly how far it is from the center of town.

PLANNING YOUR TIME

The biggest mistake you can make on Maui is skimping on your time in Hana. Ideally, Hana

Previous: rugged shoreline of Kipahulu; Kaupo. **Above:** rainbow eucalyptus on the Road to Hana.

East Maui

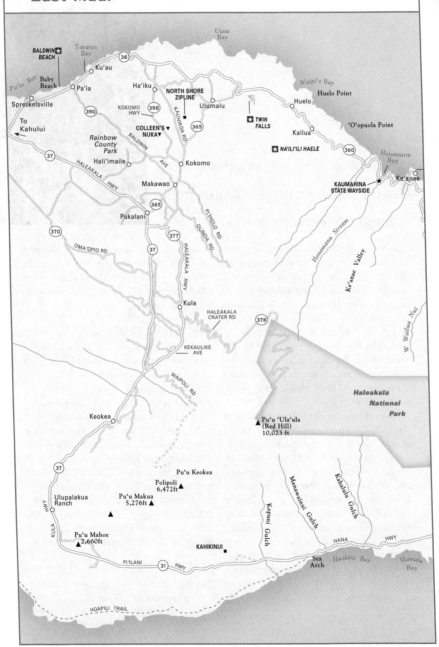

Uaoa Bay

BALDWIN BEACH ★

Tavares Bay

Ku'au

36

Pa'ia Bay

Baby Beach

Pa'ia

Spreckelsville

Ha'iku

NORTH SHORE ZIPLINE

Waipi'o Bay

Huelo Point

390

KOKOMO HWY

398

Ulumalu

Huelo

To Kahului

Rainbow County Park

COLLEEN'S NUKA▼

365

★ **TWIN FALLS**

'O'opuola Point

Kailua

37

Hali'imaile

BALDWIN AVE

Kokomo

★ **NA'ILI'ILI HAELE**

360

Honomanu Bay

Makawao

PI'IHOLO RD

KAUMAHINA STATE WAYSIDE ↘

Ke'anae

365

Pukalani

Honomanu Stream

370

377

OLINDA RD

HALEAKALA HWY

Ke'anae Valley

OMA'OPIO RD

37

Kula

HALEAKALA CRATER RD

378

W Wailua Nui

KEKAULIKE AVE

WAIPOLI RD

Haleakala National Park

Keokea

37

▲ Pu'u 'Ula'ula (Red Hill) 10,023 ft

Pu'u Keokea

Polipoli 6,472ft ▲

Ulupalakua Ranch

Pu'u Makua 5,276ft ▲

▲

Kepuni Gulch

Manawainui Gulch

Kahakulu Gulch

KULA HWY

Pu'u Mahoe 2,660ft ▲

KAHIKINUI ■

HANA HWY

PI'ILANI 31 HWY

Sea Arch

Huakini Bay

Mamalu Bay

HOAPILI TRAIL

Pa'ia

is worth three full days. Choosing to spend the night here allows more time for exploring. If you only have a day to experience the Road to Hana, devote the entire day so you can see it without feeling rushed. Pa'ia is a nice place for breakfast on the way to Hana and is worthy of at least half a day. Visit Pa'ia separately from Hana, or if you're spending the night in Hana, spend the morning at the beach in Pa'ia and then spend the afternoon enjoying the Road to Hana, when there aren't as many cars.

Driving the Road to Hana

Ah, yes, the Road to Hana—the most loved and loathed section of the island divides visitors into two camps: those who swear it's heaven on earth and those who swear never to drive it again. Most people who don't enjoy the trip didn't know what they were getting themselves into. Three words will make or break your trip: Don't rush Hana.

Devote a full day to the experience at minimum. You're visiting one of the most beautiful places on earth; two or three days are even better. Don't expect to breeze through and see it quickly, and don't expect to be back on the other side of the island to make dinner reservations. If you're staying in Ka'anapali or Wailea, it will take you 3.5 hours just to reach the Pools of 'Ohe'o (aka the Seven Sacred Pools). That's not including stops, and the stops are what make the journey worthwhile.

No one should endure a journey to Hana without knowing exactly where the next waterfall, hiking trail, ATM, food cart, or restroom is going to be. Since sights can spring up in an instant—and making a U-turn isn't possible—be prepared. A mile-by-mile rundown of what you'll see along the side of the road

Your Best Day in East Maui

Get a good night's sleep, because this is going to be a long day. Start with a stroll on **Baldwin Beach** around 7:30am, followed by crepes and coffee at **Café des Amis.** Since you'll be spending the day driving to Hana, leave Pa'ia at 9:30am at the latest. If you want to leave earlier, get breakfast on the go from **Pa'ia Bay Coffee.**

Embark on the famous **Road to Hana,** and remember to stop often to hike, swim, and drink in the beauty of the coast. Grab a bite to eat at **Nahiku Marketplace,** and then choose a visit to either **Kahanu Garden** or **Ka'eleku Caverns.** Your next stop is **Wai'anapanapa** for a look at the black-sand beach, taking time for a short dip in the underground freshwater pools.

Continue to Hana for food at **Braddah Hutts,** or if it's a weekend, **Pranee,** and stock up on water, snacks, and gas around Hasegawa General Store. If you have time, make a stop at **Hamoa Beach** for a quick splash in the waves before continuing on to the **Pools of 'Ohe'o** at **Haleakala National Park.** You'll want to leave by 4:30pm for the drive around the back of the mountain, and if you've somehow made it here by 2pm, consider hiking the **Pipiwai Trail** up to 400-foot-high **Waimoku Falls.**

Rainy Day? Either visit Hana in the rain (there will definitely be less traffic) or spend the day shopping in Pa'ia, escaping the rain with pizza at **Flatbread** and a drink at the happening bar.

follows, with specific sights and places worth stopping to linger described in greater detail.

- **Mile Marker 7:** Start in the town of Pa'ia, located around mile marker 7 on the Hana Highway (Hwy. 36). Grab breakfast from **Café des Amis** or **Pa'ia Bay Coffee,** or go for a stroll on Baldwin Beach as the water shines turquoise in morning.

- **Mile Marker 8.8:** Ho'okipa Beach Park. In winter, stop to check out the large crashing surf and the daredevil surfers who ride it. Windsurfing picks up at 11am, but if you're trying to visit Hana in one day, you should definitely be past here by then.

- **Mile Marker 10.3:** Maliko Gulch, start of the famous Maliko Run (page 107).

- **Mile Marker 13.5:** Turnoff for **Pe'ahi,** also called **Jaws**—quite possibly the most famous surf break on the planet. If Jaws is breaking, there will be dozens of cars parked along the side of the highway. The best thing to do is park near the highway and hitch a ride to the bottom of the hill. The viewing area is from a coastal bluff at the bottom of a 4WD road, and the chances of hitching a ride increase tenfold if you barter a six-pack of beer.

- Begin Highway 360.

- **Mile Marker 0:** Note the change in mile markers at the junction of Hana Highway and Kaupakalua Road.

- **Mile Marker 0.3:** Congratulations, your first waterfall! Just joking. They get much better than this.

- **Mile Marker 2:** Twin Falls and Wailele Farm Stand.

Twin Falls

When you round the hill by mile marker 2 (remember that the mileage markers started over at the junction of Kaupakalua Road), you'll be amazed at the large gravel parking lot on the right side of the road packed with cars. **Twin Falls** is the first set of waterfalls you encounter on the Road to Hana, and thus is the closest to many hotels. The 20-minute hike to the falls is relatively easy (page 231).

- **Mile Marker 2.8:** Your first taste of the turns that you're going to experience for the next 20 miles.

- **Mile Marker 3.4** Jungle Zipline (page 236)

- **Mile Marker 4.5: Huelo Lookout** (7600 Hana Hwy., 808/280-4791, www.huelolookout.coconutprotectors.com, daily), the first and most official of the many fruits stands you'll find on the Road to Hana. Enjoy fresh fruit, smoothies, and coconut candy at the coastal lookout a few steps behind the stand. They also sell local arts and crafts.

- **Mile Marker 4.9:** Your first narrow bridge crossing.

- **Mile Marker 6.5:** Naʻiliʻili Haele (Bamboo Forest), one of the most popular hikes in East Maui. Thundering waterfalls spill through a dense bamboo forest. Slippery rocks and flash-flood conditions have been known to cause injuries here (page 231).

- **Mile Marker 6.7:** Rainbow eucalyptus trees.

Rainbow Eucalyptus Trees

Just past the trailhead for the Naʻiliʻili Haele hike is a grove of rainbow eucalyptus trees, silently rising from the green pasturelands. One of the most photographed sights on the Road to Hana, these trees have bark that drips with pastel red, pink, orange, green, and gray, the strokes running the length of each narrow tree.

Unlike trees with cork-like bark, rainbow eucalyptus have a smooth, hard exterior constantly in regrowth. As a section of tree undergoes exfoliation and sheds a section of bark, the young exposed wood has a deep green hue. As the new bark ages in the sun, the wood changes from green to blue to purple to orange, eventually dying again to reveal the green growth below, starting the cycle anew. Parking can be found either at the trailhead for the Naʻiliʻili Haele hike (mile marker 6.5) or at a small pullout for a hunting road, 100 yards past the trees.

- **Mile Marker 8.1:** First scenic view of a valley looking out toward the ocean.

- **Mile Marker 8.5:** Sweeping view of dense swaths of bamboo crawling their way up the eastern flank of the mountain.

- **Mile Marker 9.5: Waikamoi Ridge Trail.** This small picnic area provides a relaxing place to stretch your legs or enjoy a roadside snack, although there are no restrooms

waterfalls on the Road to Hana

or other facilities. There's a short loop trail that gains 200 vertical feet in the surrounding forest (page 233).

- **Mile Marker 10:** Waikamoi Falls, the first roadside waterfall and swimming hole.

Waikamoi Falls

Simple, elegant, and easily accessible, Waikamoi Falls is a convenient place to take a dip. A small trail leads down to the pool, and a second waterfall is accessible above the first pool by wading across the streambed. The only inconvenience here is the lack of parking.

- **Mile Marker 10.5:** The Garden of Eden botanical garden and Coconut Café food cart.

Garden of Eden

Up the road 0.5 mile from Waikamoi Falls is the enticing **Garden of Eden** (808/572-9899, www.mauigardenofeden.com, 8am-4pm daily, $15 adults, $5 children), an ornately manicured 26-acre rainforest utopia. In 1991, Alan Bradbury, the state's first ISA-certified

Road to Hana

arborist, began clearing the hillside and re-planting native trees. It was truly a labor of love: After two decades of work, the Garden of Eden now has over 600 individually labeled plants.

You may recognize this view of the coast: The opening scene of *Jurassic Park* was filmed here. Those with a keen interest in botany and landscaping will appreciate the sanctuary, and it makes a great spot for a picnic. The entrance fee is a little steep but worth it if you're into plants. If you're traveling on a budget, you can get a similar experience at the Ke'anae Arboretum, six miles down the road. The food truck here, **Coconut Café** (8:30am-4pm daily, $8-12), has tasty fish tacos, refreshing drinks, and even a Wi-Fi hot spot.

- **Mile Marker 11.5: Haipua'ena Falls.** Parking can be limited, and it's on the Hana side of the bridge. A short trail leads down to a pool that's nice for a refreshing dip, but you don't need to spend more than 20 minutes.

- **Mile Marker 12.2: Kaumahina State Wayside Park.** Finally—restrooms. This is the first place you'll find any official facilities.

- **Mile Marker 14: Honomanu Bay,** a gorgeous gray-sand beach in a valley that's accessible by 4WD. If you have a low-clearance vehicle, find a parking space at the top of the road and visit the beach on foot.

- **Mile Marker 16.5: Ke'anae Arboretum.** A great spot to stretch your legs and enjoy a free walk in the forest. A 30-minute paved, wheelchair-accessible trail winds back into the lush landscape. After 10 minutes of walking, the paved trail becomes dirt as you make pass a fence. If you make a left once inside the boundary and head toward Pi'ina'au Stream, you'll find a small hidden swimming hole. Reaching it requires a scramble down the rocks.

- **Mile Marker 16.6:** Turnoff for Ke'anae village.

★ Ke'anae Peninsula

When you turn off the highway at mile marker 16.6, you pass through a portal to a way of life that many forgot once existed. The peninsula is a mosaic of green taro fields, vital to the livelihood of Keʻanae. Taro, also known as *kalo,* isn't just a crop, it's a representation of indigenous Hawaiian heritage. In Hawaiian mythology, a child named Haloa was stillborn and, upon being buried, turned into a taro plant. Haloa's brother became the ancestor of the Hawaiian people.

Indigenous Hawaiians thus have a blood relationship to the plant that provides them with sustenance. It's a staple of the Aloha ʻAina movement currently sweeping the state, that we humans are but stewards of the land, placed on this earth to protect it—ensuring its health as we would our own family's, and protecting it for future generations.

In addition to the taro fields, you can watch the powerful surf crash onto the rugged volcanic shore. There aren't any beaches on the Keʻanae Peninsula, and you'll often encounter locals fishing. Stop in at **Auntie Sandy's** (808/248-7448, 9am-2:30pm daily) for a warm loaf of banana bread.

- **Mile Marker 17:** Keʻanae Overlook.
- **Mile Marker 17.3:** Store and ATM. The accurately named **Halfway to Hana** (www.halfwaytohanamaui.com, 8:30am-4pm daily, $2-6, cash only) is located between the Keʻanae Overlook and the turnoff for

Wailua. It's basically a hot-dog, sandwich, and shave-ice stand with an ATM around the corner, making it the closest thing to a store around Keʻanae. Ask about the freshly baked banana bread.

- **Mile Marker 18:** Turnoff for Wailua village and **Uncle Harry's** food stand.
- **Mile Marker 18.5:** Taro *loʻi* (fields) and small waterfalls coming down the road.
- **Mile Marker 18.7:** Wailua Valley State Wayside Park offers a panoramic vista looking out over the town of Wailua, a good place to stretch your legs and get a unique photo. Once in the designated parking area, look to the right for a hidden set of stairs to access the lookout. There's also a lookout in 0.1 mile on the left side of the road.
- **Mile Marker 19.6:** Upper Waikani Falls is also called Three Bears Falls. This is a great place to stop for a swim, and there is a narrow rough trail on the Hana side of the bridge.
- **Mile Marker 21:** Wailuaiki Falls
- **Mile Marker 22.6:** Puaʻa Kaʻa State Wayside Park has restrooms and a small picnic pavilion on the *mauka* (mountain) side of the highway looking out over the stream. A short three-minute walk leads

taro fields on Keʻanae Peninsula

from the road up the stream to an underrated swimming pool and waterfall.

- **Mile Marker 24.1:** Painted Little Green Shack.
- **Mile Marker 25:** Pullout for view of Makapipi Falls. Look down from the top of the bridge!
- **Mile Marker 27.5: Coconut Glen's** (808/248-4876, www.coconutglens.com, 10:30am-5pm daily) ice cream stand, an eccentric and uplifting outpost that serves vegan ice cream made with fresh coconut milk. Much of the building is made from recycled materials gathered around East Maui, and the ice cream is served in *lilikoi* or coconuts to eliminate waste.
- **Mile Marker 28.3:** Banana bread stand.
- **Mile Marker 28.7:** Nahiku Marketplace, a warm and welcoming strip mall in the forest with a surprising selection of food. **Nahiku Café** has good coffee made with a proper espresso machine, and **Up In Smoke BBQ** has heaping bowls of kalua pig and chili ($6-9).
- **Mile Marker 29.7:** View of the Hana Airport.
- **Mile Marker 31:** Turnoff for Ka'eleku Caverns and Kahanu Garden.

Ka'eleku Caverns

As you make your way from Nahiku Marketplace, the first sights you'll encounter are a few miles before "downtown" Hana. At mile marker 31 you'll see the signs for **Ka'eleku Caverns** (808/248-7307, www.mauicave.com, 10:30am-4pm daily, $12.50 pp). Turn down 'Ula'ino Road to visit this two-mile subterranean network of lava tubes, the 18th largest in the world and the only lava tubes on Maui that are navigable and open to the public. Cave explorers are given a flashlight to examine the stalactite-encrusted surroundings. On your way out, navigate through the maze of red *ti* leaves that create the only such maze anywhere on the planet. Walking the caverns at an average pace will take about

30 minutes. There are no garbage cans or restrooms, so pack out your trash.

- **Mile Marker 31.2:** Only a few miles before the town of Hana, the legendary **Hana Farms Banana Bread Stand** (mile marker 31.2, 8am-7pm daily) features six different types of banana bread as well as a full range of fruits, coffee, sauces, and flavorings. There will be more fruit stands between Hana and Kipahulu, but none are like this. Stop for a coffee, banana bread (get a loaf with chocolate chips), and advice on your Hana adventure.

★ Kahanu Garden and Pi'ilanihale Heiau

On 'Ula'ino Road, the pavement gradually gives way to a potholed dirt road leading to **Kahanu Garden** (808/248-8912, www.ntbg.org, 9am-4pm Mon.-Fri., 9am-2pm Sat., $10, free under age 13). This 464-acre property is in Honoma'ele, an area ceded in 1848 to Chief Kahanu by King Kamehameha III. The land has remained largely unchanged since the days of ancient Hawaii. The sprawling gardens focus on species integral to Polynesian culture. You're greeted by a massive grove of *ulu* (breadfruit), and there are groves of bananas, coconuts, taro, sweet potato, sugarcane, and *'awa*. A self-guided tour details the history of the plants and the uses they had for Polynesians.

Towering **Pi'ilanihale Heiau,** a massive multitiered stone structure, is the largest remaining *heiau* in Hawaii. The walls stretch 50 feet high in some places, and the stone platforms are the size of two football fields. Multiple archaeological surveys have determined that the temple was most likely built in stages and dates as far back as the 14th century. To learn about the *heiau* and the property, you can arrange ahead of a time for an hour-long guided tour ($20 pp). To get really involved, lend a hand by volunteering (9am-noon Wed. and Fri.)—you could end up pulling taro with locals at neighboring Mahele Farms.

10 Tips for Driving the Road to Hana

One of the most beautiful activities on Maui is driving the Road to Hana. Weaving 52 miles around 600 curves and 56 one-lane bridges, it's the most loved and loathed stretch of road on the island. Here's how to plan a visit to Hana that will leave you poring over a photo album instead of searching for a divorce lawyer.

1. Hana is not a destination, but a journey. Visitors who race to the sleepy village of Hana are left saying, "This is it?" With a population of around 1,800, Hana is a place to get away from it all.

2. The Road to Hana doesn't end at Hana. The famous Road to Hana is the 52-mile stretch between Kahului Airport and the town of Hana, but many of the natural treasures are in the 10 miles beyond Hana town. Hamoa Beach, consistently voted one of the top beaches in the country, is a few miles past Hana, as is Waioka Pond, a hidden pool on the rocky coast. Thirty minutes beyond Hana town are the Pools of 'Ohe'o (the Seven Sacred Pools), with a series of cascading waterfalls falling directly into the Pacific.

3. Don't drive back the way you came. Your rental-car contract may tell you the road around the back of the island is for 4WD vehicles only, but that's not true. Parts are bumpy, and a few miles are dirt road, but unless there's torrential rain, the road is passable with a regular vehicle. Following the back road all the way around the island grants new views as the surroundings change from lush tropical rainforest to arid windswept lava flows.

4. Don't make dinner reservations. Too many people try to squeeze Hana into half a day or end up feeling rushed. Hana is a place to escape the rush, not add to it. If you're planning a day trip to Hana, block off the entire day, leave early (7am), and see where the day takes you.

5. Stop early and stop often. Take a break for a morning stroll or for breakfast at a tucked-away café. Pick up some snacks and watch the waves. Stop and swim in waterfalls, hike through bamboo forests, and pull off at roadside stands for banana bread or locally grown fruit. If the car behind you is on your tail, pull over and let it pass—there isn't any rush.

6. If you're not a confident driver, take a guided tour. Local guides provide insights into Hawaiian history and culture and offer personal anecdotes that add humor to the lengthy drive. The downside is that you're on someone else's schedule.

7. Bring a bathing suit and hiking shoes. Hana is a land of adventure: Pack the necessary wardrobe and equipment for your activity of choice.

8. If you see a sign that says *kapu,* **"keep out."** Move along and enjoy a spot more accessible to the public.

9. Don't drive home in the dark—especially if you're going the back way. Driving on narrow one-lane roads with precipitous drop-offs is difficult enough in daylight. Leave by 4pm to ensure a well-lit journey home.

10. Stay overnight. Camp at the Pools of 'Ohe'o, or stay at a bed-and-breakfast, or at the Travaasa Hana hotel. In the morning you'll have beaches and swimming holes all to yourself before the day-trippers arrive, usually around 11am.

- **Mile Marker 31.4:** Turnoff for Hana Airport and powered hang gliding lessons.
- **Mile Marker 32:** Turnoff for Wai'anapanapa State Park.

★ Wai'anapanapa State Park

Rugged **Wai'anapanapa State Park** is also known as "black-sand beach." At the beach overlook is one of the most iconic vistas on the drive to Hana. Take it slow on the 0.5-mile road down to the park; there are often small children playing. Once you reach the park, turn left at the parking lot and follow the road to the end, where you can access the black sand of Pa'iloa Beach and its freshwater caves.

Made of crushed black lava rock, the sand is as black as Hana's night sky. Lush green foliage clings to the surrounding coast, and dramatic sea arches and volcanic promontories jut into the frothy sea. Since it faces almost

Hana and Environs

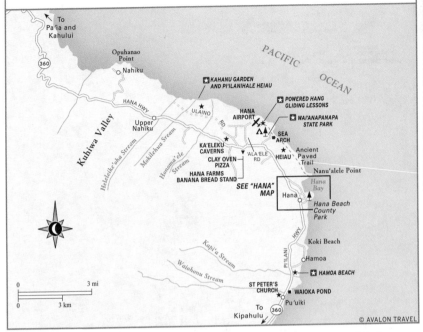

directly east, this is a popular venue for sunrise weddings, and if you spend the night in Hana, I highly recommend getting up early to come here for sunrise.

On the main paved trail by the parking lot overlook, you'll see a trail that runs in the opposite direction of the beach; this is the beginning of a popular coastal hike. One of the more popular stops along this trail is a blowhole that erupts on days with large surf. Maintain a safe distance; people have been swept into the ocean here.

The other main draw of Wai'anapanapa is the system of freshwater caves hidden in a grotto not far from the parking area. Following the cave trail from the parking lot, you'll see a sign that details the legend of the caves. Go left at the sign and travel downhill on a short loop trail. After a three-minute walk you'll reach the cave entrance. The clear water is crisp and cold, and if you swim back in either direction, you'll find some hidden caves. Bring a waterproof light, and don't go so far that you can't find your way back!

- **Mile Marker 32.7:** Hana school.

- **Mile Marker 34:** Fork in the road; stay left. The road rejoins the main highway in 1.5 miles via a right turn at the softball field in Hana town.

HANA TOWN

Before the arrival of Western explorers, Hana was a stronghold that was conquered and reconquered by the kings of Maui and the Big Island. The most strategic and historically rich spot is Ka'uiki Hill, the remnant of a cinder cone that dominates Hana Bay. It's said that the demigod Maui transformed his daughter's lover into Ka'uiki Hill and turned her into the gentle rains that bathe it to this day.

Hana was already a plantation town in 1849 when sea captain George Wilfong started producing sugar here on 60 acres. After sugar production faded in the 1940s, San Francisco

Hana

To Kahului,
Hana Airport (4 Miles), and
Wai'anapanapa State Park (2 Miles)

HANA COMMUNITY HEALTH CENTER
HANA FRESH MARKET
360
POLICE STATION
FIRE STATION

Kawaipapa Stream

King's Road Trail

Nanu'alele Point

WAIKOLOA RD

UAKEA RD

HANA HWY

KA'UIKI ST

Waikaloa Beach

Hana Bay

JOE'S RENTALS
HANA KAI MAUI RESORT
ALAU ST
HANA BAY HALE
KEANINI DR
HANA CULTURAL CENTER

LIGHTHOUSE

PARKING LOT
HANA COAST GALLERY
LUANA SPA RETREAT
KEAWA PL

QUEEN KA'AHUMANU'S BIRTHPLACE

FAGAN MEMORIAL

THE PRESERVE KITCHEN AND GRILL
TRAVAASA HANA
Hana Bay
THAI FOOD BY PRANEE
BAREFOOT CAFE

CATHOLIC CHURCH
HANA RANCH STORE
TENNIS COURTS
BALL PARK
Ka'uiki Hill

SHAKA POPS
WANANALUA CHURCH
HAU'OLI RD
HANA COMMUNITY CENTER

POST OFFICE
HANA TREASURES
SURFING BURRO
Kaihalulu (Red Sand Beach)

BANK OF HAWAII
HANA RANCH RESTAURANT AND SNACK BAR
HASEGAWA'S STORE

Jogging Trail

STABLES
CHEVRON
ONO FARMS FRUIT STAND
DA CHOW WAGON
To 'Ohe'o Gulch and Hamoa Beach
BRADDAH HUTT'S BBQ GRILL

0   0.2 mi
0   0.2 km

© AVALON TRAVEL

industrialist Paul Fagan bought 14,000 acres of what was to become the **Hana Ranch.** Today, Hana's population of 1,200 continues to be predominantly Hawaiian. There are far more sights in the Hana area than you can see in a single day.

Fagan Memorial

Once you finally roll in to Hana town, one of the most prominent sights is a massive cross above the village. Set on the 545-foot summit of Pu'u O Kahaula (Lyon's Hill), the **Fagan Memorial** was constructed to honor the town's modern founder, Paul Fagan, after he died in 1960. Fagan is credited with the creation of modern Hana when he started Hana Ranch and opened the Ka'uiki Inn, which in 1946 was the island's first resort, today called the Travaasa Hana.

The memorial is accessible by following a steep walking path from the parking lot of the Travaasa Hana hotel. Atop the summit you're

Beyond Hana

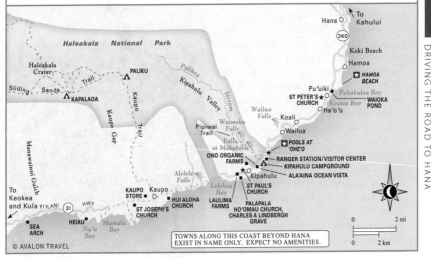

TOWNS ALONG THIS COAST BEYOND HANA
EXIST IN NAME ONLY. EXPECT NO AMENITIES.

© AVALON TRAVEL

treated to the best view in Hana, with a panoramic vista over Hana Bay and 'Alau Island in the distance.

Hana Cultural Center

While it might not look like much from the outside, the humble yet informative **Hana Cultural Center** (4974 Uakea Rd., 808/248-8622, www.hanaculturalcenter.org, 10am-4pm Mon.-Fri., $3) provides the historical backbone for the town. Over the course of Maui's history, Hana has been a unique eastern outpost. See ancient Hawaiian artifacts excavated from the Hana region, such as stone adzes and hand-woven fishnets, and walk around the **Hana Courthouse,** listed on the National Register of Historic Places. The one-room courthouse still hosts proceedings the first Tuesday of each month, and in a testament to the island's multicultural heritage, they can take place in 24 different languages. When court isn't in session, the courthouse serves as a somber museum where Hana residents recount the morning of the 1946 tsunami, which devastated the eastern end of the island.

- **Highway 330:** Technically, Highway 360 ended at Hana Bay and Highway 330 started back at the fork in the road by the fire station. Once you drive past the center of Hana town at Hasegawa General Store and the gas station, you are on Highway 330, although the mileage markers don't start again for a couple of miles When they do, they count down instead of up. The turnoff for **Hamoa Beach** and **Koki Beach** is at the first turnoff for Haneo'o Road, about 1.5 miles past the center of Hana town, which is before the mileage markers begin again. There are two turnoffs for Haneo'o Road; take the first one, as this is the direction that local traffic naturally flows.

HANA TO KIPAHULU

- **Mile Marker 51:** Mileage markers restart.
- **Mile Marker 48:** Waioka Pond, gorgeous cliff-jumping right by the sea.

Waioka Pond (Venus Pool)

Hidden at mile marker 48, **Waioka Pond,** or **Venus Pool,** is a local favorite. You have to cross a private pasture to get to the oceanfront pool, and because it's such a popular spot, the landowners haven't yet restricted access.

The first challenge is finding a legal parking spot. Because the *mauka* side of the road is lined with residential homes, the only parking is along a fence on the *makai* (ocean side) of the road. In order for you to park legally—facing the correct direction—you have to cross the bridge past the mile marker 48 sign, pull off the road, do a U-turn, and drive back toward Hana town. Once you're facing the right way, park along the grass bordering the thin metal fence.

Once you've parked, follow the fence line toward the bridge, where you'll notice an opening in the fence. Walk through and then follow the thin dirt trail down toward the shore. Make a right through the trees at the concrete structure and you'll emerge at a cliff face looking out over a large pool. This first overlook is a popular cliff-diving spot among locals. To reach the pool without jumping, clamber down the rocks to the right. The pool is fed by both a stream and saltwater washing in from the ocean. There's a small island in the middle of the pool; swim over for a view of the rocky shore.

- **Mile Marker 47.5:** Fruit and flower stand popular with tour buses.

- **Mile Marker 46.3:** Karen Davidson Fine Art.

- **Mile Marker 45.3:** The road becomes narrow and offers dramatic views of the coast.

- **Mile Marker 45:** Laura Mango art gallery.

- **Mile Marker 44.8:** Wailua Falls, an 80-foot cascade that may be the most photographed on Maui. The best way to experience it is to take the short trail down to the base and take a dip in the swimming pools, away from the crowds.

- **Mile Marker 43.2, 42.9:** Old bridges dating to 1910.

- **Mile Marker 42.1:** 'Ohe'o Stream and bridge looking over the misnamed Seven Sacred Pools.

cliff-jumping at Waioka Pool

★ Pools of 'Ohe'o

The fabled **Pools of 'Ohe'o**, inside **Haleakala National Park** (808/248-7375, www.nps.gov/hale, $15 per vehicle), are one of the island's most popular attractions. The name **Seven Sacred Pools** is the largest misnomer on the island. There are far more than seven, and there's no record in history of them having been sacred. The name likely began as a marketing ploy by hoteliers in the 1940s. The name stuck and is used to this day. The real name is 'Ohe'o (pronounced oh-HEY-oh); locals will appreciate you using it.

This part of the island is truly stunning and a highlight of visiting Maui. The first taste you'll get of the park is crossing over 'Ohe'o Gulch on a bridge at mile marker 42.1, but try not to linger too long as you'll stop traffic. The entrance to the park is 0.4 mile down the road, and if you have visited Haleakala National Park within the last three days, your receipt will still gain you entry.

Once inside the park you'll notice a large parking lot next to an informative visitors

- **Mile Marker 41.7:** Entrance to Haleakala National Park.
- **Mile Marker 41.2:** Ono Organic Farms.

Ono Organic Farms

There are numerous organic farms in Kipahulu, but the granddaddy of them all is 50-acre **Ono Organic Farms** (808/248-7779, www.onofarms.com), 0.5 mile past the entrance to Haleakala National Park. If you're a fan of exotic produce, you'll be blown away by the selection. In addition to producing 3,000 pounds of bananas *every week,* Ono also grows durians, cacao, coffee, tea, star fruit, Surinam cherries, and 60 other tropical and exotic fruits. Tours (1:30pm Mon.-Fri., $35, free under age 10) last two hours.

The tour offers a culinary journey in certified organic and GMO-free produce directly from the land. A genuine spirit of aloha permeates the farm. It's easiest to take the tour if you're staying overnight in Hana. The driveway up to the farm is part of the adventure.

- **Mile Marker 40.9:** Ho'onanea Farms fruit and coffee stand.
- **Mile Marker 40.8:** Turnoff for Palapala Ho'omau Church, the final resting place of historic aviator Charles Lindbergh.
- **Mile Marker 40.6:** Laulima Farm fruit stand and kitchen, a sprawling compound growing a wealth of organic produce and a roadside kitchen.
- **Mile Marker 39.2:** Lelekea Bay.
- **Mile Marker 39:** The road begins to deteriorate and becomes narrow, with precipitous drop-offs. This is where you should turn around if you don't want to drive around the back of the island. As a point of reference, from this point it's 50 miles to Kahului Airport via the back side, which takes about two hours without stops. If you choose to return the way you came, it's 60 miles, about 2.5 hours without stops. While bumpier, the back road is much straighter and has less traffic.

Pools of 'Ohe'o in Kipahulu

center. It's the best place on this side of the island to gain an understanding of the history, culture, and unique environment of the Kipahulu region. Rangers here are the best source of information on current trail and waterfall conditions in the park.

The visitors center is also where you begin the Kuloa Point Loop Trail leading down to the famous pools. Along the 10-minute walk, you'll go through groves of *hala* trees and past a number of historic sites. Eventually the trail emerges at a staircase down to the pools and one of the most iconic vistas in Hawaii.

The three main pools are open most days for exploring and swimming, although they're closed during heavy rains and flash floods. Reaching the uppermost pools requires some rock scaling; it's worth the effort, but be careful on the slippery rocks.

- **Mile Marker 41.9:** Trailhead for Pipiwai Trail and the 400-foot Waimoku Falls (parking for trailhead is inside park) (page 234).

- **Mile Marker 38.8:** Trailhead for Alelele Falls, a 60-foot waterfall requiring a 10-minute hike (page 234).
- **Mile Marker 38.5:** Highway 31 begins.
- **Mile Marker 38.4:** The scariest section of road. If you make it past this without a heart attack, you'll be fine the rest of the way.
- **Mile Marker 37.8:** Road turns to dirt.
- **Mile Marker 36:** Surroundings morph from tropical and lush to windswept and arid. Welcome to Kaupo!
- **Mile Marker 34.6:** Kaupo Store.

Kaupo Store

No other store on the island will amaze you quite like **Kaupo Store** (mile marker 34.6, 10am-5pm Mon.-Sat., cash only), squirreled away inside a building constructed in 1925 in surroundings that feel like the end of the earth. Inside, find cold drinks and gourmet ice-cream bars, and stock up on water and snacks for the long, winding, beautiful drive.

- **Mile Marker 33.5:** Kaupo Gap warrants a stop for the sweeping view. At the upper rim of the gap is the 6,800-foot floor of Haleakala Crater.

- **Mile Marker 31.8:** The most amazing view of Haleakala you will see. If you thought the stretch between Kipahulu and Kaupo was desolate, you're in for a treat. The southeastern flank of Haleakala opens up into the dramatic panorama—a pristine expanse of wide-open country where visitors gawk at the desolate beauty. The road is exceptionally bumpy. After Manawainui Gulch, with its overly engineered bridge in the middle of nowhere, the road begins its gradual climb away from the coast to 3,000 feet elevation in Keokea.

- **Mile Marker 31.1:** The gate to Nu'u Bay, a rocky beach popular for fishing and scenic coastal hiking.
- **Mile Marker 30.1:** Huakini Bay.
- **Mile Marker 29:** You survived the worst part of the road—smooth pavement begins.
- **Mile Marker 28.7:** Beautiful view of a lava-rock sea arch.
- **Mile Marker 27.3:** Manawainui Bridge and Gulch.

From this point the road climbs in elevation through the rural communities of Kahikinui and Kanaio before wrapping around to Maui Wine in Ulupalakua. If

historic Kaupo Store

it's before 5pm, toast to your success at the winery and grab a bite at the Ulupalakua Ranch Store. The closest gas is 5.2 miles down the road in Keokea.

Beaches

Beaches in East Maui are blissfully undeveloped, though due to the trade winds there isn't much snorkeling, and the water can be rough and choppy. Mornings offer the calmest conditions for a jog, a quick dip, or to commune with nature.

PA'IA

★ Baldwin Beach

The long, wide, and mostly empty **Baldwin Beach** is a popular local bodysurfing spot, although the waves can get large during winter. At the far western end, farthest from Pa'ia, is a small cove known as **Baby Beach,** where a fringing reef creates a natural pool perfect for wading with young ones. Instead of walking the length of Baldwin, you can access Baby Beach by turning on Nonohe Place off Hana Highway, followed by a right on Pa'ani Place, and a quick left onto Kealakai Place. There aren't any restrooms or showers, but you can drive to the shower a mile down the road at

the main entrance. On the far eastern end of Baldwin, closest to Pa'ia, a small trail leads around the point and connects with a hidden beach next to Pa'ia Bay. This little-known stretch of sand is often occupied by sun-worshipping nudists, affable hippies, and locals passing around the *pakalolo* (marijuana). If you visit during the afternoon and the wind is howling, the cove on the far eastern end of Baldwin is sheltered and offers calm swimming most of the year.

Pa'ia Bay

The closest beach to the center of town, **Pa'ia Bay** is as active as Baldwin is calm, with a basketball court in a small park area and overflow parking for the town. The skate park at the Pa'ia Youth Center teems with area youth. Bodyboarders and surfers flock here for the waves, and a number of downhill bike companies finish tours here after descending the mountainside. There are restrooms, a beach

morning stroll down Baldwin Beach

shower, and an ever-changing cast of entertaining and colorful characters.

Kuau Cove

This beach is the scenic backdrop for **Mama's Fish House,** where many take a sunset photo. This small cove has a smattering of sand and an intriguing system of tide pools great for exploring with small children. The beach shrinks at high tide, so low tide is best for poring over the rocks to see all the slippery critters. There are a few parking spots near Mama's Fish House; the spaces with blue cones are designated as beach parking.

Ho'okipa Beach Park

The global epicenter of the windsurfing world, **Ho'okipa** also offers a thin, sandy beach that's better for tanning than swimming. A fringing reef creates a small pond nice for small children, and a wide range of people can usually be found hanging out on shore. Mornings are usually calm at Ho'okipa, and when the surf isn't too high, it's possible to snorkel in front of the rocks and find numerous *honu* (sea turtles). Every night in the hour before sunset, at least half a dozen haul out on shore in front of the pavilions. Sea turtles are protected, and it's illegal to touch them.

Rather than the pavilion area, the best place is on the stretch of sand on the left side of the beach. Parking can be tight—especially when the surf is up.

HANA TOWN
Pa'iloa Beach (Black-Sand Beach)

The **Black-Sand Beach** at Wai'anapanapa State Park is the most popular beach in Hana. Just a few miles before the sleepy center of Hana and just past the turnoff for Hana Airport, dense foliage and black lava rock abut the crashing blue surf. The water along the shore is often rough, particularly in the afternoon. The beach is formed of crushed black lava rock, the result of the tumultuous wave erosion. The color of the sand is as black as the night sky.

Landing on Red or Black?

When it comes to choosing a beach in Hana, this question has nothing to do with roulette but rather the color of the sand. You'll be awed by the beauty of both. The red sand of **Kaihalulu (Red-Sand Beach)** is formed by the crushed red cinder of towering Ka'uiki Hill, and is one of the island's most photographed and unique sections. On the outskirts of town by Wai'anapanapa State Park, **Pa'iloa Beach (Black-Sand Beach)** is formed from crushed black lava rock, more like black pebbles than fine powder. Can't decide between the two? Hana is small enough that you can visit both.

To reach the shore, walk down a paved path from the parking lot of the state park. When you reach the bottom, you'll notice some sea caves you can explore at low tide. Since the sand is formed from lava rock, it isn't very comfortable; bring a blanket or a towel if you plan to hang out. Back at the parking lot, don't leave without checking out the freshwater caves. You can also walk the trail winding along the shore that leads to a thundering blowhole.

Hana Bay

Hana Bay is a laid-back crescent of gray sand in the middle of Hana town. Tucked in the lee of Ka'uiki Head, the working-class bay has a crumbling boat ramp where visitors end up when they "can't find Hana." It's nice enough for a picnic and a dip, but if you're looking for the nicest beach in Hana, keep driving out to Hamoa.

For a short, adventurous, and scenic hike, follow the trailhead at the end of the road as it snakes off into the trees. You'll reach a spot where it looks like the trail ends, but look across the narrow ravine and you'll see it on the other side. Follow this trail to a tiny red-sand beach, and eventually all the way to the plaque that commemorates the birthplace of Queen Ka'ahaumanu. The snorkeling can be fantastic in the morning. The best way to see it is with **Hana Bay Kayaks** (808/248-7711, www.hanabaykayaks.com).

Kaihalulu Beach (Red-Sand Beach)

Before visiting **Kaihalulu**, be aware that **Red-Sand Beach** is a nude beach. It can also be dangerous to access, as there are rockslides, slippery scree slopes, and sheer drop-offs. If you're up for it, this is one of the coast's most famously scenic spots. This cavernous cove hidden in the mountainside offers decent swimming inside the rocks, and the red sand gets its color from the cinder cone.

To find the trail for Red-Sand Beach, find a legal parking area on Uakea Road by the ballpark (don't park facing the wrong direction), and walk toward an open grass field where the road dead-ends by the community center. Walk across the grass field, keeping an eye on the bushes on your right for a couple of narrow trails.

Wading for a minute through waist-high grass, you'll eventually emerge at a small dirt trail that snakes down the roots of a tree. The footing can be slippery, so bare feet or closed-toe shoes are better than rubber slippers. The thin trail continues to the left up and over a bluff, where landslides can leave a lot of scree on the trail. Once at the top of the bluff, you'll be greeted with your first photo op of the stunning cove. From here it's a one-minute walk along a cliff until you emerge on the red shore.

HANA TO KIPAHULU
Koki Beach

To reach Hana's two famous beaches, travel 1.5 miles past the center of town (the Hana Ballpark) and then make a left on Haneo'o Road. Going downhill, first is **Koki Beach,** a favorite hangout of local surfers. On the left side of the beach, you can scramble over some rocks to reach some hidden sections of sand. Access to these smaller beaches is only possible only at low tide, so most people stay on the main section of the beach. The dark-red sand is a product of a cinder cone known as Ka Iwi O Pele (The Bones of Pele). According to legend, this is where Pele, the volcano goddess, met her end. Her bones were stacked high on the shore before her spirit traveled southeast to the Big Island.

★ Hamoa Beach

Continuing along Haneo'o Road, paralleling the ocean, the snowcapped peak of Mauna

Red-Sand Beach is beautiful.

Kea on the Big Island is occasionally visible in the distance. At low tide you can also see the remnants of the ancient Haneoʻo Fishpond, although access is via private land. As the road rounds back to the right, you'll finally catch glimpses of **Hamoa Beach,** which Mark Twain considered one of the most beautiful in the world.

Parking is tight. Park only on the right side of the road so that traffic flows smoothly on the left. You might have to drive past the beach before you find a space. Access to the beach is down the stone stairway. The park area at the bottom of the stairs is property of the Travaasa Hana hotel, but the sandy beach is public property.

This is the best spot in Hana for a relaxing day at the beach. On the calmest of days it's possible to snorkel along the rocky coast, though most prefer to bodysurf the consistent playful shore-break. This can also be one of the best surf breaks in the area.

Surfing

Surfing in East Maui is for intermediate and advanced surfers. Hoʻokipa Beach Park and Hamoa Bay can see surf at any time of year, and this stretch of coast roars to life from October to April with North Pacific swells. This is some of the largest, heaviest surf on the planet. Even watching from the shore, you can feel the rush of waves large enough to shake the ground beneath you.

Paʻia
SURF SPOTS
Although it's rarely surfed, a break in front of the lifeguard tower at **Baldwin Beach** offers fun longboarding before the afternoon wind picks up. If the surf is too large at places such as Hoʻokipa or Paʻia Bay, there is a reform on the shallow reef here that can offer a long ride.

If you're renting a board in Paʻia, the closest beach break is **Paʻia Bay.** While the inside section is popular with bodyboarders, there is a second peak a little farther out that is better for surfing. Mornings are best before the

windswept Koki Beach in Hana

Jaws

Pe'ahi, also called **Jaws,** can see 70-foot waves, but only a few days a year from October through April. The waves are created by massive storms in the North Pacific that churn between the Aleutian Islands and Japan. Since the North Pacific is calm during summer, it's only in winter that you stand a chance of seeing the large surf at Jaws.

Thanks to the wonders of surf forecasting, the massive waves can be predicted up to a week ahead of time. If Jaws is "going off," a high surf warning will have been issued. The warning requires wave heights of 25 feet or greater on the island's North Shore. This differs from a high surf advisory, issued when waves are 15 feet or greater. If a high surf advisory is issued, there aren't going to be 70-foot waves at Jaws.

If a high surf warning has been posted, ask a local what they've heard about the waves at Jaws—your concierge, a surf shop staffer, or any boat crew. Since island surfers watch the surf forecast like a trader watches stock futures, they'll be in the know. If Jaws is going to be breaking, get there in the morning. By the time the wind comes up in the afternoon, most of the surfers have left.

wind blows the wave to pieces. Since the wave can be fast and steep, it's best for intermediate surfers.

The epicenter for surf on the island's North Shore will forever be **Ho'okipa Beach Park,** three miles past the town of Pa'ia, a legendary windswept cove. For surfers, Ho'okipa has four sections: **Pavilions (Pavils), Middles, The Point, and Lanes.** If you are standing on the beach, Pavilions is the break that's the farthest to the right and can pick up wrapping wind swell even during the summer. Since it's the most consistent, it can also be the most localized, so beginners should be wary.

In the center of the beach, **Middles** is a big A-frame that breaks in deep water and can get board-shatteringly heavy during the winter. The wave can accommodate a larger crowd than Pavils, although you should still be skilled to paddle out. On the left side of the beach is the Point, a heavy right that's popular with windsurfers. Finally, Lanes is a left-hand wave that breaks in the cove to the west of Ho'okipa, but it's a long paddle.

A surfer throws buckets at Ho'okipa Beach Park.

SURFBOARD RENTALS

Both **HI-Tech Maui** (58 Baldwin Ave., 808/579-9297, www.surfmaui.com, 9am-6pm daily) and **Sailboards Maui** (22 Baldwin Ave., 808/579-8432, www.sailboardsmaui.com, 9:30am-7pm Mon.-Sat., 9:30am-6pm Sun.) offer casual board rentals ($20 per day). Both shops have a full range of longboards, shortboards, and fun boards. They are an affordable option for playing in the waves of Pa'ia Bay or on a multiday safari to Hana.

SURF SCHOOLS

Given the advanced surf conditions of the island's North Shore, there aren't as many surf schools in East Maui as in Lahaina or Kihei. Professional longboarder **Zack Howard** (808/214-7766, www.zackhowardsurf.com) is one of the few instructors who offers lessons ($200 private, $240 for 2, and $90 pp for 3 or more) to surf on Maui's North Shore. While most of his lessons are conducted at locations on the south shore on the road to Lahaina, advanced surfers can paddle out on the North Shore if the conditions are right.

Hana
SURF SPOTS

The two main Hana surf breaks frequented by visitors are **Koki Beach** and **Hamoa Beach,** both on Haneo'o Road 1.5 miles past the town of Hana. Because of its easterly location, Hana gets waves any time of the year. Since the waves are often the result of easterly wind swell, conditions can be rougher than elsewhere on the island. The steepness of the wave here is better suited for shortboards than longboards. Koki is where many of Hana's *keiki* (children) first learn how to pop up and ride.

Around the corner at Hamoa, the protected bay offers a respite from the trade winds. Koki breaks fairly close to shore, but the wave at Hamoa breaks farther out over a combination of sand, reef, and rocks. On moderate days, this is a good place for riding a longboard or a stand-up board, since the wave isn't as steep,

Watch for windsurfers at Ho'okipa Beach Park.

but the largest waves are for experts. There are no lifeguards at either beach in Hana.

WINDSURFING

The world's best flock in droves to **Ho'okipa Beach Park** to combine the trade winds with waves that reach 20 feet in winter. Don't expect to see windsurfers on a morning drive to Hana, as windsurfing is prohibited before 11am. A better bet is to see them on the drive back in the afternoon. Parking can be difficult at Ho'okipa, so if you're coming to watch the windsurfers, park up along the highway and leave the spots closer to shore for those who need to move gear.

Windsurfing Rentals

Although most of the windsurfing rental shops are in Kahului, **Simmer Style** (137 Hana Hwy., 808/579-8484, www.simmerhawaii.com, 10am-7pm daily) is the closest shop to Ho'okipa and the best spot on the North Shore for windsurfing rentals and supplies.

Hiking and Biking

HIKING
Road to Hana
★ **TWIN FALLS**

At mile marker 2, which is 11.4 miles past Pa'ia, **Twin Falls** is one of the easiest and shortest waterfall hikes in East Maui. It's also the first series of waterfalls on the Road to Hana. Much of the area is private land (respect the *Kapu*, or "Keep Out" signs on driveways), and most of the "trail" is a gravel road that is wide and easy to stroll. In a few spots the footing can be tricky, but this is a good choice for a tame walk into the rainforest. Occasionally, the trails to the upper waterfalls can be closed due to hazardous conditions. If there are signs posted that say the trails are closed, respect the landowners' wishes.

An outdoor playground peppered with waterfalls, the only downside is the crowding. During the midmorning hours, as visitors make their way toward Hana, there can be 50 cars parked along the side of the road. To visit with smaller crowds, stop on your drive back from Hana; come really early, before everyone else has arrived; or make a separate trip here in the late afternoon. Bring mosquito repellent.

Although there are myriad waterfalls at Twin Falls, two main ones are most accessible. The 1.3-mile trail begins in the gravel parking lot and leads through a small gate in a lush and forested orchard. There are portable toilets on the right side of the trail, and visitors are encouraged to leave a donation for their maintenance and upkeep. After five minutes of walking along the gravel road, you'll hear some waterfalls off to the left. These are nice for a quick photo, but the main waterfalls are still farther down the trail.

After 10 minutes of walking, you'll come to a stream crossing that can flood during heavy rain. If the trail is closed, it will be here, and if the water appears to be rushing violently, it's best to turn around. Five minutes past

the stream crossing is a three-way fork in the road; go straight. After five more minutes is another fork, where the trail to the left has a wooden plank crossing a small stream. Go straight, and after two minutes of clambering around an irrigation flume, you'll find a waterfall that has a small pool for swimming. While this waterfall is nice enough, there's a second waterfall, known as Caveman, that is far more dramatic, although it can be more difficult to reach.

To get to Caveman, turn around and go back to the fork in the trail with the wooden plank. Cross the wooden plank, ascend a small hill, take the fork to the left, and then take a right 50 yards later. You'll be walking downhill, and a few minutes later you'll reach a concrete irrigation structure with steps leading up and over it. From here you'll begin to see the waterfall in the distance. To reach the base of the falls, wade across a stream that is usually about knee-deep. If the stream is manageable, a short scramble past it will bring you to a cavernous waterfall begging you to take your photo behind it. Since the water isn't clear enough to see the bottom, don't even think about jumping off the top.

Adjacent to the pool at Caveman is a thin trail that switchbacks up the hill, leading to more pools and waterfalls, although since it's easy to get lost back here, it's best to have a guide to venture any farther. On your way out from Caveman, after you climb up and over the irrigation structure and ascend the hill, follow the trail to the right when it forks to end up at the three-way fork in the trail you originally encountered on your walk in, ultimately making a full loop. From here it's a short walk back to the parking lot.

★ **NA'ILI'ILI HAELE**

The waterfalls of **Na'ili'ili Haele** (Bamboo Forest) are one of the highlights of the Road to Hana, but this hike has steep, slippery slopes and stream crossings prone to flash floods. In the past few years firefighters have made hundreds of rescues. Access to the hike may soon be restricted because it has become so popular. If you decide to visit, only do so if it hasn't been raining.

At mile marker 6.5, you'll know you're approaching the trailhead by the enormous hairpin turn flanked by a rock wall. The road narrows, and parking can be difficult. You can park on the right side against the bamboo. If all these spots are taken, there are more pull-outs within 0.25 mile.

The correct trailhead is marked by a lone metal pole in a break in a wire fence. On the other side of the fence, the trail is narrow at first and winds downhill. After two minutes of walking is an intersection where you turn left to a steep scramble down a hill. This area can become slick, so use your hands to avoid slipping. At the bottom of the hill is a stream crossing with a wooden plank over a gap. On the other side of the stream, continue straight through a tunnel of bamboo before the path wraps around to the left and you rejoin the main trail. Make a right and follow the trail for another two minutes until you come to a major stream crossing.

It is easy to get turned around at the stream crossing because the trail ends. Across the stream is a downed tree slightly to the left. Follow the tree trunk to its base—this is the continuation of the trail. The trail parallels the water upstream. This section has some of the densest bamboo, and even when the sun is high in the sky, the thick grove blocks out the sun. A few minutes into the bamboo is a clearing off to the left. After a few more minutes is a second clearing. When you come to a third clearing on the left, you will hear the rush of a waterfall. Turn left to cross the stream again; this leads to the first waterfall, where there's a small pool.

Beyond this point the trail gets exponentially more challenging and treacherous. Should you want to continue, trace the edge of the pool to the far side of the streambed, where a thin rope dangles over a slippery rock face. This is where the trail continues; shimmy up the slick rock using the rope.

The trail flattens out and passes through more bamboo before arriving at another pool, larger and less crowded than the first. Slip off your shoes and slide in for a dip. There are additional pools and waterfalls upstream, but this is where the majority of accidents occur, so venture here only with a guide.

family hiking adventures in Hana

WAIKAMOI RIDGE TRAIL

The **Waikamoi Ridge Trail** (mile marker 9.5) provides a calming respite to stretch your legs on a 30-minute loop trail that takes you just far enough from the road that the only sounds you hear are the birds and the creak of swaying bamboo. The trail gains 200 vertical feet and consists of two parts: the loop trail and the spur trail to the upper picnic area. Hike in a counterclockwise direction, since this is the best-maintained section of trail. The second half of the loop, heading back downhill toward the parking lot, isn't as well maintained and is a lot muddier than the platform steps on the way up.

If you take the spur trail to the upper picnic area, there is an open clearing to explore. The trail to the upper picnic area takes about 10 minutes and is covered in *lauhala* leaves and slippery roots. At the end of the trail is a simple picnic area where a covered pavilion provides a relaxing place for a snack and a rest. Pack mosquito repellent if you plan on stopping to eat here.

Hana Town
KING'S HIGHWAY COASTAL TRAIL

One of the few hiking options in East Maui that doesn't involve a waterfall, the three-mile **King's Highway Coastal Trail** between Wai'anapanapa State Park and the northern tip of Hana Bay is one of the few navigable remnants of the ancient King's Highway that once circled the island. Today, only scarce remnants of this ancient trail are evident, but the most prominent section is here on the coast south of Wai'anapanapa. Parking for the trailhead is in the main lot of the state park. Along the course of this three-mile trail, you'll weave around azure bays flanked by black sand, pass beneath dense groves of dry *lauhala* trees, and gaze upon lava rock arches carved from the coast by the tumultuous sea.

Wear hiking boots, as the jagged *'a'a* lava can rip rubber slippers to pieces. Carry plenty of water, as there are no facilities along the trail. As you get closer to Hana Bay, the trail becomes a little more treacherous. Most people start from the Wai'anapanapa trailhead and hike about halfway before turning back. To take the road less traveled, continue north of Wai'anapanapa past a series of smaller black-sand coves before eventually emerging near the Hana Airport. Expect to devote at least three hours to this trail round-trip from the trailhead.

For a quick and easy hike that still offers a rewarding view, the trail leading from the

cooling off in Wai'anapanapa Caves

Travaasa Hana parking lot up to **Fagan's Cross** takes about 20 minutes and has a steep enough grade to offer a good leg workout. Watch for fresh guavas in the trees, as well as fresh cow pies left by the free-range cattle.

A two-mile **walking trail** leads from the trail to Fagan's Cross south toward Hamoa Beach. The track is little more than flattened grass through the pasturelands, but you'll have the coastal views all to yourself.

Kipahulu and Beyond
PIPIWAI TRAIL

Hands down, **Pipiwai Trail** is the best in Maui. It is in the upper portion of 'Ohe'o Gulch in the area known as Seven Sacred Pools. While most visitors to 'Ohe'o only pay a cursory visit to take photos, the Pipiwai Trail, which runs on the *mauka* side of the highway, is the undisputed highlight of the Kipahulu section of Haleakala National Park.

At four miles, the trail is long enough to be adventurous and short enough to be accessible, and it maintains a moderate grade. The last 0.5 mile of the trail winds through bamboo so thick it blocks out the sun, and just when you think the scenery couldn't get any more tropical, the trail emerges at the base of 400-foot Waimoku Falls. This two-hour expedition justifies the winding drive to get here. The best way to experience the trail is to camp overnight at the Kipahulu campground and hit the path before the throngs of day-trippers arrive.

To find the trailhead, drive 30 to 40 minutes past the town of Hana to mile marker 41.7, where you enter the Kipahulu section of Haleakala National Park. Parking for the trailhead is within the park boundaries. You'll have to pay the $15 park entry fee. Walk back to the road and 100 yards toward Hana, where you'll see signs for the trailhead on the left. The trail climbs steeply up a rocky slope to a sign outlining trail distances. Much of the Pipiwai Trail parallels 'Ohe'o Gulch, and you can hear the rush of the water as you make your way uphill toward the falls. It's not safe to access the pools or waterfalls in the river.

There may be days when you could get to the river by scrambling down a hillside or undefined trail, but a number of people have been swept to their deaths in flash floods. The National Park Service advises against any attempt to access the stream.

After 10 minutes on the trail is the lookout for Makahiku Falls, a 200-foot plunge that can be anything from a trickle during drier months to a violent torrent. Past the falls, the trail begins gaining elevation for another five minutes before emerging in the shade of a beautiful banyan tree. The section between the tree and the first bridge has multiple spur trails that lead to waterfall overlooks offering views of the canyons and pools.

Ten minutes past the tree is the first of two bridges that zigzag across the stream. This is a great place to snap pictures of the waterfalls and the first bamboo forest. After crossing the second bridge, when the trail turns into stairs that climb steeply toward the bamboo, there's an opening in the railing on the left side where a path leads down to a rocky streambed. This is the Palikea Stream, and if you rock-hop up the riverbed for about 15 minutes, you'll emerge at a waterfall that is less dramatic—but also less visited—than neighboring Waimoku Falls. The waterfall here trickles down the towering canyon walls, and the pool at the bottom is occasionally used by nude bathers.

Back on the main trail, continuing up the stairs, a boardwalk leads through the densest bamboo on the island. As you emerge from the creaking cavern, five more minutes of rock-hopping brings you to the pièce de résistance, 400-foot Waimoku Falls. This is one of the most beautiful corners of the island.

ALELELE FALLS

Few people make the short hike back to 60-foot **Alelele Falls,** with a refreshing pool in winter that can go dry in summer. Located on the fabled back road about three miles past the Pools of 'Ohe'o, the trailhead is at Alelele Bridge, at mile marker 38.8; park in one of the few parking spots available on the Kaupo side of the bridge.

Alelele Falls

hiking is **Hike Maui** (808/879-5270, www. hikemaui.com, $124-199), with knowledgeable guides who will take you hiking in a private area hidden behind Twin Falls. Group sizes are usually small. What makes these hikes worthwhile is not only being taken directly to the trailhead but also learning about the island's flora, fauna, history, and mythology from guides who love what they do.

BIKING

The town of Pa'ia connects two of the most popular rides on the island: the frigid ride down Haleakala and the winding journey out toward Hana. As a cycling hub, there are a few bike shops around town.

Pa'ia

One of the most comprehensive cycling experiences on Maui is at **Maui Cyclery** (99 Hana Hwy., 808/579-9009, www.gocycling-maui.com, 8am-6pm Mon.-Fri., 8am-4pm Sat., 8am-noon Sun.), a small but thorough shop in the heart of Pa'ia. In addition to offering rentals (from $30 per day), parts, services, and sales, the staff offer guided tours for some of the island's best rides.

Ha'iku

In the Ha'iku Cannery, **Haleakala Bike Company** (810 Ha'iku Rd., Suite 120, 808/575-9575, www.bikemaui.com, 8:30am-5pm Mon.-Sat., 9am-4pm Sun.) specializes in tour groups making the ride down Haleakala Volcano. You can rent a bike (from $40 per day), and if you arrange your own transportation to the top, you'll be able to ride from the summit of the volcano.

If you have the energy left for a 10-minute hike through the jungle, the reward is a waterfall that offers just the right amount of seclusion. Although parking for the trailhead is on the Kaupo side of the bridge, the trailhead is back on the Kipahulu side, at the spot where the bridge begins. Follow this well-defined trail and cross the stream a couple of times, passing ancient lava-rock walls before emerging at the base of the pristine falls.

Hiking Tours

While many private adventure tours will take you hiking as part of the experience, (page 243) one group that focuses specifically on

Adventure Sports

ZIPLINING
Ha'iku

Most adventure sports along Maui's North Shore are in the water, but **North Shore Zipline Company** (2065 Kauhikoa Rd., 808/269-0671, www.nszipline.com, Mon.-Sat.) has seven ziplines that run through the trees of rural Ha'iku in a onetime military base. The course is family-friendly and caters mainly to first-time zippers. Children as young as five can participate as long as they're accompanied by an adult. Don't think that you won't still get a rush, however, as you can hit speeds of up to 40 mph on the last line of the course, and the viewing platforms provide a unique vantage over the rural mountainside.

If you're short on time and want to combine a zipline adventure with a day trip to Hana, **Jungle Zipline** (50 E. Waipio Rd., 808/573-1529, www.junglezip.com, 8am-4pm daily), on the Road to Hana, is a great way to take a break from the car. The full course ($149) is seven lines and takes 2.5 hours. To merge this with driving the Road to Hana, opt instead for a morning tour on the abbreviated, four-line course ($112). It takes 1.5 hours, so you still have time to reach Hana. The minimum age is eight, and maximum weight is 250 pounds.

RAPPELLING

If you want to get all Navy SEAL on your Maui vacation, **Rappel Maui** (808/445-6407, www.rappelmaui.com, $200) will teach you how to strap on a harness and walk down waterfalls. The company has exclusive access to waterfalls behind the Garden of Eden, and while the first descent is a dry run on a dirt hillside, eventually you're leaning backward over a waterfall with a 60-foot drop. The guides are professional and completely committed to your safety. You could end up getting the best photo of your vacation. Weight limits are 70 to 250 pounds. Don't look down!

Walk down waterfalls with Rappel Maui.

★ HANG GLIDING IN HANA

This is the way to see the Hana coast. On an instructional lesson with **Hang Gliding Maui** (808/572-6557, www.hangglidingmaui.com), you meet your instructor, Armin, at his man-cave hangar at the Hana Airport. All flights are private, since the hang glider only has two seats, and he teaches you the basics of steering the glider as well as lift, wind speed, and direction.

This ultralight trike has wheels and a motor, so you take off down the Hana runway as you would in a regular plane, but when you reach a cruising altitude of 2,000 to 3,000 feet, you cut the engine and hang-glide back down, listening only to the wind. The view from here is life-changing, and there aren't even windows like a helicopter—just you, Armin, and the sky. Lessons are 30-minute ($190), 45-minute ($250), and one-hour ($310) flights and are offered Monday-Tuesday and Thursday-Friday.

GLIDING AND SKYDIVING

To get even higher, another option is **Skyview Soaring** (Hana Airport, 808/244-7070, www.skyviewsoaring.com, from $165), a self-powered glider where your pilot, Hans, takes you as high as 10,000 feet before killing the engines and gliding back to the airport. This isn't for the faint of heart, although the views afforded of Haleakala Crater and the eastern flank of the mountainside surpass any from along the highway. Bring your camera, as you glide silently past towering waterfalls and above the shore of Wai'anapanapa State Park. Flights are either 30 minutes or an hour.

On the longer trip you soar all the way to the rim of Haleakala Crater, reaching speeds of 50 to 100 mph on the ride down.

POWERED GLIDER FLIGHTS

If you'd rather jump out of the plane, **Skydive Hana** (400 Alalele Rd., 808/637-4121, www.skydivehana.com, 8am-3pm Sat.-Sun., from $329 pp) opened in 2015 at the Hana Airport as the island's first commercial skydive operation. The minimum age is 18, and maximum weight is 240 pounds, with a $2 per pound surcharge for those over 200 pounds.

Shopping

PA'IA

Once known for hippies, surf culture, and sugarcane, Pa'ia now features some of the island's trendiest boutiques and arguably the island's best shopping, with bikini shops, beachwear boutiques, and craft galleries populating the one-stoplight town.

Art Galleries

For amazing fine-art underwater photography from around the Hawaiian Islands, the **Cesere Brothers** (83 Hana Hwy., 808/268-4405, www.ceserebrothers.com) have a small gallery on the walk toward Pa'ia Bay where you'll find everything from colorful nudibranchs to photos of enormous tiger sharks. On the other end of Pa'ia's main strip, on the Hana side of the stoplight, **Indigo** (149 Hana Hwy., 808/579-9199, www.indigopaia.com, 10am-6pm daily) has gorgeous and inspiring photos from far-flung corners of the globe.

Surf Shops

For surf, skate, or even snowboard wear, visit **HI-Tech Maui** (58 Baldwin Ave., 808/579-9297, www.surfmaui.com, 9am-6pm daily), **Sailboards Maui** (22 Baldwin Ave., 808/579-8432, www.sailboardsmaui.com, 9:30am-7pm

Mon.-Sat., 9:30am-6pm Sun.), **Hana Highway Surf** (149 Hana Hwy., 808/579-8999, www.hanahwysurf.com, 10am-7pm daily), and **Honolua Surf Company** (115 Hana Hwy., 808/579-9593, 9am-9pm Mon.-Sat., 9am-7:30pm Sun.), all offering apparel in America's happiest surf town.

Clothing and Swimwear

The only genre that rivals surf gear in Pa'ia is women's clothing boutiques and bikini stores. Along Baldwin Avenue, **Alice in Hulaland** (19 Baldwin Ave., 808/579-9922, www.aliceinhulaland.com, 9:30am-8pm daily) offers a snarky range of clothing and accessories, and **Mahina** (23 Baldwin Ave., 808/579-9132, www.shopmahina.com, 9:30am-8pm Mon.-Sat., 10am-6pm Sun.) offers trendy women's clothing that can also be found in its sister stores all around the island. On the finer end of apparel are **Nuage Bleu** (76 Hana Hwy., 808/579-9792, www.nuagebleu.com, 9:30am-6pm daily) and **Tamara Catz** (83 Hana Hwy., 808/579-9184, www.tamaracatz.com, 10am-6pm daily), along Hana Highway toward the entrance to town. These are two of the more elegant and fashionable clothing boutiques.

When it comes to bikinis, sun-seekers

will love bouncing between Pakaloha (151 Hana Hwy., 808/579-8882, www.pakalohamaui.com, 10:30am-6pm daily) and San Lorenzo Bikinis (115 Hana Hwy., 808/873-7972, www.sanlorenzobikinis.com, 9:30am-9pm daily), in the center of town. The bikinis are skimpy, almost Brazilian, but that's the North Shore. Even more bikinis are at Maui Girl (12 Baldwin Ave., 808/579-9266, www.maui-girl.com, 9am-6pm daily) and Letarte (24 Baldwin Ave., 808/579-6022, www.letarteswimwear.com, 10am-6pm daily), both with bikinis featured in *Sports Illustrated*'s swimsuit edition.

Jewelry

While Pa'ia doesn't have as many jewelry stores as Lahaina, Studio 22K (161 Hana Hwy., 808/579-8167, www.studio22k.com, 10am-6pm Tues.-Sat.), on the far Hana side of town, is a small studio that specializes in handmade 22-karat-gold items with metal malleable enough to morph into all sorts of twisting shapes and designs.

If sterling silver is more what you're looking for, Oceania Maui (96 Hana Hwy., 808/579-6063, www.oceaniamaui.com, 9am-7pm Mon.-Sat., 10am-6pm Sun.) has over 400 designs that are crafted on Maui.

ROAD TO HANA
Gifts and Souvenirs

The best place for real shopping along the Road to Hana is at Nahiku Ti Gallery (mile marker 28.7, 808/248-8800, 10am-5pm daily), a small gallery within the Nahiku Marketplace. This curious strip mall in the rainforest is already strange in that it offers legitimate food options in the middle of nowhere, and the art gallery rivals those in Ka'anapali and Wailea. While nowhere near as large as the south shore shopping venues, the gallery has a varied selection of jewelry, crafts, paintings, pottery, and a surprising collection of art.

HANA TOWN
Art Galleries

By far the most comprehensive gallery in Hana, the Hana Coast Gallery (5031 Hana Hwy., 808/248-8636, www.hanacoast.com, 9am-5pm daily) might be the nicest art gallery on the island. A freestanding building within the Travaasa Hana hotel, the Hana Coast Gallery features fine works by Hawaiian artists. Oil paintings, ceramics, and wooden sculptures are on display in this sophisticated space, and the depth of knowledge of the staff on the intricacies of individual pieces provides an educational component to this fine-art experience.

Gifts and Souvenirs

Within the same complex as the post office and the Hana Ranch Restaurant is the small Hana Treasures (5031 Hana Hwy., 808/248-7372, 10am-5pm Mon.-Fri., 10am-3pm Sat.-Sun.), selling clothing, trinkets, and "Thank God for Hana" bumper stickers.

For Hawaiian-themed souvenirs and resort wear, visit Noe Noe (Travaasa Hana, 5031 Hana Hwy., 808/359-2401, 9am-7pm daily), inside the hotel. It has a selection of island-infused apparel to help you look fashionable down at Hamoa Beach. For a full-range of Hawaiian beauty products, it's a short walk down to the spa.

Although the selection is more utilitarian than artistic, you can also pick up basic gifts and souvenirs at the Hasegawa General Store (5165 Hana Hwy., 808/248-7079, www.hanamaui.com, 7am-7pm Mon.-Sat., 8am-6pm Sun.) in the center of town. Offerings include tank tops, hats, Hana-themed stickers, and merchandise.

HANA TO KIPAHULU
Art Galleries

Along the road between Hana and Kipahulu, on the ocean side of the highway, Karen Davidson Fine Art (mile marker 46.3, 808/248-4877, www.karendavidson.net, by appointment) focuses on the unique art of handcrafted paper. Many of the works are either oil paintings on handmade paper or an array of paper collages. There's a Hawaiian and Polynesian theme coursing through much of the artwork, unique and relevant to Hana.

The studio opens to the Hana shore. If you are more interested in fine art than tumbling waterfalls, call ahead to arrange a visit.

Entertainment

LIVE MUSIC
Pa'ia

The de facto late-night watering hole for all of the North Shore continues to be **Charley's** (142 Hana Hwy., 808/579-8085, www.charleysmaui.com, until 2am), where there's live music most nights and the only place in Pa'ia where you can dance. There can also occasionally be live music in the courtyard of intimate **Café des Amis** (42 Baldwin Ave., 808/579-6323, www.cdamaui.com, until 8:30pm).

Hana

The most happening show in town is at the hotel **Travaasa Hana** (5031 Hana Hwy., 808/359-2401, www.travaasa.com) Wednesday and Thursday evening at the Preserve Kitchen and Bar. Local people put on their finest and come for a drink and entertainment. You

never know what talent might play, as many famous Hawaiian artists have Hana roots.

It also isn't uncommon to have a local person jump out of a chair mid-meal to dance hula to a favorite song before sitting back down to finish the meal. More so than at any other establishment on the island, the evening entertainment is rich with community and a feeling of aloha, and an evening experiencing the live entertainment at the Travaasa can be more of a cultural experience than any resort luau.

Live music can also be found at the **Hana Ranch Restaurant** (5031 Hana Hwy., 808/270-5280, 7:30pm-9:30pm Tues.) one night a week. A scheduled band plays the first hour, followed by an hour of open mike. You'd be surprised how much inspiring talent a small community can foster without modern technology. Ukulele, hula, and song are ways of life in this community.

Food

HA'IKU

The town of Ha'iku is mostly residential, and aside from tropical bed-and-breakfasts has little for visitors. The exception is food, with a couple of restaurants worth the drive.

The best restaurant in Ha'iku is ★ **Nuka** (780 Haiku Rd., 808/575-2939, www.nuka-maui.com, 10am-1:30pm and 4:30pm-10pm Mon.-Sat., 4:30pm-10pm Sun., $9-19), with hand-rolled sushi that can rival the best on Maui. **Colleen's** (810 Haiku Rd., 808/75-9211, www.colleensinhaiku.com, 6am-10pm daily, $8-28) is a longtime local favorite for breakfast and a boozy brunch (Bloody Marys!), and is the perfect spot for lunch if you've just

biked down the volcano with Haleakala Bike Company next door.

PA'IA
American

Charley's (142 Hana Hwy., 808/579-8085, www.charleysmaui.com, 7am-10pm daily, $8-14) is as integral to Pa'ia as dawn patrol at Ho'okipa or bodysurfing at Baldwin Beach. Known as "Willie's Place" because Willie Nelson frequently dines here, Charley's has a colorful cast of characters. The saloon exterior exudes a gritty vibe, but inside it's a jovial, comfortable spot with locally sourced ingredients. Top off an early morning surf session with macadamia nut pancakes. A classic "bacon and blue" burger for lunch is filling and won't break your budget.

The fanciest food in central Pa'ia is at **Hana Ranch Provisions** (71 Baldwin Ave., 808/868-3688, www.hanaranchprovisions. com, 7am-2pm and 5pm-9pm daily, lunch $15, dinner $20-35), where organic produce from Hana Ranch is paired with sustainably sourced ingredients from local Maui farmers. The menu changes around what's fresh and in season.

Coffee Shops

For a morning coffee on the way out to Hana, **Pa'ia Bay Coffee** (115 Hana Hwy., 808/579-3111, www.paiabaycoffee.com 7am-5:30pm daily) is in a hidden courtyard behind San Lorenzo Bikinis. Walk through the bikini store to get to this local favorite, and if the store isn't open yet, there's an entrance around the back of the building. In addition to coffee, there's a filling selection of bagels and sandwiches ($6-9).

Italian

As the name of ★ **Flatbread Pizza Co.** (89 Hana Hwy., 808/579-8989, www.flatbread-company.com, 11am-10pm daily, $16-22) implies, you won't find any Chicago-style deep dish here. All of the pizzas use organic, locally sourced ingredients and are fired in an open *kiawe* (mesquite) wood oven. Try the Mopsy (free-range kalua pork, organic mango barbecue sauce, organic red onions, Maui pineapple, and goat cheese from Surfing Goat Dairy), or Coevolution (kalamata olives, organic and local rosemary, red onions, goat cheese from Surfing Goat Dairy, sweet red peppers, and organic herbs), both made with organic dough. A lively bar scene fills the place nightly; get there early or expect a wait. Tuesday nights, the restaurant hosts benefits for the local community, but the crowds are intense.

Mediterranean

The most relaxing place for a meal in Pa'ia is at ★ **Café des Amis** (42 Baldwin Ave.,

pizza to-go box—Hana style

808/579-6323, www.cdamaui.com, 8:30am-8:30pm daily), where you can sit in a tucked-away outdoor courtyard with Italian coffee and crepes. Lunch has exceptional Indian curries, in addition to savory crepes, and happy hour is 4pm-6pm daily.

Mexican

On the corner of Pa'ia's only stoplight, separated by the bustling crosswalk, ★ **Milagros** (3 Baldwin Ave., 808/579-8755, www.mila-grosfoodcompany.com, 11am-10pm daily, $10-19) is known for Mexican fare with a funky island twist, enormous portions, and the best happy hour in town. The black-bean nachos, ahi burrito, and blackened ahi tacos are all local favorites. Get a seat at the outdoor patio, which has some of the best people-watching in Pa'ia.

Natural Foods

Mana Foods (49 Baldwin Ave., 808/579-8078, www.manafoodsmaui.com, 8am-8:30pm daily) is the epicenter of the island's

healthy cuisine at Maka by Mana

and who caught it. Call well in advance for reservations, timing your meal for sunset if possible. Lunch is an affordable alternative.

While your hotel concierge will recommend Mama's, local surfers will point you to ★ **Pa'ia Fish Market** (100 Baldwin Ave., 808/579-8030, www.paiafishmarket.com, 11am-9:30pm daily, $11), on the corner of the only stoplight in town. Lines stretch out the door for the popular ono and mahimahi burgers. My personal favorite is the ahi burger, paired with a Hefeweizen on draft. The fish tacos and seafood pasta are shockingly good as well.

ROAD TO HANA

There's a myth that you won't find any food while driving the Road to Hana. Stores in Pa'ia and as far away as Ka'anapali offer "Road to Hana picnic lunches" as a means of staving off starvation, even though the longest stretch without any food options is under seven miles. The best plan for food when driving the Road to Hana is to start with lunch in Pa'ia, and then make frequent stops for snacks at stands on the side of the road. As long as it's a weekday, there will be plenty of options for food when you get to Hana. For detailed info on the food stops en route, see the Road to Hana mileage guide in the beginning of this chapter.

HANA

On weekdays Hana has many lunch options. Dinner options are sparse, however, and only a handful of lunch venues are open on weekends.

American

A longtime staple, the **Hana Ranch Restaurant** (5031 Hana Hwy., 808/270-5280, 11am-8:30pm daily, $9-29) is on the mountain side of the road in the "center of town." There are *shoyu* chicken plate lunches, fish and chicken sandwiches, and soothing bowls of *saimin* noodles to calm your stomach. The take-out window is open 11am-4pm daily. The inside seating area stays open as one of Hana's only dinner options.

health-conscious, with a selection of organic and natural offerings. There's a hot bar as well as a deli section where you can build your own picnic lunch for the Road to Hana, or pick up filling and affordable sandwiches ($7).

For a restaurant experience with the same great food, ★ **Maka By Mana** (115 Baldwin Ave., 808/579-9125, www.makabymana.com, 10am-8pm daily, $11) is a vegan raw bar with healthy, affordable options. Start the day on the right foot with a *kalo* coconut kefir bowl with taro and topped with *poha* berries, fresh bananas, and coconut cream.

Seafood

★ **Mama's Fish House** (799 Poho Place, 808/579-8488, www.mamasfishhouse.com, 11am-9pm daily, $20-55) is synonymous with Maui fine dining. Its cult-like followers claim that if you haven't been to Mama's, you've never been to Maui. The oceanfront location and romantic ambience are unbeatable, and the fish is so fresh that the menu tells you where your fish was caught that morning

Farmers Market

One of the best Hana lunch options is **Hana Fresh Market** (4590 Hana Hwy., 10am-2pm Mon.-Fri.), located in the parking lot of the Hana Health Clinic between Wai'anapanapa and the center of town. Proceeds support the Hana Health Clinic, and many of the vegetables and fresh produce are grown in a greenhouse on the property. There is an ample selection of filling lunch options ($8-12), such as ham, apple, and brie *paninis*, Italian sausage pasta, and lemon caper mahimahi. You can also get a tasty *poke* bowl with brown rice, and wash it all down with a fruit smoothie or a cup of Hana-grown coffee.

Food Trucks

Lunch in Hana is defined by food trucks, the most popular of which is **Braddah Hutts** (808/264-5582, 10am-3pm Mon.-Fri., $8-12) just past Hasegawa General Store. The smoky flavor of the kalua pig tacos is magic. Try the macaroni salad.

Another great choice is **Da Chow Wagon** (808/281-0023, 10am-4pm Mon.-Fri., $10-12), next to the gas station, which has local classics like chicken *katsu* and teriyaki beef.

On the other side of Hasegawa General Store, closest to Travaasa Hana, **Surfing Burro** (no phone, 8am-7pm Wed.-Sun., $6-9) has filling and affordable breakfast burritos, and is one of the only places open for breakfast if you've spent the night in Hana.

For a cool treat on a hot day, pick up frozen juice on a stick from **Shaka Pops** (808/442-2926, www.shakapopsmaui.com, noon-4pm Mon.-Fri., $4.75) across from Hasegawa General Store. The frozen treats are made here on Maui using small-batch, freshly squeezed juices.

Hawaiian Regional

The fanciest, freshest, and best meal in Hana is at the Travaasa Hana hotel, where ★ **The Preserve** (5031 Hana Hwy., 808/359-2401, 7:30am-9pm daily, $20-48) restaurant has fine dining rivaling the best on the island. The staff is friendly and happy to talk, and the atmosphere is welcomingly casual. Take the waiter's suggestion for the evening and order the fish of the day, which was likely caught earlier that morning in waters just off Hana. The rest of the menu features the freshest local ingredients. It's a great spot for a filling breakfast after watching the Hana sunrise.

Italian

Next door to the Hana Farms fruit stand, ★ **The Clay Oven** (mile marker 31.2, 808/248-7371, 4pm-8pm Fri.-Sat., $14-17) is the best thing to happen to the Hana dinner scene in a long time. Don't be fooled by the appearance of this outdoor pizza kitchen in the rainforest or the "pizza box" of fresh banana leaves. You'll be surprised to find a full menu of seven different pizza options, including classic margherita and creative potato and pesto. The pizzas are filling enough for two. Large groups can enjoy sitting in "the fireside lounge," a tent behind the open-air kitchen. It's a few miles past Wai'anapanapa heading back toward Kahului, and is only open on Friday and Saturday evenings.

Thai

Hana isn't a place you'd expect to find mouthwatering Thai, but ★ **Thai Food by Pranee** (5050 Uakea Rd., no phone, 10:30am-4pm Sat.-Tues., $10-12) is a culinary gem in the humblest of locations. Little more than a glorified food truck across from the Hana Ballpark, this open-air restaurant gets packed for lunch—especially since it's open on weekends. The filling portions of pad thai and green curry are worth the wait, and if the food is too spicy you can ask them for coconut milk to bring the heat down. Parking is along Uakea Road, and be sure to park facing the correct direction, since violators are often ticketed.

KIPAHULU AND BEYOND

If you plan on driving the back road to the other side of the island, the only real food option is **Kaupo Store** (mile marker 34.6, 10am-5pm Mon.-Sat., cash only) in the dusty Kaupo hinterlands. If you're planning on venturing from Hana to 'Ohe'o (Seven Sacred Pools) and then continuing around the back side of the island, stock up on water and snacks at **Hasegawa General Store** (5165 Hana Hwy., 808/248-7079, www.hanamaui.com, 7am-7pm Mon.-Sat., 8am-6pm Sun.), lest you end up marooned with no water or food.

Getting There and Around

CAR

There aren't any rental car operators in East Maui, so plan on driving here yourself or taking a guided tour.

Gas

There are two gas stations within walking distance of each other in **Pa'ia**. Be sure you have close to a full tank if you're going to be taking the long, winding journey out to Hana. Neither of the stations has a public restroom; the closest ones are at Pa'ia Bay.

Tucked away on a back road that visitors only end up on if they're lost, the only gas station in **Ha'iku** can be found at **Hanzawa's Store** (1833 Kaupakalua Rd., 808/298-0407, 6am-8pm Mon.-Sat., 7am-7pm Sun.) about halfway between Hana Highway and the town of Makawao.

In all of **Hana** there is only one gas station: the **Chevron** (808/270-5299, 7am-8:30pm Mon.-Sat., 7am-6pm Sun.) across from Hasegawa General Store. It has a few auto supplies, snacks, and a telephone, although for a public restroom you're better off going down to the Hana ball field. Gas in Hana is expensive: $0.50 per gallon higher than elsewhere on the island. Fill up before leaving town, because the nearest gas station west is in Pa'ia; going south around the bottom of the island, the closest is in Keokea in Upcountry, and it isn't open in the evening.

GUIDED TOURS

Despite how much fun it is to craft your own Hana adventure, you can visit Hana as part of a private tour.

The best option is **Valley Isle Excursions** (808/661-8687, www.tourmaui.com, $151 adults, $119 children), the only guided Hana tour that's part of the Hawaii Ecotourism Association. Guides are professional, knowledgeable, and funny, and the company has gone to exceptional lengths to eliminate waste from their tours.

Temptation Tours (808/877-8888, www.temptationtours.com, from $219) offers small group tours in "limo vans" and has a number of different options for visiting Hana. One of the tours explores the recesses of Ka'eleku Caverns, and a Hana picnic tour has a similar itinerary but much nicer vans. The top choice, however, is the Hana Sky Trek ($345 pp), driving the Road to Hana and then hopping aboard a helicopter at the Hana Airport for the ride back to Kahului. During the flight you'll zip by towering waterfalls you would never see from the road, and buzz over the multihued cinder cones of Haleakala Crater.

For smaller, private, customized tours, **Awapuhi Adventures** (808/269-6031, www.awapuhiadventures.com) and **Open Eye Tours** (808/572-3483, www.openeyetours.com) provide personalized experiences that are the best and most expensive. Pono Fried, an exceptional guide at Open Eye Tours, has deep respect for the culture and can offer an educational journey unlike any other.

To include hiking, adrenaline, excitement, and adventure, **Maui Easy Riders** (808/344-9489, www.mauieasyriders.com, $250 for 1 person, $500 for 7 or more) offers a day in Hana. A similar tour operator is **Blue Soul Maui** (808/269-1038, www.bluesoulmaui.com, $950 for 2-3 people), offering high end, customizable adventures.

Understanding "The Back Road"

There's a romance to Hana's "back road."

The back road from Hana (Hwy. 31) is unlike any other stretch of road on the island. On this wind-swept plain, it feels like you've journeyed to the edge of the earth. Panoramic views stretch to the horizon, and the back of Haleakala opens up as it plunges from summit to sea.

At the beginning of the drive, past the Pools of 'Ohe'o, the terrain changes from a lush paradise laden with waterfalls to grasslands. Past Kaupo Store the road straightens, and the last half of the drive, between Manawainui and Kanaio, is one of the nicest stretches of pavement on the island. You may like this section of road better than the famous front section.

The biggest misconception about the Road to Hana is that the back road around Kaupo is only accessible with a 4WD vehicle, and you'll be told that driving this section of road violates your rental-car policy. Neither of these common opinions is accurate, and on almost every day of the year, the back road is passable in any vehicle, including a regular passenger car. The road is unpaved but well-graded dirt for five miles, and at some points it is only one lane wide and has precipitous drop-offs, but at no point is 4WD essential. The only time you would need 4WD is during a torrential rainstorm—and in that situation, you should stay off the road altogether. Your rental car company won't penalize you because you drove out here, but if something goes wrong, they aren't going to come out and help you either. Luckily, island locals are some of the friendliest people you'll meet, and if you have problems, you won't have any trouble flagging someone down for help.

That said, preparation is key to enjoying a drive around the back side of Maui. Make sure that you have plenty of gas—at least half a tank when leaving Hana. Driving this road at night can be dangerous, and is pointless since you miss the expansive views. Keep an eye out for free-range cattle on the road. Other than Kaupo Store, there isn't anywhere to get food or water. If you're not a confident driver, the narrow sections and steep drop-offs may be too much. The road periodically closes due to construction, landslides, or flooding, so call the Road Closure Advisory Line (808/986-1200, ext. 2), for the latest information. Finally, no matter what your cell phone or GPS map says, there's no road from Ulupalakua back down to Kihei or Wailea.

BUS

The **Maui Bus** provides regular service between Pa'ia, Ha'iku, the Kahului Airport, and Queen Ka'ahumanu Center in Kahului, where you can connect with buses to anywhere else on the island. The rate is $2 per boarding or $4 for a day pass, and pickups begin in Pa'ia at 5:53am daily headed toward Ha'iku and 6:29am daily headed toward Kahului. The route also makes stops at the Ha'iku Marketplace and Ha'iku Community Center, with the final bus going from Ha'iku to Kahului departing the community center at 7:47pm daily.

FLIGHTS

At the small Hana Airport, you can swap the nausea-inducing three-hour drive for the convenience of a 20-minute flight. Of course, you'll miss out on all the sights along the Road to Hana, but if your focus is on getting to Hana and relaxing at the resort, **Mokulele** (866/260-7070, www.mokuleleairlines.com, 7am-7pm daily) operates flights twice daily between Kahului Airport and the landing strip in Hana. Often the Travaasa Hana hotel runs specials with the airfare included with a stay of three nights or more. If you fly to Hana, however, remember that there aren't any rental-car agencies here, so you'll have to arrange your own transportation from the airport before you get on the flight.

Where to Stay

With so many options, finding accommodations in Maui can be overwhelming.

Regardless of where you choose to stay, the rates listed here don't include the 13.42 percent tax added at checkout. If you're staying in a condo, be sure to read the fine print about additional cleaning fees. In large resorts, resort fees are $20-40 per day, and parking can be upward of $25 per day. Since Maui is spread out, consider spending your time in two separate lodgings instead of being tied to one area. Rates are lowest May-October, and resort room rates can double in winter.

CONDOS AND VACATION RENTALS

There are literally hundreds of independently owned condos and vacation rentals on Maui. Oftentimes these might be a better fit than a resort or a B&B. The best place to begin your search is on **VRBO** (www.vrbo. com). In West Maui, check out **Maui Travel Partners** (651/271-8103, www.mauitravel-partners.com). Another option is **Chase N' Rainbows** (808/611-6022, www.westmaui-condos.com), a management company with dozens of properties. For houses in East Maui check out **Hana's Finest Rentals** (www. hanasfinestrental.com) or **Island Style Vacations** (www.islandstylevacations.com) for Pa'ia and Ha'iku.

Previous: the luxurious Kapalua shoreline; Banana Bungalow Hostel Hotel in Wailuku. **Above:** Escape Upcountry to rural Star Lookout.

West Maui

KAPALUA, NAPILI, AND HONOKOWAI
Over $150

The largest and best-known resort on the northwestern side is the ★ **Ritz-Carlton Kapalua** (1 Ritz-Carlton Dr., 808/669-6200 www.ritzcarlton.com, $429-5,000), offering the amenities expected of a Ritz-Carlton. Also offered are several cultural and environmental programs, such as the acclaimed Ambassadors of the Environment. It can often be windy and wetter than in central Lahaina, but showers often pass quickly.

Also in Kapalua is the ★ **Montage Kapalua Bay** (1 Bay Dr., 808/2-6600, www.montagehotels.com, $705-2,500), with 56 residences laid out like luxurious homes. It's pricey, but you'll feel like a rock star.

Condominiums

On the point between Napili and Kapalua Bays, the ★ **Napili Kai Beach Resort** (5900 Lower Honoapi'ilani Rd., 808/669-6271, www.napilikai.com, $350-825) is a West Side classic that offers individually owned condos in a family-friendly resort setting. This is a great option for families who want to stay in one place and play on the beach. There is a miniature putting course, multiple swimming pools, and a weekly mai tai party. Many of the units have recently been renovated and are the nicest they've ever been.

An affordable spot on Napili Bay, **Napili Village** (5425 Lower Honoapi'ilani, 808/669-6228, www.napilivillage.com, $119-139) is the area's best value. These studios and one-bedroom apartments include air-conditioning, maid service, and full kitchens. The rooms aren't as luxurious as some of the other options on the beach, but being steps from Napili Bay, it's hard to argue with the price.

In Honokowai, the **Maui Kai** (106 Ka'anapali Shores Place, 808/667-3500, www.mauikai.com, $239-400) is at the boundary of Honokowai and Ka'anapali, so it's possible to take a long morning stroll down the beach to the center of the Ka'anapali strip. All units have full kitchens, gas barbecues, and the convenience of being just steps from the beach. Parking and Wi-Fi are included in the rates. This is an affordable place for families who want to be near Ka'anapali without the resort rates.

KA'ANAPALI
Over $150

As the slogan says, ★ **Ka'anapali Beach Hotel** (2525 Ka'anapali Pkwy., 808/661-0011, www.kbhmaui.com, $195-325) is Maui's "most Hawaiian hotel." A genuine feeling of aloha permeates this laid-back resort, and while it's not nearly as lavish as its neighbors, KBH occupies prime oceanfront real estate a two-minute stroll from Pu'u Keka'a (Black Rock). The open lawn is the perfect place to relax in the shade of an *ulu* tree, and while there is no hot tub, there is a swimming pool next to the popular tiki bar, a welcoming place for families. On the lawn is an outrigger sailing canoe crafted by employees of the resort, and free hula shows are held each night on the hotel's outdoor stage. Guests are made to feel like *'ohana* (family), and the rates are much more affordable.

In front of Pu'u Keka'a is the 503-room **Sheraton Maui Resort** (2605 Ka'anapali Pkwy., 808/661-0031, www.sheraton-maui.com, $303-8,000), the original Ka'anapali resort that celebrated its 50th anniversary in 2013. This luxurious beach resort is tucked into the sacred cliff face, and despite being the "oldest" hotel on the strip, it has been renovated numerous times and feels brand-new. There is a large oceanfront pool, tennis courts, spacious rooms, and a spa, and a few of the rooms are on top of the legendary Ka'anapali promontory.

On the far southern end of the Ka'anapali

$360-950) combine the luxury of an ocean-front resort with the convenient amenities of a condo. The 1,029 villas are huge and great for groups and families, and most of the villas have full kitchens and are just steps from Kahekili Beach. There's also a fascinating cultural center—the only one of its kind at any Maui resort.

LAHAINA

While there are no large resorts in Lahaina, the town's accommodations range from historic inns and modern condos to a handful of budget options.

Over $150

The **Pioneer Inn** (658 Wharf St., 808/661-3636, www.pioneerinnmaui.com, $159-229) is the oldest hotel on Maui, and it was the only hotel in West Maui until 1963. Now a Best Western hotel, the PI is across the street from Lahaina Harbor and right in the center of the action. Food, drinks, and live music are served downstairs at the popular bar.

On the northern end of town, one of Lahaina's most basic but affordable ocean-front accommodations is the **Makai Inn** (1415 Front St., 808/870-9004, www.makaiinn.net, $110-190), an old concrete apartment building that was turned into vacation rentals. The garden setting is surprisingly pleasing, ocean-front rooms have their own private lanai, and you're right on the water for watching the sunset from your balcony or the inn's open courtyard. Rates are affordable considering you're on the oceanfront, and this laid-back Hawaiian setting is a practical option for basing yourself near Lahaina.

Bed-and-Breakfasts

Couples looking for a romantic retreat will love the ★ **Plantation Inn** (174 Lahainaluna Rd., 808/667-9225, www.theplantationinn.com, $187-265), a hidden little pocket of calm that manages to retain its 19th-century charm in otherwise frantic Lahaina. On Lahainaluna Road, just a one-minute walk from Front Street, this 19-room getaway has a swimming

pool at the Westin Maui

strip is the **Hyatt Regency** (200 Nohea Kai Dr., 808/661-1234, www.maui.hyatt.com, $289-2,500), with the best pool system in Ka'anapali. This is a favorite of families who want to spend the day by the pool, and the best place along the strip to grab a drink from a bar tucked behind a waterfall or ride a twisting waterslide. This southern end of the beach is also sheltered from the afternoon trade winds, although the sand in front of the resort has been steadily eroding for years.

The **Royal Lahaina** (2780 Keka'a Dr., 808/661-3611 www.royallahaina.com, $189-550), on the northern side of Pu'u Keka'a, offers rooms for tighter budgets. In addition to the oceanfront tower are a number of individual cottages scattered around the property, where the Ka'anapali golf course runs right through the resort. A little more laid-back than some of the glitzier resorts, this is one of Ka'anapali's best oceanfront values.

Just down the beach, the **Westin Ka'anapali Ocean Resort Villas** (6 Kai Ala Dr., 808/67-3200, www.westinkaanapali.com,

Where to Stay in West Maui

Name	Type	Price	Features	Why Stay Here?	Best For
'Aina Nalu Resort	condo	$129–400	pool, kitchen	location	couples
Camp Olowalu	camping	$20–70	restrooms, oceanfront	location, affordable	budget travelers
Ho'oilo House	B&B	$339	pool, breakfast	quiet, view	couples, honeymooners
Hyatt Regency	resort	$289–2,500	waterslides, oceanfront	location, pools	families
★ Ka'anapali Beach Hotel	hotel	$195–325	free hula show	location	families, couples
Lahaina Shores Beach Resort	condo	$199–300	pool, oceanfront	location	couples
Makai Inn	inn	$110–190	oceanfront, gardens	location, affordable	budget travelers
Maui Kai	condo	$239–400	kitchens, oceanfront	location	families, couples
★ Montage Kapalua Bay	resort	$705–2,500	kitchens, oceanfront, spa, pool	full-service resort	couples, families, honeymooners, luxury-lovers

pool, included parking and Wi-Fi, and daily maid service. Breakfast is served daily until 9:30am and features French-inspired cuisine from chef Gerard Reversade, whose acclaimed restaurant on the same property gives hotel guests a discount.

Condominiums

Right on the water by 505 Front Street, the **Lahaina Shores Beach Resort** (475 Front St., 808/661-4835 www.lahainashores.com, $199-300) is a six-story condo with individually owned units. This is a convenient base to take a surf lesson, stroll down the beach, access Lahaina Harbor, or walk from town.

Smack in the center of town, a block off Front Street, is the 188-room **'Aina Nalu Resort** (660 Waine'e St., 800/367-5226, www.

outriggercondominiums.com, $129-400), a modern condo complex in a garden atmosphere that has the benefit of being right in town. Rooms are spacious and recently renovated, and a swimming pool provides a respite from the heat.

The best condo complex in Lahaina is ★ **Puamana** (from $175), a 28-acre private community on the southern edge of town. There is a sandy beach in front of the complex good for swimming, and a luxurious pool out on a point surrounded by the ocean. There are tennis courts and a beautiful old clubhouse. It's just a 10-minute stroll to central Lahaina. The oceanfront rentals are much nicer than those along the highway, and reservations are available through various West Side rental

Name	Type	Price	Features	Why Stay Here?	Best For
★ Napili Kai Beach Resort	condo	$350–825	pool, oceanfront	full amenities	families, couples
Napili Village	condo	$119–139	oceanfront	location, rates	families, couples
Pioneer Inn	hotel	$159–229	garden, pool	location	couples, budget travelers
★ Plantation Inn	B&B	$187–265	pool, breakfast	location, zquiet	couples, honeymooners
★ Puamana	condo	$175–600	pool, oceanfront	location, quiet	families, couples
★ Ritz-Carlton Kapalua	resort	$429–5,000	golf, spa	full-service resort	luxury-lovers, honeymooners
Royal Lahaina	hotel	$189–550	oceanfront, tennis	location	couples
Sheraton Maui	resort	$303–8,000	pool, oceanfront	full-service resort	families, honeymooners
Westin Ka'anapali Ocean Resort Villas	resort	$360–950	pool, oceanfront	full-service resort	families, couples

agents, including **Puamana Vacations** (www.puamanavacations.com).

SOUTH OF LAHAINA
Bed-and-Breakfasts

In the residential community of Launiupoko, above the beach park of the same name, the **Ho'oilo House** (138 Awaiku St., 808/667-6669, www.hooilohouse.com, $339, 3-night minimum) is one of the most luxurious B&Bs on the island's West Side. The views are toward Lana'i and offer panoramic sunsets on a nightly basis. Everything about this house, from its Thai-inspired architecture to its furnishings and outdoor garden area, says comfort and relaxation. Six suites are decorated in unique style, a continental breakfast is served daily, and guests can make use of the swimming pool and lounge area with a view over the water. Only two adults per room.

Camping

The camping spot with the nicest facilities is **Camp Olowalu** (800 Olowalu Village Rd., 808/661-4303, www.campolowalu.com), with tent spaces ($20 adults, $5 children), and "tentalows" ($70) that have beds and outdoor showers. There's a beautiful beach here hidden from the road that consequently isn't very crowded, and it's a convenient option for travelers on a budget who still want a little comfort.

Central Maui

WAILUKU
Hostels

The most affordable places to stay in Wailuku are the two hostels in the funkier, older part of town. While they are by no means a beach resort, they are practical, centrally located, and provide an affordable base for exploring the island. All non-US residents must show a valid passport and a ticket off the island as a prerequisite for booking a bed.

The ★ **Banana Bungalow** (310 N. Market St., 808/244-5090, www.mauihostel. com, $41-126) has free daily tours. There isn't a more affordable way to experience Maui, and while it's expected that you leave a tip for the guides, that is the only cost for tours to Hana, Haleakala, 'Iao Valley, or Little Beach. The rooms are basic and the garden is relaxing, but the hostel is in an unattractive part of the island, and it can often be a party scene, although "quiet hours" start at 10pm. Rates are $41 for a dorm bed, $93 for a private single, $104 for a double, and $126 for a triple. Linens are included, towels aren't, and surfers are always welcome.

Closer to the center of Wailuku is **Northshore Hostel** (2080 W. Vineyard St., 808/986-8095, www.northshorehostel.com, $33-99). The rooms are clean, and breakfast, Wi-Fi, airport transfers, shuttles to Kanaha Beach, and linens are all included. There aren't any private baths, but the rates are reasonable at $33 for a dorm bed and $79-99 for a private room. It's also within walking distance of Market Street and Wailuku's best restaurants and shops.

Bed-and-Breakfasts

The nicest place to stay in historic Wailuku is the ★ **Old Wailuku Inn at Ulupono** (2199 Kaho'okele St., 808/244-5897, www. mauiinn.com, $165-195, 2-night minimum), built in 1924 and listed on the Hawaii Register of Historic Places. The 10 rooms are filled with period furniture that evokes the feeling of Grandma's house. Although it sounds like marketing, this really is Maui's most Hawaiian bed-and-breakfast. Wi-Fi is included, and each room has a private bath. A filling gourmet breakfast is served at 8am daily. Most rooms are set up for double occupancy.

For peace and serenity in 'Iao Valley, the ★ **Iao Valley Inn** (80 'Iao Valley Road, 808/633-6028, www.iaovalleyinn.com) is a spectacular B&B on 37 lush acres, a true sanctuary that's just minutes outside Wailuku. There are two guest rooms ($100-160) and a separate cottage ($180-275) that can sleep up to four.

KAHULUI
$100-150

A hotel with the name **Maui Beach Hotel** (170 Ka'ahumanu Ave., 808/954-7421, www. mauibeachhotel.net, $139-159) sounds like the epitome of paradise, but here the beach is on the inside of Kahului Harbor, and you're in an industrial part of town. Still, it's a convenient spot just minutes from the airport, and there's an airport shuttle included in the rates.

Over $150

The **Courtyard Marriott** (532 Keolani Place, 808/871-1800, $200-300) is the newest and nicest hotel in Kahului. It's just an airport hotel, and the rates are high for an uninspiring view. Nevertheless, the hotel is modern and conveniently located near the airport.

Where to Stay in Central Maui

Name	Type	Price	Features	Why Stay Here?	Best For
★ Banana Bungalow	hostel	$41–126	free tours	affordable	budget travelers
Courtyard Marriott	hotel	$200–300	modern fitness room, swimming pool	location	business travelers
★ Iao Valley Inn	B&B	$100–275	quiet, breakfast	location, affordable	couples
Maui Beach Hotel	hotel	$139–159	airport shuttle	affordable	budget travelers
Northshore Hostel	hostel	$33–99	quiet	affordable	budget travelers
★ Old Wailuku Inn at Ulupono	B&B	$165–195	breakfast, quiet	historic	couples

South Maui

South Maui is the island's sunniest area and one of the most popular places for visitors. Ma'alaea and Kihei are dominated by condos with few hotels or cottages. Wailea offers the island's most luxurious resorts and some moderately priced condos.

MA'ALAEA

The only accommodations in Ma'alaea are condos, all of which are found along Hauoli Street. The benefits of staying in Ma'alaea include the central location within walking distance of Ma'alaea Harbor, the ability to cook your own meals, and some of the most affordable ocean views on the island. **Maalaea Bay Rentals** (808/244-5627 or 808/244-7012, www.maalaeabay.com) has an office at the Hono Kai Resort (280 Hauoli St., Ma'alaea) and manages more than 140 units in most of the condos along this road. All units are fully furnished with complete kitchens, TVs, phones, and a lanai, and each property has a pool and laundry facilities. Rates range $150-300 mid-December to mid-April, but summer and fall rates can be as low as $100. Many of the condos have a three-night minimum, or

longer during the Christmas holidays. For month-long stays, rates are reduced by 10 percent.

KIHEI
$100-150

The most affordable hotel option in South Kihei is the **Days Inn** (2980 S. Kihei Rd., 808/879-7744, www.daysinn.com, $139-280), on the north end of Keawakapu Beach. Rooms are small, there is air-conditioning and a small fridge, and while it might be basic, it's tough to argue with the price, considering the location. Wi-Fi, parking, and outdoor grills are included. Oceanfront suites can stretch up to $250.

Over $150

On the northern edge of South Kihei is the ★ **Maui Coast Hotel** (2259 S. Kihei Rd., 808/874-6284, www.mauicoasthotel.com, $169-435), a 265-room high-rise that is a three minutes' walk from the beach. You'll find tennis courts, a fitness room, and a swimming pool. Rooms have air-conditioning. Parking,

Where to Stay in South Maui

Name	Type	Price	Features	Why Stay Here?	Best For
Aston Maui Hill	condo	$165–400	pool, kitchen	location, amenities	couples, families
Days Inn	hotel	$139–280	oceanfront, barbecue	affordable, location	budget travelers
★ Fairmont Kea Lani	resort	$459–1,775	pool, oceanfront	romantic, luxury	families, couples, honeymooners
Four Seasons Resort	resort	$600–10,000	pools, spa, oceanfront	romantic, luxury	couples, honeymooners, luxury-lovers
★ Grand Wailea	resort	$564–3,370	waterslides, spa, oceanfront	romantic, luxury, pools	families, couples, honeymooners
Hale Pau Hana	condo	$260–380	oceanfront, kitchen	location, amenities	couples, families
Hotel Wailea	hotel	$499–1400	pool, spa, amenities	boutique, romantic	couples, luxury-lovers
Maalaea Bay Rentals	condo	$100–300	pool, kitchen, laundry	location, ocean view	families, extended stay
Mana Kai Maui	condo	$240–500	kitchen, oceanfront	location, water sports	couples, families

Wi-Fi, and a resort shuttle around the South Kihei and Wailea area are included.

Condominiums

One of the several condos at the far north end of Kihei is **Sugar Beach Resort** (145 N. Kihei Rd., 808/879-2778, www.crhmaui.com, $150-425), an oceanfront building with individually owned units as well as a swimming pool, spa, and sundries shop. The beach outside is great for a long walk, but afternoons are windy.

In North Kihei, across from Mai Poina 'Oe Ia'u Beach Park, is the **Maui Sunseeker** (551 S. Kihei Rd., 808/879-1261, www.mauisunseeker.com, $165-499) resort, a gay-friendly adults-only property featuring 16 rooms in a small and quiet setting. A sundeck with a hot tub is on the roof, there are kitchenettes in the rooms, and laundry facilities are available on-site.

Sandwiched between the Cove and Kamaole I, **Maui Vista** (2191 S. Kihei Rd., 808/879-7966, www.mauivistacondo.com, $210-325) is a 10-acre condo complex on the *mauka* (mountain) side of South Kihei Road. There are three swimming pools, six tennis courts, and barbecue grills, and most rooms have kitchens and air-conditioning. It's also a short walk to Charley Young Beach, which is just on the other side of the street.

Right on the sands of Kamaole II, the **Hale Pau Hana** (2480 S. Kihei Rd., 808/879-2715, www.hphresort.com, $260-380) is one of the best options for condos on the water. Parking and Internet access are included, as are grilling facilities, a full kitchen, a swimming pool,

Name	Type	Price	Features	Why Stay Here?	Best For
★ Maui Coast Hotel	hotel	$169–435	pool, fitness center, shuttle	full amenities	couples, business travel
★ Maui Mango Cottages	cottages	$295–395	kitchen, gardens	location, amenities	couples, families
Maui Sunseeker	LGBT resort	$165–499	kitchenette, hot tub	quiet, location	couples
Maui Vista	condo	$210–325	pool, tennis, kitchen	location, practical	couples, families
Nona Lani Cottages	cottages	$140–205	gardens, kitchenette	quiet, affordable, location	couples
Ocean Breeze Hideaway	B&B	$109–139	gardens, breakfast	quiet, affordable	couples
Sugar Beach Resort	condo	$150–425	pool, spa, kitchen	oceanfront	couples, families
Wailea Beach Marriott	resort	$331–900	pool, spa, luau	oceanfront, watersports	families, couples
Wailea Beach Villas	condo	$850–2,500	pool, oceanfront	romantic, luxury	luxury-lovers
★ Wailea Ekolu Village	condo	$260–425	kitchen, amenities	location, affordable	couples, families

and a private lanai in each room. Rates vary by season. This is a good location in a happening part of town.

Within walking distance of Kamaole III, Kihei Boat Ramp, and Keawakapu Beach is the **Aston Maui Hill** (2881 S. Kihei Rd., 808/879-6321, www.astonmauihill.com, $165-400), an upbeat condo with a Spanish motif. This quality condo resort is high on a hill and a nice alternative to expensive Wailea. There is a tennis court, swimming pool, putting green, and Wi-Fi, and each room comes equipped with a kitchen. Parking is free and there's no resort fee.

Closer to the water, the eight-story **Mana Kai Maui** (2960 S. Kihei Rd., 808/879-1561, www.manakaimaui.com, $240-500) offers the nicest resort accommodations in South Kihei.

This 50-unit complex is on the north end of Keawakapu Beach and offers snorkeling and water activities right out the front door. The Five Palms restaurant is one of Kihei's best, and there are full kitchens in the units. Rates are $240 for a standard hotel room and $500 for suites with private balconies.

Cottages

Cottages provide affordable charm not found at large condos or hotels. On the north end of Kihei, **Nona Lani Cottages** (455 S. Kihei Rd., 808/879-2497 www.nonalanicottages.com, $140-205) has eight cottages in a garden setting. The property is a refreshing throwback to simpler times, and is across the street from Kalepolepo Beach in North Kihei.

On the southern end of Kihei, the ★ **Maui**

Mango Cottages (45 Kilohana Dr., phone number provided upon booking, www.maui-mangocottages.com) are just steps from Keawakapu Beach and were completely remodeled in 2015. The two-bedroom cottage ($295) sleeps 4-5, and the three-bedroom cottage ($395) can accommodate 6. This is as close to Wailea as you can get for these rates. Wailea Beach Walk is a 10-minute stroll from the front door. The cottages have kitchens, and in summer, mangos dangling from the trees.

Bed and Breakfast

In North Kihei, the **Ocean Breeze Hideaway** (808/879-0657, www.hawaiibednbreakfast.com, $109-139) is a comfortable and affordable bed-and-breakfast just minutes from Sugar Beach. Included are Wi-Fi, breakfast each morning, and organic fruits in the garden.

WAILEA

Wailea hotels are expensive, fancy, and meant to provide indulgence. The northernmost and oldest of the Wailea resorts is **The Wailea Beach Marriott** (3700 Wailea Alanui Dr., 808/879-1922, www.marriott.com, $331-900), a 497-room oceanfront property that has been extensively restored. Families will enjoy the large system of pools, and the snorkeling and sand of Ulua Beach is a few steps away. Parking is $25 per day, Internet is $15 per day, and rates begin around $330 during the slow seasons. There are also plans for a Residence Inn by Marriott to open in fall 2016, which should have rates about $60 cheaper than the resort rooms on the ocean.

Not far from the Marriott are the ultra-luxurious **Wailea Beach Villas** (3800 Wailea Alanui Dr., 808/891-4500, www.drhmaui.com, $850-2,500), fronting the beach and steps from the Shops at Wailea. Grab a private cabana overlooking the shore, relax in the oceanfront infinity pool, and bask in the aura of extravagant luxury at Wailea's nicest accommodations.

Directly in front of Wailea Beach are two of Wailea's largest resorts, the sprawling pink ★ **Grand Wailea** (3850 Wailea Alanui Dr., 808/875-1234, www.grandwailea.com, $564-3,370) and the ultra-luxurious **Four Seasons Resort** (3900 Wailea Alanui Dr., 808/874-8000, www.fourseasons.com, $600). While both resorts offer the highest quality, the Grand Wailea is famous for its pool system and the largest corporate art collection in Hawaii. Families will enjoy navigating the

the unforgettable Grand Wailea pool

waterslides, rope swings, lazy river, and water elevator. In recent years the resort has instituted numerous cultural programs. Next door at the Four Seasons, the pool scene is much more reserved, but the cream villas looking out over the water redefine island luxury. Rooms are expensive and amenities lavish.

Around the southern end of Wailea Point are the twirling white spires of the ★ **Fairmont Kea Lani** (4100 Wailea Alanui, 808/875-4100, www.fairmont.com, $459-1,775). Located on the sands of Polo Beach, the property has undergone extensive renovations and appears nicer now than ever before. Each room is arranged like a one-bedroom suite, and the resort is involved in a number of eco-conscious initiatives to protect the island environment. The resort has an exclusive feel since it's off on its own.

If you'd rather have a boutique hotel experience than an oceanfront mega-resort, the **Hotel Wailea** (555 Kaukahi St., 808/874-0500, www.hotelwailea.com, $499-1,400) is a Relais & Châteaux property that's recently been beautifully renovated. The hillside location provides sunset views from the comfort of a private lanai, and there's a wine social each evening around the exclusive pool. Watch whales jump while you walk on the treadmill, and with only 72 suites on 16 acres, there's a peaceful garden feel. While it isn't oceanfront, there's a free resort shuttle down to the beach, a three-minute drive.

Condominiums

To be walking distance from the beaches of Wailea without the hefty price tag, look into some of the affordably priced condos on the northern edge of the resort. The ★ **Wailea Ekolu Village** (808/891-6200, www.drhmaui.com, $260-425) offers one- and two-bedroom condos with included parking and Internet, and kitchens. You can often get hefty discounts with advance reservations.

Upcountry

Upcountry is completely free of resorts, different from most Maui experiences. Peace and tranquility replace mai tais and swimming pools, and the cool mountain area is a refreshing change from the sunbaked shores below. Most accommodations are 20 minutes from the beach, although most are also conveniently located within an hour of Haleakala Volcano. Rustic, cool, and blissfully laid-back, Upcountry is where visitors come to relax, although if you plan to scuba dive, you probably shouldn't stay here since many of the accommodations are over 3,000 feet elevation. Aside from these listings, there are many accommodations in Upcountry that are small and privately owned, so **VRBO** (www.vrbo.com) and **AirBNB** (www.airbnb.com) are good places to check.

MAKAWAO

★ **Lumeria** (1813 Baldwin Ave., 855/579-8877, www.lumeriamaui.com, $300-459) is a luxurious, holistic retreat center between Makawao and Pa'ia. Housed in a brilliantly restored plantation building and with its own organic garden, Lumeria focuses on educational vacation experiences with rejuvenation and wellness. All 24 rooms are decorated differently, and Asian accents punctuate the courtyard. Lumeria is popular for yoga retreats, and there are regularly scheduled classes and workshops.

In the forest above Makawao town are the intimate ★ **Aloha Cottage** and **Thai Tree House** (808/573-8555, www.alohacottage.com, $239-279), two peaceful spots down a quiet country lane off rural Olinda Road. The only neighbors are the horses in the pastures beyond the distant fence. On a five-acre estate, the Aloha Cottage has a panoramic view from

Where to Stay in Upcountry

Name	Type	Price	Features	Why Stay Here?	Best For
★ Aloha Cottage	cottage	$239–279	hot tub, kitchen, lanai	quiet, peaceful, romantic	couples
Banyan Bed and Breakfast	B&B	$175–220	kitchen, breakfast	quiet, location	couples
G and Z Upcountry Bed and Breakfast	B&B	$149	kitchenette, breakfast	quiet, affordable	budget travelers, couples
★ Hale Ho'okipa Inn	B&B	$125–175	breakfast, garden	quiet, historic	couples
Hale Ho'omana	B&B	$119–139	breakfast, spa, wellness	location, quiet, affordable	couples, budget travelers
★ Kula Lodge	inn	$170–245	fireplace, lanai	location, romantic, quiet	couples, hikers
Kula Sandalwoods	cottage	$169–209	lanai, views	quiet, location, retreat	couples
★ Lumeria	hotel	$300–459	yoga classes, garden courtyard	meditative retreat	solo travelers, couples, groups
Peace of Maui	inn	$85–175	kitchen	affordable	budget travelers
Polipoli Springs State Recreation Area	camping	$18–90	none	quiet, wilderness	budget travelers, adventure travelers
★ Star Lookout	vacation rental	$250	kitchen, views	location, quiet, romantic	couples
Upcountry Bed and Breakfast	B&B	$150	fireplace, views, breakfast	quiet, peaceful	couples

the deck of the octagonal structure. Use the two-person hot tub on the cool Olinda nights, and wake each morning to birdsong from the surrounding forest. Rates vary depending on length of stay, and there is a $100 cleaning fee.

Bed-and-Breakfasts

Built in 1924 and used by a Portuguese family to raise 13 children, the five-bedroom plantation house ★ Hale Ho'okipa Inn (32 Pakani Place, 808/572-6698, www.maui-bed-and-breakfast.com, $125-175) has been turned into a lovely B&B with bedrooms ($125-155) and

a two-bedroom suite ($175), within walking distance of Makawao town. While improvements have been made, it still has the feel of an old-fashioned country home, and the accommodating owners provide tips and insight into Maui life. Organic fruits from the garden are served.

Up Pi'iholo Road, in the cool eucalyptus forest about 10 minutes above Makawao, Hale Ho'omana (1550 Pi'iholo Rd., 808/573-8256, www.hoomanaspamaui.com, $119-139) is a spa retreat with two affordably priced cottages in a peaceful part of the island.

Down the hill 0.5 mile from Makawao town, the **Banyan Bed and Breakfast** (3265 Baldwin Ave., 808/572-9021, www.bed-break-fast-maui.com, $175-220) is an old plantation bungalow with adjoining cottages that provides laid-back accommodations in a country setting. The complex is shaded by a monkey-pod and banyan, with swings hanging from the wide boughs to complete the rural feel. All cottages and suites have kitchens or kitchenettes, breakfast is included, and Makawao town is a short walk away.

Down near the intersection of Hali'imaile Road and Baldwin Avenue is the guesthouse **Peace of Maui** (1290 Hali'imaile Rd., 808/572-5045, www.peaceofmaui.com, rooms $85, cottage $175), centrally located between Makawao and Pa'ia. Peace of Maui overlooks the pineapple fields, and while the rooms aren't extravagant, they are clean and affordable. Rooms in the main lodge share a kitchen and baths. For a private bath, rent the two-bedroom cottage, which also provides access to the jetted tub.

KULA

The ★ **Kula Lodge** (15200 Haleakala Hwy., 808/878-1535, www.kulalodge.com, $170-245) is Upcountry's most popular option. On Highway 377 at 3,200 feet elevation, the air is crisp, cool, and more comfortable than on the coast. There are five detached chalets that have recently been renovated, and all feature private lanais and electric fireplaces. The rustic yet comfortable setting makes a perfect base for visiting Haleakala Crater.

Just up the road, the **Kula Sandalwoods** (15427 Haleakala Hwy., 808/878-3523, www.kulasandalwoods.com, $169-209) is another Kula classic that is far more laid-back than its popular neighbor. These stand-alone cottages are on a hillside and offer sweeping views of the island's central valley. Wi-Fi and morning coffee are included; the cottages are otherwise free of appliances. The summit of Haleakala is only a 45-minute drive from this location at 3,300 feet elevation.

Bed-and-Breakfasts

In Lower Kula, on the drive to Keokea, **Upcountry Bed and Breakfast** (4925 Lower Kula Rd., 808/878-8083, www.upcountrybandb.com, $150) has rooms in a relaxing Upcountry setting. The owner is a wealth of information on everything island-related, and locally grown Upcountry fruit is served with each morning's breakfast. Wi-Fi and fireplaces in winter are included, and there are sweeping sunset views. Guests must be 21 and older, and there's a strict quiet time from 9pm.

Out by the Kula Country Farms stand, where Highway 377 meets Highway 37, **G and Z Upcountry Bed and Breakfast** (808/224-6824, www.gandzmaui.com, $149) is on a beautiful six-acre farm with exceptionally welcoming owners. John and Marsha have lived in Maui since the 1960s and can tell you every tidbit about the island. The B&B opened in 2014 and has a separate entrance, a king bed, and a queen sofa bed. There's a barbecue grill on the private lanai you can use while watching the sunset. Continental breakfast is included each morning, and Haleakala Crater is under an hour away. There is a $25-per-child surcharge up to a maximum of two children.

KEOKEA AND ULUPALAKUA

For rural tranquility in a cool Upcountry setting, the ★ **Star Lookout** (622 Thompson Rd., 907/346-8028, www.starlookout.com, $250, 2-night minimum) is on Thompson Road just minutes from Grandma's Coffee House. This single cottage is a ranch-style retreat with views over the Keokea pastureland to the South Maui shore. From the "Star Bed," fall asleep gazing out at the stars through the enormous picture window. Advance reservations are required as it's Upcountry's most desirable spot.

Camping

The rugged can camp in **Polipoli Springs State Recreation Area** (permits 808/984-8109 or www.camping.ehawaii.gov, $18). The dirt road to the campground requires a 4WD vehicle. You can also book a backcountry wilderness cabin ($90); permits are issued by phone.

HALEAKALA NATIONAL PARK

Spending a night in Haleakala Crater is a unique adventure on Maui. Cold, arid, and beneath a blanket of stars, it's a backcountry trip you'd never expect on a tropical island. The warmest and most accessible campsite is **Hosmer's Grove,** at 6,800 feet elevation as you enter the park. No permit is necessary for camping at Hosmer's Grove, and you can drive to the campground. Barbecues and toilets are available.

For the three backcountry campsites, you have to obtain a free permit and watch a short safety video at **Park Headquarters** (808/572-4400, 7am-3:45pm daily). All gear must be packed in and out on an arduous trail. **Holua** campsite is cold and dry, **Paliku** campsite is a few degrees warmer and set in a lush forest. There are also three backcountry cabins (reservations: www.recreation.gov, $75) with basic cooking facilities and bunk beds. Reservations for cabins are required about six months in advance.

East Maui

PA'IA
Under $100

A short walk above Pa'ia, the **Aloha Surf Hostel** (221 Baldwin Ave., 808/8680117, www.alohasurfhostel.com) offers dorm rooms ($39) or private rooms ($80-125). There is a communal kitchen and Wi-Fi is included, and the hostel offers free daily tours.

$100-150

Tucked away in Spreckelsville and within walking distance of Baby Beach, **Sprecks Plantation House** (phone number provided upon booking, www.sprecksplantationhouse.com, $95-150) is an affordable option on the outskirts of trendy Pa'ia. Rooms are basic, very clean, and arranged in a single-level apartment style. If you're here to windsurf, you can even ride a bike to Kanaha and Kite Beach in under 20 minutes.

Over $150

In the center of town, the ★ **Pa'ia Inn** (93 Hana Hwy., 808/579-6000, www.paiainn.com, $199-999) is a trendy and chic boutique hotel steps from the beaches of Pa'ia. The decor has a dark-wood Balinese tone, and each individually designed room offers a luxurious private getaway in the middle of Pa'ia's bustle.

Also in the center of town is the **Nalu Kai Lodge** (18 Nalu Place, 808/385-4344, www.paiahotel.com, $135-175), offering simple and comfortable accommodations just steps from Pa'ia Bay. There is a second-story deck with ocean views as well as outdoor showers and a tiki bar.

Right on Kuau Cove, ★ **The Inn at Mama's Fish House** (799 Poho Place, 808/579-9764, www.mamasfishhouse.com, adults only, $250-850) is an impossibly romantic boutique hotel in one of the North Shore's best settings. The suites, studios, and cottages feature amenities such as full kitchens, maid service, and 15 percent off at the restaurant. The real perk, however, is the location, as there's nothing like staying where people lust over the dinner.

Bed-and-Breakfasts

Between Pa'ia and Ho'okipa Beach Park, the **Kuau Inn** (676 Hana Hwy., 808/579-6046, www.kuauinn.com, $125-145, 2-night minimum) is a four-room house that offers clean B&B accommodations just minutes from the shore. Breakfast and Wi-Fi are included. There is a full kitchen, covered lanai, and communal living room. The cleaning fee is $25.

Up in Ha'iku, **Maui Tradewinds** (808/573-0066, www.mauitradewinds.com, $229-422) is only 10 minutes' drive to the beaches in Pa'ia but is secluded, quiet, and has sweeping views of the island's North Shore. Rates decrease with length of stay, and there is a $100 cleaning fee.

ROAD TO HANA

Not far from Twin Falls is **Windward Garden B&B** (435 Ho'olawa Rd., 808/268-3874, http://windwardgardenbandb.com, $165-192), a gorgeous property within walking distance of beautiful coastal bluffs, with nature, yoga, surfing, and a green healthy lifestyle 20 minutes east of Pa'ia. Individual suites share baths.

Also near Twin Falls is the **Tea House Cottage** (800/215-6130, www.roadtohanacottages.com, $175). This B&B is "off the grid," with solar power and a rain catchment system. It's quiet, with no distractions, and from here you have broad views of the ocean. A tunnel through the trees leads to the house, and walkways run throughout the property, one to a small stupa built in 1976 by a Tibetan monk. The private Tiara Cottage ($100), also on the property, is an East Maui steal.

In Huelo you'll find the ★ **Huelo Point Lookout** (808/573-0914, www.maui-vacationrentals.com, $250-405), a collection of five vacation rentals in a lush and heavenly section of the island, not for the resort-loving crowd. These five separate vacation rentals provide sweeping views of the Huelo coast and are a place to escape from it all. There is no beach outside your door, but there is a blanket of stars every night and outdoor hot tubs from which to enjoy them.

HANA

The east end of the island is another place where booking engines like **VRBO** (www.vrbo.com) display many privately owned options that don't have formal websites.

Under $100

Budget-friendly and basic, **Joe's Rentals** (4870 Uakea Rd., 808/248-7033, www.joesrentals.com, $50-60, cash only) is close to Hana Bay and walking distance from the center of town. This home has been split into eight guest rooms, with shared ($50) or private ($60) bath. There's kitchen access, a communal TV room, and daily towel change, but if a

Spoil yourself with a night at Travaasa.

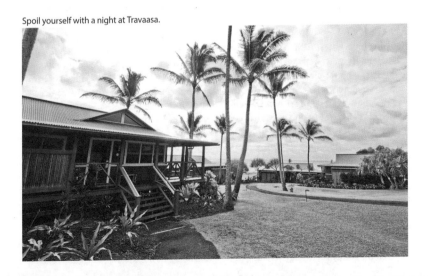

Where to Stay in East Maui

Name	Type	Price	Features	Why Stay Here?	Best For
Ala'aina Ocean Vista	B&B	$221–231	gardens, hot tub, barbecue	quiet, peaceful	couples
Aloha Surf Hostel	hostel	$30–125	kitchen	affordable, location	budget travelers
★ Bamboo Inn	B&B	$195–265	ocean-view lanai, breakfast	location, romantic	couples
Haleakala National Park: Kipahulu	camping	$15	pit toilets, barbecue	location, affordable	budget travelers
Hana Bay Hale	vacation rental	$145–245	kitchens	location, amenities	couples, families, groups
Hana Kai Maui Resort	condo	$200–300	kitchen, lanai, oceanfront	location, quiet	couples
Hana Lani Treehouses	treehouse	$135–210	gardens, cooking facilities	quiet, unique	couples
★ Huelo Point Lookout	vacation rental	$250–405	hot tub, ocean view	location, quiet, peaceful	couples
Joe's Rentals	inn	$50–60	kitchen	location, affordable	budget travelers

little dirt and the occasional bug bother you, you might want to look elsewhere.

Over $150

The boutique hotel ★ **Travaasa Hana** (5031 Hana Hwy., www.travaasa.com, $400-1,200) is the nicest place in Hana, a luxurious compound in the center of town that was the island's first resort hotel when it opened in 1946. Since that time it has continued as the island's best resort. In addition to the standard amenities of tennis courts, a swimming pool, a fitness center, and spa, Travaasa helps guests forge a meaningful connection with Hana's Hawaiian culture. Resort experiences include throw-net fishing, coconut husking, lei making, hula dancing, and ukulele classes as well as adventure activities such as horseback riding booked through the resort's concierge. Wellness and

culture permeate the resort, and for a real splurge, book one of the Ocean Bungalows with lanais facing the water. The resort has Wi-Fi but no TVs, as you're supposed to unwind, relax, untether, and breathe.

Closer to town, the funky, ultra-relaxing ★ **Bamboo Inn** (808/248-7718, www.bambooinn.com, $195-265) offers three oceanfront rooms that look out over the water toward Waikoloa Beach. A thatched-roof hut serves as the centerpiece for the property. The owner, John, is a wealth of information on Hana history and culture, and this is a modern, soothing place to fall asleep to the crash of the waves. Wi-Fi is available in the courtyard, and breakfast is included.

Condominiums

The **Hana Kai Maui Resort** (1533 Uakea Rd., 808/248-8426, www.hanakaimaui.com,

Name	Type	Price	Features	Why Stay Here?	Best For
Kuau Inn	B&B	$125–145	kitchens, lanai	location, affordable	couples, budget travelers
Maui Tradewinds	B&B	$229–422	lanai, kitchen	quiet, romantic	couples, honeymooners
Nalu Kai Lodge	inn	$135–175	oceanfront, tiki bar	location, affordable	couples
★ Pa'ia Inn	inn	$199–999	oceanfront, gardens	location, boutique	couples
Sprecks Plantation House	apartment	$95–150	kitchenette	affordable, location	budget travelers, couples
Tea House Cottage	B&B	$100–175	off the grid, gardens	location, quiet, peaceful	couples
★ The Inn at Mama's Fish House	inn	$250–850	kitchens, oceanfront	location, romantic	couples, honeymooners
★ Travaasa Hana	resort	$400–1,200	spa, pool, activities	location, luxury, amenities	couples, honeymooners
Windward Garden B&B	B&B	$165–192	lanai, gardens	location, quiet, peaceful	couples

$200-300) is the only condo in Hana. The 18 rental units are well maintained and offer a lot for the price, especially considering the condo is near the sands of Hana Bay.

Vacation Rentals

For a unique and "out there" experience, the Hana Lani Treehouses (808/248-7241, www.hanalani.maui.net, $135-210, 2-night minimum) are screened-in bungalows up in the trees, with the paths lit only by tiki torches. If you mind a few bugs, this isn't for you. This "camping with a roof" is available in these three-level "treetop" houses ($135-145) or in a more traditional bed-and-breakfast cottage ($210) that has its own electricity. Two-night minimum is usually required, but one-night stays are possible for an additional $20. The driveway down

to the property is an adventure in itself and can often be pretty bumpy.

The Hana Bay Hale (808/248-4999, www.hanabayhale.com, $145-245) looks out over Hana Bay and features three separate suites: the Kauiki and Waikoloa one-bedroom units ($145 plus $25 for 1-night stays), with kitchenettes, and the two-bedroom Hana Bay suite ($245 plus $35 for 1-night stays), with a full kitchen. The units can be combined into a single house if traveling in a large group.

KIPAHULU

One of the best parts of staying in Kipahulu is waking in the morning and having the Pools of 'Ohe'o virtually all to yourself. One of the most peaceful accommodations in this area is the Ala'aina Ocean Vista (808/248-7824, www.hanabedandbreakfast.com, $221-231 plus $50 less than 3 nights), a tropical bed-and-breakfast on four lush acres that is the exact opposite of the Ka'anapali resort experience. Birds chirp in the nearby treetops, there is a barbecue area for those who want to cook their own dinner, and a large assortment of various fruit trees sustain the daily breakfast. The bamboo forest of the Pipiwai Trail is only a short walk away. This is a romantic getaway set out in the country for those who just want to unwind. Directions to the location are provided upon booking.

Camping

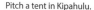

Some of Maui's best camping is in the **Kipahulu Campground** ($15 per vehicle) of Haleakala National Park. There are few things better than falling asleep to the sound of crashing surf, then waking in the morning to walk to the pools before anyone else has arrived. There are pit toilets at the campground and grassy campsites. The best sites are hidden beneath *lauhala* trees on the trail leading toward the pools. Rates for camping also cover the entrance fee to the national park. If you didn't pack camping gear, contact **Hana Camp Gear** (800/332-4022, www.hanacampgear.wordpress.com), or consider heading to Hana in an old VW camper bus you can rent from **Aloha Campers** (800/482-2070, www.alohacampers.com).

Pitch a tent in Kipahulu.

Lana'i

Look for ★ to find recommended
sights, activities, dining, and lodging.

Highlights

★ **Lana'i Culture and Heritage Center:**
Artifacts from wooden spears used in ancient
battles to old photographs of Lana'i's plantation
days adorn this cultural resource (page 268).

★ **Keahiakawelo (Garden of the Gods):**
An otherworldly landscape of tortured earth is
dotted with red boulders that appear to have
fallen from the sky (page 269).

★ **Keomoku Village:** Little more than a collection of old homes and a haunting abandoned
church, this stretch of shore shows what life on
Lana'i must have been like a century ago (page
270).

★ **Kaunolu Village:** Explore a complex that
was once the home of King Kamehameha I, virtually untouched since the 19th century (page
272).

★ **Hulopo'e Beach Park:** This crescent of
white sand has the island's best snorkeling when
the ocean is calm and its best surf on a southern
swell (page 274).

★ **Kaiolohia (Shipwreck Beach):** The
fringing reef ringing the island's northwest coast
has been the demise of dozens of ships, including the World War II Liberty ship that provides
a dramatic backdrop for this windswept beach
(page 275).

★ **Polihua Beach:** Escape to what feels like
the end of the earth on the island's northern

coast. This is the place to make the only set of
footprints in the sand (page 277).

★ **Munro Trail:** This 12.8-mile hiking trail
winds to the island's 3,370-foot summit (page
280).

I t's hard to find an outdoor playground more stunning than Lana'i, home to a mere 3,500 residents and crisscrossed by just 30 miles of paved roads.

The late 1980s saw this island's cash crop transition from the world's largest pineapple plantation to high-end tourism. With the construction of the luxurious Four Seasons Resort, the island instantly became one of Hawaii's most exclusive getaways. In 2012, Oracle CEO Larry Ellison purchased 98 percent of the island, and while a range of projects, including a winery, a college, and a tennis center, has been discussed for the tiny island, as of yet the largest change has been the spectacular renovation of the Four Seasons Resort.

Resort life aside, visitors come to enjoy the snorkeling at Hulopo'e Beach Park, and the plantation-era charm of cozy Lana'i City—the island's only town. Choose to explore a little deeper, however, with morning hikes on pine-shrouded mountain trails, off-roading through otherworldly moonscapes, and surfing empty waves along an empty beach.

Lana'i is an island of unparalleled luxury, but it's also about 4WD trucks with deer skulls mounted to the bumper, aging Filipino plantation workers "talking story" in Dole Park, and

petroglyphs scattered across rock faces that predate any of the island's modern history. It's a tight-knit community where townsfolk greet each other with first names and a smile.

ORIENTATION

The island's only town, **Lana'i City,** is in the middle of the island at about 1,700 feet elevation, 20 minutes from **Manele Harbor** and the **Four Seasons Resort Lana'i** and about 10 minutes from the **Lana'i Airport.** **Hulopo'e Beach** Park is a 10-minute walk from the harbor, and with the exception of the restaurants and shops at the resort, all of the island's stores and facilities are in Lana'i City. The rest of the island is a network of dirt roads perfect for off-road exploring, with many sights 45 minutes to an hour outside Lana'i City.

PLANNING YOUR TIME

Most people visit Lana'i as a day trip from Maui. If you take the 6:45am ferry from Lahaina Harbor, you have 8 to 10 hours

---

Previous: Keahiakawelo, or Garden of the Gods; sunset at Kaunolu. **Above:** Spinner dolphins are a common sight on the southwestern coast of Lana'i.

Lana'i

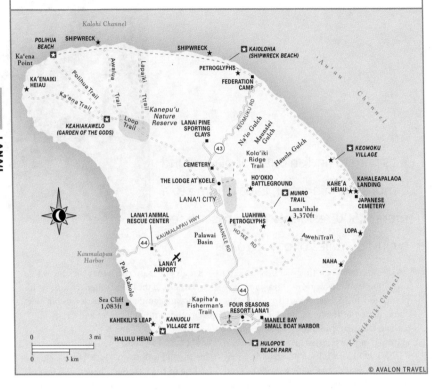

© AVALON TRAVEL

to explore the island before catching the ferry back. You'll have enough time to visit Hulopo'e Beach and do some snorkeling, hiking, and sunbathing, as well as time to rent a Jeep and explore the island's east shore. If you spend a couple of nights on Lana'i, you'll have enough time to explore the island's remote and isolated spots and still be able to relax and enjoy the island's slow pace.

Sights

★ LANA'I CULTURE AND HERITAGE CENTER

There's no better place to learn about the history of Lana'i than at the **Lana'i Culture and Heritage Center** (730 Lana'i Ave., 808/565-7177, www.lanaichc.org, 8:30am-3:30pm Mon.-Fri., 9am-1pm Sat., free admission). Started in 2007 in a building adjacent to the Hotel Lana'i, the exceptionally informative little museum features displays pertaining to the days of ancient Hawaii through the end of the Dole plantation. Black-and-white photos from Lana'i's ranching days are joined by stone adzes, poi pounders, and a 10-foot-long 'ihe pololu wooden spear used as a weapon similar to a jousting lance. More than just a collection

Your Best Day on Lana'i

If you're visiting Lana'i as a day trip from Maui, get an early start by taking the 6:45am ferry. Make ferry reservations beforehand, and arrange for a 4WD vehicle to use on Lana'i for the day. When you arrive on Lana'i at 7:45am, take the shuttle to Lana'i City if you're renting a Jeep from **Dollar,** or if you've rented a Jeep through a local company, it might be waiting at the harbor.

Grab breakfast at **Coffee Works** by 8:30am, and pick up water and snacks at **Richard's Supermarket.** Drive to **Shipwreck Beach** and then make your way down the eastern shore to **Keomoku Village.** It's five more minutes to **Kahalepalaoa** and an empty white-sand beach, and 15 more minutes to **Lopa** beach, better protected from the wind.

Once you've left your footprints in the sand, drive for an hour back to Lana'i City for a late lunch at **Blue Ginger.** Spend 30 minutes strolling **Lana'i City** to check out the local shops, and if you rented from Dollar, return the Jeep and take the shuttle down to Manele Harbor (there's usually a shuttle around 3:30pm). Instead of going to the harbor, however, see if they can drop you at **Hulopo'e Beach Park,** where you'll swim, sunbathe, and if you brought gear, snorkel at the nicest beach on Lana'i.

If you're feeling festive, head up to the **Four Seasons Resort** for a drink at the ocean-view pool bar, or hike to **Pu'u Pehe Overlook** as the sun sinks low in the sky. It's a 10-minute walk to Manele Harbor, where the 6:45pm ferry will take you back to Lahaina.

Rainy day? Take the rain as an opportunity to explore Lana'i City in depth. Just like a sunny day, start with breakfast and coffee at **Coffee Works,** and then walk off breakfast by exploring the **shops** that circle around Dole Park. Grab lunch at **Blue Ginger,** and then head to **Lana'i Culture and Heritage Center** for a dose of the island's history. Finish with dinner at Lana'i City Grille inside of Hotel Lana'i.

of historical photos and artifacts, the center also highlights how the culture of Lana'i has been influenced by historical events.

KANEPU'U PRESERVE

Six miles down Polihua Road, just before reaching Keahiakawelo (Garden of the Gods), **Kanepu'u Preserve** is the only remaining dryland forest of its kind in Hawaii. Thanks to a fence erected in 1918 by Lana'i Ranch manager George Munro, this 590-acre preserve is home to 48 species of native Hawaiian plants that covered most of the island prior to the arrival of the invasive *kiawe* tree and root-destroying goats and sheep. Managed by the Nature Conservancy, the preserve features a short, self-guided trail where visitors can see native hardwoods such as *lama* (Hawaiian ebony) and *olopua* (Hawaiian olive). The trail only takes about 15 minutes to walk, and it makes a nice stop before exploring the Garden of the Gods.

★ KEAHIAKAWELO (GARDEN OF THE GODS)

Although we've successfully put a rover on Mars, **Keahiakawelo** is the closest most of us will ever get to walking on the red planet. Despite being only seven miles from the pine-lined streets of Lana'i City, the Garden of the Gods looks like a moonscape. Erosion created ravines and rock spires in deep reds, purples, and sulfuric yellows. The best time to visit this dry, dusty, and often windswept area is at sunset, when the rich palette of color is enhanced by the afternoon light.

Keahiakawelo is almost completely devoid of vegetation, but the strangest part of the panorama is the expanse of boulders that tumble over the barren hillside. It's unclear how they got here, but the ancient Hawaiians had a number of theories. According to legend, the rocks were dropped by gods as they tended their heavenly gardens, providing the site's English name, Garden of the Gods.

Keahiakawelo remains a must-see for the

consuming sense of seclusion. The road here can be rutted and rough, and a 4WD vehicle is needed if you're visiting after a heavy rain. To reach the site, take a left just after the Lodge at Koele and travel seven miles on Polihua Road, taking the right at the fork after the Koele Stables.

KA'ENA IKI HEIAU

On the dusty stretch of road between Keahiakawelo and Polihua Beach, a side road branches off to the left and leads to the island's westernmost promontory, Ka'ena Point. The deep waters off Ka'ena make this a favorite among islanders for fishing. The main reason to venture down Ka'ena Trail, however, is to see **Ka'ena Iki Heiau,** a large stone platform constructed in the 17th century and the largest remaining *heiau* on Lana'i. It doesn't take long to explore the area around the *heiau,* but it makes a nice side trip.

★ KEOMOKU VILLAGE

There isn't much to see in the abandoned village of **Keomoku,** but driving through this coastal ghost town provides a feeling of Lana'i's recent past. It also makes a great stop if you are heading out to the beach at Lopa.

Before the arrival of Europeans, it's believed there were thousands of indigenous Hawaiians living along Lana'i's eastern shore. *Heiau* were constructed as places of worship, and petroglyphs such as those found at Kaiolohia depict basic scenes from this ancient time. By the time Frederick Hayselden chose Keomoku as the site for his Maunalei Sugar Company in 1899, however, the island's population had dwindled to fewer than 200. Water was routed from Maunalei Valley, a locomotive was installed to move cargo, and Keomoku bustled like any other Hawaiian plantation town. Problems arose when the water turned brackish, and the supply at Maunalei quickly dried up.

In one of the state's shortest-lived sugar ventures, the Maunalei Sugar Company closed in 1901 after only two years in operation. Indigenous Hawaiians living in the area attribute the company's demise to the stones from ancient *heiau* being used in constructing the plantation. This, it would seem, did not sit well with Hawaiian deities. In 1951 the last resident of Keomoku—Daniel Kaopuiki—begrudgingly moved his family into the uplands, and Keomoku, once the pulse of the island of Lana'i, was officially abandoned.

Keomoku remains abandoned, and there are a couple of places where you can see

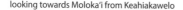

looking towards Moloka'i from Keahiakawelo

The Myth of the "Private Island"

A pesky myth needs to be dispelled: Lana'i is not a private island. It's true that the island has historically had only one main landowner, and today 98 percent of the island is owned by Oracle CEO Larry Ellison. However, the state of Hawaii retains ownership of certain parcels, such as the Manele Small Boat Harbor, and many local families own their own homes. You do not need to ask permission from the primary landowner to come here. There is a public airport and regular ferry service, and there are 3,500 full-time residents.

Imagine that you live in a neighborhood where there are 100 homes and you somehow manage to buy 98 of them. You still live in a neighborhood that's in a U.S. state and subject to its laws. Even on a mostly private island, you can't just do whatever you want. There are police officers, firefighters, a public school, a county council member, and myriad laws that apply. Under Hawaii state law, all shores from the ocean up to the line of vegetation is for public use. Consequently there is no such thing as a private beach in Hawaii. On this "private island," anyone can freely walk the shore.

the remnants of its past. Driving the sandy 4WD road through the former plantation town is a tour through Lana'i's history. Simple beachfront fishing shacks dot the sandy road, their yards ringed with fishing nets.

The number-one attraction in Keomoku is **Ka Lanakila Church,** 5.5 miles from where the pavement ends on Keomoku Highway. The hauntingly beautiful wooden structure was constructed in 1903 to house a Hawaiian-speaking congregation. Abandoned for years, the church is currently in the process of being restored, and special sermons are still intermittently conducted in Hawaiian throughout the year.

Behind the church, a small trail leads for 10 minutes to remains of the Maunalei Sugar Mill, and across the street, a trail passes through the coconut grove to the wooden Lahaina passenger boat that has sat in the mud for more than a century. A small shrine 1.5 miles past the church honors the Japanese field laborers who died on Lana'i in the few short years of the sugar plantation's existence, and 0.5 mile beyond the shrine is the

Ka Lanakila Church in Keomoku Village

abandoned pier at Kahalepalaoa, which offers good fishing and sweeping views of neighboring Maui.

LUAHIWA PETROGLYPHS

The good thing about the **Luahiwa Petroglyphs** is they are only 10 minutes from Lana'i City and accessible with a regular car. The bad part is they have been permanently scarred by modern graffiti, and they no longer resemble the rock art they once were. There are nearly 1,000 drawings at Luahiwa, and stepping from one rock to another reveals different tales emblazoned on the out-of-place boulder formations. While 95 percent of the drawings date before Western contact, some etchings, such as those featuring horses, suggest that the petroglyphs are a multigenerational canvas that records Lana'i's varied history.

To reach the Luahiwa Petroglyphs, head south on Manele Road from Lana'i City as if you're driving down toward Hulopo'e Beach Park. After 1.5 miles, turn left at a small building on the left side of the road. When you find a locked gate, proceed to the dirt road that immediately parallels it on the left side. Head down this road for 0.7 mile until you reach a Y-junction, at which point you go left again. After 0.3 mile, make an extreme right turn, almost doubling back the way you came, up onto a higher road. If you're unsure if this is the correct turn, look for a rock just after the intersection that has the name "Luahiwa Petroglyphs" emblazed on it facing the opposite direction. Proceed for 0.4 mile on the upper road until you reach another rock that says "Luahiwa," and park in the small dirt pullout. The petroglyphs are on the large boulders at the base of the hill, and a 30-second scramble through the bushes will bring you face-to-face with the ancient rock carvings.

★ KAUNOLU VILLAGE

Kaunolu is difficult to reach, but it is a historically significant place, and its isolation has kept it undeveloped and virtually untouched. Follow Highway 440 south from Lana'i City.

Lost on Lana'i

If you need a helping hand trying to plan an outing to Lana'i, the locally based **Lost On Lana'i** (808/215-0201, www.lostonlanai. com) is a one-stop shop for booking activities and ferry transportation to the island. They offer combo deals that you won't find elsewhere and can also answer questions about the island. With over 300 miles of dirt roads leading every which way, you want to make sure you don't actually end up getting lost on Lana'i.

Just past the airport turnoff is a large boulder inscribed with "Kaunolu." Turn left on the smooth, dusty road, accessible to any vehicle provided it hasn't rained heavily. After two miles is a historical marker and another sign pointing toward Kaunolu. Make a right down this road, which is steep, eroded, and rough. Dollar allows their Jeeps to go to the top of the road but not all the way to the bottom. To reach the bottom, you can chance it with the Jeep and hope for the best, procure a private vehicle that has no restrictions, or drive until the road gets too rough and then get out and walk, which is probably the best option. It's three miles from here to the shore.

At the bottom of the road is a Y-junction. The road to the left leads to a set of fishing shacks used by locals who come to drink beer and fish, but turn right instead. The road abruptly ends at a wooden picnic table beneath a tree, marking the entrance to Kaunolu. This shore was home to a thriving population from the 15th century until it was abandoned in the late 19th century. Notice that except for the wind and the waves, Kaunolu is completely silent.

The sandy ravine fronting the beach is the only successful canoe launch between here and Hulopo'e. To reach the remains of the ancient canoe *hale* (house), look for a trail that leads down the hill from where the road ends. After a rocky scramble to the dry riverbed, and follow the trail toward the water, passing

Lana'i City

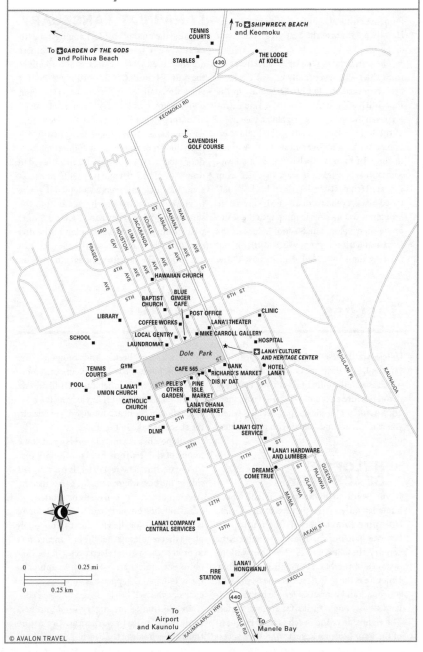

TENNIS COURTS

To ★SHIPWRECK BEACH and Keomoku

To ★GARDEN OF THE GODS and Polihua Beach

STABLES

THE LODGE AT KOELE

430

KEOMOKU RD

CAVENDISH GOLF COURSE

3RD
FRASER AVE
GAY AVE
HOUSTON AVE
ILIMA AVE
JACARANDA AVE
KOELE AVE
LANAII AVE
MAHANA AVE
NANI ST
ST
ST
ST

4TH AVE

HAWAIIAN CHURCH

5TH AVE

BAPTIST CHURCH

BLUE GINGER CAFE

6TH ST

LIBRARY

COFFEE WORKS

POST OFFICE

LANA'I THEATER

CLINIC

SCHOOL

LOCAL GENTRY

MIKE CARROLL GALLERY

HOSPITAL

LAUNDROMAT

Dole Park

ST

★LANA'I CULTURE AND HERITAGE CENTER

PUULANI PL

KAUNAOA

TENNIS COURTS

GYM

CAFE 565

BANK

HOTEL LANA'I

POOL

LANA'I UNION CHURCH

8TH

PELE'S OTHER GARDEN

PINE ISLE MARKET

RICHARD'S MARKET

DIS N' DAT

ST

CATHOLIC CHURCH

LANA'I OHANA POKE MARKET

POLICE

9TH

LANA'I CITY SERVICE

ST

DLNR

10TH

11TH

LANA'I HARDWARE AND LUMBER

ST

ST

QUEENS

DREAMS COME TRUE

PALAWAI

OLAPA

AHA

MANA

12TH

ST

LANA'I COMPANY CENTRAL SERVICES

13TH

AKAHI ST

LANA'I HONGWANJI

FIRE STATION

AKOLU

440

KAUMALAPAU HWY

MANELE RD

To Airport and Kaunolu

To Manele Bay

© AVALON TRAVEL

0   0.25 mi

0   0.25 km

some petroglyphs. An interpretive placard points out the canoe *hale*. This is the base of the Halulu *heiau*, a place of worship and of immense cultural significance to indigenous Hawaiians. It's also the best preserved *heiau* on Lana'i.

The trail bends to the right as it climbs up from the rocks, eventually crossing a footbridge toward the top of the *heiau*. Up the short hill is a Y-junction. Go left to find petroglyphs in the rocks, or go right to a viewpoint of the Kaholo Pali sea cliffs, the highest on Lana'i, with some over 1,000 feet. A notch in the cliff here is labeled Kahekili's Leap. Kahekili was a fearless warrior chief from the late 18th century, with half his body tattooed black, eyelids and tongue included. He brought warriors here to jump into the sea to prove their valor. The 80-foot height of the *lele kawa* (cliff jumping) wasn't difficult, but clearing the 15-foot ledge at the base of the cliff was. Medical help is far away; don't even consider jumping.

LANA'I CAT SANCTUARY

While some might consider hanging out with cats as a weird way to spend a vacation, others are enamored with the dozens of fur balls at the quirky **Lana'i Cat Sanctuary** (808/215-9066, www.lanaianimalrescue.org, 11am-3pm daily). Known as the "Little Lions" of Lana'i, all of these felines are rescues that were once feral on Lana'i, today exchanging petting for purr-filled moments at their comfortable outdoor sanctuary. Volunteers are encouraged to drop by and help pet and play with the cats—some of which can even be adopted if you're interested in taking one home. To find the sanctuary, drive from Lana'i City 0.6 mile past the airport, and make a left at the dirt road with the "Kaunolu" sign on the rock. Just after you make the turn, the sanctuary is on the right.

Beaches

Unless you have a 4WD or high-clearance vehicle, Lana'i only has one accessible beach, which is also the only one with any facilities. If you procure a Jeep or a local's truck, there are a number of undeveloped beaches where you can run around naked with no one there to care.

★ HULOPO'E BEACH PARK

If you want to make your friends back home jealous, snap a picture of this beach. **Hulopo'e Beach Park** is the undisputed favorite hangout for islanders, named the country's best beach in 1997. Within walking distance of the Manele Small Boat Harbor, Hulopo'e is the only beach on the island with restrooms and showers. Despite being the island's most popular, it's far from crowded. The right side of the beach is used by guests of the Four Seasons Resort, who have access to the white umbrellas and lounge chairs. Similarly, guests of Trilogy Excursions' snorkel tour from Maui inhabit the left-hand side of the beach Monday-Friday, leaving the middle section of the beach for visitors to relax in the shade or bake in the sun.

Hulopo'e Bay is a marine reserve and home to one of the few reefs in Maui County that isn't in decline. The reef extends over the left side of the bay, where colorful parrotfish the size of your forearm can easily be spotted and heard nibbling on the vibrant corals. Hulopo'e is also famous for the Hawaiian spinner dolphins that regularly enter the bay. In an effort to protect the natural sleep cycles of the dolphins, swimmers are asked not to approach them. If dolphins happen to swim toward you, consider yourself lucky.

In addition to the sugary sand and perfectly placed palm trees, there are two nature trails on each side of the beach. The **Kapiha'a**

Fisherman's Trail departs from the right side of the bay, and the **Trail to Pu'u Pehe Overlook** starts from the left side. There is also a fantastic system of tide pools stretching around the left point of the bay, and one is even deep enough to teach young children to snorkel. The easiest way to get to the tide pools is to use the stairway on the trail to Pu'u Pehe Overlook.

★ KAIOLOHIA (SHIPWRECK BEACH)

The most popular beach among island visitors after Hulopo'e is **Kaiolohia,** also called **Shipwreck Beach.** To get to Shipwreck, drive past the Lodge at Koele and down Lana'i's windswept "back side" by following the switchbacking, but paved, Keomoku Highway. The views as you descend this winding road stretch all the way to neighboring Maui. A favorite pastime of island teenagers during the plantation days was to flash their headlights at family members on Maui at a prearranged time, then wait eagerly for their cousins to flash them back (Did I mention life on Lana'i can be slow?).

Once you reach the bottom of the paved highway, a sign points left toward Shipwreck Beach. Follow the sandy road (4WD recommended) for 1.5 miles before it deadends in a parking area. When you pass the shacks built out of driftwood and fishing floats, you've arrived.

Traditionally this area was known as Kaiolohia. The current moniker originates with the unnamed World War II Liberty ship that was intentionally grounded on the fringing reef. Numerous vessels have met their demise on this shallow stretch of coral, but this concrete oil tanker has deteriorated more slowly than most. Stoic in its haunted appearance, the ship remains firmly lodged in the reef as a warning to passing vessels of the dangers.

Because of the persistent northeasterly trade winds, Kaiolohia is rarely suitable for snorkeling or swimming. Your time is better spent combing the beach for flotsam: Japanese glass balls used as fishing floats are the beachcomber's ultimate reward. To reach the Liberty ship is about a mile's walk along the sandy shore, although numerous rocks interrupt the thin strip of sand to give the appearance of multiple beaches. From here it's technically possible to walk all the way to Polihua Beach, but unless you have arranged a ride at the other side, it's a 16-mile round-trip venture in an area with no services or

Splash in the tide pools of Hulopo'e Beach Park.

LANA'I
BEACHES

Lana'i's Other Shipwreck Beach

Besides Shipwreck Beach, a second wreck off Lana'i, the Navy ship YO-21, is hardly ever visited. Take your 4WD vehicle seven miles out along Polihua Road to Keahiakawelo (Garden of the Gods), and make a right onto Awalua Road. This steep, eroded trail offers sweeping views across the Kalohi Channel to neighboring Moloka'i before you arrive, three miles later, at a coastal outpost known as Awalua. The Dollar Jeep rental company doesn't recommend going down this road, so if you choose to drive to Awalua, you're doing so at your own risk—stay out of the deep sand. There are multiple pullouts on the side of the road if you want to drive part of the way and walk to the beach. The reward is a narrow stretch of coast where you'll be the only person, and the chance to view a rusting ship that was stationed at Pearl Harbor on the morning of the Japanese bombing in 1941. Just like at the better-known Shipwreck Beach, photographing the ship and beachcombing are safer options than trying to swim.

Aside from the wrecks at Awalua and Kaiolohia, hundreds of ships have met their demise on this remote stretch of reef. In 1826 the U.S. ship *London* sank here with a large amount of gold and silver aboard, only a portion of which was ever recovered. No divers have ever come back carrying gold bullion, however, so whatever treasure may remain has been lost to the sea.

shade. Walking as far as the ship gives you ample time to explore.

Make a side trip to visit the **petroglyphs** on your way back to the car. About 0.25 mile after the road ends, you'll encounter the concrete base of what was once a lighthouse. If you're uncertain whether you're at the right place, check the concrete base, where names were inscribed in 1929. From the base of the lighthouse, turn directly inland and rock-hop for 300 yards until you'll see a large rock with "Do not deface" written on it. A white arrow points to a trail behind the rock that leads to petroglyphs of dogs, humans, and a drawing known as "The Birdman."

KAHALEPALAOA

When you reach the bottom of Keomoku Highway, where the pavement ends, take a right at the fork in the road, which leads to a rugged coastal track that ranks as one of the best drives on the island. A 4WD vehicle is

the famous shipwreck of Kaiolohia

LOPA

Just over one mile past Kahalepalaoa is **Lopa,** a protected stretch of sand that is the nicest on Lana'i's back side. Although the beach isn't that different from Kahalepalaoa, Lopa faces south, so it's more protected from the northeasterly trade winds, which makes reading a book in a beach chair infinitely more enjoyable. Lopa is a popular camping spot for locals, and a couple of picnic tables have been placed beneath the thorn-riddled *kiawe* (mesquite) grove lining the beach. Although the swimming and snorkeling are poor compared to Hulopo'e Beach Park, Lopa is the perfect place for longboard surfing or paddling along the shore in a kayak (if you brought one). The chances of encountering anyone else on Lopa are higher on the weekend, when locals come to camp and fish, but as at many of Lana'i's beaches, if there happens to be anyone else, it's considered crowded.

kayaking waves off Lopa

recommended, as the deep sand patches can drift onto the road, and depending on recent rains, the road can become rutted and rough. Nevertheless, some of Lana'i's nicest beaches are down this road, and provided there aren't enormous puddles, anyone with a Jeep or SUV should be able to navigate it.

While there are a number of small pullouts along the side of the road leading to narrow windswept beaches, the first beach of any size is **Kahalepalaoa,** 7.5 miles from where the pavement ended. The name translates to "House of the Whale Ivory"; whale bones are believed to have washed ashore and were then used to build a dwelling. In more recent times this spot was also the site of a Club Med-style day resort named Club Lana'i. The booze-fueled excursion from Maui no longer operates, but the coconut grove that once housed the venue marks the start of a long white-sand beach that's perfect for casual strolling.

★ POLIHUA BEACH

Polihua is so remote that even Lana'i residents consider it "out there." A vast, windswept, and often completely empty stretch of sand, Polihua is utterly unrivaled in its seclusion. If you've ever fantasized about placing the only set of footprints on a deserted beach, this is the place to do it. The name Polihua derives from a Hawaiian term for "eggs in the bosom," a reference to the green sea turtles that haul out on the sand to bury eggs on the isolated shore.

The strong currents at Polihua make the water unsafe for swimming, and oftentimes the afternoon trade winds turn the entire beach into a curtain of blowing sand. The morning hours are best for a relaxing stroll through the sand dunes, and by sunset the winds have usually died down enough to watch the sun sink behind the northwest horizon. With views that stretch across the Kalohi Channel toward Moloka'i, this is one of the last beaches in Hawaii where it's still possible to feel alone.

A 4WD vehicle is imperative to reach Polihua. Travel seven miles from Lana'i City on Polihua Road to Keahiakawelo. Continue on the same road for another 25 minutes as it switchbacks down the rutted dirt track before reaching its terminus a few yards short of the beach. There are no services, so if you visit Polihua, remember to bring water and food, and to pack out everything you brought with you.

Snorkeling and Diving

SNORKELING

When it comes to snorkeling, **Hulopo'e Beach Park** easily trumps any other place on the island for the health of the reef, clarity of the water, and variety of fish. Thanks to its protected status as a marine preserve, the reef is in better shape than other places on the island, and snorkelers will revel in the large schools of *manini* (convict tang) and vibrant *uhu* (parrotfish) that flit around the shallow reef. The best snorkeling in the bay is on the left side of the beach. Since Hulopo'e faces south, it can be prone to large surf and shorebreak April to October. The shore-break can make entry and exit to the water a little challenging, and the visibility won't be as good as on days that are calmer.

Nevertheless, even a mediocre day at Hulopo'e is better than a good day at many other places. The reef never gets deeper than 25 feet. Occasionally Hawaiian spinner dolphins venture into the bay, although they usually hang out over the sand on the right, closer to the hotel.

Not far from Hulopo'e but equally as gorgeous is the vibrant reef at **Manele Bay.** Don't confuse this with snorkeling in Manele Harbor; that would be disgusting. The reef at Manele Bay is on the opposite side of the break wall between the harbor and the cliffs. Entry from shore can be tricky, since you have to come off the rocks, but if you follow the driveway of the harbor all the way to the far end, there is a little opening in the rocks where it's possible to make a graceful entry. Schools of tropical reef fish gather in abundance, and the spinner dolphins sometimes hang out in this area as well. Although Manele Bay is 0.25 mile from Hulopo'e Beach, it's still part of the marine preserve, so the same rules apply: Don't stand on the coral, and don't feed the fish. It's best not to touch anything at all.

There isn't anywhere on Lana'i to rent snorkeling equipment for the day, so your best bet is to bring your own. The snorkeling equipment at Hulopo'e Beach is only for Trilogy's day guests who come from Maui, and the gear at the Four Seasons beach kiosk is exclusively for hotel guests.

If you want to explore the island's remoter reefs, only accessible by boat, **Trilogy Excursions** (1 Manele Harbor Dr., 808/874-5649, $250 pp) provides the only snorkel charter service operating on Lana'i. The 3.5-hour snorkeling and sailing excursion usually heads around the southwestern coast to the towering sea cliffs of Kaunolu, also known as Shark Fin Cove due to the dorsal fin-shaped rock in the middle of the bay. There can occasionally be other boats from Maui here, but more often than not this trip provides the opportunity to snorkel the waters of the historic fishing village with only a handful of others. Given that Kaunolu is exposed to the deeper waters offshore, snorkelers intermittently see pelagic species such as spinner dolphins, bottlenose dolphins, eagle rays, manta rays, and whale sharks. If there's wind on the way back to Manele, the crew will hoist the sails, and since bookings are sporadic due to the low numbers on Lana'i, call the Maui office ahead of time to inquire about a charter.

SCUBA DIVING

Lana'i has some of the best diving in the state, with 14 named dive sites along the school of *manini* at Hulopo'e Beach Park

southwestern coast. The most famous are **First** and **Second Cathedrals.** At First Cathedral, just offshore from Manele Harbor, the cavern entrance is at 58 feet. Inside, beams of sunlight filter down through the ceiling like light passing through a stained-glass window. There have even been a few underwater weddings here.

The best way to exit the cathedral is via a hole in the wall known locally as The Shotgun, where divers place their hands on the sides of the cathedral and allow the current to wash through a narrow opening. In addition to the main cathedral, there are a number of other swim-throughs and arches where you can catch a glimpse of spiny lobsters, frogfish, colorful parrotfish, and if you're lucky, a pod of spinner dolphins passing overhead.

Down the coast at Second Cathedral, the underwater dome is about the same size but intersected by so many openings it looks like Swiss cheese. Divers can pass in and out of the cathedral from a variety of different entry points. The highlight is a rare black coral tree that dangles from the cathedral ceiling. Large schools of *ta'ape* (blue-striped snapper) congregate on the back side of the cathedral, and you can swim through a school that numbers in the hundreds. Visibility at both of these sites regularly reaches 80 to 120 feet, and the water can be so clear that you see most of the dive site standing on the pontoon of the boat.

The most affordable way to dive off Lana'i is with a boat from Maui. The island's only dive operator, **Trilogy Excursions** (808/874-5649), only offers private charters with high prices, mainly as an amenity for the Four Seasons Resort. Check with dive operators in Lahaina about the best way to dive off Lana'i.

Surfing

SURF SPOTS
Hulopo'e Beach Park
Hulopo'e Beach Park is the island's most popular surf spot. Since it faces south, it's exposed to southerly swells, which means April to October are the best for finding surf. This left point break can be challenging, however, and it's not for beginners. The wave breaks over a shallow coral reef and the takeoff can be steep, although when Hulopo'e is firing, it can be one of the best summer waves in Maui County. The long lefthander will hold its size 2 to 12 feet. Be careful of the inside section, which can carry you straight into the shore-break.

Lopa
Lopa is the island's preeminent beginner wave, and just because it's user-friendly doesn't mean that it can't be a great ride. A beach break with multiple peaks, the waves at Lopa aren't usually as steep and are

better suited for longboards and nose-riding. Winter months can be flat, but on summer days there's almost always something to ride. You'll have to bring your own board and provide your own transportation. To reach Lopa, take Keomoku Highway to where the paved road ends, then take a right and proceed for nine miles.

RENTAL OPERATORS

Although things might change in the near future now that the resort is open again, there currently isn't anywhere to rent a board on Lana'i. You can either bring your own on the ferry, or call the Lana'i Ambassador desk (808/565-2388) at the Four Seasons Resort to inquire.

Hiking and Biking

HIKING
★ Munro Trail

Munro Trail doesn't look like anywhere else on Lana'i, or in Hawaii. This 12.8-mile dirt road is more like the Pacific Northwest than the tropics. Wandering around the stands of Cook pines is one of Lana'i's most iconic adventures. Get up early, throw on a light jacket, and head into the uplands, where the smell of eucalyptus wafts through an understory of ironwoods and pines. For clear skies and dry conditions, it's best to hike Munro Trail in the morning hours before enveloping clouds blow in on the trades.

To reach Munro Trail, travel past the Lodge at Koele on Keomoku Highway until you reach a sign for Cemetery Road, where you make a right just before the first mile marker. On Cemetery Road, the pavement turns to dirt and then branches off to the left, bringing you to the start of the trail. Technically Munro Trail is a single-lane dirt road navigable by anyone with a 4WD vehicle. The Dollar Jeep rental company doesn't allow its Jeeps to go on the steep and potentially muddy track, and even Hummers occasionally get stuck. The other option is to park at the trailhead and make the 5.5-mile (one-way) hike to the summit, stopping at lookouts along the way.

The first lookout, starting from Cemetery Road, is Koloiki Ridge, about 2.5 miles into the trail. A small red-and-white sign on the left side of the trail points the way to the ridge, and after a brief 0.25-mile jaunt, you are rewarded with grandiose views back into Maunalei Gulch and out to the islands of Maui and Moloka'i. This lookout is also accessible as part of the Koloiki Ridge Trail hike, which starts behind the Lodge at Koele.

Back on the main trail, continue for a couple of miles beneath a shroud of forest until you pass some communication towers. Just past the towers is Ho'okio Gulch, a place that forever transformed Lana'i. In 1778 Kahekili, ruler of Lana'i and Maui, was besieged by Kalaniopu'u, a powerful chief from the Big Island whose army featured a fearless young warrior named Kamehameha. In the battle at Ho'okio, Kahekili and his warriors attempted to defend the island from the invading warriors by slinging stones down from the hilltop and hiding in crevasses carved into the cliff face. Ultimately, Kahekili and his men were defeated, and the ensuing occupation of Lana'i by Kalaniopu'u and his army drove the resource-strapped island into famine, which decimated much of the population. It's said that the spirits of those who perished in the battle still reside in the cool forests and keep watch over the eroded gulches and canyons.

Finally, after you've climbed an uphill section of trail, 5.5 miles from the end of Cemetery Road you'll find the 3,370-foot summit of Lana'ihale, or The Hale, as it's known to locals. This is the only point in Hawaii where it's possible to see five other islands on the clearest days, and during winter even the snowcapped peaks of Mauna Kea and Mauna Loa on the Big Island can be seen, over 100 miles southeast. If you continue the length

Lana'i on Horseback

Lana'i is steeped in its ranching heritage. The island was once a huge sheep and cattle ranch where *paniolos* roamed the terrain on horseback. Cattle no longer roam, but the island's ranching heritage lives on at the **Stables at Koele** (1 Keomoku Hwy.), where local guides who are authentic *paniolos* offer guided trail rides (1.5 hours, $190 pp) through the Lana'i City hinterlands. Keep an eye out for axis deer or mouflon sheep as you ride at your own pace on excursions geared to your skill level. The knowledgeable guides fortify the excursion with tales of the island's history. Rides are booked through the activities desk at the Four Seasons Resort (808/565-2000).

of the trail, it descends for seven miles down the southern side of the ridge, past turnoffs for the Awehi and Naha trails, and eventually emerges in the remains of old pineapple fields at Highway 440 (Manele Rd.).

Pu'u Pehe Overlook

This often photographed sea stack is an iconic symbol of Lana'i and is one of the most scenic places on the island. It's not possible to climb onto Pu'u Pehe, but the **Pu'u Pehe Overlook Trail** offers hikers a sweeping panorama of the rock and the surrounding coast. To reach the overlook, take the dirt road at the south end of Hulopo'e Beach Park (the side opposite the resort) and follow it for 100 yards until it reaches a set of stairs leading down to the tide pools. From here the road becomes a trail that wraps left across the headland before reaching a hidden sandy cove popular with bodyboarders and nudist sunbathers. To get down to this sandy cove, known as Shark's Bay, requires a scramble through a chute in the rocky cliff that involves some risk.

To reach the overlook, carefully follow the edge of the cliff until it reaches a promontory about 100 feet above the shimmering reef below. Aside from the sweeping vista, it's also possible to get a good view from here of the *heiau* that stands atop Pu'u Pehe, an archaeological site that is a mystery given that it's nearly impossible to access the top of the rock.

Kapiha'a Fisherman's Trail

The **Kapiha'a Fisherman's Trail** begins on the side of Hulopo'e Beach in front of the Four Seasons Resort and meanders past the mega-mansions on the point. Well-marked

LANA'I
HIKING AND BIKING

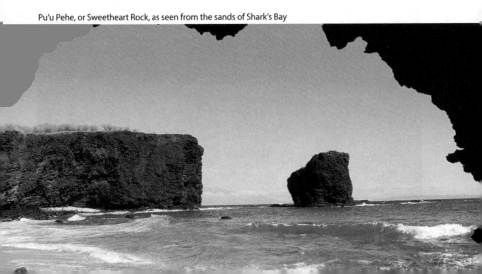

Pu'u Pehe, or Sweetheart Rock, as seen from the sands of Shark's Bay

by a natural stone walkway, this 1.5-mile trail hugs the rocky coast as it weaves its way through the ancient village of Kapiha'a. Little remains of the village today, but various historical markers point out the location of *heiau* still visible in the area.

Even though this trail catches the coastal breezes off the surrounding water, there is little shade. Given the rugged nature of the path, wear closed-toe shoes. After the trail reaches a dramatic terminus atop sea cliffs on the back nine of the golf course, an easier return route is to follow the cart path back to the golf clubhouse.

Koloiki Ridge Trail

An offshoot of the Munro Trail, the **Koloiki Ridge Trail** is a five-mile out-and-back hike that begins directly behind the Four Seasons Koele Resort. On a nice day, this is the perfect way to spend two or three hours. Walking the trail is like taking a historical tour through Lana'i's past.

To reach the trailhead, go to the main entrance of the Four Seasons Koele Resort and then follow the service road toward the golf clubhouse. Once you reach the main clubhouse, another paved service road running behind the fairway ultimately leads to the

trailhead. Along the initial paved section of trail, you'll encounter white-and-red signs on the trail as part of an interpretive map available at the hotel's concierge desk.

Once the dirt trail begins, you'll find yourself walking beneath a canopy of ironwood trees and Cook pines that predate the luxury hotels. Planted in 1912 by the botanist George Munro, the pines were used as a means of securing water by trapping moisture from the passing clouds, and even today they still play a major role in providing water for the island's residents.

Making a right at the red-and-white sign marked "10" places you directly on the Munro Trail. About 0.5 miles down Munro Trail at sign number 17, an arrow points the way down to the dramatic Koloiki Ridge. Once out from beneath the canopy of trees, you'll notice that the ridge is flanked on both sides by dramatic gulches. From this often windy vantage point at the end of the trail, the islands of Moloka'i and Maui appear on the horizon beyond the deep blue Pailolo Channel. When facing the islands, on the left side of the ridge is Naio Gulch, a dry rock-strewn canyon where you can occasionally catch a glimpse of the island's elusive mouflon sheep. On the right is Maunalei Gulch, a deep cleft in the island

Maunalei Valley from the Koloiki Ridge Trail

that once had the island's only free-flowing stream. If you look closely on the valley floor, you can still see an old service road leading to a pump house. Water from Maunalei once fed the island's sugar plantation.

BIKING

Unless you brought your own bicycle over on the ferry, the best option for biking on Lana'i is with **Lanai Cycles** (808/563-0565, www.lanaicycles.com), where a three-hour guided sunrise tour involves winding down the backside of Lana'i with only a handful of other people. Unlike the bike tours on neighboring Maui that can involve hundreds of people, here a small group rides on roads that are virtually empty. An 8am start time can be arranged if you're arriving on the ferry from Maui; otherwise tours start 20 minutes before sunrise in Lana'i City.

UTV RIDING

An alternative to renting a Jeep for the day is to tour the island's bumpy back roads on a Polaris UTV. These all-terrain vehicles are a thrill to drive and can handle the challenging terrain. The two-hour tours can be booked directly through the Four Seasons Resort activity desk (808/565-2000, $248 pp, $395 per couple).

Golf

Effective in 2016, unless you're a guest of the Four Seasons Resort or have a Hawaii ID, you can't golf at the famous Jack Nicklaus-designed **Manele Golf Course** (1 Manele Bay Rd., 808/565-2000). If you are able to play, prepare for a round with sweeping ocean views and tee shots over the water, and a 19th-hole clubhouse where you can often see dolphins splashing in the bay. The golf course in Koele may open in 2017, but it will likely also be reserved exclusively for Four Seasons guests.

While the two courses are private, there's a third course on Lana'i that's open to everyone. More of the no-shirt, no-shoes, beer-a-hole type of course, the nine-hole **Cavendish Golf Course** is suited for recreational golfers who want a quick practice round. Best of all, the course is free.

How do you expect to putt with that view?

LANA'I
GOLF

283

Constructed in 1947 as a recreational option for island pineapple workers, the Cavendish still operates as a place for islanders to practice their game and casually unwind. Although the fairways and tee boxes can be speckled with crabgrass and patches of dirt, the greens are still properly maintained. There are no carts or cart paths, so you get a workout walking the course's moderate elevation changes.

To reach the first tee box for the Cavendish course, make a right as if going to the Koele golf clubhouse off Keomoku Highway. Just after the turn is an open field on the right side of the road with a small flag fluttering in the distance. Welcome to the Cavendish. You'll have to supply your own clubs, balls, tees, and beer.

Shopping

Lana'i is the only Hawaiian Island where you could visit every store on the island without having to move the car. With the exception of the small stores within the Four Seasons Resort, every shop is within walking distance of the parking area around Dole Park.

CLOTHING AND SOUVENIRS

The only gas station on the island, the **Lana'i Plantation Store** (1036 Lana'i Ave., 808/565-7227, 6am-10pm daily) offers a great selection of island souvenirs and clothing along with the usual snacks and beverages. It's open later than most.

By Dole Park, the **Hula Hut** (418 8th St., 808/565-9170, 10am-5:30pm Mon.-Sat.) sells everything from hand-painted ceramic ornaments to women's jewelry and wind chimes. The Balinese woodwork gives an exotic feel to the interior. Facing the park, **The Local Gentry** (363 7th St., 808/565-9130, 10am-6pm Mon.-Fri., 10am-5pm Sat., 10am-2pm Sun.) offers a larger men's selection as well as a full range of women's clothing and Olu Kai shoes.

In the Four Seasons Resort, Makakae, Pilina, and Mua Loa offer high-end apparel and luxury boutiques that are curated by Seaside Luxe.

ART AND JEWELRY

The most prominent gallery on the island is **Mike Carroll Gallery** (443 7th St., 808/565-7122, www.mikecarrollgallery.com, 10am-5:30pm Mon.-Sat., 9am-2pm Sun.), between Canoes restaurant and the Lana'i City theater. There's a good chance that you'll find Mike painting right in the store. Many of his pieces focus on the simple yet captivating beauty of Lana'i. He is an in-demand artist who is constantly crafting original works. The gallery will occasionally feature visiting artists who come to relax and hone their craft in this charming plantation-style studio.

For a look at local artwork, visit the **Lana'i Art Center** (339 7th St., 808/565-7503, www.lanaiart.org, hours vary) to see just how much talent exists on an island of only 3,500 people. Fine photography and handmade jewelry accompany paintings and woodwork. A portion of this nonprofit's proceeds fund local art programs for Lana'i's youth. This gallery is a worthwhile stop after the Saturday farmers market or while walking off a Blue Ginger cheeseburger.

Lana'i Nightlife

Don't visit Lana'i for the nightlife. Evening is that inconvenient stretch of darkness that brings outdoor adventure to a halt. There are no nightclubs or dinner shows, and aside from the hotels, there is only one place you can even get a beer (Pele's Other Garden). Nevertheless, there is still a semblance of activity on certain nights of the week—just don't expect it to stretch past 10pm. On Wednesday, the party is at **Pele's Other Garden,** where live music rocks the bistro 7pm-10pm. Live music can also be enjoyed at the **Lana'i City Grille** 6:30pm-9:30pm on Fridays. Occasionally music will also be featured on Thursdays at the Grille, although the schedule is intermittent.

Food

AMERICAN

Pele's Other Garden (811 Houston St., 808/565-9628, www.pelesothergarden.com, lunch 11am-2pm Mon.-Fri., dinner 4:30pm-8pm Mon.-Sat., $7-19) is the hangout of anyone hankering for a good sandwich or a cold draft beer. The bistro also whips up healthy and affordable food options, ranging from avocado and feta wraps to pizza and chicken parmesan.

Just down the road from Richard's Supermarket, **Café 565** (408 8th St., 808/565-6622, 10am-3pm and 5pm-8pm Mon.-Sat.) is great for groups that can't agree on what they want. This hole-in-the-wall offers Italian, American, and standard local fare with calzones ($9-12), pizza ($16-22), and sub sandwiches ($6-10) as well as burgers ($7) and plate lunch options ($9). Grab a seat on the outdoor picnic tables: You can access the free Wi-Fi out here and people-watch on the street.

For a quick and easy grab-and-go option, **Lana'i City Service** (1036 Lana'i Ave., 808/565-7227, 6am-10pm daily) has a soup-and-sandwich bar as well as enormous shave ice.

COFFEE SHOPS

Even sleepy Lana'i City needs help waking up in the morning, and **Coffee Works** (604 Ilima Ave., 808/565-6962, 7am-3pm Mon.-Sat.) is the island's only full-time java establishment. Breakfast bagels and lunch sandwiches accompany the usual range of coffee offerings, and the outdoor porch is a great place for watching the mellow town slowly spring to life.

FARMERS MARKET

Even though it's no longer a sprawling pineapple plantation, the red dirt of Lana'i still manages to produce some locally grown crops. The **Lana'i City Farmer's Market** (Dole Park and behind Richard's Supermarket, 6am-11am Sat.) is the best place for fresh items such as corn, papaya, and pineapple. It's a great weekend activity in the island's only town.

HAWAIIAN REGIONAL

The fanciest meal in Lana'i City is at ★ **Lana'i City Grille** (828 Lana'i Ave., 808/565-7211, www.hotellanai.com, 5pm-9pm Wed.-Sun., $15-38). The fare is more expensive than at hole-in-the-wall plate-lunch stands, but when the waiter serves a plate of miso-marinated sea bass with mushroom potato hash, cost seems less important. The Grille has the island's most comprehensive wine list. Reservations are strongly recommended, particularly on Friday evenings, when the live jazz band provides the best entertainment in town.

LOCAL STYLE

While the exterior might not look like much, at ★ **Blue Ginger** (409 7th St., 808/565-6363, www.bluegingercafelanai.com, 6am-8pm Thurs.-Mon., 6am-2pm Tues.-Wed., $6-11, cash only) the swinging screen door and funky plantation-style appearance are all part of the hole-in-the-wall charm. Breakfast

Where Is All the Pineapple?

More than 20 years have passed since the last pineapple was picked on Lana'i, but some still think of it as "Pineapple Island." The 16,000-acre pineapple plantation was the world's largest, supplying nearly 75 percent of the world's pineapples, but rising production costs led Dole to close its Lana'i operation and focus on the Philippines and Thailand. The only remnants of the Dole plantation days still visible are the ubiquitous scraps of black plastic sprouting from the red dirt and fluttering in the breeze. Pieces of the plastic are believed to go down as far as six feet.

Even though the high school boys' basketball team is still known as "The Pine Lads," Lana'i has shifted from an agricultural economy to tourism. For an in-depth look at the history of the pineapple on Lana'i, and to see some of the island's lone remaining pineapple plants, visit the **Lana'i Culture and Heritage Center** (730 Lana'i Ave., 808/565-7177, www.lanaichc.org, 8:30am-3:30pm Mon.-Fri., 9am-1pm Sat.) in sleepy Lana'i City.

is heaping *loco moco* plates of fried eggs, hamburger meat, rice, and gravy, and the homemade hamburger patties are the lunchtime draw that has kept patrons coming in from Dole Park since 1991. It's a true local hideout.

Neighboring **Canoes** (419 7th St., 808/565-6537, 6:30am-1pm Sun.-Thurs., 6:30am-8pm Fri.-Sat.) offers up their own special hamburger recipe, a staple of Lana'i cuisine since 1953. Canoes has the usual selection of local plate lunches and items off the grill, although a special treat is the heaping breakfast portions, available until 1pm.

When you've had your fill of plate lunches, infuse your diet with some fresh fish at the ★ **Lana'i Ohana Poke Market** (834 Gay St., 808/559-6265, 10am-3pm Mon.-Fri., $7-17, cash only), which, in classic Lana'i fashion, is either open until 3pm or until they run out of fish. While the *poke* alone can be expensive, the best bet for a cheap and filling lunch is a *poke* bowl: one-third of a pound of fish served with two scoops of white or brown rice. Simple outdoor picnic tables provide the seating for this hole-in-the-wall take-out stand.

RESTAURANTS AT FOUR SEASONS RESORT LANA'I

If you've only made it as far as the pool by lunch and have no intention of leaving, order some food poolside from ★ **Kailani** (11am-4pm and 6pm-9:30pm daily, $18-40), where you can get fish tacos of blackened mahimahi or a filling plate of falafel. Prices are well above average ($31 for 3 fish tacos), but chalk it up to having a table at one of the world's most exclusive pools. For slightly lower prices and a view of the bay, **Views** (11am-3pm daily, $20) restaurant at the golf clubhouse has burgers, sandwiches, and local beer.

For dinner, ★ **Nobu Lana'i** (6pm-9:30pm daily, $35), has a selection sushi from famed chef Nobu Matsuhisa, and **One Forty** (6:30am-10:30am and 6pm-9pm daily, $40-65) has exceptional plates of Hawaiian Regional cuisine. The ahi *poke* appetizer served with dinner can compete with the best in the islands, and the hand-cut steaks and plates of fresh fish are the best that you'll find on Lana'i. For breakfast, start your day with seared ahi Benedict ($31).

Where to Stay on Lana'i

Name	Type	Price	Features	Why Stay Here?	Best For
Apo's House	vacation rental	$195	kitchen	affordable, location	couples, families
Dreams Come True	vacation rental	$141	kitchen	affordable, location	couples, budget travelers
★ Four Seasons Resort Lana'i	resort	from $960	pool, golf, oceanfront	luxury, romantic	couples, honeymooners, luxury-lovers
★ Hotel Lana'i	hotel	$174–254	lanai, breakfast	romantic, location, historic	couples
Hulopo'e Beach Park	camping	$30 + $15 pp	restrooms, water, oceanfront	location, affordable	budget travelers, groups, families

Where to Stay

While Lana'i is home to one of the most luxurious resorts in the state—and perhaps two once Koele reopens—there are a handful of more affordable options if you want to stay in the town. Lately, almost every vacation rental option on Lana'i has gone on **VRBO** (www.vrbo.com), the first place to check to find a little plantation home on the hill. There are still a few you can book directly by phone or through their own sites.

HOTELS

Small and historic ★ **Hotel Lana'i** (828 Lana'i Ave., 808/565-7211, www.hotellanai.com, $174-254) is in the center of tranquil Lana'i City. This was the island's first hotel, built in 1923 for visiting guests of the ruling Dole Pineapple Company. While you won't find the same amenities as at the more expensive resorts, the 10 rooms of this plantation-style building retain a historic feel without sacrificing comfort. The best rooms are those with their own private lanai, and there is also a cottage removed from the main building. Wi-Fi and breakfast are both complimentary, and shuttle service to the harbor is available for $10 pp.

Lavish, luxurious, and delightfully over the top, the ★ **Four Seasons Resort Lana'i** (1 Manele Bay Rd., 808/565-2000, www.fourseasons.com/lanai, from $960) is one Hawaii's most exclusive. New owner Larry Ellison devoted millions of dollars to major renovations when he took over from David Murdock, and the Asian decor that once dominated the hotels has been replaced by Hawaiian designs. The massive tech infusion, such as futuristic Toto toilets, makes every part of staying here an experience unto itself. Sit beachfront by the pool and sip on a cocktail while gazing at Hulopo'e Bay as spinner dolphins splash in the distance and pool staff clean your sunglasses. You'll feel like a celebrity. The Manele resort opened in February 2016, and the Koele should be open by the middle of 2017.

BED-AND-BREAKFASTS

The **Dreams Come True** (808/565-6961 www.dreamscometruelanai.com, $141) guesthouse has four rooms. The house dates to 1925 and was largely renovated in 2000 with hardwood floors and Italian marble in the baths. The local owners have a wealth of island knowledge. Breakfast is included in the rates, as is Internet access.

VACATION RENTALS

In town, **Apo's House** (www.lanaicityrental.com, $195) is a three-bedroom, two-bath, fully furnished house with a full kitchen. It's an older plantation home, but you have the convenience of walking into Lana'i City and the feeling that you're integrated in the local community.

CAMPING

The island's only official campground is at **Hulopo'e Beach Park** (reservations: info@lanaibeachpark.com, 3-day permit $30 plus $15 pp per night), and it's more expensive than you'd expect for camping. You do get to wake up steps from one of the nicest beaches in the country, and it's still cheaper than any room in town. A two-night stay for two people, for example, would cost $60 for the first night and

Lahaina-Lana'i Ferry Schedule

DEPART LAHAINA HARBOR (MAUI)

- 6:45am
- 9:15am
- 12:45pm
- 3:15pm
- 5:45pm

DEPART MANELE HARBOR (LANA'I)

- 8am
- 10:30am
- 2pm
- 4:30pm
- 6:45pm

$30 for the second. The campground is within walking distance of the ferry dock, and having a cooler with wheels is a big help for carrying supplies.

Getting There and Around

GETTING THERE
Air

Flying into Lana'i requires a jump from neighboring Honolulu. **Ohana by Hawaiian** (800/367-5320, www.hawaiianairlines.com) operates turboprop planes with 25-minute flights from Honolulu (HNL) that run a couple of times per day.

Ferry

Traveling from Maui, the easiest and most practical way to get to Lana'i is the **Expeditions Ferry** (808/661-3756, www.

go-lanai.com, one-way $30 adults, $20 children), which runs five times daily between Lahaina and Manele harbors. Travel time is usually about an hour, and during whale season (Dec.-Apr.), you can frequently spot humpback whales from the outdoor seating of the upper deck. Although you can buy tickets at the harbor kiosk in Lahaina the morning of your journey, make reservations ahead of time, particularly for the early morning trip. Don't be late; this is one ferry that doesn't wait around.

GETTING AROUND

If you're staying at the Four Seasons Resort, there's shuttle service to Lana'i City, the airport, and the harbor. Rates from the airport are $45 pp for a shuttle, or $195 for a luxury SUV. From Manele Harbor, rates are $20 pp, or $85 per SUV (5 people maximum). There are complimentary shuttles to Lana'i City, and if you're staying at Hotel Lana'i, there is shuttle service to the resort. If you're staying elsewhere or visiting for the day, you'll have to rent a vehicle or take a cab.

Rentals

The longest-running and most reputable Jeep rental company on the island, **Dollar Lana'i Rent a Car** (1036 Lana'i Ave., 808/565-7227, www.visitlanai.com, 7am-7pm daily) provides 4WD Jeeps (2-door $139 per day, 4-door $169 per day). The company requests that the vehicles be returned by 5pm, so if you come from Maui on the early morning ferry, you will arrive at the harbor by 7:45am, be at the rental car counter by 8:15am, and on your way with your Jeep by no later than 8:45am, giving you more than seven hours to explore the island. Dollar provides you with a map of the island and clearly states which roads are off-limits. If you end up requiring a tow from someplace "out of bounds," it's going to cost you $500. Aside from the driver, extra passengers cost $10 pp for a shuttle from the ferry to Lana'i City.

Lanai Cheap Jeeps (800/311-6860, www.lanaicheapjeeps.com) also has rentals ($124), and **Aloha Adventure Rentals** (www.alohaadventurerentals.com) has H2 Hummers ($187) that can handle the rugged terrain.

Taxi

The island's only taxi service is **Rabaca's Limousine Service** (808/565-6670), which connects the airport, harbor, and Lana'i City for $10 pp.

Gas

There is only one station on the entire island: **Lana'i City Service** (1036 Lana'i Ave., 808/565-7227, 6am-10pm daily) supplies fuel for all 3,500 residents. Don't worry about the price; you're better off just not looking, as it's often $1 to $1.50 more per gallon than on Maui. Then again, with only 30 miles of paved roads, it isn't uncommon for a tank of gas to last a month or more.

directions, Lana'i style

Moloka'i

Visitors often mistake Moloka'i's lack of typical resort activities for a lack of things to do.

But the protected vibe is incomparably relaxed and epitomizes "old Hawaii," where you find yourself talking to strangers as you would with an old friend. Moloka'i is a step back to simpler times when life was slower. That doesn't mean it's boring. Imagine surfing perfect waves off an empty white-sand beach, or hiking through rainforests to thundering falls in Hawaii's original settlement. Ride mules down a steep switchbacking trail with sweeping views of the coast, or tattoo the sand with a string of footprints on a sunset stroll.

Moloka'i is Hawaii's most "Hawaiian" island in that it has the highest percentage of ethnic Hawaiians and is one of the last places you might hear Hawaiian spoken on the street. It's a place where culture and ancient tradition are preferred over modern progress.

ORIENTATION

Though the airport is located in Ho'olehua, **Kaunakakai** is the island's main town and the hub of everyday life. It's the location of the island's only gas stations and the bulk of the restaurants, and also the Hotel Moloka'i, the island's largest. The western shore is about 30 minutes away and is best for beaches and sunsets. Eastern Moloka'i has oceanfront cottages and lush **Halawa Valley.** Central Moloka'i, near **Kualapu'u,** has a handful of sights, a restaurant, and it's on the way to the misty uplands and **Kalaupapa Trail.**

PLANNING YOUR TIME

In general, 4-5 days is enough time to properly visit the island, though you can visit most of the island's highlights in a very efficient two days. Many people visit from Maui for the day, although this limits what you can do. When scheduling your trip, plan on one day for Halawa Valley and East Moloka'i, and a second day for Kalaupapa. A third day could be spent at the west end beaches or hiking Mo'omomi or the Bog, and a fourth and fifth day provide nice buffers if activities are canceled by rain.

To visit Moloka'i in two days, head to the west end to catch the sunset after a morning in Kalaupapa, and the next day go hiking in Halawa Valley before dinner at Hale Kealoha. By staying in the vicinity of Kaunakakai, most places are within a 30-minute drive, and an hour to Halawa Valley.

Previous: family sunset in West Moloka'i; Decorate coconuts at the Ho'olehua "Post a Nut." **Above:** Kapuaiwa Coconut Grove.

Look for ★ to find recommended
sights, activities, dining, and lodging.

Highlights

© AVALON TRAVEL

★ **Moloka'i Forest Reserve:** This is one of the few places in the state with an ecosystem identical to what the Polynesians first found over 1,500 years ago. Nearly 98 percent of the plant species are indigenous to Moloka'i (page 293).

★ **Kalaupapa Peninsula:** The Kalaupapa Peninsula fuses some of Moloka'i's darkest moments with its most dramatic surroundings. The former leper colony is now home to the most scenic mule ride on the planet (page 296).

★ **Papohaku Beach:** Nearly three miles long and virtually deserted, Papohaku Beach is the island's best spot for watching a fiery sunset (page 300).

★ **Mo'omomi:** Wild and secluded, Mo'omomi feels like Moloka'i's lost coast (page 301).

★ **Private Tour of the Northern Sea Cliffs:** Embark with an adventure guide for an unforgettable ocean tour of the tallest sea cliffs in the world (page 304).

★ **Guided Paddleboard and Kayaking Tours:** Enjoy a downwind paddle off the island's southern coast (page 305).

★ **Cultural Hike into Halawa Valley:** Travel to the roots of Hawaiian culture on a cultural hike and swim at the base of a waterfall (page 308).

Your Best Day on Moloka'i

If you only have a day to spend on the Friendly Isle, start with a hearty breakfast at Mana'e Goods & Grindz before continuing on to Halawa Valley for the 9am cultural hike. Make the long drive past town to Kualapu'u Cookhouse, where a late lunch will break up the drive to Papohaku Beach, where a fiery sunset and vast stretch of sand helps bring the day to a close.

If you're still hungry once back in town, or want to relax with a drink, get an oceanfront table at Hale Kealoha and enjoy the live local music. Feeling really ambitious? Get dessert at Hot Bread Lane behind Kanemitsu Bakery. This is a lot of driving for a single day, but it hits many of Moloka'i's highlights.

Rainy Day? Grab a warm drink from Coffees of Hawaii and sit on the covered front porch before heading to the Post-a-Nut in Ho'olehua to mail yourself a coconut. Pick up souvenirs at Beach Break, Blue Monkey, or the strip of stores in town, and strike up conversation while listening to live music at the Hotel Moloka'i bar. Sometimes if it's raining in town it is sunny on the west end of the island for tanning or watching the sunset, so ask a local if they know what the weather is like out west.

Sights

People who claim that there isn't a lot to do on Moloka'i have more than likely never visited. Sure, Moloka'i is a place to decompress and generally kick back and relax, but in addition to the hiking, biking, snorkeling, diving, surfing, and eating, there are also traditional sightseeing and activities.

KAUNAKAKAI
Kapuaiwa Coconut Grove
Planted in 1860 by King Kamehameha V, the Kapuaiwa Coconut Grove once sported over 1,000 waving palms. It makes a beautiful picture from the road.

Moloka'i Plumeria Farm
Have you ever wanted to make your own lei and be surrounded by the scent of plumeria? Just west of town on Highway 460, as the road starts heading uphill, is Moloka'i Plumeria Farm (808/553-3391, www.molokaiplumerias.com), where you can tour the property (10:30am daily, $25), pick your own flowers, and make a plumeria lei. Tours require advance reservations.

TOPSIDE
★ Moloka'i Forest Reserve
As you head west from Kaunakakai, slowly gaining elevation, the turnoff for the Moloka'i Forest Reserve is just before mile marker 4. Turn right before the bridge, and after a few hundred yards you'll pass the Homelani Cemetery, where red-dirt Maunahui Road winds way into the mountains. Your car rental agency will tell you that this road is impassable except in a 4WD vehicle, and that's true if it has rained recently. The road is rough even when it's dry and requires at least a high-clearance truck or jeep. Follow the rutted road up into the hills into a deep forest of 'ohi'a, pine, eucalyptus, and giant ferns planted in the early 1900s. The cool, pleasant air carries the rich, earthy smells of the forest. At 5.5 miles you enter the Moloka'i Forest Reserve.

After nine miles is the Sandalwood Measuring Pit, a depression in the ground in the shape of a ship's hull. Now bordered by a green pipe fence, it's not worth the drive out here in itself. Hawaiian chiefs had the pit dug to measure the amount of sandalwood necessary to fill the hold of a ship, and traded the

Moloka'i

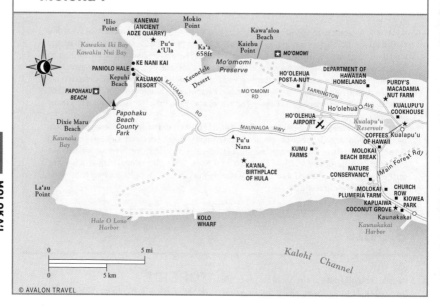

aromatic wood to Yankee captains for whiskey, guns, and tools. The traders carried the wood to China, where they made huge profits. The trade was so lucrative that the male population of entire villages were forced into the hills to collect it. It took only a few years to denude the mountains of their copious stands of sandalwood, even more incredible when you consider that all the work was done by hand.

One mile after the Sandalwood Pit is the **Waikolu Overlook,** a precipitous 3,700-foot drop that's frequently lined with waterfalls. Waikolu Overlook is as far as most vehicles can go. Continuing farther is the **Kamakou Preserve** and the hike to **Pepe'opae Bog** (page 306). The road is so bad that the only way forward is to park at Waikolu and walk.

Purdy's Na Hua O Ka 'Aina Farm (Macadamia Nut Farm)

A popular visitor stop is **Purdy's Na Hua O Ka 'Aina Farm** (808/567-6601, www.molokai.com/eatnuts, 9:30am-3:30pm Tues.-Fri.,

10am-2pm Sat., free) behind the public high school on Lihi Pali Avenue. This is the island's only macadamia nut farm, where you'll learn everything you wanted to know about macadamias. An informal tour led by the jovial owner teaches how to crack open the hard nut, how the nuts are grown, and how to pick out the good ones. There are no pesticides, herbicides, or other chemicals used in this 50-tree grove. While samples are included with the free tour, a small gift shop sells everything from macadamia-nut honey to mac nut-themed clothing.

Kumu Farms

If you're into healthy, organic produce, **Kumu Farms** (Hua Ai Rd., 808/351-3326, www.kumufarms.com, 9am-4pm Tues.-Fri., free) is the place for the island's best produce. Despite the recent explosion of farm-to-table cuisine, this working farm has been growing crops since 1981 and is the best place on the island to pick up fresh veggies straight from the *kumu,* or source.

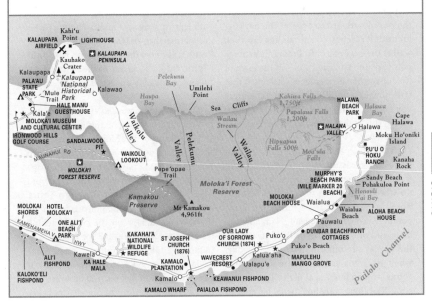

Visitors can peruse the outdoor market for certified organic and non-GMO produce and glean some expert culinary advice from recipes and cookbooks around the shop. Five minutes west of the airport on Hua Ai Road, an easy turn from Highway 460, this rapidly expanding farm now produces over 20,000 pounds of papaya every week. Pick up a bag of frozen basil and macadamia-nut pesto for a homemade pasta dinner.

Ho'olehua Post-A-Nut

Never have kids loved going to the post office more than in Ho'olehua. A simple one-room building on arid homesteading land, the **Ho'olehua Post Office** (Pu'u Pila Ave., 808/567-6144, 8:30am-4pm Mon.-Fri.) is home to the popular Post-A-Nut, where you can decorate a coconut and ship it anywhere in the world. Postmaster Gary has shipped coconuts to Kathmandu, Namibia, Kyrgyzstan, and Antarctica (twice). Rates to the U.S. mainland run $10-14.

Moloka'i Museum and Cultural Center

Off Highway 470, two miles north of Kualapu'u, is the **Moloka'i Museum and Cultural Center** (808/567-6436, 10am-2pm Mon.-Sat., $5 adults, $1 students), a simple museum focused on the history of Kalaupapa. There's a small exhibit on Hawaiian artifacts as well as a basic gift shop, but most informative are the documentary videos and old newspaper articles about life on the Kalaupapa Peninsula. On the same grounds, behind the museum, is the **R. W. Meyer Sugar Mill**, constructed in 1878 during the island's short-lived sugar era.

Pala'au State Park

Above the residential town of Kala'e and past the mule barn, Highway 470 eventually deadends in the parking lot of **Pala'au State Park.** The park offers decent camping, and there are public restrooms at the parking lot, but no potable water and only basic facilities. The air is noticeably cooler than at the shore, and by midmorning the northeasterly trade winds are usually blowing.

To reach **Kalaupapa Overlook,** follow the paved path at the edge of the parking lot until it reaches a terminus at a low rock wall at the edge of a cliff. From this vantage point are unobstructed views of the town of Kalaupapa, the former leper settlement that still houses a handful of patients. Unless you booked a mule ride or a permit to hike down, this is the closest to Kalaupapa that you can get.

Back at the parking lot, an unpaved trail leads 200 yards through a cool canopy of trees before emerging at a sacred spot named **Ke Ule O Nanahoa,** also called **Phallic Rock** for reasons that are immediately apparent. According to legend, Nanahoa, the male god of fertility, once lived nearby in the forests surrounding Pala'au. One day, when Nanahoa sat to admire a beautiful young woman looking at her reflection in a pool, Kawahua, Nanahoa's wife, became so jealous that she attacked the young woman by yanking on her hair. Nanahoa was outraged in turn and struck his wife, who rolled over a nearby cliff before turning to stone. Nanahoa also turned to stone, in the shape of an erect penis, and sits here today.

★ KALAUPAPA PENINSULA

This isolated peninsula is where people with leprosy were sent to die. The story goes deeper than that, and touring the **Kalaupapa Peninsula,** now the **Kalaupapa National Historical Park,** is one of the most powerful and scenic adventures you can experience in Hawaii.

There are three ways to visit the national historical park: hiking in, riding a mule, and flying. All are possible Monday-Saturday, and the minimum age is 16. Unfortunately, due to the timing, it isn't possible to visit Kalaupapa the same day you arrive on the ferry from Maui. To hike in, contact **Damien Tours** (808/567-6171) (page 306). To ride a mule down to Kalaupapa on the switchbacking trail, contact **Kalaupapa Rare Adventure** (808/567-6088, www.muleride.com, 8am-3:30pm daily, $199). Don't do the mule ride if you have a fear of heights, and be aware that the rides can sometimes be canceled for heavy rain. The maximum weight for riders is 250 pounds.

To fly to Kalaupapa, **Makani Kai Air** (808/834-1111, www.makanikaiair.com) has flights from the Moloka'i airport to the Kalaupapa airstrip ($75 one-way). Flight time

empty beach at Kalaupapa National Historical Park

Kaunakakai

© AVALON TRAVEL

SCALE NOT AVAILABLE

is 15 minutes, and in order to make the 10am tour, book the 9:20am flight that arrives at 9:35am. For the return journey, there's a 2:15pm flight back. Planes only hold nine people, so advance reservations are a must. Maximum weight is 249 pounds.

For a combo tour where you hike down and fly back, or any other Kalaupapa logistics, either **Kalaupapa Rare Adventure** (808/567-6088, www.muleride.com) or **Molokai Outdoors** (808/553-4477, www.molokai-outdoors.com) can explain all the options.

Whichever way you choose to arrive, the only way to tour the peninsula is with **Damien Tours** (808/567-6171), who share Kalaupapa's history and discuss its uncertain future, and take you to sights like the Kalawao lookout and St. Philomena Church.

WEST MOLOKA'I

The only sights in West Moloka'i are the fiery sunsets and the procession of isolated beaches that line the western coast.

In 1897 a group of wealthy Honolulu businesspeople purchased 70,000 acres of land in the western half of Moloka'i and named it Moloka'i Ranch. It attempted a number of ventures until finally succumbing in 2008 to public pressure over proposed development. Closing the ranch's hospitality operations eliminated 120 jobs, and the area has yet to recover.

Over the years the ranch supported sugarcane, pineapples, sweet potatoes, wheat, cattle, safari tours, a luxury lodge, an 18-hole golf course, a movie theater, and rustic accommodations on Kaupoa Beach, colloquially known as "tentalows." With ranch operations mostly on hold, the small residential town of **Maunaloa** is all that remains. Occasionally there are still rodeos in town. The ranch may rise again, but for the time being it's an abandoned hinterland of isolated ghost-town confusion.

EAST MOLOKA'I

Since the arrival of the Polynesians, eastern Moloka'i has supported most of the island's population. The mountains provide the water, farmland, and pigs, and the ocean provides fish that have been sustainably managed for over 1,000 years. Many of the residents maintain this subsistence-based lifestyle, where the people are stewards of the land that nourishes them.

Many of the historic sites in this area have limited access because they are on private land. Sites that landowners have not opened to visitors, such as 'Ili'iliopae, the largest *heiau* on the island, are not included here. Nevertheless, a day trip to the east end of the island is easily Moloka'i's best road trip, with views toward Maui and humble historical sights. The white-sand beaches are nice for a picnic or a quick dip to cool off, and the road to Halawa rivals Maui's Road to Hana when it comes to magnificent views.

Ali'i Fishpond

Driving east from Kaunakakai, you'll come to **Ali'i Fishpond** at mile marker 3, just before One Ali'i Beach Park. The 35-acre fishpond was originally constructed with rocks carried by hand 10 miles over the adjacent mountain. Having fallen into disrepair, the Ali'i Fishpond has been painstakingly brought back to life by Ka Honua Momona (www.kahonuamomona.org), a nonprofit organization dedicated to sustainable land practices on Moloka'i. If you pull in to the parking lot and staff members are working on the property, they will happily show you around. Workers are usually here in the morning before the wind picks up, and if no one is around, it's best to admire the fishpond from a distance.

View from the Heights

Since the coastal road doesn't have great views, drive up to the **Kawela Plantation** to get a panoramic photo of the fringing reef and coast. Just a few minutes east of One Ali'i Beach Park, turn *mauka* (toward the mountain) into the Kawela Plantation I

Moloka'i Fishponds

At one time there were 60 stone fishponds lining the shore of Moloka'i's southern coast. Some have been restored and are in use today. Indigenous people who inhabit the area still eat the way their ancestors did for centuries.

Constructed of lava rock and large blocks of coral, the fishponds represent a system of aquaculture that serves as one of early Hawaii's greatest feats of engineering. Most of the fishponds are believed to be 700 to 800 years old, and although some have been overtaken by coastal mangroves, there are still a few that are possible to visit. If you go, don't walk on the walls or disturb any of the stones.

development, drive past rows of plumeria trees, and make the first left. From here, follow the steep hill until it dead-ends in a cul-de-sac. This is the best view of the southern coast until mile marker 20.

St. Joseph's Church

Driving along Highway 450, **St. Joseph's Church** is around mile marker 10. Although Father Damien is famous for reaching out to the patients of Kalaupapa, he would also frequently make the arduous trek over the mountains to the southern coast where, in 1876, he constructed St. Joseph's Church. A statue of Damien stands outside this small, recently restored building. To look inside, check the doors; they are often unlocked.

In an effort to convert Hawaiians to Christianity, it's believed that Father Damien purposely chose this spot in Kamalo to provide an alternative to the Puili *heiau*, which lies just inland.

Pu'u O Hoku Ranch

Past mile marker 20 and Waialua and Murphy's Beaches, the road narrows and runs near the sea. Honk your horn as you come around tight corners, and if you feel queasy from the drive, there's a sandy cove past mile

Father Damien

Roman Catholic priest Joseph de Veuster, aka Father Damien, came from Belgium to Hawaii. His brother, also a priest, was originally slated for the trip, but he fell ill and Father Damien took his place. Damien spent several years on the Big Island of Hawaii, building churches and learning the language and ways of the people, before traveling to Kalaupapa in 1873.

Damien saw the people with leprosy at Kalaupapa as deserving of life and comfort. When they hid under a bush at his approach, he pulled them up and stood them on their feet. He carried water to the sick and dying, bathed their wounds, and built shelters with his own hands. When clothing or food ran short, he walked topside to ask for more. Other church factions opposed his actions, and the government gave him little aid, but he persevered.

Father Damien modified St. Philomena Church, originally built in Honolulu in 1872, and shipped it to Moloka'i in segments. He invited his charges inside, but those grossly afflicted could not control their mouths, so spittle would drip to the floor. They were ashamed to soil the church, so Damien cut squares in the floor through which they could spit onto the ground. Slowly, the authorities began to take notice. Damien eventually contracted leprosy himself and died in 1889 at age 49. In 1936 the government of Belgium asked that his remains be returned. His body was exhumed and sent home, but a memorial still stands where he was once interred at Kalaupapa. After lengthy squabbles with the Belgians, Father Damien's right hand was returned to Kalaupapa in 1995 and has been interred as a religious relic. He was beatified by Pope John Paul II in 1994 and canonized by Benedict XVI in 2009.

marker 21 where you can rest. This far out on the island is very rural, and often you'll encounter groups of residents just hanging out and fishing. Be sure you have more than a quarter tank of gas if you plan to venture farther, as there are no facilities as you continue east.

Once Highway 450 starts gaining in elevation, the sweeping pasturelands of **Pu'u O Hoku Ranch** (808/558-8109, www.puuohoku.com) come into view. This 14,000-acre working ranch and farm dominates the eastern tip of the island. You've driven so far north and east that it's possible to see Maui's northern coast. There's a basic store at the ranch headquarters that sells its own products, such as organic honey, dried banana fingers, kale, chard, eggplant, cherry tomatoes, and sweet apple bananas. The ranch is also one of the only places that produces and sells 'awa, a traditional Polynesian medicinal and painkilling drink, and it also sells ranch-raised beef and venison. Driving through the ranch, watch for nene geese in the pastures and on the road. The ranch also has a number of lodging options to get away from it all.

Halawa Valley

At the end of Highway 450, after utopian plantation homes, single-lane turns, and the ranchland's windswept bluffs, **Halawa Valley** suddenly appears when you reach a hairpin turn. At the lookout, you can snap a shot of Moa'ula Falls, toward the back of the valley. This is the best possible view of the falls unless you take a Halawa Valley guided hike (page 308).

Halawa is believed to be Hawaii's first settlement, circa AD 650, with some evidence suggesting settlement as early as AD 300. This is the "old Hawaii," where mythology, nature, and residents commune in a way not found in modern society. The handful of residents who still inhabit this valley live a subsistence lifestyle that parallels their ancestors. Electricity is scarce, there's no cell phone reception, and taro lo'i (fields) weave their way up the verdant valley floor. Aside from swimming at the sandy beach or joining the guided hike, there is little to do in Halawa but snap photos and enjoy the beauty.

Beaches

If having a beach to yourself seems like your kind of afternoon, then pack a beach chair and a good book. Moloka'i's beaches are meant for sunbathing rather than snorkeling or swimming, as northwesterly swells bring large surf in winter and a reef lines the southern coast. You won't find beachside tiki bars or activity agents—in Moloka'i it's just you, the sand, the vast blue Pacific, and a fiery sunset each night.

WEST MOLOKA'I

The west end of Moloka'i has the island's best beaches, usually spared the relentless trade winds that buffet the eastern coast. Summer months are best for swimming, with the exception of Papohaku, which is always dangerous. In winter surf turns the western coast into a cauldron of white water. The empty shores are always good for sunbathing, and the sunsets are the best on the island.

★ Papohaku Beach

Over two miles long and nearly 100 yards wide, **Papohaku Beach** is easily Moloka'i's most scenic and popular. Six people is considered a crowd, and while parts of the beach are dotted with homes, the majority of Papohaku is undeveloped with empty sand for strolling. Swimming is a terrible idea, as the rip currents and undertow are overwhelming year-round. Instead, take a morning jog or watch the sunset over the lights of Honolulu, 32 miles away.

To get here, follow Highway 460 toward the town of Maunaloa, and take a right on Kaluakoi Road. Follow Kaluakoi to sea level until it wraps around to the left. The beach park has multiple entrances on the right side of the road. For extended stays, **camping** is possible at Papohaku if you obtain a permit from the County Parks Department (808/553-3204).

Kepuhi Beach

Kepuhi Beach fronts the Kaluakoi Villas and the abandoned Sheraton resort. It's an ideal beach for swimming during the summer, and the sunset each night is the kind that ends up on your Christmas card. To reach Kepuhi Beach, follow the signs for Kaluakoi Villas off Kaluakoi Road. Public beach parking is available.

huge Papohaku Beach

The Birthplace of the Hula

Western Moloka'i history is deeply rooted in Hawaiian culture. Not far from Maunaloa, in an area known as Ka'ana, legend speaks of the goddess Laka being the first to dance the hula, having "given birth" to the dance at a hill known as Pu'u Nana. Fanning out from Ka'ana, Laka subsequently journeyed throughout Hawaii, teaching the dance to anyone who wanted to learn. To this day traditional *hula halau* (hula schools) will prepare an offering or altar to Laka, goddess of the hula, as part of their performance and ceremony. It's believed that after sharing her dance with the people of Hawaii, Laka returned to Moloka'i, where her remains are buried at Pu'u Nana overlooking the western shores. Today, the **Ka Hula Piko** (www.kahulapiko.com), an annual festival held at the end of May or beginning of June, celebrates the roots of hula and perpetuation of the craft.

Kapukahehu (Dixie Maru)

Named after a fishing boat that sank near the bay, **Dixie's** is at the southern end of the road. From Papohaku Beach Park, follow Kaluakoi Road until it reaches Pohakuloa, turn *makai* (toward the sea), and follow it to the end of the cul-de-sac. The narrow alleyway that looks like a driveway is the beach access, and there's a small parking area about 100 yards down. For an even smaller, more hidden beach, there's a small trail through the *kiawe* (mesquite) trees that eventually leads over a fence. Follow this trail for 10 minutes, and it will bring you to sandy **Kaunala Beach,** frequented by surfers, nudists, and locals, but you'll often have it all to yourself.

Kawakiu and Pohaku Mauliuli Beach

Between Kepuhi and 'Ilio, a number of hidden, sandy coves provide splendid isolation. To reach **Kawakiu Beach,** follow the signs to the Paniolo Hale condominium complex from Kaluakoi Road by making a right on Kaka'ako and then turning left down Lio Place, following the pavement to the end. A rudimentary sign here points the way to the beach, and when the dirt road ends in a parking lot, it's a short walk to the shore. If you don't have a high-clearance or 4WD vehicle, consider parking near the end of the pavement and walking along the dirt road. While the first beach is nice, it's nothing compared to Kawakiu, so continue north by scrambling over some rocks until you arrive

at **Pohaku Mauliuli.** From here, a dirt road runs along the bluff and leads to Kawakiu. If the tide is low and the surf is calm, walk along the shore. The protected cove is idyllic in summer, tumultuous in winter, and almost always empty. If you prefer to bathe in the buff, this is the place to do it. Bring lots of water as well as proper footwear for lava rocks and thorns.

Hale O Lono

Hale O Lono is incredibly remote and rarely visited. With the closing of Moloka'i Ranch, the dirt roads once used by ranch guests now are only sporadically used. **Hawela Beach,** on the east side of the old harbor entrance, is the most accessible and most protected. Rough conditions can persist at any time of the year, but on days with light winds and flat surf, the swimming and sunbathing at Hawela are on par with anywhere on the island. To find Hale O Lono, follow Highway 460 to its terminus in the town of Maunaloa. From here, Mokio Street leads to a sloping, rutted, seven-mile dirt road running to the shore. Regular vehicles with high clearance can handle this road if it hasn't been raining; a 4WD vehicle is needed if it's wet.

★ Mo'omomi

If you crave adventure, head to **Mo'omomi.** You'll need a 4WD vehicle to get to this coast, which is pristine. Its seclusion is revered and in some cases protected by local indigenous Hawaiians. Mo'omomi is currently open to visitors, but it's imperative to be respectful and keep on established trails. In the past, access has ranged from total freedom to discussion of erecting a gate. Contact **The Department of Hawaiian Home Lands** (600 Maunaloa Hwy., 808/560-6104) to inquire about current restrictions. The western portions of Moʻomomi are run by the Nature Conservancy, and visitors are asked to stay out of the dunes because of the fragile ecosystem.

To reach the Moʻomomi pavilion from Hoʻolehua, follow Farrington Avenue until the road becomes dirt, and keep right at the fork. Once parked, walking along the shore leads to a series of underwhelming beaches, but once you get back on the dirt road, the beauty of windswept **Kawaʻaloa Beach** opens up before you. Swimming is only possible in summer, as large north swells create dangerous rip currents the rest of the year. The best activity at Kawaʻaloa is strolling. For a unique way to visit, contact **The Nature Conservancy** (808/553-5236, hike_molokai@tnc.org), which hosts monthly hikes March to October.

EAST MOLOKAʻI

The eastern beaches are the most popular among residents, and morning hours offer the calmest conditions before the trade winds arrive. Like a South Pacific postcard, white-sand coves ringed by lazy palms are dotted by colorful fishing boats, and more than anywhere else on the island, there's a sense of enveloping calm. The swimming and snorkeling are best at high tide, the beachcombing and sunbathing are better at low tide, and everything is better before the afternoon wind.

Pukoʻo Beach

Just east of the Manaʻe Goods & Grindz, by mile marker 16, a small beach access sign points down a dirt driveway to hidden **Pukoʻo Beach.** You'll find water that's clear, protected, and good for swimming. It's a good spot for enjoying a casual plate lunch or taking a dip to cool off.

Waialua Beach

Waialua Beach is a narrow ribbon of sand 18.5 miles east of Kaunakakai, with some of the island's best swimming. As with other beaches in the area, the wind gains in strength throughout the day, and at high tide the sand almost disappears completely. Be sure to watch for coral heads exposed at low tide.

Pukoʻo Beach

Kumimi Beach

Also known as Twenty-Mile Beach or Murphy's Beach, **Kumimi Beach** is by mile marker 20 on Highway 450 and is the last stretch of sand before the road narrows to one lane. This is arguably East Moloka'i's most popular beach and has sweeping, spectacular views. It also has wide sand, is a nice spot for snorkeling, and in the afternoon hours you might see kitesurfers running laps down the coast.

Simple and small, **Sandy Beach** is past mile marker 21 on the winding drive toward Halawa. The beach is protected from the trade winds and, most of the time, from the surf. The beach is small, with just enough room to put down a towel. You might also share space with kids wading in the shallows or locals selling bananas out of the back of a truck.

Halawa Bay

After weaving 10 miles over the rocky coast and down through the lush eastern valleys, the two beaches that form **Halawa Bay** are like gold at the end of a rainbow. At the terminus of Highway 450, Kama'alaea Bay is the more protected beach on the far side of the stream. This is the best option for swimming and escaping the wind. Kawili Beach, at the bottom of the cliff, is more exposed to the currents and the trade winds. It's a surreal feeling to hang out on the shores of a place considered one of the oldest settlements in Hawaii. The only facilities are two portable toilets and a single trashcan by the pavilion at the end of the road.

Snorkeling and Diving

Don't tell anybody, but Moloka'i has some of the best snorkeling and diving in Hawaii. With the exception of a few protected areas, Moloka'i's dive and snorkel spots can only be accessed by boat. **Dixie Maru Beach** on the west shore and **Kumimi Beach** on the east shore usually have calm conditions and are the only two bays to snorkel from shore. The island's southern shore is home to Hawaii's longest fringing reef, and dive outfitters have 40 named spots along its outer edge. **Moku Ho'oniki**, off the eastern tip, is known for hammerhead sharks and occasionally some larger pelagic species, from tiger sharks to whales.

CHARTERS, TOURS, AND RENTAL SHOPS

With an office right on a corner on Kaunakakai's main thoroughfare, literally inside the gas station, **Molokai Fish and Dive** (53 Ala Malama Ave., 808/553-5926, www.molokaifishanddive.com, hours vary, usually 6am-7:30pm Mon.-Sat., 6am-7pm Sun.) offers three-hour snorkeling trips ($79 pp) and scuba trips ($145) to the reef or Moku Ho'oniki ($295). This shop is the only **PADI** operation on the island and can accommodate a variety of snorkel and dive excursions. Prices and open hours can vary, so call for rates and availability.

For snorkeling only, **Moloka'i Ocean Tours** (40 Ala Malama Ave., Suite 107, 808/553-3290 or 808/298-3055, www.molokaioceantours.com) can accommodate up to six passengers on the 40-foot catamaran *Manu Ele'ele* for snorkeling excursions to Kaunakakai ($75 pp). This boat visits the south shore's fringing reef, and trips usually leave around 7:30am. Rent full snorkel sets ($9 per day, $30 per week). If the downstairs office is closed, check upstairs at the sister shop, **Something For Everybody** (40 Ala Malama Ave., Suite 201, 808/553-3299, 10am-6pm Mon.-Fri., 9am-1pm Sat., www.allthinsmolokai.com) for rentals and more info.

★ Private Tour of the Northern Sea Cliffs

Local adventure guide Walter Naki runs **Moloka'i Action Adventures** (808/558-8184) and is one of the only people who regularly takes visitors to the tallest sea cliffs in the world. The trip is only possible when conditions allow, and since conditions are so variable, call for rates and availability. If it works out, it's guaranteed to be the most memorable day of your vacation.

Surfing, Paddling, and Kayaking

WEST MOLOKA'I

Remote and empty, West Moloka'i is best in winter when the swells that send waves to O'ahu come crashing onto this coast. The difference is that there aren't 200 people vying for the same wave, and traffic on the highway is nonexistent. While the quality isn't as good as O'ahu's, the surf in western Moloka'i can be heavy, and only experienced surfers should paddle out on big-wave days.

The best-known and consequently most crowded spot on this end of the island is **Sheraton's** at Kepuhi Beach, named after the defunct resort that fronts the beach. Access is sandy and easy, but be wary of occasional shallow boulders while paddling out. The wave is on the left side of the beach, and on better days can be an A-frame that holds to 10 feet. Sheraton's is a decent spot for intermediate surfers if it's small, and only for experts if it's pumping.

If Sheraton's is too big, drive south to **Dixie Maru** where a right point break wraps into the bay at sizes half of Sheraton's. If Dixie's is crowded, meaning more than three people, or if you're up for a little adventure, a goat trail leads back into the *kiawe* trees and to **Kaunala Beach,** where another right break bends in toward the shore. The takeoff can be a little difficult since you sit off the rocks,

stand-up paddling the southern coast

but it's a fun wave to get a few turns in when Sheraton's is all closed out.

On the southern end of the island, the beaches around **Hale O Lono** harbor are able to pick up swells any time of year and can often be heavy in winter. The wind can be fierce in the afternoon, and the murky conditions conjure fears of toothy predators, but there's a 95 percent chance you'll have the waves to yourself. If the wind is down, the waves are up, and the water is clear, the beaches off Hale O Lono can offer some of the most adventurous surf on Moloka'i. Follow the dirt road from Maunaloa town straight downhill to the shore, seven miles later. A 4WD vehicle is recommended.

KAUNAKAKAI

Since Kaunakakai faces directly south, the best waves are from May through September. Despite the fact that the area boasts miles of shoreline, the majority is blocked by the fringing reef, which makes paddling out virtually impossible. Nevertheless, locals still flock to

Kaunakakai Wharf during the big swells of summer. Expect a long paddle, since you have to get out past the reef to get to the waves, but the long paddle is rewarded by Moloka'i's best summer wave. Expect a very local crowd, as well as lots of "spongers" (bodyboarders).

EAST MOLOKA'I

The only place for beginners to surf in East Moloka'i is **Waialua Beach,** where gentle rollers provide enough push to practice getting up on two feet. While the waves can be fun, it can be shallow at low tide. More advanced surfers can ride waves at **Halawa,** which can be powerful and barreling on the largest swells of winter. If a group of locals paddles out, head back to shore.

Rental Shops and Tour Operators

If you don't bring a board on the ferry from Maui (airlines only allow boards up to six feet), the best place to rent is at **Beach Break** (2130 Maunaloa Hwy., 808/567-6091, 10am-4pm Mon.-Sat.) at the Holomua Junction, between Kaunakakai and the airport. They have the largest selection on the island, and the owner, Zack, can provide info on where you should and shouldn't paddle out. Rent longboards

($30 per day, $150 per week), shortboards ($24 per day, $120 per week), a full range of boogie boards, beach gear, stand-up paddleboard equipment, and accessories. Check out the surf art, shot right here on Moloka'i.

In central Kaunakakai, rent Soft Top surfboards ($25 per day, $100 per week) from **Moloka'i Ocean Tours** (40 Ala Malama Ave., Suite 107, 808/553-3290 or 808/298-3055, www.molokaioceantours.com).

★ Guided Paddleboard and Kayaking Tours

Inside Hotel Moloka'i, the desk staff for **Moloka'i Outdoors** (808/553-4477, www.molokai-outdoors.com, 8am-10am and 3pm-5pm daily) can line you up with a Soft Top surfboard ($17 per day, $68 per week), fiberglass surfboard ($22 per day, $88 per week), stand-up paddleboard, paddle, or kayak. They offer **Guided Paddleboard and Kayaking Tours** (Mon. and Wed.-Fri.) of the island's southeastern coast that range 5-8 miles and visit the island's fringing reef—the longest of its kind in the United States. You'll paddle by fishponds, oceanfront homesteads, and colorful sections of reef, and gain fascinating insight on sustainable practices and Moloka'i's rural way of life.

tranquil coves on the eastern shore

MOLOKA'I SURFING, PADDLING, AND KAYAKING

Hiking and Biking

Even for Maui residents, Moloka'i's hiking trails are shrouded in mystery. Often the trails require a 4WD vehicle to access or permission from private landowners, although there are still a number that are accessible to the public.

HIKING
Topside

Bathed in the scent of eucalyptus and pine, the "topside" of central Moloka'i feels like the mountains. With trails ranging 1,500 to 4,000 feet in elevation, the air is cooler, and once you enter the **Kamakou Preserve,** the weather turns wetter and the surroundings more lush. Songs of native *i'iwi* birds ring from the tree-tops while mist hangs in the silence of deeply carved valleys.

KALAUPAPA OVERLOOK

The easiest walk is the 1,500-foot paved walkway to the **Kalaupapa Overlook,** which starts at the end of the road in Pala'au State Park. Take Highway 470 past the mule barn for the Kalaupapa trail rides and continue until it dead-ends in a parking lot. There are basic restrooms here but no potable water. Be prepared for high winds that can blow your hat off, and get your camera ready for the best views of the Kalaupapa Peninsula.

KALAUPAPA TRAIL

For good reason, the **Kalaupapa Trail** (Mon.-Sat.) is the most popular hike on Moloka'i. It descends 1,700 vertical feet over the course of 3.2 miles and 26 switchbacks. There are photo-worthy views of the sea cliffs and the gorgeous, empty white-sand beach at the bottom. This trail was hand-cut into the mountain in 1886 by Portuguese immigrant Manuel Farinha to establish a land connection with the residents living topside. The trail is still in good shape, and you need to be too: Everything that goes down must come back

up. Expect the hike down to take 1.5 hours, and close to 2 hours for the return.

Since this is part of **Kalaupapa National Historical Park,** which has caps on the number of visitors, a permit is required to tour the peninsula. If you want to hike to Kalaupapa instead of riding a mule, contact **Damien Tours** (808/567-6171) in advance. They meet hikers at the bottom of the trail at 10am and provide a four-hour guided tour ($50 pp) of the Kalaupapa Peninsula and the national historical park. Pay them at the bottom (cash works best), and call the day before to let them know you'll be coming.

You can also book the hike through **Kalaupapa Rare Adventure** (808/567-6088, www.muleride.com, $69), optionally including a sandwich. Pick up your meal ticket and permit to the national historical park at the mule barn before hiking down. In order to be at the bottom by 10am, you should begin hiking by 8:30am at the latest. To reach the trailhead, drive 200 yards past the mule barn on Highway 470 and park on the right side of the road. Be sure to bring rain gear and a good pair of shoes, and while there's a small store in Kalaupapa where you can restock on water and snacks, it's best to pack enough food and water that you don't have to rely on the store.

PEPE'OPAE BOG

Constantly shrouded in cloud cover and dripping in every color of green imaginable, if ever there were a place to visualize Hawaii before the arrival of humans, it is **Pepe'opae Bog.** Ninety-eight percent of the plant species here are indigenous to Moloka'i, and 219 of the species are found nowhere else on earth. Following Highway 460 from Kaunakakai, make a right before the bridge at the Homelani Cemetery sign and follow the dirt road for 10 miles to the parking area at Waikolu Overlook.

Making it to Waikolu Overlook in a regular vehicle requires high clearance and the best road conditions, and you will get stuck if you go any farther. If you have a 4WD vehicle, you can drive another 2.6 miles to the trailhead, but this is precarious at best and requires advanced driving skills. The best option is to park at Waikolu and hike.

From the road, follow the signs for Pepe'opae Bog. Once the trail begins, stay on the metal boardwalk. If you step off, expect to sink shin-deep into the soggy moss and mud. The boardwalk runs for 1.5 miles through some of the most pristine rainforest left in the state. Hikers who make it to the end are rewarded with a view into **Pelekunu Valley,** plunging 4,000 feet through the uninhabited, untouched wilderness below. Hikers can attempt the climb on their own, and **The Nature Conservancy** (808/553-5236, hike_molokai@tnc.org) leads hikes into Pepe'opae once per month March to October; advance reservations are required.

PU'U KOLEKOLE

On the same 4WD road leading to the Pepe'opae trailhead, hikers who take the fork to the right will reach the start of the **Pu'u Kolekole Trail,** a two-mile hike to the 3,951-foot summit of Pu'u Kolekole. The view overlooks the southern shore and fringing reef, the island's best view of the southern coast.

West Moloka'i

Given western Moloka'i's lack of mountains, and that the land is privately owned, all of the hikes on this side of the island follow the isolated coast.

KAWAKIU AND 'ILIO POINT

A nice walk from the condo complexes of Kaluakoi follows either the coast or a dusty dirt road to the secluded beauty of **Kawakiu Beach.** From Maunaloa Highway (Hwy. 460), take the Kalukaoi Road exit and follow it to the bottom of the hill before making a right on Kaka'ako Road. A left on Lio Place leads to the Paniolo Hale parking lot, where you can follow the signs for the beach, crossing over the fairway of the old golf course

MOLOKA'I
HIKING AND BIKING

mossy and green Pepe'opae Bog

before you reach the shore. Make a right, and it's 45 minutes of walking along the coast to Kawakiu.

If the tide or surf is too high to walk along the coast, turn inland past **Pohaku Mauliuli Beach** (Make Horse Beach). After a few minutes, you'll be on a dirt road that leads north and deposits you at Kawakiu. About 100 yards before the road drops onto the sand at Kawakiu, there's an ancient Hawaiian *heiau* out on the rocky point. To continue on to 'Ilio Point, follow the coast for another 30 minutes, where you'll eventually encounter an old Coast Guard LORAN station and refreshingly little else. Be sure to bring plenty of water, and let someone know where you're going beforehand, since this area is exceptionally remote.

MO'OMOMI COASTAL TRAIL

Hikers with a 4WD vehicle can visit **Mo'omomi** (page 301) where a coastal trail connects a string of beaches with a windswept series of dunes. Each month March to October, **The Nature Conservancy** (808/553-5236, hike_molokai@tnc.org) leads guided hikes through the area, and while the trail is open year-round, due to the fragile ecosystem, it's imperative that hikers stay on the trail to protect the natural surroundings.

★ Cultural Hike into Halawa Valley

You heard it here first: The **Cultural Hike into Halawa Valley** (808/542-1855 or 808/551-5538, www.halawavalleymolokai.com, $75, $45 under age 12) is the best activity in Hawaii. The caveat is that you have to be interested in Hawaiian culture, as this hike is about more than walking through a rainforest to a beautiful waterfall; it's an educational experience and a journey back in time, where you are welcomed into one of Hawaii's most sacred valleys.

You'll pass numerous *heiau*, the temples that have sat here silently for centuries, and crush *kukui* nuts straight from the trees to

Hike to waterfalls in historic Halawa Valley.

feel the healing oils. Depending on the season, your guide might pick *lilikoi* (passionfruit) or guava from the trees to share as a snack on the trail, and if it begins to rain back in the valley, just grab an enormous elephant ear leaf as a natural umbrella. You'll learn about taro and how it's cultivated, learn how residents hunt pigs with knives, and hear stories of the 1946 tsunami from the last remaining resident. At the end of the hike is Moa'ula Falls, a multi-tiered 250-foot waterfall that spills toward a plunge pool, where the rocks are dotted with ancient petroglyphs. This is the real Hawaii, and if you schedule the hike, bring along a *ho'okupu,* or offering—pieces of fruit or items you'd use around the house.

To book the trip, phone and leave a message, or book through the **Moloka'i Outdoors** (808/553-4477, www.molokaioutdoors.com) desk in Hotel Moloka'i or through **Moloka'i Fish and Dive** (53 Ala Malama Ave., 808/553-5926, www.molokaifishanddive.com). You can also just show up around 9am at the pavilion at the end of

Don't Change Moloka'i

Nowhere in the islands do the war drums against development beat louder than in Moloka'i, often with regard to development around the island's beaches. It's a complex and sensitive issue, but a popular bumper sticker on the island describes local sentiment: "Moloka'i: not for sale. Just visit. Our lifestyle and economy depend on it." Some visitors assume residents of Moloka'i are anti-tourism, but Moloka'i vendors know tourism is integral to the struggling island economy.

But a glance across the Pailolo Channel to the resorts of Ka'anapali demonstrates what Moloka'i wants to avoid becoming. Most of the island is majority indigenous Hawaiian, and in many ways it is the last holdout of ancient Hawaiian culture. With development comes modernization and loss of culture, as seen in countless indigenous societies across the globe.

The concept of land ownership has never existed in traditional Hawaiian culture. We are stewards of the land, not its owners. Given this belief, Moloka'i residents don't instantly buy in to Western concepts of property rights, real estate, and development. The people of Moloka'i are happy to welcome visitors to share their culture and aloha, but not outsiders who want to put up housing developments, wind farms, or piers to accommodate cruise ships. As another popular bumper sticker says, "Don't change Moloka'i; let it change you," which is really all that needs to be said.

the road and hope for a last-minute spot (usually $60 pp). Be sure to pack mosquito repellent, water, snacks, and clothes that can get wet and muddy.

BIKING

The best mountain biking in Moloka'i is on the roads of the Moloka'i Forest Reserve, and road cyclists enjoy miles of open road with minimal traffic. The ride east from Kaunakakai to Halawa Valley is comparable to Maui's ride to Kahakuloa.

In central Kaunakakai, **Moloka'i Bicycle** (80 Mohala St., 808/553-5740 or 808/553-3931, www.mauimolokaibicycle. com, 3pm-6pm Wed., 9am-2pm Sat.) caters to every bike need: rentals (one-day $32 plus $20 per day thereafter, $120 per week), parts, and advice on good rides. They can arrange free pickups and drop-offs from a number of Moloka'i hotels, and $20-25 pickups from the airport and hotels such as Wavecrest and Kaluakoi.

Other Recreation

BIRD-WATCHING

Many of Hawaii's original bird species are extinct, but there are a number of rare species that cling to existence on Moloka'i. The last known sightings of the *oloma'o* (Moloka'i thrush), for example, as well as the *kakawahie* (Moloka'i creeper), were both in the forests of **Kamakou Preserve,** a rugged and wet mountain area that requires a 4WD vehicle to access. **The Nature Conservancy** (808/553-5236, hike_molokai@tnc.org) leads trips into the preserve once per month March through October.

Closer to town, if you're interested in volunteering in one of Moloka'i's wetlands or learning more about the island's endangered bird species, contact **Nene O Moloka'i** (808/553-5992 or 808/553-9029, www.nene. net, nene@aloha.net), a nonprofit organization dedicated to protecting Moloka'i's endangered waterfowl.

The 45-acre **Kakahai'a National Wildlife Refuge,** 5.5 miles east of Kaunakakai, is not open to independent visitors but can be visited on a tour through the **Maui County National Wildlife Refuge office**

(808/875-1582). The refuge is home to endangered *ae'o* (Hawaiian stilts) as well as endangered *'alae ke'oke'o* (Hawaiian coots).

During the fall and winter it's common to see *kolea* (Pacific golden plover) scuttling across the shore and grassy areas of the island. These birds migrate to the Arctic Circle during summer before returning to Hawaii for the winter. Once the *kolea* are seen in the islands, locals know that the humpback whales aren't far behind.

FISHING

Fish are central to Moloka'i's culture, and it's the only island where fishing is sustainably managed around the Hawaiian lunar calendar. Fishing is a way of life on the island, and aside from the fishponds along the southern coast, many houses have traditional fishing nets hanging and drying in the yard. Offshore, the Penguin Banks between Moloka'i and O'ahu are some of Hawaii's best fishing grounds, although fishing near shore is good as well. As a general rule, the earlier you depart, the better your chances for success.

Charters

The best place in Kaunakakai for buying fishing accessories is **Moloka'i Fish and Dive** (53 Ala Malama Ave., 808/553-5926, www.molokaifishanddive.com, 7:30am-6pm Mon.-Sat., 8am-2pm Sun.), which also operates four-hour trips ($695 plus $125 per additional hour) on the 38-foot Delta cruiser *The Coral Queen.*

To throw out some lines with one of Hawaii's best fishers, book a charter with captain Mike Holmes of **Fun Hogs Fishing** (808/567-6789 or 808/336-0047, www.molokaifishing.com), an avid canoe racer and sailor. Aboard the 27-foot *AHI,* Holmes takes guests trolling for blue-water game fish such as mahimahi, ono, ahi, and marlin on four-hour charters ($450) or very reasonably priced full-day eight-hour charters ($600). Fun Hogs can also arrange seasonal whale-watching trips ($70 adults), private snorkeling charters, or any other sort of outing for six or fewer passengers.

Also based at Kaunakakai is Captain Joe Reich of **Alyce C. Sportfishing** (808/558-8377, www.alycecsportfishing.com), who similarly offers half-day, three-quarter-day, and full-day charters aboard his 31-foot cruiser. Call for rates, and expect fresh fish for dinner.

For a unique Moloka'i shore-based adventure, **Molokai Ocean Tours** (40 Ala Malama Ave., 808/553-3290, www.molokaioceantours.com) offers **evening torch fishing** off the Kapuaiwa Coconut Grove, as well as standard deep sea charters ($500-625).

GOLF

If you like your golf casual (meaning bring your own six-pack), the island's only golf course is the nine-hole **Ironwood Hills Golf Club** (Kalae Hwy., 808/567-6000, www.molokaigolfcourse.com, 7am-5:30pm daily, $18) in the cool eucalyptus groves of Kala'e. The course is at 1,200 feet elevation not far from Pala'au State Park, and the $18 greens fees are easy on the pocket. Carts are $9, club rentals are $10, and the driveway is a bumpy dirt road. Last tee off is at 4pm.

Shopping

If your idea of vacation is spending time at the mall, you won't find the experience here. Most shops on Moloka'i are utilitarian general stores, some with worthy souvenirs.

KAUNAKAKAI

Shopping in Kaunakakai, you don't have to go very far: All the stores are on the same street. You can park on Ala Malama Avenue and walk to every shop in town.

Imports Gift Shop (82 Ala Malama Ave., 808/553-5734, 9am-6pm Mon.-Sat., 9am-1pm Sun.) offers a small selection of imported gifts and locally made items in addition to clothing, souvenirs, and snacks.

Kalele Bookstore and Divine Expressions (64 Ala Malama Ave., 808/553-5112, www.molokaispirit.com, 10am-5pm Mon.-Fri., 9am-2pm Sat.) offers books, locally crafted artwork, jewelry, wooden bowls, and even advice on touring Moloka'i. It's an eclectic and worthwhile stop for some crafts and Moloka'i tales.

Moloka'i Art from the Heart (64 Ala Malama Ave., 808/553-8018, www.molokaigallery.com, 10am-5pm Mon.-Fri., 9am-2:30pm Sat.) is a consignment boutique where 136 local artists are able to showcase and sell their products. Find anything from sarongs to CDs to original paintings. It's a great stop to support the local community.

By the gas station at the end of the road, **Moloka'i Fish and Dive** (61 Ala Malama Ave., 808/553-5926, www.molokaifishanddive.com, 7:30am-6pm Mon.-Sat., 8am-2pm Sun.) provides basic gear for the beach as well as camouflage hunting clothing, stickers, souvenirs, and a surf shop.

Toward the wharf, upstairs from the American Savings Bank, **Something For Everybody** (40 Ala Malama Ave., 808/553-3332, www.allthingsmolokai.com, 10am-6pm Mon.-Fri., 9am-1pm Sat.) is where you'll find *na mea Moloka'i,* "all things Moloka'i," from

clothing and stickers to custom-made hats as well as fantastic advice about the island.

On the more practical side, **Moloka'i Drugs** (28 Kamoi St., 808/553-5790, 8:45am-5:45pm Mon.-Fri., 8:45am-2pm Sat.), in the Kamoi Professional Center, covers medicinal needs and can fill prescriptions.

TOPSIDE

In Kualapu'u, the gift shop **Coffees of Hawaii** (1630 Farrington Ave., 808/567-9490, 9am-4pm Mon.-Sat.) has aloha shirts, coffee, island themed gifts, and staff who can explain the history of coffee on the island.

At the Holomua Junction, **Blue Monkey** and **Beach Break** (2130 Maunaloa Hwy., 808/567-6091, 10am-4pm Mon.-Sat.) combine to create the island's largest retail space. Part surf shop and part craft boutique, this modern store has clothing, art, gifts, and island souvenirs. This is a must-stop for shopping on Moloka'i, as it combines the flavor of every other store on the island.

WEST MOLOKA'I

With the 2008 closing of Moloka'i Ranch, a lot of Maunaloa businesses closed too, so options for shopping are limited.

A Maunaloa staple since 1980, the **Big Wind Kite Factory** (120 Maunaloa Hwy., 808/552-2364, www.bigwindkites.com, 8:30am-5pm Mon.-Sat., 10am-2pm Sun.) is an eclectic hodgepodge of handmade kites and woodwork from Bali. As the only store left in the town, by process of elimination, it's worth a look. The owner, Jonathan, will give free factory tours of where the kites are made, help you fly a kite in the park, or even make a kite for any children you may have with you. The store has the largest collection of books found on the island. It's possible to visit repeatedly and still find something new. Look for the rainbow stairs in what is left of central Maunaloa.

MOLOKAʻI
FOOD

Entertainment

For a truly authentic island experience, visit the **Coffees of Hawaii Espresso Bar** (1630 Farrington Ave.) for the weekly *kanikapila* jam session (10:30am Tues.), where a collection of locals strum ukulele and dance hula on the porch.

Paddler's Inn (10 Mohala St., 808/553-3300, www.molokaipaddlersinn.com) has a "Ladies Night" (8pm-midnight Wed.), and often has live music other nights of the week. Rolling Rock draft beer is $3 all day, and you'll find evening drink specials and football on the TV. Check the website for an up-to-date schedule.

The musical group Na Ohana Hoaloha can usually be found at **Hotel Molokaʻi** (1300 Kamehameha V Hwy., 808/660-3397) 3pm-5pm Sunday. The best show of the week is long-running *Na Kupuna* (4pm-6pm Fri.). Far more than live music by the ocean, it's an evening of stories and song with some of the island's most respected *kupuna* (elders) and the tight-knit local community. Other nights of the week have live music until 9pm and a lively scene at the bar.

Food

Food on Molokaʻi is mostly "local style," meaning stick-to-the-ribs plate lunches, but recent years have seen a welcome increase in culinary diversity. The options are sparse outside Kaunakakai, so be sure you have a plan for food if you venture away from town.

KAUNAKAKAI
American

The island's only restaurant to serve resort-quality food is ★ **Hale Kealoha** (1300 Kamehameha V Hwy., 808/660-3400, 7am-9pm daily, $14-24), which also has Molokaʻi's only restaurant tables with an oceanfront view. A kitchen fire closed the restaurant for four years, and it finally reopened in November 2015 in a huge leap forward for the entire Molokaʻi culinary scene. Hale Kealoha uses fresh ingredients sourced on the island, including shrimp from Keawa Nui Farms and an *ulu* (breadfruit) turkey burger. You'll also find pasta dishes, omelets, burgers, steaks, and salads, and since it's the island's only spot with a hotel liquor license, you can order a cocktail from the oceanfront bar and enjoy the nightly live music.

In the center of Kaunakakai, ★ **Paddler's Inn** (10 Mohala St., 808/553-3300, 11:30am-9pm daily, $10-16) has the best chicken *katsu* you'll find on Molokaʻi. The closest thing to a sports bar on the island, Paddler's has multiple TVs and ice-cold beer on tap, with occasional live music in the afternoon and happy hour (2pm-6pm daily) plus $3 Rolling Rocks all day. In summer, Paddler's is the place to be for the canoe races, and the fish-and-chips, burgers, plate lunches, and sandwiches are some of the best on the island. Order from the window inside, and grab a seat on the patio.

Finally, even sleepy Kaunakakai has a takeout burger joint, and the patties at **Molokaʻi Burger** (20 Kamehameha V Hwy., 808/553-3533, 7am-9pm Mon.-Sat., $5-9) don't disappoint. Little more than a drive-through shed next to Molokaʻi Pizza Café, this place has budget burgers big enough to fill you up. For a local treat, skip the bun and spring for a *loco moco*, a hamburger patty served with two eggs, white rice, and gravy.

Coffee Shop
While it isn't exactly a coffee shop, **Home**

Town Groceries (93 Ala Malama Ave., 808/553-3858) serves Moloka'i's earliest cup of coffee, beginning at 5am daily.

Farmers Market

If you happen to be in town on a Saturday morning, the **Farmers Market** (7am-noon Sat.) is held on the sidewalk in front of the banks, and it is as much a social event as a shopping experience for fresh, locally grown food. Don't be surprised if you find fisherfolk selling their catch from the back of a truck.

Filipino

Big Daddy's (67 Ala Malama Ave., 808/553-5841, 8am-6pm daily, under $9), along the main Ala Malama Avenue strip, serves a variety of inexpensive Filipino food and Hawaiian fare, in addition to the eggs and omelets for breakfast and local-style plate lunches. Next door is Big Daddy's Market, for a limited selection of groceries, some prepared foods, and a few true Filipino delicacies such as *balut*.

Ice Cream

To step back in time to the days of dessert at the general store, **Kamoi Snack-n-Go** (28 Kamoi St., 808/553-3742, 10am-9pm Mon.-Fri., 9am-9pm Sat., noon-9pm Sun.) has tubs of ice cream like succulent Kona mud pie, which you can get in a waffle cone. There are fresh chocolate chip cookies baked daily, as well as free Wi-Fi, an assortment of gifts, and the old-school charm of a drugstore counter.

Local Style

In central Kaunakakai, ★ **Kanemitsu Bakery** (79 Ala Malama Ave., 808/553-5855, 5:30am-6:30pm Tues.-Sun., $5-9, cash only) isn't just a restaurant; it's a Moloka'i institution that has served baked goods and bread since 1922. Breakfast and lunch are plate-lunch fare, but what catapults the bakery to legendary status is **Hot Bread Lane** (8pm-11pm Tues.-Sun.), where their famous hot bread is served from a window in a dingy, dimly lit alley out back. The experience feels

illicit, trading cash for gargantuan loaves of cream cheese- and strawberry-filled bread. Other flavors include cinnamon and butter, or a blueberry with cream cheese. Loaves ($7-8) are big enough for two or three people.

For a quick plate lunch at a local favorite, check out **Maka's Corner** (35 Mohala Place, 808/553-8058, 7am-9pm Mon.-Fri., 8am-1pm Sat.-Sun., $7-10) in the middle of town, where you'll find hamburger steak, teriyaki chicken, and heaping bowls of *saimin.*

Markets

Friendly Market (Ala Malama Ave., 808/553-5595, 8:30am-8:30pm Mon.-Fri., 8:30am-6:30pm Sat.) stays open later than most places in town and is a great spot to pick up picnic supplies for a beach day.

If the Friendly Market doesn't have what you need, **Misaki's Groceries and Dry Goods** (Ala Malama Ave., 808/553-5505, 8:30am-8:30pm Mon.-Sat., 9am-noon Sun.), a few doors down, should be able to fill the gap.

Natural Foods

If you simply can't handle another plate lunch and need healthy fare, head to **The Store House** (145 Puali Place, 7am-5pm Mon.-Fri., 9am-3pm Sat., $5-10) for mango or strawberry tropical bowls ($5.75) topped with almonds, granola, coconut, banana, and honey. You'll also find kale and protein smoothies ($7.50) as well as salads, *kombucha,* and BLT sandwiches. This small spot is family run, and the fresh food is an oasis in a town of rice and mac salad.

Pizza

The de facto Moloka'i pizza spot is **Moloka'i Pizza Café** (15 Kaunakakai Place, 808/553-3288, 10am-10pm Mon.-Thurs., 10am-11pm Fri.-Sat., 11am-10pm Sun., $10-25, cash only), in the last building on the road toward the ferry dock. Pizzas are served either whole or by the slice ($2.60), and there's also a decent selection of pasta dishes as well as rides and games for the kids.

TOPSIDE
Coffee Shop
For a morning or afternoon pick-me-up, **Coffees of Hawaii Espresso Bar** (1630 Farrington Ave., 808/567-9490, 6am-5pm Mon.-Fri., 8am-8pm Sat., 8am-5pm Sun.) is a happening spot to grab a coffee, mocha, or glazed guava pretzel. The coffee is grown and processed right across the street. Try the Moloka'i Mule Skinner, the island's signature blend.

Local Style
A longtime Moloka'i classic, ★ **Kualapu'u Cookhouse** (1700 Farrington Ave., 808/567-9655, 7am-2pm Mon., 7am-8pm Tues.-Sat., 9am-2pm Sun., $8-14, cash only) is a swinging-screen-door plate-lunch institution where life moves slowly. Order inside at the counter and sit outside on the open-air lanai. You'll get your food when it's ready—no sooner, no later, no worries. Try the chicken *katsu* or *loco moco*, and if you're really hungry, order your plate "*kanaka*-style" for an additional $7.

WEST MOLOKA'I
Since the Moloka'i Ranch shuttered its operations, there are no restaurants on this side of the island. If you want to put together a picnic for the beach, **Maunaloa General Store** (200 Maunaloa Hwy., 808/552-2346, 9am-6pm Mon.-Sat., 9am-noon Sun.) has basic grocery items. If you're hanging out on the beach in Kaluakoi and need an overpriced snack, there's a **sundry store** (9am-5pm daily) in the otherwise abandoned resort.

EAST MOLOKA'I
The only restaurant on the east end is ★ **Mana'e Goods & Grindz** (mile marker 16, Hwy. 450, 808/558-8498, 6:30am-4pm Mon.-Fri., 7:30am-4:30pm Sat.-Sun., $6-9), where a takeout window serves everything from chicken *katsu* to freshly made fruit smoothies. If the banana pancakes happen to be on the menu, don't even hesitate—just order them.

Where to Stay

Moloka'i is gloriously free of resorts, and no building on the island is taller than a palm tree. The closest thing you'll find to a resort is laid-back Hotel Moloka'i, which has a concierge, an oceanfront restaurant, a bar, and daily maid service. Most of the island's accommodations are condos, and both **Moloka'i Vacation Properties** (808/553-8334, www.molokai-vacation-rental.net) and **Friendly Isle Realty** (808/553-3666, www.molokairealty.com) have a wide selection of options. Like elsewhere in the islands, check **VRBO** (www.vrbo.com) for deals on privately owned condos.

WEST MOLOKA'I
Staying in West Moloka'i means you're really far from everything—except beaches and sunsets. The weather has a tendency to be drier, but it's a 25-minute drive to Kaunakakai and the closest restaurant or gas. While the abandoned Sheraton complex is endlessly creepy, there are still a large number of condo units in the surrounding vicinity of Kaluakoi, as well as a handful of privately owned condos that are closer to Dixie Maru Beach.

One of the largest in West Moloka'i is the **Ke Nani Kai** (50 Kepuhi Place, 800/490-9042, www.kenanikai.com, $100-200), an expansive complex that has a swimming pool, one- and two-bedroom units, and affordable rates.

Closer to the beach, the **Paniolo Hale** offers similar accommodations just steps from the shore. Units here rent for $110-225 per night with a two- to three-night minimum, although some units have longer minimum stays.

complex on a tiny sliver of a beach with a large number of individually owned units as well as others managed by Castle Resorts (808/553-5944). The three-story complex has a large open courtyard with barbecue facilities and a swimming pool. The trade winds here are strong in the afternoon, and the swimming out front is marginal, but this is a convenient option toward the center of the island.

EAST MOLOKA'I

Along this eastern section of the island are the bulk of vacation rentals, cottages, and B&Bs. Afternoons are punctuated by brisk trade winds, and the setting is more tropical than arid West Moloka'i.

Bed-and-Breakfasts

Ka Hale Mala (808/553-9009, www.molokai-bnb.com, $80, with breakfast $90, cash only) is less than five miles east of Kaunakakai on Kamakana Place, on the ground floor of a family house set amid a tropical garden. There is a large living room, a full kitchen, a full bath, a separate bedroom, and a laundry room, plus use of snorkel gear.

Condominiums

The largest condo on the east end of the island is the **Wavecrest Resort** (808/558-8101, $100-200), at mile marker 13, with individually owned units. General amenities include a swimming pool, a tennis court, laundry facilities, and a nicely manicured five-acre setting. One- and two-bedroom units have full kitchens and look across the Pailolo Channel toward Maui. There is a front desk (7:30am-1:30pm Mon.-Fri.).

Vacation Rentals

The ★ **Aloha Beach House** (808/828-1100 or 888/828-1008, www.molokaivacation.com) is a great little two-bedroom cottage on the beach near Waialua, with a full kitchen, washer and dryer, and a view looking across to Maui. Best of all, a swimmable beach is just out the front door. Rates are $250 with a three-night minimum, plus a $175 cleaning fee.

Hotel Moloka'i under the light of a full moon

CENTRAL MOLOKA'I

Refreshingly basic and in the nontouristy cool uplands of Kala'e, near the Kualapu'u Coffee Farms and Kalaupapa Peninsula, **Hale Manu Guesthouse** (808/567-9136, www.halemalu-molokai.com, cash only) is a small, relaxed place with two guest rooms ($55) and a small cottage ($80). Guest rooms share a bath, and all rooms have access to a full kitchen in the main house. Discounts are available for longer stays.

Near Kaunakakai, ★ **Hotel Moloka'i** (808/660-3408, www.hotelmolokai.com, $175-250) is on the water and offers A-frame rooms in a resort-style setting, with a swimming pool, activities desk, included Wi-Fi, and live entertainment every night. The rooms, refurbished numerous times, have fridges and microwaves. This is a convenient, comfortable, and relaxing option. Rates vary by room size and season, and it's home to the island's only oceanfront restaurant and bar.

Near Kaunakakai, the **Molokai Shores** (1 and 2 bedrooms $190-250) is a condominium

Where to Stay on Moloka'i

Name	Type	Price	Features	Why Stay Here?	Best For
★ Aloha Beach House	vacation rental	$250	oceanfront, kitchen	location, romantic	couples, groups, families
Dunbar Beachfront Cottages	vacation rental	$190	oceanfront, kitchen	location, quiet	couples
Hale Manu Guesthouse	vacation rental	$55–80	kitchen	location, affordable	budget travelers, solo travelers, couples
★ Hotel Moloka'i	hotel	$175–250	kitchenette, pool, breakfast	modern, activities desk	couples, families
Ka Hale Mala	B&B	$80–90	gardens, kitchen	quiet, affordable	budget travelers, couples, solo travelers
Ke Nani Kai	condo	$100–200	pool, kitchen	close to beach, location	couples, families
Molokai Beach House	vacation rental	$250	oceanfront, kitchen	location, full amenities	couples, groups, families
Molokai Shores	condo	$190–250	pool, barbecue, kitchen, oceanfront	location	families, couples
Pala'au State Park	camping	$18	restrooms, pavilion	affordable, location	budget travelers
Paniolo Hale	condo	$110–225		oceanfront, kitchen	location, quiet
Papohaku Beach Park	camping	$10–20	toilets, water	oceanfront, quiet	budget travelers
★ Pu'u O Hoku Ranch	cottages	$200–300	kitchen, views	quiet, retreat	couples, honeymooners, families
Waikolu	camping	$18	toilets, picnic tables	quiet, nearby hiking	budget travelers, adventure travelers
Wavecrest Resort	condo	$100–200	pool, tennis, amenities	oceanfront, modern	couples, families

The two neat and trim two-bedroom **Dunbar Beachfront Cottages** (808/558-8153, www.molokai-beachfront-cottages.com, cash only) are on a secluded section of beach, each with a full kitchen, living room, laundry, and deck. These are quiet surroundings but you still have TV and free Wi-Fi. Cottages can sleep up to four. Rates are $190 with a three-night minimum, plus an $85 cleaning fee.

Also near Waialua is the **Molokai Beach**

House (808/261-2500, www.molokaibeach-house.com), a three-bedroom, two-bath oceanfront home with all amenities. There is a large yard with a picnic table on the ocean side, and inside is a big living room, a full kitchen, and a laundry room. The house sleeps up to six. Rates are $250 with a three-night minimum, or $1,600 per week, with a $125 cleaning fee.

At the far eastern end of the island high on the eastern hillside is 14,000-acre ★ **Pu'u O Hoku Ranch** (808/558-8109, www.puuohoku. com). The lodge and three cottages are some of the best and remotest on the island. This is a working ranch that's minutes away from the shore at Halawa Bay. Wi-Fi is available in a few spots, but most accommodations are "un-plugged." Check in at the ranch office along the highway at mile marker 25, where there is a small sundries store that sells basic food and gift items.

The two-bedroom Sunrise Cottage ($225) has a full kitchen and a covered lanai and sleeps up to four. The larger, four-bedroom Grove Cottage ($300 for 4, plus $30 pp additional guests) can sleep up to eight. From this cottage there are ocean views to Maui with amazing whale-watching in winter. Five miles closer to Kaunakakai along the main highway, the one-bedroom Sugar Mill cottage ($200) sleeps four, has a full kitchen, and is walking distance from one of the island's nicest beaches.

CAMPING

There are a couple of campgrounds scattered across Moloka'i for travelers on a budget.

The **Papohaku Campground** ($10 pp Mon.-Thurs., $20 pp Fri.-Sun.) at Papohaku Beach in West Moloka'i requires a permit from the Department of Parks and Recreation office (90 Ailoa St., 808/553-3204, 8am-1pm and 2:30pm-4pm Mon.-Fri.) in Kaunakakai, inside the Mitchell Pauole Center.

For the **Waikolu Campground**, near the Pepe'opae Bog, and the **Pala'au Campground**, within walking distance of the trailhead for the hike to Kalaupapa and accessible only with a 4WD vehicle, obtain permits online at least seven days in advance from the Hawaii Department of Land and Natural Resources (www.camping.ehawaii. gov, $18 for up to 6 people).

Getting There and Around

GETTING THERE
Air
When flying to Moloka'i, don't expect a big plane or a smooth ride. The small aircraft are vulnerable to the brisk trade winds, although the flights are scenic. Often flights from Maui provide views of Moloka'i's dramatic northern sea cliffs as well as aerial views of the Kalaupapa Peninsula. From Maui, sit on the left side of the aircraft for the best chance of waterfall and coastal views.

The largest planes are with **Ohana** (800/367-5320, www.hawaiianairlines.com), a subsidiary of Hawaiian Airlines, with 37-seat aircraft and multiple flights per day from both Kahului and Honolulu.

Both **Makani Kai Air** (808/834-1111, www. makanikaiair.com) and **Mokulele Airlines** (808/567-6381 or 866/260-7070, www. mokuleleairlines.com) offer direct flights from Honolulu and Kahului; any other city will require a connecting flight. Fares are often cheaper than the ferry, but be sure to check the baggage restrictions, since there isn't much space on the planes.

Moloka'i Airport
The **Moloka'i Airport** (MKK, 3980 Airport Loop, 808/567-9660) at Ho'olehua is a small open-air facility where you still walk out on the runway to board your plane. There's a single coffee shop (6am-6:30pm daily), and

the only rental car operator, **Alamo** (808/567-6381, www.alamo.com, 6am-8pm daily), has offices across the street.

FERRY

Though the **Moloka'i Ferry** (877/500-6284, www.molokaiferry.com, $62 adults, $31 ages 4-12, free under age 4) used to be the most convenient way to get to the island, it's now more expensive and less comfortable than the short 30-minute flights. Occasionally the ferry is still cheaper, especially if traveling with children, and it's also the best option if you're traveling with cargo or bringing longboards (the maximum surfboard length on flights is six feet). The ferry departs from Lahaina (6am Tues. and Thurs.-Sat.) and returns from Moloka'i (5pm Tues. and Thurs.-Sat.). The crossing takes 1 hour and 45 minutes, and while the ride over is pleasant, the return trip can be rough.

GETTING AROUND
Car Rental

The only rental-car agency with a booth at the airport is **Alamo** (808/567-6381, www.alamo.com, 6am-8pm daily), which has a large fleet of cars and 4WD Jeeps. If you rent from Alamo, don't lose your key—they don't have extras. For an affordable cruiser, check out **Molokai Car Rental** (105 Ala Malama St., 808/336-0670, www.molokaicars.com), a casual locally owned company that can deliver the car to the airport or ferry dock. They don't have 4WD vehicles, but ask about their room-and-car package at Hotel Moloka'i. The only place besides Alamo to get a 4WD vehicle, **Moloka'i Outdoors** (808/553-4477, www.molokai-outdoors.com) occasionally rents SUVs for stays of three days or longer. Finally, if you're taking the **Moloka'i Ferry** (877/500-6284, www.molokaiferry.com), ask about their cruise and car package deal.

Gas

There are only two gas stations on the island,

right next to each other in Kaunakakai. Be sure you have at least half a tank of fuel before heading out on an day trip to Halawa or Papohaku. **Rawlins Chevron** (Hwy. 450 and Kaunakakai Place, 6:30am-8:30pm Mon.-Thurs., 6:30am-9pm Fri.-Sat., 6:30am-6pm Sun.) has longer hours and more supplies, though it costs at least $0.75 more per gallon than on Maui.

Taxi

The best option for taxis on Moloka'i is **Hele Mai Taxi** (808/336-0937 or 808/646-9060, www.molokaitaxi.com), also offering private tours of the island. Expect to pay about $32 from the airport to Hotel Moloka'i, and $30 from the ferry to Kalaupapa Trail. Also available is **Mid-Nite Taxi** (808/658-1410 or 808/553-5652), although service can be spotty.

Shuttle Bus

If you're on a budget, the **MEO public shuttle bus** (www.meoinc.org) operates three routes across the island—but you need to be flexible with your schedule, and there's no service on weekends. Shuttle stops include Hotel Moloka'i and in front of Misaki's Market in central Kaunakakai. The Maunaloa shuttle stops at the airport, and the shuttle runs six times Monday-Friday to Maunaloa, and eight times Monday-Friday to Puko'o in East Moloka'i. Along the routes the driver will usually let you get off wherever you want. Although it's free, donations to keep the shuttle going are accepted. For schedules visit the website.

Tours

Moloka'i Outdoors (808/553-4477, www.molokai-outdoors.com) offers an Island Tour package ($150 adults, $78 children) from Halawa Lookout all the way to Papohaku Beach. Operating three times per week, these tours cover the island in an air-conditioned van and usually carry a small group of only 4-8.

Background

The Landscape

GEOGRAPHY

The island of Maui is 727 square miles, making it the second largest island in Hawaii behind the massive 4,029-square-mile Big Island of Hawaii. There are 120 miles of coastline. At its widest point, the island is 26 miles from north to south and 48 miles from east to west.

Known as the "Valley Isle," Maui is the product of two volcanoes—Haleakala and the older Mauna Kahalawai—that merged together into a central isthmus to form the island we know today. At 10,023 feet above sea level, Haleakala is estimated to be about 750,000 years old, making it half as old as Mauna Kahalawai, otherwise known as the West Maui Mountains, which have stood for 1.5 million years. In looking at the two mountains, it's evident that Mauna Kahalawai—with its deeply eroded valleys and dramatically carved peaks—has been exposed to the forces of nature longer than smooth Haleakala. Haleakala's aging is visible in the ravines of Kipahulu, the Kaupo Gap, and the cleft in the mountainside towering above Ke'anae.

Although the islands of Maui, Lana'i, Moloka'i, and Kaho'olawe are four separate landmasses today, all were once connected in an island known as Maui Nui (Great Maui). This massive island was larger than the modern-day Big Island, and it's estimated that the islands were joined until as recently as 20,000 years ago when sea levels were lower as a result of an ice age.

If you look at a map of Hawaii, you will notice that the islands align northwest to southeast. The islands were formed by volcanoes over a consistent hot spot in the mantle of the earth. The tectonic plate in the crust containing the islands drifts northwest at 3-5 inches per year, essentially creating an "island conveyer belt." Over the course of millions of years, islands bubble up from the ocean floor and drift off the hot spot. Their cores then become extinct volcanoes and they drift northwest, steadily eroding until they become shorter, smaller, and more dramatically sculpted. This explains why the Big Island of Hawaii, which has 500 new acres of land in its most recent eruption, is the largest island with the tallest mountains, and why Maui, next in the chain, is the second largest with the second tallest mountain. Kaua'i is the oldest in the chain at four million years, and of the 132 islands that make up the state of Hawaii, tiny Midway and Kure atolls are the northwestern reaches.

A seamount known as Lo'ihi is believed to be the next Hawaiian island in the long Pacific chain. Researchers estimate that the island of Lo'ihi will surface southeast of the Big Island in 10,000 years.

Rivers and Lakes

Maui has no navigable rivers, but there are hundreds of streams. Two of the largest are **Palikea Stream,** which runs through Kipahulu Valley, forming 'Ohe'o Gulch, and **'Iao Stream,** which has sculpted the amazing monoliths in 'Iao Valley. The two largest natural bodies of water are the 41-acre **Kanaha Pond** on the outskirts of Kahului and 500-acre **Kealia Pond** on the southern shore of the isthmus. Be aware that streams and rivulets can quickly turn from trickles to torrents, causing flash floods in valleys that were nearly dry only minutes before.

Previous: scenic viewpoint at historic Kalawao; oceanfront spot to say "I Do."

Hawaiian Archipelago

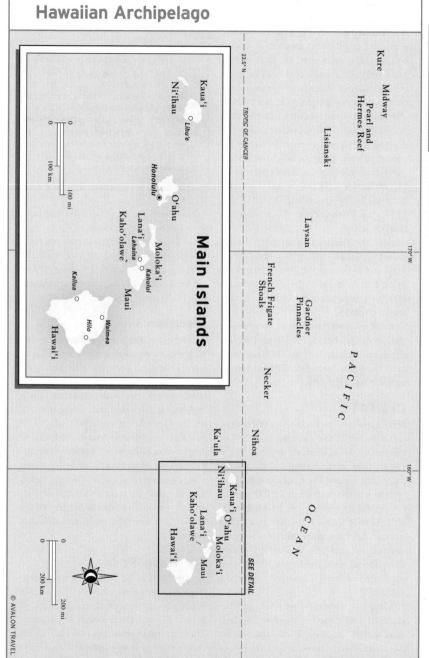

Main Islands

Kaua'i
Ni'ihau
Lihu'e

Honolulu
O'ahu
Lana'i
Lanaina
Kaho'olawe
Moloka'i
Kahului
Maui

Kailua
Waimea
Hilo
Hawai'i

Kure
Midway
Pearl and
Hermes Reef

Lisianski

Laysan

French Frigate
Shoals
Gardner
Pinnacles

Necker

Nihoa

Ka'ula

Kaua'i
Ni'ihau
O'ahu
Lana'i
Moloka'i
Kaho'olawe
Maui
Hawai'i

SEE DETAIL

PACIFIC

OCEAN

23.5° N
TROPIC OF CANCER

170° W

160° W

0   0
100 km   100 mi

0   0
200 km   200 mi

© AVALON TRAVEL

NATURAL DISASTERS

Maui has experienced a number of events that remain fresh in recent memory, the most dramatic being the 1946 **tsunami** that swept entire villages away along the flank of East Maui and flooded much of Halawa Valley on the eastern tip of Moloka'i. More recently, the tsunami that struck Japan on March 11, 2011, also caused a big mess in Maui. There was no loss of life, but Lahaina Harbor completely drained, and the returning water was strong enough to sink numerous boats and destroy the docks at many of the island's harbors. At Manele Harbor on Lana'i, the end of the ferry dock was finally repaired early in 2016.

The last **hurricane** to affect Maui was Hurricane Iniki in 1992, and while Maui avoided the billions in damage the storm caused on Kaua'i, waves destroyed the pier at Mala and sank numerous boats. Hurricane Iwa in 1982 crept close to the islands, although Maui is outside the hurricane belt, usually spared direct hits.

Although **earthquakes** are rare, a large temblor on October 15, 2006, caused enough damage to close the back road to Hana for almost two years due to landslides and structural damage to bridges.

CLIMATE

Maui, Lana'i, and Moloka'i have weather similar to the rest of the Hawaiian Islands. The weather on Maui depends more on where you are than on the season, and the average daily temperature along the coast is about 78°F in summer and about 72°F in winter. On Haleakala summit, the average is 43-50°F, although snow can fall in rare winter storms. The lowest temperature ever recorded on Maui was atop Haleakala in 1961, when it dropped well below freezing to 11°F. In contrast, sunny Kihei has recorded a blistering 98°F.

Maui has wonderful weather, and because of near-constant breezes, the air is usually clear and clean. Traffic and weather conditions never create smog, although on days when the winds blow from the south, a

The Tsunami Siren

If you are visiting Maui on the first workday of the month, don't be alarmed when you hear a loud siren around noon. This is the island's tsunami warning system. The sirens are systematically tested once a month. The loud wailing will last about 30 seconds, after which the regular peace and tranquility will resume. If you hear the tsunami siren at any other time, ask your hotel about potential tsunami evacuations, which have occurred three times since 2011.

volcanic haze, known as "vog," drifts up from the volcano on the Big Island.

On Lana'i, the average summer temperature along the coast is about 80°F, while the average winter temperature is about 70°F. It can be as much as 10 degrees cooler in Lana'i City, in the cooler uplands.

Precipitation

It's raining somewhere on Maui every day while other areas experience drought. A dramatic example is comparing Lahaina with Pu'u Kukui, both in West Maui and separated by only seven miles. Lahaina, which translates as "Merciless Sun," is hot, arid, and gets only 15 inches of rainfall annually, while Pu'u Kukui can receive close to 400 inches of precipitation. Other leeward towns get a comparable amount of rain as Lahaina, but as you move upcountry and around the north coast, the rains become more frequent. In Hana, rainfall is about five times as much as on the leeward side, averaging more than 80 inches per year.

The Trade Winds

Temperatures in the 50th state are both constant and moderate because of the trade winds, a breeze from the northeast that blows at 10 to 25 mph. These breezes are so prevalent that the northeast sides of the islands are always referred to as **windward,** regardless of where the wind happens to be blowing on

Polynesian Triangle

HAWAI'I

PACIFIC
OCEAN

Johnston Atoll

Palmyra Atoll

Baker   Christmas Island

EQUATOR

Phoenix Islands

Tuvalu   Marquesas

Samoa

Society
Islands   Tuamotu
Archipelago

Tahiti

Tonga   Cook
Islands   Austral Islands

Pitcairn

Easter Island

New Zealand

0   1000 mi
0   1000 km

© AVALON TRAVEL

any given day. You can count on the trades an average of 300 days per year, rarely missing a day during summer and occurring half the time in winter. Although usually calm in the morning, they pick up during the heat of the afternoon and weaken at night.

Kona Winds

Kona means "leeward" in Hawaiian, and when the trades stop blowing, these southerly winds often take over. To residents of Hawaii, *kona wind* is a euphemism for bad weather because it brings in hot, sticky air. Luckily, kona

winds are most common October to April, when they appear roughly half the time. The temperatures drop slightly during the winter, so these hot winds are tolerable, and even useful for moderating the temperature.

A kona storm is another matter. These subtropical low-pressure storms develop west of the Hawaiian Islands, and as they move east, draw winds from the south. Usually occurring only in winter, they can cause heavy rainfall and considerable damage, often continuing for the better part of a week. For locals, this is "winter."

Maui Ocean Conditions

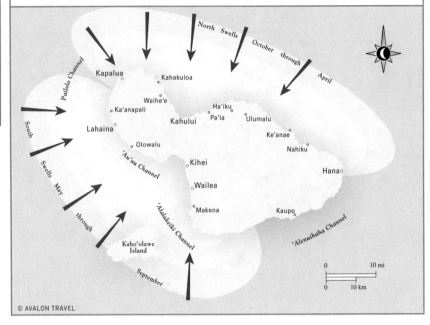

© AVALON TRAVEL

Plants and Animals

Anyone who loves a mystery will be intrigued by the speculation about how plants and animals first came to Hawaii. More than 2,000 miles from any continent, Hawaii is isolated from the normal ecological spread of plants and animals. Even the most tenacious flora and fauna would have trouble crossing the mighty Pacific. Those that made it by chance would find a totally foreign ecosystem where they had to adapt or perish. Survivors evolved quickly, and many plants and birds became so specialized that they were limited not only to specific islands in the chain but to habitats that frequently consisted of a single isolated valley. After traveling so far and adapting to a niche, they didn't budge again.

Before settlement, Hawaii had no fruits, vegetables, coconut palms, edible land animals, conifers, mangroves, or banyans. The early Polynesians brought 27 varieties of plants they needed for food and other purposes. About 90 percent of the plants on the Hawaiian Islands today were introduced after Captain Cook first set foot here. Tropical flowers, wild and vibrant as we know them today, were relatively few. In a land where thousands of orchids now brighten every corner, there were only four native varieties, the fewest in any of the 50 states. Today, the indigenous plants and animals have the highest rate of extinction anywhere on earth. By the beginning of the 21st century, native plants growing below 1,500 feet in elevation were almost completely extinct or totally displaced by introduced species. The land and its life have been greatly transformed by humans and agriculture.

The Forbidden Island

It's understandable that after a five-hour plane ride with a view of only water, many visitors to Maui are geographically disoriented. Seeing other islands looming on the horizon only makes it more confusing. If you are in South Maui facing the water, the island in the distance to the right is Lana'i. But what's that other island sitting silently to the left?

That mysterious island has a fascinating history of crime, death, destruction, and rebirth. **Kaho'olawe** (Ka-HO-OH-LAW-vay), with no residents and no hotels, is a dry island in the rain shadow of Haleakala. Kaho'olawe was only sporadically settled during ancient times. During the mid-1800s, after Christian missionaries convinced Queen Ka'ahumanu to abolish capital punishment, the barren island was used as a penal colony, where life was difficult and miserable; many prisoners died of starvation. In 1841 a band of banished criminals swam from Kaho'olawe to Makena on Maui, raided a settlement, loaded some canoes with food, and then paddled victoriously back to their emaciated fellow prisoners. With food now in hand, the marooned prisoners focused on solving their second problem: the lack of women. A team paddled across the channel to Lana'i and returned with a boatful of volunteers from the women-only penal colony there. Suddenly, all on Kaho'olawe was right again.

Once the penal colony was closed, there were a number of failed attempts at ranching on the island. After the Japanese invasion of Pearl Harbor in 1941, Kaho'olawe was placed under martial law, and over the next 50 years the forbidden island served as a practice bombing range for the military. Longtime residents remember the island glowing orange in the evening due to the explosions.

Legions of indigenous Hawaiian activists protested the bombing of a major Hawaiian island. The protests intensified in 1976 when a group of activists headed to Kaho'olawe. On the way to the island, their boats were stopped by a U.S. Coast Guard helicopter. Nine people landed and spent a few hours on the island before being detained. Kaho'olawe became a catalyst for change that indigenous Hawaiian activists rallied around. The bombing finally ceased in 1990. Some island residents believe that the billions of dollars in real estate investments on the nearby Wailea shore were the real reason it stopped: a political donation here, an old friend there, and *voila!*, no more bombing.

Today, the island of Kaho'olawe is owned by the state of Hawaii, although it exists under the stewardship of organizations such as the Kaho'olawe Island Reserve Commission and Protect Kaho'olawe Ohana. No commercial activities are permitted, and long-term goals such as clearing the island of ordnance and replanting native foliage have already begun. The U.S. Navy spent $400 million clearing the island of millions of pounds of military debris—the largest ordnance removal in the nation's history. Despite these efforts, vast unknown quantities of debris remain. There are also hundreds of recorded archaeological sites, ensuring that Kaho'olawe will forever be dedicated to Hawaiian culture.

PLANTS
Introduced Species

The majority of flora considered exotic was introduced either by the original Polynesians or by later settlers of European origin. The Polynesians who colonized Hawaii brought foodstuffs, including coconuts, bananas, taro, breadfruit, sweet potatoes, yams, and sugarcane. Non-Hawaiian settlers brought mangoes, papayas, passion fruit, pineapples, and the other tropical fruits and vegetables. The flowers, including protea, plumeria, anthuriums, orchids, heliconia, ginger, and most hibiscus species, have come from every continent on earth.

Native Trees

Koa and 'ohi'a are two indigenous trees still seen on Maui. Both have been greatly depleted by the foraging of introduced cattle and goats and through logging and forest fires. The **koa**, a form of acacia, is Hawaii's finest native tree. It can grow to more than 70 feet and has a strong, straight trunk that can

Microclimates

The weather in Maui can be confusing. Often it can be raining at your hotel but sunny two miles down the road, and the wind can be blowing 30 knots at one beach but completely still at another.

On the mainland frontal storm systems can stretch for thousands of miles, but weather on Maui is regulated by microclimates. Since the trade winds blow from a northeasterly direction, towns on the northern or eastern coasts are on the windward side of the island and are prone to more wind and rain. Towns on the southern and western shores are in the lee of the steep mountains and are consequently drier and calmer. This explains why parts of the island such as Kapalua, Napili, and Hana are wetter and drier than Lahaina or Kihei. Conversely, during the hot summer months when Lahaina can swelter in 90°F heat, the northern areas of Napili and Kapalua can be 10 degrees cooler and blessed with a cooling breeze.

Many visitors only check the weather forecast on sites such as Weather.com, which only displays the forecast for the Kahului Airport, on the windier and wetter windward side of Maui. Consequently the forecast will almost always call for showers. Don't be discouraged: Chances are resort areas such as Wailea, Kihei, Lahaina, or Ka'anapali are experiencing a completely different, often sunnier, forecast. For a more accurate weather forecast, see local weather sites such as www.mauiweathertoday.com, which breaks down the island's forecasts by microclimates.

Microclimates don't vary from each other all the time. October to April, Maui can be affected by large cold fronts in the same way that the mainland is. If a large cold front in the North Pacific, which will eventually drop snow and rain on the U.S. West Coast, decides to swing south, the front can move across the islands and bring heavy rain everywhere. While these fronts often dissipate over Kaua'i and O'ahu before reaching Maui, thereby make Kaua'i and O'ahu wetter than Maui, occasionally the front will envelop the entire state and bring up to a week of rain.

For locals, this is what's known as "winter." The island might not get snow (except atop Haleakala), but Maui is still prone to winter storms that bring a lot of rain. No one wants to have a week of rain on their vacation, but a "normal" winter day in Hawaii can be 78°F and sunny, or 74°F and rainy—but at least it's warm.

If you're staying in Kapalua, Napili, or Ka'anapali and it's windy and rainy at your hotel, don't assume it's raining everywhere. If you are planning a vacation in winter, particularly January or February, cross your fingers that you'll enjoy some midwinter sun.

---

measure more than 10 feet in circumference. The Hawaiians used koa as the main log for their dugout canoes, and elaborate ceremonies were performed when a log was cut and dragged to a canoe shed. Koa wood was also preferred for paddles, spears, and surfboards, and today, fine Hawaiian galleries across the islands sell koa wood bowls and crafts.

The 'ohi'a is a survivor and therefore the most abundant of all the native Hawaiian trees—though a recent outbreak of 'ohi'a disease is currently ravaging the forests. The 'ohi'a produces a tuft-like flower—usually red, but occasionally orange, yellow, or white, the latter being rare and elusive—that resembles a pompon. The strong, hard wood was used to make canoes, poi bowls, and temple images. 'Ohi'a logs were also used as railroad ties and

shipped to the mainland from Pahoa on the Big Island. It's believed that the golden spike finally linking the rail lines spanning the U.S. East and West Coasts in Ogden, Utah, was driven into a Puna 'ohi'a log.

'Ahinahina (Silversword)

Found on the high alpine slopes of Haleakala above the 6,000-foot level, the 'ahinahina plant is an iconic symbol for the beauty of Haleakala Crater. The plant may live for only a few years or for nearly a century, but each ends its life by sprouting a gorgeous stalk of hundreds of purplish-red flowers before withering from a majestic six-foot plant to a flat, gray skeleton. 'Ahinahina bloom mostly in July and August, but they can bloom as early as

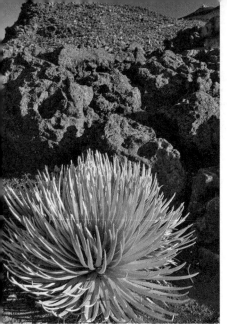
a silversword, or *'ahinahina,* in Haleakala Crater

May and as late as November. An endangered species, *'ahinahina* are completely protected.

Protea

The slopes of leeward Haleakala between 2,000 and 4,000 feet elevation have perfect growing conditions for protea. The days are warm, the nights are cool, and the well-drained volcanic soil has the right minerals. Protea make excellent gifts that can be shipped anywhere, and although they are beautiful as fresh-cut flowers, they have the extra benefit of drying superbly: just hang them in a dark, dry, well-ventilated area. You can see protea, along with other botanical specialties, at the gardens, flower farms, and gift shops in Kula.

ANIMALS
Birds

One of the great tragedies of natural history is the continuing demise of Hawaiian bird life. Perhaps only 15 original species of birds remain of the more than 70 indigenous species that thrived before the coming of humans. Since the 1778 arrival of Captain Cook, 23 species have gone extinct, with 31 more in danger. Hawaii's endangered birds account for 40 percent of those officially listed as endangered or threatened by the U.S. Fish and Wildlife Service. In the last 200 years, more than four times as many birds have become extinct in Hawaii as in all of North America.

Despite the threats, a few cling to life in the remote reaches of the East Maui rainforest, with the *'akohekohe, 'i'iwi,* and *'amakihi* some of the notable varieties. While visitors aren't likely to encounter many of the island's forest birds, those interested in these fragile species should contact the **Maui Forest Bird Recovery Project** (www.mauiforestbird.org) for more information and ways to volunteer.

Other than forest birds, two water birds found on Maui are the **Hawaiian stilt** (*ae'o*) and the **Hawaiian coot** (*'alae ke'oke'o*). The stilt is about 16 inches tall and lives on Maui at Kanaha and Kealia Ponds, with a black body, white belly, and distinctively pink legs.

At Haleakala Crater, the dark-rumped petrel is found around the Visitors Center about one hour after dusk May to October. The *nene* **goose**—the Hawaiian state bird—is a close cousin of the Canada goose and can be found in large numbers in the grass around Paliku Cabin.

Mammals

Hawaii's only two indigenous land mammals are the Hawaiian monk seal and the hoary bat; all other mammals have been introduced. While **monk seals** are sometimes sighted along island shores and reefs, the most famous mammals are the whales and dolphins that ply the waters offshore. The channels among the islands of Maui County are home to the world's largest population of **humpback whales.** These acrobatic, aerial cetaceans are a delight for winter visitors, and there are few things like the thrill of a 45-ton animal erupting out of the water before your eyes. Humpbacks migrate to the islands from November to May to mate, give birth, and care

BACKGROUND
PLANTS AND ANIMALS

No Land Predators

Maui can be a hiker's dream, and not just because of the scenery. Unlike other parts of the world, where bears, mountain lions, and snakes are a concern, Maui has no land predators. Remote sections of the island are home to wild boars, axis deer, and mountain goats, although all flee at the sound of human footsteps. There are centipedes and a small number of scorpions, but unless you're hiking through a compost pile, you're not likely to encounter them. When you set off on a hike, there is nothing to worry about in the way of natural predators.

for their young, and during the course of their four-month stay, they don't eat anything at all.

While whales are only observed during the winter, **dolphins** are year-round residents and a common sight around the islands. There are three distinct pods of Hawaiian spinner dolphins residing along West Maui, South Maui, and the southwestern coast of Lana'i. The acrobatic spinners can complete up to seven full rotations in the air before splashing back down into the water. Larger bottlenose dolphins are also occasionally seen, while pan-tropical spotted dolphins are confined to deeper waters.

PLANTS AND ANIMALS OF LANA'I

Most of Lana'i's flora and fauna have been introduced. The **Cook pine** and the **mouflon sheep** were a human intervention to improve the natural, often barren habitat. These species have adapted so well that they now symbolize Lana'i in the way that the pineapple once did. Besides the mouflon, Lana'i boasts **axis deer, Rio Grande turkeys,** and a number of **ring-necked pheasants.** Like the other islands of Hawaii, Lana'i, unfortunately, is home to native birds that are headed for extinction, although the recent rediscovery of a colony of *'ua'u* (Hawaiian petrels) on the summit of Lana'ihale has given hope that all is not yet lost.

PLANTS AND ANIMALS OF MOLOKA'I

The *kukui,* or candlenut tree, is common to all the Hawaiian Islands, and while it's the official tree for the state, its tiny white blossom is Moloka'i's official flower. The *kukui,* introduced centuries ago by the early Polynesians, grows on lower mountain slopes, is distinguished by its pale green leaves, and dominates the valleys of lush eastern Moloka'i.

Land animals on Moloka'i, such as **pigs, goats,** and **axis deer,** were introduced by humans. Moloka'i's feral pigs of the upper wetland forests of the northeast, indiscriminate in their relentless hunt for food, are ecological nightmares that virtually bulldoze the rainforest into fetid pools and gouged earth, where mosquitoes and other introduced species thrive while driving out the indigenous species. Today, pigs are hunted and fences keep them out of some fragile areas.

Offspring from a pair of goats left by Captain Cook on the island of Ni'ihau spread to all the islands and were well adapted to life on Moloka'i. Originally from the arid Mediterranean, goats could live well without any surface water, a condition prevalent over most of Moloka'i. Today, they're found primarily in the mountainous area of the northeast.

History of Maui

DISCOVERY OF THE ISLANDS

It is unknown exactly when the first Polynesians arrived in Hawaii, but the great deliberate migrations from the southern islands seem to have taken place AD 400 to 800, although anthropologists keep pushing the date back as new evidence appears. They arrived through an uncanny ability to sail and navigate without instruments, using the sun by day and the moon and stars by night. The first planned migrations were from the Marquesas, a group of 11 islands in eastern Polynesia, and for five centuries the Marquesans settled and lived peacefully on the new land.

It appears that in the 12th century, a deliberate exodus of warlike Tahitians arrived and subjugated the settled islanders. A Tahitian priest named Pa'ao introduced the warlike god Ku and the rigid *kapu* system of laws, forever altering the religious and social landscape. Voyages between Tahiti and Hawaii continued for about 100 years, and Tahitian customs, legends, and language became the Hawaiian way of life. Suddenly, for reasons not recorded, the voyages discontinued, and Hawaii returned to isolation.

CAPTAIN COOK

On January 18, 1778, Captain Cook's 100-foot flagship HMS *Resolution* and its 90-foot companion HMS *Discovery* first caught sight of the island of O'ahu. Two days later, Cook ventured ashore at the town of Waimea to reprovision his ships, and from this moment, life would never be the same for the Hawaiians. He didn't stay long in Waimea, but Cook noted in his diary that the Hawaiians looked similar to other peoples of the Pacific he had encountered, specifically those of New Zealand.

Once the seafarers were on shore, brass medals were traded for a mackerel, and Cook noted that the Hawaiians were quite enamored with the ships. Sailors immediately took to mixing with the women, bringing the first sexually transmitted diseases to the island. They would later ravage the population.

When Cook returned a year later, his impact would become much more significant. Cook had named Hawaii "the Sandwich Islands" in honor of one of his patrons, John Montague, the Earl of Sandwich. On his return voyage he spotted Maui, on November 26, 1778. After eight weeks seeking a suitable harbor, the ships bypassed the island and finally found safe anchorage at Kealakekua Bay on the Kona coast of the Big Island. Fortunately Mr. Anderson, the ship's chronicler, left a handwritten record of the strange and tragic events that followed.

When Cook landed on the Big Island it was the time of the *makahiki,* a celebration dedicated to the beloved god Lono. For a few days, as Cook circled the island, the Hawaiians circled it too, parading a structure that resembled a ship's mast: a crossbeam held overhead with two flowing white sheets of tapa. On January 16, 1779, as the Hawaiians reached Kealakekua Bay, Lono's sacred harbor, Cook's ship came into the port. Because of the timing with the *makahiki,* the Hawaiians believed Cook to be a god and welcomed him to shore with respect.

In the following weeks the Englishmen overstayed their welcome, but when they left, the *Resolution* broke down at sea. Cook returned to Kealakekua but was no longer well received. As the Hawaiians stole random items from the sailboat, the sailors became violent. When the Hawaiians stole a cutter that had been moored to a nearby buoy, Cook lost his temper—a reaction that would ultimately cost him his life. He went ashore with backup, intending to take Chief Kalaniopu'u hostage for ransom. When the violence escalated, Cook was killed. A bitter, protracted argument ensued over the return of Cook's bones (he was ceremoniously roasted to remove the bones from the flesh), and upon finally receiving the bones of their leader, Cook's men sailed back to England.

At the time of Cook's visit, Hawaii was in political turmoil. In the 1780s the islands were divided into three kingdoms: Kalaniopu'u ruled the Big Island and the Hana district of Maui; Kahekili ruled the rest of Maui, Kaho'olawe, Lana'i, and eventually O'ahu; and Kaeo ruled Kaua'i. Soon after, the great warrior Kamehameha conquered all the islands and brought them under one rule, a dynasty that would last 100 years until the Hawaiian monarchy fell forever.

With regard to Western explorers, however, it became known that Hawaii was a convenient stop on routes to the Pacific Northwest and China, leading to an influx of Westerners and increased foreign trade. Hawaii, it seemed, was no longer a secret.

THE OLOWALU MASSACRE

In 1790, as Western traders were still beginning their forays to the islands, the U.S. merchant ship *Eleanora,* commanded by Yankee captain Simon Metcalfe, was looking for a harbor after a long voyage from the Pacific Northwest. Following a day behind was the *Fair American,* a tiny ship sailed by Metcalfe's son, Thomas. While the elder Metcalfe's ship was anchored off the southern coast of Maui, some natives slipped close in their canoes and stole a small boat, killing a sailor in the process.

Upon learning that the perpetrators were from the village of Olowalu, about five miles south of Lahaina, Metcalfe decided to sail there and trick the Hawaiians by first negotiating a truce and then unleashing full fury upon them. Signaling he was willing to trade, he invited canoes of innocent natives to visit his ship. In the meantime, he ordered that all cannon and muskets be readied with scatter shot. When the canoes were within hailing distance, he ordered his crew to fire at will.

More than 100 people were slain, and the Hawaiians remembered this killing as "the Day of Spilled Brains." Metcalfe then sailed away to Kealakekua Bay and, in an unrelated incident, succeeded in insulting a ruling chief named Kameiamoku who vowed to annihilate the next *haole* ship he saw.

Fate sent him the *Fair American* and young Thomas Metcalfe. The little ship was overrun by superior forces, and in the ensuing battle, the mate, Isaac Davis, so distinguished himself by open acts of bravery that his life alone was spared. Kameiamoku later turned over both Davis and the ship to Kamehameha. Meanwhile, while harbored at Kealakekua, the senior Metcalfe sent John Young to reconnoiter. Kamehameha, having learned of the capture of the *Fair American,* detained Young so he could not report, and Metcalfe, losing patience, marooned his own man and sailed off to Canton. Kamehameha quickly realized the significance of his two captives and the *Fair American* with its brace of small cannons. He appropriated the ship and made Davis and Young trusted advisers, eventually raising them to the rank of chief. They would all play a significant role in the unification of Hawaii.

KAMEHAMEHA'S UNIFICATION OF THE ISLANDS

Kamehameha was born on the Big Island of Hawaii, after a prophecy that he would become a "killer of chiefs." Because of this, other chiefs ordered the child to be killed, so his mother had to sneak off to the royal birthing stones near Mo'okini Heiau on the island's Kohala coast. After giving birth, she gave the child to a servant, who took him down the coast to raise him in solitude. As he grew and matured, Kamehameha proved himself a fierce and hardy warrior, and in due time became one of the strongest chiefs on the island.

In 1790, Kamehameha invaded Maui with the assistance of cannons from the captured *Fair American.* In the Battle of Kepaniwai at 'Iao Valley, Kamehameha killed so many commoners it's said that he dammed the stream waters with their bloody bodies. After his decisive victory on Maui, Kamehameha was drawn back to the Big Island to quell uprisings on his home island. When the king of Maui, Kahekili, sailed to the Big Island to exact revenge for the slaughter at ʻIao, he was thoroughly beaten by Kamehameha's forces at the Battle of Waimanu Valley. Demoralized and defeated, Kahekili succumbed to the rule of Kamehameha, and the battle for Maui had been won.

By the time Kamehameha had won the Big Island and Maui, Hawaii was becoming a regular stopover for ships seeking the lucrative sandalwood trade with China. In February 1791, Captain George Vancouver, who had originally sailed on Cook's ill-fated voyage, returned to Kealakekua and was greeted by a throng of 30,000. The captain at once recognized Kamehameha, who was wearing a Chinese dressing gown that he had received in tribute from another chief, who in turn had received it directly from the hands of Cook himself. Captain Vancouver became a trusted adviser of Kamehameha and told him about the Westerners' form of worship, and the captain gave him gifts of beef cattle, fowl, and breeding stock of sheep and goats. The Hawaiians were cheerful and outgoing, and they showed remorse for the earlier incident when they indicated that the remainder of Cook's bones had been buried in a temple close to Kealakekua. Young, by this time firmly entrenched in Hawaiian society, made no request to sail away with Vancouver. During the next two decades of Kamehameha's rule, the French, Russians, English, and Americans discovered the great whaling waters off Hawaii, and their increasing visits shook the ancient religion and social order of *kapu.*

Kamehameha's final victories over the other islands would come later, with a decisive conflict in 1794 on the island of Oʻahu. Kamehameha and 16,000 of his troops pushed Kalanikupule—the leader of Oʻahu—back into the mountains of Nuʻuanu to the edge of towering cliffs that form the backdrop of Honolulu. After fierce fighting, Kamehameha's men drove Kalanikupule's warriors over the cliffs, and with the dramatic victory, Kamehameha now took control of Oʻahu. In 1796 Kamehameha put down a revolt on Hawaii, and Kaumualiʻi, the king of Kauaʻi, recognizing his strength, gave up the island rather than suffer attack. For the first time in history, Kamehameha became the sole ruler of all of the islands in Hawaii.

Under Kamehameha, social order was medieval, with *aliʻi* (nobility) owing their military allegiance to the king and the serf-like *makaʻainana* paying tribute and working the lands.

The great king ruled until his death on May 8, 1819. Hawaii knew a peaceful rule under Kamehameha. After years on Maui, he returned to his home in Kona on the Big Island where he eventually died. To this day, his burial place is unknown. His son, Liholiho, gained the kingdom (and would become Kamehameha II), although Kamehameha's wife Kaʻahumanu had a strong influence and power.

NO MORE *KAPU*

As Kaʻahumanu used her strength to counsel Kamehameha's son and successor, Liholiho, she knew that the old ways would not carry Hawaii into the future. In November 1819 she inspired Liholiho to eliminate the *kapu* system of laws that had so rigidly dominated Hawaiian society. Men eating with women had been prohibited under *kapu,* as was women eating certain foods, such as bananas and particular fish. To exhibit the end of the *kapu* system, Kaʻahumanu and Liholiho ate together in public, thereby shattering these important taboos and marking the demise of the old ways. As the first morsels passed Kaʻahumanu's lips, the ancient gods of Hawaii tumbled. Throughout the land, revered *heiau* were burned and abandoned and idols knocked to the ground. Now the people had nothing but their weakened inner selves to rely on. Nothing and no one could answer their prayers; their spiritual lives were in shambles.

MISSIONARIES AND WHALERS

The year 1819 was of the utmost significance in Hawaiian history. It marked the death of Kamehameha, the overthrow of the ancient *kapu* system, the arrival of the first whaler in Lahaina, and the departure of Calvinist missionaries from New England, determined to convert the heathen islands. With the *kapu* system and all of the ancient gods abandoned (except for the fire goddess Pele of Kilauea), a great void existed in the souls of the Hawaiians.

Missionaries

Into this spiritual vortex sailed the brig *Thaddeus* on April 4, 1820. Coming ashore in Kailua-Kona, the Reverends Bingham and Thurston were granted a one-year trial missionary period by King Liholiho. They established themselves on the Big Island and O'ahu and from there began the transformation of Hawaii. By 1824 the new faith had such a foothold that Chieftess Keopuolani, the first wife of Kamehameha and mother of Kamehameha II, climbed to the fire pit atop Kilauea and defied the volcano goddess Pele. This was even more striking than the previous breaking of the food *kapu* because the strength of Pele could be seen. Keopuolani ate forbidden 'ohelo berries and cried out, "Jehovah is my God."

The year 1824 also marked the death of Keopuolani, who was given a Christian burial. She had set the standard by accepting Christianity, and several of the *ali'i* had followed the queen's lead. Liholiho had sailed off to England, where he and his wife contracted measles and died. During these years, Ka'ahumanu allied herself with Reverend Richards, pastor of the first mission in the islands, and together they wrote Hawaii's first code of laws based on the Ten Commandments. Foremost was the condemnation of murder, theft, brawling, and the desecration of the Sabbath by work or play. The

early missionaries had the best of intentions, but they were blinded by the single-mindedness that was also their greatest ally. *Anything indigenous* was felt to be inferior, and they set about wiping out all traces of the old ways. In their rampage they reduced the Hawaiian culture to ashes—more so than the diseases brought in by the whalers.

Whalers

A good share of the common sailors of the early 19th century came from the lowest levels of the Western world. Many a lecherous drunkard had awoken from a stupor and found himself on the pitching deck of a ship, discovering to his dismay that he had been "pressed into naval service." These sailors were uneducated and lawless. Their present situation was dim, their future hopeless, and they would live to be 30 if they were lucky and didn't die from scurvy or a thousand other miserable fates. They snatched brief pleasure in every port and jumped ship at any opportunity, especially in an easy berth such as Lahaina. In exchange for aloha they gave drunkenness, sloth, and insidious death by disease. By the 1850s the population of native Hawaiians had tumbled from the estimated 300,000 reported by Captain Cook in 1778 to barely 60,000. Common conditions such as colds, flu, sexually transmitted diseases, and sometimes smallpox and cholera decimated the Hawaiians, who had no natural immunity to these foreign ailments.

Two Worlds Collide

The 1820s were a time of confusion for the Hawaiians. When Kamehameha II died, the kingdom passed to Kauikeaouli (Kamehameha III), who made his residence in Lahaina. The young king was only nine years old when the title passed to him. His childhood was during the cusp of the change from old ways to new, and he was often pulled in two directions by vastly differing beliefs. Since he was royal born, he was bound by age-old Hawaiian tradition to mate and produce an heir with the highest ranking *ali'i* in

The Hawaiian Written Word

Prior to the arrival of the missionaries, the Hawaiian language—like all other Polynesian languages—had no written form. All information was passed along orally through song, chant, or dance. The missionaries, however, found it difficult to convert Hawaiians to Christianity without the ability to read, write, or create a Hawaiian-language Bible, so the missionaries took on the task of creating a Hawaiian orthography and establishing a written form of the language.

With a 12-letter alphabet in place (14 if the *okina* and *kahako* characters are included), the island's first printing press was shipped from Honolulu and housed here in Hale Pa'i in 1834. Not long after its arrival, the first printed newspaper west of the Rocky Mountains—a four-page publication called *Ka Lama Hawaii*—was printed on Valentine's Day of the same year. Along with the press came myriad other benefits of written language, such as hymn books, written laws, and a Hawaiian Constitution. In the course of a single lifetime in the 19th century, the indigenous Hawaiians went from having no form of written communication to boasting one of the highest literacy rates in the world.

the kingdom. This mate happened to be his younger sister, Princess Nahi'ena'ena. To the old Hawaiian advisers, this arrangement was perfectly acceptable. To the influential missionaries, incest was an unimaginable abomination. The young king could not stand the mental pressure imposed by conflicting worlds, and he became a teenage alcoholic too royal to be restrained.

Meanwhile, Nahi'ena'ena was under even more pressure because she was a favorite of the missionaries, having been baptized into the church at age 12. At times she was a pious Christian, at others she drank all night. As the prince and princess grew into their late teens, they became even more attached to each other, and whenever possible, they lived together in a grass house built for the princess by her father.

In 1832 the great Ka'ahumanu died, leaving the king on his own, and in 1833 Kamehameha III fell into total drunken confusion, one night attempting suicide. After this episode he seemed to straighten up a bit and mostly kept a low profile. In 1836, Princess Nahi'ena'ena was convinced by the missionaries to take a husband, and though she married Leleiohoku, a chief from the Big Island, she continued to sleep with her brother. It's uncertain who fathered the child, but Nahi'ena'ena gave birth to a baby boy in September 1836, though the young prince survived for only a few hours and Nahi'ena'ena never recovered.

She died in December 1836 and was laid to rest in Lahaina. After the death of his sister, Kamehameha III became a sober and righteous ruler, and he governed longer than any other king until his death in 1854.

Missionaries Take Over

In 1823 the first mission was established in Lahaina, and within a few years many of the notable *ali'i* had been converted to Christianity. Construction began on Waine'e Church in 1828, while a struggle brewed between missionaries and whalers centering on public drunkenness and the servicing of sailors by indigenous women. The missionaries placed a curfew on sailors and prohibited local women from boarding ships. The sailors were outraged. In 1825 the crew of the *Daniel* attacked the home of Reverend Richards, and in 1827, sailors from the whaler *John Palmer* fired their cannon at his house, prompting the construction of the Lahaina fort.

The Great Mahele

In 1840, Kamehameha III instituted a constitutional monarchy, bringing about the Hawaiian Bill of Rights. The most far-reaching change was the transition to private ownership of land, although the Hawaiians did not think in terms of "owning" land. No one could *possess* land, one could only *use* land, and its ownership was a strange foreign concept. As a

The "Lawful Hawaiian Government"

At Ho'okipa Lookout and Maliko Gulch you will notice signs proclaiming that the land is under the jurisdiction of the "Lawful Hawaiian Government." While the issue of Hawaiian sovereignty is lengthy and complex, here are the basics about the ongoing movement.

The kingdom of Hawaii was formed in 1810 when King Kamehameha united all the islands under a single rule, and it lasted until 1893 when the monarchy was illegally overthrown in a bloodless coup by a group of Western businesspeople. While the kingdom existed under a monarchial system of rule from 1810 to 1840, a notable change took place in 1840 when King Kamehameha III changed the system of governance to a constitutional monarchy similar to those found in modern-day Spain, Thailand, or Sweden. A congress was established, there were recognized officials, and a constitution was drafted that outlined the laws of the nation. Due to the efforts taken to create a legitimate form of government, the kingdom of Hawaii was officially recognized by England and France in 1843, and the United States followed suit in 1846. Hawaii had embassies in dozens of countries; there was a Hawaiian embassy in Washington DC as well as consulates in New York and San Francisco.

In 1893, however, Western business interests overthrew Queen Lili'uokalani and formed the Republic of Hawaii, which was governed by Sanford Dole. A motion was put forth to be annexed by the United States, but it failed when President Grover Cleveland ruled through an investigation of the takeover that it was not performed through legal means. Another annexation attempt would be put forth in 1897, but this too would be shot down due to a letter of protest from Queen Lili'uokalani, who remained under house arrest, along with tens of thousands of Hawaiian signatures. Finally, with the outbreak of the Spanish-American War in 1898, U.S. congressional legislation decided that Hawaii would be occupied by U.S. military forces as a strategic military base in the Pacific. Once the war was over, the occupiers remained, and Hawaii stayed a territory to the United States despite the end of the hostilities (it would later become a state in 1959). Since Hawaii was never formally annexed by either treaty or war, however, the Hawaiian offices of government were consequently never abolished, and when Queen Lili'uokalani died in 1917, the offices sat vacant.

In 1993, President Bill Clinton signed the Apology Resolution, which basically said that the

result, naive Hawaiians gave up their lands for a song to unscrupulous traders, and land ownership issues remain a basic and unrectified problem to this day. In 1847, Kamehameha III and his advisers separated the lands of Hawaii into three groupings: crown land (belonging to the king), government land (belonging to the chiefs), and the people's land (the largest parcels). In 1848, there were 245 *ali'i* who entered their land claims in the *Mahele Book,* assuring them ownership. In 1850 the commoners were given title in fee simple to the lands they cultivated and lived on as tenants, not including house lots in towns. Commoners without land could buy small *kuleana* (farms) from the government for $0.50 per acre. In 1850, foreigners were also allowed to buy land in fee simple, and the ownership of

Hawaii from that day forward slipped steadily from the hands of its indigenous people.

SUGAR

While the first successful sugar plantation was on Kaua'i, Maui wasn't far behind when it came to refining the sweet stuff. Many of the successful sugar barons were sons of New England missionaries, and by the mid-1800s sugar mills were springing up from Hana to Lahaina. Labor was the main issue, however. Upon realizing their contracts amounted to indentured servitude, many of the Hawaiians refused to work. Chinese laborers were brought in, but rather than slaving for $3 a month, they often abandoned their contracts and went on to start other businesses. Japanese laborers were then tried, and they

United States was sorry for overthrowing the Hawaiian monarchy, recognizing officially that it had done so. It was at this time that sovereignty leaders realized that even though the monarchy had ceased to exist with the death of Queen Liliʻuokalani, the Hawaiian framework of government established had never actually disappeared. Since the framework was still in place, it simply needed to be reinstated with new officers, citizens, and elections.

Using the old electoral processes established in the 1864 constitution, elections began being held in 1999 to once again establish a congress for a kingdom that had never disappeared. Henry Noa was elected prime minister, there are now representatives to the congress from 24 districts across the state, and elections take place among the Hawaiian Kingdom citizens. In order to become a citizen of the Hawaiian Kingdom, you must swear an oath of allegiance to the kingdom and renounce your citizenship to the United States. As of July 2011, there were 400 citizens in the Hawaiian Kingdom, with 7,000 citizenship applications being processed. In addition to the elected offices, there are also a Department of Health and Department of Transportation. There is a slight chance you might see a vehicle displaying a Hawaiian Kingdom license plate on both the front and back of the car during your time on the island.

Citizens of the Hawaiian Kingdom are quick to point out, however, that they are not seceding from the United States, because the kingdom of Hawaii was never formally ceded in the first place. At no point did the offices and system of government cease to exist, and after a 107-year vacancy the positions are being filled once again. This reinstated government has been officially recognized in numerous international proceedings, notably at the International Criminal Court in 2012. No U.S. government grants are involved in the funding of the nation, and you will often see *huli huli* chicken stands (especially in the Wahikuli section of Lahaina) that help raise funds for reinstating the lawful Hawaiian government.

Proponents of the Hawaiian Kingdom do not hope to seek "nation within a nation" status such as those granted to Native Americans because this would mean formally ceding the nation to the overall governance of the United States. Instead, they would prefer to continue with their sovereignty, which was never formally abolished.

worked 10-hour days, six days a week, for $20 a month plus housing.

Eventually sugar was doing so well the industry seemed promising to foreigners who needed work. Boatloads of immigrants from Japan, Portugal, Germany, and Russia came to the islands, and their religions, foods, customs, and cultures mixed together in the multiethnic plantation communities. As the sugar industry boomed, the plantation owners became the new "chiefs" of Hawaii who would carve up the land and dispense favors. With the power of the sugar barons growing with each year, the writing was on the wall that the Hawaiian monarchy would soon be eliminated.

END OF THE MONARCHY

As with the Hawaiian people themselves, the Kamehameha dynasty was dying from within. King Kamehameha IV (Alexander Liholiho) ruled from 1854 to 1863, and his only child died in 1862. He was succeeded by his older brother Kamehameha V (Lot Kamehameha), who ruled until 1872. With his passing, the Kamehameha line ended. William Lunalilo, elected king in 1873 by popular vote, was of royal, but not Kamehameha, lineage. He died after only a year in office and, being a bachelor, left no heirs. He was succeeded by David Kalakaua, known far and wide as the "Merrie Monarch," who made a world tour and was well received wherever he went. Kalakaua died in 1891 and was replaced by his sister, Lydia Liliʻuokalani, last of the Hawaiian monarchs.

When Liliʻuokalani took the throne in 1891, the native population was at a low of 40,000. When the McKinley Tariff of 1890 brought a decline in sugar profits, she made no attempt to improve the situation, and planters saw her as an obstacle to economic growth. Lorrin Thurston, a Honolulu publisher, gathered a group of 30 men and challenged the Hawaiian monarchy. Naturally, the conspirators could not have succeeded without some solid assurances from a secret contingent in the U.S. Congress as well as outgoing President Benjamin Harrison, who favored Hawaii's annexation. Marines from the *Boston* went ashore to "protect American lives," and on January 17, 1893, the Hawaiian monarchy came to an end. As for Liliʻuokalani, she remained staunchly loyal to her people until her death in 1917, and her struggles are documented in *Hawaii's Story*, a powerful read detailing the history of the era.

ANNEXATION

In relinquishing the throne, Liliʻuokalani surrendered not to the conspirators, but to U.S. ambassador John Stevens. She believed that the U.S. government, which had assured her of Hawaiian independence and had signed numerous friendly treaties, would be outraged by the overthrow. Indeed, incoming President Grover Cleveland was appalled at the events that had transpired in Hawaii, and he sent a delegation to the islands to research their legality, with hopes of transferring lands back to the queen. Meanwhile, when the conspirators brought the movement for annexation to Congress, it failed to pass, given the shaky ground on which it stood. Not to be deterred, they refused to reinstate Liliʻuokalani, and instead continued to operate as a republic with Sanford Dole at the helm.

An unsuccessful countercoup was staged in 1895. After a cache of weapons was found in the queen's garden, Liliʻuokalani was relegated to house arrest in a bedroom of ʻIolani Palace. Over the next couple of years, two more annexation movements would be offered to the U.S. Congress, although after witnessing the stiff resistance of the Hawaiian people to formal annexation (a petition of over 30,000 signatures known as the Kuʻe Petition opposed joining the union), the movement failed in Congress three times.

Circumstances changed, however, when the United States was drawn into the Spanish-American War in 1898. Recognizing that Hawaii was strategically situated for fighting the Spanish in the Philippines and that Pearl Harbor would make the perfect naval port, a joint resolution of Congress was signed that deemed it acceptable to annex Hawaii as a circumstance of the impending war known as the Newlands Resolution.

There remains great debate today over the legality of the situation. In many ways it appears that since no formal annexation treaty was signed—particularly one pertaining to international lands that are extraterritorial of immediate borders—that Hawaii technically may never have been annexed through proper and constitutional channels. Furthermore, whatever documents were in fact signed were done so as an agreement with the Republic of Hawaii, and at no point was an agreement made with the original Hawaiian kingdom representing more than 90 percent of the population. Even now, over 120 years later, it remains a hotly contested issue, and as time marches on, there is growing support for the kingdom that may have never ceased to exist.

Nevertheless, as Hawaii entered the 20th century, it became largely Americanized. Hawaiian language, religion, and culture were nearly gone. Everyone dressed like Westerners and practiced Christianity, and Asians made up 75 percent of plantation workers. By 1900 everyone was encouraged to attend school, and almost 90 percent of Hawaiians were literate. Interracial marriages were accepted, and Hawaii became a true melting pot.

Pearl Harbor Attack

On December 7, 1941, the Japanese carrier *Akagi* launched the attack on Oʻahu. At the end of the day, 2,325 U.S. military members and 57 civilians were dead, 188 planes were destroyed,

18 major warships were sunk or heavily damaged, and the United States was in World War II. It roared on for four years through the Nagasaki and Hiroshima bombings, and when it was over, in the hearts of a nation, Hawaii was an integral part of the United States.

Statehood

During World War II, Hawaii was placed under martial law, but no serious attempt to intern the Japanese population was made. Many Japanese-Americans went on to gain the respect of the American people through their outstanding fighting record during the war. Hawaii's own 100th Battalion became the famous 442nd Regimental Combat Team, which would be the most decorated battalion in all of World War II. When these GIs returned home, no one was going to tell them that they were not loyal Americans. Many of these Americans of Japanese Ancestry (AJAs) took advantage of the GI Bill and received higher education. They also rallied grassroots support for statehood. When the vote finally occurred, approximately 132,900 voted in favor of statehood with only 7,800 votes against. Congress passed the Hawaii State Bill on March 12, 1959, and on August 21, 1959, President Eisenhower announced that Hawaii was officially the 50th state.

History of Lana'i

There was a time when the island of Lana'i was believed to have been dominated by spirits. Abandoned and considered taboo, the island was opened to settlement in the 1400s when a chief by the name of Kaka'alaneo banished his mischievous son Kaulula'au there, only to find that when Kaulula'au's campfire could be seen burning from Maui each night, it meant that the spirits had been driven out.

Lana'i went through the next few hundred years as a satellite of Maui. Its population of 3,000 indigenous people was ravaged in 1778 by Kalaniopu'u, aging king of the Big Island. The pillaging sent the population of the island into decline so that by the start of the 20th century only a handful of Hawaiians remained. The old order ended completely in 1900 when one of the last traditional *kanaka,* a man named Ohua, hid the traditional fish-god Kunihi and died shortly thereafter in his grass hut.

No one knows his name, but all historians agree that a Chinese man tried his luck at raising sugarcane on Lana'i in 1802. He brought boiling pots and rollers to Naha on the east coast, but after a year of hard luck gave up and moved on. About 100 years later a large commercial sugar enterprise was attempted at Maunalei. This time the sugar company built a narrow-gauge railroad to carry the cane, but again sugar cultivation was foiled. Religious scholars today suggest that since stones from indigenous *heiau* were used to build the railroad, the desecration of a sacred place is what ultimately turned the water brackish and caused the plantation to fail.

Meanwhile, in 1854 a small band of Mormon elders tried to colonize Lana'i by starting a "City of Joseph" at Palawai Basin. Walter Murray Gibson came to Palawai to lead an idyllic settlement for the Latter-Day Saints. While he set to work improving the land with funds from Utah, the Mormon Church discovered that the acreage at Palawai was not registered to the church at all, but to Gibson himself! He was excommunicated, and the bilked settlers relocated.

A few other business ventures proved uneconomical, and Lana'i languished. The last big attempt at cattle raising produced the Lana'i Ranch (1874-1951), part of the lands that make up the Cavendish Golf Course and the Lodge at Koele in Lana'i City. This enterprise did have one bright note in the New Zealander George Munro, who was hired as ranch manager. He imported all manner of seeds and cuttings in his attempt to foliate the island and create a watershed. Although the ranch eventually failed, Munro's legacy of Cook pines stands as a testament to this amateur horticulturist.

THE RISE AND FALL OF PINEAPPLES

In 1922 James D. Dole purchased much of Lanaʻi from the Baldwin family for $1.1 million, just $12 per acre. Dole had experienced success with canning pineapple on other islands, and the expansive Palawai Basin seemed perfect for growing his business.

With pineapple well established on the world market, Lanaʻi finally had a firm economic base. From a few thousand fruits in the early days, the flow at its peak reached a million fruits per day. They were shipped from the port at Kaumalapau, which was specially built in 1926 to accommodate Lanaʻi's "pines."

At the industry's height, Lanaʻi had 18,000 acres of pineapples under cultivation, the largest single pineapple plantation in the world. Virtually the entire island was operated by the Dole Co., whose name had become synonymous with pineapples. In one way or another, everyone on Lanaʻi owed his or her livelihood to pineapples. As time wore on, however, the tiny island struggled to compete with foreign operations, particularly those in the Philippines, and due to continual economic problems, Dole Co. made the decision to cut its losses. In 1986 David Murdock, the CEO of Castle & Cooke, acquired all of Dole's holdings on the island and started the transition to luxury tourism.

THE CASTLE & COOKE ERA

While Murdock absorbed Dole's struggling pineapple operation on Lanaʻi, plans were put into place to create a more sustainable economy. By the time that the last pineapple was picked in 1992, the glitzy new Manele Bay Resort had been open for a year, with the equally luxurious Lodge at Koele built where the Lanaʻi Ranch headquarters once stood. Suddenly, with the introduction of the resorts and the addition of more than 1,000 resort employees and personnel, the island's population nearly doubled, from around 1,700 to close to 3,000. Today, with the resort also having developed some private homes on the point around Hulopoʻe Bay, the island's population is around 3,300.

In addition to more and cleaner jobs, the resorts brought a different way of life to once homey little Lanaʻi. During the plantation days the island offered a simple, family-oriented way of life. Many of the island's old-timers long for those times. Despite the coming of multisource capitalism, however, the community remains tight-knit. Lanaʻi City is still the island's only town, although change is evident in refurbished homes and residential developments built to accommodate the swelling population.

THE LARRY ELLISON ERA

Just as soon as Lanaʻi residents had adjusted to life under Murdock, however, the Castle & Cooke CEO sold his stake in the island to Larry Ellison in June 2012 for upward of $500 million. Once again, the fate of the island hangs in the balance. Ellison received 98 percent of the island of Lanaʻi in the deal; the other 2 percent is federal and state property such as the boat harbors as well as personal plots of land owned by residents.

While official releases have pointed to Lanaʻi becoming a "model of sustainability," other rumblings have included a third hotel being built along the shore in Kahalepalaoa, the airport being expanded to accommodate direct flights from the mainland, and even talk of making the island a winter training ground for the Oracle fleet of racing sailboats. From an organic winery to a massive tennis center, rumors for the future abound. Nevertheless, in the first phases of his ownership, Ellison has done much to spruce up the island, including repaving the parking lot at Hulopoʻe Beach Park, renovating the restrooms, reopening the public swimming pool in Lanaʻi City, and renovating the Four Seasons Resort after a lengthy eight-month closure.

History of Moloka'i

Since the days of ancient Hawaii, Moloka'i has been steeped in mysticism and lore. It's believed to be the home of Laka, goddess of the hula, and Halawa Valley is believed to be one of the oldest settlements in Hawaii. Human sacrifices were performed at the 'Ili'ili'opae Heiau. Even today the power and *mana* of this little-known island is evident everywhere.

Captain James Cook first spotted Moloka'i on November 26, 1778, but because it looked bleak and uninhabited, he bypassed it. Eight years later Captain George Dixon sighted the island and decided to land, although little about this first encounter was recorded in his ship's log. Moloka'i slipped from the attention of the Western world until Protestant missionaries arrived at Kalua'aha in 1832 and reported the indigenous population at approximately 6,000.

CHANGING TIMES

From the time the missionaries arrived until the 1850s, Moloka'i remained almost unchanged. The Great Mahele of 1848 provided for private ownership of land, and giant tracts were formed into the Moloka'i Ranch. About 1850, German immigrant Rudolph Meyer came to Moloka'i and married a high chieftess named Dorcas Kalama Waha. Together they had 11 children, with whose aid he turned the vast lands of the Moloka'i Ranch into productive pastureland. In 1875, Charles Bishop bought half of the 70,000 acres of Moloka'i Ranch, and his wife, Bernice, a Kamehameha descendant, inherited the remainder. In 1898, the Moloka'i Ranch was sold to businesspeople in Honolulu for $251,000. This consortium formed the American Sugar Co. But after a few plantings, the available water on Moloka'i turned brackish, and once again Moloka'i Ranch was sold. Charles Cooke bought controlling interest from the other businesspeople in 1908 and remained in control of the ranch until 1988.

In 1921, Congress passed the Hawaiian Homes Act, which set aside 43,000 acres on the island for people who had at least 50 percent Hawaiian blood. By this time, however, all agriculturally productive land in Hawaii had already been claimed. The parcels given to the Hawaiians were poor and lacked adequate water. Many Hawaiians had long since left the land and were raised in towns and cities. Now out of touch with the simple life of the taro patch, they found it difficult to readjust. However, to prevent the Hawaiians from selling their claims and losing the land forever, the Hawaiian Homes Act provided that the land be leased to them for 99 years. Making a go of these 40-acre (*kuleana*) parcels was so difficult that successful homesteaders were called "Moloka'i Miracles."

In 1923 Libby Corporation leased land from Moloka'i Ranch at Kaluakoi and went into pineapple production. Del Monte followed in 1927 at Kualapu'u. Both built company towns and imported Japanese and Filipino field laborers, swelling Moloka'i's population and stabilizing the economy. Many of the indigenous Hawaiians subleased their *kuleana* tracts to the pineapple growers, and the Hawaiian Homes Act seemed to backfire. Instead of the homesteaders working their own farms, they were given monthly checks and lured into a life of complacency. Those who grew little more than family plots became, in effect, permanent tenants on their own property. More significantly, they lost the psychological advantage of controlling their own future and regaining their pride, as envisioned in the Hawaiian Homes Act.

MODERN TIMES

For the next 50 years life was quiet. The pineapples grew, providing security. Another large ranch, **Pu'u O Hoku** (Hill of Stars) was formed on the eastern tip of the island. It was originally owned by Paul Fagan, the

San Francisco entrepreneur who later developed the Hana Ranch on Maui. In 1955, Fagan sold Puʻu O Hoku to George Murphy, a Canadian industrialist, for a meager $300,000. The ranch, under Murphy, became famous for beautiful white Charolais cattle, a breed originating in France.

In the late 1960s, things quietly started happening on Molokaʻi. The Molokaʻi Ranch sold 6,700 ocean-side acres to the Kaluakoi Corp., which it controlled along with the Louisiana Land and Exploration Company. In 1969 the long-awaited Molokaʻi reservoir was completed at Kualapuʻu; finally West Molokaʻi had plenty of water. Shortly after Molokaʻi's water problem appeared to finally be under control, Dole Co. bought out Libby in 1972, lost millions in the next few years, and shut down its pineapple production at Maunaloa in 1975. By 1977 the acreage sold to the Kaluakoi Corp. was starting to be developed. The Molokai Sheraton (later called the Kaluakoi Hotel, but now closed) opened along with low-rise condominiums and 270 fee-simple homesites ranging 5 to 43 acres. Plans for this area included two more resorts, additional condominiums, shopping facilities, bridle paths, and an airstrip (it's only 20 minutes to Honolulu). It seemed that sleepy Molokaʻi with the tiny Hawaiian Homes Act farms was now prime real estate and worth a fortune.

To complicate the picture even further, Del Monte shut down its operations in 1982, throwing more people out of work. In 1986 it did resume planting 250-acre tracts, but now all of the pineapple is gone. Recently, coffee has been put into production near the old pineapple town of Kualapuʻu, some experimental plots of fruits and vegetables have been planted, and the Molokaʻi Ranch has brought in sheep and cattle. After Brierly Investments (now known as GuocoLeisure) bought the Molokaʻi Ranch in 1988, other changes started, including a total face-lift for the town of Maunaloa and a greater emphasis on tourism. An 18-hole golf course was built, the town of Maunaloa surged, and luxury accommodations throughout West Molokaʻi breathed life into the struggling economy.

All of that changed, however, in April 2008, when the ranch decided to cease all operations amid heavy opposition from locals critical of plans to develop Laʻau Point with over 200 luxury homes. Everything from the movie theater to the golf course to the hotels was closed, and over 120 employees lost their jobs. Today, the businesses still remain vacant. Though the ranch has claimed in recent years that the focus of growth will be on sustainable energy and agriculture, much of the island continues to struggle to find an economic foothold.

Government and Economy

GOVERNMENT

The government of Hawaii is limited to two levels, the state and the county, of which the islands of Maui, Moloka'i, Lana'i, and Kaho'olawe make up Maui County. Politics and government were at one time taken seriously in the Aloha State, which once consistently turned in the best national voting record per capita. For example, in the first state elections, 173,000 of 180,000 registered voters cast ballots—a whopping 94 percent of the electorate. These days, however, although there is still great voter turnout for state and local elections, Hawaii boasts one of the worst voter turnouts for national presidential elections. In the 2012 election, Hawaii saw a measly 62 percent of registered voters cast ballots, which gave it the distinction of having the lowest turnout in the nation. Because of Hawaii's location in the far west, when presidential elections are held, the results are often known before many in the state have time to cast their ballots. There is also a vocal minority that sees no point voting in elections for a nation they would rather not be a part of.

Hawaii is the only state to have just a single school district. A packed schoolroom in downtown Honolulu falls under the same set of guidelines as a one-room schoolhouse in West Moloka'i. Consequently, the idea of moving to a neighborhood where the schools are better isn't part of Hawaiian life.

ECONOMY

Today, tourism and the military are the two prime sources of income for Hawaii. Tourists come in anticipation of endless golden days on soothing beaches, while the military is provided with the strategic position of an unsinkable battleship. Each economic sector nets Hawaii billions annually. Also contributing to the state revenue are, in descending proportions, manufacturing, construction, and agriculture.

Tourism

Maui is the second most frequently chosen Hawaiian destination after O'ahu and welcomes more than two million visitors annually. On any given day about 40,000 visitors are enjoying the island. Maui's most popular attractions are Haleakala National Park, Lahaina town, the Maui Ocean Center, the Whalers Village Museum, 'Iao Valley, and Hana.

Agriculture

Maui generates agricultural revenue through cattle, pineapples, coffee, and flowers, along with a substantial subculture for *pakalolo* (marijuana). Cattle grazing occurs on the western and southern slopes of Haleakala, where 30,000 acres are owned by the Haleakala Ranch and more than 18,000 acres by the Ulupalakua Ranch. The upper slopes of Haleakala around Kula are a gardener's dream, where delicious onions, potatoes, and all sorts of garden vegetables are grown.

Maui's lone remaining sugar mill will close at the end of 2016, and while definitive plans are yet to be made as to what will replace the acreage, theories abound, from cattle to hemp to small organic farming. Hali'imaile Pineapple Company grows pineapples between Pa'ia and Makawao on the lower slope of Haleakala. Since Maui's last cannery closed in 2007, the only way to buy pineapples is in the form of a whole fruit.

Meanwhile, renegade entrepreneurs grow patches of *pakalolo* wherever they can find a spot that has the right vibes and is away from the prying eyes of authorities. Deep in the West Maui Mountains and along the Hana coast are favorite areas of island growers.

Military

The small military presence on Maui comprises a tiny U.S. Army installation near Kahului, the U.S. Coast Guard facility at Ma'alaea, and an Air Force tracking station on top of Haleakala.

People and Culture

POPULATION

Hawaii is a true ethnic melting pot where more than 50 diverse groups are represented. With 144,000 residents, Maui has the third largest island population in Hawaii, with about 7,000 residents on Moloka'i and 3,500 on Lana'i. Maui's population density is 210 people per square mile, with Moloka'i and Lana'i at 27 and 24 per square mile, respectively. The Kahului-Wailuku area has the island's greatest population with nearly 58,000 people, and the South Maui zip code is one of the island's largest, with over 29,000 residents in Kihei and Wailea. The Upcountry population is just over 39,000, including Pa'ia and Ha'iku, and West Maui has 21,000. In East Maui about 5,000 live along the Hana Highway, although fewer than 2,000 reside in Hana itself. For Maui County, 78 percent are urban while 22 percent live rurally. The ethnic breakdown of Maui County's 163,000 people is 36 percent Caucasian, 29 percent Asian, 23 percent mixed, 11 percent Hawaiian, and 1 percent other.

PEOPLE
Hawaiians

Any study of the indigenous Hawaiians is ultimately a study in tragedy because it nearly ends in their demise. When Captain Cook first sighted Hawaii in 1778, there were an estimated 300,000 Hawaiians living in relative harmony with their ecological surroundings; within 100 years a scant 50,000 demoralized and dejected Hawaiians existed almost as wards of the state. Today, although more than 240,000 people claim varying degrees of Hawaiian blood, experts say that fewer than 1,000 are pure Hawaiian, and this might be stretching it.

It's easy to see why people of Hawaiian lineage could be bitter over what they have lost, being strangers in their own land, much like Native Americans. The good news is Hawaiians are gradually reclaiming some parcels originally lost, with many families now owning homes through the Department of Hawaiian Home Lands. The movement for independent rule is continuing to gain strength, and a Hawaiian cultural awakening continues to grow by the year.

POLYNESIAN ROOTS

The Polynesians' original stock is muddled and remains an anthropological mystery, but it's believed that they were nomadic wanderers who migrated from both the Indian subcontinent and Southeast Asia through Indonesia, where they learned to sail and navigate on protected waterways. As they migrated, they honed their sailing skills until they could take on the Pacific. As they moved, they absorbed people from other cultures and races until they had coalesced into the Polynesians.

THE CASTE SYSTEM

Hawaiian society was divided into rankings by a strict caste system determined by birth and from which there was no chance of escaping. The highest rank was the *ali'i*—the chiefs and royalty. Ranking passed from both father and mother, and custom dictated that the first mating of an *ali'i* be with a person of equal status.

A *kahuna* was a highly skilled person whose advice was sought before any major project was undertaken, such as building a house, hollowing a canoe log, or even offering a prayer.

Besides this priesthood of *kahuna*, there were other *kahuna* who were not *ali'i* but commoners. The two most important were the healers (*kahuna lapa'au*) and the black magicians (*kahuna 'ana'ana*). The *kahuna lapa'au* had a marvelous pharmacopoeia of herbs and spices that could cure more than 250 diseases common to the Hawaiians. The *kahuna* 'ana'ana could be hired to cast a love spell over a person or cause his or her untimely death.

The common people were called the *maka'ainana*, "the people of land"—the farmers, craftspeople, and fishers. The land that they lived on was controlled by the *ali'i*, but they were not bound to it. If the local *ali'i* were cruel or unfair, the *maka'ainana* had the right to leave and live on another's lands. The *maka'ainana* mostly loved their local *ali'i* much like a child loves a parent, and the feeling was reciprocal. All *maka'ainana* formed extended families called *ohana* who usually lived on the same section of land, called *ahupua'a*. Those farmers who lived inland would barter their produce with the fishers who lived on the shore, and thus all shared equally in the bounty of land and sea.

A special group called *kauwa* was an untouchable caste confined to reservations. Their origins were obviously Polynesian, but they appear to have been descendants of castaways who had survived and become perhaps the aboriginals of Hawaii before the main migrations. It was *kapu* for anyone to go onto *kauwa* lands, and doing so meant instant death. If a human sacrifice was needed, the *kahuna* would summon a *kauwa*, who had no recourse but to mutely comply. To this day, to call someone *kauwa*, which now supposedly means only "servant," is still considered a fight-provoking insult.

HAWAIIANS TODAY

Many of the Hawaiians who moved to the cities became more and more disenfranchised. Their folk society stressed openness and a giving nature but downplayed the individual and the ownership of private property. Ni'ihau, a privately owned island, is home to about 120 pure-blooded Hawaiians, representing the largest concentration of them, per capita, in the islands. The Robinson family, which owns the island, restricts visitors to invited guests only.

The second-largest concentration is on Moloka'i, where 2,700 Hawaiians, living mostly on 40-acre *kuleana* of Hawaiian Home Lands, make up 40 percent of that island's population. The majority of mixed-blood Hawaiians, 240,000 or so, live on O'ahu, where they are particularly active in the hotel and entertainment fields.

Chinese

Next to Yankees from New England, the Chinese are the oldest migrant group in Hawaii, and their influence has far outshone their meager numbers. They brought to Hawaii, along with their individuality, Confucianism, Taoism, and Buddhism, although many have long since become Christians. The Chinese population of 56,000 makes up only 5 percent of the state's total, but the vast majority live on O'ahu. The first Chinese were brought to Hawaii in 1852 to work on sugar plantations. They were contracted to work for $3 a month plus room and board. After working 12-hour days six days a week, the Chinese nearly always moved on when their contracts were done and started their own businesses or shops.

Japanese

The first Japanese to come to Hawaii were ambassadors sent to Washington DC by the shogun, who stopped in Honolulu on the way in 1860. A small group came eight years later to work on the plantations, and a large influx came in 1885. After a migration of Japanese farmers who were sent over because of a famine, from 1897 to 1908 there was a steady influx. By 1900 there were more than 60,000 Japanese in the islands.

Caucasians

Next to Hawaiians themselves, Caucasians have the longest history in Hawaii. They settled in earnest since the missionaries of the 1820s and were established long before any other migrant group. Caucasians have a distinction separating them from all other ethnic groups in Hawaii in that they are lumped together as one. A person can be anything from a Protestant Norwegian dockworker to a Greek Orthodox shipping tycoon, but if his

Local Custom: No Shoes in the House

One of the local customs visitors often find shocking is the removal of shoes before entering a house. Unless you're directly told otherwise, no shoes in the house is a definite rule. There are a few theories about where the custom came from. Some say it's common sense not to track added dirt and germs inside, while others say it's a Japanese custom relating to not following in other people's shoes (or paths, or footsteps).

Whatever the origins might be, follow it if you visit a local's home. It's even usually requested by the management of vacation rentals. This rule doesn't extend to hotels or businesses, but if you notice a pile of shoes at the door of a small business, it's probably a sign that the owner prefers the no-shoes rule. If you are a fan of the custom or already practice it at home, locally made Please Remove Shoes signs and tiles can be purchased around the island.

or her skin is light, in Hawaii, he or she is a *haole*. What's more, a person could have arrived at Waikiki from Missoula, Montana, in the last 24 hours, or his or her *kama'aina* family can go back five generations, but again, if the person is Caucasian, he or she is a *haole*.

The word *haole* has a floating connotation that depends on the spirit in which it's used. It can mean everything from a derisive "honky" or "cracker" to nothing more than "white person." The exact Hawaiian meaning is clouded, although it largely has to do with the fact that when white people first arrived, they lacked any true *ha*, which means "spirit," or "breath." Europeans did not "share breath" in the same way that many Polynesian cultures would (such as the traditional greeting of pressing noses rather than hands), and this lack of "breath" lives on today in the semi-derogatory term.

Portuguese

Between 1878 and 1887, around 12,000 Portuguese came to Hawaii. Later on, 6,000 more arrived between 1906 and 1913. They were put to work on plantations and gained a reputation as good workers. Although they were European, for some reason they weren't *haole*, but somewhere in between. Nearly 27,000 Portuguese made up 11 percent of Hawaii's population by 1920. They intermarried, and the Portuguese remain an ethnic group in Hawaii today. One item they brought in that would influence local culture was the

cavaquinho, a stringed instrument that would evolve into the ukulele.

Filipinos

The Filipinos who came to Hawaii brought high hopes of amassing personal fortunes and returning home as rich heroes, but for most it was a dream that never came true. Filipinos had been U.S. nationals ever since the Spanish-American War of 1898 and as such weren't subject to immigration laws that curtailed the importation of other Asian workers. The first to arrive were 15 families in 1906, but a large number came in 1924 as strikebreakers. From the first, Filipinos were looked down on by other immigrant groups and were considered particularly uncouth by the Japanese. The value they placed on education was the lowest of any group, and even by 1930 only about half could speak rudimentary English, the majority remaining illiterate. They were billeted in the worst housing, performed the most menial jobs, and were the last hired and first fired.

One big difference between Filipinos and other groups was that the men brought no Filipino women to marry, so they clung to the idea of returning home. In 1930 there were 30,000 men and only 360 women. Many of these terribly lonely bachelors would feast and drink on weekends and engage in cockfighting on Sundays. When some did manage to find wives, their mates were inevitably part Hawaiian. Filipino workers continued to be imported, although sporadically, until 1946, so even today there are a few old Filipino bachelors who never managed to get home.

Other Groups
About 10 percent of Hawaii's population is a conglomerate of small ethnic groups. Of these, one of the largest and fastest growing is Korean, with 23,000 individuals. About 30,000 residents consider themselves Puerto Rican, and 22,000 residents identify as black. Another fast-growing group is Samoans, with 16,000 currently settled in Hawaii and more on the way. Other lesser represented ethnic groups include 3,500 Native Americans, 4,000 Tongans, 7,000 other Pacific Islanders, and 8,000 Vietnamese.

FOOD
Although modern Hawaiian food is extremely meat-based, traditionally Hawaiians were nearly vegetarian, reserving meat for celebrations rather than daily meals. Traditional Hawaiian food can still be found, but a lot of it now is simply considered "local food" and blended with food from other cultures.

With ancient Hawaiians, the ocean was a great source of food, and they cultivated successful land crops such as taro, sweet potatoes, breadfruit, and sugarcane. They raised pigs and chickens for celebratory meals, although they wouldn't make use of the eggs.

The taro root was the staple crop, and it was the first thing they got going when settling the island. Taro would mostly be pounded into poi, which is another staple often eaten with other foods. Women avoided the starch while pregnant in hopes of avoiding growing a large baby.

Another treat is *haupia,* a custard-like substance made from coconut and usually served as a dessert. *Lau lau* is a luau food that is served as a small package of meat, fish, or vegetables all wrapped in *ti* leaves and then baked or steamed. For fish, a local favorite is ahi *poke,* a dish served at many delis and supermarkets mixed with soy sauce, onions, seaweed, and other flavors and enjoyed as a snack or a meal.

THE ARTS
Since everything in old Hawaii had to be fashioned by hand, almost every object was either a genuine work of art or the product of a highly refined craft. With the "civilizing" of the indigenous population, most of the old ways disappeared, including the old arts and crafts. Most authentic Hawaiian art by master craftspeople exists only in museums. But with the resurgence of connecting to Hawaiian roots as part of the Hawaiian Renaissance, many old arts are being revitalized, and their legacy lives on in a number of proficient artists.

Hula
The hula is more than an ethnic dance; it's the soul of Hawaii expressed in motion. It began as a form of worship during religious ceremonies and was danced only by highly trained men. As time went on, however, women were allowed to learn the hula, and today both genders perform the dance equally.

During the 19th century, the hula almost vanished because the missionaries considered it vile and heathen. King Kalakaua saved it during the late 1800s by forming his own troupe and encouraging the dancers to learn the old hula. Many of the original dances had been forgotten, but some were retained and are performed to this day.

Hula is art in swaying motion, and the true form is studied rigorously and taken seriously. Today, hula *halau* (schools) are active on every island, teaching hula and keeping the old ways and culture alive. Ancient hula is called *hula kahiko,* and modern renditions are known as *hula auana.* Performers still spend years perfecting their techniques. They show off their accomplishments during the fierce competition of the Merrie Monarch Festival in Hilo every April.

Canoes
The most respected artisans in old Hawaii were the canoe makers. With little more than a stone adze and a pump drill, they built sleek and seaworthy canoes that could carry 200

people and last for generations. The main hull was usually a gigantic koa log, and the gunwale planks were minutely drilled and sewn to the sides with sennit rope. Apprenticeships lasted for years, and a young man knew that he had graduated when one day he was nonchalantly asked to sit down and eat with the master builders. Small family-size canoes with outriggers were used for fishing and perhaps carried a spear rack; large oceangoing double-hulled canoes were used for migration and warfare. On these, the giant logs had been adzed to about two inches thick. A mainsail woven from pandanus was mounted on a central platform, and the boat was steered by two long paddles. The hull was dyed with plant juices and charcoal. The entire village helped launch such a canoe.

Carving

Wood was one of the primary materials used by Hawaiian craftspeople. They almost exclusively relied on koa because of its density, strength, and natural luster. It was turned into canoes, wood ware, calabashes, and furniture used by the ali'i. Temple idols were another major product of wood carving. A variety of stone artifacts were also turned out, including poi pounders, mirrors, fish sinkers, and small idols.

Weaving

Hawaiians became the best basket makers and mat weavers in all of Polynesia. Ulana (woven mats) were made from lauhala (pandanus) leaves. Once the leaf was split, the spine was removed and the fibers stored in large rolls. When needed these would be soaked, pounded, and then fashioned into various floor coverings and sleeping mats. Intricate geometric patterns were woven in, and the edges were rolled and well fashioned. Coconut palms were not used to make mats in old Hawaii, but a wide variety of basketry was fashioned from the aerial root 'ie'ie.

Featherwork

This highly refined art was practiced only on the islands of Tahiti, New Zealand, and Hawaii, but the fashioning of feather helmets and idols was unique to Hawaii. Favorite colors were red and yellow, which came only in limited supply from a small number of birds such as the 'o'o, 'i'iwi, mamo, and 'apapane. Professional bird hunters in old Hawaii paid their taxes to the ali'i in prized feathers. The feathers were fastened to a woven net of olona cord and made into helmets, idols, and beautiful flowing capes and cloaks. These resplendent garments were made and worn only by men, especially during battle, when a fine cloak became a great trophy of war. Featherwork was also employed in the making of kahili and lei, which were highly prized by the ali'i women.

Lei Making

Any flower or blossom can be strung into a lei, but the most common are orchids or the lovely-smelling plumeria. Lei, like babies, are all beautiful, but special lei are highly prized by those who know what to look for. Of the different stringing styles, the most common is kui—stringing the flower through the middle or side. Most "airport-quality" lei are of this type. The humuhumu style, reserved for making flat lei, is made by sewing flowers and ferns to a ti, banana, or sometimes hala leaf. A humuhumu lei makes an excellent hatband. Wili is the winding together of greenery, ferns, and flowers into short, bouquet-type lengths. The most traditional form is hili, which requires no stringing at all but involves braiding fragrant ferns and leaves such as maile. If flowers are interwoven, the hili becomes the haku style, the most difficult and most beautiful type of lei.

Tapa Cloth

Tapa, cloth made from tree bark, was common throughout Polynesia and was a woman's art. A few trees such as the wauke and mamaki produced the best cloth, but a variety of other types of bark could be used. First, the raw bark was pounded into a feltlike pulp and beaten together to form strips (the beaters had distinctive patterns that helped make the cloth supple). The cloth was decorated by stamping (a form of block printing) and dyed with natural colors from plants and sea animals in shades of gray, purple, pink, and red. They were even painted with natural brushes made from pandanus fruit, with an overall gray color made from charcoal. The tapa cloth was sewn together to make bed coverings, and fragrant flowers and herbs were either sewn or pounded in to produce a permanent fragrance.

Festivals and Events

For such a small island, there is always something happening on Maui. From sporting events to film festivals and rodeos to wine festivals, Maui is a flurry of community fervor. Dates are rarely constant, however, so check local listings and websites for up-to-date information. While many events are annual affairs, the most consistent festive occasion is the **Friday Town Parties** (www.mauifridays.com), which take place every Friday night. Rotating between Wailuku, Lahaina, Makawao, Kihei, and on the rare fifth Friday, Lana'i, these are great community events that are free to attend.

For other events of all sorts throughout the state, visit the calendar of events listing on the Hawaii Visitors Bureau (HVB) website (www.calendar.gohawaii.com), or check out the weekly schedule of events on the *Maui Time* website (www.mauitime.com/calendar), or the fantastic daily calendar of events that's featured on Maui Now (www.mauinow.com/events).

MAUI
January
The PGA golf tour kicks off each year with the **Hyundai Tournament of Champions** (www.kapalua.com) held during the first week of January at the Kapalua Plantation Course.

February
Chinese New Year (www.visitlahaina.com) celebrations are held in the evening along Front Street in Lahaina and include a lion dance, martial arts demonstrations, live music, food, and, of course, firecrackers.

For artists, the **Maui Open Studios** (www.mauiopenstudios.com) takes place during each weekend in February, showcasing the talent of the island's local art community.

The **Maui Whale Festival** (www.mauiwhalefestival.org) is sponsored by the Pacific Whale Foundation and features live music, festivals, fun runs, and community activities through the month of February. The annual **World Whale Day** takes place at Kihei's Kalama Park and is the largest event of the festival.

Seeing as February is the peak of whale season, it only makes sense that another event, **Whales Tales** (www.whaletrust.org), is held during the busy month. The event at the Ritz-Carlton Kapalua resort supports local whale research teams such as the Whale Trust, Center for Whale Studies, and Hawaii Whale Research Foundation.

March
The month usually kicks off with more whale-related events at the **Lahaina Whale and Ocean Arts Festival** (www.visitlahaina.com) held in central Lahaina.

March 26 is **Prince Kuhio Day,** a public state holiday observed in remembrance of Prince Kuhio, heir to the throne of the Hawaiian monarchy.

Toward the end of the month, the **Celebration of the Arts** (www.celebrationofthearts.org) at the Ritz-Carlton Hotel in Kapalua is a four-day event that spotlights various indigenous art forms and cultural traditions. It's an absolute must-visit if you are in town.

Whale Season: Thar She Blows!

December to May, the waters of Maui County house the largest population of humpback whales found anywhere in the world. If whale-watching is high on your list of Maui experiences, it's important to time your visit during the peak of whale season, not summer.

Officially, whale season in Maui runs December 15 to May 15, although the first sighting is usually mid-October, and whales can linger through the end of May. For whale-watching, however, the peak season is the 10-week span of January 15 to March 31. During the month of April, there are noticeably fewer whales by the day. Whale-watching tours will usually operate December 15 to April 20, after which time there is no guarantee of seeing whales. Boats often advertise "whale searches" rather than whale-watching at the beginning and end of the season, which is a way of saying you probably won't encounter whales, but your money will gladly be accepted.

During the peak of the season, anyone setting out on a charter is guaranteed to see whales. The question becomes which whales you should look at since you'll end up being surrounded.

April

Usually held on the first weekend in April at the Maui Tropical Plantation, the **Maui County Agricultural Festival** (www.mauicountyfarmbureau.org), aka the "Maui Ag Fest," celebrates the rich heritage of farming and agriculture on Maui.

The **East Maui Taro Festival** (www.tarofestival.org) is celebrated in Hana with traditional ceremonies, music, food markets, symposia, demonstrations, and exhibitions to honor one of the island's most basic food sources and the resurgence of Hawaiian cultural traditions.

In Lahaina, April 20-24 is the approximate date of the **Banyan Tree Birthday** (www.visitlahaina.com) celebration for the town's famous banyan tree.

April 22 is **Earth Day,** and there are numerous environmental cleanups and festivals across the island where visitors can get involved.

Upcountry, the **Haiku Ho'olaulea and Flower Fest** (www.haikuhoolaulea.org) is held at the Ha'iku Community Center with live music, auctions, "talk story" sessions, vendors, and a welcoming atmosphere that defines this rural town.

May

May 1 is **Lei Day** in Hawaii. There are usually large lei day celebrations held in Wailea and various other places around the island.

At Whalers Village in Ka'anapali, the **Maui Onion Festival** (www.whalersvillage.com) celebrates everything about the Maui onion with food vendors, craft booths, recipe contests, chef demonstrations, and live entertainment.

Upcountry in Makawao, the **Seabury Hall Craft Fair** (www.seaburyhall.org) is held on the Saturday before Mother's Day and features Hawaiian craft vendors from across the state. With live music, food booths, and hundreds of artists, it's the perfect place to pick up a gift for mom.

At the Maui Arts and Cultural Center, the **Maui Brew Fest** (www.mauiarts.org) celebrates the culture of craft brewing and the love of good beer.

June

The annual **Upcountry Fair** at the Eddie Tam Center, Makawao, is an old-fashioned farm fair right in the heart of Maui's *paniolo* country. Crafts, food, and competitions are all part of the fair, as are the county 4-H championship and auctions.

In Kapalua, foodies flock to the **Kapalua Wine and Food Festival** (www.kapaluawineandfoodfestival.com), a three-day event featuring some of the state's top sommeliers and chefs.

June 11 is **King Kamehameha Day** in Lahaina. Festivities include a parade through town, crafts, and lots of food and entertainment.

The annual **Slack-Key Guitar Festival** (www.slackkeyfestival.com) at the Maui Arts and Cultural Center in Kahului features some of Hawaii's best musicians.

The **Maui Film Festival** (www.mauifilmfestival.com) shows films at both the Maui Arts and Cultural Center as well as the Celestial Cinema on the golf course lawn in Wailea.

The **Da Kine Classic Windsurfing Event,** a professional windsailing competition for men and women, is held at Kanaha Beach, and is part of the summer-long Maui Race Series.

July

Over the July 4 weekend, head for the coolness of Makawao for the annual **Makawao Rodeo.** *Paniolo* are an old and important tradition in Hawaiian life. Held at the Oskie Rice Arena, this old-time Upcountry rodeo can't be beat for fun and entertainment. It's accompanied by the Paniolo Parade through town.

The **Fourth of July** brings the best fireworks display on Maui to the Lahaina Roadstead, and thousands congregate for the show.

July also has numerous Buddhist festivals taking place across the island, with one of the largest being the **Obon Festival** at the Mantokuji Soto Temple in Pa'ia.

September

The Valley Isle Road Runners (virr.com) sponsor the numerous races throughout September, including the **Hana Relay** (www.hanarelay.com) and **Maui Marathon** (www.mauimarathonhawaii.com). The Hana Relay sees over 1,200 people run in costume from Kahului Airport to the downtown ballpark in Hana. The next week, the marathon takes runners from the Queen Ka'ahumanu Center in Kahului, down to Ma'alaea, and then along the ocean to Whalers Village in Ka'anapali. The weekend is also punctuated by the **Front Street Mile** event, where some of the world's top mileage runners tackle the flat course of Front Street.

October

The **Maui County Fair** at the Wailuku War Memorial Complex brings out the kid in everyone. An old-fashioned fair with western and homespun flavor, this popular event caters to more than 100,000 people every year and offers rides, booths, exhibits, and games, plus plenty of music and food.

In Lahaina, the **Lahaina Plantation Days** (www.lahainarestoration.org) is hosted by the Lahaina Restoration Foundation and features live music, food booths, and movies held under the smokestack.

The **XTERRA World Championships** (www.xterraplanet.com) are held in Kapalua. This is an off-road triathlon that combines a 1.5-mile ocean swim, 19-mile mountain-bike ride, and a 7-mile trail run.

During the second half of October, the **Ka'anapali Fresh** (www.kaanapalifresh.com) food and wine festival features cuisine and demonstrations from some of the island's top chefs and sommeliers.

At the end of the month, wild costumes and outlandish behavior set the mood for **Halloween** in Lahaina, the largest celebration of Halloween in Hawaii, often called the "Mardi Gras of the Pacific."

November

The **Maui Invitational Basketball Tournament** (www.mauiinvitational.com) holds a preseason college team playoff at the Civic Center in Lahaina.

Each year the Ka'anapali Beach Hotel hosts **Hula O Na Keiki,** the state's only children's solo and partner hula contest. Two days of competition make this an entertaining event for everyone.

December

The **Holiday Lighting of the Banyan Tree** takes place in Lahaina, as well as decorating the Old Courthouse for Christmas.

MOLOKA'I

While there are numerous smaller festivals that take place on Moloka'i, the following are some of the larger annual events. For specific dates and more information, visit www.molokaievents.com.

January

The **Ka Moloka'i Makahiki Festival** is held for one day each January to celebrate the *makahiki,* a traditional time following the harvest when wars would cease in favor of arts, crafts, competition, and merriment. This tradition is carried on today at the Mitchell Pauole Center in Kauanakai.

May

The **Moloka'i Ka Hula Piko** (www.kahulapiko.com) festival is perhaps the largest annual event on the island and celebrates the history of the hula at its legendary birthplace in West Moloka'i.

September

Moloka'i is well known for its outrigger canoe races, when the island buzzes with visitors from across the Pacific. The **Pailolo Challenge** (www.pailolo.com) features paddlers who race from Maui to Kauanakakai, and the **Na Wahine O Ke Kai** features all-women paddle crews who race from Hale O Lono Harbor to the neighboring island of O'ahu.

October

More famous than the Pailolo is the **Moloka'i Hoe** (www.molokaihoe.com) outrigger canoe race, in which paddlers race from West Moloka'i to O'ahu. More than 1,000 paddlers compete in the event. It's an exciting time to be visiting West Moloka'i.

The **Festivals of Aloha** is a community event taking place for more than 50 years in the city of Kaunakakai.

LANA'I

Many of the annual events of Lana'i went dormant when the Four Seasons closed, and now that it's open again, it remains to be seen how many events will follow. Many of the events are small in scope and akin to a community potluck.

November

While there are numerous races throughout the year, the largest event of the **TriLanai** (www.trilanai.com) race series is the off-road sprint triathlon that takes place in November.

Essentials

maui bus

Transportation

GETTING THERE
Air

You'll likely land at the **Kahului Airport** (OGG, 1 Kahului Airport Rd., 808/872-3830, www.hawaii.gov), which is 30 to 45 minutes by car from the resort areas of Wailea and Ka'anapali. Kahului has direct flights to a host of mainland cities and a handful of international destinations, and it's served by most major carriers.

Other than Kahului, there are two small airstrips in Kapalua and in Hana. They have no direct flights to the mainland, but there are seven flights per day from the **Kapalua Airport** (JHM, 4050 Honoapi'ilani Hwy., 808/665-6108, www.hawaii.gov) to Honolulu on neighboring O'ahu.

GETTING AROUND
Car
CAR RENTAL

Rental cars are the easiest way to get around and explore the island. While there are a number of large corporate car-rental companies operating within the airport, there are also a number of locally owned companies that can provide better rates and more "authentic" looking cars. A shiny new rental car is nice to drive around in, but the downside is that rentals are car thieves' preferred target. Having a car that looks like a local's can potentially save you the cost of a break-in.

Most local car-rental companies offer free transportation to the airport if arranged ahead of time. Check **Maui Vans** (190 Papa Place, 808/877-0090, www.mauivans.com), **Kimo's Rent a Car** (440 Alamaha St., 808/280-6327, www.kimosrentacar.com), **Kihei Rent a Car** (96 Kio Loop, 808/879-7257, www.kiheirentacar.com), and **Manaloha**

Rent a Car (200 Waiehu Beach Rd., 808/283-8779, www.manaloharentacar.net).

Book ahead if you're traveling during the peak season, and know that drivers who are under 25 will often incur extra fees. To save some money, only rent a 4WD vehicle for the days you'll need it rather than for the duration of your trip.

TAXI

More than two dozen taxi companies operate island-wide service on Maui, and besides providing normal taxi service, they will also run tours all over the island. Taxis are expensive and metered by the distance traveled. From Kahului Airport, the fare to Lahaina should be roughly $65, and $80 to Ka'anapali, $100 to Kapalua, and $55 to Wailea. Expect $5-10 in and around Kahului, and about $14 to the hostels in Wailuku. Any taxi may drop off at the airport, but only those with permits may pick up there.

Those in need of a taxi can call **Surf Taxi** (807/870-9974, www.surftaximaui.com), **West Maui Taxi** (808/661-1122, www.westmauitaxi.com), **Kihei Taxi** (808/298-1877, www.kiheitaxi.com), **Aloha Maui Taxi** (808/661-5432, www.alohamauitaxi.com), or **MJ Taxi** (808/283-9309, www.mjtaxi.com).

SHUTTLES

Robert's Hawaii (866/293-1782, www.robertshawaii.com) connects the Kahului Airport to virtually anywhere on the island and operates daily during flight arrival and departure times. With this door-to-door service, pickup can be either from the airport or from any hotel or condo if you're going to the airport. **Executive Airport Shuttle** (808/669-2300 or 800/833-2303) offers virtually the

---

Pacific Crossroads

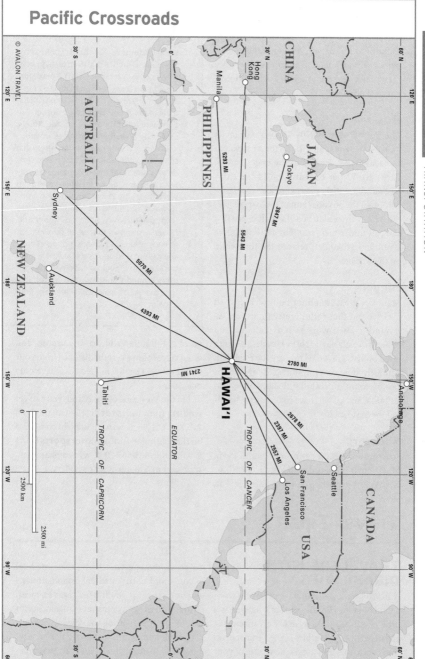

© AVALON TRAVEL

CHINA

JAPAN

PHILIPPINES

AUSTRALIA

NEW ZEALAND

HAWAI'I

USA

CANADA

Manila
Hong Kong
Tokyo
Sydney
Auckland
Tahiti
Anchorage
Seattle
San Francisco
Los Angeles

5293 MI
5543 MI
3847 MI
5070 MI
4393 MI
2741 MI
2780 MI
2678 MI
2397 MI
2557 MI

TROPIC OF CANCER
EQUATOR
TROPIC OF CAPRICORN

2500 km
2500 mi

same service to and from the airport and to points around the island for marginally better rates, which average around $50 pp from Kahului to Ka'anapali. Although these companies will pick you up as soon as they can, they prefer several hours' or even 24 hours' notice if possible.

Bus

The **Maui Bus** (808/270-7511, www.co.maui.hi.us) system has eight routes for an inexpensive way to get around to the major towns. Fares are $2 per boarding or $4 for a day pass, and monthly passes are also available. Although the bus does run to the airport, riders are not allowed to board with luggage that can't fit under their seat. For a full listing of island bus schedules, refer to the timetables on the website.

Bicycle

Maui is a great island for both serious road cyclists and those who prefer to just cruise around town. Towns such as Lahaina and Kihei are easily navigable by bicycle, although often cyclists are forced to share the road with similarly slow-moving traffic. Rental shops can be found in Kahului, Pa'ia, Kihei, and Lahaina, and all will have island maps detailing the best rides.

Scooters

Scooters are great for running around town. Most rental operators will ask for a cash or credit card deposit. You must be at least 18

Drive with Aloha

Local customs come into play behind the wheel. You'll notice that even on highways, drivers cruise along slowly. The maximum speed limit anywhere on Maui is 55 mph, and in many places it's 30 to 45 mph. Off the main roads, it's essential to go slow in residential neighborhoods or on side streets, especially when there are homes around.

Going fast can result in an angry fist shaken at your car or a call for you to slow down. Aside from speed, car horns are only used in an emergency (or when your friend walks by), aggressive driving is severely frowned upon, and it's common courtesy to stop and allow waiting cars into traffic. Drivers are known to wave or throw *shakas* at each other, and there's a good chance you'll see at least one "Slow Down! This ain't the Mainland!" bumper sticker during your drive around the island. You're probably here to relax, so leave earlier and take time to enjoy the ride.

years old, have a valid driver's license, and often stay within a certain distance from your rental office. Legally, mopeds can have only one rider.

On the West Side of the island, you can get scooters from **Motoroshi** (129 Lahainaluna Rd., 808/661-0006, www.motoroshi.com), and on the south side **Aloha Motorsports** (2463 S. Kihei Rd., 808/667-7000, www.alohamotorsports.com), among other providers.

Travel Tips

TRAVELERS WITH DISABILITIES

A person with a disability can have a wonderful time in Hawaii; all that's needed is a little planning. Make as many arrangements ahead of time as possible: Tell the transportation companies and hotels the nature of your disability so they can make prearrangements to accommodate you. Bring your medical records and notify medical establishments of your arrival if you'll need their services. Travel with a friend or make arrangements for an aide on arrival. Bring your own wheelchair if possible and let airlines know if it is battery-powered. Boarding interisland carriers sometimes requires steps. Wheelchairs are boarded

Kahului Airport

COMMUTER TERMINAL

AIR CARGO BUILDING

CAR RENTAL BOOTHS

KAYA ST.

To Kanaha Beach

CAR RENTAL BASE YARDS

PARKING

ARRIVAL TERMINAL/ BAGGAGE CLAIM

CENTRAL BUILDING

PARKING

DEPARTURE TERMINAL

To Kahului

TARMAC

SCALE NOT AVAILABLE

© AVALON TRAVEL

early on special lifts, but they must know in advance that you're coming. Most hotels and restaurants easily accommodate people with disabilities, but call ahead to make sure.

Information

The state Commission on Persons with Disabilities was designed to aid disabled people. It is an invaluable source of information and distributes self-help booklets, published jointly by the Disability and Communication Access Board and the Hawaii Centers for Independent Living. Any person with disabilities heading to Hawaii should write first or visit the office of the **Hawaii Centers for Independent Living** (414 Kuwili St., Suite 102, Honolulu, HI 96817, 808/522-5400). On Maui, contact the **Maui Center for Independent Living** (220 Imi Kala St., Suite 103, Wailuku, HI 96793, 808/242-4966). Additional information is available on the **Disability and Communication Access Board website** (www.hawaii.gov/health).

LGBT TRAVELERS

Gay and lesbian travelers are welcome throughout Hawaii. While acceptance is part of the general state of mind, Maui has a smaller gay and lesbian community in terms of nightclubs, bars, or other gathering places than O'ahu does, for example. In 2011, Hawaii was the seventh state to legalize civil unions for same-sex couples, well before national marriage equality was established.

For a lodging option specifically geared

Interisland Air Routes

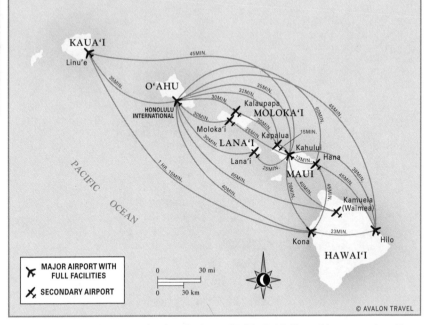

toward LGBT travelers in North Kihei, check out the **Maui Sunseeker** (551 S. Kihei Rd., North Kihei, 808/879-1261 or 800/532-6284, www.mauisunseeker.com).

For LGBT-related information for Maui, the website of **Maui Pride** (www.mauigay-info.com) has a listing of upcoming events, and **Pride Guide Hawaii** (www.gogayhawaii. com) has detailed listings of dining, nightlife, and lodging options. Another source is the **International Gay and Lesbian Travel Association** (954/630-1637, www.iglta.org), which can connect you with gay-friendly organizations and tours.

Health and Safety

Every year Hawaii ranks among the healthiest states. People here live longer than those anywhere else in the country, with an average life span of about 80 years. Lifestyle, heredity, and diet help with these figures, but Hawaii is still an oasis in the middle of the ocean, and germs just have a tougher time getting here. There are no cases of malaria, cholera, or yellow fever, and because of strict quarantine laws, rabies is nonexistent.

Due to the perfect weather, soothing negative ionization from the sea, and the carefree lifestyle, everyone seems to feel better in the islands. Hawaii is just what the doctor ordered: a beautiful, natural health spa. The food and water are perfectly safe, and the air quality is the best in the country.

On the other hand, tooth decay, perhaps because of the wide use of sugar and the enzymes present in certain tropical fruits, is 30

Traveling with Children

Traveling with children on Maui can be a memorable experience. Consider the kind of trip you want and book activities accordingly.

Other than the beach, one of the best sites on the island for kids is the **Maui Ocean Center,** full of hands-on activities and educational experiences. To sneak away for a romantic dinner, the best service on the island for a short-term sitter is **The Nanny Connection** (808/875-4777, www.thenannyconnection.com), where professional sitting staff will meet you at your hotel and take care of children in your absence.

percent above the national average. Obesity and related heart problems, as well as hard-drug use—especially crystal meth, or "ice"—are prevalent among native Hawaiians.

WATER SAFETY

Hawaii has a sad claim to fame: More people drown here than anywhere else in the world. Moreover, there are dozens of scuba, snorkeling, and boarding accidents yearly, with broken necks and backs or other injuries. These statistics shouldn't keep you out of the water. The best remedy is to avoid situations you can't handle, and ask lifeguards or beach attendants about conditions and follow their advice. If local people refuse to go in, there's a good reason. Even experts can get in trouble in Hawaiian waters, and while some beaches are calm and gentle, others can be frothing giants.

While beachcombing and especially when walking out on rocks, never turn your back to the ocean. Always be aware of what is going on with the water. Undertows (the water drawing back into the sea) can knock you off your feet and pull you into the shore-break. Observe the water carefully before you go in. Study it for rocks, breakers, and reefs. Look for ocean currents, especially those within reefs that

can cause riptides when the water washes out a channel. Note where others are swimming or snorkeling, and go there. Don't swim alone, if possible, and obey all warning signs. When snorkeling, come ashore before you get tired.

When the wind comes up, get out. Stay out of the water during periods of high surf. High surf often creates riptides, powerful currents that can drag you out to sea. Mostly they peter out not far from shore, and you can often see their choppy waters on the surface. If you get caught in a "rip," don't fight by swimming directly against it; you'll only exhaust yourself. Swim diagonally across it, while letting it carry you, and try to stay parallel to the shore until you are out of the strong pull.

When bodysurfing, never ride straight in with your hands out in front you. This is the number one cause of broken necks in Hawaii. Instead, ride the wave at a 45-degree angle, and try to kick out the back of the wave instead of letting it slam you into the sand. Remember, waves come in sets, and little ones can be followed by giants, so watch for a while before jumping in. Standard procedure is to duck under a breaking wave. You can survive even thunderous oceans using this technique. Don't try to swim through a heavy froth, and never turn your back and let it smash you.

Sharks and Marinelife

Some visitors fear that the moment their feet can no longer touch the sand they will be immediately attacked by **sharks.** The reality is that the chances of even seeing a large shark are remarkably slim, and since Hawaiian sharks have plenty of fish, they don't usually bother with unsavory humans. Still, try to avoid the mouths of rivers, murky water, and swimming around dawn and dusk.

Portuguese men-of-war and other jellyfish put out long, floating tentacles that sting if they touch you. It seems that many floating jellyfish are blown into shore by winds on the 8th, 9th, and 10th days after the full moon. Don't wash a sting off with freshwater—this will only aggravate it. Hot saltwater will take away the sting, as will alcohol, aftershave

Maui for Free

Maui can be expensive, but it doesn't have to be. A number of Maui activities don't cost a thing:

- A morning stroll on the Kapalua Coastal Trail or Baldwin Beach
- Bodysurfing at D. T. Fleming Beach Park
- Watching the sunset at Haleakala and staying to watch the stars come out
- Free hula performances at the Lahaina Cannery Mall
- Hiking in Polipoli, Makena, or Hana
- Watching fisherfolk sell their catch at Lahaina Harbor
- Swimming beneath a waterfall on the Road to Hana
- People-watching beneath the banyan tree

lotion, or meat tenderizer. After rinsing, soak with a wet towel. Antihistamines may also bring relief. Expect to start to feel better in about half an hour.

Coral can give you a nasty cut and is known for causing infections because it's a living organism. Wash the cut immediately and apply an antiseptic. Keep it clean and covered, and watch for infection. With coral cuts, it's best to have a professional look at it.

Poisonous **sea urchins** found in tide pools and shallow reefs can be beautiful creatures, but if you step on them, their spines will enter your foot, break off, and burn like blazes. This is known to locals as *wana* ("vah-na"). Soaking a couple of times in vinegar for half an hour or so should stop the burning, or if that's not possible, the Hawaiian solution is urine. It might seem gross, but it should put the fire out. Don't worry—the spines will die in a few days, and there are generally no long-term effects.

Hawaiian reefs also have their share of **moray eels.** These creatures are ferocious in

Always respect the power of the ocean.

- A morning swim off Ka'anapali Beach
- Free evening entertainment at Whalers Village
- Volunteering with a local environmental organization
- Watching the surfers at Lahaina or Honolua Bay
- Watching the windsurfers at Kanaha Beach Park or Ho'okipa
- "Talking story" with a local
- Free talks at islands resorts, such as the free art tours and cultural talks that are held at the Grand Wailea, or the Sense of Place tours (10am Fri.) at the Ritz-Carlton at Kapalua
- Whale-watching from the Pali Lookout between Ma'alaea and Lahaina

appearance but will never initiate an attack. You'll have to poke around in their holes while snorkeling or scuba diving to provoke them. Sometimes this is inadvertent on the diver's part, so be careful where you stick your hands while underwater.

Present in streams, ponds, and muddy soil, **leptospirosis** is a freshwater-borne bacteria, deposited by the urine of infected animals. From 2 to 20 days after the bacteria enter the body, there will be a sudden onset of fever accompanied by chills, sweats, headache, and sometimes vomiting and diarrhea. Preventive measures include staying out of freshwater sources and mud where cattle and other animals wade and drink, not swimming in freshwater if you have an open cut, and not drinking stream water. Leptospirosis may be fatal in some cases if left untreated.

SAFETY IN THE OUTDOORS
Hiking

Other than bodysurfing and swimming, the most common way that visitors end up hurt or in trouble is taking unnecessary risks while hiking. Remember that wet rocks are slippery, and that stream crossings can be dangerous since flash floods can occur without warning. Stay away from the tops of waterfalls, where something as unpredictable as a gust of wind

can send you one step farther than you had originally planned. If you are doing any cliff-jumping, be sure you've scouted the landing zone for rocks and that it's been verified as safe by someone in the know. When hiking along the sea, remember that large surf can unpredictably crash onto the shore, so keep a safe distance from turbid seas and slippery rocks.

While elastic bandages and disinfectants are great for cuts and scrapes, the most important thing to pack with you before heading out on an adventure is a dose of common sense; don't go out in conditions with which you're unfamiliar, and never push yourself outside of your comfort zone when wandering off your own. As the motto says, "If in doubt, don't go out." Remember that the moment you set foot on a trail—in the mountains, the rainforest, or along the shore—every action is a direct result of choices you made. It isn't the fault of the landowner that wet rocks on the property are slippery, so be prepared to accept personal responsibility for keeping yourself safe while exploring.

Sun

Many can't wait to strip down and lie on the sand, but the tropical sun will burn you to a crisp if you aren't diligent about sunscreen. Burning rays come through more easily in

Dengue Fever

Dengue Fever, a mosquito-borne tropical disease, is not endemic to Hawaii, but in 2015 it came to the Big Island with an infected traveler. As of early 2016 there were over 200 cases of dengue fever identified on the Big Island—the majority among residents rather than visitors. Waipio Valley on the Big Island was closed to visitors to minimize the potential for new cases. Infected individuals are usually asymptomatic, but symptoms may include fever, joint pain, headache, and rash.

The best way to avoid Dengue is to avoid be bitten by mosquitoes. Stay away from high-risk areas and check the Hawaii Department of Health (http://health.hawaii.gov/docd/dengue-outbreak-2015) for more information. If you are visiting a higher-risk area, be sure to cover your skin, especially around sunrise and sunset, when mosquitoes are most active, and to use bug spray with DEET. *(Contributed by Bree Kessler, author of* Moon Big Island of Hawaii*)*

Hawaii because of the sun's angle, and you don't feel them as much because there's always a cool breeze. The worst part of the day is 11am to 3pm. Even though Maui is at about 21 degrees north latitude, not even close to the equator, it's still hundreds of miles south of sunny Southern California.

While spray-on sunscreens might be convenient, they stain the decks of boats, end up in your neighbor's mouth, and can ignite your skin if you stand next to an open flame (yikes!). The best, albeit most expensive, option is a sunscreen that isn't petroleum-based so that the chemicals don't wash off in the water and damage the coral. The best local sunscreen is **Doc Martin's,** developed by a local dermatologist and surfer to be highly water-resistant and great for covering your face.

Be aware of dehydration. The sun and wind sap your energy and your store of liquid. Bottled water in various sizes is readily available in all parts of Hawaii., or better yet, carry a reusable water bottle.

MOSQUITOES, ROACHES, AND CENTIPEDES

While Hawaii isn't infested with a wide variety of bugs, it does have its share. Mosquitoes were unknown in the islands until their larvae stowed away in the water barrels of the *Wellington* in 1826 and were introduced at Lahaina. They bred easily in the tropical climate and rapidly spread to all the islands.

They are a particular nuisance in the rainforests. Be prepared, and bring a natural repellent such as citronella oil, available in most health food stores on the islands, or a commercial product available in grocery and drugstores. Campers will be happy to have mosquito coils to burn at night.

Cockroaches are a common sight in Hawaii and are nothing to worry about. They love the climate like everyone else, and it's difficult to keep them under control.

Perhaps the most dangerous island critters are the fearsome-looking centipedes, which wiggle their way into dark places, particularly after the grass is mowed or the neighboring field harvested. Centipedes can deliver a nasty bite, and juveniles pack more venom than adults. The best way to deal with them is with the old rubber slipper.

While you aren't likely to encounter too many spiders while on vacation, brown spindly cane spiders can grow to be about the size of your hand, although their bite isn't dangerous.

HAOLE ROT

A peculiar skin condition caused by the sun and damp towels is referred to locally as *haole* rot because it supposedly affects only people of European descent, but you'll notice some dark-skinned folks with the same condition. Basically, the skin becomes mottled with white spots that refuse to tan. You get a blotchy effect, mostly on the shoulders and back. Dermatologists have a name for it, and they'll give you a prescription with a high price tag to cure it. It's common knowledge throughout the islands, however, that Selsun Blue shampoo has an ingredient that stops the white mottling effect. Just rub the lather over the affected areas, and it should clear up.

MEDICAL SERVICES
Hospital
Between central Kahului and central Wailuku, **Maui Memorial Medical Center** (221 Mahalani St., 808/244-9056) is the only full-service hospital on the island.

Medical Clinics
Several clinics dot the island. In South Maui, visit **Urgent Care Maui/Kihei Physicians** (1325 S. Kihei Rd., Suite 103, 808/879-7781) or **Kihei-Wailea Medical Center** (808/874-8100) in the Pi'ilani Village Shopping Center. **Kaiser Permanente** has clinics in Lahaina (910 Waine'e, 808/662-6800), Wailuku (80 Mahalani St., 808/243-6800), and Kihei (1279 S. Kihei Rd., 808/891-6800). In West Maui, **Urgent Care West Maui** (808/667-9721, www.westmauidoctors.com, 8am-9pm daily) is in the Ka'anapali Fairway Shops, and in Hana, the **Hana Community Health Center** (808/248-8294) is along the highway as you enter town.

Information and Services

VISITOR INFORMATION
Free Travel Literature
Free travel literature is loaded with tips, discounts, maps, happenings, and more. Found at the airport arrival lounge and on some street stands, they include the narrow-format *This Week Maui, Maui Gold, Maui Magazine, Maui Beach and Activity Guide, Maui Activities and Attractions,* and the magazine-style *Maui Drive Guide,* with excellent maps and tips, provided free by many car rental agencies. A great resource for activities is *101 Things to Do in Maui;* it also has money-saving coupons.

Visitors Bureaus
The **Hawaii Visitors Bureau** (HVB, www.gohawaii.com) is a top-notch organization providing help and information to Hawaii's visitors. Anyone contemplating a trip to Hawaii should visit a nearby office or check out its website for specific information that might be helpful or required.

The best information on Maui is dispensed by the **Maui Visitors Bureau** (1727 Wili Pa Loop, Wailuku, HI 96793, 808/244-3530 or 800/525-6284, www.visitmaui.com). For

Moloka'i, check out the **Moloka'i Visitors Association** (P.O. Box 960, Kaunakakai, HI 96748, 808/553-5221, www.visitmolokai.com). Additional online information pertaining to Maui County can be found at the official **County of Maui website** (www.co.maui.hi.us).

Weather Reports and Surfing Conditions
Remember that Maui has microclimates with weather unlike that on the mainland. To check what the weather is going to be in a certain part of the island, refrain from using large national websites such as Weather.com and instead opt for a local site more in tune with the island nuances. For weather, the best site around is www.mauiweathertoday.com by Glenn James, which offers both weather and surf conditions, with surf heights in the Hawaiian scale.

Consumer Protection
If you encounter problems with accommodations, bad service, or downright rip-offs, try the following: **Maui Chamber of Commerce** (313 Ano St., Kahului, HI 96732,

808/871-7711, www.mauichamber.com), the state **Office of Consumer Protection** (808/984-8244 or 808/587-3222, www.hawaii. gov), or the **Better Business Bureau** (Oʻahu, 877/222-6551).

MONEY
Currency

U.S. currency is among the drabbest in the world. It's all the same size, with little variation in color; those unfamiliar with it should spend some time getting acquainted to avoid making costly mistakes. Coinage in use is one cent (penny), five cents (nickel), 10 cents (dime), 25 cents (quarter), 50 cents (half dollar), and $1; paper currency is $1, $2 (uncommon), $5, $10, $20, $50, and $100. Since 1996 new designs have been issued for the $100, $50, $20, $10, and $5 bills, although both the old and new bills are accepted as valid currency.

Traveler's Checks

Traveler's checks are accepted throughout Hawaii at hotels, restaurants, car rental agencies, and in some stores and shops. However, to be readily convertible, they should be in U.S. currency. Some larger hotels that frequently have Japanese and Canadian guests will accept those currencies. Banks accept foreign-currency traveler's checks, but it'll mean an extra trip and inconvenience. It's best to get most of your traveler's checks in $20 or $50 denominations; anything larger may be hard to cash at shops and boutiques, although not at hotels.

Credit Cards

Credit cards are accepted for virtually all business transactions in Maui. Almost every form of lodging, shop, restaurant, and amusement takes them, although a handful of local mom-and-pop shops only accept cash.

COMMUNICATIONS AND MEDIA
Telephone

The telephone system on the main islands is

Book Online

If you want to save some serious cash when booking activities on Maui, virtually every activity operator on the island offers discounts for booking directly online. Oftentimes these discounts are in the range of 10 to 15 percent, which saves them money in the long run since concierge commissions can be as high as 30 percent (really). Granted, concierges work hard to earn that commission by educating themselves on exactly which activity will be right for you and your family, but if you've already decided on the activity you want, bust out that laptop and save some money by making your own reservation. Be sure to read the fine print: Sometimes the deal is only valid if booked at least seven days in advance.

modern and comparable to any system on the mainland. For landlines, any phone call to a number on that island is a local call; it's long-distance when dialing to another island or beyond the state.

Cell (mobile) phone reception is good throughout Hawaii. Like anywhere, however, there are pockets where reception is poor or nonexistent.

For directory assistance, dial 1-411 (local), 1-555-1212 (interisland), 1-area code/555-1212 (mainland), 1-800/555-1212 (toll-free).

The area code for all of Hawaii is 808.

Newspapers

The major local newspaper available on Maui is the daily *Maui News* (www.mauinews. com), which has decent coverage and a good listing of local events. The *Lahaina News* (www.lahainanews.com) is a weekly community paper with news, feature stories, and entertainment listings. Free local weekly and biweekly newspapers include *Maui Time* (www.mauitime.com), focusing heavily on island entertainment options and political commentary, and *Maui Weekly* (www.maui-weekly.com).

Volunteering Opportunities

WEST MAUI: HONOKOWAI VALLEY

Spend a Saturday with Maui Cultural Lands (808/276-5593, www.mauiculturallands.org) in the magical Honokowai Valley for one of the best volunteering experiences on the island. Away from the highway and back in a valley that's been forgotten by time, the remains of an ancient Hawaiian village are slowly being brought back to life. The structures here, including rock walls and lo'i, are over 600 years old. The village was abandoned in the 1800s when the water was diverted for sugar. Today, spending a morning volunteering in Honokowai Valley is one of the most culturally authentic and meaningful experiences you can have in West Maui. In most cases, groups meet at 9:15am on Saturday morning at the bottom of Pu'ukoli Road across from Kahekili Beach Park.

UPCOUNTRY: HALEAKALA

For the chance to stay in a wilderness cabin inside Haleakala Crater, volunteer with Friends of Haleakala (www.fhnp.org) on one of their monthly service trips. The majority of these backpacking trips are free, and a few cost $15. During the three-day trip you'll clean the cabins and remove invasive species. You'll need to pack your own sleeping bag as well as food, water, and supplies, and participants are required to be physically fit and comfortable hiking at altitude. Space is limited, so check out the website for service dates and ways you can volunteer.

WEIGHTS AND MEASURES

Hawaii, like the rest of the United States, employs the U.S. system of measurements. Dry weights are in ounces and pounds; liquid measures are in ounces, quarts, and gallons; and distances are measured in inches, feet, yards, and miles. The metric system is known but not in general use.

Electricity

The same electric system is in use in Hawaii as on the U.S. mainland. The system functions on 110 volts, 60 hertz alternating current (AC); type A (two-pin) and type B (three-pin) plugs are used. Appliances from Japan will work, but there is some danger that they will burn out, while those requiring the normal European 220 volts, with other types of plugs, will not work.

Time Zones

There is no daylight saving time in Hawaii. In winter, Hawaii is 2 hours earlier than the West Coast's Pacific standard time, 4 hours earlier than central standard time, 5 hours earlier than eastern standard time, and 11 hours earlier than Germany. During the mainland's daylight savings time, Hawaii is 3 hours earlier than Pacific daylight time, and 6 hours earlier than eastern standard time.

Because Hawaii is just east of the International Date Line, it is almost a full day behind Asian and Pacific cities. Hawaii is 19 hours earlier than Japan, 18 hours earlier than Singapore, 21 hours earlier than Sydney, and 23 hours earlier than New Zealand and Fiji.

Resources

Glossary

HAWAIIAN

There was once a time when it was illegal to speak Hawaiian. The language was relegated to the home, children were punished for speaking it in school, and a census performed in 1983 determined there were only 50 island youths who could speak their native tongue. It wasn't until 1978 that the language began a monumental comeback as part of a greater movement known as the Hawaiian Renaissance, and today, Hawaiian is fluently spoken by nearly 25,000 people, not counting the tens of thousands of residents who pepper their daily speech with Hawaiian loan words.

While English is the official language of tourism and daily life, the following list provides a basic vocabulary of words you are likely to hear. You might even discover some Hawaiian words that are so perfectly expressive they'll become regular parts of your vocabulary.

'a'a: rough clinker lava; *'a'a* has become the geological term to describe this type of lava found anywhere in the world.

'ae: yes

ahupua'a: pie-shaped land divisions running from mountain to sea that were governed by *konohiki*, local *ali'i* who owed their allegiance to a reigning chief

aikane: friend; pal; buddy

'aina: land; the binding spirit to all Hawaiians. Love of the land is paramount in traditional Hawaiian beliefs.

akamai: smart; clever; wise

akua: a god, or divine

ali'i: a Hawaiian chief or noble

aloha: the most common greeting in the islands; can mean both hello and good-bye, welcome and farewell. It can also mean romantic love, affection, or best wishes.

anuenue: rainbow

'a'ole: no

'aumakua: a personal or family god, often an ancestral spirit

auwe: alas; ouch! When a great chief or loved one died, it was a traditional wail of mourning.

halakahiki: pineapple

halau: school, as in hula school

hale: house or building; often combined with other words to name a specific place, such as Haleakala (House of the Sun)

hana: work; combined with *pau* means end of work or quitting time

hanai: literally "to feed." Part of the true aloha spirit. A *hanai* is a permanent guest, or an adopted family member, usually an old person or a child. This is an enduring cultural phenomenon in Hawaii, in which a child from one family (perhaps that of a brother or sister, and quite often one's grandchild) is raised as one's own without formal adoption.

haole: a word that at one time meant foreigner, but which now means a white person

hapa: half, as in a mixed-blooded person being referred to as *hapa haole*

hapai: pregnant; used by all ethnic groups when a *keiki* is on the way

haupia: a coconut custard dessert often served at a luau

he'enalu: surfing

heiau: A platform made of skillfully fitted

Hawaiian Language Pronunciation Guide

The Hawaiian language can appear baffling. Seemingly chaotic chains of vowels blend to create extremely long words. Confronted with the task of pronouncing words like *Honoapi'ilani* (aka Hwy. 30) or *Kealaikahiki,* many give up.

Vowels are not pronounced like those in English but as in Spanish: "aw, eh, ee, oh, ooh." Take the word *la* (sun), pronounced phonetically as "law," as opposed to "lah." The word *ala* (which means "road" or "path") is pronounced as "aw-law."

Much like in German, long words are easier to understand as several smaller words run together. Take, for example, *Haleakala,* Maui's famous mountain. Break it into smaller words: *hale a ka la,* phonetically "haw-lay-aw-kaw-LAW." Broken down, the meaning of the name is also easier to parse. *Hale* means "house," *a* means "of," *ka* means "the," and *la* means "sun," so, "House of the Sun."

Honoapi'ilani breaks down to *hono a Pi'ilani: hono* (bay) *a* (of) *Pi'ilani* (an ancient king of Maui), or completely, "the bays of Pi'ilani." This is a fitting name for highway, seeing as Pi'ilani once created a footpath around much of the island as a way of connecting all the parts of his domain.

Kealaikahiki breaks down to *ke ala i kahiki: ke* (the) *ala* (road) *i* (to) *kahiki* (Tahiti), or completely, "the road to Tahiti." The "k" and "t" sounds are interchangeable in many Polynesian languages, and lacking a "t" in modern Hawaiian, the "k" is substituted. The name refers to the channel between Lana'i and Kaho'olawe, which points south, so it makes sense that "the road to Tahiti" is the direction canoes would head when journeying back to their ancestral homeland.

rocks, upon which temporary structures were built as temples and offerings made to the gods

hono: bay, as in Honolulu (Sheltered Bay)

honu: green sea turtle; endangered

ho'olaule'a: any happy event, but especially a family outing or picnic

huhu: angry; irritated

hui: a group; meeting; society; often used to refer to Chinese businesspeople or family members who pool their money to get businesses started

hukilau: traditional shore fish-gathering in which everyone lends a hand to *huki* (pull) the huge net

hula: indigenous Hawaiian dance in which the rhythm of the islands is captured by swaying hips and stories told by lyrically moving hands. A *hula halau* is a hula group or school.

huli huli: barbecue, as in *huli huli* chicken

imu: underground oven filled with hot rocks and used for baking. The main cooking method featured at a luau, used to steam-bake pork and other succulent dishes. The tending of the *imu* was traditionally for men only.

ipo: sweetheart; lover; girlfriend or boyfriend

kahuna: priest; sorcerer; doctor; skillful person. In old Hawaii *kahuna* had tremendous power, which they used for both good and evil. The *kahuna ana'ana* was a feared individual who practiced black magic and could pray a person to death, while the *kahuna lapa'au* was a medical practitioner bringing aid and comfort to the people.

kai: the sea. Many businesses and hotels employ *kai* as part of their names.

kalua: roasted underground in an *imu.* A favorite island food is *kalua* pork.

kama'aina: a child of the land; an old-timer; a longtime island resident of any ethnic background; a resident of Hawaii or native son or daughter. Hotels and airlines often offer discounts called "*kama'aina* rates" to anyone who can prove island residency.

kanaka: man or commoner; later used to distinguish a Hawaiian from other races

kane: man, but used to signify a relationship such as husband or boyfriend. Written on a restroom door, it means "men's room."

kapu: forbidden; taboo; keep out; do not touch

Understanding the *Okina*

Notice what appears to be a backward apostrophe in the middle of Hawaiian words such as Lana'i and Ka'anapali. This character is the *okina*, used to indicate pronunciation. To a linguist the *okina* denotes a glottal stop, meaning the voice stops briefly between two vowel sounds. An example in English is the hyphen in "uh-oh." *Lana'i* is pronounced "lah-NA-ee," the final *a* and the *i* each pronounced distinctly. Incorrect pronunciation would be to blend the two final vowels together as "lah-nai," which in the Hawaiian language means "a porch," written *lanai*.

Similarly, *Ka'anapali* is correctly pronounced with two distinct *a*'s, phonetically "kah-ah-naw-PAW-lee." Incorrect pronunciation would be to blend the vowels together as "KAW-nah-paw-lee," or the dreaded "Ka-NAH-poli." The *okina* points out that the vowels are pronounced individually and not blended. *Lahaina*, written with no *okina*, is correctly pronounced with the blended vowels as "law-HIGH-nah."

kaukau: slang word meaning food or chow. Some of the best food in Hawaii comes from the *kaukau* wagons, trucks that sell plate lunches and other morsels.

keiki: child or children; used by all ethnic groups. "Have you hugged your *keiki* today?"

kiawe: an algaroba or mesquite tree from South America commonly found in Hawaii along the shore. It grows nasty long thorns that can easily puncture a tire. Legend has it that the trees were introduced to the islands by a misguided missionary who hoped the thorns would coerce Hawaiians into wearing shoes. Actually, they are good for fuel, as fodder for hogs and cattle, and for reforestation, none of which you'll appreciate if you step on one of the thorns or flatten a tire.

kokua: help. "Your *kokua* is needed to keep Hawaii free from litter."

kolohe: rascal

kona wind: a muggy subtropical wind that blows from the south and hits the leeward side of the islands. It usually brings sticky hot weather and is one of the few times when air-conditioning will be appreciated.

ko'olau: windward side of the island

kukui: a candlenut tree whose pods are polished and then strung together to make a beautiful lei. Traditionally the oil-rich nuts were strung on the rib of a coconut leaf and used as a candle.

kuleana: home site; the old homestead; small farms. Especially used to describe the small spreads on Hawaiian Home Lands on Moloka'i.

Kumulipo: ancient Hawaiian genealogical chant that records the pantheon of gods, creation, and the beginning of humankind

kupuna: a grandparent or old-timer; usually means someone who has gained wisdom. The statewide school system now invites *kupuna* to talk to the children about the old ways and methods.

la: the sun. Often combined with other words to be more descriptive, such as Lahaina (Merciless Sun) or Haleakala (House of the Sun).

lanai: veranda or porch. You'll pay more for a hotel room if it has a lanai with an ocean view.

lani: sky or the heavens

lauhala: traditional Hawaiian weaving of mats, hats, etc., from the prepared fronds of the pandanus (screw pine)

lei: a traditional garland of flowers or vines. One of Hawaii's most beautiful customs. Given at any auspicious occasion, but especially when arriving or leaving Hawaii.

lele: the stone altar at a *heiau*

limu: edible seaweed of various types. Gathered from the shore, it makes an excellent salad. It's used to garnish many island dishes and is a favorite at luau.

lolo: crazy, as in *lolo buggah* (stupid or crazy guy)

lomilomi: traditional Hawaiian massage; also, raw salmon made into a vinegared salad with chopped onion and spices *lua:* the toilet; the bathroom

luakini: a human-sacrifice temple. Introduced to Hawaii in the 13th century at Waha'ula Heiau on the Big Island.

luau: a Hawaiian feast featuring poi, *imu*-baked pork, and other traditional foods. Good ones provide gastronomic delights.

luna: foreman or overseer in the plantation fields. They were often on horseback and were renowned for either their fairness or their cruelty. Representing the middle class, they served as a buffer between plantation workers and white plantation owners.

mahalo: thank you. *Mahalo nui* means "big thanks" or "thank you very much."

mahele: division. The Great Mahele of 1848 changed Hawaii forever when the traditional common lands were broken up into privately owned plots.

mahimahi: a favorite eating fish. Often called "dolphin," but mahimahi is a true fish, not a cetacean.

mahu: similar to transvestite or transgendered person; often used derisively

maile: a fragrant vine used in traditional lei. It looks ordinary but smells delightful.

maka'ainana: a commoner; a person "belonging" to the *'aina* (land), who supported the *ali'i* by fishing and farming and as a warrior

makai: toward the sea; used by islanders when giving directions

make: dead; deceased

malihini: what you are if you have just arrived: a newcomer; a tenderfoot; a recent arrival

malo: the native Hawaiian loincloth. Not worn except at festivals or pageants

mana: power from the spirit world; innate energy of all things animate or inanimate; the grace of god. Mana could be passed on from one person to another, or even stolen. Great care was taken to protect the *ali'i* from having their mana defiled. Commoners were required to lie flat on the ground and cover their faces whenever a great *ali'i* approached. *Kahuna* were often employed in the regaining or transference of mana.

manini: small; stingy; tight

mauka: toward the mountains; used by islanders when giving directions

mauna: mountain. Often combined with other words to be more descriptive, such as Mauna Kea (White Mountain).

mele: a song or chant in the Hawaiian oral tradition that records the history and genealogies of the *ali'i*

Menehune: the legendary "little people" of Hawaii. Like leprechauns, they are said to shun humans and possess magical powers.

moa: chicken; fowl

moana: the ocean; the sea

moe: sleep

mo'olelo: ancient tales kept alive by the oral tradition and recited only by day

nani: beautiful

nui: big; great; large; as in *mahalo nui* (thank you very much)

'ohana: a family; the fundamental social division; extended family. Now often used to denote a social organization with grassroots overtones.

oli: chant not done to a musical accompaniment

'ono: delicious; delightful; the best.

'opihi: a shellfish or limpet that clings to rocks and is gathered as one of the islands' favorite pupu. Custom dictates that you never remove all of the *'opihi* from a rock; some are always left to grow for future generations.

'opu: belly; stomach

pahoehoe: smooth, ropy lava that looks like burned pancake batter. It is now the geological term used to describe this type of lava found anywhere in the world.

pakalolo: "crazy smoke"; marijuana

pake: a Chinese person. Modified from the Chinese word meaning "uncle." Can be derisive, depending on the way it's used.

pali: a cliff; precipice. Hawaii's geology makes them quite common. The most famous are the *pali* of O'ahu, where a major battle was fought.

paniolo: a Hawaiian cowboy. Derived from Spanish. The first cowboys brought to Hawaii during the early 19th century were Mexicans from California.

pau: finished; done; completed. Often combined into *pau hana,* which means the end of work or quitting time.

pilau: stink; bad smell

pilikia: trouble of any kind, big or small; bad times

poi: a glutinous paste made from the pounded corm of taro, which ferments slightly and has a light sour taste. Purplish in color, it's a staple at luau, where it is called one-, two-, or three-finger poi, depending on its thickness.

pono: righteous or excellent

pua: flower

puka: a hole of any size. *Puka* is commonly used by island residents, whether talking about a pinhole in a rubber boat or a tunnel through a mountain.

pupu: an appetizer; a snack; hors d'oeuvres; can be anything from cheese and crackers to sushi. Often, bars or nightclubs offer complimentary pupu.

pupule: crazy; nuts; out of your mind

pu'u: hill, as in Pu'u 'Ula'ula (Red Hill)

tapa: a traditional paper cloth made from beaten bark. Intricate designs were stamped in using beaters, and natural dyes added color. The tradition was lost for many years but is now making a comeback, and provides some of the most beautiful folk art in the islands. Also called *kappa.*

taro: the staple of old Hawaii. A plant with a distinctive broad leaf that produces a starchy root. It was brought by the first Polynesians and was grown on magnificently irrigated plantations. According to the oral tradition, the life-giving properties of taro hold mystical significance for Hawaiians, since it was created by the gods at about the same time as humans.

ti: a broad-leafed plant that was used for many purposes, from plates to hula skirts. Especially used to wrap religious offerings presented at the *heiau.*

tutu: grandmother; granny; older woman. Used by all as a term of respect and endearment.

ukulele: *uku* means "flea" and *lele* means "jumping," so "jumping flea," the way the

Hawaiians perceived the quick finger movements used on the banjo-like Portuguese folk instrument called a *cavaquinho*

wahine: young woman; female; girl; wife. Used by all ethnic groups. When written on a restroom door, it means "women's room."

wai: freshwater; drinking water

wela: hot.

wiki: quickly; fast; in a hurry. Often seen as *wiki wiki* (very fast), as in Wiki Wiki Messenger Service

USEFUL PHRASES

Aloha ahiahi Good afternoon

Aloha au ia 'oe I love you

Aloha kakahiaka Good morning

E komo mai Welcome

Ha'uoli la hanau Happy Birthday

Ha'uoli makahiki hou Happy New Year

Mahalo nui loa Thank you very much

Mele Kalikimaka Merry Christmas

PIDGIN

More so than Hawaiian, Pidgin is the language spoken around the islands. A mix of words from English, Hawaiian, and a host of other languages, it has a lilt, cadence, and grammar entirely its own. Even though it uses a lot of English, to nonresidents, Pidgin can be completely undecipherable. It can take years to fully understand Pidgin, but for the *keiki* who were raised here it is a natural native tongue. While you probably won't become fluent, here are some basic phrases to get by.

an' den and then? big deal; so what's next?

auntie respected elderly woman

bumbye Later; after a while

blalah from *brother,* but refers to a large, heavy-set, good-natured Hawaiian man

brah brother; pal. All the bros in Hawaii are brahs. Used to call someone's attention. One of the most common words even among people who are not acquainted. After a fill-up at a gas station, a person would say "Tanks, brah."

chicken skin goose bumps

choke lots of something

cockaroach steal; rip off

da kine a catchall word of many meanings that epitomizes the essence of Pidgin. *Da kine* is a euphemism for Pidgin and is substituted whenever the speaker is at a loss for a word or just wants to generalize.

geev um Give it to them; Give them hell; Go for it. Can be used as an encouragement. If a surfer is riding a great wave, the people on the beach might yell, "Geev um, brah!"

grinds food

hana hou again. Especially after a concert, the audience shouts "hana hou" (one more!).

hele on Let's get going.

howzit? as in "Howzit, brah?" What's happening? How's it going? The most common greeting, used in place of the more formal "How do you do?"

lesgo Let's go! Do it!

li'dis an' li'dat like this or that

lolo stupid, crazy

mo' bettah A better way of doing something.

pakalolo "crazy smoke," meaning marijuana

pau finished; done; over and done with. A Hawaiian word. *Pau hana* means end of work or quitting time. Once used by plantation workers, now used by everyone

seestah sister, female

shaka hand wave where only the thumb and baby finger stick out, meaning "Thank you, all right!"

shoots whatever, sure, in agreement. Example: "What, you like go Makena today?" "Shoots!"

rubbah sleepah rubber slippers, sandals, flip-flops. Referring to slippers as "sandals" is only something that mainlanders would do.

stink eye basically, frowning at someone; using facial expression to show displeasure. Hard looks. What you'll get if you give local people a hard time.

talk story spinning yarns; shooting the breeze; throwing the bull; a rap session. If you're lucky enough to be around to hear *kupuna* (elders) talk story, you can hear some fantastic tales in the tradition of old Hawaii.

tanks, brah thanks, thank you

to da max all the way

wea stay? literally, "where stay," to ask a location. Examples: "Wea the car stay?," "Wea you stay?," or the glorious "Wea you stay going?" (Where are you going?)

We go Let's go! Usually used in conjunction with *shoots,* as in "shoots we go!"

Suggested Reading

There are many books on Hawaii. Publishers that focus on Hawaiian topics include the **University of Hawaii Press** (www.uhpress. hawaii.edu), with the best overall general list of titles on Hawaii. The **Bishop Museum Press** (www.bishopmuseum.org/press) puts out many scholarly works on Hawaiiana, as does **Kamehameha Schools Press** (http:// kspress.ksbe.edu). Also good, with a more general-interest list, are **Bess Press** (www. besspress.com), **Mutual Publishing** (www. mutualpublishing.com), and **Petroglyph Press** (www.basicallybooks.com). In addition, a website specifically oriented toward books on Hawaii, Hawaiian music, and other things Hawaiian is **Hawaii Books** (www.hawaiibooks.com).

ASTRONOMY

Rhoads, Samuel. *The Sky Tonight—A Guided Tour of the Stars over Hawaii.* Honolulu: Bishop Museum, 1993. Four pages per month of star charts—one each for the horizon in each cardinal direction. Exceptional!

COOKING

Choy, Sam. *Cooking from the Heart with Sam Choy*. Honolulu: Mutual Publishing, 1995. This beautiful hand-bound cookbook contains many color photos by Douglas Peebles.

Wong, Alan. *New Wave Luau*. Berkeley, CA: Ten Speed Press, 1999. With his book, a prized Hawaiian chef shares wonderful recipes across the board of Hawaiian and local food.

CULTURE

Hartwell, Jay. *Na Mamo: Hawaiian People Today*. Honolulu: 'Ai Pohaku Press, 1996. Profiles 12 people practicing Hawaiian traditions in the modern world.

Kamehameha Schools Press. *Life in Early Hawaii: The Ahupua'a*. 3rd ed. Honolulu: Kamehameha Schools Press, 1994. Written for schoolchildren to better understand the basic organization of old Hawaiian land use and its function, this slim volume is a good primer for people of any age who wish to understand this fundamental societal fixture.

Kirch, Patrick V. *Feathered Gods and Fishhooks: An Introduction to Hawaiian Archaeology and Prehistory*. Honolulu: University of Hawaii Press, 1997. This scholarly, lavishly illustrated, yet readable book gives new insight into the development of precontact Hawaiian civilization. It focuses on the sites and major settlements of old Hawaii and chronicles the main cultural developments while weaving in the social climate that contributed to change.

McBride, Likeke. *Petroglyphs of Hawaii*. Hilo, HI: Petroglyph Press, 1997. A revised and updated guide to petroglyphs found in the Hawaiian Islands. A basic introduction to these old Hawaiian picture stories.

McBride, L. R. *Practical Folk Medicine of Hawaii*. Hilo, HI: Petroglyph Press, 1975. An illustrated guide to Hawaii's medicinal plants as used by the *kahuna lapa'au* (medical healers). Includes a thorough section on ailments, diagnosis, and the proper folk remedy. Illustrated by the author, a renowned botanical researcher and former ranger at Hawaii Volcanoes National Park.

ANIMALS

Fielding, Ann, and Ed Robinson. *An Underwater Guide to Hawaii*. Honolulu: University of Hawaii Press, 1987. If you've ever had a desire to snorkel or scuba the living reef waters of Hawaii and be familiar with what you're seeing, get this small but fact-packed book. The amazing array of marinelife in the archipelago is captured in glossy photos with accompanying informative text. Both scientific and common names are given. This book will enrich your underwater experience and serve as a reference guide for years.

Hoover, John P. *Hawaii's Fishes: A Guide for Snorkelers and Divers*. Honolulu: Mutual Publishing, 2007. The definitive resource for identifying the fish of Hawaii.

Kay, Alison, and Olive Schoenberg-Dole. *Shells of Hawaii*. Honolulu: University of Hawaii Press, 1991. Color photos and tips on where to look.

PLANTS

Kepler, Angela. *Hawaiian Heritage Plants*. Honolulu: University of Hawaii Press, 1998. A treatise on 32 utilitarian plants used by the early Hawaiians.

Miyano, Leland. *A Pocket Guide to Hawaii's Flowers*. Honolulu: Mutual Publishing, 2001. A small guide to readily seen flowers in the state. Good for the backpack or back pocket.

Teho, Fortunato. *Plants of Hawaii—How to Grow Them.* Hilo, HI: Petroglyph Press, 1992. A small but useful book for those who want their backyards to bloom into a tropical paradise.

Valier, Kathy. *Ferns of Hawaii.* Honolulu: University of Hawaii Press, 1995. One of the few books that treat the state's ferns as a single subject.

HISTORY

Ashdown, Inez MacPhee. *Recollections of Kahoʻolawe.* Honolulu: Topgallant Publishing, 1979. The tortured story of the lonely island of Kahoʻolawe by a member of the family who owned the island until it was turned into a military bombing range during World War II. This is a first-person account of life on the island and is rife with myths, legends, and historical facts about Kahoʻolawe.

Barnes, Phil. *A Concise History of the Hawaiian Islands.* Hilo, HI: Petroglyph Press, 1999. An examination of the main currents of Hawaiian history and its major players, focusing on the important factors in shaping the social, economic, and political trends of the islands. An easy read.

Davenport, Kiana. *Shark Dialogues.* New York: Penguin Books, 1995. A fictional account of Hawaii's history based on historical events. A captivating read, and told from the perspective of Hawaiians.

Daws, Gavan. *Shoal of Time: A History of the Hawaiian Islands.* Honolulu: University of Hawaii Press, 1974. A highly readable history of Hawaii dating from its "discovery" by the Western world to its acceptance as the 50th state. Good insight into the psychological makeup of influential characters who forged Hawaii's past.

Ellis, William. *A Narrative of an 1823 Tour through Hawaii.* Reprint. Honolulu: Mutual Publishing, 2004. Reprint of the 1825 journal by an early missionary of a journey around the island of Hawaii and impressions of the land and its people. One of the first descriptions of Hawaii for the West.

Fornander, Abraham. *An Account of the Polynesian Race; Its Origins and Migrations, and the Ancient History of the Hawaiian People to the Times of Kamehameha I.* Rutland, VT: C. E. Tuttle, 1969. This is a reprint of a three-volume opus originally published from 1878 to 1885. It is still one of the best sources of information on Hawaiian myth and legend.

Ii, John Papa. *Fragments of Hawaiian History.* Honolulu: Bishop Museum, 1959. Hawaii's history under Kamehameha I as told by a Hawaiian who actually experienced it.

Joesting, Edward. *Hawaii: An Uncommon History.* New York: W. W. Norton, 1978. A truly uncommon history told in a series of vignettes relating to the lives and personalities of the first Caucasians in Hawaii, Hawaiian nobility, sea captains, writers, and adventurers. Brings history to life.

Kamakau, S. M. *Ruling Chiefs of Hawaii,* revised edition. Honolulu: Kamehameha Schools Press, 1992. A history of Hawaii from the legendary leader ʻUmi to the mid-Kamehameha dynasty, from oral tales and a Hawaiian perspective.

Liliʻuokalani. *Hawaii's Story by Hawaii's Queen.* Reprint. Honolulu: Mutual Publishing, 1990. Originally written in 1898, this moving personal account recounts Hawaii's inevitable move from monarchy to U.S. Territory by its last queen, Liliʻuokalani. The facts can be found in other histories, but none provides the emotion or point of view expressed by Hawaii's deposed monarch. This is a must-read to get the whole picture.

Nickerson, Roy. *Lahaina, Royal Capital of Hawaii.* Honolulu: Hawaiian Service, 1978.

The story of Lahaina from whaling days to present, spiced with ample photographs.

Tabrah, Ruth M. *Ni'ihau: The Last Hawaiian Island.* Kailua, HI: Press Pacifica, 1987. Sympathetic history of the privately owned island of Ni'ihau.

Takaki, Ronald. *Pau Hana: Plantation Life and Labor in Hawaii.* Honolulu: University of Hawaii Press, 1983. The story of immigrant labor and the sugar industry in Hawaii until the 1920s from the workers' perspective.

LANGUAGE

Elbert, Samuel, and Mary Pukui. *Hawaiian Dictionary.* Honolulu: University of Hawaii Press, 1986. The best dictionary available on the Hawaiian language. The *Pocket Hawaiian Dictionary* is a less expensive, condensed version of this dictionary and adequate for most travelers with a general interest in the language.

Pukui, Mary Kawena, Samuel Elbert, and Esther T. Mookini. *Place Names of Hawaii.* Honolulu: University of Hawaii Press, 1974. The most current and comprehensive listing of Hawaiian and foreign place names in the state, giving pronunciation, spelling, meaning, and location.

MYTHOLOGY, LEGEND, AND LITERATURE

Beckwith, Martha. *Hawaiian Mythology.* Reprint. Honolulu: University of Hawaii Press, 1976. Originally printed in 1940, this work remains the definitive text on Hawaiian mythology. Beckwith compiled this book from many sources, giving exhaustive cross-references to genealogies and legends expressed in the oral tradition. If you are only going to read one book on Hawaii's folklore, this should be it.

Beckwith, Martha. *The Kumulipo.* Reprint. Honolulu: University of Hawaii Press, 1972. Translation of the Hawaiian creation chant, originally published in 1951.

Kalakaua, His Hawaiian Majesty, King David. *The Legends and Myths of Hawaii.* Edited by R. M. Daggett, with a foreword by Glen Grant. Honolulu: Mutual Publishing, 1990. In this book, originally published in 1888, Hawaii's own King Kalakaua draws upon his scholarly and formidable knowledge of the classic oral tradition to bring alive ancient tales from precontact Hawaii. A powerful yet Victorian voice from Hawaii's past speaks clearly and boldly, especially about the intimate role of pre-Christian religion in the lives of the Hawaiian people.

Pukui, Mary Kawena, and Caroline Curtis. *Tales of the Menehune.* Honolulu: The Kamehameha Schools Press, 1960. Compilation of legends relating to Hawaii's "little people."

Internet Resources

Maui County
www.co.maui.hi.us
Includes information on city government, the county-sponsored bus system, disability access, and a calendar of events.

Hawaii Visitors and Convention Bureau
www.gohawaii.com
The official site of the state-run tourism organization has information about all of the major Hawaiian Islands: transportation, accommodations, eating, activities, shopping, Hawaiian products, an events calendar, a travel planner and resource guide for a host of topics, as well as information about meetings, conventions, and the organization.

Maui Information Guide
www.mauiinformationguide.com
A large, informative, and modern website that offers insights into everything from activities and trip planning to helpful tips and safety guidelines.

Alternative Hawaii
www.alternative-hawaii.com
Alternative source for ecofriendly general information and links to specific businesses, with some cultural, historical, and events information.

Hawaii Ecotourism Association
www.hawaiiecotourism.org
Lists goals, members, and activities, and provides links to member organizations and related ecotourism groups.

Hawaii Visitors Bureau Calendar of Events
http://calendar.gohawaii.com
Events listings for events of all sorts happening throughout the state. Information can be accessed by island, date, or type.

State Foundation of Culture and the Arts
www.state.hi.us/sfca
This site of the State Foundation of Culture and the Arts features a calendar of arts and cultural events, activities, and programs held throughout the state.

Hawaiian Music Island
www.mele.com
Check out the Hawaiian music scene at one of the largest music websites focusing on Hawaiian music, books, and videos related to Hawaiian music and culture, concert schedules, Hawaiian music awards, and links to music companies and musicians. Others with broad listings and general interest information are www.nahenahe.net and www.hawaii-music.com.

University of Hawaii Press
www.uhpress.hawaii.edu
This University of Hawaii Press website has the best overall list of titles for books published on Hawaiian themes and topics.

Hawaii Museums
www.hawaiimuseums.org
This site is dedicated to the promotion of museums and cultural attractions in the state, with links to member sites on each of the islands.

Maui News
www.mauinews.com
Website of Maui's largest newspaper. It has a concentration of news coverage about Maui, but also covers major news from the neighboring islands.

Office of Hawaiian Affairs
www.oha.org
Official site for the state-mandated organization that deals with indigenous Hawaii-related affairs.

Reinstated Hawaiian Government
www.reinstated.org
Site of one of the organizations of native Hawaiians advocating for sovereignty and independence.

Index

disabilities, travelers with: 354-355
Dixie Maru Beach: 301, 303, 304
Dollar Lana'i Rent a Car: 269, 280, 289
D. T. Fleming Beach Park: 15, 19, 40-41, 58
Dumps: 147
East Maui and the Road to Hana: 207-245; map
   210-211
economy: 341
electricity: 363
emergencies: 361

F

Fagan Memorial: 220-221
Fagan's Cross: 234
Farmacy, The: 96, 122
Father Damien: 23, 299
fauna: 327-328
featherwork: 346
festivals and events: 347-350
First Cathedral: 17, 279
fish/fishing: Lana'i 272; Moloka'i 310; South Maui
   158; West Maui 44, 67-68
5 Caves: 152
Five Graves: 146, 152
505: 43
Flatbread: 213, 240
flightseeing tours: 113-114
flora: 325-327
food: 345
food trucks: 121
Fort at Lahaina: 33, 36
Four Seasons Resort Lana'i: 13, 269, 286, 287
Fourth Friday: 165
Friday Town Party: 82

GH

Garden of Eden: 214-215
Gazebo, The: 14, 29, 83
geography: 320
golf: Central Maui 114-115; Lana'i 283-284;
   Moloka'i 310; South Maui 160-161; West Maui
   74-75
government: 341
Grandma's Coffee House: 14, 179, 205-206
Grandma's surf break: 60
Guardrails: 60
Ha'iku: 235, 236, 239
Haipua'ena Falls: 215
Halawa Bay: 303, 305
Halawa Valley: 21, 293, 299, 308-309
Haleakala and Upcountry: 14, 175-206; map 178
Haleakala Crater: 179
Haleakala National Park: 13, 20, 179-183, 188, 190-
   195, 196-197, 213, 222; map 189
Haleakala Ridge Trail: 192

Hale Kealoha: 293, 312
Haleki'i and Pihana Heiau: 100-101
Halemau'u Trail (Switchback Trail): 190
Hale O Lono: 301, 304
Hale Pa'ahao: 37
Hale Pa'i Printing Museum: 38
Hali'imaile Distillery: 179, 183
Hali'imaile General Store: 179, 203-204
Hamoa Beach: 14, 16, 20, 213, 221, 227-228, 230
Hana: 16, 22, 219-221, 226-227, 230, 233-234, 236,
   238, 239, 241-242; maps 219, 220
Hana Bay: 226-227
Hana Courthouse: 221
Hana Cultural Center: 221
Hanakao'o Beach (Canoe Beach): 44, 55
hang gliding: 236
haole rot: 360-361
Hawaiian Islands Humpback Whale National
   Marine Sanctuary Visitors Center: 128, 130-131
Hawaiian Music Series: 82
Hawaiian Paddle Sports: 18, 60, 63, 64, 152, 157
Hawaiian Sailboard Techniques: 18, 108
Hawela Beach: 301
health: 356-361
helicopter rides: 112-113
hiking: general discussion 20-21, 359; Central
   Maui 99, 108-110; East Maui 219, 226, 231-235;
   Lana'i 13, 280-283; Moloka'i 294, 306-309;
   South Maui 139, 158-160; Upcountry 188, 190-
   192; West Maui 69-73
historical and cultural sites: 22-23
history: 329-340
Hoapili Trail: 20, 128, 159-160
honeymoon hotspots: 22
Honokowai: 29-31, 39-42, 45-47, 54-55, 57-58, 61,
   63, 69-71, 74, 75, 76, 78-79, 83-85
Honokowai Beach Park: 40
Honolua Bay: 13, 14, 17, 19, 30, 45-46, 54, 58
Honolua Store: 29, 83
Honolua Valley: 29
Honomanu Bay: 215
Ho'okio Gulch: 280-281
Ho'okipa Beach Park: 19, 226, 229, 230
Ho'olehua Post-a-Nut: 293, 295
horseback riding: Central Maui 111; Lana'i 281;
   South Maui 162; Upcountry 196
Hosmer's Grove: 180, 181, 196-197
Hosmer's Grove Nature Trail: 190
hospitals: 361
Hot Bread Lane: 293, 313
Hotel Moloka'i: 293, 315
Huelo Lookout: 213
Hui No'eau Visual Arts Center: 183
Hui O Wa'a Kaulua Canoe Hale: 22, 43
hula: 345
Hula Grill: 13, 80, 86

List of Maps

Photo Credits

Title page photo: © Kristin Belew
page 4 © Kyle Ellison; page 6 (top left) © Jenna Strubhar, (top right) © Kristin Belew, (bottom) © Alexandra Baackes; page 7 (top) © Kyle Ellison, (bottom left) © Kyle Ellison, (bottom right) © Heather Ellison; page 8 (top) © Kristin Belew, (bottom) © Kyle Ellison,; page 9 (top) © Jenna Strubhar, (bottom left) © Kyle Ellison, (bottom right) © Kyle Ellison; page 10 © Kyle Ellison; page 13 (top left) © Heather Ellison, (top right) © Kyle Ellison; page 15 © Heather Ellison; page 16 (bottom left) © Kristin Belew, (bottom right) © Kyle Ellison; page 18 © Heather Ellison; page 19 © Mark Driessen; page 21 (top left) © Jenna Strubhar, (top right) © Heather Ellison; page 22 © Mark Driessen; page 23 © Kyle Ellison ; page 25 (top) © Heather Ellison, (bottom) © Kyle Ellison; page 27 © Kristin Belew; page 30 © Mark Driessen; page 40 © Kyle Ellison; page 43 © Kyle Ellison; page 44 © Jenna Strubhar; page 48 © Kyle Ellison; page 53 © Kyle Ellison; page 61 © Kyle Ellison; page 64 © Kyle Ellison; page 67 © Alexandra Baackes; page 68 © Kyle Ellison; page 71 © Kyle Ellison; page 72 © Kyle Ellison; page 92 (top) © Kyle Ellison, (bottom) © Kyle Ellison; page 93 © Kyle Ellison; page 98 © Kyle Ellison; page 101 © Kyle Ellison; page 106 © Kyle Ellison; page 107 © Heather Ellison; page 109 © Kyle Ellison; page 114 © Kyle Ellison; page 124 (top) © Kyle Ellison, (bottom) © Jenna Strubhar; page 125 © Jenna Strubhar; page 129 © Jenna Strubhar; page 130 © Jenna Strubhar; page 131 © Kyle Ellison; page 136 © Kyle Ellison; page 138 © Jenna Strubhar; page 140 © Kyle Ellison; page 145 © Kyle Ellison; page 146 © Kyle Ellison; page 148 © Kyle Ellison; page 150 © Kyle Ellison; page 155 © Kyle Ellison; page 157 © Kyle Ellison; page 159 © Kyle Ellison; page 175 (top) © Jenna Strubhar, (bottom) © Kyle Ellison; page 177 © Heather Ellison; page 180 © Kyle Ellison; page 183 © Kyle Ellison; page 185 © Kyle Ellison; page 186 © Alexandra Baackes; page 192 © Jenna Strubhar; page 193 © Alexandra Baackes; page 196 © Kyle Ellison; page 197 © Alexandra Baackes; page 200 © Kyle Ellison; page 202 © Kyle Ellison; page 205 © Kyle Ellison; page 207 (top) © Kyle Ellison, (bottom) © Heather Ellison; page 209 © Jenna Strubhar; page 214 © Jenna Strubhar; page 216 © Kyle Ellison; page 222 © Mark Driessen; page 223 © Jenna Strubhar; page 224 © Kyle Ellison; page 225 © Kyle Ellison; page 227 © Heather Ellison; page 228 © Heather Ellison; page 229 © Kyle Ellison; page 230 © Kyle Ellison; page 232 © Jenna Strubhar; page 233 © Heather Ellison; page 235 © Kyle Ellison; page 236 © Kyle Ellison; page 240 © Kyle Ellison; page 241 © Jenna Strubhar; page 244 © Kyle Ellison; page 246 (top) © Jenna Strubhar, (bottom) © Alexandra Baackes; page 247 © Heather Ellison; page 249 © Kyle Ellison; page 256 © Alexandra Baackes; page 261 © Kyle Ellison; page 264 © Kyle Ellison; page 265 (top) © Kyle Ellison, (bottom) © Heather Ellison; page 267 © Kristin Belew; page 270 © Kyle Ellison; page 271 © Kyle Ellison; page 275 © Heather Ellison; page 276 © Kyle Ellison; page 277 © Kyle Ellison; page 279 © Kristin Belew; page 281 © Kyle Ellison; page 282 © Kyle Ellison; page 283 © Kyle Ellison; page 289 © Kyle Ellison; page 290 (top) © Heather Ellison, (bottom) © Kyle Ellison; page 291 © Kyle Ellison; page 296 © Kyle Ellison; page 300 © Mark Driessen; page 302 © Heather Ellison; page 304 © Heather Ellison; page 305 © Heather Ellison; page 307 © Kyle Ellison; page 308 © Mark Driessen; page 315 © Kyle Ellison; page 319 (top) © Kyle Ellison, (bottom) © Jenna Strubhar; page 327 © Mark Driessen; page 351 (top) © Kyle Ellison, (bottom) © Kyle Ellison; page 358 © Kyle Ellison